The truth is . . . we never planned to do another *Jewish Catalog*. The success of *Catalog 1* and the deluge of requests from you, the reader, for additional information caused us to reconsider. And so we embarked on a second *Catalog* venture. Midway through, we realized we could not put everything into only one more volume. So we've decided to complete a trilogy, with yet another volume soon to come—a third (and *final*) *Catalog!*

By now it is common knowledge that *Catalog 1* grew out of the havurah community. In many ways, however, the whole enterprise has moved beyond that community into a community that includes the many people who took *Catalog 1* seriously, yet had never even seen a havurah. Indeed, some of the ideas/concepts in *Catalog 1* have spread into the wider community so that there are now havurot in many synagogue settings. While these may be less intense than our ideal would have it, certainly the entire venture has taught us that there are more people "out there" than we had ever realized. In fact, the movement itself has taken many new forms and shapes. It is our hope that the *Catalog* has been a part of that and that this new volume will also play a vital role in the movement's future.

In a very real sense, this movement is reflected in our own personal experiences over the past two years—years of great joy and equally great pain, much of it connected with the success of *Catalog 1*. During this period, we've grown as people and as Jews, and the *Catalog* has/should have grown, too. We hope and believe that this book probes more deeply, and is a more serious effort, than *Catalog 1*. Yet at the same time, we hope that it is even more joyful and accessible, and thus on both accounts as approachable as its predecessor. Perhaps there is also more concern with proper ways to act rather than the simple how-to of doing Jewish things—more attention to the community, less to the self. But above all, we still believe in the same value that permeated the first book—the need for a community to be Jewish with.

Sharon and Michael Strassfeld

Some notes on how to use this book:

1. Read the introduction to *Catalog 1*—it's a good overall background to who we are, what we've tried to do, where you can plug in.

2. Even more than for *Catalog 1*, you will need a Bible and a siddur as you amble your way through this book.

3. The *Encyclopaedia Judaica* is a very valuable resource and a good way to continue to explore areas we touch upon.

4. Seek out teachers in various areas who can help/guide you in new paths.

5. Find yourself a community to share your searches with.

6. Go beyond this book. Follow your own needs and don't be deterred by people who would write you out of the community because of their own particular "definitions" of what does or does not constitute a Jew.

More notes:

1. Bibliographic suggestions for the chapter on Talmud Torah may be found in *Catalog 1*, pp. 227 and 235.

2. We have spent a great deal of time struggling with the women's issue. It is an ongoing struggle—an unresolvable one—that gets more complicated as each new factor is added to the stew (careers, children, etc.). There are no easy answers. But certainly we believe that the move toward equality of the sexes (whether you read "equal" as separate-but-equal or as exactly the same is irrelevant here) should be reflected in the language we use. We therefore invented (only to find that others had invented long before us) nonsexist forms for written language: s/he and wo/man. These are only literary forms—not meant to be spoken. They reflect our belief that the language we use embodies and reflects underlying assumptions about roles, status, etc. and is one of the crucial ways in which these philosophies and ideas are transmitted.

W9-BJM-001

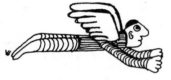

sources & resources

with editorial help from
Mark Nulman
Nessa Rapoport
Levi Kelman

The Jewish Publication Society of America
Philadelphia

ILLUSTRATIONS: *Stuart Copans*
DESIGN: *Adrianne Onderdonk Dudden*

the second Jewish catalog

compiled and edited by
Sharon Strassfeld
Michael Strassfeld

Take to heart these instructions with which I charge you this day. Impress them upon your children.
Deuteronomy 6:6-7

We dedicate this book to our parents, who brought us up with an understanding of Ahavas Torah and Ahavas Yisrael—a love for Torah and a love for the people of Israel. May we be able to convey these values to our child, Kayla Judith.

"editors" refers to Sharon Strassfeld and Michael Strassfeld

1   Life Cycle
In the beginning

The middle years

Accord and discord

Where love is, no room is too small.

Yiddish Proverb
Trans. Leo Rosten

May God who blessed our fathers Abraham, Isaac, and Jacob and our mothers Sarah, Rivkah, Leah, and Rachel bless
Kay Powell, Adrianne Onderdonk Dudden, Chaim Potok, Stu Copans,
Mark Nulman, Steven Fialkoff, David Szyoni, Rebecca Ziplonsky,
Lionel Koppman, Lester Waldman, Judy Barick, Temima Gazari,
Aviva Cantor Zuckoff, Henya Pulitzer, Leslie Kane, Lenny Levin,
Lauri Wolff, Ralene Levy, Irv Leos
for their assistance and encouragement in the preparation of this Catalog. May ha-Kadosh Barukh Hu send blessing and prosperity on all the work of their hands together with all those who work for peace. AMEN.

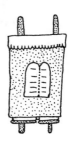

Robert Agus is a founder of the Farbrengen in Washington, where he currently devotes himself to hazzanut music and to contemplating the creation of a holistic Jewish community.

Albert Axelrad has just celebrated his tenth anniversary as Hillel director at Brandeis University.

Fred Berk is the head of the Jewish Dance Division of the 92nd Street YM/YWHA in New York City and the director of the Israeli Folk Dance Department of the American Zionist Youth Foundation.

Daniel Boyarin teaches Talmud at the Jewish Theological Seminary and divides his time equally between studying and wishing he were studying.

Marsha Bryan teaches Jewish music in addition to her musical and administrative duties with the Zamir Chorale of New York.

David M. Feldman is the author of *Birth Control in Jewish Law* and *Judaism and the Sexual Revolution,* and he is rabbi of the Bay Ridge Jewish Center in Brooklyn, N.Y.

Leslie Gottlieb is active in public relations, political affairs, and Jewish organizations. BA cum laude from Syracuse University; MA from American University.

Lynn Gottlieb is the rabbi of Temple Beth Or of the Deaf, a group of the New York Society for the Deaf. She is a member of the New York Havurah, a puppeteer at the Jewish Museum, and director of Bat Kol Players–Portraits of Women.

Arthur Green is a founder of Havurat Shalom and currently teaches in the Religion Department at the University of Pennsylvania.

Kathy Green is a founding member of Havurat Shalom who works in Jewish education and is concerned with bringing the values of humanistic education and of Jewish spirituality to bear on the Jewish educational process.

Jeffrey and Resna Hammer are the parents of Rachel and Tamar, and members of the Farbrengen in Washington. Resna is a Montessori instructor and Jeff is the deputy director of Special Volunteer Programs for ACTION.

Sy Hefter (MSW U. Conn and MS CCNY) is the educational director of the Jewish Community Center of Wyoming Valley; he searches for and develops ideas that will help in the perpetuation and enrichment of Judaism and the Jewish people in an open society.

Richard J. Israel is the director of the Bnai Brith Hillel Foundations of Greater Boston. He is a bee keeper and a Boston Marathon runner and lives in Newton with his wife and four children.

William Kavesh is a member of Havurat Shalom and a physician at the South Boston Medical Center. In his spare time he is a carpenter.

Levi Kelman is a rabbinical student at the Jewish Theological Seminary.

Naamah Kelman has a BA in Urban Studies–Community Organizing. She has done work for a variety of community organizations, including teaching folk dance to the blind.

Arthur Kurzweil is a writer, philatelist, genealogist, and librarian—depending on who asks. Presently his goal is to find the names of his paternal great-great-great-grandparents.

Harvey Lerner is an art director of Lerner-Newhoff Advertising and is a designer for Torah Toys. He also is actively involved in Torah study.

Michael Levy, who is blind, is a rabbinical student at the Jewish Theological Seminary, where he also graduated from the Teachers' Institute. He has worked for the Jewish Braille Institute.

Deborah E. Lipstadt is assistant professor of history and comparative religion at the University of Washington, where she serves as assistant chairperson of the Jewish Studies Committee. She has contributed to *Jewish Reflections on Death, Jewish Catalog 1, Jewish Social Studies, Review of Books on Religion,* and a variety of other publications.

Daniel Margolis is the principal of the Solomon Schechter school in Newton, Mass. He and **Patty Margolis** are the parents of Ariel.

Hershel Jonah Matt has served as rabbi in Nashua, N.H., Troy, N.Y., and Metuchen and Princeton, N.J., and has given special attention in his congregational work and in his writing to issues of prayer, ethics, ritual, theology, and interfaith dialogue.

Sabra Wakefield Morton is a Yankee, yogini, and free-lance writer. She also bakes bread for Tony, Michael, and Evan.

Stanley Newhoff is a professional writer and a principal in his own advertising agency—Lerner-Newhoff Advertising. He is deeply involved in the development of Torah Toys.

Contributors

Mordecai Newman holds an MFA from Yale Drama School. He has acted and directed in New York and has directed amateur productions at Camp Ramah and for USY groups.

Mark Nulman is working toward his master's in business at NYU.

Miriam Oles is a psychotherapist living in Berkeley, Calif., and is active in the unorthodox Orthodox Berkeley Jewish community.

Pinchas Peli is the former editor of *Panim el Panim* and currently heads Mosad Heschel in Israel.

Nessa Rapoport is the former managing editor of *Conservative Judaism* and is now living in Israel.

Sharon Pucker Rivo has been the director of the Jewish Media Service since the creation of the project in 1973. She is married to Dr. Elliott Rivo and they have three children—Lisa, Steven, and Rebecca.

Mae Shafter Rockland is a craftsperson residing with her family in Princeton, N.J. Her books include *The Work of Our Hands* and *The Hanukkah Book*.

Joel Rosenberg (Toys) is a cultural anthropologist in educational technology. He was the director of a drug rehabilitation program for Chabad House in L.A. and left this to help found Torah Toys.

Joel Rosenberg (Devar Torah) has written frequently for *Response, Judaism, Moment, Davka,* and other periodicals. He lives in the Boston area and is earning his doctorate in the history of consciousness (with an emphasis on Hebrew and comparative literature) from the University of California at Santa Cruz.

Dona Rosenblatt is a graduate of the Cleveland Institute of Art with a major in weaving and a minor in ceramics. She was an assistant director and choreographer for Shalhevet, an Israeli folk dance group of the JCC of Cleveland. She has just formed a performing Israeli dance group in Montreal.

Chip Rosenthal has only recently become interested in Judaism. He is now active in his temple's programs and in the formation of a Jewish youth group.

Gita Rotenberg, having equipped herself with appropriate degrees from Barnard, the Jewish Theological Seminary, and Bank Street College, is, with her husband, raising four perfect children in Montreal. Editing and writing fill her many leisure hours.

Shulamit Saltzman teaches dance at Trinity College and in Manhattan.

Joseph Schiff is the former executive director of the West Side Jewish Community Council and his particular concern is inner-city Jewish life.

Seymour Siegel teaches at the Jewish Theological Seminary and City College of New York. He is chairperson of the Committee on Jewish Law and Standards of the Rabbinical Assembly of the Conservative movement. He has participated in many gittin (as a witness and dayan, of course).

Mel Silberman is associate professor in the Department of Psychoeducational Processes, Temple University.

Shoshana Silberman is educational director at Congregation Beth Tikvah–Bnai Jeshurun. Both Shoshana and Mel have been active in alternative Jewish activities such as the Germantown Havurah and Minyan.

Bea Stadtler is the registrar at the Cleveland College of Jewish Studies. She is a member of the Executive Committee of the National Council for Jewish Education and has written numerous articles, films, and books—among them *The Holocaust: A History of Courage and Resistance,* which won the 1975 Schwartz Award from the National Jewish Book Council.

Steven Stroiman is the coordinator of the Jewish Educational Workshop, and facilitator of the Unstructured Synagogue. He is also instructor of Jewish education at Gratz College and at the Reconstructionist Rabbinical College.

Judith Targan is a member of Havurah Derech Reut and of the Upper West Side Minyan in New York. She lives in New York, where she is pursuing two careers—one in Jewish education and one in learning disabilities.

Moshe Waldoks is the Hillel director at Tufts University. He is also a doctoral candidate in Near Eastern and Judaic Studies at Brandeis University. His interests include theater, Jewish humor, and the Messiah and Messianists, in particular Reb Hillel Zeitlin.

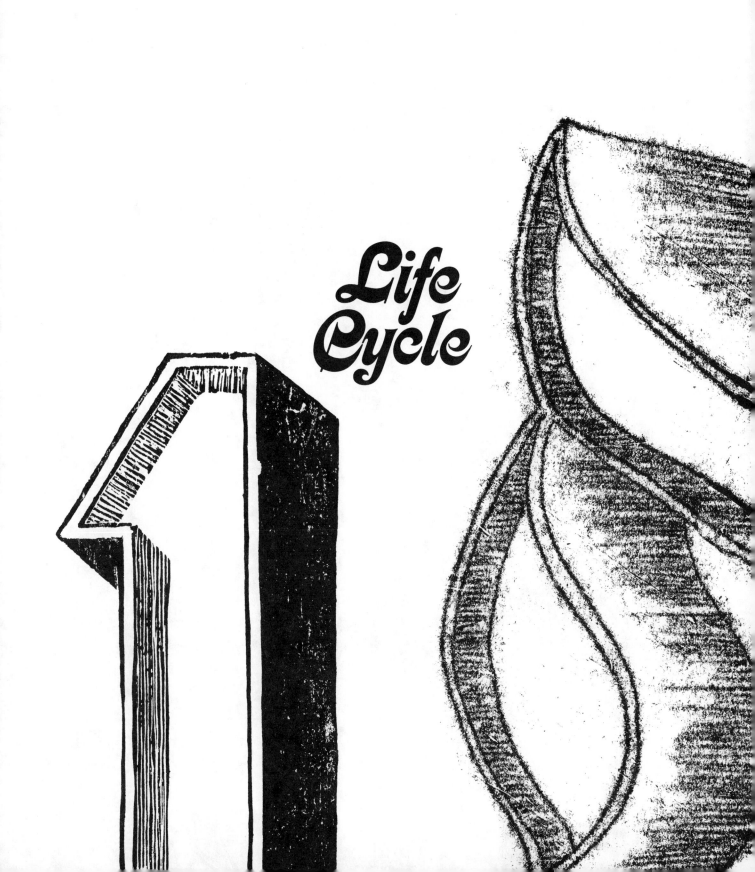

Life
Cycle

1

in the beginning

Birth

Introduction

Whether it's one, two, five, or six years after the wedding, the questions of when? how many? how far apart? get asked—usually by Bobbeh and Zaydeh, who begin to prod about two months after the wedding! In any event, sooner or later the question cannot be put off—especially from yourselves. It is, after all, the first mitzvah—commandment: "Peru urevu—be fertile and increase."

(I am not going to present here all the pertinent reasons why Jews should have children—lots of them! I take it as a given that if you are reading this section you must have made a decision already. But if you haven't, leaving aside the fact that Jews as a people have a lot of catching up to do, if you were, God forbid, to miss the incredible joy, contentment, and pure satisfaction that our own child, Ariel, gives to us, you would be missing the height and the depth of the soul's pleasure.)

Making the decision

The psychology of having a child doesn't begin or end with the considerations of parental responsibilities toward the new addition. It is a rational decision for which everyone must be completely prepared. Take advantage of being a couple and savor the memories, then be ready to give that condition up for a long time . . . in exchange for other joys, satisfactions, schedules, trials, redefined relationships with each other, and "THE KID," and dirty diapers—all of which are the least of the day-to-day practical problems. Don't be afraid to study other families, take an active interest in their methods, and read the books (see the Bibliography at the end of this chapter). Talk it out, make decisions . . . "We're going to do it this way" . . . and know that you'll change your minds.

Become familiar with agencies that can be helpful: Planned Parenthood, La Leche League, etc. Consult trustworthy sources on pregnancy, abortion, childbirth, and so forth. Face the issues. For halakhic views and information some rabbis may be good to talk to. Above all, for God's sake, learn about Jewish genetic diseases. Read the chapter in this book. Take

Starting a mishpochoh (mishpahah)

"How long have you been married?"
"A little over two years."
"How many kids do you have?"
"None . . . yet."
"Oh? . . . Hmmm." (Don't even begin to think of what's going on in this head!)

Another typical exchange:

"Let's see: if it's a boy, we'll name him Christopher after my great-aunt's second husband, Hayim."
"Yeah, and if it's a girl, we'll name her Megan Fern after my father's father, Moishe, and my mother's second cousin Fayge."

The mitzvah of being fruitful and multiplying exists so the earth will be settled. And it is a great mitzvah . . . because of it, all the others exist (*Shulhan Arukh,* Even ha-Ezer 1).

מִצְוָה פְּרָיָה וּרְבִיָה – כְּדֵי שֶׁיִּהְיֶה
הָעוֹלָם מְיוּשָׁב, וְהִיא מִצְוָה גְדוֹלָה
שֶׁבִּסְבָתָה מִתְקַיְמוֹת כָּל הַמִצְווֹת
בָּעוֹלָם.

the Tay-Sachs test. There is no excuse for ignorance, especially when a child's life may be at stake.

Some pointers:

1. Choose either a good hospital (it's good because someone you know/trust says so) or a good obstetrician (same criterion); either way you'll get from one to the other—AND PUT *YOURSELVES* (yes, both of you) in his/her hands. You'll have plenty questions, so, nu . . . at physician's prices, ASK!

2. Check your medical insurance at least a year before you hope for/want the baby.

3. It's one thing to want to have "natural" or "prepared" childbirth, i.e., under the supervision of a competent doctor, nurse, or other pro, and a completely different story to have childbirth "au naturel," on the living room rug, biting a war surplus bullet, "just like the kitty cat did!" The latter is quaint, but insanity!

4. Many hospitals now have "family-centered maternity" services, where the husband and wife can be together through labor and delivery, where the father can have virtually twenty-four hour visiting privileges, and where "rooming in" (having the baby with you in the same room, usually not advised) is permitted. In these hospitals the care is good (and even better in "teaching" hospitals), and the nurses are usually outstanding.

5. In fact, nurses can frequently be more helpful than doctors, and always more helpful and useful than "Tante Shuske," either mother (in-law) or the girl next door in the hospital (who invariably has a phonograph in her room blasting out Mozart to "start my child out early with the finer things"). There are years and years of their advice ahead, most of it interesting, some useful—but only when you're able to weigh it rationally.

Note: It is interesting that very few agencies of the Jewish community take an active interest in newborns or expanding Jewish families. An occasional synagogue and an even rarer Jewish center or Jewish family service recognizes the arrival with something more than an announcement.

Traditions

Despite all modern trappings, expenses, two o'clock feedings, and complete disruption of happily married life, the birth of a child is a berakhah—blessing. Besides the two of us, the Torah says so:

"God blessed them and God said to them, 'Be fertile and increase, fill the earth and master it' " (Genesis 1:28).

וַיְבָרֶךְ אֹתָם אֱלֹהִים וַיֹּאמֶר לָהֶם פְּרוּ וּרְבוּ וּמִלְאוּ אֶת הָאָרֶץ וְכִבְשֻׁהָ.

The Talmud reinforces the obligation:

"A person must not refrain from having children, unless he already has some! Shammai's school says: At least two sons [based on the example of Moses, who left Tzipporah after the birth of his two sons]. And Hillel's school says: At least one son and one daughter, because it is written (in Genesis 5:2) 'Male and female He created them' " (Mishnah Yevamot 6).

לֹא יְבַטֵּל אָדָם מִפְּרִיָּה וּרְבִיָּה אֶלָּא אִם כֵּן יֶשׁ לוֹ בָנִים. בֵּית שַׁמַּאי אוֹמְרִים שְׁנֵי זְכָרִים וּבֵית הִלֵּל אוֹמְרִים זָכָר וּנְקֵבָה שֶׁנֶּאֱמַר זָכָר וּנְקֵבָה בְּרָאָם.

Concern in this area does not end with the number of children you have or when you have them; there are also responsibilities parents have toward their children which should be understood before entering into this virgin territory. Sure, the Ten Commandments puts an onus on the child by saying: כַּבֵּד אֶת אָבִיךָ וְאֶת אִמֶּךָ "Honor your father and your mother" (Exodus 20:12 and Deuteronomy 5:16); but the Talmud also says:

"Anyone who does not teach his son a skill or profession may be regarded as if he is teaching him to rob" (Kiddushin 29a).

כָּל שֶׁאֵינוֹ מְלַמֵּד אֶת בְּנוֹ אוּמָנוּת כְּאִלּוּ מְלַמְּדוֹ לִיסְטוּת.

Another practical obligation:

"The father is obligated to marry off his sons and daughters . . . to provide his daughter with appropriate clothes and a dowry" (*Shulhan Arukh*, Even ha-Ezer 71).

הָאָב חַיָּב לְהַשִּׂיא אֶת בָּנָיו וּבְנוֹתָיו . . .וּלְהַלְבִּישׁ אֶת בִּתּוֹ לְפִי כְּבוֹדָהּ וְלָתֵת לָהּ נְדוּנְיָא.

Prospective parents must also be prepared to take an active role in the development of their children's moral character:

"The father must rebuke his child to improve his behavior, but he should do so pleasantly and not cruelly, and he is forbidden to hit his older son" (Otzar Dinim u-Minhagim 1). (Could this be the source of the "middle child syndrome"?) And:

עַל הָאָב לְיַסֵּר אֶת בְּנוֹ כְּדֵי לְהֵטִיב דַּרְכּוֹ אֲבָל בְּדֶרֶךְ נוֹעַם וְלֹא בְּאַכְזָרִיּוּת וְאָסוּר לְהַכּוֹת אֶת בְּנוֹ הַגָּדוֹל.

"A father should be careful to keep his son from lies, and he should always keep his word to his children" (Talmud, Sukkah 46b).

יִזָּהֵר הָאָב לְהַרְחִיק אֶת בְּנוֹ מִשֶּׁקֶר וְהוּא בְּעַצְמוֹ יְקַיֵּם אֶת הַבְטָחָתוֹ לְבָנָיו.

Being a successful model and being conscious of this responsibility is an awesome responsibility.

Keeping Lilith away and other bubeh meisehs

Aside from the many beautiful rituals associated with the birth of a Jewish child, a magnificent folklore has grown up around the event. Because of the many great dangers that used to be inherent in childbirth, the newborn and the new mother had to be guarded from all evil. From these early folk practices of two thousand years ago many customs have developed, some quaint, some strange, and some that even today sound reasonable.

Lilith, the feminine evil spirit, is the natural enemy of newborns. Amulets, talismans, closed or open windows, and the lel shimmurim, the night of watching preceding a brit milah—circumcision—prevented her from causing harm to mother or child. Drawing a magic chalk circle around the labor bed, blowing the shofar in the labor room, and calling the child by a "code name" instead of his/her real name—these, too, prevented the demons from performing their tasks. Your doctor may think that all these are foolish, but you might point out that s/he carries malpractice insurance!

Jewish superstitions and folklore also had their beautiful aspects. Quite a lovely legend is told of the attainment of man's highest stage of his spiritual life, not when he is full grown, but while he is still in his mother's womb. Louis Ginzberg, ז״ל tells it in *Legends of the Bible* (Philadelphia: Jewish Publication Society, 1956), and Hayim Schauss tells it in *The Lifetime of a Jew* (New York: Union of American Hebrew Congregations, 1957) (slightly different versions: we've chosen a little from each).

In his chapter entitled "Beliefs concerning Birth," Schauss writes:

In talmudic times (the first centuries of the Common Era) the belief was current among Jews that man's soul was independent of his body, existing eternally in the past and in the future. Only for a short, limited time is it placed in the body of a certain human being. All the souls of the world

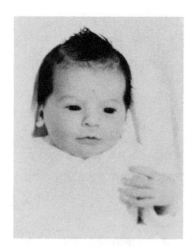

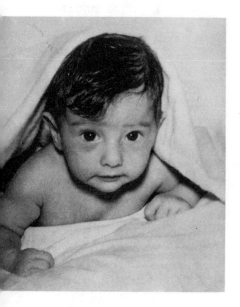

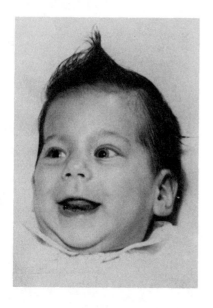

preexist in heaven in a kind of a spiritual reservoir and at first have no desire to enter the human bodies on earth. They do it only by force. God decrees that a certain soul shall enter a certain body, and God also decrees the moment when the soul shall leave the body.

In this realm of belief, the vanishing mortal body plays an insignificant role in comparison with the pure and eternal soul. Accordingly, man attains the highest stage in his spiritual life not after the full growth of his body, but before he is projected in the form of a human being into the light of the world. (In his prenatal existence in his mother's womb, a light burns over his head, and he sees from one end of the world to the other. He sees there much more than a human being is capable of seeing during the course of his entire life.)

According to this belief, a special angel is appointed to supervise the souls. He receives an order from God to place a certain soul in a certain child at the time of its conception. At first the pure soul recoils from entering the foul body. It yields only to the force of God's decree. The angel brings the soul into the womb and joins it with the embryo.

In his chapter entitled "Adam," Ginzberg continues the legend:

Two angels are detailed to watch that she shall not leave it, nor drop out of it, and a light is set above her, whereby the soul can see from one end of the world to the other. In the morning an angel carries her to paradise, and shows her the righteous, who sit there in their glory, with crowns upon their heads. The angel then says to the soul: "Dost thou know who these are?" She replies in the negative, and the angel goes on: "These whom thou beholdest here were formed, like thee, in the womb of their mother. When they came into the world, they observed God's Torah and His commandments. Therefore they became the partakers of His bliss, which thou seest them enjoy. Know also thou wilt one day depart from the world below, and if thou wilt observe God's Torah, then wilt thou be found worthy of sitting with these pious ones. But if not, thou wilt be doomed to the other place."

In the evening, the angel takes the soul to hell, and there points out the sinners whom the angels of destruction are smiting with fiery scourges, the sinners all the while crying out Woe! Woe! but no mercy is shown unto them. The angel then questions the soul as before: "Dost thou know who these are?" and as before the reply is negative. The angel continues: "These who are consumed with fire were created like unto thee. When they were put into the world, they did not observe God's Torah and His commandments. Therefore have they come to this disgrace which thou seest them suffer. Know thy destiny is also to depart from the world. Be just, therefore, and not wicked, that thou mayest gain the future world."

Between morning and evening the angel carries the soul around and shows her where she will live and where she will die, and the place where she will be buried, and he takes her through the whole world, and points out the just and the sinners and all things. In the evening, he replaces her in the womb of the mother, and there she remains for nine months.

When the time arrives for her to emerge from the womb into the open world, the same angel addresses the soul: "The time has come for thee to go abroad into the open world." The soul demurs: "Why dost thou want to make me go forth into the open world?" The angel replies: "Know that as thou wert formed against thy will, so now thou wilt be born against thy will, and against thy will thou shalt give account of thyself before the King of kings, the Holy One, blessed be He." But the soul is reluctant to leave her place. Then the angel fillips the babe on the nose, extinguishes the light at his head, and brings him forth into the world against his will. Immediately the child forgets all his soul has seen and learnt, and he comes into the world crying, for he loses a place of shelter and security and rest.

There are other customs, legends, and folklore that surround birth. We will list a few of the ones we know about. We will not, however, try to explain their rationale, since much of the logic behind them is unknown and many of the customs were simply borrowed from other cultures:

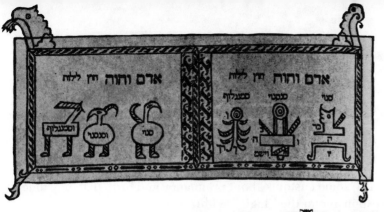

1. Yemenites hang a hamsikah—amulet—in the shape of outstreched palms over the crib to protect the mother and infant. Mae Rockland's instructions for making your own hamsikah can be found in "Folk Art." East European Jews had an amulet called a kimpetzetel ("a note for a child's bed"). This amulet petitioned for protection from the child-stealing demoness Lilith. It would often contain Psalm 121 because of verse 6: "By day the sun will not strike you,/Nor the moon by night." (For an interesting history of this amulet's origin, see Theodor Gaster, *Customs and Folkways of Jewish Life* [New York: William Sloan, 1955].)

2. Yemenites also used to hide sweets under the bed so that evil spirits would be occupied eating them.

3. The mother would pray at the graves of her family or of pious people to ensure a safe delivery.

4. To ensure an easy delivery, all ties and knots in the woman's clothes would be undone and the doors (and/or windows) of the house would be opened.

5. Sometimes if the labor was a difficult one, the circumference of the cemetery walls would be measured and a number of candles would be donated to the synagogue according to their length.

6. Garlic was frequently hung in the baby's room (to deodorize the diapers and protect the infant).

7. One final interesting custom. To ensure an easy pregnancy, a string was measured seven times around the grave of a renowned rabbi and then bound around the stomach of a pregnant woman. (Presumably thereafter she maintained strong ties with the pious one—or at least with the string!)

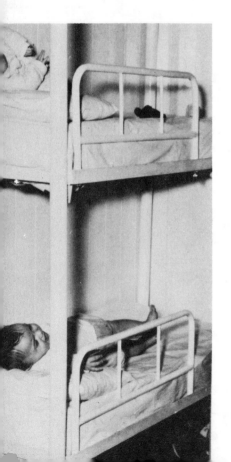

זבני ישראל פרו וישרצו

AND THE CHILDREN OF ISRAEL MULTIPLIED AND GREW IN NUMBER...

Rabbi and Mrs. Richard Israel joyfully announce the birth of a son David Noam - February 25

There are also some customs about pregnancy and birth that may touch chords more responsive to the "logic" within us:

1. There is a *very* strong custom not to purchase or acquire clothes, furniture, toys, equipment, etc. for a new child before it is born. The logic behind this is one based on concern for the sensitivities of a couple who might lose their baby and should not have to confront the tangible evidence of their happy expectations.

2. It is regarded as frivolous to respond seriously to the question, "Do you want a girl or boy?" The traditional answer is simply, "A healthy child."

Mikveh after birth: a problematic halakhah

It is written in Leviticus 12:1-5:

The Lord spoke to Moses, saying: Speak to the Israelite people thus: When a woman at childbirth bears a male, she shall be unclean seven days; she shall be unclean as at the time of her menstrual infirmity. On the eighth day the flesh of his foreskin shall be circumcised. She shall remain in a state of blood purification for thirty-three days: she shall not touch any consecrated thing, nor enter the sanctuary until her period of purification is completed. If she bears a female, she shall be unclean two weeks as during her menstruation, and she shall remain in a state of blood purification for sixty-six days.

Since the destruction of the Temple, the longer waiting periods required for blood purification are no longer observed (although a few still do observe this custom). What we are left with from this passage then are two facts:

1. After bearing a male child, a mother must count seven days of "impurity" and then seven additional "clean" days. Then she should go to the mikveh.

2. After bearing a female child, a mother must count fourteen days of "impurity" and then again seven additional "clean" days. Then she should go to the mikveh.

The inevitable question arises: Is a woman punished for bearing a girl child by having to wait longer before going to the mikveh?

The next question ought to be (but too often isn't): What was the nature of the society to which the Torah directed itself?

I offer no solutions or explanations. I refer this whole discussion to Rachel Adler's chapter in *Catalog 1 (The Jewish Catalog*, Philadelphia: Jewish Publication Society, 1973) titled "Tumah and Taharah—Mikveh" (especially page 171). Rachel has a very beautiful, very moving explanation of this ritual, which will go far in helping us to reconcile what cannot be ignored as preferential treatment given for boys with our own concerns for tradition and with our own contemporary sensitivities. I urge everyone to read it.

Names

There are two conflicting customs about choosing an appropriate name for a baby. The Ashkenazic custom is to name a child in memory of someone who has died—thus creating a continuous community by perpetuating the names of all who have been members. The Sephardic custom is to name a new child in honor of a living relative.

In certain Ashkenazic families, people have gone to great lengths to find some relative with a name that bears some resemblance to a preferred "modern" name. While there is no "right way" for choosing a name—no halakhah about it—there is a certain amount of common sense that should enter the decision. Certain names have clear non-Jewish associations and perhaps ought to be avoided (e.g., Christopher, Luke, Sean, Jan, etc.—no offense intended). Other Hebrew names could be undesirable because of the nature of the personalities who originally bore them—Job, Ishmael, Esau, Cain, etc.

The practice of giving two sets of names, one civil (English) and one Jewish (Hebrew or Yiddish), began in European communities around the thirteenth century. Frequently the lack of ingenuity in converting one name to another language or in converting a female name to a male one and vice versa created some rather strange combinations.

In fact, however, there are no real stipulations in tradition, although customarily there are three sources for the names of a newborn:

1. The expression of an idea—e.g., Devorah means bee, Yonah means dove, etc.—or celebration of an event—e.g., Sinaya after the Six-Day War; Amihayim during the Yom Kippur War; Esther or Mordecai during the Purim season. The origin of this custom is biblical: "So she named him Joseph, which is to say, 'May the Lord add another son for me'" (Genesis 30:24).

2. The preservation of the memory or the name of a family ancestor, as mentioned. The origin of this custom is Semitic, dating from around the fifth or fourth century B.C.E., and it spread through Jewish communities from Elephantine to Palestine.

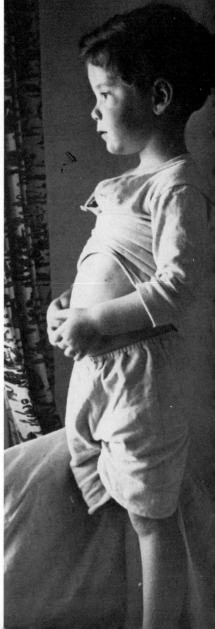

3. Traditional names or combinations of common contemporary names with true Hebrew/Yiddish equivalents.

Despite the fact that there are no laws concerning names, this area can be of the greatest concern to people, who besiege their rabbi with questions. All the hysteria is unnecessary. It is important to know your own Hebrew names, as this will be used in the ketubbah—marriage contract—as well as when you are called up to the Torah and like occasions. There is a custom to help you to remember your name. After the daily Amidah some prayer books have lists of Hebrew names, which are followed by a biblical verse whose first and last letter (in Hebrew) is the same as the first and last letter of the Hebrew name. So *David* is remembered by *Dirshu . . . tamid* (Psalms 105:4). The custom is to recite this daily so you won't forget your name.

You should also know your father's name, since in the above-mentioned circumstances you are known as, say, Moshe ben (son of) Shlomo rather than Moshe Nulman. Some people have begun to use their mother's name also, e.g., Moshe ben Shlomo ve-Rahel (and Rachel). Besides the honor due your mother, it is important traditionally to know your mother's name for certain ritual occasions, especially for a mi-she-berakh—general prayer for blessing (often a prayer for health), where it is customary to use the mother's name—e.g., Moshe ben Rahel.

All of the above holds true for a woman, and she would be called Hadassah bat (daughter of) Hillel if, for example, she were to receive an aliyah.

Traditionally it is also important to know whether you are a kohen (a member of the priestly tribe), levi (a Levite was a Temple functionary), or a yisrael (all other Jews). This appellation is added to the end of your name—e.g., David ben Hillel ha-kohen or ha-levi (in the case of a yisrael, the title is assumed and not mentioned): David son of Hillel "the priest" or "the Levite."

The following is a list of possible Hebrew names and their English equivalents. It is taken from the rabbi's guide of the Orthodox movement.

You might also check Alfred J. Kolatch's *The Name Dictionary: Modern English and Hebrew Names* (New York: Jonathan David, 1967). It's quite good.

Boys

א

Abba	אבא
Avigdor	אביגדור
Abiezer	אביעזר
Abishalom	אבישלום
Abraham	אבלי, ראה אברהם
Abraham	אברהם
Abram	אברם
Abraham	אברמקא, ראה אברהם
Absalom	אבשלום
Ada	אדא
Ahubiah	אהוביה
Aaron	אהרן
Uri	אורי
Oshiah	אושיעה
Judah	אידל, ראה יהודה
Isaac	איזה (יצחק המכונה איזה)
Isaac	איטשע, ראה יצחק
Isaac	אייזמן (יצחק המכונה אייזמן)
Isaac	אייזיק (יצחק המכונה אייזיק)
Israel	איסר (ישראל המכונה איסר)
Israel	איסרל, ראה איסר
Isaac	איצל, ראה אצל
Isaac	איצק, ראה יצחק
Ithamar	איתמר
Elhanan	אלחנן
Alter	אלטער
Elijah	אליה
Elijah	אליהו
Elimelech	אלימלך
Eliezer	אליעזר
Eliakim	אליקים
Alexander	אלכסנדר
Elazar	אלעזר
Elkanah	אלקנה
Asher	אנשיל (אשר המכונה אנשיל)
Isaac	אצל (יצחק המכונה אצל)

Aaron	ארון, ראה אהרן
Arieh	אריה
Asher	אשר

ב

Buna	בונא
Jehiel	בונין (יחיאל המכונה בונין)
Benjamin	בונש (בנימין המכונה בונש)
Avigdor	ביגדור, ראה אביגדור
Beinush	בינוש
Ben Zion	בן ציון
Benjamin	בנימין
Baruch	בענדיט (ברוך המכונה בענדיט)
Dov-ber	בער (דוב המכונה בער)
Isaac	בערא (יצחק המכונה בערא)
Dov-ber	בעריל, ראה בער
Dov-ber	בערע, ראה בער
Bezalel	בצלאל
Baruch	ברוך

ג

גאטליב (ידידיה המכונה גאטליב)	Jedidiah
גבריאל	Gabriel
גד	Gad
גדיל (גד המכונה גדיל)	Gad
גדליה	Gedaliah
גדליהו	Gedaliah
גוטליב (אהוביה המכונה גוטליב)	Ahubiah
גוטמן (טוביה המכונה גוטמן)	Tobiah
גוטקינד (טוביה המכונה גוטקינד)	Tobiah
גומפיל, ראה גימפל	Mordecai
גימפל (מרדכי המכונה גימפל)	Mordecai
געדיל (גד המכונה געדיל)	Gad
געץ (אליקים המכונה געץ)	Eliakim
געצל, ראה געץ	Eliakim
גרונם (שמואל המכונה גרונם)	Samuel
גרוסמן (גדליה המכונה גרוסמן)	Gedaliah
גרשם	Gershom
גרשן	Gershon

ד

דוב	Dov
דוב בער	Dov-Ber
דוד	David
דן	Dan
דניאל	Daniel

ה

האשקא (יהושע המכונה האשקא)	Joshua
הונא	Huna
הושיל, ראה העשיל	Joshua
הושמן (יהושע המכונה הושמן)	Joshua
הושע	Hosea
הושקא, ראה האשקא	Joshua
הילל	Hillel
הילמן (שמואל המכונה הילמן)	Samuel
הירץ (נפתלי המכונה הירץ)	Naphthali
הירש צבי או נפתלי (המכונה הירש)	Zevi or Naphthali
הירשל, ראה הירש	Zevi or Naphthali
הנדיל (מנוח המכונה הנדיל)	Manoah
הענדיל, ראה הנדיל	Manoah
הענוך (חנוך המכונה הענוך)	Enoch
הענעך, ראה הענוך	Enoch
הערמאלן (אהרן המכונה הערמלן)	Aaron
הערץ (נפתלי המכונה הערץ)	Naphthali
הערצקא (נפתלי המכונה הערצקא)	Naphthali
הערש, ראה הירש	Zevi or Naphthali
העשיל (יהושע המכונה העשיל)	Joshua
העשל, ראה העשיל	Joshua

ו

וואלף זאב או בנימין (המכונה וואלף)	Zev-Wolf
ווייבר (אליקים המכונה ווייבר)	Eliakim

ז

זאב	Zev
זאוול, ראה זבל	Zavl
זאלקין (יצחק המכונה זאלקין)	Isaac
זאלקינד (שלמה המכונה זאלקינד)	Solomon
זבולון	Zebulun
זבל	Zavl
זונדל (חנוך המכונה זונדל)	Enoch
זוסא (אליעזר, אלכסנדר, יהושע, יואל, יקותיאל, ישראל, משלם, עזריה או שניאור המכונה זוסא)	Zussa
זוסל	Zussle
זוסלין (יצחק המכונה זוסלין)	Isaac
זוסמן (אליעזר, יואל, משלם, עמנואל או עזריאל המכונה זוסמן)	Zussman
זימל	Ziml
זימלין (שניאור המכונה זימלין)	Shneiur
זיסא	Zissa
זיסל	Zissl
זיסקינד (שניאור המכונה זיסקינד)	Shneiur
זכאי	Zakkai
זכריה	Zechariah
זלא (שלמה המכונה זלא)	Shneiur
זלמן (לרוב שניאור המכונה זלמן)	Shneiur
זנוויל (נתן או שמואל המכונה זנוויל)	Nathan or Samuel
זעליג	Zelig
זעליקמן (חזקיה המכונה זעליקמן)	Hezekiah
זעמל (משלם המכונה זעמל)	Meshulam
זרח	Zarah

ח

חביה, ראה רחביה	Rehabiah
חזקאל, ראה יחזקאל	Ezekiel
חזקיה	Hezekiah
חיאל, ראה יחיאל	Jehiel
חייא	Hiyya
חיים	Hayyim
חמיה, ראה נחמיה	Nehemiah
חנא, ראה חנן	Hanan
חנוך	Enoch
חנן	Hanan
חננאל	Hananel
חניה	Hananiah
חניהו	Hananiah
חצקאל, ראה יחזקאל	Ezekiel

ט

טביה, ראה טוביה	Tobiah
טוביה	Tobiah
טודרוס (מנחם המכונה טודרוס)	Menahem
טרייטל (יהודה המכונה טרייטל)	Judah

י

יאנטל, ראה יום טוב	Yom Tob
יאנקל, ראה יעקב	Jacob
יאסל, ראה יוסף	Joseph
ידידיה	Jedidiah
יהואש	Jehoash
יהודה	Judah
יהונתן	Jonathan
יהושע	Joshua
יואל	Joel
יואש	Joash
יודה, ראה יהודה	Judah
יודל (יהודה המכונה יודל)	Judah
יוחנן	Johanan
יוזל, ראה יהושע, יוסף	Joshua or Joseph
יופל, ראה יוסף	Joseph
יום טוב	Yom Tob
יונה	Jonah
יונתן	Jonathan
יוסל, ראה יוסף	Joseph
יחזקאל	Ezekiel
יחיאל	Jehiel
יידל (יהודה המכונה יידל)	Judah
יעקב	Jacob
יעקל (יעקב המכונה יעקל)	Jacob
יצחק	Isaac
יקותיאל	Jekuthiel
יקיר	Jakkir
ירוחם	Jeruham
ירחמיאל	Jerahmiel
ירמיה	Jeremiah
יששכר	Issachar
ישמעאל	Ishmael
ישעיה	Isaiah
ישראל	Israel
יששכר	Issachar

כ

כהנא	Kahana
כלב	Caleb
כרמי (משה המכונה כרמי)	Moses
כתריאל	Kathriel

ל

לזר (אלעזר או אליעזר המכונה לזר)	Elazar or Eliezer
לוי	Levi
ליב	Leib
ליב (יהודה המכונה ליב)	Judah

  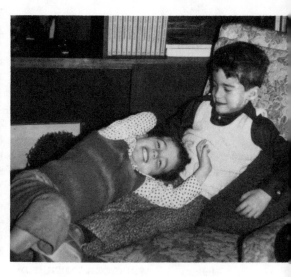

Left column	**Middle column**	**Right column**

Judah — ליבא (יהודה המכונה ליבא)
Eliezer *or* — ליברמן (אליעזר או
Judah — יהודה המכונה ליברמן)
Elazar *or* — ליזר (אלעזר או אליעזר
Eliezer — המכונה ליזר)
Uri, Eliezer, — ליפמן (אורי, אליעזר,
or — או יום טוב המכונה
Yom Tob — ליפמן)
Lippa — ליפע
Lemml — לעמל
Lappidoth — לפידות

מ

Mordecai — מאטע (מרדכי המכונה מאטע)
Meir — מאיר
Menahem — מאן (מנחם המכונה מאן)
Menahem — מאניש, מאניש (מנחם המכונה מאניש)
Mordecai — מונא (מרדכי המכונה מונא)
Mordecai — מונין (מרדכי המכונה מונין)
Mordecai — מייזול (מרדכי המכונה מייזול)
Michael — מיכאל
Micah — מיכה
Michael — מיכל, ראה מיכאל
Melech — מלך
Menahem — מן (מנחם דמתקרי מן)
Manoah — מנוח
Menahem — מנחם
Mannie — מני
Menahem — מניס (מנחם המכונה מניס)
Manasseh — מנשה
Menahem — מענדל (מנחם המכונה מענדל)
Mordecai — מרדכי
Moses — משה
Meshulam — משלם
Mattathias — מתתיה
Mattathias — מתתיהו

נ

Nathan — נאטע, ראה נתן
Noah — נח
Nahum — נחום
Nehemiah — נחמיה
Nahaman — נחמן
Nathan — נטע, ראה נתן
Nissim — ניסים
Nissan — ניסן
Naphtali — נפתלי
Nathan — נתן
Nethanel — נתנאל

ס

Sinai — סיני
Sander — סנדר
Sonderman — סנדרמאן
Saadiah — סעדיה
Sander — סענדר
Sanderman — סענדרמאן

ע

Obadiah — עבדיה
Abraham — עבריל (אברהם המכונה עבריל)
Abraham — עברמן (אברהם המכונה עברמן)
Obadiah — עובדיה
Ozer — עוזר
Uzziel — עזיאל
Ezra — עזרא
Azriel — עזריאל
Azariah — עזריה
Amiel — עמיאל
Amihud — עמיהוד
Aminadab — עמינדב
Emanuel — עמנואל
Amram — עמרם
Akiba — עקיבא
Akiba — עקיבה

פ

Fybush — פייבש
Fyvish — פייוויש
Fytl — פייטל
Phinehas — פינחס
Pinie — פיניע
Fishl — פישל
Fishka — פישקע
Palti — פלטי
Paltiel — פלטיאל
Pesah — פסח
Perez — פרץ
Pethahiah — פתחיה

צ

Zevi — צבי
Zadok — צדוק
Bezalel — צלאל, ראה בצלאל
Zemmah — צמח

ק

Jacob — קאפל (יעקב המכונה קאפל)
Karpl — קארפל
Kehath — קהת
Jekuthiel — קויפמן (יקותיאל או משלם המכונה קויפמן)
Koppilman — קויפילמן
Jekuthiel — קוסא (יקותיאל המכונה קוסא)
Jekuthiel — קושא (יקותיאל המכונה קושא)
Jekuthiel — קותיאל, ראה יקותיאל
Akiba — קיבא, ראה עקיבא
Kolonymus — קלונימוס
Kolonymus — קלמן (קלונימוס המכונה קלמן)
Moses — קעציל (משה המכונה קעציל)
Nathan — קרפיל (נתן המכונה קרפיל)

ר

Reuben — ראובן
Raphael — רפאל

<table>
<tr><td>ש</td><td></td><td>Shalom</td><td>שלום</td><td>Shemariah</td><td>שמריה</td></tr>
<tr><td>Saul</td><td>שאול</td><td>Meshullam</td><td>שלם (משלם דמתקרי שלם)</td><td>Samson</td><td>שמשון</td></tr>
<tr><td>Shevah</td><td>שבח</td><td>Solomon</td><td>שלמה</td><td>Isaiah</td><td>שעיה, ראה ישעיה</td></tr>
<tr><td>Sabbatai</td><td>שבתי</td><td>Shammai</td><td>שמאי</td><td>Sabbatai</td><td>שעפטיל (שבתי המכונה שעפטיל)</td></tr>
<tr><td>Saul</td><td>שואל, ראה שאול</td><td>Samuel</td><td>שמואל</td><td></td><td></td></tr>
<tr><td>Shahor</td><td>שחור</td><td>Simcha</td><td>שמחה</td><td>Sabbatai</td><td>שעפסיל (שבתי המכונה שעפסיל)</td></tr>
<tr><td>Joshua</td><td>שיע, ראה יהושע</td><td>Shemariah</td><td>שמערל, ראה שמריה</td><td></td><td></td></tr>
<tr><td>Joshua</td><td>שיקע, ראה יהושע</td><td>Simeon</td><td>שמעון</td><td>Shraga</td><td>שרגא</td></tr>
<tr><td>Schachna</td><td>שכנא</td><td>Shemaiah</td><td>שמעיה</td><td>ת</td><td></td></tr>
<tr><td>Issachar</td><td>שכר, ראה יששכר</td><td>Shneiur</td><td>שניאור</td><td>Tanhum</td><td>תנחום</td></tr>
</table>

Girls

<table>
<tr><td>א</td><td></td><td>ג</td><td></td><td>ה</td><td></td></tr>
<tr><td>Abigail</td><td>אביגיל</td><td>Golda</td><td>גאָלדא</td><td>Hoda</td><td>האָדא</td></tr>
<tr><td>Eidl</td><td>אידל</td><td>Gutta</td><td>גוטא</td><td>Hodl</td><td>האָדל</td></tr>
<tr><td>Eidla</td><td>אידלע</td><td>Gutl</td><td>גוטל</td><td>Hagar</td><td>הגר</td></tr>
<tr><td>Itta</td><td>איטא</td><td>Gitta</td><td>גיטא</td><td>Hodes</td><td>האָדס</td></tr>
<tr><td>Alte</td><td>אלטע</td><td>Gittl</td><td>גיטל</td><td>Hadassah</td><td>הדסא</td></tr>
<tr><td>Asnah</td><td>אסנה</td><td>Geilah</td><td>גילה</td><td>Hinda</td><td>הינדא</td></tr>
<tr><td>Asenath</td><td>אסנת</td><td>Ginendl</td><td>גינענדל</td><td>Hindl</td><td>הינדל</td></tr>
<tr><td>Esther</td><td>אסתר</td><td>Glicka</td><td>גליקא</td><td>Hena</td><td>הענא</td></tr>
<tr><td>ב</td><td></td><td>Ginendl</td><td>גענדיל</td><td>Hendl</td><td>הענדל</td></tr>
<tr><td>Bithiah</td><td>באסיע, ראה בתיה</td><td>Gnessia</td><td>גנעסיא</td><td></td><td></td></tr>
<tr><td>Bithiah</td><td>באָשע, ראה בתיה</td><td>Gella</td><td>געלא</td><td>ו</td><td></td></tr>
<tr><td>Buna</td><td>בונא</td><td>Gruna</td><td>גרונא</td><td>Vichna</td><td>וויכנא</td></tr>
<tr><td>Bunia</td><td>בוניא</td><td>ד</td><td></td><td>ז</td><td></td></tr>
<tr><td>Beila</td><td>בילא</td><td></td><td></td><td></td><td></td></tr>
<tr><td>Beilka</td><td>בילקא</td><td>Doba</td><td>דאָבא</td><td>Zussa</td><td>זוסא</td></tr>
<tr><td>Bluma</td><td>בלומא</td><td>Dabrush</td><td>דאברוש</td><td>Zissl</td><td>זיסל</td></tr>
<tr><td>Blimela</td><td>בלימלא</td><td>Dabrusha</td><td>דאברושא</td><td>Zissla</td><td>זיסלא</td></tr>
<tr><td>Broyna</td><td>ברוינא</td><td>Deborah</td><td>דבורה</td><td>Zlatta</td><td>זלטא</td></tr>
<tr><td>Breina</td><td>ברײנא</td><td>Deborah</td><td>דוואָסא (דבורה המכונה דוואסא)</td><td>Zilpah</td><td>זלפה</td></tr>
<tr><td>Breindl</td><td>ברײנדל</td><td></td><td></td><td>Zelda</td><td>זעלדא</td></tr>
<tr><td>Berochah</td><td>ברכה</td><td>Deborah</td><td>דוואָשא (דבורה המכונה דוואשא)</td><td>Selma</td><td>זעלמא</td></tr>
<tr><td>Bath-Sheba</td><td>בשא (בת שבע המכונה בשא)</td><td>Dinah</td><td>דינה</td><td>ח</td><td></td></tr>
<tr><td>Bithiah</td><td>בתיא</td><td>Dreiza</td><td>דרײזא</td><td>Hassia</td><td>חאסיא</td></tr>
<tr><td>Bath-Sheba</td><td>בת שבע</td><td>Dreizl</td><td>דרעזיל</td><td>Hasha</td><td>חאשא</td></tr>
</table>

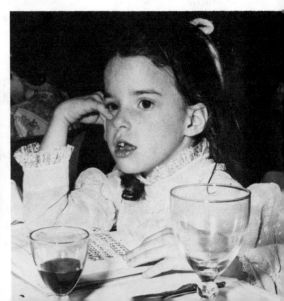

Eva	חוה
Hvolas	חוואלס
Hvolash	חוואלש
Hayyah	חיה
Hena	חיענא
Hannah	חנה
Hasidah	חסידה

ט

Toltza	טאלצא
Tamara	טאמאַרא
Tana	טאנא
Toyba	טויבא
Tila	טילא
Toltza	טלצא
Temma	טעמא
Troyla	טרוילא
Treina	טרינא
Charna	טשאַרנא
Cherna	טשערנא

י

Jochebed	יאכא (יוכבד המכונה יאכא)
Jochebed	יאכלו (יוכבד המכונה יאכלו)
Jochebed	יאָכא (יוכבד המכונה יאכא)
Jochebed	יאכנא (יוכבד המכונה יאכנא)
Judith	יהודית
Judith	יוטא
Jochebed	יוטלין (יוכבד המכונה יוטלין)
Jochebed	יוכבד
Yetta	יטא
Yenta	ינטא
Yenta	יענטא

ל

Leah	לאה
Loytza	לויצא
Libba	ליבא
Libka	ליבקא
Lipka	ליפקא

מ

Mattl	מאַטל
Mattla	מאַטלא
Mariasha	מאַריאשא
Mahlah	מחלה
Michlah	מיכלה
Milcah	מילכה
Minna	מינא
Mindl	מינדל

Minka	מינקא
Mirra	מירא
Mirl	מירל
Malkah	מלכה
Menuhah	מנוחה
Mary	מערע
Margolith	מרגלית
Miriam	מרים

נ

Nuhah	נוחה
Nehamah	נחמה
Nehamah	נעכא (נחמה המכונה נעכא)
Nehamah	נעכול (נחמה המכונה נעכול)
Nehamah	נעכלא (נחמה המכונה נעכלא)
Naomi	נעמי

ס

Sossia	סאַסיא
Simma	סימא
Slava	סלאַווא
Slova	סלאַווא

ע

Etta	עטא
Ethel	עטל
Achsah	עכסה
Ella	עלא
Elka	עלקא

פ

Foygl	פויגל
Feigu	פיגו
Feiga	פייגא
Peya	פייע
Pessa	פעסע
Pessia	פעסיע
Pessl	פעסל
Perl	פעריל
Pesha	פעשא
Fradl	פראַדל
Fruma	פרומא
Fridl	פרידל
Freida	פריידא
Freidl	פריידל

צ

Tzartl	צאַרטיל
Tzartl	צאַרטל

Tziviah	צביה
Tzinna	צינא
Tzippa	ציפא
Tzirl	צירל
Zipporah	צפורה

ק

Keila	קילא
Clara	קלאַרא
Kendl	קענדל
Kroyna	קרוינא
Kreindl	קרינדל

ר

Rhoda	ראדא
Ralla	ראלא
Rashl	ראשל
Rebecca	רבקה
Rosa	רויזא
Ruth	רות
Rachel	רחל
Ruhamah	רחמה
Rebecca	ריבה, ראה רבקה
Reizl	ריזל
Rycha	רייכא
Rychl	רייכל
Ryna	ריינא
Rytza	רייצא
Rytzl	רייצל
Rissa	ריסא
Rickl	ריקל
Rickla	ריקלא
Rella	רעלא
Reshka	רשקא

ש

Sheba	שבע
Shulamith	שולמית
Sheina	שינא
Sheindl	שינדל
Shelomith	שלומית
Simhah	שמחה
Shiphrah	שפרה
Shprintza	שפרינצא
Shprintzl	שפרינצל
Sarah	שרה

ת

Tamar	תמר
Tirzah	תרצה

Synagogue naming ceremony

Today, when both girl and boy babies are frequently introduced to the covenant with brit ceremonies, we either have to discard the old custom of a shul naming or renew it. While it was true that only girls were named in this way, there is no reason why both girls and boys couldn't be named again after the brit in front of the entire synagogue community. The following prayer-blessing is used for this occasion:

FOR A GIRL CHILD
(mother's and father's name)

מִי שֶׁבֵּרַךְ אֲבוֹתֵינוּ אַבְרָהָם יִצְחָק וְיַעֲקֹב הוּא יְבָרֵךְ אֶת
(*for both parents* בְּתָּם) וְאֶת בִּתּוֹ (*mother's and/or father's name*)
הַנּוֹלְדָה לוֹ (לָהֶם *for both parents*) וְיִקָּרֵא שְׁמָהּ בְּיִשְׂרָאֵל
(*child's name*) אָנָּא בָּרֵךְ אֶת אָבִיהָ וְאֶת אִמָּהּ וְיִזְכּוּ לְגַדְּלָהּ
לְיִרְאָתֶךָ – לְתוֹרָה לְחֻפָּה וּלְמַעֲשִׂים טוֹבִים וְנֹאמַר אָמֵן.

"May He who blessed our fathers Abraham, Isaac, and Jacob bless (parent[s]) and his/her/their daughter/son born to him/her/them. May his/her name be known in Israel as——; guard and protect his/her father and mother and may they live to rear him/her in the fear of God, study of the Torah, for the wedding canopy, and for a life of good deeds. And let us say Amen."

FOR A BOY CHILD
(mother and/or father's name)

מִי שֶׁבֵּרַךְ אֲבוֹתֵינוּ אַבְרָהָם יִצְחָק וְיַעֲקֹב הוּא יְבָרֵךְ אֶת
(*for both parents* בְּנָם) וְאֶת בְּנוֹ (*mother and/or father's name*)
הַנּוֹלָד לוֹ (לָהֶם *for both parents*) וְיִקָּרֵא שְׁמוֹ בְּיִשְׂרָאֵל
(*child's name*) אָנָּא בָּרֵךְ אֶת אָבִיו וְאֶת אִמּוֹ וְיִזְכּוּ לְגַדְּלוֹ
לְיִרְאָתֶךָ – לְתוֹרָה לְחֻפָּה וּלְמַעֲשִׂים טוֹבִים וְנֹאמַר אָמֵן.

Brit ceremonies

Introduction

In general, a brit refers to a covenant—a pledge of obligation between two parties which is sometimes accompanied by a token signifying the brit. Historically there have been three signs that point out the three major covenants between God and people.

The first is Shabbat, which was given to serve as a sign of creation: "The Israelite people shall keep the Sabbath, observing the Sabbath throughout the ages as a covenant for all time: it shall be a sign for all time between Me and the people of Israel" (Exodus 31:16-17).

The second is the rainbow, which was given to symbolize the renewal of mankind after the Noah flood: "God further said, 'This is the sign that I set for the covenant between Me and you, and every living creature with you, for all ages to come. I have set My bow in the clouds, and it shall serve as a sign of the covenant between Me and the earth. When I bring clouds over the earth, and the bow appears in the clouds, I will remember My covenant between Me and you and every living creature among all flesh, so that the waters shall never again become a flood to destroy all flesh'" (Genesis 9:12-15).

And the last is the circumcision brit, which was established as the sign signifying the beginning of the Hebrew nation: "Such shall be the covenant between Me and you and your offspring to follow which you shall keep: every male among you shall be circumcised. You shall circumcise the flesh of your foreskin, and that shall be the sign of the covenant between Me and you" (Genesis 17:10-11).

Circumcision came to be regarded as the unique sign of our covenant and gradually emerged as a physical symbol of a child's joining the community of Israel.

Brit milah for boys

Apologists claim the brit milah has African tribal origins or real health values; some relate it to blood rituals, castration acts, or initiation rites. Whatever these roots, Judaism has transformed the brit milah into one of the most significant experiences in the life of a family—profoundly moving for the new father and mother, other children, relatives, and friends.

The "ceremony" can either be performed perfunctorily in a hospital room or doctor's office by a physician or in an elaborate home or synagogue setting full of moving symbols, sounds, gestures, emotions—surrounded by community. While obstetricians routinely perform "circs," few bring to the operation any religious significance. Brit milah—that first introduction of a child into his community—must be done by a mohel—ritual circumciser (i.e., any person who is trained in the physical operative procedures as well as Jewish ritual). A good mohel will be:

1. clean;

2. trained (some communities sponsor training courses with local boards of rabbis and hospitals);

3. concerned for the parents (the mother, especially; we found that the brit was an even more trying time for Patty than for me, and our wonderful mohel, Rabbi Arnold Wieder, had obviously anticipated this and was adept at calming both of us);

4. willing to visit the child to examine him and explain the procedure to the parents at least once before the event;

5. thorough (he will return at least once afterward to check his handiwork on the baby and answer questions; and

6. entertaining: your guests should be able to follow what he is doing, and he should be a real "master of the ceremony."

By the way, traditionally one doesn't hire the mohel, but simply asks him to act as the father's shaliah—representative—in performing the mitzvah of milah. In reality the mohel usually has a set fee scale.

THE EVENT

The brit milah is always held during the eighth day after the child is born—frequently in the morning—even if the eighth day occurs on a Shabbat or holiday. Remember, however, that the Jewish day begins in the evening of "the day before" rather than at midnight (see the chapter in *Catalog 1* on "The Calendar" for a full explanation). So if the child is born, let us say, on Monday night, his brit will be a week later on Tuesday. If the child is born during the day, the same day the next week is the day the brit takes place (i.e., if he is born Monday afternoon, the brit takes place the following Monday).

SOME LAWS AND CUSTOMS

1. While it is customary for the father to be the "agent" for the brit, there is no reason the mother should not participate equally. We take this as a given. Unfortunately, some mohalim will not accept this easily. Nearly all, if not all, mohalim are Orthodox, since the Conservative, etc. movements have failed to train their own mohalim. Many mohalim will allow the mother in the room (traditionally she is in another room). This major stride was made when mohalim realized there was little reason to fear that the mother would faint (it's usually the father who faints—for good Freudian reasons), and some mohalim will even allow the mother to read things she has prepared on her own. However, many object to the mother saying the blessings with the father at the brit. Leaving aside the general nonliberation of mohalim, this attitude is based on the fact that halakhically the

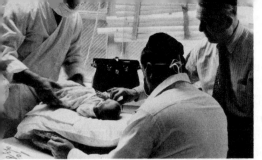
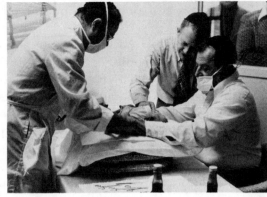
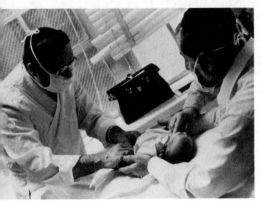

responsibility to circumcise the child belongs to the father, who delegates the mohel to act for him. The mother does not have, and so cannot delegate, the authority and therefore has "no right" to say the blessings.

You can try pointing out to the mohel that your saying the blessing is unrelated to your husband's delegating the authority to him. At worst, you are uttering God's name in vain ("a wasted blessing"), which is *your* responsibility not his. Even if he agrees, this might not satisfy you totally, since it is extremely unlikely that he will allow *you* and your husband to delegate to him the authority to circumcise. But this is the best that can be expected. Shoshana and Mel Silberman of Philadelphia spoke with a number of mohalim until they got one to agree even to the simultaneous blessings.

2. There is a custom to make a feast of fruits and beverages on the Erev Shabbat before the day that the brit takes place. This is seen as a feast held in honor of performing a mitzvah (see Yoreh Deah 265:12, gloss) and is called a shalom zakhor. Similarly, there is a custom to stay awake studying all night before the circumcision, to protect the child from demons, etc. It is obviously the last chance for the demons to get the child before circumcision makes him safe. This is called lel shimmurim—the night of watching.

3. One should not circumcise an infant who is weak, sick, or premature when medical opinion indicates that the circumcision might be dangerous. The brit, in this case, is postponed until a later date.

4. Although a brit may normally be held on Shabbat or a festival—even on Yom Kippur—if the brit has been postponed because of the health of the child, it should not take place on any of those days.

5. It is customary to light candles in the room where the brit is to take place.

6. Another custom is to set aside a chair for the prophet Elijah (who is called the angel of covenant and is reputed to be the protector of little children).

For those concerned, pressure should be exerted on the Powers-That-Be (no, *not* God) to train non-Orthodox mohalim.

7. It is also a custom to put the infant on the chair before the actual circumcision.

8. Whenever possible, the brit should take place with a minyan—quorum of ten people.

9. It is customary for everyone but the godfather who is holding the baby to remain standing during the ceremony.

10. The parent (or both parents when possible) should hand the knife to the mohel and stand by him while he performs the milah to indicate that the mohel is the agent of the parent(s) (see No. 1 above).

The basic elements of the brit milah ceremony are below. There is great historical precedent for adding meaningful readings, songs, statements, etc.—whatever the parents are into. While psalms, poetry, music, group readings are appropriate within the context of the traditional brit milah, you should check nonetheless with the mohel you'll be using. He's also sharing in the ceremony and deserves consideration.

It is also nice to have copies of the service available for your guests: photocopy machines are very handy toys.

ORDER OF CIRCUMCISION

Candles are lit in the room where the circumcision is to be performed.

A chair is set aside in honor of the prophet Elijah, and the following is said:

This chair is devoted to Elijah the prophet, may his remembrance be for the good.

When the infant is brought in to be circumcised, all present rise and say aloud:

May he who cometh be blessed.

All present must remain standing to the end of the ceremony. The circumciser takes the infant from the one who brought him in, and joyfully says:

The Holy One, praised be He, said to our father Abraham: "Walk thou before Me and be thou perfect."

I am ready and willing to perform the precept which the Creator, praised be He, commanded us concerning circumcision.

If the father himself performs the circumcision, he says:

I am ready . . . which the Creator, praised be He, commanded me to circumcise my son.

The circumciser places the infant upon the chair set aside for the prophet Elijah, and recites:

This chair is devoted to Elijah, may his remembrance be for the good.

For Thy salvation I have waited, O Lord.

I have hoped for Thy salvation, O Lord, and Thy commandments have I fulfilled.

Elijah, thou angel of the covenant, lo, thine is before thee. Do thou stand at my right and sustain me.

I have hoped for Thy salvation, O Lord.

I rejoice at Thy word, as one that findeth great spoil.

Great peace have they who love Thy law; and there is no stumbling for them.

Happy is he whom Thou choosest and bringest nigh that he may dwell in Thy courts.

Those present respond:

May we be satisfied with the goodness of Thy house, the holy place of Thy temple.

ה. סדר ברית מילה

מדליקים נרות בבית המילה.
מכינים כסא לכבוד אליהו הנביא, ואומרים:

זֶה הַכִּסֵּא שֶׁל אֵלִיָּהוּ הַנָּבִיא זָכוּר לַטּוֹב.

כשמביאים את הרך הנימול לבית המילה, קמים הנאספים על רגליהם ואומרים:

בָּרוּךְ הַבָּא.

ועומדים הנאספים על רגליהם עד סוף סדר המילה.
המוהל לוקח את התינוק מיד המביא אותו, ואומר בשמחה:

אָמַר הַקָּדוֹשׁ בָּרוּךְ הוּא לְאַבְרָהָם אָבִינוּ, הִתְהַלֵּךְ לְפָנַי וֶהְיֵה תָמִים.

הִנְנִי מוּכָן וּמְזוּמָּן לְקַיֵּם מִצְוַת עֲשֵׂה שֶׁצִּוָּנוּ הַבּוֹרֵא יִתְבָּרַךְ לָמוֹל.

וכשהאב בעצמו מל את בנו, יאמר:

הִנְנִי מוּכָן ... שֶׁצִּוָּנוּ הַבּוֹרֵא יִתְבָּרַךְ לָמוֹל אֶת־בְּנִי.

וישים את התינוק על כסא שהוכן לאליהו הנביא ויאמר:

זֶה הַכִּסֵּא שֶׁל אֵלִיָּהוּ זָכוּר לַטּוֹב.
לִישׁוּעָתְךָ קִוִּיתִי יְיָ.

שִׂבַּרְתִּי לִישׁוּעָתְךָ יְיָ, וּמִצְוֹתֶיךָ עָשִׂיתִי.
אֵלִיָּהוּ מַלְאַךְ הַבְּרִית, הִנֵּה שֶׁלְךָ לְפָנֶיךָ, עֲמוֹד עַל יְמִינִי וְסָמְכֵנִי.
שִׂבַּרְתִּי לִישׁוּעָתְךָ יְיָ.
שָׂשׂ אָנֹכִי עַל אִמְרָתֶךָ כְּמוֹצֵא שָׁלָל רָב.
שָׁלוֹם רָב לְאֹהֲבֵי תוֹרָתֶךָ וְאֵין לָמוֹ מִכְשׁוֹל.
אַשְׁרֵי תִּבְחַר וּתְקָרֵב יִשְׁכּוֹן חֲצֵרֶיךָ.

הנאספים עונים:

נִשְׂבְּעָה בְּטוּב בֵּיתֶךָ קְדֹשׁ הֵיכָלֶךָ.

The performer of the circumcision places the infant upon the lap of the godfather, and before performing the circumcision says the following benediction:

Praised be Thou, O Lord our God, King of the Universe, who hast sanctified us with Thy commandments, and commanded us concerning the rite of circumcision.

The circumcision is performed.

And immediately after the circumcision, before the uncovering is performed, the father, or the god-father if there is no father, says:

Praised be Thou, O Lord our God, King of the Universe, who has sanctified us by Thy commandments, and hast bidden us to make him enter into the covenant of Abraham our father.

Those present respond:

As he has been entered into the covenant, so may he be introduced to the study of the Law, to the nuptial canopy, and to good deeds.

After the performance of the circumcision, the circumciser takes a goblet of wine, and continues:

Praised be Thou, O Lord our God, King of the Universe, who hast created the fruit of the vine.

Praised be Thou, O Lord our God, King of the Universe, who hast sanctified the well-beloved (Isaac) from the womb and hast set Thy statute in his flesh, and hast sealed his offspring with the sign of the holy covenant. Therefore, because of this, O living God, our Portion and our Rock, deliver from destruction the dearly beloved of our flesh, for the sake of the covenant Thou hast set in our bodies. Praised be Thou, O Lord our God, who hast made the covenant.

Our God and God of our fathers, preserve this child to his father and to his mother, and let his name be called in Israel —— son of ——. Let the father rejoice in his offspring, and let the mother be glad with her children; as it is written: "Let thy father and thy mother rejoice, and let her that bore thee be glad." And it is said: "And I passed by thee, and I saw thee weltering in thy blood, and I said unto thee: 'In thy blood thou shalt live.' Yea, I said: 'In thy blood thou shalt live.'" (*A little wine is put in the mouth of the infant when the last two sentences are repeated.*) And it is said: "He hath remembered His covenant forever, the word which He commanded to a thousand generations; (the covenant) which he made with Abraham, and His oath unto Isaac, and confirmed the same unto Jacob for a statute, to Israel for everlasting covenant." And it is said: "And Abraham circumcised his son Isaac when he was eight days old, as God commanded him." O give thanks unto the Lord; for He is good; for His loving-kindness endureth forever. The little child, ——, may he become great. As he has been entered into the covenant, so may he be introduced to the study of the Law, to the nuptial canopy, and to good deeds.

הַמּוֹהֵל לוֹקֵחַ אֶת הַתִּינוֹק וּמַנִּיחַ אוֹתוֹ בְּחֵיק הַסַּנְדָּק, וְלִפְנֵי הַמִּילָה מְבָרֵךְ:

בָּרוּךְ אַתָּה יְיָ, אֱלֹהֵינוּ מֶלֶךְ הָעוֹלָם, אֲשֶׁר קִדְּשָׁנוּ בְּמִצְוֹתָיו, וְצִוָּנוּ עַל הַמִּילָה.

אַחַר כָּךְ יַחְתּוֹךְ אֶת הָעָרְלָה.

וּמִיָּד קוֹדֶם הַפְּרִיעָה מְבָרֵךְ הָאָב, וְאִם אֵין לַתִּינוֹק אָב, מְבָרֵךְ הַסַּנְדָּק:

בָּרוּךְ אַתָּה יְיָ, אֱלֹהֵינוּ מֶלֶךְ הָעוֹלָם, אֲשֶׁר קִדְּשָׁנוּ בְּמִצְוֹתָיו, וְצִוָּנוּ לְהַכְנִיסוֹ בִּבְרִיתוֹ שֶׁל אַבְרָהָם אָבִינוּ.

וְהַנֶּאֱסָפִים עוֹנִים:

כְּשֵׁם שֶׁנִּכְנַס לַבְּרִית, כֵּן יִכָּנֵס לְתוֹרָה וּלְחֻפָּה וּלְמַעֲשִׂים טוֹבִים.

אַחַר הַפְּרִיעָה וְהַמְּצִיצָה לוֹקֵחַ הַמּוֹהֵל כּוֹס וּמְבָרֵךְ:

בָּרוּךְ אַתָּה יְיָ, אֱלֹהֵינוּ מֶלֶךְ הָעוֹלָם, בּוֹרֵא פְּרִי הַגָּפֶן.

בָּרוּךְ אַתָּה יְיָ, אֱלֹהֵינוּ מֶלֶךְ הָעוֹלָם, אֲשֶׁר קִדֵּשׁ יְדִיד מִבֶּטֶן וְחֹק בִּשְׁאֵרוֹ שָׂם, וְצֶאֱצָאָיו חָתַם בְּאוֹת בְּרִית קֹדֶשׁ. עַל כֵּן בִּשְׂכַר זֹאת, אֵל חַי, חֶלְקֵנוּ, צוּרֵנוּ, צַוֵּה (נ"א צִוָּה) לְהַצִּיל יְדִידוּת שְׁאֵרֵנוּ מִשַּׁחַת, לְמַעַן בְּרִיתוֹ אֲשֶׁר שָׂם בִּבְשָׂרֵנוּ. בָּרוּךְ אַתָּה יְיָ, כּוֹרֵת הַבְּרִית.

אֱלֹהֵינוּ וֵאלֹהֵי אֲבוֹתֵינוּ, קַיֵּם אֶת הַיֶּלֶד הַזֶּה לְאָבִיו וּלְאִמּוֹ וְיִקָּרֵא שְׁמוֹ בְּיִשְׂרָאֵל (פְּלוֹנִי בֶּן פְּלוֹנִי). יִשְׂמַח הָאָב בְּיוֹצֵא חֲלָצָיו, וְתָגֵל אִמּוֹ בִּפְרִי בִטְנָהּ. כַּכָּתוּב, יִשְׂמַח אָבִיךָ וְאִמֶּךָ, וְתָגֵל יוֹלַדְתֶּךָ. וְנֶאֱמַר, וָאֶעֱבֹר עָלַיִךְ וָאֶרְאֵךְ מִתְבּוֹסֶסֶת בְּדָמָיִךְ, וָאֹמַר לָךְ בְּדָמַיִךְ חֲיִי, וָאֹמַר לָךְ בְּדָמַיִךְ חֲיִי (נוֹתֵן בָּאֶצְבַּע מֵהַיַּיִן בְּפִי הַתִּינוֹק). וְנֶאֱמַר, זָכַר לְעוֹלָם בְּרִיתוֹ, דָּבָר צִוָּה לְאֶלֶף דּוֹר. אֲשֶׁר כָּרַת אֶת אַבְרָהָם, וּשְׁבוּעָתוֹ לְיִשְׂחָק. וַיַּעֲמִידֶהָ לְיַעֲקֹב לְחֹק, לְיִשְׂרָאֵל בְּרִית עוֹלָם. וְנֶאֱמַר, וַיָּמָל אַבְרָהָם אֶת יִצְחָק בְּנוֹ בֶּן שְׁמוֹנַת יָמִים, כַּאֲשֶׁר צִוָּה אוֹתוֹ אֱלֹהִים. הוֹדוּ לַיְיָ כִּי טוֹב, כִּי לְעוֹלָם חַסְדּוֹ. (פְּלוֹנִי) זֶה הַקָּטָן גָּדוֹל יִהְיֶה. כְּשֵׁם שֶׁנִּכְנַס לַבְּרִית, כֵּן יִכָּנֵס לְתוֹרָה וּלְחֻפָּה וּלְמַעֲשִׂים טוֹבִים. (אָמֵן).

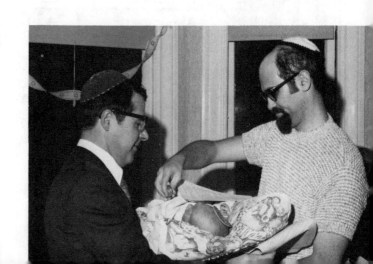

The circumciser then recites the following prayer while standing:

Creator of the universe! May it be Thy gracious will to regard and accept this (performance of circumcision), as if I had brought this infant before Thy glorious throne. And Thou, in Thy abundant mercy, through Thy holy angels, give a pure and holy heart to ——, the son of ——, who was just now circumcised in honor of Thy great Name. May his heart be wide open to comprehend Thy holy Law, that he may learn and teach, keep and fulfill Thy laws.

Special prayer for the circumcised infant:

May He who blessed our fathers Abraham, Isaac, and Jacob bless this tender infant who was circumcised, and may He grant him a perfect cure. May his parents [or: relatives] deserve to raise him up to the study of the Law, to the nuptial canopy, and good deeds. Let us say, Amen.

All present now recite Alenu Leshabeah (It Is Our Duty to Praise). After that the hands are washed for the feast, the benediction over bread is pronounced, and the feast is enjoyed.

ORDER OF GRACE AFTER MEALS

A song of Ascents
When the Lord brought back those that returned to Zion,
We were like unto them that dream.
Then was our mouth filled with laughter,
And our tongue with singing.
Then said they among the nations:
"The Lord hath done great things with these."
The Lord hath done great things with us;
We are rejoiced.
Turn our captivity, O Lord,
As streams in the dry land.
They that sow in tears
Shall reap in joy.
Though he goeth on his way weeping that beareth the measure of seed,
He shall come home with joy, bearing his sheaves.

אַחַר כָּךְ יַעֲמֹד הַמּוֹהֵל וְיִתְפַּלֵּל תְּפִלָּה זוֹ:

רִבּוֹנוֹ שֶׁל עוֹלָם, יְהִי רָצוֹן מִלְּפָנֶיךָ שֶׁיְּהֵא זֶה חָשׁוּב וּמְרֻצֶּה וּמְקֻבָּל כְּאִלּוּ הִקְרַבְתִּיהוּ לִפְנֵי כִסֵּא כְבוֹדֶךָ. וְאַתָּה בְּרַחֲמֶיךָ הָרַבִּים, שְׁלַח עַל יְדֵי מַלְאָכֶיךָ הַקְּדוֹשִׁים נְשָׁמָה קְדוֹשָׁה וּטְהוֹרָה לְ (פב״פ) הַנִּמּוֹל עַתָּה לְשִׁמְךָ הַגָּדוֹל, וְשֶׁיִּהְיֶה לִבּוֹ פָּתוּחַ כְּפִתְחוֹ שֶׁל אוּלָם בְּתוֹרָתְךָ הַקְּדוֹשָׁה, לִלְמוֹד וּלְלַמֵּד, לִשְׁמוֹר וְלַעֲשׂוֹת.

מִי שֶׁבֵּרַךְ לַיֶּלֶד אַחַר הַמִּילָה:

מִי שֶׁבֵּרַךְ אֲבוֹתֵינוּ, אַבְרָהָם, יִצְחָק וְיַעֲקֹב, הוּא יְבָרֵךְ אֶת הַיֶּלֶד הָרַךְ הַנִּמּוֹל וִירַפֵּא אוֹתוֹ רְפוּאָה שְׁלֵמָה, וְיִזְכּוּ אֲבוֹתָיו (קְרוֹבָיו) לְגַדְּלוֹ לַתּוֹרָה וּלְחֻפָּה וּלְמַעֲשִׂים טוֹבִים. וְנֹאמַר אָמֵן.

אוֹמְרִים "עָלֵינוּ לְשַׁבֵּחַ". אַחַר כָּךְ נוֹטְלִים אֶת הַיָּדַיִם, וּמְבָרְכִים בִּרְכַּת "הַמּוֹצִיא", וְאוֹכְלִים מִן הַסְּעוּדָה.

סֵדֶר בִּרְכַּת הַמָּזוֹן:

שִׁיר הַמַּעֲלוֹת:

בְּשׁוּב יְיָ אֶת־שִׁיבַת צִיּוֹן
הָיִינוּ כְּחֹלְמִים.
אָז יִמָּלֵא שְׂחוֹק פִּינוּ
וּלְשׁוֹנֵנוּ רִנָּה.
אָז יֹאמְרוּ בַגּוֹיִם:
הִגְדִּיל יְיָ לַעֲשׂוֹת עִם אֵלֶּה.
הִגְדִּיל יְיָ לַעֲשׂוֹת עִמָּנוּ
הָיִינוּ שְׂמֵחִים.
שׁוּבָה יְיָ אֶת־שְׁבִיתֵנוּ
כַּאֲפִיקִים בַּנֶּגֶב.
הַזֹּרְעִים בְּדִמְעָה,
בְּרִנָּה יִקְצֹרוּ.
הָלוֹךְ יֵלֵךְ וּבָכֹה נֹשֵׂא מֶשֶׁךְ הַזָּרַע
בֹּא יָבֹא בְרִנָּה נֹשֵׂא אֲלֻמֹּתָיו.

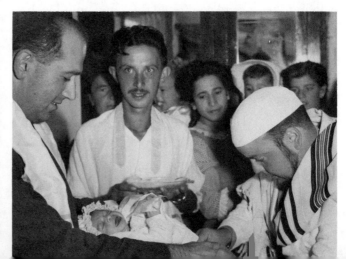

He that leads in Grace, says:

Let us say Grace.

Those present say:

Praised be the name of the Lord henceforth and forever.

The one that leads in Grace thereupon says:

Praised be the name of the Lord henceforth and forever.

Let us give thanks to Thy Name amidst the faithful. Blessed are ye of the Lord.

Those present repeat:

Let us give thanks to Thy Name amidst the faithful. Blessed are ye of the Lord.

The one who leads in Grace continues:

With the sanction of the fear-inspiring and revered God, who is a refuge in time of trouble, the God girded with strength.

All repeat: "Let us give thanks," etc.

With the sanction of the holy law, pure and clear, which Moses the servant of the Lord gave us as heritage.

All repeat: "Let us give thanks," etc.

With the sanction of the priests and Levites I will call upon the God of the Hebrews, I will declare His glory in all regions; I will bless the Lord.

All repeat: "Let us give thanks," etc.

With the sanction of all these honored guests, I will open my mouth with song, yea, my very bones shall declare, Blessed is he that cometh in the name of the Lord.

All repeat: "Let us give thanks," etc.

(Continue the normal order of Grace, adding the prayers below where the Harahaman for Shabbat and holiday are normally added.)

May the All-merciful bless the father and the mother of the child; may they be worthy to rear him, to initiate him in the precepts of the Law, and to train him in wisdom; from this eighth day and henceforth may his blood be accepted, and may the Lord God be with him.

May the All-merciful bless the godfather who has observed the covenant of circumcision, and rejoice exceedingly to perform this deed of piety; may He reward him for his act with a double recompense, and ever exalt him more and more.

May the All-merciful bless the tender infant that has been circumcised on his eighth day; may his hands and his heart be firm with God, and may he become worthy to appear before the Divine Presence three times in the year.

If the circumciser leads in the Grace, one of the company present recites the following paragraph:

May the All-merciful bless him who has circumcised the flesh of the foreskin, duly fulfilling each part of the precept. The service would be invalid of one who is timid and fainthearted, or who failed to perform the three essentials of the ceremony.

רַבּוֹתַי, נְבָרֵךְ.

המסובים עונים:

יְהִי שֵׁם יְיָ מְבוֹרָךְ מֵעַתָּה וְעַד עוֹלָם.

המברך על המזון אומר:

יְהִי שֵׁם יְיָ מְבוֹרָךְ מֵעַתָּה וְעַד עוֹלָם. נוֹדֶה לְשִׁמְךָ בְּתוֹךְ אֱמוּנַי, בְּרוּכִים אַתֶּם לַיְיָ. המסובים חוזרים ואומרים נודה וכו'.

המברך:

בִּרְשׁוּת אֵל אָיוֹם וְנוֹרָא, מִשְׂגָּב לְעִתּוֹת בַּצָּרָה, אֵל נֶאְזָר בִּגְבוּרָה, אַדִּיר בַּמָּרוֹם יְיָ. נודה

בִּרְשׁוּת הַתּוֹרָה הַקְּדוֹשָׁה, טְהוֹרָה הִיא וְגַם פְּרוּשָׁה, צִוָּה לָנוּ מוֹרָשָׁה, מֹשֶׁה עֶבֶד יְיָ. נודה

בִּרְשׁוּת הַכֹּהֲנִים וְהַלְוִיִּם, אֶקְרָא לֵאלֹהֵי הָעִבְרִיִּים, אֲהוֹדֶנּוּ בְּכָל אִיִּם, אֲבָרְכָה אֶת יְיָ. נודה

בִּרְשׁוּת מָרָנָן וְרַבָּנָן וְרַבּוֹתַי, אֶפְתַּח פִּי בְּשִׁיר וּשְׁפָתַי, וְתֹאמַרְנָה עַצְמוֹתַי, בָּרוּךְ הַבָּא בְּשֵׁם יְיָ. נודה

הָרַחֲמָן, הוּא יְבָרֵךְ אֲבִי הַיֶּלֶד וְאִמּוֹ, וְיִזְכּוּ לְגַדְּלוֹ וּלְחַנְּכוֹ וּלְחַכְּמוֹ, מִיּוֹם הַשְּׁמִינִי וָהָלְאָה יֵרָצֶה דָמוֹ, וִיהִי יְיָ אֱלֹהָיו עִמּוֹ. הָרַחֲמָן, הוּא יְבָרֵךְ בַּעַל בְּרִית הַמִּילָה, אֲשֶׁר שָׂשׂ לַעֲשׂוֹת צֶדֶק בְּגִילָה, וִישַׁלֵּם פָּעֳלוֹ וּמַשְׂכֻּרְתּוֹ כְפוּלָה, וְיִתְּנֵהוּ לְמַעְלָה לְמָעְלָה. הָרַחֲמָן, הוּא יְבָרֵךְ רַךְ הַנִּמּוֹל לִשְׁמוֹנָה, וְיִהְיוּ יָדָיו וְלִבּוֹ לָאֵל אֱמוּנָה, וְיִזְכֶּה לִרְאוֹת פְּנֵי הַשְּׁכִינָה שָׁלֹשׁ פְּעָמִים בַּשָּׁנָה.

כשהמוהל מברך, יתן כוס של ברכה לאחר, ויאמר: -

הָרַחֲמָן, הוּא יְבָרֵךְ הַמָּל בְּשַׂר הָעָרְלָה, וּפָרַע וּמָצַץ דְּמֵי הַמִּילָה, אִישׁ הַיָּרֵא וְרַךְ הַלֵּבָב עֲבוֹדָתוֹ פְּסוּלָה, אִם שָׁלָשׁ אֵלֶּה לֹא יַעֲשֶׂה לָהּ.

May the All-merciful, regardful of the merit of them that are akin by the blood of the circumcision, send us His anointed to give good tidings and consolation to the people that is scattered and dispersed among the nations.

May the All-merciful send us the righteous priest, who remains withdrawn in concealment until a throne, bright as the sun and radiant as the diamond, shall be prepared for him, the prophet who covered his face with his mantle and wrapped himself therein, with whom is God's covenant of life and of peace.

May the All-merciful make us worthy of the days of the Messiah, and of the life of the world to come. Great salvation giveth He to His king; and showeth loving-kindness to His anointed, to David and to his seed, forevermore. He who maketh peace in His high places, may He make peace for us and for all Israel; and say ye, Amen.

הָרַחֲמָן, הוא יִשְׁלַח לָנוּ מְשִׁיחוֹ הוֹלֵךְ תָּמִים, בִּזְכוּת חֲתַן לַמוּלוֹת דָּמִים, לְבַשֵּׂר בְּשׂוֹרוֹת טוֹבוֹת וְנִחוּמִים, לְעַם אֶחָד מְפֻזָּר וּמְפוֹרָד בֵּין הָעַמִּים.

הָרַחֲמָן, הוא יִשְׁלַח לָנוּ כֹּהֵן צֶדֶק אֲשֶׁר לֻקַּח לְעֵילוֹם, עַד הֻכַן כִּסְאוֹ כַּשֶּׁמֶשׁ וְיַהֲלוֹם, וַיָּלֶט פָּנָיו בְּאַדַּרְתּוֹ וַיִּגְלוֹם, בְּרִיתִי הָיְתָה אִתּוֹ הַחַיִּים וְהַשָּׁלוֹם.

הָרַחֲמָן, הוא יְזַכֵּנוּ לִימוֹת הַמָּשִׁיחַ וּלְחַיֵּי הָעוֹלָם הַבָּא. מַגְדִּיל יְשׁוּעוֹת מַלְכּוֹ וְעֹשֶׂה חֶסֶד לִמְשִׁיחוֹ, לְדָוִד וּלְזַרְעוֹ עַד עוֹלָם. עֹשֶׂה שָׁלוֹם בִּמְרוֹמָיו, הוא יַעֲשֶׂה שָׁלוֹם עָלֵינוּ וְעַל כָּל־יִשְׂרָאֵל, וְאִמְרוּ אָמֵן.

THE ORDER AND OTHER ASPECTS OF THE BRIT MILAH

Food
The brit ceremony, like most Jewish festivities, provides the opportunity for celebration with food and drink. Preparing for it ahead of time and freezing the goodies can keep the expectant parents busy during the last few weeks of waiting. But realize that this is a ploy to keep you active and don't overdo. Caterers, friends, and family can/should be asked to help out too.

It is the custom to invite people to share your joy during a simha—celebration—by giving them special, honored roles during the ceremony. You may decide to honor a number of your guests by choosing a:

1. Kvatterine (female, like "godmother"), who takes the baby from the mother to the

2. Kvatter (male, like "godfather"), who takes the baby to Elijah's Chair.

3. Two males: one to take the baby and place him on the pillow on the chair, and another to take the baby and hand him to the

4. Sandak (male, the real Jewish godfather), who, seated, with the baby on his lap or with his knees touching the bottom of the table on which the milah will be performed, assists the mohel by holding the infant throughout the ceremony. Being the sandak is the greatest honor in the brit milah ceremony aside from being the mohel!

5. The standing sandak holds the baby during the berakhah—borei peri hagaffen (wine), and

6. A female takes the infant from the mohel or sandak and returns him to the mother.

7. Many other people can be honored with ha-Motzi—the blessing over bread—or various parts of the Birkat ha-Mazon—Grace after Meals.

Oh boy, it's a girl!!!

Traditionally the arrival of a baby girl was noted when the father was given an aliyah to the Torah in the synagogue approximately one month after his daughter's birth. It was then possible that the mother could also come to shul, and possibly even the baby girl. After the services there would be a festive Kiddush for the entire congregation. While this is still practiced, today the girl is usually named as soon after birth as possible, and the celebration may take place in the home as well as in the synagogue. In

Sephardic communities, however, the girl is named only at home, to which guests are invited for a meal and the announcement of the name. It is clear that in recognizing the arrival of a boy baby, Judaism makes adequate or even more than adequate provisions for marking the occasion and celebrating it. Many people feel, however, that not enough of an opportunity is provided by Jewish tradition to mark the birth of a girl.

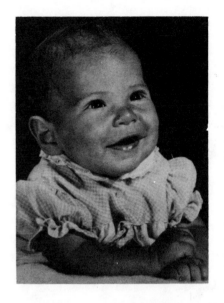

There are many good and valid reasons for seeking to create a ritual event that marks the entrance of a girl baby into the brit. The conceptual framework of the covenant was never meant to exclude women totally, and what may have been perfectly reasonable for women historically seems unnecessarily exclusionary to modern sensitivities.

With the new interest in Jewish feminism, many people have reassessed their needs and values and have written their own brit ceremonies. We include some of the many sent to us with the hope that they inspire other parents to explore the tradition and their own Jewish needs. Though to date none have been adopted as accepted ritual by any recognized religious group, this should not prevent anyone from working on his/her own version. Remember that there isn't a lot of time from the birth of the baby to the time of the brit (if you intend to observe the girl's brit on the eighth day), so you might think ahead and consider using biblical passages from Shir Hashirim and Psalms and selections featuring the female heroines (the seven prophetesses: Sarah, Miriam, Devorah, Hannah, Abigail, Huldah, and Esther) or other women of note in the Bible.

Some naming ceremony is appropriate, perhaps something analogous to the wedding ceremony, where the woman keeps the ketubbah— marriage contract—as her own. In this case the baby's name might be inscribed on a beautifully drawn parchment signed by witnesses during the brit, perhaps with a drop of wine spilled on an appropriate spot and maybe even the baby's fingerprint or footprint or a Polaroid photograph attached to the document. (A Shabbat brit might be a problem, but then you don't have to have the ceremony on the eighth day.) Naturally, wine, the She-heheyanu, and other common elements can be included as well.

The following are some samples and suggestions from people who have been working on this idea:

1. A brit ceremony was created by Rabbis Dennis and Sandy Sasso of New York and was published in *Moment* magazine (May 1975).

2. Another version, called Brit Kedusha (Holiness Covenant), was written by Ellen and Dana Charry of Philadelphia. The Charrys include Psalm 98, the She-heheyanu berakhah, the naming ceremony (changed slightly from the brit milah), wine, and the priestly blessing in their version.

3. Rabbi Paul Swerdlow, creator of Brit ha-Nerot (the Brit of Candles), cites the passage from Deuteronomy 29:9-14, which specifically includes others besides men in the Sinai brit: children, strangers, woodchoppers, waterdrawers, AND WIVES (not all women or girls, interestingly). In Swerdlow's version, lighted candles and wine take the place of the cutting in the brit milah. Naming is similar.

Brit ha-Nerot is available at $1.50 a copy:

Rabbi Paul Swerdlow
12 Selwyn Dr.
Broomall, Pa. 19008

4. Mary Gendler, of Andover, Mass., has written an article called "Sarah's Seed: New Ritual for Women." She explores circumcision and its historical and folkloric roots and devises an equivalent ceremony for baby

That our sons may be as plants grown up in their youth; that our daughters may be as corner stones, polished after the similitude of a palace...
Psalm 144

I know its a nice verse, but how will our liberated readers feel about it?

girls. Having checked with many physicians to ascertain that the proposal is a perfectly healthy one, she suggests a ritual rupturing of the hymen soon after birth. The operation would be performed by a trained and competent woman.

Mary acknowledges that her proposal will probably arouse dismay, anxiety, and disapproval. She sees the underlying spiritual meaning of circumcision as involving a marking and opening of the generative organ and a consecration to God of the seed that will issue from it. Since there is no comparable ritual "opening" for women, her proposal is to create one, thereby creating parallel (in spirit) brit ceremonies for both boys and girls.

Mary's article was printed in the Winter 1975 issue of *Response* magazine, which is available by sending $2 to:

Response
523 W. 113th St.
New York, N.Y. 10025

5. The following is a brit ceremony written by Mel and Shoshana Silberman of Philadelphia. They write that their brit ceremony was based on several sources, which they mention both because it is proper to give credit and because they believe that the sharing of ideas can help to create new Jewish rituals and liturgy. They credit

    a. the traditional brit milah ceremony for boys,

    b. Ellen and Dana Charry's ceremony,

    c. Sandy and Dennis Sasso's,

    d. their own sensitivities and needs.

The ceremony is as follows:

BRIT CEREMONY

"This is the day that the Lord has made— let us exult and rejoice on it" (Psalms 118:24).

זֶה הַיּוֹם עָשָׂה יְיָ נָגִילָה וְנִשְׂמְחָה בוֹ.

"Blessed is the Lord God, God of Israel, who alone does wondrous things; Blessed is His glorious name forever, and let His glory fill the whole world; Amen and Amen" (Psalms 72:18-19).

בָּרוּךְ יְיָ אֱלֹהִים אֱלֹהֵי יִשְׂרָאֵל עֹשֵׂה נִפְלָאוֹת לְבַדּוֹ. וּבָרוּךְ שֵׁם כְּבוֹדוֹ לְעוֹלָם וְיִמָּלֵא כְבוֹדוֹ אֶת כָּל הָאָרֶץ אָמֵן וְאָמֵן.

"God spoke to him [Abram] further, 'As for Me, this is My covenant with you: You shall be the father of a multitude of nations. And you shall no longer be called Abram, but your name shall be Abraham. . . . As for your wife Sarai . . . her name shall be Sarah . . . she shall give rise to nations'" (Genesis 17:3-6, 15-16).

"All the generations, even those unborn, were at Sinai and participated in the covenant making. Today our daughter formally becomes a part of the covenant of Israel.

"The Sabbath has been the sign of the covenant for generations. It is written in Exodus 31:16: 'The Israelite people shall keep the Sabbath, observing the Sabbath throughout the ages as a covenant for all time: it shall be a sign for all time between Me and the people of Israel.'

"So we, on this Sabbath, bring our daughter into the covenant of Israel. May she be led to a life of Torah, service, and good deeds."

"Sustain this child along with her mother and father. Her name shall be called in Israel: ——."

קַיֵּם אֶת הַיַּלְדָּה הַזֹּאת לְאָבִיהָ וּלְאִמָּהּ וְיִקָּרֵא שְׁמָהּ בְּיִשְׂרָאֵל.

"The father of a righteous man will exult;
he who begets a wise son will rejoice in him.
Your father and mother will rejoice;
she who bore you will exult" (Proverbs 23:24-25).

יִשְׂמַח הָאָב בְּיוֹצֵא חֲלָצָיו

וְתָגֵל הָאֵם בִּפְרִי בִּטְנָהּ

כַּכָּתוּב: יִשְׂמַח אָבִיךָ וְאִמֶּךָ

וְתָגֵל יוֹלַדְתֶּךָ.

"Praised are You, God, who makes parents rejoice with their children."

בָּרוּךְ אַתָּה יְיָ מְשַׂמֵּחַ הוֹרִים עִם הַיְלָדִים.

"It is written (Judah b. Illai: Lamentations Rabbah 1:6:33): 'See how precious children are: The Shekhinah did not go with the Sanhedrin and priestly watches into exile, but it did go with the children.'"

"May the life of this child be one of happiness and wisdom.
"Help us to lead our daughter in the footsteps of the great leaders of Israel, whose deeds continue to shine across the ages of our people.
"We praise You, God, whose Torah links the generations one to another."

אֱלֹהֵינוּ וֵאלֹהֵי הוֹרֵינוּ, גַּדֵּל אֶת הַיַּלְדָּה הַזֹּאת לְחַיִּים שֶׁל שִׂמְחָה, חַיִּים שֶׁל טוֹבָה חַיִּים שֶׁל חָכְמָה.

"We praise You, who has created the fruit of the vine." (*All present drink from wine cup.*)

בָּרוּךְ אַתָּה יְיָ אֱלֹהֵינוּ מֶלֶךְ הָעוֹלָם בּוֹרֵא פְּרִי הַגָּפֶן.

Parents, grandparents, siblings recite:

"Blessed are you, Lord our God, King of the Universe, who has given us life, sustained us, and brought us to this moment."

בָּרוּךְ אַתָּה יְהֹוָה אֱלֹהֵינוּ מֶלֶךְ הָעוֹלָם שֶׁהֶחֱיָנוּ וְקִיְּמָנוּ וְהִגִּיעָנוּ לַזְּמַן הַזֶּה.

"Bless us, God—all of us together—with the light of Your countenance."

בָּרְכֵנוּ אָבִינוּ כֻּלָּנוּ כְּאֶחָד בְּאוֹר פָּנֶיךָ.

6. We also include the brit ceremony written by Daniel and Myra Leifer for their daughter, Ariel Hanna. Ariel was born at home with the help of a midwife, a doctor, and Daniel. The Leifer ceremony was printed in *Response's* special issue, Summer 1973 (no. 18), entitled "The Jewish Woman: An Anthology." It is available for $2 from *Response* (see address above).

Two hours after Ariel's birth, when the physician and midwife had left and all three of us were together in our bed and Ariel had nursed for the first time, we said together the following seven berakhot in Hebrew and English (our own translations) with a cup of wine from which we all drank. These blessings were chosen from the blessings for various occasions and the seven wedding blessings. We chose those blessings that had general and particular personal meaning for us. We deliberately paralleled these blessings in number and content with the wedding blessings, because we saw in the birth of our child one of the fulfillments of our marriage and because of the fullness and sacral quality of the number seven in Jewish tradition.

"Praised are You, Adonai, our God, Lord of the Cosmos, Creator of the mystery of creation."

בָּרוּךְ אַתָּה יְיָ אֱלֹהֵינוּ מֶלֶךְ הָעוֹלָם עֹשֶׂה מַעֲשֵׂה בְרֵאשִׁית.

"Praised are You, Adonai, our God, Lord of the Cosmos, Creator of everything for Your glory."

בָּרוּךְ אַתָּה יְיָ אֱלֹהֵינוּ מֶלֶךְ הָעוֹלָם שֶׁהַכֹּל בָּרָא לִכְבוֹדוֹ.

"Praised are You, Adonai, our God, Lord of the Cosmos, Creator of humanity."

בָּרוּךְ אַתָּה יְיָ אֱלֹהֵינוּ מֶלֶךְ הָעוֹלָם יוֹצֵר הָאָדָם.

"Praised are You, Adonai, our God, Lord of the Cosmos, who created human beings in Your image and Your likeness, and out of their very selves You prepared for them a perpetual spiritual being. Praised are You, Lord, Creator of humanity."

בָּרוּךְ אַתָּה יְיָ אֱלֹהֵינוּ מֶלֶךְ הָעוֹלָם, אֲשֶׁר יָצַר אֶת הָאָדָם בְּצַלְמוֹ, בְּצֶלֶם דְּמוּת תַּבְנִיתוֹ, וְהִתְקִין לוֹ מִמֶּנּוּ בִּנְיַן עֲדֵי עַד. בָּרוּךְ אַתָּה יְיָ יוֹצֵר הָאָדָם.

"Praised are You, Adonai, our God, Lord of the Cosmos, who has such as these Your creatures in Your world."

בָּרוּךְ אַתָּה יְיָ אֱלֹהֵינוּ מֶלֶךְ הָעוֹלָם שֶׁכָּכָה לוֹ בְּעוֹלָמוֹ.

"Praised are You, Adonai, our God, Lord of the Cosmos, rememberer of the covenant and steadfastly faithful in Your covenant, keeping Your promise."

בָּרוּךְ אַתָּה יְיָ אֱלֹהֵינוּ מֶלֶךְ הָעוֹלָם זוֹכֵר הַבְּרִית וְנֶאֱמָן בִּבְרִיתוֹ וְקַיָּם בְּמַאֲמָרוֹ.

"Praised are You, Adonai, our God, Lord of the Cosmos, who has sustained us in life and being and brought us to this very moment."

בָּרוּךְ אַתָּה יְיָ אֱלֹהֵינוּ מֶלֶךְ הָעוֹלָם שֶׁהֶחֱיָנוּ וְקִיְּמָנוּ וְהִגִּיעָנוּ לַזְּמַן הַזֶּה.

These blessings were followed by the blessing over wine.

"Praised are You, Adonai, our God, Lord of the Cosmos, Creator of the fruit of the vine."

בָּרוּךְ אַתָּה יְיָ אֱלֹהֵינוּ מֶלֶךְ הָעוֹלָם בּוֹרֵא פְּרִי הַגָּפֶן.

Perhaps most important of all, in our efforts to celebrate the birth of our daughter with the same equality and dignity with which the birth of a son is traditionally celebrated, was our decision to have a pidyon ha-bat—a redemption of our firstborn daughter (see the section below on "Pidyon ha-Ben" for a full explanation of the ritual). We wished to retain the awe and gratitude for a peter rechem—fruit of the womb—child that is reflected in the traditional ceremony. We followed the traditional text and format of the ceremony, changing, adapting, adding so as to create what we hoped would be a ritual that took our tradition forward unabused but invigorated. The ceremony itself took place within the community of the regular members of the University of Chicago Hillel's "Upstairs Minyan." The text of our ceremony follows. The English translations are our own.

CEREMONY OF REDEMPTION AND HALLOWING OF A DAUGHTER
1. Myra read a poem: *Natasha* by Barbara Friend (*Ms.*, December 1972, p. 87).
2. Daniel explained the origin and meaning of the ritual.
3. A woman friend read some of the relevant biblical passages: Numbers 3:11–13, 18:13–16.
4. Ariel's godmother read Deuteronomy 29:9–14 (all the generations, even those unborn, were at Sinai and participated in the covenant making) and two rabbinic passages about children: Canticles Rabba 1:24 and

Pesikta de R. Kahana 121a. Both can be found in Nahum N. Glatzer's *The Rest Is Commentary* (Beacon, 1961), pp. 218 and 229.

35

Birth

5. Ritual (a cup of wine and a loaf of hallah are present):

a. Statement by parents—Daniel and Myra:

"This is our firstborn daughter. She opened, freed, and liberated the womb of her mother. Holy is she to Adonai, as it is written, 'Consecrate to me every firstborn; man and beast, the first issue of every womb among the Israelites is Mine' (Exodus 13:1). Now it is good in our eyes and our desire to redeem her. And here is the money of her redemption and hallowing."

זֹאת בִּתֵּנוּ בְּכוֹרָתֵנוּ הִיא. פֶּטֶר רֶחֶם לְאִמָּהּ. קֹדֶשׁ הִיא לַיהֹוָה, כַּכָּתוּב, „קַדֶּשׁ לִי כָל בְּכוֹר פֶּטֶר כָּל רֶחֶם בִּבְנֵי יִשְׂרָאֵל בָּאָדָם וּבַבְּהֵמָה לִי הוּא". וְטוֹב בְּעֵינֵינוּ לִפְדוֹתָהּ וְהִנֵּה כֶּסֶף פִּדְיוֹנָהּ וְקִדּוּשָׁהּ.

b. Setting aside of the money for tzedakhah contributed in Ariel's name.

c. Blessings said by parents—Daniel and Myra:

"Praised are You, Adonai, Our God, Lord of the Cosmos, who has made us holy through Your commandments and commanded us to bring our daughter into the covenant of the people of Israel."

בָּרוּךְ אַתָּה יְיָ אֱלֹהֵינוּ מֶלֶךְ הָעוֹלָם אֲשֶׁר קִדְּשָׁנוּ בְּמִצְוֹתָיו וְצִוָּנוּ לְהַכְנִיסָהּ בִּבְרִיתוֹ שֶׁל עַם יִשְׂרָאֵל.

"Praised are You, Adonai, Our God, Lord of the Cosmos, who has made us holy through Your commandments and commanded us to redeem every firstborn, the first issue of every womb among the Israelites."

בָּרוּךְ אַתָּה יְיָ אֱלֹהֵינוּ מֶלֶךְ הָעוֹלָם, שֶׁהֶחֱיָנוּ וְקִיְּמָנוּ וְהִגִּיעָנוּ וְצִוָּנוּ עַל פִּדְיוֹן כָּל בְּכוֹר פֶּטֶר רֶחֶם בִּבְנֵי יִשְׂרָאֵל.

"Praised are You, Adonai, who makes parents rejoice with their children."

בָּרוּךְ אַתָּה יְיָ מְשַׂמֵּחַ הוֹרִים עִם הַיְלָדִים.

"Praised are You, Adonai, our God, Lord of the Cosmos, who has sustained us in life and being and brought us to this very moment."

בָּרוּךְ אַתָּה יְיָ אֱלֹהֵינוּ מֶלֶךְ הָעוֹלָם אֲשֶׁר קִדְּשָׁנוּ בְּמִצְוֹתָיו לַזְּמָן הַזֶּה.

Statement and blessing of the representative of the community—read by Ariel's godfather:

"This tzedakhah instead of this child, this in exchange of that, this money redeems this firstborn. May this daughter, Ariel Hanna, daughter of Michal and Daniel Isaac, enter into life, Torah, and the awe of the Divine. May it be God's will that just as she has entered into redemption and the covenant, so may she enter into the study of Torah, under the marriage canopy, and into the doing of good deeds. Amen."

זֹאת תַּחַת זֹאת. זֹאת חִלּוּף זֹאת. זֹאת מְחוּלָה עַל זֹאת. וְתִכָּנֵס זֹאת הַבַּת אֲרִיאֵל חַנָּה בַּת מִיכַל וְדָנִיאֵל יִצְחָק לְחַיִּים, לְתוֹרָה וּלְיִרְאַת שָׁמָיִם.

" 'O sister! May you grow into thousands of myriads' (Genesis 24:60).
May God make you as our mothers Sarah, Rivka, Rachel, and Leah.
Adonai bless you and keep you..
Adonai make His face to shine upon you and be gracious to you.
Adonai lift up His face to you and grant you peace."

אֲחוֹתֵנוּ אַתְּ הֲיִי לְאַלְפֵי רְבָבָה.
יְשִׂימֵךְ אֱלֹהִים כְּשָׂרָה, רִבְקָה, רָחֵל וְלֵאָה.
יְבָרֶכְךָ יְיָ וְיִשְׁמְרֶךָ.
יָאֵר יְיָ פָּנָיו אֵלֶיךָ וִיחֻנֶּךָּ.
יִשָּׂא יְיָ פָּנָיו אֵלֶיךָ וְיָשֵׂם לְךָ שָׁלוֹם.

"Praised are You, Adonai, our God, Lord of the Cosmos, Creator of the fruit of the vine."

בָּרוּךְ אַתָּה יְיָ אֱלֹהֵינוּ מֶלֶךְ הָעוֹלָם בּוֹרֵא פְּרִי הַגָּפֶן.

"Praised are You, Adonai, our God, Lord of the Cosmos, who brings bread out of the earth."

בָּרוּךְ אַתָּה יְיָ אֱלֹהֵינוּ מֶלֶךְ הָעוֹלָם הַמּוֹצִיא לֶחֶם מִן הָאָרֶץ.

(1)   "How happy are those whose way is blameless,
    who follow the teaching of the Lord."

אַשְׁרֵי תְמִימֵי דָרֶךְ הַהֹלְכִים בְּתוֹרַת יְהֹוָה.

(156)   "Your mercies are great, O Lord,
    as is Your rule, preserve me."

רַחֲמֶיךָ רַבִּים יְהֹוָה כְּמִשְׁפָּטֶיךָ חַיֵּנִי.

(73)   "Your hands made me and fashioned me;
    give me understanding that I may learn your
    commandments."

יָדֶיךָ עָשׂוּנִי וַיְכוֹנְנוּנִי הֲבִינֵנִי וְאֶלְמְדָה מִצְוֹתֶיךָ.

(8)   "I will keep Your laws;
    do not utterly forsake me."

אֶת חֻקֶּיךָ אֶשְׁמֹר אַל תַּעַזְבֵנִי עַד מְאֹד.

(90)   "Your faithfulness is for all generations;
    You have established the earth and it stands."

לְדֹר וָדֹר אֱמוּנָתֶךָ כּוֹנַנְתָּ אֶרֶץ וַתַּעֲמֹד.

(58)   "I have implored You with all my heart;
    have mercy on me, in accordance with Your
    promise."

חִלִּיתִי פָנֶיךָ בְכָל לֵב חָנֵּנִי כְּאִמְרָתֶךָ.

(109)   "Though my life is always in danger,
    I do not neglect Your teaching."

נַפְשִׁי בְכַפִּי תָמִיד וְתוֹרָתְךָ לֹא שָׁכָחְתִּי.

(37)   "Avert my eyes from seeing falsehood;
    by Your ways preserve me."

הַעֲבֵר עֵינַי מֵרְאוֹת שָׁוְא בִּדְרָכֶךָ חַיֵּנִי.

7. At the last moment we received a copy of an interesting brit ceremony written by Margarita Freeman and Leonard Levin. They pick up on the idea of the covenant at Sinai, when all Israel heard the word of the Lord, and include an ear-piercing ceremony (or, in an alternate version, a pair of earrings is placed on the ear of the child). Here is an excerpt from this ceremony:

Praise be You, O Lord, our God, King of the Universe, who makes heard His covenant in the ears of all Israel, as it is said: Then He took the book of the covenant and He read it into the ears of the people. And they said: All that the Lord has spoken we will do and hear [obey]. And it is said: And now, O Israel, hear the laws and rules which I am instructing you to observe, so that you may live to enter and occupy the land that the Lord, the God of your fathers, is giving you. And it is said: Hear O Israel! The Lord our God, the Lord is One. Praised are You, O Lord, who establishes the covenant.

8. Finally, the Strassfelds have been thinking over the problem of girls' brit ceremonies. While agreeing with part of the thrust of Mary Gendler's arguments, we would favor a different approach, since what is needed is a ceremony with substance that reflects the differences between male and female.

To us, the essential part of circumcision is that it marks the entering into the covenant of Israel—for males in a physical ritual involving the sexual organs. And it is this symbol of procreation that serves as a covenantal reminder of that person's role in continuing the chain of generations of Israel.

The Talmud teaches us that the Israelites in the desert entered the covenant by the performance of three rituals: (1) circumcision, (2) bringing a sacrifice, and (3) ritual immersion (mikveh). Because of this, converts (who are like the newborn) traditionally require circumcision and immersion to become a new member of Israel. It would seem to us, then, that an appropriate brit ceremony for a female child would be ritual immersion. The mikveh has become a symbol for women's sexuality—a sexuality that is marked in a cyclical fashion (see *Catalog 1*, Rachel Adler's article on mikveh). Male sexuality is of a different nature and so is marked in a different way—as a permanent mark on the sexual organ. The woman's is both less and more permanent; less since it is not always "there," more since there is a real remembrance on a periodic basis, while circumcision is an easily forgotten thing. (That the whole area of mikveh needs some rethinking and redefinition is clear, and perhaps assigning this new role to mikveh would aid in the process.) Thus there seems good basis for use of the mikveh as a ceremony for entering the covenant, since the connection between the mikveh and women's sexuality is also clear. It is not surprising, then, that the Meiri (a medieval commentator) comments on Yevamot 46a, saying that when Abraham was circumcised and thus entered the covenant (Abraham's circumcision is, significantly, the source of milah for men), Sarah was ritually immersed to enter the covenant. It seems time to follow Sarah's example.

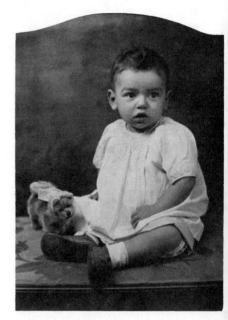

Birkat ha-Gomel

Interestingly, the brit ceremony traditionally offers one of the rare occasions when a woman can perform a mitzvah—commandment—in a minyan. A woman is not exempt from reciting Birkat ha-Gomel—the blessing of thanks said after being delivered from mortal danger or after recovery from an illness. The blessing should be said in a minyan, and the brit ceremony affords the perfect opportunity. A short service has been created for that purpose and can be found in the Hertz prayer book; here is an excerpt:

What can I render the Lord for all His benefits toward me? I will offer to you the sacrifice of thanksgiving and will call upon the Name of the Lord. I will pay my vows to the Lord in the presence of all His people; in the courts of the Lord's house, in the midst of you, O Jerusalem. Hallelujah.

מָה אָשִׁיב לַיְיָ כָּל תַּגְמוּלוֹהִי עָלָי. לְךָ אֶזְבַּח זֶבַח תּוֹדָה וּבְשֵׁם יְיָ אֶקְרָא. נְדָרַי לַיְיָ אֲשַׁלֵּם נֶגְדָה נָּא לְכָל עַמּוֹ. בְּחַצְרוֹת בֵּית יְיָ בְּתוֹכֵכִי יְרוּשָׁלָם. הַלְלוּיָהּ.

The blessing is:

"Blessed are You, Lord our God, King of the Universe, who does good to the undeserving and who has dealt kindly with me."

בָּרוּךְ אַתָּה יְיָ אֱלֹהֵינוּ מֶלֶךְ הָעוֹלָם, הַגּוֹמֵל לְחַיָּבִים טוֹבוֹת, שֶׁגְּמָלַנִי כָּל טוֹב.

The community responds by saying:

"May He who has shown you kindness deal kindly with you forever."

מִי שֶׁגְּמָלְךָ כָּל טוֹב, הוּא יִגְמָלְךָ כָּל טוֹב סֶלָה.

In general it might be good to explore the forgotten or forsaken customs of the tradition for other opportunities for participation in the birth of a child by women or jointly by the mother and father. For example, Rabbi Arnold Wieder, the Brookliner mohel, tells me that it is a mitzvah for both husband and wife to recite the following berakhah—blessing—for the birth of each child:

"Blessed are You, Lord our God, King of the Universe, who is good and who does good."

בָּרוּךְ אַתָּה יְיָ אֱלֹהֵינוּ מֶלֶךְ הָעוֹלָם הַטּוֹב וְהַמֵּטִיב.

Pidyon ha-ben–
redemption of the firstborn

The special significance of the male firstborn is recognized by the pidyon ha-ben ceremony, which could also be developed for a girl baby. (Though after one solid month of getting up for two A.M. feedings and six A.M. feedings, and the radical realization that a "tiny child shall henceforth determine your life," you may not *want* to redeem your beloved firstborn from the unsuspecting kohen.) Still, there is indeed a special feeling for the first child. Besides, the pidyon ha-ben is another occasion Judaism provides for a natural, organic celebration. Once again, food, song, honors distributed to the guests, at a time when the new mother may feel more able to prepare and participate, all mark a significant event in the Jewish community.

The firstborn in biblical society had a special status. Like the firstfruits, the firstborn was seen as more favorable—perhaps because both are the first products of the procreative process. Therefore the firstborn received a double portion of his father's estate. And that is why the last plague in Egypt struck so deeply—it killed the firstborn.

Tradition tells us that because the firstborn of Israel were spared during this plague, God consecrated them to His service: "For every firstborn among the Israelites . . . is Mine. . . . I consecrated them to Myself at the time that I smote every firstborn in the land of Egypt" (Numbers 8:17). Later, as punishment for worshiping the golden calf, this privilege/duty was taken away from the firstborn and given to the tribe of Levi. (Scholars have seen this latter story as an attempt to explain the more gradual change from the Temple's being serviced by the firstborn to its being serviced by the Levites.)

Because at one time the firstborn were consecrated to God, it was necessary to redeem them from Temple service—with five shekels, according to the biblical command. Despite the subsequent destruction of the Temple, this practice of redemption continued and still exists today.

The ceremony should take place on the thirty-first day after the child's birth (thirty days being seen as a sign of a child's full viability).

The ceremony follows:

You shall have the firstborn of man redeemed. . . . Take as their redemption price, from the age of one month up, the money equivalent of five shekels (Numbers 18:15-16).

HAND OVER THOSE SHEKELS.

SERVICE FOR THE REDEMPTION OF THE FIRSTBORN
(PIDYON HA-BEN)

סֵדֶר פִּדְיוֹן הַבֵּן

The father, presenting his child to the kohen, makes the following declaration:

"This, my firstborn son, is the firstborn of his mother, and the Holy One, blessed be He, hath given command to redeem him, as it is said, And those that are to be redeemed of them from a month old shalt thou redeem, according to thine estimation, for the money of five shekels, after the shekel of the sanctuary, the shekel being twenty gerahs; and it is said, Sanctify unto Me all the firstborn, whatsoever openeth the womb among the children of Israel, both of man and of beast: it is Mine."

זֶה בְּנִי בְכוֹרִי הוּא פֶּטֶר רֶחֶם לְאִמּוֹ. וְהַקָּדוֹשׁ בָּרוּךְ הוּא צִוָּה לִפְדּוֹתוֹ. שֶׁנֶּאֱמַר וּפְדוּיָו מִבֶּן חֹדֶשׁ תִּפְדֶּה בְּעֶרְכְּךָ כֶּסֶף חֲמֵשֶׁת שְׁקָלִים בְּשֶׁקֶל הַקֹּדֶשׁ עֶשְׂרִים גֵּרָה הוּא. וְנֶאֱמַר קַדֶּשׁ־לִי כָל־בְּכוֹר פֶּטֶר כָּל־רֶחֶם בִּבְנֵי יִשְׂרָאֵל בָּאָדָם וּבַבְּהֵמָה לִי הוּא.

The father then places before the kohen silver to the amount of five selaim or shekels (five silver dollars), and the kohen asks:

"Which wouldst thou rather, give me thy firstborn son, the firstborn of his mother, or redeem him for five selaim, which thou art bound to give according to the Torah?"

מַאי בָּעֵית טְפֵי לִתֵּן לִי בִּנְךָ בְּכוֹרְךָ שֶׁהוּא פֶּטֶר רֶחֶם לְאִמּוֹ. אוֹ בָּעֵית לִפְדּוֹתוֹ בְּעַד חָמֵשׁ סְלָעִים כִּדְמְחַיָּבַתְּ מִדְּאוֹרַיְתָא.

The father replies:

"I desire rather to redeem my son, and here thou hast the value of his redemption, which I am bound to give according to the Torah."

חָפֵץ אֲנִי לִפְדּוֹת אֶת־בְּנִי. וְהֵילָךְ דְּמֵי פִדְיוֹנוֹ כִּדְמְחַיַּבְתִּי מִדְּאוֹרַיְתָא.

The kohen receives the redemption money and returns the child to his father, whereupon the latter says the following blessing:

"Blessed art thou, O Lord our God, King of the Universe, who hast hallowed us by Thy commandments and given us command concerning the redemption of the firstborn son.

בָּרוּךְ אַתָּה יְיָ אֱלֹהֵינוּ מֶלֶךְ הָעוֹלָם, אֲשֶׁר קִדְּשָׁנוּ בְּמִצְוֹתָיו וְצִוָּנוּ עַל פִּדְיוֹן הַבֵּן.

"Blessed art thou, O Lord our God, King of the Universe, who hast kept us in life and hast preserved us and enabled us to reach this season."

בָּרוּךְ אַתָּה יְיָ אֱלֹהֵינוּ מֶלֶךְ הָעוֹלָם, שֶׁהֶחֱיָנוּ וְקִיְּמָנוּ וְהִגִּיעָנוּ לַזְּמַן הַזֶּה:

The kohen then takes the redemption money and, holding it over the head of the child, says:

"This is instead of that, this in commutation for that, this in remission of that. May this child enter into life, into the Torah and the fear of heaven. May it be God's will that even as he has been admitted to redemption, so may he enter into the Torah, the nuptial canopy, and into good deeds. Amen."

זֶה תַּחַת זֶה. זֶה חִלּוּף זֶה. זֶה מָחוּל עַל זֶה. וְיִכָּנֵס זֶה הַבֵּן לְחַיִּים לַתּוֹרָה וּלְיִרְאַת שָׁמָיִם: יְהִי רָצוֹן שֶׁכְּשֵׁם שֶׁנִּכְנַס לַפִּדְיוֹן כֵּן יִכָּנֵס לַתּוֹרָה וּלְחֻפָּה וּלְמַעֲשִׂים טוֹבִים. אָמֵן.

The kohen places his hand upon the head of the child and pronounces the following benediction:

"God make thee as Ephraim and Manasseh. The Lord bless thee, and keep thee: the Lord make His face to shine upon thee, and be gracious unto thee: the Lord turn His face unto thee, and give thee peace.

יְשִׂמְךָ אֱלֹהִים כְּאֶפְרַיִם וְכִמְנַשֶּׁה. יְבָרֶכְךָ יְיָ וְיִשְׁמְרֶךָ. יָאֵר יְיָ פָּנָיו אֵלֶיךָ וִיחֻנֶּךָּ. יִשָּׂא יְיָ פָּנָיו אֵלֶיךָ וְיָשֵׂם לְךָ שָׁלוֹם.

"The Lord is thy guardian: the Lord is thy shade upon thy right hand. For length of days, and years of life and peace shall they add to thee. The Lord shall guard thee from all evil; He shall guard thy soul. Amen."

יְיָ שֹׁמְרֶךָ יְיָ צִלְּךָ עַל־יַד יְמִינֶךָ. כִּי אֹרֶךְ יָמִים וּשְׁנוֹת חַיִּים וְשָׁלוֹם יוֹסִיפוּ לָךְ. יְיָ יִשְׁמָרְךָ מִכָּל־רָע. יְיָ יִשְׁמֹר אֶת־נַפְשֶׁךָ. אָמֵן.

Traditionally, if a female child is born first, then no subsequent male child is considered a firstborn and therefore none of the children are redeemed.

Some laws and customs

1. The law of redemption applies to firstborn children. In fact, it applies to the firstborn of the mother. Therefore, if a man is married more than once, the firstborn of each wife must be redeemed.

2. The ceremony should take place on the thirty-first day, unless it's Shabbat or yom tov, in which case it should be postponed a day.

3. If the woman has previously miscarried a fetus more than forty days old, the new child is not considered the firstborn. A child delivered by Caesarian section is not considered a firstborn. In cases with these and similar complications, it is best to ask a rabbi.

4. Five dollars, particularly five silver dollars, are used in place of the five shekels. The kohen may return the money after the ceremony is over,

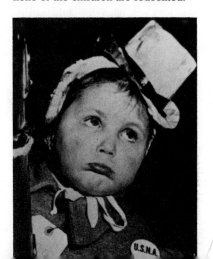

Consider the following biblical passages:
Devorah: Judges 4:8-9
Miriam: Exodus 15:21 "And Miriam . . . triumphed gloriously"
Hannah: 1 Samuel 1:5, 15, 16; 2:1-10

Other nice things to do

1. It has been traditional in certain communities to mark the birth of a child by planting a tree. The parents may choose to do this physically, with a real tree here, or spiritually, with one in Israel. If you have no yard or garden, perhaps the synagogue or center has an area that can be used for this purpose. Norfolk pines make good house plants for many years. In any event, a cedar is the customary tree to plant for a boy, a pine for a girl. When the child marries, it is a lovely custom to use wood from these trees as part of the huppah—the wedding canopy.

2. Sabra Morton has written to us about a minhag—custom—we had never heard of. She has made her own for her children and we are intrigued by the possibilities of this tradition—the wimpel.

but this cannot be a precondition; otherwise it is not considered to be a valid transaction.

Despite this, it is sometimes customary to give the kohen money for doing the ceremony, particularly if the kohen is in financial need. In fact, it was customary to look for a kohen who needed the money and ask him to do the ceremony.

5. There is a custom of placing the baby on a specially embellished tray during presentation to the kohen.

6. If a father never redeemed the firstborn or died before he could do so, then the firstborn should redeem himself and say the two blessings when he comes of age.

7. The firstborn whose father is a kohen or Levite or whose mother is the daughter of a kohen or Levite is exempt from redemption.

Traditionally this whole ceremony is very male oriented—only the father, the kohen (male priest), and a male firstborn are involved. Yet, as can be seen from Nos. 1 and 7 above, the status of the firstborn depends on the mother, not the father (it is her firstborn), and the mother's being the daughter of a kohen frees the parents from an obligation to do the ceremony. Recently some people have included the mother in the ceremony (both parents reciting the blessing together) and/or have used a female kohen (i.e., the daughter of a male priest). Others have done a pidyon ha-bat—that is, a similar redemption ceremony for a female firstborn (see the Leifer ceremony earlier in this chapter). If you have one, you should be careful of the grammatical language used in the traditional ceremony, changing son (ben) to daughter (bat), etc.

The young girls of the Bible don't provide terribly attractive models for this event (Tamar, Dinah). But perhaps the emphasis for the celebration of the birth of the first girl should be based on Miriam for her music and song, Devorah for her courage and leadership, and Hannah for her dedication to her child. The initials of these three women spell the Hebrew word hemed—desire or delight. What an appropriate name: Tekes Hemed— טֶקֶס חֶמֶד the Ceremony of Delight!

The wimpel

A beautiful birth ritual from the Germanic lands, one that was nearly extinguished by the Holocaust, continues in many Jewish communities today. (While it was traditionally done for boys only, here is another instance of a ritual that is adaptable for girls too.) A mappah—Torah binder—which is called a wimpel in German (in Yiddish you pronounce it "vimpel") is made of the cloth used to swaddle an infant at the brit. The fabric is carefully cleaned, then cut and sewn into a strip seven or eight inches wide and nine to twelve feet long. Painted or embroidered on it are the child's name, the parents' names, and the date of birth, followed by a Hebrew inscription:

"The little one (name of child) of —— was born with mazel on (date). May God bless him/her to grow up to the study of Torah, to the marriage canopy, and good deeds. Amen. Selah."

The maker of the wimpel might be the child's mother or father, another relative, a friend, or a Torah scribe. The traditional text and pictures inspire lovely embellishments, and the binder often is very colorful and imaginative: an open Torah can show an appropriate quotation, and the gaily bedecked huppah sometimes shelters several members of the bridal party. It is the custom for the child's zodiac sign to be emblazoned near the birth date. The child's name itself can often suggest decoration: e.g., Aryeh ben Judah—Aryeh literally means "lion"—must have at least one lion. Other animals and flowers often are added, and biblical scenes and quotations are commonly used.

The size, colorfulness, and the very personal quality of this kind of mappah explain its German name: wimpel means "banner."

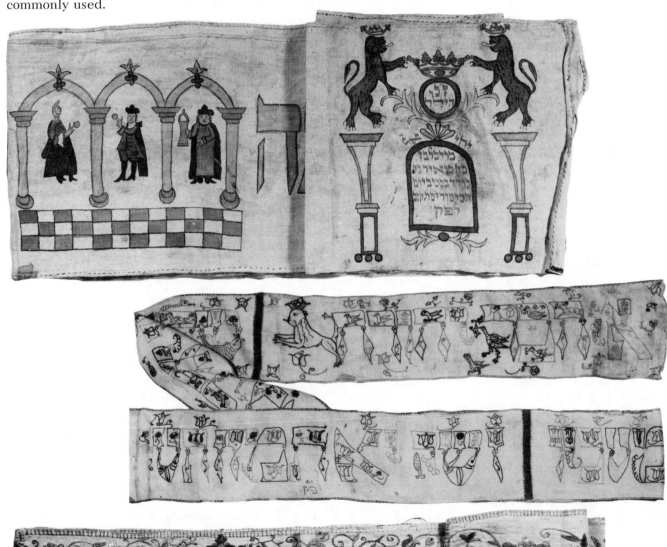

When the child's parents take him/her to the synagogue on the Shabbat closest to the child's first birthday (not the Hebrew birthday, but the one closest to a year after birth), the new wimpel is used on the Torah. The child helps to hold the Torah while one of the parents binds the Torah and recites a special berakhah:

"I will give thanks unto the Lord with my whole heart, in the council of the upright of the congregation. For this child I prayed, and the Lord has granted me my petition which I asked of Him. As for me, in the abundance of Your loving-kindness will I come to Your house. The child which You have given to Your servant is weaned; support him, confirm him, strengthen him with the Tree of Life. May his heart be pure and doubly firm in the spirit of grace. Draw him near to Your Torah, instruct him in Your commandments, teach him Your ways, turn his heart to love and awe of Your Name. Train the boy in Your way, and even when he is old he will not depart from You. Alive, alive, he will know You as I do today. A father will teach Your truth to his sons. Blessed are You, Lord our God, King of the Universe, who has granted us life, sustenance, and permitted us to reach this season."

אוֹדֶה יְיָ בְּכָל לֵבָב בְּסוֹד יְשָׁרִים וְעֵדָה. אֶל הַנַּעַר הַזֶּה הִתְפַּלָּלְתִּי וַיִּתֵּן יְיָ לִי אֶת שְׁאֵלָתִי אֲשֶׁר שָׁאַלְתִּי מֵעִמּוֹ. וַאֲנִי בְּרֹב חַסְדְּךָ אָבוֹא בֵיתֶךָ הַיֶּלֶד אֲשֶׁר חָנַנְתָּ אֶת עַבְדְּךָ גָּמוּל מֵחָלָב, נָעֳתָק מִשָּׁדַיִם; תָּמְכֵהוּ, אַשְּׁרֵהוּ, הַחֲזִיקֵהוּ בְּעֵץ חַיִּים. לֵב טָהוֹר יְהִי נָכוֹן בְּרוּחַ חֵן פִּי שְׁנַיִם. קָרְבֵהוּ לְתוֹרָתֶךָ, לַמְּדֵהוּ מִצְוֹתֶיךָ, הוֹרֵהוּ דְרָכֶיךָ, הַט לִבּוֹ לְאַהֲבָה וּלְיִרְאָה אֶת שְׁמֶךָ. חֲנוֹךְ לַנַּעַר עַל פִּי דַרְכּוֹ; גַּם כִּי יַזְקִין לֹא יָסוּר מִמֶּךָּ. חַי, חַי יוֹדֶךָ כָּמוֹנִי הַיּוֹם. אָב לַבָּנִים יוֹדִיעַ אֶת אֲמִתֶּךָ. בָּרוּךְ... שֶׁהֶחֱיָנוּ וְקִיְּמָנוּ וְהִגִּיעָנוּ לַזְּמַן הַזֶּה.

The berakhah contains, among other biblical quotations, part of Hannah's prayer when she took the young Samuel to the Temple.

The wimpel remains on the scrolls until the next reading from the Torah, after which it generally is given to the synagogue as a present. Some congregations have the custom of using a boy's wimpel again when he becomes Bar Mitzvah.

I said bring a wimpel, not a wimpie

Resources

1. If you want to read about wimpels, you can find some information in *Embroideries and Fabrics for Synagogue and Home* (Lillian S. Freehof and Bucky King, Great Neck, N.Y.: Hearthside Press, 1966). This book also has a number of excellent photographs of old and modern wimpels.

2. Should you want to see some, seek out a congregation of German background and call its secretary; most synagogues are proud of their collections and will arrange for you to visit. When traveling keep your eyes open in museums or ask a curator. Many wimpels can be found in the mappah collections of:

The Jewish Museum
1109 Fifth Ave.
New York, N.Y. 10022

The Jewish Museum
Upper Woburn Pl.
London WC 1, England

The Israel Museum
Jerusalem, Israel

To make a wimpel

If, best of all, you would like to make one, the possibilities are nearly unlimited. Halakhah doesn't say anything about wimpels, so all you need think of—or not!—is custom. Traditionally the four pieces that are sewn together to form the length are of equal size, and if you incorporate the usual inscription, either in Hebrew or in English, you'll have the special feeling of being part of a chain of tradition that's about four hundred years old. It tends to root you yet a little deeper. But it's possible too to do your own things, and perhaps you can originate a custom that someday will also be four hundred years old!

Here are a few practical considerations:

a. Although there are no halakhic specifications about fabric, you may want to observe the regulations of shatnez (see *Catalog 1,* page 51) for the cloth that is wrapped, garmentlike, around the child. (Shatnez is the prohibition against mixing linen and wool.)

b. Choose a material that is suitable for the type of decoration you want to use. Fine wool, linen, silk, and many synthetics are excellent for crewel embroidery; an even-weave fabric is good for almost anything and will be best for sketching in the lettering. If you're planning to paint, why not experiment with various media? Out of consideration for the generations to come, you might want to avoid impermanent water-base paints. Remember that the material should be lightweight enough to be tied.

c. Flat-fell seams are a traditional way of putting the ends of the four pieces together, and these are both easy and neat. You can do them by hand or on a sewing machine. It is customary to put a binding around all four sides, usually in a brightly contrasting color, and this is much simpler than hemming all that length.

    d. You can use the cloth to swaddle the baby just after it is born or else you can plan a first birthday Shabbat service or party. Share the loving labor: an artistic father can make his child's wimpel, and it might be nice for the mother to say the berakhah. After all, Hannah did.

    3. Finally, Mel and Shoshana Silberman of Philadelphia, in addition to the brit ceremony they wrote for their daughter, have written a weaning ceremony (with the amount of birth stuff they're turning out, you'd think they have *ten* kids instead of *three!*).

You may ask: "How did this tradition get started?" I'll tell you: I don't know—Tevyeh.

A *Jewish weaning ceremony*

Nursing an infant is a beautiful experience. It sensitizes one to the work of creation. It is indeed a miracle that a woman's body is able to sustain her offspring. Nursing provides benefits to both mother and child. The mother receives great personal satisfaction from the physical closeness she feels to her baby. The mutual regulation of the mother's and infant's bodily needs is an important step in the development of trust and psychological well-being. The child, of course, receives the health benefits of the mother's milk. Weaning is the end of a unique relationship between mother and child.

"And the child grew up, and was weaned, and Abraham held a great feast on the day that Isaac was weaned" (Genesis 21:8).

וַיִּגְדַּל הַיֶּלֶד וַיִּגָּמַל וַיַּעַשׂ אַבְרָהָם מִשְׁתֶּה גָדוֹל בְּיוֹם הִגָּמֵל אֶת יִצְחָק.

From the biblical text we learn that there was a celebration at the time of Isaac's weaning. We suggest that this custom be reintroduced in our day with special blessings for the occasion. Weaning a child is an important time for both the family and the child, and there should be a Jewish ceremony to mark the event.

    We believe that a Jewish ceremony should be created for this occasion that would be significant for not only the mother, but also the father. The mother can celebrate her ability to provide sustenance to her child. It would be appropriate for her to recite a blessing for having been able to

nurse. In addition, a weaning ceremony provides a way for the father to express his appreciation for the care of the infant. Having witnessed this miracle of nature, he might express gratitude for God's loving-kindness. Finally, it is also a time for both the mother and father to recognize their new responsibilities as Jewish parents.

It seems to us that the Shabbat following the actual weaning would be an appropriate time for a ceremony. The mother might be honored with an aliyah at the Torah service. It would be nice to bring the baby to the bimah—the platform where the Torah is read—at that time for a mi-she-berakh. The father should be responsible for the "feast," which could be held as the second or third Shabbat meal. At this time selections from Psalm 104 could be said (it is traditional to read this psalm on Shabbat afternoon between Simhat Torah and Pesah):

"Bless the Lord, O my soul;
　O Lord, my God, You are very great; . . .
You make springs gush forth in torrents;
　they make their way between the hills,
　giving drink to all the wild beasts;
　the wild asses slake their thirst.
The birds of the sky dwell beside them
　and sing among the foliage.
You water the mountains from Your lofts;
　the earth is sated from the fruit of Your work.
You make the grass grow for the cattle
　and herbage for man's labor,
　that he may get food out of the earth—
　wine that cheers the hearts of men
　oil that makes the face shine,
　and bread that sustains man's life.
The trees of the Lord drink their fill,
　the cedars of Lebanon, His own planting,
　where birds make their nests;
　the stork has her home in the junipers.
The high mountains are for wild goats;
　the crags are a refuge for rock-badgers.

He made the moon to mark the seasons;
　the sun knows when to set.
You bring on darkness and it is night,
　when all the beasts of the forests stir.
The lions roar for prey,
　seeking their food from God.
When the sun rises, they come home
　and couch in their dens.
Man then goes out to his work,
　to his labor until the evening.

How many are the things You have made, O Lord;
　You have made them all with wisdom;
　the earth is full of Your creations."

The mother says:

"Blessed are You, God, Ruler of the Universe, who has made me a woman."

בָּרוּךְ אַתָּה יהוה אֱלֹהֵינוּ מֶלֶךְ הָעוֹלָם שֶׁעָשַׂנִי אִשָּׁה.

"Blessed are You, God, Ruler of the Universe, who has enabled me to nurse."

בָּרוּךְ אַתָּה יהוה אֱלֹהֵינוּ מֶלֶךְ הָעוֹלָם שֶׁנָּתַן לִי לְהָנִיק.

The father says:

"Blessed are you, God, Ruler of the Universe, who sustains life with loving-kindness."

בָּרוּךְ אַתָּה יהוה אֱלֹהֵינוּ מֶלֶךְ הָעוֹלָם הַמְכַלְכֵּל חַיִּים בְּחֶסֶד.

The mother and father together say:

"Blessed are You, God, Ruler of the Universe, who creates the fruit of the vine."

בָּרוּךְ אַתָּה יהוה אֱלֹהֵינוּ מֶלֶךְ הָעוֹלָם בּוֹרֵא פְּרִי הַגָּפֶן.

After the parents drink the wine, they give the child a small sip. This symbolizes the end of the child's dependence on his mother's milk. Then they say:

"Blessed are You, God, Ruler of the Universe, who has sustained us and preserved us and brought us to this occasion.

בָּרוּךְ אַתָּה יהוה אֱלֹהֵינוּ מֶלֶךְ הָעוֹלָם שֶׁהֶחֱיָנוּ וְקִיְּמָנוּ וְהִגִּיעָנוּ לַזְּמַן הַזֶּה.

"May we, in love, continue to give sustenance to this child and provide for his/her physical needs. May we provide spiritual sustenance through examples of goodness and loving-kindness and by teaching the insights of the Torah and the traditions of our people."

(In honor of this occasion, it would be appropriate for the parents to make a charitable donation. In Eastern Europe it was customary to make a donation equal to the weight of the child.)

"Blessed are You, God, Ruler of the Universe, who brings forth bread from the earth."

בָּרוּךְ אַתָּה יהוה אֱלֹהֵינוּ מֶלֶךְ הָעוֹלָם הַמּוֹצִיא לֶחֶם מִן הָאָרֶץ.

(It was customary in Eastern Europe for a neighbor to give the child the first food he received after weaning. This tradition can be continued by someone other than the parents giving the child a piece of bread before the guests partake of the motzi.)

"Just as Abraham and Sarah rejoiced at the weaning of their son Isaac, our hearts, too, are glad that (child's name) has grown into full childhood sustained in good health by God's precious gift of milk."

"Bless us, God—all of us together—with the light of Your countenance."

בָּרְכֵנוּ אָבִינוּ כֻּלָּנוּ כְּאֶחָד בְּאוֹר פָּנֶיךָ.

All of these are our ideas for the weaning ceremony we'll use when Gabriel gets himself ready to "get on the bottle." (Right now he shows little sign of it!) Just as Abraham believed it was important to mark this event, our hope is that this time of thanksgiving will be given a modern Jewish expression.

Bibliography

Mark Nulman of Providence, R.I. has compiled this brief bibliography on birth:

Brazelton, T. Berry. *Infants and Mothers: Differences in Development.* New York: Delacorte, 1969.

Donin, Hayim Halevy. *To Be a Jew.* New York: Basic Books, 1972.

Gaster, Theodor. *Customs and Folkways of Jewish Life.* New York: William Sloane, 1955.

Guttmacher, Alan. *Pregnancy and Birth.* New York: Viking, 1956.

Koltach, Alfred J. *The Name Dictionary: Modern English and Hebrew Names.* New York, N.Y.: Jonathan David, 1967.

Schneid, Hayyim. *Family.* Jerusalem: Keter, 1973.

Shulman, Albert, *Gateway to Judaism.* 2 vols. New York: Thomas Yoseloff, 1971.

Spock, Benjamin. *Baby and Child Care.* Des Moines: Meredith, 1968.

In conclusion

There can be no conclusion to this section... because birth is a beginning. It's a whole new world... a whole new life... in so many different and wondrous ways. It's the most affirmative of actions in a time when such actions seem hardest to make. And for that reason, it is so Jewish a decision... affirming life and goodness and innocence and learning and love and responsibility and obligation, when it is not easy to do so. Mazel tov! And may your children successfully enter the brit with our people Israel, the world of the Torah and its riches, the wedding canopy and its joys and sorrows as they create a house among the community of Israel, and the world of good deeds for all of us in need.

To the Parents and the Kids

It occurs to us that the gap between the chapter on Birth and the chapter on Bar/Bat Mitzvah leaves thirteen years unaccounted for. Quite a long time in growth and development to leave anyone out of Judaism! In fact, however, a great tradition surrounds the raising of children and including them in the Jewish life of the family and the community. The following are some of the customs with which we were raised and which, looking back, cause us to feel laughter, nostalgia, and incredible joy.

To the parents

1. Because the Evil Ones were particularly desirous of capturing the souls of little boys, an interesting custom arose to prevent this. The hair of the boy is allowed to grow until he is three years old—thus rendering him indistinguishable from a little girl, with whom the Evil Ones disdain involvement! When the child turns three, his hair is cut amid great celebration.

2. The Talmud urges the mother to breast-feed her children for the first twenty-four months! (Ketubbot 60b, Yevamot 43a).

3. As a minor, a child is not held responsible for performing religious rituals, although in the talmudic period the custom arose of introducing children to rituals as soon as they were able to understand their significance (Sukkot 42a).

4. According to the same Talmud passage, a child's education is expected to begin as soon as he begins to speak clearly.

5. The first day of school for a child is a time for great celebration. To make the association a positive one for the child, the custom arose to strew the child's first book with candy and raisins. Others spread the letter alef (the first letter of the alphabet) with honey, which the child could lick after learning his/her first letter.

6. Parents are encouraged to take their children with them to the synagogue or to the "junior congregation" (for "junior people") of their school, where children are encouraged to participate in or lead certain rituals:

    a. Children are encouraged to sip the wine after Kiddush.

b. A child frequently leads the community in reciting Birkhot ha-Shahar—the early portion of prayers; and in singing "Ein ke-Eloheinu" or "Anim Zemirot" at the end of the service.

c. Further, a child is permitted to dress the Torah scroll (the ceremony is called gelilah) after the reading of the Torah.

7. Certain times in the celebration cycle are especially reserved for the participation of children. This was seen as an incentive for the child to study and as an expression of the wish that the words of the Torah would be sweet to the child's lips:

a. Children are blessed by the father (and mother) on Friday night (see *Catalog 1*, page 108).

b. The Mishnah suggests that children gradually be trained to fast on Yom Kippur (Yoma 8:4).

c. The Talmud suggests that a child be given a lulav on Sukkot as soon as he is able to understand the ritual (Sukkah 42a).

d. Simhat Torah is a particularly auspicious celebration, for children are given Israeli flags adorned with apples, which they wave as they circle the room (hakafot) with the Torah. In addition, it is the custom to call together all the children under a spread tallit, where they are given a collective aliyah called Kol ha-Nearim—All the Children.

e. Hanukkah and children! Who has to ever *talk* about Hanukkah and children? Leaving aside the presents, each child is customarily given his/her own menorah to light. In addition, the favorite game of dreidel, while played by adults, is supposed to be for children (a little Kiddie Lib here! Claim your rights!).

f. The most notable holiday celebration for children is, of course, Passover. Here the entire structure of the Seder—each ritual, each tale—is designed to provoke the child's curiosity about the event.

g. Girls (boys if you/they are into it) should have their own candles to light on Shabbat and holy days.

To underage Jews

1. The obligation of a person before Bar/Bat Mitzvah is to honor his/her parents and teacher (Deuteronomy 5:16). (That goes for *after* too!)

2. You are further enjoined to provide needy parents or teachers with food or dress when these are necessary (Kiddushin 31b).

3. Also—and watch out for this one!

If a man has a wayward and defiant son, who does not heed his father or mother and does not obey them even after they discipline him, his father and mother shall take hold of him and bring him out to the elders of his town at the public place of his community. They shall say to the elders of his town, "This son of ours is disloyal and defiant; he does not heed us. He is a glutton and a drunkard." Thereupon the men of his town shall stone him to death (Deuteronomy 21:18–21).

But this last practice was virtually abolished by the rabbis of the Talmud, who realized that since all children are defiant, if we persisted in stoning them there soon wouldn't *be* any children! Most likely it was abolished when extreme forms of capital punishment were abolished.

4. Your father is required to teach you how to swim (Kiddushin 29a). The Talmud also says if a father doesn't teach his son a trade, it's as though he taught him to be a robber.

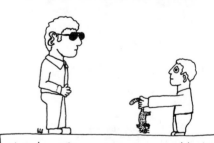

About his children, every parent is blind.
YIDDISH PROVERB   TRANS. LEO ROSTEN

Also, according to *strong* tradition, the parents must ransom the afikoman matzah on Passover from the child (assuming they're clever enough to find the hiding place) for *whatever you want!* Kids, if your parents protest, point out that a minhag in Judaism is the equivalent of A LAW!

It is easier to have children than to raise them.
YIDDISH PROVERB   TRANS. LEO ROSTEN

Adoption

It is written that God created the world so that it would continue the process of creation. So too with people. On the sixth day God created man and woman in the image of God, and in that image endowed them with the gift to create generations.

In all that God provides there is a blessing and a curse. The divine will is evident even in barrenness, for it was only through God's intervention that Abraham and Sarah, Isaac and Rebecca, and Jacob and Rachel were able to bear children. And perhaps it was the recognition of God's intention in all that occurs that led the rabbis to consider anyone who rears an orphan the same as if he had begotten the child.

Adoption is a difficult topic to write about. We are put off by the enormousness of the task. Yet we recently adopted our daughter Tamar and feel so unutterably blessed and validated that we are moved to share our experiences with you. Adoption is such a very personal life decision that it seems an affront to try to write a clinical article about it. What follows, then, is a story—our story—liberally laden with the fruits of our Jewish study and our investigations into halakhah.

Even before we were married we faced the medical certainty that we would never have children, and therefore from the beginning we planned to adopt a family. When our first daughter, Rachael Anne, was born in our home on the eighth of Av, we shared not only the ecstasy of birth but the additional miracle that, contrary to medical prediction, we had created another human being.

Several years passed, and despite a series of doctors, tests, thermometers, pills, charts, and more doctors, it became evident that there would not be another child. Whereas the original decision to adopt had been relatively easy, the presence of Rachael was now a very real consideration: we wondered if we could love an adopted child as much as we loved our own.

In thinking about adoption, we had assumed that the child we would adopt would be Jewish. On Yom Kippur, for some inexplicable reason, the rabbi of our shul spoke of adoption, recommending that the child come from *non-Jewish* parents. The concept, seen in the light of halakhah, has two related advantages: (1) there is no question of mamzerut—the problem of nonlegitimate children who are created through the Jewishly adulterous

relationship of a married woman and a man other than her Jewishly legal husband (although the status of mamzerut rarely prevails outside of Orthodox circles); and (2) it reduces the probability of the child's ever entering into an incestuous marriage.

On the other hand, adoption of a non-Jewish child necessitates conversion and raises the question of the validity of a minor's conversion. Most rabbis feel that the bet din (court), which acts as a father to all orphans, does not require consent when its action is for the benefit of the individual. Nonetheless the general feeling is that the child must validate any conversion that occurred prior to a certain age—usually that of Bar/Bat Mitzvah. If the child denies the conversion, it is considered not to have taken place.

Before you adopt any child it is essential to consult a rabbi as well as a lawyer. In American law the tendency has been to confer the same legal rights on an adopted child as on natural issue, and their status is indistinguishable. (The critical legal area usually is that of inheritance.) Moreover, when the adoption becomes final, the court issues a new birth certificate to create the fiction of parenthood.

It is precisely this last point that differentiates American law from talmudic law: halakhah makes no provision for transferring title of a child from one human being to another. Therefore defining the term adoption by American standards is inappropriate when applied to halakhah, which offers no mechanism, legal or fictional, to establish a relationship corresponding to that of natural issue. However, the bet din may exercise its authority to appoint a guardian, who to all intents and purposes assumes the responsibilities inherent in adoption.

An individual's status under Jewish law, unlike his status in American society, is entirely hereditary. Although the child may assume the family

Blessed art Thou oh Lord our G-d, who hast given a life into our care.

A converted child must go through the normal conversion ritual, i.e., circumcision (for males) and mikveh—ritual bath—for both male and female. The latter is postponed until it is safe to immerse the child (when it's about a year old usually). (See Birth.)

Children without childhood are a dark and fearsome spectacle. —Mendele

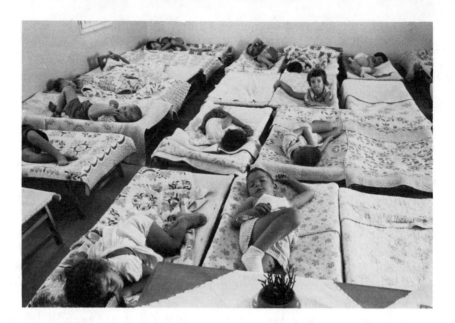

name, the privileges and obligations of being a kohen or a Levite are dependent solely upon birth. Conversely, the child retains the priestly classification irrespective of the adopted family's origin. It is also important to ascertain if the infant is a firstborn, in which case it needs a pidyon ha-ben/bat (see Birth). For the same reason, marriage to the natural members of the adopted family is permissible because it would not violate the prohibition against incest—though this is discouraged. Once adopted, the child is treated as if it is a natural child. Because of this, the child should revere his/her adoptive parents. The child should observe all the laws of mourning, say Kaddish, etc.

Although it may take several years to adopt a child, the time varies from case to case. Adoption agencies do not function on a first come, first served basis, but rather attempt to match the child and the family. (This assumes that there are children available at the agencies—see "Finding a Child.")

In our own case, we requested an infant male, believing that the age and sex difference would be more acceptable to Rachael. As time passed the sex became less important, and we doubled the probability of finding a child by changing our request to one for an infant.

Adoption policies, procedures, and costs vary from agency to agency, as does the availability of children. Our initial inclination was to approach a Jewish agency, which would be able to assist us with a brit—circumcision—and/or conversion (for explanations, see Birth). However, because of the lack of Jewish children, they referred us to a public agency, which, in the end, posed no problem.

Despite policy variations, all agencies require endless interviews and forms. We were interviewed as a family, as a couple, and as individuals. The caseworker was particularly interested in Rachael, who, after all, demonstrated the best proof of our suitability as parents. The discussions focused primarily around our motivations, future plans, and early childhood experiences. After a home interview, we received certification of acceptability.

The process up to the point of certification was relatively abstract; reality hit when the agency called to inform us that they had found an infant. Despite months of preparation, we were confronted with the fact that a live human being would be joining our family and that within a few weeks our lives would be changed forever.

We went to the agency with the full expectation that, after filling out a few more forms, we would be returning home with a long-anticipated child. Nothing had prepared us for the possibility that the child would not be right for us, but after an hour we looked at each other, drew a deep breath, and admitted to ourselves and each other that this frail infant was not what we had expected.

That evening we slept little, talking until the early hours of dawn. How could we have rejected an infant? What was it that was not right? Would the agency find another child or did this experience demonstrate that we were not suitable? Did it mean that subconsciously we did not really want another child? What kind of people *were* we? There were no answers, and for weeks we were haunted by feelings of shame and guilt. There are no answers today except that whatever chemistry exists between people did not exist between this infant and us.

Just when the sensations were beginning to numb, our anxiety was again raised to a peak by another call from the agency. The guilt, the shame, and all the feelings we had experienced reasserted themselves. Even worse was the fear that this could possibly be our last opportunity.

Just as we were unable to explain the first experience, we do not understand why this infant was ours from the first moment; but we knew that our souls were matched. There is no doubt that Tamar Shulamit is our daughter, and we found the answer to our original question: it *is* possible to love an adopted child as if it were your own because, indeed, the child *becomes* your own.

Finding a child

There is an unfortunate discrepancy between the supply and demand for adoptive parents and children. There is no shortage of loving parents, childless couples, and singles who wish to share their lives with unwanted children. However, the number of children available for adoption is down to a trickle. This is a recent development stemming from the easy availability of contraception and abortion. Therefore the adoptive process can be a bureaucratic nightmare—dehumanizing and frustrating. But here is how to find a child:

1. *Agencies:* These sectarian groups used to be the most common facility for adoption. However, since agencies do not pay the natural mother, most pregnant women will not go to them. Because of this, most agencies have closed their waiting lists. This method is the most responsible channel for adoption. They screen and match children and potential parents carefully, and provide counseling for the natural mother. This is also the least expensive method.

2. *Lawyers:* There are now lawyers who specialize in adoption. The reason they are able to find the children is that they offer to pay the mothers. The going rate for adoption through a lawyer is from $7,000 to $20,000 ($3,000 to $10,000 goes to the natural mother). Agencies claim that these lawyers are creating a marketplace attitude and are not concerned about the emotional effects of the adoption on the natural mother or the proper placement of the child. The lawyers claim that the agencies are not being realistic. The mothers feel they lose money by having a child (by losing pay or being fired), and in the long run it's cheaper for them to have an abortion.

If you plan to adopt through a lawyer, have your own lawyer spread the word for you until you find one who specializes in adoption.

3. *Physicians:* Doctors do not generally specialize in adoption, but they will occasionally treat a mother who does not want her child. Doctors are usually more sensitive to the adoption process than lawyers are, from the point of view of both the natural mother and the adoptive parent(s). Ask your own doctor or check with clinics, gynecologists, obstetricians, etc.

4. *Rabbis:* Through their counseling work, a clergyperson may come in contact with a mother looking for someone to adopt her child. Speak confidentially to your rabbi and explain your needs and problems.

Note: There is much debate over this method of adoption. It lends itself to financial exploitation and a number of illegalities. On the other hand, for most people this is the only way to find an infant to adopt. The legislatures of a number of states have begun to consider laws to regulate or eliminate this practice. Many states have laws limiting the amount of money that can be involved in adoptions, but as yet it is not illegal for a lawyer to handle an adoption. Nonetheless, lawyers' fees for these transactions are exorbitant, and the whole procedure is shady at best. (Because of this, we, the editors of the *Catalog,* have very mixed feelings about having added the above to Jeff and Resna's chapter.)

Some advice

1. For specific legal advice, consult a rabbi as well as a lawyer when you begin the process. Jewish law rates in importance with American law.

2. Talk to people who have done it. You may think you don't know anyone who has adopted, but in your extended circle of friends there is sure to be someone.

3. Make sure the agency you choose is a reputable one. Check around.

4. If you don't want to/can't adopt children but have a love for children *and* if you have the time (perhaps even if you don't) you might look into being a Jewish big brother/sister. The Jewish Big Brother Association is always in need of volunteers and can point you toward local Jewish children who are fatherless. Contact the national agency and ask them about local Jewish agencies that deal with this problem.

Big Brothers of America
220 Suburban Station Bldg.
Philadelphia, Pa. 19103

Generally: Spread the word that you are interested in adopting a child to all the professionals mentioned and more. Something is bound to turn up.

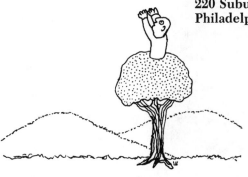

Jewish Genetic Diseases

 From early times Jewish scholars had a keen eye for diseases that might be hereditary in nature. The Talmud (Yevamot 64b) forbids circumcision of a baby if his two brothers bled to death following the procedure; if two sisters each lose a son after circumcision, a baby boy born to the third should not be circumcised.

The rabbis had made two very important discoveries that are borne out by modern studies: hemophilia is hereditary and it is transmitted through the female.

Other factors are known to play a role in the transmission of disease, but it is hard to assess their relative weight. Sorcery, demonology, and other divine and nondivine interventions were seriously considered at various times in history. The latter, especially, was blamed by both Jews and non-Jews for Jewish illness. The biblical plagues and pestilences were an obvious sign of divine displeasure.

But the most fascinating example of a disease purported to have a theological basis is hemorrhoids. Even before Portnoy's father, Jews always suspected that they were afflicted with hemorrhoids out of proportion to the general population. R. Isaac Abravanel, the fifteenth-century Jewish statesman who wrote the first commentary to appear in a Haggadah, also left us the following legacy: "It is always found that Jews suffer from acute fever, pestilence, and hemorrhoids more than any other nation" (Zimmels, p. 92—see the Bibliography at the end of this chapter for full references). Although Abravanel does not attempt an explanation of this phenomenon, a certain Bernard de Gordon, writing in Latin a hundred years earlier, suggests three reasons (quoted by Friedenwald): "They are generally sedentary . . . they are usually in fear and anxiety and therefore the melancholy blood becomes increased," and finally, to get to the theological point referred to earlier, "it is the divine vengeance against them (as written in Psalms 78:66); and 'He beat back [in the hinder parts] His foes,/Dealing them lasting disgrace.'"

So much for divine influences. Environmental factors such as our overprocessed food seem to be the main villains in the production of hemorrhoids, and recent thinkers see no specific Jewish predisposition. But we can learn something constructive from this little historical vignette, namely, the difficulty in separating out factors other than heredity in the transmission of disease. Take environment, for example. Nahmanides blamed "contamination of the air" for shortening men's lives. With the predilection of Jews for polluted urban environments, Jews would have more lung diseases than the general population simply because more of them live in cities. (This would also aggravate any possible Jewish hereditary tendencies toward lung diseases; however, none are known of, despite one medieval reference to them.) Therefore we have to be very careful in interpreting figures.

Assuming we forget about environmental factors—which might explain a predisposition of Jews to depression, for example—all hereditary diseases start with a spontaneous mutation (change) of a gene (or a group of genes, known as a chromosome). There is no point in trying to understand Jewish hereditary diseases if we do not understand what genes are and what they do.

Genes

A gene carries genetic information to tell a cell how to develop. Mutations of genes occur all the time, but the body often repairs them or they result in such abnormal changes that the cell dies. Even if the cell lives, the mutation does not affect heredity unless it occurs in the sperm or egg cells, because these are the only cells that can pass the mutation from generation to generation. The sperm and egg cells together carry all the genetic information necessary to make a new person. Each provides one gene for each characteristic of the new person. Thus when the sperm and egg combine they provide two genes for each characteristic. For example, there is a gene for eye color. If the egg provides the color blue and the sperm provides the color blue, then the eyes are guaranteed to be blue. If the egg provides brown and the sperm provides blue, the color of the eyes depends on which gene has the stronger effect. If blue has the stronger effect, we say it is dominant. If blue is dominant, you need only one gene of blue to get blue eyes. If it has the weaker effect, we say it is recessive. This means that you need two genes of blue to get blue eyes.

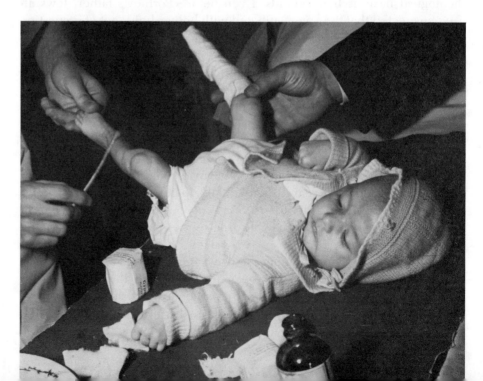

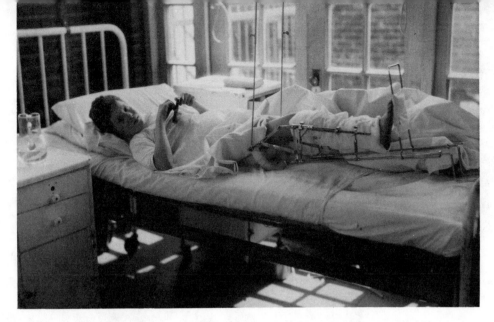

Tay-Sachs disease is carried by a recessive gene. This means that a person can have one gene for Tay-Sachs and still not get the disease. Such a person is called a carrier. If two carriers marry, the odds are that each will provide a Tay-Sachs gene in half their sperms and eggs. Therefore, on the average, one-quarter of their offspring will get Tay-Sachs disease. This is why it is important to know if you are a carrier of Tay-Sachs disease—or indeed other Jewish diseases, for which there are carrier tests.

With this preliminary knowledge, let's consider three specific diseases of Jews. All of them result from an inherited absence of a specific enzyme within the cells that keeps the concentration of certain normally occurring fats (known as lipids) at the proper level. In each of these diseases, a different enzyme is missing or present in very low concentrations, resulting in the abnormal accumulation of a particular lipid. When the level of the lipid gets too high, it is poisonous to the whole body and can ultimately result in death. The curious thing about these three diseases is that the families of almost everyone affected can be traced back to one area: the northeastern provinces of Poland and the Baltic states.

Jewish diseases

Tay-Sachs disease

The best-known of the Jewish diseases is Tay-Sachs, a lethal disorder of excess fat storage in the central nervous system. It causes progressive mental deterioration and death by five years of age. Because of modern technology it is now, in some sense, a "controllable" disease. There is a simple blood test available to determine if a person is a Tay-Sachs carrier. One in thirty Ashkenazic Jews is a carrier (and one in thirty-six hundred is actually afflicted with the disease). If both parents are carriers, the fetus can be tested in utero (in the uterus) at the end of fourteen weeks of pregnancy; if the fetus is found to have Tay-Sachs disease, the parents can then decide whether or not they want an abortion. Thus parents can, if they so choose, be spared the agonizing heartbreak of bearing a child suffering from Tay-Sachs disease.

The test for Tay-Sachs carriers is a simple blood test—brief, inexpensive, and painless. There is no excuse for any Jew of childbearing age to avoid having such a blood test—for Tay-Sachs or any other Jewish disease that is preventable.

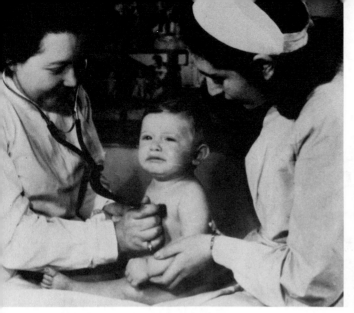

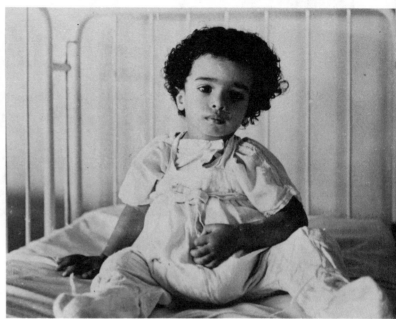

Niemann-Pick disease

This disease too results in the abnormal accumulation of fats within the body. It is a condition similar to Tay-Sachs and has a similar lethal course resulting in early death. It is a very rare disease with a frequency of one in forty thousand people. It can be detected in utero, at which point the parents can decide whether to abort if the fetus is found to have the disease.

Gaucher's disease

This is the only one of these fat-storage diseases that can be compatible with a relatively long life. The accumulations of fat occur primarily in the spleen and bones, resulting in anemia, easy bleeding, and fractures. Although it is not nearly as well known as Tay-Sachs disease, it is in fact the most prevalent of the three: one case per twenty-five hundred Jews. It too can be detected in utero, but there seems to be very little point in subjecting a woman to the interuterine test: the abortion of fetuses with Gaucher's disease is not usually recommended since the disease is not fatal in childhood like Niemann-Pick and Tay-Sachs.

Other diseases affecting Jews more than non-Jews are too numerous to mention. We will only include some of the more significant ones.

Dysautonomia (Riley-Day syndrome)

Dysautonomia is a rare children's disease affecting the nervous sytem, causing blood pressure problems, recurrent pneumonia, emotional difficulties, and other serious problems. In one study 99 percent of the affected children were found to be Jewish. Even more striking, "326 of the 328 Jewish parents [of these children] have ancestry derived from the area of the Jewish Pale in Eastern Europe" (Shiloh and Selavan, p. 79). The Pale of Settlement—the area to which Jews were confined after Russia took over eastern Poland in 1792 and 1796—is essentially the same area noted to be the source of the fat storage diseases mentioned above.

Dysautonomia is a recessive disease, so both parents have to have the gene for the offspring to be affected. Unfortunately, there is no way to learn whether a parent is a carrier or to detect the disease in utero, so parents who have one child with the disorder are faced with the difficult choice of deciding whether to have more children—25 percent of whom are likely to be afflicted.

Ulcerative colitis and Crohn's disease

These are inflammatory conditions of the bowels, producing bloody and/or frequent diarrhea. Both diseases predominantly affect Ashkenazic Jews. No adequate explanation for this phenomenon has been put forth.

Familial Mediterranean fever

Among non-Ashkenazic Jews, a number of diseases occur with increased frequency. Familial Mediterranean fever is a relatively rare condition afflicting Arabs, Armenians, and Sephardic Jews with periodic episodes of fever, abdominal and chest pains, and arthritis. How it came to affect these three groups is a question whose answer might provide an incentive to peace in the Middle East.

Glucose–6–phosphate dehydrogenase deficiency

This abnormality is easier to describe than to pronounce. It is characterized by a lack of a certain enzyme needed for stability of the red blood cells. When patients with this condition are given any of many common drugs and other agents that stress red blood cells, the red blood cells break down and cause anemia. This condition occurs in less than one-half of one percent of Ashkenazic Jews, but is present in 25 percent of Iraqi Jews and 58 percent of Kurdish Jews. It also affects a substantial number of American blacks.

Psychological afflictions

Depression and various neuroses have been attributed to Jews in excess, and studies have supported this contention. Schizophrenia, on the other hand, is said to be much rarer among Jews than among the general population.

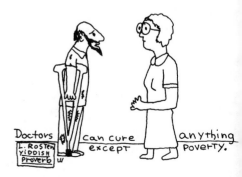

Doctors can cure anything except poverty.
L. Rosten Yiddish Proverb

Many other Jewish diseases mentioned in the medical literature have a pattern of hereditary transmission that is not fully understood. Even so, what is striking is their prevalence among a particular group of people—Jews—and especially among a particular subgroup of Jews such as Ashkenazic Jews from eastern Poland in the case of Tay-Sachs, dysautonomia, Niemann-Pick, and Gaucher's disease. Why these mutations occurred is impossible to explain. The perpetuation of the disease presumably is somewhat favorably affected by inbreeding, at least in early generations of it. But there are also factors working the other way. Parents who have one child with Tay-Sachs disease may be so afraid of having another child with the disease (even though the odds of one in four are certainly in favor of their having a normal child) that they cease having children altogether.

Other factors are also apparently at work. One study, for example, suggests that Tay-Sachs carriers seem to have a higher birthrate than noncarriers; thus the loss of children to the disease is offset by the increased production of carriers. Another study noted that grandparents of children with Tay-Sachs disease had significantly fewer cases of tuberculosis than grandparents of other children. This suggests that carriers of the Tay-Sachs gene may have had certain health advantages contributing to their perpetuation.

Whatever the reasons for their appearance and perpetuation, all these diseases of Jews are likely to be with us for some time. It behooves us to learn as much as we can about them to prevent as much family anguish as possible.

Resources

1. There is an organization devoted specifically to research of dysautonomia. Ninety percent of the money raised goes directly to research, and there are chapters of the organization in Detroit, Montreal, California, New Jersey, Boston, Worcester, Mass., New York City, Long Island, and Brooklyn. They provide numerous pamphlets and brochures to both doctors and parents. The main office for information about these chapters and about dysautonomia in general is:

Dysautonomia Foundation
370 Lexington Ave.
Room 1508
New York, N.Y. 10017

2. There is also an organization devoted specifically to Tay-Sachs research and control. They will tell you where the nearest center to your home is for taking the Tay-Sachs test. There are now nationwide facilities, and every major city can be depended upon to provide the test. People who live in cities without such facilities can also take the test. The Tay-Sachs Association has arranged with

Kingsbrook Jewish Medical Center
Birth Defects Center for Lipid Storage Diseases
Rutland Rd. and E. 49th St.
Brooklyn, N.Y. 11203

to send instructions to individual doctors for taking the blood sample. The specimen is then sent to Kingsbrook, which will analyze it and send back the results. Kingsbrook receives specimens from all over the world, and Ms. Fran Berkovits, who coordinates the whole program, is helpful and efficient. For more information write:

They can also give you advice about amniocentesis—the process of testing in utero to determine if a fetus has the disease. Also, talk to your own doctor for advice in all these areas.

Bibliography

1. Krikler, Dennis. "Diseases of the Jews." *Postgraduate Medical Journal* 46 (1970):287. This is a comprehensive listing and description of almost every disease known to occur in Jews, with a critical analysis of some that were once thought to occur to excess in Jews and are now known not to (e.g., hemophilia and diabetes).

2. Shiloh, Ailon, and Selavan, Ida C. *Ethnic Groups of America: Their Morbidity, Mortality and Behavior Disorders.* Vol. 1, *The Jews.* Springfield, Ill.: Charles C Thomas, 1973. A useful book but most of the articles reprinted in it are over ten years old. Recent researchers (e.g., Kolodny, see below) suggest that the mechanism of inheritance postulated in the article on Gaucher's disease is incorrect—that it is simply inherited as a recessive trait.

3. Kolodny, Edwin H. "Clinical and Biochemical Genetics of the Lipidoses." *Seminars in Hematology* 9 (1972):251.

———. *"Heterozygote Detection in the Lipidoses."* In *The Prevention of Genetic Disease and Mental Retardation,* by Aubrey Milunsky. Philadelphia: W. B. Saunders and Co., 1975.

Both these articles are very useful for those interested in learning more about Tay-Sachs, Niemann-Pick, and Gaucher's diseases, but only if you understand medical and biochemical terminology.

4. Greene-Hamilton, James. "The Use of Genetic Markers in Oriental Jewish Historical Studies." *Jewish Quarterly Review,* April 1972.

An interesting application of the knowledge of Jewish diseases in the determination of Jewish migrations.

5. Friedenwald, Harry. *The Jews in Medicine.* Baltimore: Johns Hopkins, 1944.

6. Zimmels, H. J. *Magicians, Theologians, and Doctors.* New York: Philip Feldheim, 1952.

Origin

It will certainly seem strange to many people that the origins of the Bar/Bat Mitzvah, that ceremony which vies in the minds of many Jews with the brit milah—circumcision—for the position of THE rite of passage in Judaism, are shrouded in mystery, controversy, and scholarly debate.

The reason for the lack of precise information is clear. The Bible fails to mention either a Bar Mitzvah celebration or to give any indication that thirteen was considered the demarcation line between the status of child and that of adult. In fact, when a particular age is cited in the Bible as a test or requirement for full participation in the community's activities, the age given is twenty, not thirteen. At age twenty, one could bear arms and was obliged to pay the half-shekel for the support of the Temple (Exodus 30:14; Leviticus 27:3-5; Numbers 1:3, 20).

Though the Bible makes no specific references to the age of thirteen as the time when the child passes into adulthood, there are strong indications that it is not a recent innovation. By the first century C.E., thirteen for a boy and twelve for a girl were recognized as the ages when they were obliged to fully observe the commandments and to participate in the rituals of the community. (Often the Talmud will only mention thirteen when discussing the age of majority. The rabbinic authorities have generally interpreted any mention of age thirteen as age twelve in the case of a female.) At these ages, a minor's word was now valid in a court of law.

The Talmud (Mishnah Niddah 5:6) states that when a vow is made by someone age thirteen or above, it is a valid vow. In another section (Ketubbot 50a) it is mentioned that a boy of thirteen and a girl of twelve must fast for a full day on the holiday of Yom Kippur. The obligation to fast on this day was and is something that is required of adults only (though the Talmud cites certain rabbis who believed children should begin fasting for part of Yom Kippur prior to reaching the age of twelve or thirteen, so that they would be prepared to observe the fast when they were required to do so according to the halakhah—Jewish law). The clearest and most explicit recognition of thirteen as the age when a child was considered to be a fully responsible member of the community is the statement in the Talmud (Avot 5:21): "At age thirteen one becomes subject to the commandments."

There is a wide variety of opinions on the reason for the choice of the

This chapter will attempt to treat the Bar Mitzvah and the Bat Mitzvah as one entity. Recognizing, however, that in Judaism the religious role of the male has historically been far more pronounced and that certain of the rites associated with the Bar Mitzvah are, in most cases, performed only by men (the use of tefillin—phylacteries—being a prime example), in certain sections the Bar and Bat Mitzvah are separated one from the other.

twelfth and thirteenth year. Some ascribe it to foreign influences present in Palestine in the first century B.C.E., and others feel it to be a throwback to earlier puberty rites that were practiced by many groups in ancient times. In any case, there is little question that by the time of the redaction of the Talmud (approximately the sixth century C.E.), and probably long before that, the rabbis universally recognized twelve and thirteen as that time when the individual was obligated to observe all the commandments and was responsible for his/her actions.

Changes in role of the Bar Mitzvah

The question of when and why the twelfth and thirteenth years were chosen as the point of adulthood is not the only nebulous area one encounters in examining the history of the Bar Mitzvah celebration. It is clear that, while not biblical in origin, twelve and thirteen were recognized as special points in one's life nineteen hundred years ago. BUT the Bat/Bar Mitzvah celebration as we know it today is not simply the time when a child becomes obliged to observe the commandments; it is the time when children are first *allowed* to participate in and perform the various rituals associated with full membership in the community. Prior to this time the child dons no tefillin—phylacteries, is not accorded the privilege and honor of being called up at services to make a blessing over the Torah, cannot serve as one of the ten adults needed to comprise a minyan—the quorum necessary for community prayer, cannot act as the hazan or baal koreh—the individual who leads the congregation in prayer, and in certain congregations does not wear a prayer shawl (the traditions associated with the latter custom vary widely).

Talmudic sources make it quite clear that this was once *not* the case. While a child was obligated to perform these rituals by thirteen, if he understood their significance prior to that time and was considered capable of performing them, he could do so—*even though he had not yet reached the age of majority.* The Talmud (Sukkah 42a) explicitly states: "If a minor knows how to wrap himself in the tallit he is subject to the obligation . . . if he knows how to look after tefillin his father must acquire them for him." This is not the sole talmudic source which indicates that the rituals we associate with the Bar Mitzvah were observed prior to thirteen: "All are qualified to be among the seven [who read from the Torah], even a minor" (Megillah 23a). (I would cheat you if I did not point out that this same portion of the Talmud goes on to state that women were also allowed to read from the Torah but nonetheless should not do so.)

It is obvious, then, that while thirteen was the age of entry into the adult community for the child, it was not associated with the performance of particular religious rituals. If a child had been wearing phylacteries for a number of years and had read from the Torah on numerous occasions prior to his thirteenth birthday, to do so at age thirteen could not have been a great event or even an innovation. The *religious* distinction between a minor and a major in talmudic times was, it appears, primarily theoretical.

In the Middle Ages, sometime between the fourteenth and sixteenth centuries, the Bar Mitzvah concept and the celebration that accompanied it took on a form different from what is indicated in the Talmud and became quite close to the more essential elements of contemporary practice. The

exact time of change is another area of debate but one that we need not pursue here. Suffice it to say that the innovations occurred in Germany and Poland but, as Solomon B. Freehof points out ("Ceremonial Creativity among the Ashkenazim," in *Beauty in Holiness,* ed. Joseph Guttman [New York: Ktav, 1963]), they were quickly and universally adopted by Jews of both Ashkenazic and Sephardic backgrounds.

Traditions

As one might expect, there are subtle differences in the traditions as observed by Ashkenazim and Sephardim. There are, in addition, variations within each group depending on the land of origin. (This is particularly apparent vis-à-vis customs surrounding tefillin.)

At some time in the Middle Ages minors were deprived of the religious rights that had been theirs in talmudic times. Minors no longer wore tefillin or received aliyot prior to Bar Mitzvah. This served to heighten the significance and momentous nature of reaching the Bar Mitzvah age.

Over the years five major facets of the Bar Mitzvah celebration evolved, all of which still exist in some form today—often in a form quite close to the original:

1. *Aliyah* (the blessing over the Torah): The child was—and is—called up to recite the blessings over the Torah. In addition, in certain congregations s/he reads the prophetic portion of the week, the haftarah; in others

s/he reads the entire biblical portion—the sidra; and in others s/he reads none of the above. It was, and is, the custom in certain congregations for the child to lead services.

2. *Parental blessing:* Upon being called up to the Torah to recite the blessing over it, the parents of the child add: "Barukh she-petarani mean-sho shel zeh—Blessed is He who has freed me from responsibility for this child's conduct."

The text of the blessing, found in a midrash on Genesis (Genesis Rabbah 63:10), symbolizes the fact that from that day on the parent is no longer responsible for the education of the child or for the child's misdeeds. The child now must bear the responsibility for his/her own actions.

3. *The derashah or Bar Mitzvah speech:* The child prepares, with the aid and assistance of a teacher, a derashah (also called a devar Torah)—a speech concerning some issue or point of Jewish law. The derashah is either delivered at services, immediately thereafter (this was the custom in Germany in the Middle Ages), or at the time of the Afternoon Service. In many communities this custom is still observed. In certain congregations it has been replaced with a prayer read by the child.

4. *Seudah or Bar Mitzvah feast:* At some time, usually on the Shabbat of the Bar Mitzvah, a seudah—festive meal—was given by the parents in honor of the child's having reached the age of Bar Mitzvah. The concept of a meal to accompany a particularly momentous event is popular in Judaism. Such a meal is called a seudat mitzvah—a meal celebrating a commandment. This is the original and primary reason for the feast that accompanies the wedding ceremony, the circumcision, and the siyyum—the ceremony marking the conclusion of study of a section of the Talmud. The meal at each of these occasions constitutes a seudat mitzvah. Often the derashah was delivered at this meal. Of all the various facets of the Bar/Bat Mitzvah celebration, it is this one that is most scrupulously observed by every segment of the Jewish community. In the true rabbinic tradition of "placing a fence around the mitzvah," that is, expanding upon the commandment lest it be minimized or violated in any way, the Bar Mitzvah feast has been expanded to proportions beyond anything the Talmud ever dreamt possible or even acceptable (see "A Note on Sumptuary Laws").

5. *Tefillin or Phylacteries:* Upon the occasion of the Bar Mitzvah the child begins to don tefillin, which are worn when saying the morning prayers on weekdays. They are not worn on Shabbat and yom tov, and are therefore not worn at the Bar Mitzvah (if it is held on the Shabbat). There are a variety of customs as to the exact date one commences wearing the tefillin. There are those who begin a month before the thirteenth birthday. Some begin closer to it, some the day after, and others a full year prior to that date.

It should be noted that the Bar Mitzvah ceremony does not have to be held on Shabbat, but can take place on any day when the Torah is read at the service. This would include Mondays, Thursdays, or Rosh Hodesh—first day(s) of a new month.

Until recently, among certain Sephardic groups in Israel the wearing of tefillin was begun two full years prior to the Bar Mitzvah (see *Keter Shem Tov*, vol. 1, IV, page 13). Among the Sephardim the day when the child first begins to don tefillin is of major importance. Yom Tefillin—the Day of Phylacteries—has come to assume the quality of a celebration in its own right.

A note on sumptuary laws

During the Middle Ages the rabbis enacted a series of decrees that have come to be called sumptuary laws. These forbade various practices and were enacted to limit conspicuous consumption at a time when there was anti-Jewish criticism that charged ostentatious and overly luxurious living.

These laws generally limited the size of feasts at celebrations, as well as the dress and jewelry that could be worn. For example, the Rhenish synods of 1202–23 decreed that only those who participated in the accompanying religious ceremony could participate in the banquet. The 1615–16 conference in Poland declared that people could only wear two rings on weekdays, four on Shabbat, and six on holidays. Neither men nor women were allowed to wear precious stones except for pregnant women, who were allowed to wear a diamond because it was believed to have curative powers.

Because of the diversity of dress customs among different communities the Spanish decree of 1432 could not make general rules in this area. It was decided, though, that each community was required to create its own ordinances, which would be incumbent on community members.

The entire rationale of the sumptuary laws can be summed up in the first nine words of the Lithuanian decree of September 4, 1637:

Inasmuch as people are spending too much money unnecessarily on festive meals, every Jewish community and settlement that has a rabbi is expected to assemble its officers and rabbi to consider the number of guests which it is suitable for every individual in view of his wealth and the occasion, to invite to a festive meal. . . . In a settlement where there is no rabbi, the nearest Jewish court will enact such an ordinance for them.

There is no point in beginning a diatribe here against lavish Bar Mitzvah banquets or other areas of conspicuous consumption. Suffice it to say that if anyone is interested in beginning a campaign to institute sumptuary laws in contemporary Jewish life . . . they'll have our support.

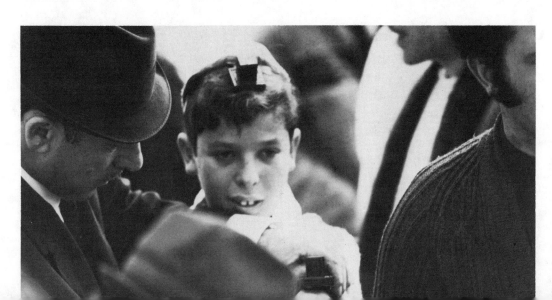

The Bat Mitzvah celebration

The Bat Mitzvah ceremony or celebration varies greatly depending on where it is observed. In Europe it was customary, particularly among the Germans, to give a party or seudah in honor of the girl's having reached the age of majority. The seudah was held on the twelfth birthday, and often the girl recited a derashah. In certain places it was customary for her parents to say the Barukh she-petarani blessing. Today as a twentieth-century innovation in some communities—particularly in Conservative and Reform congregations in North America—the Bat Mitzvah celebration is observed in the same manner as the Bar Mitzvah, and the young woman reads from the Torah and/or the prophetic portion of the Bible. Other congregations celebrate Bat Mitzvah but limit the celebration to Friday night services. While in certain places the Bat Mitzvah has been moved up to the age of thirteen, in others it is still observed at the age of twelve. It is safe to assume that in view of contemporary society's awareness of the role of woman, the Bat Mitzvah (both its significance as a milestone in the girl's life and the ceremonies that accompany it) will be expanded in importance in years to come.

The significance of the Bar / Bat Mitzvah

It is essential that one realize that being Bar/Bat Mitzvah and *becoming* a Bar/Bat Mitzvah (one who is obligated to perform the commandments) do not have a cause-and-effect relationship. In other words, one is a full-fledged member of the Jewish community, able to participate in all aspects of its religious expression and existence even if one has never had a Bar/Bat Mitzvah celebration. All that is necessary is that one be twelve years old if a female and thirteen if a male. It is common to hear people lament the fact that they did not have the opportunity to celebrate a Bar/Bat Mitzvah. Belated Bar/Bat Mitzvahs have become increasingly common in recent years; (see "Belated Bar/Bat Mitzvahs"). Many an individual who did not

have the opportunity to have one at the proper age has chosen to observe this rite of passage at a later date. While these ceremonies are quite moving experiences and the efforts to study and prepare for them should be lauded and encouraged, it is important that one remember that the essence of Bar/Bat Mitzvah is the *age* of the individual. The obligations and responsibilities become theirs whether there is a formal celebration or not. The ceremony, which is of fairly recent origin, does not make one a Bar/Bat Mitzvah; it merely marks the time when one becomes a "son/daughter of the commandments." The real meaning of the phrase is not "son or daughter of the commandments" but "one of the commandments," i.e., one who is obligated to perform them.

There are those who would argue that the ceremony should be postponed to a later date, possibly the age of fifteen or sixteen, when a person can more fully comprehend the meaning of joining the community. I cannot help wondering if this would imply that the obligations—which are really the essential meaning of Bar/Bat Mitzvah—would also be moved to a later date. Before any shifting of the ceremony to another date is considered, efforts should be made to highlight and emphasize the significance and the importance of the Bar/Bat Mitzvah. To move a ceremony because it has been observed in the past in a manner that has clouded its essential meaning, instead of accenting it, is to accomplish little. Twelve and thirteen have been the ages observed as the age of majority for over two millennia. The tradition of "thirteen and subject to the commandments" is something to be revered. We all ought to try to return the celebration of Bar/Bat Mitzvah to its original meaning.

Actually Rabbi, we've decided to forget about the mitzvah and concentrate on the bar!

The point of it all

Exodus 15:2, "This is my God and I will enshrine Him," has prompted Jews to make particular efforts to embellish both the rituals of Jewish life and the objects associated with them. Witness the beautiful Torah covers, menorahs, candlesticks, Kiddush cups, spice boxes, and so forth. Along with the ritual items, the ceremonies take on all sorts of added elements, which, though often not essential to the rites themselves, heighten their drama, emphasize their significance, and serve to "enshrine Him."

This is particularly true of the Bar/Bat Mitzvah. No ceremony is a prerequisite for one's being obligated to observe the commandments. All concerned in any Bar/Bat Mitzvah should remember that its actual meaning is one of commencement, not conclusion, of joining, and not leaving. To observe the Bar/Bat Mitzvah as symbolic of the conclusion of one's Jewish education is to make it the antithesis of what it is supposed to represent. (A familiar refrain, heard in a multitude of households is "You HAVE to go to religious school because you have to be Bar/Bat Mitzvahed." Can one criticize children for logically assuming that once they are Bar/Bat Mitzvahed they no longer have to go or that a religious education is no longer imperative???) We must not turn the significance of Bar/Bat Mitzvah into something that is diametrically opposed to its actual function and original meaning. It is important to remember that the Bar/Bat Mitzvah has acquired such importance not only because it marks an auspicious moment in a child's lifetime but also because it offers an individual, a family, a community, and in a real sense klal Yisrael—the entire community of Israel—the opportunity to celebrate and reaffirm a centuries-old heritage and tradition in a new and vital moment.

Alternative celebrations

Many families have begun to seek alternative forms by which to celebrate a child's Bar/Bat Mitzvah. One of the increasingly popular alternatives is for the family to travel to Israel and for the child to celebrate his/her Bar/Bat Mitzvah in a synagogue there or at the Western Wall. Another alternative is for the family and friends to go to a resort, hotel, or retreat and to observe the Bar/Bat Mitzvah in a rustic, informal, and intimate setting. There are others who believe that the "correct" locale for the celebration of the Bar/Bat Mitzvah is with the community, which the child now joins as a full-fledged member. They contend that logically and symbolically the ceremony should be held not *away from* but *in* the synagogue, where the entire congregation can join in celebration.

The following are suggestions from people who took varying amounts of responsibility for doing their own celebrations; we begin with Sabra Morton of Lexington, Mass., who has now had the joy/headache of planning and executing two Bar Mitzvah celebrations for her sons Michael and Evan.

In any case, it seems to me that any change that increases the child's, the family's, and the guests' comprehension of the significance and momentous nature of this event "harei zeh meshubah"—is worthy of praise!

Well I guess he's not quite ready for Tefillin.

Rabbi Solomon Freehof has described the Bar Mitzvah as a genuine folk product—and who has a better right to be folk than you and yours and I and mine? This is a propitious time to set forth on your own: the ceremony of Bar/Bat Mitzvah, though it has accreted in recent generations, is so shallowly rooted in halakhah and even in tradition that it invites innovative observance.

No halakhah, very little in the way of old traditions . . . what then is left with which to celebrate the time when a son or daughter takes on the responsibility and privilege of observing the commandments? Three things remain: a minyan for reading Torah—easily acquired by spreading the word, berakah, and the kavvanah—intention.

Kavvanah is the hard part. What is, what will be your intention? What will you do? How? Why? If you are seeking alternatives, part of your rejection of the "usual" is probably based on what someone has called the Madison Avenue quality of Bar/Bat Mitzvah—some rather flashy advertising and heavy hoopla for a rather tenuous product. Perhaps this, then, is the place to begin: let the weight of the ceremony and the ritual balance the weight of the festivities that accompany it. Keeping this in mind, think very hard (sometimes this turns out to be meditation) about what this rite of passage really means to those immediately involved—the child, the parents, the rest of the family. Okay, let's work on it together.

How one was done (two, actually)

For a number of reasons, which may or may not be the same as yours, our family felt that we needed to remove ourselves from the more usual Bar Mitzvah observances and create a ritual and a celebration that could have special meaning and importance for us all. We did some research and a great deal of reading, and gradually something evolved. Here are a few of the things we learned about and did; possibly some of them will seem right for you. With every "Bar" please read "Bat"; it'll save paper.

When? Anytime. The age at which a young person takes on the responsibilities of the commandments depends upon—the source you're reading! We chose *Pirkei Avot* (5:24), which specifies age thirteen. Many synagogues and temples, with large numbers of children to put through the process, have of necessity begun to ignore precise thirteen-ness, and that is talmudically quite acceptable. However, we were moved by Ecclesiastes 3:1, "To every thing there is a season, and a time for every purpose under the heaven," and so it was important for us that our son become Bar Mitzvah on the Shabbat (although really you can choose any day at all on which Torah is read) closest to his thirteenth Hebrew birthday. It was Shabbat Bereshit—the beginning of the cycle—"When God began to create . . . ," a very beautiful time in the Jewish year, one filled with stories, ideas, and images upon which we could build. It was a special joy that our next son had the same Shabbat, three years later. It also was a challenge; people kept asking: "What will you do for an encore?" Of course there are ideas unlimited in every Torah portion. By the time you've dug out a service (or two) from one of them, not only will you be something of an expert on it, you'll have a new appreciation of a rabbi's weekly work.

Where? Anywhere. "In every place where I cause My name to be mentioned I will come to you and bless you" (Exodus 20:21). One of our boys became Bar Mitzvah in the Jewish chapel at Brandeis University. The service for our other son was held in our yard on a bright October day. (We had looked at several "functional rooms." Functional they might have been—but very sterile too. Another possibility, if you don't live in a huge house, is to rent a big tent.)

How? With meditation, with love, with joy. And with much labor, which can be the manifestation of these. Here is part of our how to, with some of its labors.

1. *Invitations*: Presumably you can assemble a minyan by word of mouth, but when you get down to the fact that lots of people want to share in the nachas, you'll need something written or printed. One good thing to do is to buy cards from a charity that you like to support. Or you may want to design and make invitations—by silk-screen, woodcut, whatever is beautiful and your own. You can write the message by hand, or you can have it printed by photo offset, perhaps together with your design, comparatively inexpensively. We used pictures from books (if you choose something copyrighted, you'll need the owner's permission). One of ours showed the Bet Alpha Synagogue zodiac mosaic, which we found appropriate to the theme of creation. You might want to try your design on a fold-and-mail, called in the trade a self-mailer, since envelopes are a waste of paper. Fasten it with seals from an organization you support. If you're thinking shalom, write it somewhere.

2. *The service*: Here is where your heart and head really take over and kavvanah is felt. Do what is beautiful and Jewish and important to you. We made a service for each of our boys, retaining only the Torah and haftarah readings, the Shema, and the parental blessing from the customary service.

בה

Ruthie has reached the age of קבלת-מצות, and we are marking the occasion at a שבת service when she will read the הפטרה.

Can you join us on שבת morning, May 27, at 9:30, in the Hillel Foundation building (5715 Woodlawn Avenue)?

We hope that you can be with us also for the כבוד luncheon at the foundation immediately after the service.

Max and Esther Ticktin

R.S.V.P.

Creating a service took us a long time; the first one was nearly a year in the making, the second was several months. We began by reading and reading and *reading*. From this we garnered a wide variety of writings that have some truth and importance for us and that seemed relevant to the Shabbat of Creation. These we had printed by offset in booklets, one for each guest. (Hebrew can be photocopied and pasted onto the copy before it goes to the printer.) Some of our sources included scriptural and talmudic writers, as well as Leo Baeck, Harlow Shapley, Maimonides, Anne Frank, Anne Bradstreet, letters out of the Holocaust from someone in our family, William Butler Yeats, and Pierre Teilhard de Chardin. Here are some examples of how their messages came together, on Shabbat Bereshit, as we considered the creation, our place in it, and our Jewishness in it.

"By what way is the lighted parted,
Or the east wind scattered? . . ."

"I am the wind which breathes upon the sea."

"Canst thou bind the chains of the Pleiades,
Or loose the bonds of Orion? . . .
Knowest thou the ordinances of the heavens?"

"I am a word of science."

"Who hath put wisdom in the inward parts?
Or who hath given understanding to the mind?"

"I am the God who created the fire in your head."

And the dialogue continues. The first speaker is God to Job; the response is Celtic and anonymous.

Here is a portion that speaks of our Jewishness; it is excerpted from a section that undertook to relate Jewish history to recent events.

The Egyptians ruthlessly imposed upon the Israelites the various labors that they made them perform. Ruthlessly they made life bitter for them with harsh labor at mortar and bricks and with all sorts of tasks in the field (Exodus 1:13).

Frankfort on the Main
August 18, 1942

My dear brothers and sisters,
The weather is glorious, but everybody is on the move. Today all old age homes and institutions began their journeys.... The next trip will follow very quickly.... I must expect that I will belong to the next group of travelers ... and slowly I am getting used to the idea. God the Almighty can protect us anywhere. The present destination is supposed to be not too far and its living conditions, only for the elderly and sickly, to be easier. ...

September 11, 1942
Erev Rosh Hashanah
Friday, and I am all finished with my preparations for the trip and send you once more my farewell greetings, all my dear ones. I cannot find more words today. I know that you can sense them. ... To you, all my dear ones, the best for the future under God's protection.

The booklet for the service, part single-spaced typing and part Hebrew, was twenty pages. The service took about an hour.

3. *The scroll*: But the central text, the heart of the matter, is Torah. When a boy or girl accepts the duties of the commandments, it is symbolized by the child's reading from the scroll of the commandments, usually the maftir portion. So find a Torah scroll. This isn't as hard as you might

One tactical problem we succeeded in solving is how to serve one lovely large hallah and then get it carved up for many guests in a reasonably short time. You construct a loaf that can be pulled apart, which gives you the super feeling of really breaking bread. Use a firm but gentle dough—and instead of braiding, roll dough on a floured board into a large sheet about ¼ inch thick. Using a pastry wheel, cut the dough into strips and then into squares or diamonds (you should be sort of counting at this point, because these will make the serving pieces). Dip each piece of dough into melted butter or margarine, making sure that it has cooled enough so that it won't murder the yeast. Arrange the shaped pieces in the large pan, slightly overlapping them; you'll have several layers. Let the whole thing rise again until doubled. Bake at 350 degrees F., in the lower third of the oven, about 45 minutes. Cool the loaf in the pan for ten minutes or so, then turn it out very gently. This bread freezes well. When it is quite cold, freeze it in a big plastic bag. To thaw, let it stand overnight (we are now at Erev Bar Mitzvah) in its wrapping. Any handsome cloth can be a hallah cover, and voilà—with ha-Motzi each guest can "peel" a piece of bread.

Note: There are complex rules about how to warm food on Shabbat. Check with a rabbi for clarification about how to cope with the issue.

think: many synagogues will lend you one. (When you pick it up, make sure its *yad*—pointer—accompanies it.) The synagogue either will suggest the proportions of your donation or will leave the matter up to you.

With scroll in hand, you still need to make the Torah and haftorah texts available to the participants in the service. Let's assume you're somewhere other than in a Jewish building. It's easier to incorporate these texts, in Hebrew and in English, into your printed service than it is to borrow piles of Bibles from a synagogue. Besides, while synagogues do have extra scrolls, they're likely to be using their books.

The only other things you need for the service are an appropriate setting for the Torah scroll (we used a table covered with a blue and gold silk sari) and chairs for those guests who don't want to sit on the lawn or the floor. A rental agency will deliver and pick up chairs and also various other things you may need. Read on.

4. *Music*: If you're in a Jewish building, you may be able to use the organ or hire the choir (we're assuming Conservative or Reform here). At home you're on your own. A flutist filled some spaces for us, beautifully (a flute played outdoors surely approximates the music of the spheres). You can play any portable instruments, sing traditional melodies, compose and teach a niggun or two.

5. *The Kiddush*: Do consider restricting this part of the festivity to those things that are traditionally blessed on Shabbat: bread and wine. The more opulent your menu at this point, the more complex your berakhah system over the food needs to be, and you'd have to be quite a scholar to figure out (on the spot) the berakhot to cover those little wieners and Chinese egg rolls often seen at present-day Kiddushim.

By now your guests have figured out that some unusual things are happening, so they won't object when the Kiddush wine is served in little paper cups. Pour the wine ahead of time or, if you're outdoors where there are bees, arrange to have friends help you pour when you're ready.

6. *The food*: Having gotten this far, you just might want to do the loving labor of the meal. As a Jewish mother, I know better than to try to tell others how to feed their families. Here are just a few ideas I picked up, some by negative experience.

  a. There are many good books on cooking for a crowd, and they'll tell you everything you need to know. Almost. Here are some things they may not tell you.

  Table-and-chair-rental places often have unexpected wonders to offer—linens, cutlery, *tremendous* platters, enormous bowls. Most cities have ordinances that require that these things be autoclaved, which may, for stainless steel, suit you with regard to kashrut.

  No matter how carefully you compute for potato salad, you'll have a lot left over.

  No matter how carefully you compute for lox, you won't have *any* left over.

  Have four percolators, two of them for tea. Serve from two while two are brewing in the kitchen. Neighbors have these, or they can be rented.

  Fifty adults will consume a case of wine at a buffet-then-find-a-seat meal. Sitting at tables, with wine bottles on the tables, the same people will drink two cases. You can use a plastic wastebasket filled with water and ice to chill wine very quickly.

  b. Consider the possibility of serving a cold meal. Whatever your observance of Shabbat and of kashrut, you'll find that salad and platters of sliced things can be delicious, pretty, and easy to prepare and serve. Hot rolls are easy to add; make or buy them, foil-wrap and freeze them by the dozen, then heat as needed.

c. You'll be happier with the day if you do all your cooking well ahead of time. This will involve a lot of freezer space, your own and/or a neighbor's.

d. Paper plates and cups solve a lot of dilemmas about kashrut, and if your ecological imperative permits plastic cutlery and wine glasses, you've got it made.

e. If friends offer to make things, accept! Tell them what your plans are and let them add what they like to do. Our friends provided lovely things based on their special talents: a dried arrangement for a buffet table, an immense tray of homemade pastries, a watermelon bowl with toothpick-able fruits and Friday night dinner for the mishpahah.

f. Meanwhile, back in the kitchen on The Day. This is *not* the time to accept help from friends, or you'll find *all* of them in your kitchen. If you have more than fifteen or so guests, hire some experienced help for the tasks of serving, opening wine, clearing dishes, and cleaning up. You've done everything up to now; it's time to celebrate with your friends.

Louise and Dan Franklin, of Maitland, Fla., planned a different kind of Bar Mitzvah celebration for their son Jonathan. The invitation below outlines the form they chose to use.

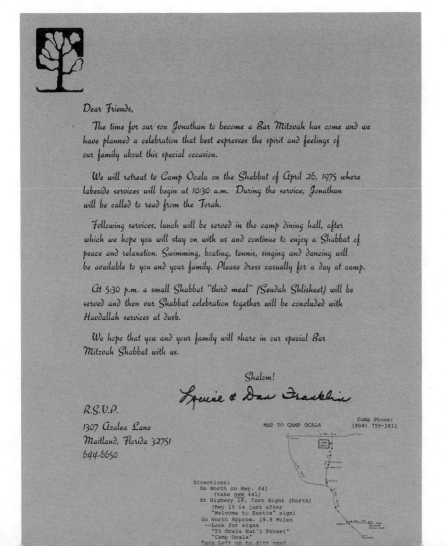

Dear Friends,

The time for our son Jonathan to become a Bar Mitzvah has come and we have planned a celebration that best expresses the spirit and feelings of our family about this special occasion.

We will retreat to Camp Ocala on the Shabbat of April 26, 1975 where lakeside services will begin at 10:30 a.m. During the service, Jonathan will be called to read from the Torah.

Following services, lunch will be served in the camp dining hall, after which we hope you will stay on with us and continue to enjoy a Shabbat of peace and relaxation. Swimming, boating, tennis, singing and dancing will be available to you and your family. Please dress casually for a day at camp.

At 5:30 p.m. a small Shabbat "third meal" (Seudah Shlisheet) will be served and then our Shabbat celebration together will be concluded with Havdallah services at dusk.

We hope that you and your family will share in our special Bar Mitzvah Shabbat with us.

Shalom!

Louise & Dan Franklin

R.S.V.P.

1307 Azalea Lane
Maitland, Florida 32751
644-6650

MAP TO CAMP OCALA

Camp Phone:
(904) 759-2811

Directions:
Go North on Hwy. 441
(take new 441)
At Highway 19, Turn Right (North)
(Hwy 19 is just after
"Welcome to Eustis" sign)
Go North Approx. 19.8 Miles
--Look for signs
"95 Ocala Nat'l Forest"
"Camp Ocala"
Turn Left on to dirt road

Some things you might think you need but don't

1. a rabbi (you're reading Torah, not seeking spiritual advice)

2. a bar (keep things simple)

3. professional musicians (any of the kids have a guitar? an accordion? a zither?)

4. vast flower arrangements (they wither anyway)

Some other things you might not need but then again you might

1. If you're not having all those expensive flower arrangements for you and yours, you might want to send an anonymous donation, perhaps a plant to someone. Cheery all around, and Maimonides, who is big on anonymous gifts, would rather like it too.

2. If your son wants at this time to fulfill the commandment of tzitzit, he needs a tallit. A daughter, though not commanded to wear a tallit, is permitted to, and she may feel very comfortable with this ritual symbol. You can make one for him/her in a number of ways (see *Catalog 1*, page 51). Our sons have tallitot with embroidered designs suitable to Shabbat Bereshit, and each has an embroidered Hebrew inscription: "When God began to create the heaven and the earth. . . ." "It is not your duty to complete the task, but neither are you free to desist from it." Genesis and *Pirkei Avot* here combine to express our wish that our sons will live creatively, will extend creation.

3. Make your own Kiddush wine. Take a minyan to a mountain. Read Torah on a retreat. When your child chants the maftir, say shalom and mazel tov and kiss him/her. Feast on hotdogs *or* ice cream; is this for the kid or isn't it?

The main thing is kavvanah, and each of you will delineate and experience your own. Shalom. Enjoy.

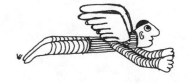

Louise adds some hindsight observations that ought to be helpful to anyone planning a retreat Bat/Bar Mitzvah (incidentally, she wrote to tell us how happy they all were to be able to share their celebration with you *Catalog* people. May we all be able to share celebration always within the community):

After the glow that is still with us even this long after the celebration, we can only urge other people to use their own personal skills and talents to create a moment that speaks to them. It was a day filled with love and warm memories—a high point in our Jewish lives. We take joy in sharing some of our experiences with you.

Above all else, the Bar Mitzvah (or Bat—that goes without saying) person should be deeply involved in all that happens. We didn't want a Bar Mitzvah doll (you know, the kind where you pull the string and out comes the prerecorded haftarah), and so were very pleased when Jonathan decided to chant his portion in English. In every phase Jonathan was involved with the decision making, and we tried to be sensitive to his requests and needs.

Some of our more concrete suggestions:

1. One of the big hangups that accompany all Bar Mitzvah celebrations is the whole food scene. We felt that we *had* to be free of all this, and so having the Bar Mitzvah at a kosher camp where there was a cook who handled all the food eliminated that problem. We avoided the usual Bar Mitzvah orgy by having simple food, and I was free to concentrate on the service itself.

2. We hired a beautiful girl (who plays guitar) to sing. She sang throughout the service, and the mood created by her ethereal voice and the

lakeside setting was one of a pristine purity. Our family is into music and chose to concentrate on this aspect. I can see many variations on our theme—if a family is into art or dance or Jewish study, their celebration could reflect these interests and strengths.

3. We planned to have everything but lunch outdoors. If we did it again we might even have lunch in a grand picnic style outside too. If the day is warm not only is the dining room stuffy, but the outdoors beckons.

4. We scheduled a bet midrash during the afternoon under a huge spreading tree. Our associate rabbi had printed commentary relating to the Torah portion and a lively discussion ensued with real exploration and sharing.

5. During the later afternoon, after people had pursued various sports activities, we gathered again to sing and sing as evening fell. Havdalah concluded a beautiful day.

6. Finally, it *does* take guts to do something different from the traditional community celebration. But our experience was invaluable to all of us. Dan and I found we had a deeper sense of parenthood and a great strengthening of the relationship between Jonathan and us. For Jonathan it was an affirmation of his capabilities, his strengths, and his commitment to his Jewish life.

Pre/post Bar / Bat Mitzvah ritual innovations

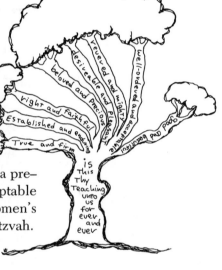

Sy Hefter of Wilkes-Barre, Pa. has some interesting suggestions for a pre–Bar Mitzvah and a post–Bar Mitzvah boy. Some of the ideas are adaptable for girls (depending on your synagogue's progress in equalizing women's roles), and he adds some general guideline possibilities for a Bat Mitzvah.

The Bar Mitzvah year

The year following the Bar Mitzvah of a boy can be designed to have special meaning. The rabbi can announce the beginning of the year as he accepts the boy into the adult Jewish world. The boy must assume more roles in the synagogue than is usually the case. The Bar Mitzvah ceremony is the beginning of the boy's fuller participation in Jewish life, and he must continue to LEARN and DO.

The Bar Mitzvah countdown

Arrangements are made for the boy to be given a tallit or to pick a piece of attractive material and sew a tallit WITHOUT TZITZIT—ritual fringes. The rabbi or teacher shows the boy how to tie the tzitzit and the boy ties them himself. In addition, tefillin should be purchased without a bag. The boy should pick out the material for the tefillin bag, and he himself or a relative or friend should sew the bag, using a simple pattern. The bag can also be woven. A bag for the tallit can be made the same way.

Days to Bar Mitzvah	minus 30	boy puts on tefillin for the first time and attends the regular daily morning service. He brings along food for a small Kiddush to mark the occasion.
	minus 7	boy reads Torah in synagogue on Saturday afternoon for the first time.
	minus 5	boy reads Torah in synagogue on Monday morning for the second time.
	minus 2	boy reads Torah in synagogue on Thursday for the third time.
	minus 1	boy leads Friday afternoon and evening services and recites Kiddush.
The Day:	Zero Hour!	boy leads entire service, reads Torah, and delivers short talk about the portion of the week.

But all this is the beginning. For the coming twelve months, the boy will be known as a Ben Mitzvah and will assume his responsibilities as an adult in five areas.

a. THE SYNAGOGUE

The boy will attend religious services regularly, every Friday evening and every Saturday morning. If he attends on Saturday mornings or at any time the Torah is read, he would be given opportunities to:

(1) serve as assistant gabbai; lead the closing hymns at the end of services

(2) be given aliyot

(3) be given a haftarah during the year, as well as his own haftarah

(4) tie the Torah

(5) take the Torah out of the ark

(6) lift up the Torah after the reading is completed

(7) if able and permitted to do so, read the Torah on either Monday or Thursday morning during the year; if he can learn the Rosh Hodesh reading, he could read it also.

The boy should undertake a commitment to perform weekly service to some person or a group for an entire year. Some possibilities:

(1) visit an elderly person, grandparent, patient in an old age home;

(2) visit hospitals or nursing home patients;

(3) tutor a child in Hebrew or English studies without pay;

(4) volunteer to help an agency serving the blind, handicapped, retarded;

(5) perform volunteer service for a person in local prison;

(6) be part of minyan at a house of mourning whenever (God forbid) the occasion arises;

(7) serve as usher in synagogue;

(8) volunteer to help in the local Jewish community center (JCC).

c. PROJECT

The boy should undertake a project that will benefit either the Jewish or general community. Suggestions:

(1) rearrange school, synagogue, or JCC library; catalog it if needed;

(2) check the tzitzit of the tallitot in a synagogue and correct them where necessary;

(3) help erect a sukkah; sound a shofar for a hospital patient or anyone homebound during the High Holidays; deliver gifts to Jewish elderly in old age home or housing project before each Jewish festival.

SHOFAR

d. VISIT

The boy should visit a number of key institutions in Jewish life; choosing three out of the following:

(1) the synagogues and temples in his community (at least one of each denomination); meet the rabbis and learn about their views of Judaism;

(2) the Jewish old age home, Jewish community center, Jewish family service agency, Jewish federation, and mikvah; meet the heads of each and discuss their services;

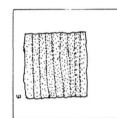

(3) in New York City: the Jewish Museum, the Statue of Liberty, a matzah factory, Lubavitch headquarters;

(4) the Touro Synagogue in Newport, Rhode Island;

(5) a place of Jewish interest one hundred miles or more from home, travel there alone, spend the day, and return.

e. ISRAEL

The boy would complete any four out of the following:

(1) view on TV or in a private showing by an organization some of the following:

(a) *Exodus* (b) *Let My People Go* (c) *The Last Chapter* (d) *Legacy of Anne Frank*

(2) read some of the following and write a review:

(a) *The Chosen* by Chaim Potok

(b) *Exodus* by Leon Uris

(c) *Story of Masada* by Yigal Yadin

(d) *Cast a Giant Shadow* by Ted Berkman

(e) *Haym Salomon* by Howard Fast

(f) *Diary of a Young Girl* by Anne Frank

(g) *To Do Justly* by Albert Vorspan

(h) *Encyclopedia of Jews in Sport* by Bernard Postal

(3) help in the annual UJA drive or raise money for another Israeli tzedakhah

(4) make a scrapbook containing pictures of five leaders of Israel, a map of Israel, pictures of ten places to visit in Israel, twenty different Israeli postage stamps, and five different coins

(5) complete a ten-week minicourse in speaking Hebrew.

A committee of the synagogue where the Ben Mitzvah and his family belong would meet regularly with the boy and hear reports of his progress. A suitable ceremony at the end of the year would mark the completion of the various studies and projects.

Synagogues that are considering instituting a new tradition for girls coming of age ought to consider building into the design of such a custom some ideas that would make the occasion a long-remembered one. Here are some ideas that can be tried on for size:

(1) utilizing mothers instead of teachers as key people to prepare girls;

(2) designing a Bat Mitzvah year (similar to the Bar Mitzvah year outlined above);

(3) utilizing some of the principles of Women's Consciousness to develop some indigenous feminine approaches to acceptance of Judaism as a young woman;

(4) writing new prayers and readings in a contemporary idiom that reflect twentieth-century approaches to the Almighty;

(5) developing ceremonies using the mother and the grandmother of the girl as well as aunts, cousins, etc.—women welcoming women to the community.

A last note: Some people sent in copies of the Bar/Bat Mitzvah services they had written for/with their children. They are willing to share advice with others who want to do their own. Some of these people are:

Mr. Yosef Yanich
American Jewish Congress
4200 Biscayne Blvd., Suite 3F
Miami, Fla. 33137

Dan and Louise Franklin
1307 Azalea La.
Maitland, Fla. 32751

Sabra and Tony Morton
3 Rolfe Rd.
Lexington, Mass. 02173

Belated Bar / Bat Mitzvah: notes on a promising program

Many people who missed their Bar/Bat Mitzvahs the first time around have begun to experiment with filling this lack when they are older. Al Axelrad, the Hillel rabbi at Brandeis University, has begun a program there to encourage people who want to, to have a belated Bar/Bat Mitzvah.

Just after Yom Kippur, 1970, Steve, a Brandeis senior visited me. After exchanging pleasantries, he finally asked sheepishly: "Rabbi, is it permissible for a Jew to become Bar Mitzvahed at the age of twenty-one?"

He found immediate comfort in the assurance that a Jew automatically becomes a Bar Mitzvah at the age of thirteen and that ceremonially one may become a Bar Mitzvah (i.e., called to the Torah for an aliyah) anytime after the age of thirteen. As a history major he took delight in learning that a number of great Jewish historical figures in fact became Bnai Mitzvah later in life. I also added that I feel that Bar Mitzvah ceremonies as we know them at thirteen are ridiculously premature and that Bar Mitzvah at an older age seriously recommends itself to me. With that for encouragement, his story began to unravel: a story not uncharacteristic in its message of alienation and estrangement.

His parents, exceedingly marginal Jews to begin with, did not practice Judaism themselves at home, nor did they expose their children intellectually or experientially to the tradition. Instead, they nominally joined a big temple, farming the children out for purposes of receiving a Jewish education. The education turned out to be minimalist, superficial, and inferior, and the temple experience was impersonal and uninspiring. Eventually, at different stages, the boys dropped out. Since their parents cared little and provided no encouragement, Steve did not undergo the Bar Mitzvah preparation and ceremony.

Not, that is, until his senior year at Brandeis. After several conversations we selected a tutor who volunteered his time, and together we mapped out a program. With Shavuot, occurring toward the very end of the academic year, as the target Bar Mitzvah date, Steve embarked on an in-depth study of the covenant concept, along with an intellectual and experiential introduction to the Shabbat and its liturgy, to Hebrew and some cantillation. He met with his tutor on a weekly basis and with me at irregular intervals. He wrote a fine paper dealing with the covenant, came to shul with some regularity, attended Shabbat dinners, and in general got on seriously with the business of becoming a relatively knowledgeable and active Jew, whatever that would eventually come to mean to him.

The Bar Mitzvah service occurred within the context of our ongoing informal, spirited, and highly participatory Shabbat morning havurah. The warmth of the service, the joy of the occasion, and the spirit of the participants blended beautifully to create a memorable experience. The participatory spirit was contagious, and Steve's thirty-some-odd friends in attendance joined in freely, joyously, and as fully as they could. For some it was their first synagogue experience in years; for several, their first ever. Woven into the singing, davening—praying, and Torah reading was an outstanding derashah on the covenant by Steve (based on his paper), my shorter devar Torah, and an open discussion followed by a Kiddush catered by Steve's friends. In addition to its religious, intellectual, and communal value, this particular service was such a moving emotional experience that by its conclusion even the eyes of the more restrained people present were moist. Of course, the greatest impact of all was on Steve, who exuded an emotional combination of pride and humility. Steve was called up for his second aliyah months later in the fall, at our communal Yom Kippur morning service, and his growth as a Jew continues.

Working out the plan

Stirred by this experience, Steve's tutor and I concluded that in all probability this case was no anomaly, that there must be many others on the campus who never did become Bar/Bat Mitzvah ceremonially: women who

have consistently been denied the equal Jewish experience open to men; Jews of both sexes who have become alienated from Jewish life by a variety of factors, including lack of exposure, familial indifference, marginality, or antagonism, Jewish malpractice at the institutional level, etc. Moreover, we agreed that thirteen is a preposterously early age for Bar Mitzvah (which should be a maturity-requiring rite of passage) and that its preparation and ceremonial celebration seemed more fitting at sixteen, eighteen, or later. In this way it would become a volitional and intensive process, born of initiative and understanding, involving in-depth learning and creativity. We thus decided to initiate a new program—Brandeis Hillel's "Belated Bar/Bat Mitzvah Program."

In the fall of 1971 a corps of tutors agreeable to giving "Bar/Bat Mitzvah lessons" as a labor of love was formed and continues. The lessons consist of a systematic introduction of Judaism, an in-depth study of a central Jewish concept or text, Shabbat and the liturgy, Hebrew, cantillation. The tutees also meet with me from time to time and occasionally they meet together, as well as attending services frequently. Most of them are complete novices, or close to it. The experience itself culminates in the writing and delivering of an original devar Torah at the service, and in the reading of the Torah/haftarah portion. The ceremony preferably occurs within the context of one of our ongoing services, e.g., the Friday evening Reform service or the Saturday morning traditional service (in which the seating is integrated and the roles of men and women are completely equal). Once in a while it occurs at a special service convened for the occasion. Thus far several undergraduates, recent alumni, and one member of the staff have experienced the "Belated Bar/Bat Mitzvah Program," while several others, including a faculty member, are currently in various stages of preparation. A number of others have chosen to go through with the tutorial preparation but not with the synagogue ceremony itself, preferring to experience a personal, individualized introduction to Judaism on an intellectual and philosophical level, without the ritual component. The program continues to grow and prosper.

Some jumping-off points

1. Our "Belated Bar/Bat Mitzvah Program" can be duplicated anywhere. Although it may function most effectively on campus with abundant Jewish resources, which makes possible a luxury such as a tutorial corps, it can be successfully duplicated by a single qualified teacher (rabbi or other), in much the same way that reading courses are offered.

2. An interesting possibility would be for a parent to experience a Bar/Bat Mitzvah ceremony for the first time along with his/her youngster. The possibility of a father/mother (usually the latter, owing to the woman's more limited role in the traditional synagogue of the past), who has never undergone the ceremony, studying along with the child in a tutorial and being called up to the Torah as a Bar/Bat Mitzvah on that occasion strikes me as potentially moving and stirring. This would make the experience even more of a family affair, although the pitfalls of contrivance and artificiality would certainly loom large in many cases.

3. Invariably the parents and sometimes extended families of the belated Bar/Bat Mitzvah have joined in the simha, even when that has meant coming from afar geographically (and often spiritually). Therein lies a delicate problem, however, requiring deft and sensitive handling. I cannot give

a formula for success but can sensitize readers to the problem, so that they can anticipate it and not be caught by surprise.

Often, the emotional reaction of the parents is mixed, ambivalent. They rejoice over their child's finding meaning in Judaism and in their child's Jewish affirmation. At the same time, however, they feel embarrassed and defensive over the inference that they had failed to impart all this to their children in the first place, earlier in life. This much is written on their faces; mostly it goes unverbalized.

It is good, then, to strive to meet the parents warmly, honor them during the service (e.g., with an aliyah, or at least with the opening of the ark, with raising or dressing the Torah scroll if they prefer a "nonspeaking" role), make them feel comfortable, and give them the assurance that this bold and meaningful initiative on the part of the belated Bar/Bat Mitzvah must be in some measure a reflection of the nourishing and nurturing that they themselves have done.

4. Reconsecration of Jews at thirteen-year intervals is another possibility perhaps worthy of experimentation. Both Jewish communal and family life would be better if we could succeed in initiating and establishing a tradition that every thirteen years following the age of thirteen each Jew would be expected to take a tutorial or other course in aspects of Judaism and prepare anew for being called to the Torah. Bar/Bat Mitzvah bet, gimmel, etc. would thus occur in the life cycle of the Jew at the age of twenty-six, thirty-nine, fifty-two, sixty-five, seventy-eight, etc. These late-in-life occasions would not partake of the rote nature of the Bar-Mitzvah-at-age-thirteen experience, but would proceed on the basis of understanding and learning in depth. The number thirteen is an obvious choice, fastening as it does on a well-established tradition. This, however, would enhance its attractiveness without detracting from its goal—i.e., striving for a knowledgeable and practicing adult Jewish citizenry.

One last vision: The impressiveness of belated Bar Mitzvah might convince rabbinic and lay leaders in Jewish religious life of the preposterousness and futility of maintaining the ceremony of Bar Mitzvah at thirteen. With the notion of the belated Bar Mitzvah as an available alternative, and with preparatory courses and ceremonies proving to be an attractive and constructive option, the age of Bar/Bat Mitzvah may be changed, initially at least, to an older, more mature age, in liberal forms of Jewish religious life. As I have said, the ages that suggest themselves to me are sixteen (certainly an age of passage on the American scene) or eighteen (voting and military service age). Sixteen is perhaps best, as youngsters are still in their family settings, whereas by eighteen they may have left home.

These visions and possible ramifications are bonuses, making the idea of belated Bar Mitzvah programs even more constructive. Having experienced a number of such moving ceremonies in the last three years and having seen the positive impact on the participants persuades me that such programs deserve to be blessed by proliferation throughout the Jewish community.

Confirmation

 In the nineteenth century, German Reform Judaism decided to substitute a confirmation ceremony, held at the age of sixteen, for the Bar Mitzvah. The feeling was that at thirteen the person could not really be considered an adult and could not really understand the full significance of the ritual.

Here in America the practice of confirmation has continued, but it is held in addition to the Bar/Bat Mitzvah rather than being a substitute for it. It is clear that, in America at least, the reasons once given for the creation of the Confirmation ceremony still obtain today. Adolescence is prolonged (sometimes into the early twenties), and the entry into the Jewish adult community at thirteen now seems premature. Perhaps a preentry at thirteen and a full entry at sixteen or eighteen could provide an alternative. In any event, the value of the Confirmation ceremony, undertaken in seriousness and with commitment, can be manifold. Chip Rosenthal, who celebrated his Confirmation in the not-too-distant past, shares his experiences.

The Confirmation services

A Confirmation service may be as interesting and unique as its participants wish it to be. I was confirmed in May 1975 with a few other people who had graduated from our temple's school. I found Confirmation to be an important and serious experience, with much more meaning to me than my Bar Mitzvah. At thirteen my Bar Mitzvah had no impact on me, since I really didn't know what I believed or where I fit in Judaism. It felt more like a regular service in which the rabbi gave me a small part. The Confirmation, however, felt like *my* service since I helped to create it.

My Confirmation class in school was given the responsibility for planning a service that would reflect our feelings. We decided to complement the usual prayers and Torah reading with poems, talks, and interpretations of traditional prayers. For example, one person liked the poem "Anyone

Lived in a Pretty How Town" by E. E. Cummings, so the rest of us agreed to use it in the service. In addition, we rewrote prayers to include the original basic idea but put them into terms that were contemporary and/or acceptable to us. For example, I agreed with the general idea of working together for worldwide peace, but I avoided the word God to conform to my agnostic ideas. Sometimes we agreed with the prayers, but more often than not we disagreed.

The most interesting part of the service, however, were the talks prepared by members of my class. They expressed our ideas about Judaism, Confirmation, life. Most important, all of us felt free to say not what someone wanted to hear, but what we thought and what we believed. I spoke of how I thought too many Jews had left their Judaism in the temples, to be produced only on Friday nights. I spoke of how I disagree with many Jewish principles, while agreeing with others, and even mentioned how and why I consider myself partially agnostic. The whole experience—the freedom to be honest and clear about our Judaism and ourselves—was an important one for all of us.

Some advice

If you are planning a Confirmation service, I would like to give a few suggestions. The first goes to the parents of confirmands-to-be: don't force your kids to enroll in a Confirmation class. They are probably old enough to decide what they want, and anyway, if you stick them into a class without any choice they will probably learn nothing and manage to slow the progress of the rest of the class. But by all means encourage your child.

Now to confirmands: you might want a theme for your service. When we were trying to come up with a theme for our service, our rabbi told us a story about two archers. One man kept missing the target with his arrows, while another kept getting bull's-eyes. When the first man asked the second for his secret, the second man showed him that after he had shot an arrow and it had landed, he drew a target around the arrowhead. What I'm trying to say is—form your theme around what you have.

Maybe the most important thing is to put a piece of yourself in the service, even if it is just a poem you read or wrote. The best idea, of course, is to give a short uncensored talk. If there is a decision to give talks, it is good to listen to suggestions, but remember that it's *your* talk.

Also, don't stifle other people's ideas. Suppose someone wants to use a poem you don't like. Before you veto it, remember that maybe s/he won't like the prayer that *you* want to use.

Leaders of Confirmation classes: you can censor a speech all you want, but that won't change a person's feelings. In today's world, wouldn't it be better to give it straight rather than to lie and cover up to make it sound nice?

The last suggestion is—don't restrict yourself to my suggestions. Your class should get together and talk about your particular service. A really good Confirmation service can make up for all the years you had to spend in Hebrew school!!

And God will say, make a path, clear the way, remove the stumbling block out of the way of My people.
—Isaiah

Honoring Parents

The Ten Commandments: an introduction

We are taught in the Ten Commandments that we are obligated to show honor to our parents: "Honor your father and your mother" (Exodus 20:12, Deuteronomy 5:16).

We know and take seriously the fact that Rabbi Akiva and Rabbi Ishmael debated whether all the commandments of the Torah which were mysteriously contained within the ten—were not somehow the prototype rules for all Jewish behavior. And so we concentrate on the ten for a moment, seeking to understand why these ten, more specifically why the fifth—honoring our parents—is given so much weight.

Let's begin by considering how the fifth commandment fits into the context of the ten. The first asserts the existence of God and makes sense both because of the intrinsic power of the statement and because it establishes the central reality of Jewish belief. Given the declaration of the first, the second and the third establish the rules of the game. They tell us not to make or worship other gods or do anything that detracts from the "I AM" of the first commandment. While the first three commands basically concern wo/man's relationship to God, there is a hint of change in the theme of the fourth. We are told in the first part of the fourth commandment to remember or observe the seventh day, which is a Shabbat unto God. Why? Because God created our universe in six days and rested on the seventh. Generations of Jews have understood the fourth commandment as an invitation to share with God in the process of creation-work-rest. Thus the first three commandments can be understood as establishing or proclaiming divinity and wo/man's relation to that divinity. While the fourth is still concerned with wo/man's relationship to the divine, God seems to be reaching out to people, as it were, and inviting participation.

Then comes the fifth commandment. It is the first of the latter commands, which seem to deal with the relationships between people rather than between God and humanity. Mysteriously, a transition has occurred in the space between the fourth and fifth commandments. But the transition is subtle. The theme of creation and of man's sharing with God is still maintained, for parenting is the most basic of human creative acts. As God created the universe, so does humanity create progeny. We observed that the earlier commandments were mitzvot bein adam la-makom—commandments concerning a person's relationship to God—and yet a subtle motif of worship can be detected in the fifth. Our rabbis explained that in the birth of any child there are three partners: mother, father, and God. So our sages taught that when a person honors a parent, God says: "I ascribe merit to them as though I had dwelt among them and they had honored Me" (Kiddushin 30b). Thus the transition from commands dealing with the relationship between God and people to commands bein adam la-havero—between people and people—is accomplished in the fifth commandment.

The parent-child relationship

It is appropriate that a series of commands dealing with the interpersonal begins with the parent-child relationship. It is the most basic of all human relationships. It is our primal relationship, through which we learn to relate to others. In each of our own personal beginnings, all females are our mothers and all males are our fathers. As an infant grows, his/her parameters expand. The child learns to differentiate. How appropriate that the first of a series of interpersonal commands begins with the primal relationship and proceeds to differentiate other relationships. Following this developmental approach, it is reasonable that the command is addressed to the child—telling the *child* how to relate to the parent rather than addressing us as parents or adults. Freudians among us should also appreciate that the very next command is "You should not murder," which they might want to see in this developmental context as a restraint of the oedipal.

The command to honor

What are we called upon to do in the fifth commandment? We are commanded to honor. What in the world does "to honor" mean? The rabbis interpreted kavod as an expression of the most desirable of all relations between two people: mutual respect for the dignity of the other.

The rabbis taught that you must extend kavod to anyone, regardless of

that person's social status or power in relationship to you. Even though there might be real inequality, the rabbis called for mutuality of respect. Furthermore, the rabbis taught that each of us must honor the other, but that no one should demand honor for him/herself. Thus God seeks honor for our parents, not they for themselves.

But what does "mutual respect for the dignity of the other" mean? Does kavod imply a relatively superficial social convention, an etiquette, a deep emotion, or a norm of human decency? By respecting the dignity of the other, am I in fact drawing away, detaching myself? Perhaps the parent-child relationship in its depths is chaotic, and by being commanded to honor we are really commanded to withdraw from the primal chaos. Respect the other; deal with the other on conscious levels of dignity; don't intrude; don't act out unconscious, chaotic drives. See the parent as a person with an identity that is separate; withdraw yourself from childish projections that do not permit you to see your parent as an other. Perhaps there can only be respect if there is separation, for if there is no other, who is the object of your kavod? It seems that separation or withdrawal is necessary for respect; but once such separation occurs then there exists space for approach on a higher level, namely, approaching the other as a person in his/her own right.

Traditional ways to show honor

While the rabbis clearly tell us that it is incumbent upon us to honor our parents, they articulate relatively few specific ways in which we should express honor. They do not concern themselves with distinctions between feeling honor and expressing honor. Perhaps they so much knew what it means to honor parents that they assumed we would also know, or perhaps, wisely, they left the matter to our own discretion.

Here are some rabbinic examples of ways of expressing the honor due parents:

1. A child should not stand or sit in a place where his parent is accustomed to standing or sitting. Rabbi Tarfon so loved and honored his mother that when she wanted to go to bed, he would make himself into a human stepladder so she could get into the bed, which was too high for her to reach otherwise. Rabbi Joseph, on hearing his mother's footsteps, would

say: "I will arise before the approaching Shekhinah" (Kiddushin 31a-b).

2. A child should not support his parents' opponents in a scholarly dispute (Kiddushin 31b; Rashi).

3. The rabbis praised Dama, a heathen, son of Netina of Ashkelon, who refused to awaken his father, although he needed a key lying under his father's pillow in order to conclude a transaction that would have brought him a profit of 600,000 gold coins (Kiddushin 31a).

4. The rabbis made it clear that honor and obedience are not necessarily synonymous: it is not permitted for a child to transgress a prohibition at his father's request, since both father and son are obligated to observe the same mitzvot (Yevamot 6a).

5. In areas of financial responsibility the rabbinic position is firm: If a parent is in need, the child is obligated to supply him/her with food, drink, clothing, blankets, and other help (Kiddushin 31b-32a; *Shulhan Arukh,* Yoreh Deah 240:5). The halakhah stresses that aid to an indigent parent must be performed with generosity of spirit on the child's part; it is stated that even if a child gives the father pheasants as food, if the act is performed grudgingly it will cause the child to lose his/her portion in the world to come.

6. Jewish law and tradition also prescribe modes for mourning the death of a parent, and such mourning is seen as a form of honoring our parents. For example, during the first twelve months after his father's death, a son is supposed to say: "Thus said my father, my teacher, for whose resting place may I be an atonement." After the initial twelve months the son should say: "His memory be for a blessing, for the life of the world to come" (Kiddushin 31b).

Contemporary sensitivity

We are beset by an incredible variety of issues in our own lives, issues that range from the psychodynamics of respect to the ethics of homes for the aged. In between, we face the reality that, for better or worse, parent-child relationships within the Jewish community are affected by the larger culture in which we live. The larger community, even after Sophie Portnoy, still harbors the image of the Jewish family as somehow stronger than other American families. We find a kind of proof for the continued existence of this image when we hear prospective converts say that they are attracted by the closeness of our families. And yet we realize that, unlike earlier generations, the son of a tailor may neither want to be a tailor nor be complimented when told he is like his father. In fact, he may be terrified by the realization that he is anything like his father.

We have learned from that uniquely Jewish profession, psychology, that adolescents must establish their own independent and separate identities and that the thrust for selfhood may require rejection of their parents or their parents' values. We have learned that subjecting our own will to that of another, even if that other be a parent, can destroy. Many of us endorse the concept of confrontation. Modern movements within psychology have helped legitimize the expression of anger. Although many of us might maintain that honoring another can only truly happen if it is done honestly, we also must admit that conflicts between our contemporary culture and the rabbinic vision of kavod do exist.

We glimpse a rabbinic utopia in which human interaction is based on mutual kavod. It is so fragile. It is as though an entire system of interaction or an entire society were based upon two people—the first two people in our lives. Our parents, then, are our first relationship. And it is there that all learning begins.

On Leaving Home: A New Rite of Passage

Pervading much of Jewish life is the injunction, "Do not separate yourself from the community." The holidays, prayers, and customs continually reaffirm one's ties with klal Yisrael—the community of Israel. Even at that point of ultimate separation—death—the individual is linked with the community.

There is a phenomenon in American life that has become so commonplace that little attention has been given to the psychological as well as the physical separation that actually occurs—the transition between high school and college. This period, more than any other in one's life, signifies a radical break from one's family, friends, and community. For those who attend college away from home, the physical move is a removal from the security and comfort of home (although it is often looked upon as a sign of weakness for one to admit this sense of loss). For those who commute to college from home, the sense of separation is lessened but still there. But it goes further than the immediacy of the present. To know that eighteen years of a familiar way of living are about to end and to step into the unknown, the unfamiliar, where one is to forge a personal life-style and make major life decisions—as exciting as this may sound—are also quite frightening. Coupled with the impending loss felt by one's parents and family, which is sometimes more intense than that felt by the graduating student, the anxiety of separation becomes even more apparent.

At one time, not long ago, the institution of marriage acknowledged the transition from adolescence to adulthood. Young people lived with their families until they were ready to marry, and they were encouraged to wed while still young. The couples set up their homes and businesses in proximity to their parents, thus reinforcing the strength of the extended family. Of course that era no longer exists. We are living in an age when geographical mobility is the norm and when adolescence is extended by postponing one's career and marriage to the mid- and late twenties.

One can argue that the ceremonies and parties revolving around high school graduation could provide a meaningful transition from high school to college. However, several factors almost prohibit the possibility. The current state of education and the devaluation of the high school diploma on the job market have downgraded the sense of achievement one has upon graduating. Yet, ironically, the overwhelming emphasis at the graduation ceremony is on academic achievement. Other factors, such as a sense of separation and transition, are alluded to in passing if at all. And the personal element is practically lost in the routinized, mass-oriented production of graduation.

What, then, can be done to help make this rite of passage a meaningful event in one's life? One suggestion is to incorporate it into the Jewish life cycle. In other words, like other periods of change (birth, puberty, marriage, death) that have been translated into the Jewish idiom, this "young adult" stage can have quite significant implications. But why make it a Jewish event? The answer is simple. If Judaism is to adapt to changing human needs, it must be able to interpret real-life events within its own sphere of values and symbols. What other life-system is as aware of the positive and negative effects of separation as Judaism? What other people puts as much emphasis on the individual in his/her family and community as the Jewish people? It seems logical, therefore, that the place to start is in the home.

Some suggestions

1. Havdalah—the ritual that "separates" Shabbat from the rest of the week—could be the most natural time to choose for a new "Ritual of Separation."

2. Perhaps the graduate would begin by sharing his/her thoughts and feelings upon leaving home. The people present could respond simply and honestly—a dialogue of feelings.

3. Appropriate poems, songs, or readings could be said/sung before the Havdalah ceremony.

4. Bread and honey (symbol of sweetness and new beginnings because of their association with Rosh ha-Shanah) could be shared.

5. Finally, those present could reinvoke the traditional Jewish blessing formula. People could put one hand on the head of the graduate and one hand on the head of the person next to them and recite:

"The Lord bless you and keep you.
The Lord make His face to shine upon you and be gracious to you.
The Lord turn His face to you and grant you peace."

accord and discord

Sex and Sexuality

Introduction *by Hershel Matt*

 Surely the sexual revolution has brought much that is good. Knowledge is generally recognized to be good—and who can deny that knowledge of sexual matters has vastly increased. We know more about what our bodies are like and how they work. The facts of conception and contraception are ever more widely known; misconceptions are more and more rare. Our knowledge of the harsher realities of sexual behavior has also vastly increased: venereal disease, premarital pregnancy, abortion, illegitimacy, prostitution, promiscuity, adultery, homosexuality—all are matters of common knowledge to adults in all segments of society, to almost all teenagers, and to many preteenagers as well. To the extent that knowledge is a good thing, the sexual revolution has surely been a boon.

Awareness also is usually considered to be a benefit—and the sexual revolution, as it has increased our knowledge, has also increased awareness. We have become much more aware of the presence and power of our own sexual needs and desires and drives, of our satisfactions and frustrations—which, we now realize, are those of all normal men and women. We have become more aware of how many areas of life and how many aspects of behavior are affected by sex. We have become more aware of how hypocritical we have been in permitting, encouraging, and practicing a double standard in various forms—as between men and women, as between people we are willing to marry and the people we merely go with or go to, as between one group or occasion or circumstance and another. And we have become more aware of our own self-righteousness in deploring, condemning, ridiculing, exposing, forbidding, and punishing those whose words we ourselves have used and whose deeds we ourselves have been guilty of engaging in.

As the sexual revolution has increased our knowledge and awareness, it has also increased what is widely considered to be a further benefit: matter-of-factness in reaction and frankness of expression. What we now have come to know and be aware of, we find ourselves able more freely to express. We are less secretive and inhibited in discussing sexual matters. We no longer feel compelled to resort to vague terms and circumlocutions when referring to parts of the anatomy, functions of our physiology, or articles of our clothing; almost nothing sexual is unmentionable. In private

conversations and in the public media, full and frank descriptions and portrayals of sexual matters occur. And what we see and read and hear presented so frankly in various entertainment and communications media, as well as in actual life, no longer angers or disgusts or shocks us.

Furthermore, the sexual revolution, as it has increased our knowledge, awareness, and frankness, has decreased many of our fears. Because of advances in technology, science, and communication, many of the fears that plagued our predecessors have diminished or disappeared: unwanted pregnancies, premarital or postmarital, can usually be avoided—and when they occur can more safely be terminated; venereal disease can be prevented—or when contracted, can usually be cured; impotence, sterility, and frigidity can often be corrected or cured. Our fears about masturbation have been all but eliminated, and our fears about homosexuality have been markedly reduced. Much of what used to be terrifying because it was called perversion has become less frightening when termed abnormal and has tended even to become acceptable, as "normality" has come to include an ever-broader range of behavior. All in all, we are less afraid of other people's sexuality and of our own.

And yet in spite of all that is good in the sexual revolution, almost all of us realize that there is much that is bad. Indeed, we sense that somehow the very things that are good in it are also themselves bad. Or, to put it more exactly, most of the changes wrought by the revolution are inherently neither good nor bad but neutral—they can lead to either good or bad results. Surely neither the increase in knowledge, awareness, and frankness, nor the decrease in fear has brought about an unmistakable growth of genuine health, happiness, and harmony—for the older generation, between the older and younger generations, or for the younger generation itself. Each gain seems ambiguous. There is much greater knowledge—but is there greater understanding? There is greater awareness—but is there greater concern? There is greater frankness—but is there greater compassion? There is less fear—but is there not also less awe?

As Jews we should assume that there are resources within our Torah tradition for drawing upon the blessing and mitigating the curse of the sexual revolution.

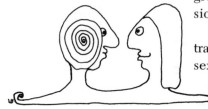

The Torah tradition

What does the Torah say concerning human sexuality?

The Torah says that "God began to create heaven and earth," the world and all that is in it—which is to say that what is often called "nature" is neither simply necessary nor simply accidental but comes as a result of God's power and wisdom and love, in accordance with His plan, for the fulfillment of His purpose. (Perhaps we should say "creation" rather than "nature.")

The Torah says that God "created man in His image" and that, since among all His other creatures "no fitting helper was found," "male and female He created them." What a strange paradox! Human beings, men and women both, are unique among God's creatures: they bear a likeness to God, who has personality but no sexuality; and they bear a likeness to animals, who have sexuality but no personality. And both the divine image and sexuality—each of them present from man's very creation—are essential to man's humanity. Furthermore, the two aspects affect each other and limit each other: on the one hand, even when man and woman are united sexually, their sexual union, though natural in the sense of normal, is not natural in the sense of a mere animal copulation. It is a distinctively human relationship—an I-Thou relationship, a relationship of two-persons-in-the-divine-image, each of infinite worth, neither one intended to be exploited as an object of the other's aggressiveness or selfish satisfaction. On the other hand, the relation between man and woman, however aesthetic and moral and spiritual, is an avenue to sexual expression.

The Torah says that "God saw all that He had made"—including man and woman—"and found it very good." Human sexuality, therefore, far from being unworthy or ugly or "dirty" or obscene or in any way evil or unpleasing to God, is good.

The Torah says that God's command to man—His very first command—was to "'Be fertile and increase, fill the earth.'" Sexual relations and human reproduction are thus a fulfillment of God's will and intention for wo/man.

The Torah says: "The Lord God said, 'It is not good for man to be alone; I will make a fitting helper for him.'... Then the man said, 'This one at last/Is bone of my bones/And flesh of my flesh, ... Hence a man leaves his father and his mother and clings to his wife, so that they become one flesh." Not only reproduction but also enduring companionship, mutuality, helpfulness—and sexual union as a regularly renewed means for their expression and nurture—are among God's prime purposes for man and woman. Furthermore, when children come of age they must break away from their parents and unite with others, founding new families of their own.

The Torah says that after the first man and woman had sinned by disobeying God's command, they "hid from the Lord God..." but "the Lord God called to man and said to him, 'Where are you?.. Did you eat of the tree from which I had forbidden you to eat?'" Whatever wo/man does is known to God; wherever wo/man goes s/he remains in God's presence.

The Torah says that at first Adam and Eve "were naked...yet they felt no shame" but that after they had disobeyed God's command—succumbing to the serpent's temptation to be like God—"the eyes of both of them were opened and they perceived that they were naked, and they sewed together fig leaves and made themselves loincloths." And still later, when they were driven from the Garden of Eden, "the Lord God made garments of skin for Adam and his wife, and clothed them." In God's original plan and in the ideal world, human nakedness occasions no shame; in the actual human situation, however, nakedness connotes immodesty.

The Torah says: "You shall not commit adultery." "Do not follow your heart and eyes in your lustful urge." "The devisings of man's mind are evil from his youth." "Sin couches at the door;/Its urge is toward you,/Yet you can be its master." Concerning the immoral sexual practices of the pagans, the Torah admonishes: "You shall not copy the practices of the land of Egypt...nor shall you follow their laws." "You shall...not...engage in any of the abhorrent practices...and you shall not defile yourselves through them." "I have put before you life and death, blessing and curse. Choose life." Wo/man is endowed with the capacity to distinguish and the ability to choose; wo/man is able to resist temptation; no wo/man always does; as Ecclesiastes says: "For there is not one good man on earth who does what is best and doesn't err."

The Torah says: "Reprove your neighbor, but incur no guilt [through your silence] because of him."

The Torah says: "You shall neither side with the mighty to do wrong." "Sweep out evil from your midst."

Drawing upon the complex of Torah teachings cited, one can arrive at this formulation of a Jewish approach to sex: *Human sexuality, like every human capacity, comes from God and is therefore holy and good—provided that it is exercised in faithful acceptance of God's purpose and in reverent awareness of His presence. The proper sexual relation is that which serves both to express and to further, on an enduring basis, the mutually responsive and responsible love of a man and woman who recognize that each has been created in God's image.*

The incest taboo may have had a eugenic purpose, but the Torah and Torah tradition speak of it in terms of sex morality alone.

The Torah tradition (*Pirkei Avot*) says: "Do not judge your fellowman until you are in his situation."

Psalms 112:1 says: "Happy is the man who fears the Lord,/Who is greatly devoted to His commandments."

The Torah—the Torah book and the Torah tradition—has many other things to say about human sexuality; about how human beings are meant to act and not to act; about those who live faithfully by God's command and those who live unfaithfully; about the consequences of sexual immorality for the individual and for society. And throughout this literature, which has been studied through the ages by old and young, there is almost always a striking frankness and explicitness. It was evidently not felt that holiness must involve prudishness or censorship, or that explicitness of sexual reference constituted a profanation of the sacred. Yet in spite of the frankness and explicitness, the Torah tradition, in both literature and life, managed to nurture and sustain in sexual matters the quality of tzeniut—an exquisite mood of delicacy, reserve, and modesty.

The scope of tradition and its application   *by David Feldman*

In the light of all this, Judaism sees sexuality and sexual expression as something positive and joyous, not obscene or inherently evil. It regards sex as a legitimate good, as a mitzvah, as an act compatible with holiness. At the same time, Judaism imposes certain restraints and discipline upon this area of life that are intended to safeguard both persons and sex itself from abuse.

In its proper setting, sex is a mitzvah. The marital sex obligation is defined by halakhah in terms both of frequency and quality. The husband may not be "pious" at his wife's expense and pursue ascetic inclinations to the neglect of the marital mitzvah. For example, when asceticism became popular among both Jewish and Christians in the Middle Ages, there was, according to Gershom Scholem, "one important difference, that nowhere among the Jewish ascetics did penitence extend to sexual abstemiousness in marital relations." Moreover, the husband has the mitzvah of quality as well; he is to "give happiness to the woman he has married" (Deuteronomy 24:5) in this matter of sex relations. The sex act itself is described in the classic Jewish sources as both good and holy.

Now, holiness is more usually perceived in terms of restraint, and this encounters understandable resistance. In the name of holiness, the Bible exhorts against following the abominations of "the land of Egypt where you dwelt, or of the land of Canaan to which I am taking you" (Leviticus 18:3). Adultery, incest, sodomy, and bestiality are called abominations; rape and seduction are likewise censured. The Talmud (Yoma 75a) imagines the initial resistance put up by the Israelites against refraining from such practices. Maimonides writes: "No prohibition in all of the Torah is as difficult to keep as that of forbidden sexual relations" (*Hilkhot Isurei Biyah* 22:18).

Adultery is severely condemned. It is both a sin (Joseph to Potiphar's wife: "How then could I do this most wicked thing, and sin before God?")—a sin that "defiles"—and a crime. Along with murder and idolatry, adultery-incest is so grave a sin that one must choose martyrdom instead:

for those three sins "let him die rather than transgress" (Sanhedrin 74a); except in these cases, Torah can be set aside to preserve life or health.

While the kind of adultery so roundly condemned is that of a married woman—with consequences to the children, who are declared mamzerim (illegitimate)—sexual relations between a married man and an unmarried woman constitute an offense of a different category. This "double standard" was quite consistent with a patriarchal system that allowed for polygamy but not for polyandry. Still, if the husband had not taken a second woman as either wife or concubine, the relationship was one of zenut (harlotry). With polygamy and concubinage losing favor on both social and moral grounds, the mutual fidelity of monogamy became the normative ideal.

John Calvin was astonished at not finding any explicit reference to fornication among the sexual prohibitions of the Torah—that is, relations between unmarried consenting adults. The halakhah, however, in Midrash and Talmud, interprets Leviticus 19:29 ("Do not degrade your daughter and make her a harlot") as referring to consensual relations without benefit of marriage.

Maimonides codified the view that declares such relationships to be harlotry and that sees the marriage bond as the Torah's advance over laws of primitive society. Only thus can the relationship become sanctified, incorporating its social and economic—and parental—responsibilities. Living together without conjugal intentions is zenut; living together *with* conjugal intentions is what makes a marriage—and it also makes the couple husband and wife, who then require a divorce to withdraw from the implicit commitment they have undertaken. The marriage ceremony and document make this commitment explicit, as it were, because society has a stake in their relationship as well. The Torah, Maimonides means to say, has institutionalized the relationship—not to shackle it, but to raise it from what it was in prebiblical and precivilization days. Marriage is an institution to protect the partners from the uncertainties of changing moods and the lure of competing claims on their affections. Marriage thus prevents the ultimate human relationship from being trivialized; it does the same for sex itself. The holy and essentially human character of the sexual relationship obtains when the sexual is part of an umbrella of relationships—physical, emotional, social. Being the most intimate, the sexual is reserved for the most total of relationships.

While the idea of living together without marriage may be attractive to lovers who are impatient with commitment or exclusivity, with social status, or with any long-run considerations, those who share society's goals and religion's ideals will see the ceremony and certificate as their allies to that end.

To keep one far from temptation and unchastity, certain preventive measures are set forth in the Talmud and codes. Among these is the decree against yihud—being alone together—with, for example, an unmarried woman or especially with the wife of another man. The force of these temptations varies, of course, so that while yihud is forbidden so as to safeguard against adultery, "Israel" says the Talmud, "is above suspicion of sodomy or bestiality"; hence no similar restriction was deemed necessary against these acts.

The modern debate as to whether homosexuality is an aberration or an illness or neither is irrelevant to the Jewish moral tradition. Actually, the recent vote by the American Psychiatric Association to exclude homosexuality from the category of mental illness only restores it to the area of

Contemporary Americans tend to regard sex as a biological necessity and to condone casual sex among consenting adults. In a sense this attitude is an extension of the "It's-okay-as-long-as-I-don't-hurt-anybody" mentality that is rampant today. Jewishly this attitude has absolutely no validity. Every act has significance, because in Judaism people are not ultimately responsible solely to themselves or even to one another. We bind ourselves to a higher law and try, insofar as we are able, to conduct our lives within those boundaries. Sex, then, is never an act devoid of significance—morally or otherwise. Sex is seen in terms of serious emotional commitment and as an ultimate human relationship, and can never, whether pre- or post-marriage, be seen as casual. Such an attitude would be anathema to every Jewish value.

moral choice. If homosexuality is not the result of compulsion, then it must be considered to be a freely chosen act. And as a freely chosen act, it is forbidden by Jewish law (Leviticus 20:13). It is a violation of the Torah's concept of sexual purpose and sexual functions, not unlike the modern biological notion that years of evolution have placed the sexual organs in a heterosexual position—evidence, we are told, that wo/man is programed for procreation, not for homosexuality.

Of course, the homosexuality spoken of as being morally repugnant, whether an illness or not, pertains not to fantasies or mere contact, but to the behavioristic act of sodomy. It is the act itself, not the actor, that is morally repugnant. We are bidden to show every compassion for the sinner—but not for the sin. Yet our compassion for the sinner need not lead us to condone something that is inimical to the Jewish concept of sex and family. The fact that Talmud and codes (Kiddushin 82a; Even ha-Ezer 24:1) say that "Jews are above suspicion" of doing that kind of thing is interesting: it means that homosexuality is not, or at least had not been, a Jewish "vice." Some claim that this rare incidence of homosexuality in the Jewish community (at least until recent times) is the result of Judaism's affirmative attitude to heterosexual sex and family life.

The value judgments are evident in the laws on birth control as well. The sexual act in marriage has two independent coequal purposes—the procreational ("peru urevu—be fertile and increase") and the relational (shalom bayit—family harmony); marital sex is integral to both. So in cases where a possible pregnancy poses a threat to the wife's health or well-being, the physical relationship must not be set aside. Likewise, if the hazards of pregnancy are avoided by sexual abstinence, then both purposes or functions of marriage, instead of just one, are subverted. If conception of children must be prevented, it would be wrong to subvert the mitzvah of marital sex at the same time. Hence contraception is mandated. Where contraception is used by choice, there are some methods that are acceptable to most authorities (see Medicine for a discussion of various contraception methods).

In abortion, too, concern for the woman's welfare is evident in Jewish ethics. Paramount in decisions about abortion is the principle that "her welfare takes precedence." But whereas this refers to the relative interests of mother vis-à-vis the potential child, the rest of the Jewish sex ethic refers to woman vis-à-vis man. In this arena, considerateness for her is as fundamental as is the abstract moral concern for the fetus, and detailed legal and moral provisions aim at preventing a "sex-object" role.

The Jewish sex ethic, then, affirms sexual pleasure in the disciplined structure of family life and holds the restraints of civilization to be the means of holiness.

Finally
All of this is necessarily inadequate. It is simply impossible to discuss fully such crucial issues within the confines of a few pages. The only possibility is to open a door and begin to understand the premises on which Jewish concern rests. And the concern that above all informs and speaks through any discussion of any sexual issue in Judaism is the affirmation of sexual pleasure and the celebration of the continuation of life as God's blessing to His people.

A contemporary approach to Jewish sexuality by Arthur Green

For the sake of honesty, it should be stated at the outset that any treatment of sexuality in this *Catalog* is necessarily problematical. The nature of the *Catalog*, from its outset, has been twofold: to be a guide to traditional Jewish living, drawn with some leeway from the traditional sources, and at the same time a reflection of the neotraditional Jewish life-style that is evolving among certain young-in-spirit American Jews, in havurot—alternative communities—and in the life patterns of concerned individuals. While these circles have tended toward traditionalism in ritual areas, have often rediscovered liturgy as a means toward personal religious expression, and have redeveloped deep Jewish ethnic loyalties, those of us who form them know that we are postmodern rather than premodern Jews, and that our life-style is hardly to be considered halakhic ("legal" within normative Jewish canons) in the full sense of that term. It is in the areas of sexuality and the place of women that this discrepancy between fully halakhic traditionalism and the neotraditionalism of these "new Jews" is most clearly seen.

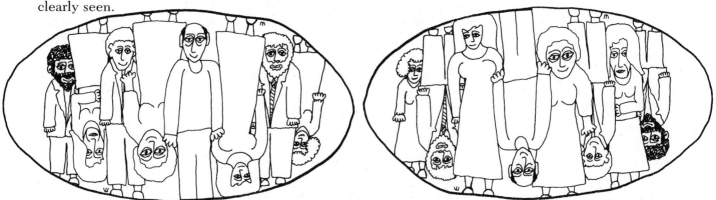

A few examples in the realm of sexual mores will serve to clarify our point. Halakhah, frowning upon any degree of sexual expression outside of marriage, has classically sought to protect its followers from sexual arousal in untoward circumstances: unmarried men and women should not dance together, touch each other, be alone in a room together. The ethic of this current group is utterly different. Short of genital sexuality, expressions of intimacy are encouraged: in matters of hugging, holding, and speaking of love, most people in the Jewish counterculture are not unlike their American post-1960s counterparts, sometimes shocking their more Orthodox associates. One of the leaders of this many-streamed movement, otherwise generally identified with a somewhat hip version of halakhic Judaism, was heard to explain it thus: our ancestors worked so one-sidedly at developing the life of the spirit that they came to be afraid of their bodies; now, when Jews have returned to the land and are discovering their rootedness to the physical, we must also return to loving God through forms of bodily expression. The brief sermon was concluded with an exhortation to get up and dance and, in the tightly-grasped circle, to know that we love one another. Rav Kook, on whose thinking such an analysis is based, would hardly have approved!

A more serious example: The halakhah has generally viewed all forms of nonmarital intercourse as beilat zenut—harlotry. Among the many young unmarrieds in groups that are close to this *Catalog*, there is hardly any thought of condemnation concerning premarital sexuality, including intercourse (even without deep love commitment!), provided it is carried on within the general bounds of interpersonal decency. Even to evoke such "liberal" halakhic standards as the legitimacy of common-law marriage is irrelevant to the lives of these Jews, who have rather guiltlessly had any number of sexual partners.

Yet another example: The halakhah has always taken a rather dim view, to put it mildly, of homosexuality. The biblical term abomination pretty well sums up the traditional attitude. When a havurah schedules a retreat and announces that "spouses and lovers" (including homosexual lovers) of haverim are welcome to attend the weekend event, it is clear that

God and Israel are lovers: Israel, the redeemed servant girl at the Red Sea, sees a vision of her young black-curled lover coming toward her. Sinai, the great revelatory event of human history, is constantly depicted in terms of love and marriage. The words of God at Sinai are kisses, and from the sublime kissing of God and Israel at Sinai, according to some Kabbalists, angels are born (Horodetzky, *Kitvei ha-Ari*). In the Tent of Meeting, a place of privacy and silence, that marriage is consummated. The highest form of prayer, say the Hasidic masters, is to be termed "intercourse with the Presence" (*Toldot Yaakov Yosef* 38d). The Sabbath is the time when God and the community of Israel meet in sexual embrace.

Passion is a master.
—Yiddish Proverb
Trans. Leo Rosten

Rather talk to a woman and think of God than talk to God and think of a woman.
—Yiddish Proverb Trans. Leo Rosten

The pursuit of passion becomes boring.
—Hasidic Saying. Trans. Leo Rosten

approval has been given to an open flouting of the halakhic norm. While remaining rather conservative in their own lives, few people in these circles are now scandalized at the *thought* of bisexual behavior.

Given this situation, which cannot simply be wished out of existence by well-meaning traditionalists, how is one to write a guide to sexual practices? To leave the issue untouched would be an unforgivable avoidance. The need for such a guide is most serious: Jews who find the old standards inoperable for them find themselves bereft of moral guidance in this area, and are in need of a new and realistic approach. What follows, then, is a stumbling outline of what might be called a sexual ethic for Jews who have found the whole traditional realm of hilkhot ishut impossible as a personal standard, and who nevertheless seek guidance from the traditional wisdom and values of Judaism.

The greatest and potentially most divine mystery accessible to most humans is the mystery of sexuality. The totality and all-embracing quality of sexual expression, including the arousal of body, mind, and emotions, has in many ways been used by our sages to symbolize the most profound secrets of the cosmos. "All of scripture is holy," says Rabbi Akiba, "but the Song of Songs is the holy of holies" (Yadayim 3:5).

Kabbalists see the very origins of the universe as a never-ceasing process of arousal, coupling, gestation, and birth within the life of a God who is both male and female, and proclaim this complex inner flow of divinity, described in the most graphic of sexual terms, to be the highest of mysteries.

All this imagery provides for the Jew an *ideal* of sexuality. While we know well that most human sexuality hardly approaches this exalted picture, it does provide us with a point of view. It indicates strongly that we Jews should stand opposed to the current moves toward the "demystification" of sexuality, which seeks to define coupling as a purely biological function. We are made most fully human by the fact that this act, shared by us with the animal kingdom, can be raised in our consciousness to the rung of raza de-yihuda—the sublime mystery of union. Sexuality at its fullest is brimming with religious kavvanah: this is a teaching that we would be fools to ignore. If we cannot fulfill the ideal, we can begin to approach it.

The sort of coupling spoken of here is impossible if it is not mutually engaging. One could hardly imagine a religiously more offensive thought than that of one person "using" another in order to reach the sublime. A high level of sexuality can only be based upon a fully developed intimacy between those involved, an intimacy that includes a daytime life together which serves as a counterpoint to the greater intimacies of the night.

The tradition has always assumed that such intimacy can exist only between two given individuals, that any person is capable of only one such intimate relationship at a particular point in life, and that these two individuals be a man and a woman. Such a relationship is sanctified by the bonds of marriage. All these assumptions are now called into question by the possibilities of open marriage, loving homosexuality, and nonmarital love situations. We can no longer insist upon the singular legitimacy of exclusive heterosexual monogamy as a key to the sexual ideal. We can, however, assert the value of deep and honest intimacy, including a full life with the other, as a sine qua non of sexuality at its highest.

This intimacy perforce involves another area of traditional Jewish concern: that of interpersonal *responsibility*. The whole area of sexuality, both in the search for partners and in the act itself, is one of tremendous personal vulnerability. The complex needs that emerge in the course of sexual giving do not permit that giving to be taken for granted, but rather call for responsible consideration on the part of the other. While we may no longer live within the traditional view, which claims that a man "possesses" a woman by virtue of having intercourse with her, our ethics should still contain a mutualized echo of that view. Despite claims of sexual liberation, we should have sufficient psychological awareness to realize that sexual involvement may be of great and sometimes traumatic significance to the other, and the feelings involved must be taken seriously. Any ethic that says that I am responsible only for myself, but not for the other, is abhorrent to Judaism.

Within marriage or other forms of steady sexual liaison there is an even greater degree of responsibility. Here the other has been led to trust, and that trust may not be violated. However open we may be with regard to alternative sexual life-styles, it should be said clearly that any Jewish ethic must remain unalterably opposed to any extramarital relationship in which the other marriage partner is deceived. A marriage that one partner unilaterally decides is "open" is in fact not open at all, and makes a mockery of the traditional values of fidelity, honesty, and responsibility.

The greater problem, however, is not that of the married but that of the unmarried. What do we say to the adult (we do not speak here of adolescents, whose problems are quite different) who has not found a person to share the depths of love, or who even feels incapable of such a relationship? What do we say to the widowed or divorced person, used to loving sexual fulfillment, who is now driven to distress partially by sexual loneliness? It is clear that *we cannot advocate celibacy for all who are not in love.* Given the world in which we live, they would simply ignore such pious pronouncements, rightly noting that it is usually the self-righteousness of the happily married that stands behind them. Living in a world where we cannot advocate either ideal sex or no sex as the alternatives, what we must begin to evolve is a *sliding scale* of sexual values. (Rabbi Zalman Schachter is owed our thanks for first having articulated the notion of the "sliding scale" in various areas of neohalakhic practice.) At the top of this scale would stand the fully knowing and loving relationship outlined above, while rape—fully unconsenting and anonymous sexuality—would stand at the bottom. Somewhere near the middle of the scale, neither glorified nor condemned, would be the relationship of two consenting persons, treating one another with decency, fulfilling the biological aspects of one another's love-needs, while making no pretense at deeper intimacy. Given such a scale, a Jew might begin to judge his/her own sexual behavior in terms of a series of challenges which s/he might want to address.

Each particular relationship will of course bring forth its own questions, and the place of any relationship on the scale of values would be determined by a combination of factors. Only at or near the bottom of the scale (rape) would we speak of sin; in other relationships we would do better to note the inadequacies of our situation than to bemoan our sins.

This kind of new halakhah, when taken seriously, is in its very liberalism more difficult and in some ways less immediately gratifying than the old. It does not remove our insecurities by telling us what we may and may not do. Rather, it leads us to self-examination and encourages growth. By maintaining the ideal of true and full sublime sexuality, we may be able to continually infuse ourselves with higher strivings, while not self-righteously condemning anyone who, through the circumstances of his/her life, stands at a different point in our flexible scale of intimate values.

Love: Is the sexuality of this relationship an expression of a depth of feeling that exists between us, or is the feeling generated only by sexual arousal itself?

Knowing: Have the partner and I really come to know one another and see one another as full human beings, or does this act remain a basically anonymous sexual encounter?

Honesty: Have I presented myself in an untrue way (by words, dress, or style) in order to win this sexual reward, thus making it more difficult for true knowing to emerge in this relationship?

Degradation: Have I had to go someplace (pickup scene, bar?) or do something (pay in cash or favors?) that I consider personally debasing in order to get this partner, thus keeping myself far from true sexual fulfillment? Could I not find a partner in some more wholesome way?

Consent: Do both of us really want this sexual contact, or has one of us fallen into it unwillingly, making it a contact in which both are disgraced?

Shidduch— The Jewish Connection

One beginning: it's all good for a laugh

The Bible has it that Adam was the first single and that God did not view this as an entirely satisfactory condition. Had it been 1976 a shidduch ad might have been placed in the personal column of the *New York Review of Books:*

Nude unself-conscious male with fruited garden apartment in Eden, desires to meet fitting helper. Object: clinging as one flesh.

But the year of creation was not a good year for singles, so God made for Adam a fashioned rib called Eve. Without divine intervention, however, we don't recommend that Jewish men and women be connected in this manner.

The question is, though, how *do* Jewish singles get it together?

Let's take a look at some historical models.

Fact: Abraham was the first Jewish parent with an unmarried child on his hands. What did he do? He commissioned his servant Eliezer to find a "significant other" for his son Isaac.

In those days the best place to meet a single woman was at a watering hole or well. Eliezer decided to hang out at the Aram-Naharayim well, where, after a while, he spotted Rebecca. Not only was she comely, but she treated him to a drink; and not only that, she also treated his camels to drinks. Eliezer was so pleased with her generosity that he ran to her father's house to draw up the contract. Sight unseen, Isaac and Rebecca were connected. This is not to say that they did not grow to love one another, but first came the contract, then the commitment.

IF you seek a faultless friend you will remain friendless.
Yiddish proverb
Trans. Leo Rosten

So what's new today?

Here in America—the "goldeneh medinah"—there are 43 million singles and at least a quarter of a million of them are Jews. Some have defiantly chosen the single condition, but most have drifted into it casually. Whether defiantly or casually, there seem to be certain factors that have facilitated this trend.

In America the "must" of Jewish living no longer obtains. Whereas in the past a Jew married to fulfill not only human needs but godly ones as well, today godly needs don't seem to loom very large. So, one does one's thing (that is, if one knows what one's thing is). Without that sense of covenant or contract, without that sense of "It's bigger than the both of us," relationships tend to be affairs rather than affirmations.

Complicating things further, we've ruled out the shadchan (the matchmaker of *Fiddler on the Roof* fame) as a reasonable way for Jews to get together. True, the idea of men and women being paired up by a glatt kosher butcher of human flesh seems less than spontaneous and romantic. But in modern society what advances have we made over the shadchan? In our infinite wisdom we have created kosher meet markets called Concord Singles Weekends and singles dances for people who would rather swing than "shuckle." Dances, feh! For $4 you get the privilege of being ignored, humiliated, or shot down. What happened to romance? Where's the spontaneity?

A key confrontation on a singles weekend arrives with Saturday breakfast. In the Concord's stadium-size dining room . . . the atmosphere is as romantic as a bottling plant—but to singles it looks like the world's largest marriage factory. Accordingly, the master of fates is maître d' Irving Cohen, who decides who sits near whom. Cohen requires seconds to size up a stag's approximate age, education and motivation, then assigns the single to a table where tastes should be compatible. To help him keep track, Cohen identifies each guest with a color coded peg stuck in a war plan of the dining room (*Newsweek*, January 15, 1968).

Or if you've exhausted the Concord, Grossingers, and your local synagogue's dances, you could always try a computer dating service (Atlanta's Jewish community has its own). The problem with that is—do you *really* want a machine to pick out a mate for you? Besides which, the questions asked are frequently of the "off-the-wall" variety.

In any case, computers leave us cold and I suspect we'd all prefer to do our own hunting.

A further problem is that in America, Jewish community values are either hard to transmit or become distorted in the translation. The Jewish ideal of married bliss as the desideratum for all has fallen by the wayside. The model of Mary Tyler Moore—Single Career Woman—is in and the old "woman of valor more precious than pearls" is out.

Wedded life may still be touted in conjunction with the myth of bliss but it has become a distinct liability in the peculiar arena of television programming. The dominant position of prime-time entertainment is now monopolized by what ad agencies might refer to as the "unmarried." . . . Granted, some of these characters may have been married at one time but now are either divorced (Kojak) or struggling alone as a widower (Lucas Tanner). But the implied message seems unmistakable: being single is more fun, or at least provides more opportunities for getting in on the fun (*New York Times*, September 10, 1974).

And added to this is the woman's movement, which quite rightly lets us know that a woman has worth independent of a man and that a Jewish woman can study at a university to *become* a doctor, not to *marry* one. All of which leads us to believe that the Jewish world for many is no longer a wedding. It's more like a catered affair. And it's clear that the Jewish community hasn't "come through" in any serious way to grapple with these vows.

Portnoy and the American Jewish Princess Computer Dating Service
Please answer the following questions:

1. What do you think Friday nights are best for?
   a. going to synagogue
   b. fulfilling the biblical injunction in Genesis 1:28
   c. eating at a Chinese restaurant
   d. making a guilt call to your parents
   e. all of the above

2. (For men) Your ideal mate should:
   a. know Martin Buber's books better than you do
   b. not get headaches
   c. know how to bake a good hallah—or know the good bakeries where you can get one

3. (For women) Your ideal mate should:
   a. be a doctor/lawyer/Indian chief/kosher butcher
   b. know how to recite the Kiddush from the prayer book without looking at the transliteration
   c. not be nagged by Portnoy's complaint

Another beginning: where have all the young Jews gone?

Okay. So the problem can be seen as light, amusing, humorous. But there's another side—the serious side felt by us singles ourselves. It is an undeniable fact that singles have been ignored, denigrated, and put down by the Jewish community.

In all honesty we have to admit that Judaism has traditionally frowned upon the single adult life-style as an institution. No doubt survival of the species must have been the prime reason why living in the unconnected and/or celibate state was discouraged. But at the same time, we'd like to believe that our progenitors were attempting to actualize the life of shidduch. The world to them *was* a wedding, full of brides, grooms, and betrothed couples. To give you an idea, take a look at "L'Kha Dodi" (Shabbat as bride) or Song of Songs (God and Israel as lovers— see rabbinic commentary), etc. If shidduch (or, if you want to wax grandly philosophical, dialogue) was the Jewish view of the world, then the single condition was not to be encouraged.

So let's call that the rationale behind the Jewish community's failure vis-à-vis the unmarried. For it is clear that not only was the community unprepared to cope with singles, it has also failed dismally to reach out and program effectively to meet singles' needs.

The fact is that most synagogues are centered around the family unit. This unit was the core of Jewish life, and synagogue programing developed to meet those needs. Sisterhoods grew up to service the needs of women

(married ones) and men's clubs to service married men's needs. But a definable gap grew up between Bar/Bat Mitzvah and betrothal. Some synagogues made meager, wary forays into programing for the single Jewish community by running Saturday night dances that were about as Jewish as leftover chow mein—and equally satisfying emotionally. So it is small wonder that Jewish singles sought identification elsewhere.

Naturally, much hand-wringing and pitiful moaning occurred in the Jewish community about the high rate of intermarriage and the lack of "young people" (are *all* singles young?) at Friday night services. It did not occur to anyone to see a cause-and-effect relationship between the drifting of Jewish singles to the contemporary watering holes and the lack of Jewish alternatives to these places. It is partly because the establishment—the synagogues, community centers, and national organizations—failed to reach singles effectively and imaginatively that these singles bars have prospered. In the few instances where interesting programs have been developed, such as those planned by the New York Federation, they have proved to be successful and well attended.

But: some advice to singles
It can be frustrating to rely on the Jewish community to respond to our needs. Change comes slowly to our family, and while we should work to promote such change, we should also realize that we have to help ourselves in the meantime. We're going to have to create our own institutions that service our own needs. So if you're concerned about single Jews having a batampte (tasteful) way of coming together, then what follows is a nicely "prepared table."

An initial suggestion

We begin by suggesting that unattached Jews use traditional Jewish structures for coming together. A focal point of the community has always been its service or interest groups, and these are a good jumping-off point. Why not form or join

1. a study group
2. a Project Ezra—i.e., a group that visits and helps the poor, elderly, infirm Jews of your city
3. a hevra for visiting the sick

**Lincoln Square Synagogue
200 Amsterdam Ave.
New York, N.Y. 10023**

has such a group called Bach-Bikur Holim (Visiting the Sick). Write to them for details.

4. a havurah (see *Catalog 1*, "Blueprint for a Havurah")
5. a UJA young leadership group

**United Jewish Appeal
1290 Avenue of the Americas
New York, N.Y. 10036**

Check with your local synagogue to see what programs exist or what programs might be started. You might also check with one of the following national Jewish organizations to see if they have a program in your area:

Note: The Task Force publishes a monthly newsletter for $3 a year, which gives information on Jewish singles events in the New York area. It is also a good resource for program ideas.

**Bnai Brith
1640 Rhode Island Ave. N.W.
Washington, D.C. 20036**

**American ORT Federation
817 Broadway
New York, N.Y. 10003**

**American Jewish Congress
15 E. 84th St.
New York, N.Y. 10028**

**New York Federation of Jewish Philanthropies
Task Force on Jewish Singles
130 E. 59th St.
New York, N.Y. 10022**

**American Jewish Committee
165 E. 56th St.
New York, N.Y. 10022**

Some further suggestions on making the connection

So there you are in Philadelphia, Atlanta, or San Franciso. The weekend's coming up and you're wondering what to do to meet some interesting new people. The bar scene isn't for you, neither is your Aunt Sarah's next-door neighbor, and there haven't been any good parties recently. You think: "Isn't it about time that someone invented a painless (maybe even fun) way to meet Jewish singles?" Relax. Somebody has.

The three programs presented below have had long-run engagements in New York City. They are presented as program models that can be adapted by existing groups or newly formed groups to suit their particular needs. They are three formats that provide social alternatives to the current singles scene and do it—most importantly—in a Jewish context. They don't guarantee instant connections, but they might at least ignite a few sparks.

The Shabbat meal

THE FORMAT

Dinner is served, Shabbat ritual is followed (Kiddush, ha-Motzi, etc.), and an Oneg Shabbat follows.

The Shabbat is a very special time of the week and a very important observance when, ideally, we try to shed the cares of the past few days and seek a sense of renewal. The program should reflect this tone (candlelight, wine, etc.). The setting should be special and the evening should flow with ease and a minimum of last-minute details. A feeling of intimacy and interaction should be fostered, which means that a limit of about thirty-five to forty people should be present.

DINNER

The traditional Shabbat meal consists of wine and hallah initially, with chopped liver, gefilte fish or soup as a first course; then chicken, vegetables, kugel, and salad as the main course, followed by tea and cake. For any galloping gourmets in the group, the menu obviously can be elaborated on or changed. The setting should include white tablecloths (linen if possible), flowers, silver, and china (again, if possible) to reflect the special quality of the evening. Different people can be assigned to make different parts of the meal, or—if the budget permits—it can be catered.

THE SERVICE

The traditional prayers such as candlelighting, blessing over the wine, and ha-Motzi—blessing over hallah—should be said before the meal. The rest of the service can be held afterward either in a sanctuary or in the same setting. One variation of the program, however, is to hold part of the service while people are still at the tables and even incorporate parts of it into the meal. A creative service or just some additions can be written by members of the group. This is an educational and interesting experience for those

Rationale
This program has many advantages. Since most singles eat alone, it provides a welcome opportunity to share food and an evening in community. Also, most singles are not affiliated with a synagogue, and thus often miss Shabbat services.

who write the service and also may make it more directly relevant for those who attend.

After the service, tea and cake are served, and people are encouraged to mingle, talk, sing, and even do Israeli folk dancing if the mood strikes.

THE DETAILS

One of the most essential elements in any successful program is attention to details and careful advance planning to ensure against last minute problems. If a creative service is to be written, allow the writers several weeks for their undertaking. A mailing should go out at least two or three weeks ahead of time asking for reservations and payment—in advance! If the responses are slow in coming in, it may be necessary to have another mailing (possibly to a larger audience) as well as a phone committee (a boring but effective way of getting a response). Based on the number of reservations, food can be made and/or ordered. The charge for the program depends in part on the cost of the food—around $5 is about right. The program can begin at sundown (which will vary depending on the time of the year) and will probably run to 10:30 or 11:00.

Group discussions

THE FORMAT

The program begins as people enter. About half an hour is allowed for light refreshments (a little wine helps) and general mingling. Name tags are filled out for each person upon entry (a necessary evil), and room assignments are made. Everyone then gathers in an auditorium, where the program of the evening is explained. A speaker talks for about twenty minutes. The speaker should not deliver a lecture. Rather, s/he should discuss interesting aspects of the evening's topic and raise stimulating questions to be followed up in the discussion groups. This part of the evening has been eliminated in some programs and people are asked to go directly to their assigned rooms. In the smaller rooms, group discussions are held for about forty-five minutes to an hour and then everyone reassembles for more refreshments and wine.

Rationale
The New York Federation Task Force on Jewish Singles has adopted this format, as have other groups, and it has proved very popular. For good reason. The program provides a stimulating social evening with the opportunity to discuss an interesting topic in a small group, where interaction and the exchange of ideas and experiences are possible.

THE GROUPS

Groups should ideally have about twelve to fifteen people (with a fairly equal distribution of men and women). A group leader whose role is to guide and facilitate the discussion has been previously assigned. But the leader should not be viewed as The Leader. Preferably s/he should have some background in group dynamics, psychology, and Jewish organizations. This person should set the tone for the conversations and stimulate discussion. Guidelines should be established at the beginning; for example, everyone is encouraged to participate—this is not a therapy session but an opportunity to share interesting ideas and experiences; people should speak in the first person and not overgeneralize; there should be no personal attacks. Group leaders should have a training session before the program and ideally a brief meeting following the program to assess the discussion and share ideas.

THE TOPICS

The topics should be chosen with two basic criteria in mind: (1) the content should be Jewishly related, and (2) it should be of interest and relevant to the people in the groups. We've used such topics as "Portnoy Meets the American Jewish Princess"; "Intermarriage"; "Christmas and Hanukkah"; "How I Feel as a Jew"; "Do You Feel Safe as a Jew Today?"; "Jewish Men/Gentile Women–Jewish Women/Gentile Men"; "Israel and Diaspora Relationships." The topics do not have to be rigidly adhered to if the group wants to go in a different direction; however, the Jewish angle should be maintained.

THE DETAILS

This kind of program requires a good deal of planning and attention to detail. Discussion leaders must be trained and assigned. Room assignments must be made in advance and the rooms must be clearly marked. The topic must be decided on in advance and advertised if possible. People must be assigned to groups as they enter. A speaker must be found if one is required. Advertising and direct mailing are important in this kind of program, since it is best to have from one hundred to three hundred people present (depending on facilities). If the programs go well, word of mouth will effectively provide future audiences. Advertising can be done in local newspapers or magazines. However, advertising has a plus and a minus effect. The plus is that it may bring new people, the minus is you cannot be sure what kind of a crowd it will bring or how many people it might attract (it may be necessary, for example, to turn people away—not *always* a bad thing). The charge for this program should be no more than $3.

Bet Café

THE FORMAT

The program is held at an established time on a set day (in New York, every other Sunday at 5 P.M.). People are greeted as they enter and are able to browse through the interesting literature that is provided, or else sit at a table and talk and drink coffee with new or old acquaintances. After an hour or so there is a more structured program, such as poetry reading, classical or folk music, an original play or skit, or a discussion on topics like Israel, the Jewish poor, Hasidism, or Jewish history. After this part of the program more time is allowed for casual conversation and refreshments.

Rationale
Bet Café programs provide an informal, casual environment that is conducive to lively discussion and talk. The aim in the Bet Café program that has been running in the Brotherhood Synagogue of New York City is to expose people to Jewish ideas and experiences. Although the goal is not a strictly social one, it provides an excellent atmosphere in which to meet people and share ideas.

THE SETUP

A table with interesting, somewhat unconventional literature is set up on one side, as is a table with coffee, tea, and soda. Since the program is free no other refreshments are provided, but people are asked to bring their own—nuts, cookies, or fruit—if they wish. Informal placement of the tables and candlelight help create a casual environment—a key to this kind of program.

THE DETAILS

Unlike the group discussion programs, the preparations required for this format are relatively simple. An announcement (giving the schedule and topics for a number of programs, if possible) can be sent out. Again, word of mouth will eventually be helpful once the program is established. Literature and simple refreshments are provided, together with a person who serves as speaker or leader for the evening's program. Aside from these basics, the evening should set its own tone and tempo.

If none of these leads are successful, then maybe you should think about starting your own group with some friends. After all, that's how Adam got it together—with a little help from his friend.

General program tips

1. Plan for and organize a program, allowing plenty of time to do it right. Project potential problems and decide how to deal with them.

2. Expand your mailing lists by having sign-up sheets at every program and encourage people to sign up themselves and their friends.

3. Decide on your program goal—to increase membership, to provide for an educational evening, to attract singles, etc. The programs outlined here have different goals and may attract different audiences. One way of looking at the differences in the tone of these programs is in terms of dress: a woman would wear a dress to the Shabbat dinner, a pants suit to the discussion groups, and jeans to the Bet Café.

Divorce

Introduction: some basic considerations

How does Judaism view divorce? The most important thing that can be said in answer to this question is that Judaism represents a religion which sanctifies *people*, and when two people can no longer share in a loving relationship, Judaism sees nothing at all humiliating or reprehensible about terminating that relationship.

There is great sadness felt for a couple who divorce, and in fact it is said: "Over him who divorces his wife of his youth, even the altar of God sheds tears" (Gittin 90b). Nevertheless, it seems clear that the possibility for divorce is itself a reflection of the importance of marriage. In the Jewish view, the relationship of marriage is seen as one of total commitment, of mutual love ("they become one flesh"—Genesis 2:24). Without this warmth and love the marriage bonds can become oppressive rather than fulfilling, and that is why Judaism creates the possibility of the dissolution of the relationship.

Judaism maintains some basic attitudes toward divorce that should be pointed out:

1. In Jewish law, divorce is the act of the parties to the marriage. Marriage itself is a freewill act, the formation of a covenant, between a man and a woman. The dissolution of the marriage is also a freewill act of the man and the woman. The court merely supervises to see that everything is done properly. Under certain circumstances the religious authorities can force a divorce, but unlike the Western legal system, where a divorce is a decree of the legal authorities, in Jewish tradition it remains an act between the man and the woman.

2. Also unlike the Western legal system, Judaism does not treat divorce as an adversary proceeding. On the contrary, under Jewish law it cannot really be effectuated unless there is *mutual consent*. Therefore it is not necessary to prove that one of the parties is "guilty" in order to make divorce possible. If there is agreement between the man and the woman that the marriage covenant should be dissolved, then the procedure can go forward.

3. The main instrument of divorce is the bill of divorcement, which is called a get. The word get, meaning "document," refers to the paper that the husband hands to the wife at the divorce proceedings. Only when the

Jewish tradition recognized the legitimacy of divorce from the very earliest times. In fact the Bible itself established the procedure for divorce:

A man takes a wife and possesses her. She fails to please him because he finds something obnoxious about her, and he writes her a bill of divorcement, hands it to her, and sends her away from his house (Deuteronomy 24:1).

Leaving aside for the moment all questions of how Jewish divorce treats women (which we'll get to later), it is clear from this passage that the institution of divorce was already well known in ancient times. Even then, the procedure centered around a bill of divorcement—sefer keritut—and was (and still remains) largely in the domain of the husband.

get is delivered into the hands of the wife does the divorce actually take place.

4. The writing of the get and its delivery to the woman is dependent upon the consent of the husband, as it is written: "... and he writes her a bill of divorcement." It is possible, however, for the woman to petition the court for a divorce. If her plea is acceptable, the court tries to persuade the husband to consent to the get. According to the talmudic authorities, it is even permissible for the court to use physical means to strengthen their persuasion: "Kofin oto ad she-yomar, 'rotseh ani'—They force him until he says, 'I consent'" (Gittin 45a). In the Diaspora, where there is no Jewish autonomy, this power of persuasion cannot be invoked, although it is possible to use other means, such as informing employers of the man's recalcitrance, etc. However, in Israel there have been cases where men have been fined or put in jail in order to "persuade" them to consent to a divorce that the court has ruled should be given. This aspect of the Jewish divorce procedures leads to many difficulties. However, when the husband refuses to give a woman a get according to traditional Jewish law, the possibilitiy exists that the wife will always remain technically married to him—an aguna, an "anchored-down" woman—unable to remarry though not actually married to her husband. (We will be speaking more about this later on.)

5. In Jewish law there are general differences in status between men and women (see *Catalog 1*), and these are pointed up most sharply in attitudes concerning marriage and divorce. For a full discussion of what we consider inequities in the law perpetrated against women vis-à-vis divorce, see "Righting an Injustice" later in this chapter. But to understand some of the discussion that comes next, certain facts must be acknowledged:

a. The Torah permits polygamy and does not permit polyandry. Accordingly, "a woman cannot be the wife of two [men]" (Kiddushin 7a; Rashi), while a man *may* contract a second marriage even if his first has not been legally dissolved according to Jewish law. While it is true that, under the herem of Rabbenu Gershom—the ban enacted by Rabbenu Gershom (an eleventh-century scholar)—polygamy is no longer permitted under Jewish law, if a husband *does* enter into another marriage it is considered legally valid (Tur, Even ha-Ezer 44). (The first wife's recourse is to take him to court to compel the husband to divorce either her *or* the other woman.) This herem, incidentally, applied only to Ashkenazic communities and not to Sephardic communities.

b. In Judaism the term adultery refers to a sexual relationship between any married woman and any man other than her husband—whether married or unmarried. Such a relationship is, according to Leviticus 20:10, deserving of the death penalty for both parties (although obviously in reality this punishment is not administered). The relationship between any man—whether married or unmarried—and an unmarried (unmarried in accordance with *Jewish* law) woman is not considered adultery and does not come under the serious prohibition that adultery does. So again the woman is at a disadvantage. If she never received a get from her first husband, she cannot, according to Jewish law, enter into a relationship with any other man because she is legally still married to her first husband.

Why you should have a Jewish as well as a civil divorce

In the Diaspora the Jewish divorce is usually sought *after* the dissolution of the marriage by the civil courts, generally because the civil divorce has implications for children, taxes, property, etc. in ways that the Jewish divorce for the most part does not. According to Jewish law, then, the woman and the man remain legally married, even after they have received their civil decree, until they obtain a get. The thinking behind this approach is that since the contracting of the marriage was a religious act conducted under the auspices of the Jewish tradition, the dissolution of the marriage should likewise be done under the authority of the Jewish law. Efforts are now being made to inform lawyers to arrange a Jewish divorce for their clients at the same time that they arrange the civil divorce. If this is done, it will remove many difficulties later on.

Reform Judaism generally does not require a get. It accepts the civil divorce as sufficient for remarriage. Reconstructionist, Conservative, and Orthodox Judaism do require the get. It should be pointed out that in the eyes of the traditionalist elements within the Jewish community, a woman's remarriage without a get is tantamount to adultery and whatever offspring are produced are technically mamzerim—illegitimate. Since the get procedure is not difficult to arrange, it is clear that all persons who are civilly divorced should arrange for a Jewish divorce so that their status, and the status of any future children in the Jewish community, will not be jeopardized.

It is crucial to obtain a get in Israel. In the Diaspora it is possible to remarry civilly or to find a rabbi who will not require that one have a get. In Israel, however, the laws of the state are the traditional Jewish laws of marriage and divorce. Therefore individuals who plan to settle in Israel, who are concerned about their status in Israel, or who are concerned about

A word about "loving your neighbor as yourself"
Both Conservative and Orthodox Judaism are committed to the requirement of a get. The procedures supervised by Orthodox rabbis and by Conservative rabbis are the same. Nevertheless, in general, Orthodox rabbis do not accept the validity of a get administered by a court of Conservative rabbis. Briefly, this is because Orthodox rabbis bind themselves to their particular approach to the halakhic system and are reluctant, in most cases, to accept the authority of those who bind themselves to a different approach to the halakhic system.

This situation is especially true in Israel, where the official authorities are all Orthodox; so persons who plan to settle in Israel or who plan to have an Orthodox rabbi officiate at their remarriage would be best advised to have an Orthodox rabbi arrange the get.

the status of any future children under Israeli law should see to it that they obtain a get.

111

Divorce

The document

Let's assume that both parties are willing to arrange for a get. The first thing to do, of course, is for one of the parties to contact a rabbi, who will be able to advise the individuals about what must be done. Since the giving of the get involves many technical procedures, many rabbis do not supervise the divorce proceedings themselves. They will usually refer the interested parties to the local bet din—rabbinical court. Every large city has a bet din; in smaller communities it may be necessary to travel to a large center in order to have the get written and delivered. There is usually a fee involved in obtaining a get, and this covers the cost of the materials involved, the time of the sofer—the scribe, and the time of the officiating rabbi. The fee runs between $100 and $175 but is waived in cases of need. Incidentally, the fee is frequently paid by whatever party requested the get, although sometimes both parties split the cost.

The get must be written by hand in Aramaic. According to the ancient regulations, the woman herself is qualified to write her own get; however, the custom has taken root that only a trained sofer can prepare the document. Because of the many technicalities involved, it is better to have an experienced scribe do the task.

The materials necessary to write the get are all prepared according to prescribed ritual and tradition. The get is written on heavy white paper (originally it was written on parchment). Special ink is used to write the text, usually with a goose quill. This ink cannot be erased, so no modifications can be introduced into the get after it is written. An old tradition ordains that the get itself should have twelve lines (the gematria— numerical equivalent—of the word get is twelve).

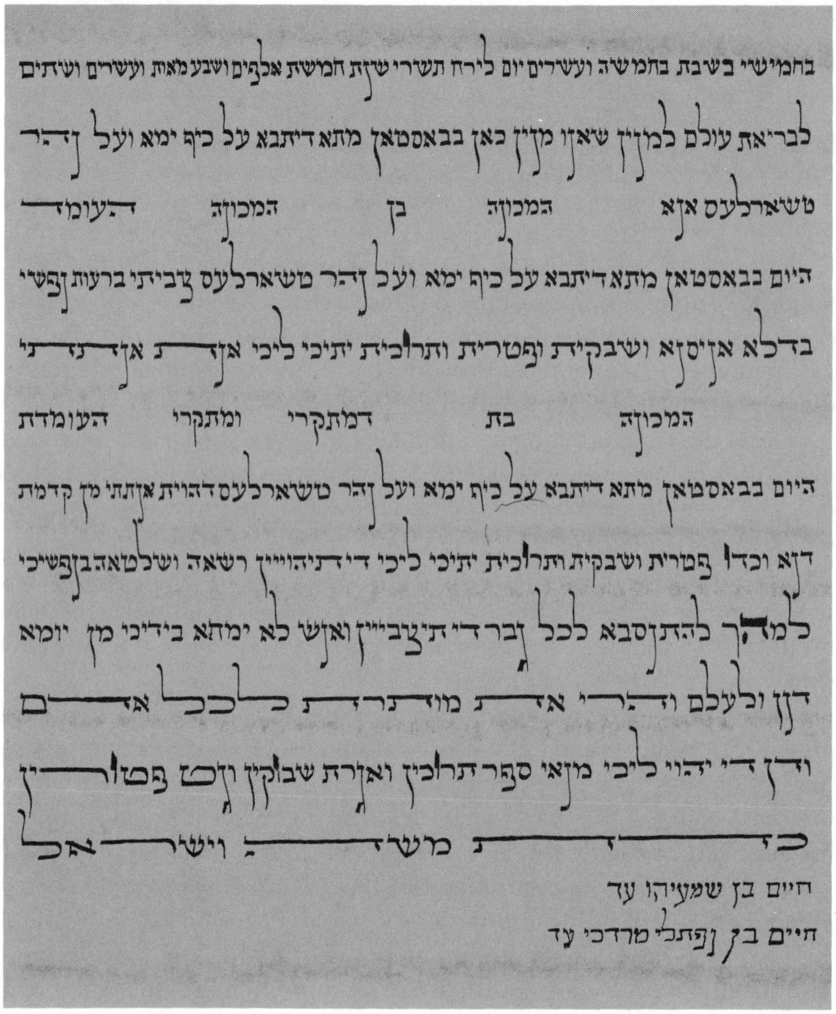

בחמישי בשבת בחמשה ועשרים יום לירח תשרי שנת חמשת אלפים ושבע מאות ועשרים ושתים

לבריאת עולם למנין שאנו מונין כאן בבאסטאן מתא דיתבא על כיף ימא ועל נהר

טשיארלעס אנא המכונה בן המכונה דיעומד

היום בבאסטאן מתא דיתבא על כיף ימא ועל זהר טשיארלעס צביתי ברעות נפשי

בדכלא אניסה ושבקית ופטרית ותרוכית יתיכי ליכי אנת אנתתי

המכונה בת דמתקרי ומתקרי העומדת

היום בבאסטאן מתא דיתבא על כיף ימא ועל זהר טשיארלעס דהוית אזתתי מן קדמת

דנא וכדו פטרית ושבקית ותרוכית יתיכי ליכי די תיהויין רשאה ושלטאה בנפשיכי

למהך להתנסבא לכל גבר די תיצבייין ואנש לא ימחא בידיכי מן יומא

דנן ולעלם ודהרי אנת מותרת לכל אדם

ודן די יהוי ליכי מנאי ספר תרוכין ואגרת שבוקין וגט פטורין

כדת משה וישראל

חיים בן שמעיהו עד

חיים בן נפתלי מרדכי עד

The following is the text of the get (translation taken from the *Encyclopaedia Judaica* article on "Divorce," vol. 6).

On the ____ day of the week, the ____ day of the month of ____ in the year ____ from the creation of the world according to the calendar reckoning we are accustomed to count here, in the city ____ (which is also known as ____) which is located on the river ____ (and on the river ____) and situated near wells of water, I ____ (also known as ____), the son of ____ (also known as ____), who today am present in the city ____ (which is also known as ____), which is located on the river ____ (and on the river ____), and situated near wells of water, do willingly consent, being under no restraint, to release, to set free, and put aside you, my wife, ____ (also known as ____), daughter of ____ (also known as ____), who is today in the city of ____ (which is also known as ____), which is located on the river ____ (and on the river ____), and situated near wells of water, who has been my wife from before. Thus I do set free, release you, and put you aside, in order that you may have permission and the authority over yourself to go and marry any man you may desire. No person may hinder you from this day onward, and you are permitted to every man. This shall be for you from me a bill of dismissal, a letter of release, and a document of freedom, in accordance with the laws of Moses and Israel.

____ the son of ____ witness
____ the son of ____ witness

One of the details the law requires is that the get be witnessed by two individuals. As in most other Jewish ritual procedures, the witnesses must be males over the age of thirteen who are not related to each other or to the divorcing husband and the about-to-be divorced wife. They should also be observant Jews.

The most crucial thing about the get, from the point of view of traditional legal requirements, is that the names of the parties and the places involved be spelled correctly. If there is any mistake about these spellings the whole get may be invalidated. Rabbis who officiate at gittin (plural of get) procedures are especially trained to know the correct spellings of names and surnames. One of the most famous stories in modern Hebrew literature is the "Kotso shel Yod" by Y. L. Gordon, in which a get is invalidated because the letter yod is not written properly in one of the names, and tragically, since the husband has disappeared, the woman becomes an aguna. The reason for this meticulousness is that in ancient times there were few means for positively identifying individuals. It was suspected that a get written for one party might fraudulently be used by another with a similar name. Therefore it was important to have the exact data included in the get.

Once the get is properly written, it is then ready to be delivered by the husband to the wife.

The procedure

The following is the Jewish divorce procedure based on the Seder Ha-get given at the end of chapter 154 of Eben ha-Ezer (the part of the *Shulhan Arukh* concerned with marriage and divorce). The English text was prepared by the late Professor Boaz Cohen (may his memory be a blessing).

Rabbi (to husband): "Do you *Ploni ben Ploni* [*So-and-so the son of So-and-so*] give this get of your own free will without duress and compulsion?"
Husband: "Yes."
Rabbi: "Perhaps you have bound yourself by uttering a vow or by making any binding statement which would compel you to give a get against your will?"
Husband: "No."
Rabbi: "Perhaps you have once made a statement which would invalidate the get, or you have uttered or done something to render the get null and void, and have forgotten it, or you were under the erroneous impression that such acts do not render the get null and void; will you therefore please make void all such remarks and acts of yours in the presence of witnesses?"
Husband: "Hear ye witnesses; in your presence I declare null and void any previous declaration that I may have made which may invalidate this get. I also declare any witness that may hereafter testify to such a statement as disqualified."
Sofer (to husband): "You, *Ploni ben Ploni*, I am presenting to you as a gift these writing materials, the paper, the pen, and the ink so that they become your property."

(Husband accepts the writing materials, lifts them up to show that he has acquired them.)

Husband: "Ye witnesses listen to what I will say to the sofer." (Then, addressing the sofer, he says): "You, sofer, *Ploni ben Ploni*, I give you this paper, ink, and pen and all the writing material and I order you that you write for me, *Ploni ben Ploni*, a get to divorce my wife, *Plonit bat Ploni*, and write this get lishmee, lishmah, uleshem gerushin [for me exclusively, for her exclusively, and for the purpose of a get exclusively], and write even as many as a hundred gittin, if necessary, until one valid get is written and signed according to the law of Moses and the children of Israel. I hereby authorize you to make any corrections in the document that may be necessary."
Sofer: "So I shall do."

Husband (to each witness in the hearing of the other): "You, *Ploni ben Ploni*, act as witness and sign the get which the sofer, *Ploni ben Ploni*, shall write specifically for me, *Ploni ben Ploni*, and for my wife, *Plonit bat Ploni*, and sign as many as a hundred gittin if necessary until one valid get is written and signed and delivered according to the law of Moses and the children of Israel."

Each witness: "So I shall do."

(Husband then hands over the writing material to the sofer.)

Sofer (to witnesses): "Hear ye witnesses: All these preparations that I make and all the writing that I shall do, I shall do in the name of the husband, *Ploni ben Ploni*, to divorce his wife, *Plonit bat Ploni*, and I am writing it lishmo, lishmah, uleshem gerushin."

The get is then written and the witnesses must be present during the writing of the first line. The witnesses, as well as the scribe, make a distinguishing mark on the get. When the get is finished and the ink is dried, the witnesses read the get.

(Before the witnesses sign it, they say to each other): "You, *Ploni ben Ploni*, witness that I am signing this get leshem [in the name of] *Ploni ben Ploni*, who ordered us to sign a get to divorce his wife, *Plonit bat Ploni*, and I am signing it lishmo, lishmah, uleshem gerushin."

Rabbi (to sofer): "You, sofer, *Ploni ben Ploni*, is this the get that you have written?"
Sofer: "Yes."
Rabbi: "Do you have any special mark by which you can identify this get?"
Sofer: "Yes and this is it" (points it out).
Rabbi: "Did *Ploni ben Ploni* give you the writing materials in the presence of the witnesses?"
Sofer: "Yes."
Rabbi: "Did the husband tell you to write the get?"
Sofer: "Yes."
Rabbi: "Did he tell you to write it lishmo, lishmah, uleshem gerushin?"
Sofer: "Yes."
Rabbi: "Did he order you in the presence of witnesses?"
Sofer: "Yes."
Rabbi: "Did you write it lishmo, lishmah, uleshem gerushin?"
Sofer: "Yes."
Rabbi: "What did you say before you started writing this get?"
Sofer: "I said: 'I write this get in the name of the husband, *Ploni ben Ploni*, to divorce with it his wife, *Plonit bat Ploni*, and I write it lishmo, lishmah, uleshem gerushin.'"
Rabbi: "Did you say so in the presence of witnesses?"
Sofer: "Yes."
Rabbi: "Were the witnesses present at least during the time you wrote the first line?"
Sofer: "Yes."
Rabbi (to witnesses): "Did you, witnesses, hear the husband, *Ploni ben Ploni*, order the sofer to write a get for his wife, *Plonit bat Ploni*, and to write it lishmo, lishmah, uleshem gerushin?"
Witnesses: "We did."
Rabbi: "Did you hear him say that he would write it lishmo, lishmah, uleshem gerushin?"
Witnesses: "We did."
Rabbi: "Were you present when he wrote the first line?"
Witnesses: "We were."
Rabbi (to each witness separately): "Is this your signature?"
Each witness: "Yes."
Rabbi: "Did you sign it lishmo, lishmah, uleshem gerushin?"
Each witness: "Yes."
Rabbi: "Did the husband tell you to do so?"
Each witness: "Yes."

Rabbi: "Did the other witness see you sign the get?"

Witness: "Yes."

Rabbi: "What did you say before you signed?"

Witness: "I said: 'I am signing this get in the name of the husband, *Ploni ben Ploni,* to divorce with it his wife, *Plonit bat Ploni,* and I am signing it lishmo, lishmah, uleshem gerushin.' So I said and so I signed."

(Rabbi repeats this with second witness. Then the get is read again to check that it is correct.)

Rabbi (to husband): "Again I wish to ask you whether you give this get of your own free will."

Husband: "I do."

Rabbi: "Did you bind yourself by any statement or by any vow in a way that would compel you to give this get against your free will?"

Husband: "No."

Rabbi: "Again I wish to ask you that perhaps you did make such a statement and have forgotten it or made it erroneously. Will you therefore cancel all such statements and declare them null and void?"

Husband: "You witnesses hear that I declare in your presence null and void all previous declarations that I have made which may invalidate this get. I also declare any witness that may testify to such a statement as disqualified."

Rabbi (to wife): "Are you accepting this get of your own free will?"

Wife: "Yes."

Rabbi: "Did you bind yourself by any statement or vow that would compel you to accept this get against your will?"

Wife: "No."

Rabbi: "Perhaps you have unwittingly made such a statement that would nullify the get. In order to prevent that, will you kindly retract all such declarations?"

Wife: "I revoke all such statements that may nullify the get, in the presence of you the witnesses."

Rabbi (to those present): "If there is anyone who wishes to protest let him do so now."

Husband (to witnesses): "You be also witnesses to the delivery of the get."

(Rabbi now tells the wife to remove all jewelry from her hands, to hold her hands together with open palms upward to receive the get. The sofer holds the get and gives it to the rabbi. The rabbi gives the get to the husband who, holding it in both hands, drops it into the palms of the wife and says: "This be your get and with it be you divorced from this time forth so that you may become the wife of any man.")

The wife receives the get, lifts up her hands, walks with it a short distance, and returns. She returns the get to the rabbi. The rabbi reads the get again with the witnesses. The rabbi again asks the sofer and witnesses to identify the get and the signatures.

Rabbi: "Hear all you present that Rabbeinu Tam has issued a ban against all those who try to invalidate a get after it has been delivered."

The four corners of the get are then cut and it is placed in the files of the rabbi. The husband and the wife receive written statements called petur, which certify that their marriage has been dissolved according to the requirements of Jewish law.

While it is true that the ceremony is archaic in nature, I believe that the strong stamp of ritual adds to the solemnity of the occasion and creates a deep feeling of tradition. The halakhic reasons for some of the procedures are complicated, but let's examine at least some of them.

1. There is great stress that the get be written lishmah, that is, with the *particular* man and woman in mind. If this is not done, the get is not valid. The requirement that the get be written lishmah is derived by the talmudic authorities from the words in the verse from Deuteronomy, "vekatav lah—he writes *her* a bill of divorcement," meaning it is *only* for her.

2. Furthermore, as is obvious from the verse in Deuteronomy, the obligation is on the husband to write the get himself. Because we now have scribes who are specially trained in the technical aspects of writing the document, the husband must turn over his obligation to the scribe. For that

reason he must formally acquire the materials (usually as a gift from the sofer) with which the get is prepared and then legally give them to the scribe, so that the scribe can serve as his agent in preparing the document.

3. The get must be conveyed from the husband to the wife, and she must indicate her possession of it by lifting her hands, etc. This is in fulfillment of the requirement that there be a valid kinyan—means of conveyance and acquisition.

4. The wife removes her finger jewelry before receiving the get so that nothing comes between the document and her whole hands' acceptance of it.

5. The "distinguishing mark" on the get is made so that if the validity of the get is later challenged, the sofer will be able, by checking for the distinguishing mark, to ascertain that it is indeed the document he prepared. For example, he might arrange the lettering of the get so that the last letter of the last three lines of the document will, if read down, spell אמן — amen.

6. The document is cut at the very end of the divorce so that it can never be reused fraudulently by any other party.

This whole procedure, including the writing of the get, usually takes no more than two hours and requires only a few participants—the couple, the rabbi, the witnesses, and the sofer.

Appointing shelihim—agents

In the procedure that has just been detailed, the husband and the wife are both present during the divorce proceedings. Frequently, however, for various reasons, both parties cannot be present. The husband may live in one place, the wife in another; or the parties may decide to forgo the emotional strain of meeting again after a sometimes bitter divorce proceeding in the civil courts. The traditional legal system has therefore made provisions for the appointment by either party of a shaliah—agent. The husband may appoint a shaliah to deliver the get to his wife, and if this agent cannot complete the task, he has the right to appoint another one, and the second agent yet another one, etc.; the wife can also appoint an agent to receive the get for her. Thus the required procedure can be effected without the parties seeing each other. The rabbi who arranges the get can arrange the documents and procedures for the appointment of the shelihim as well.

The get zikkui (get of benefit)

Under various circumstances a get zikkui (get of benefit) may be arranged. According to traditional law, the woman's consent to a divorce is not necessary, and the get can be delivered to her even against her will. But the ordinance of Rabbenu Gershom, who was known as the Light of the Exile (c. 965–1028), prohibited divorcing a woman without her consent. The question of just what constitutes consent is one that requires some understanding.

According to the talmudic authorities, "zakhin le-adam she-lo lefanav" —a benefit—can be conferred upon an individual even when s/he is not present. That is, if the procedure can be considered a benefit to a person, we assume that his/her consent would be granted were s/he to know about it. This principle is invoked, for example, in the conversion of minors. Although minors are not in a position to give consent, we assume that they would give consent if they were old enough, since becoming a Jew is a zekhut—a privilege. The same reasoning is used when a civil divorce has already been granted and the wife cannot be located or refused to accept a get. The bet din—rabbinical court—can appoint a shaliah to receive the get for her even without her explicit consent, because it is felt that a zekhut is being conferred on the wife, who can now remarry according to the halakhah without the risk of being an adulteress (which would be her status were she to remarry without a get). According to Rabbi Moses Isserles (in his glosses to the *Shulhan Arukh*, Even ha-Ezer 1:10), in cases where the wife became an apostate from Judaism, the custom was to divorce her through a get zikkui.

Any rabbi who ordinarily arranges for a get can arrange for a get zikkui. The procedure is the same as for an ordinary get, except that instead of giving the get to the wife, the husband (or his agent) gives the get to a shaliah who is appointed by the court.

The permission of the hundred rabbis–heter meah rabbanim

Any person who is mentally incompetent—owing to insanity or other afflictions—cannot, of course, participate in a legal procedure involving his/her consent. No legal procedure is valid in which one party is mentally incompetent.

The problem is extremely difficult where one partner in a marriage is struck with mental illness and the other partner wishes a divorce. Of course, it is first necessary to get a civil divorce (except in Israel, where, as mentioned, there are no civil divorces—only halakhic ones). But then what are the options for a Jewish divorce? If the husband is mentally incompetent, the authorities rule that if he enjoys even brief periods of lucidity and if he authorizes the get during these periods, the divorce can be arranged. The authorities interpret lucidity in broad terms: it is enough if he understands that he is married and that he is terminating his marriage. However, if the husband never has any periods of lucidity, or if the proper witnesses are not present during these periods, then the wife is an aguna and in

It should be pointed out that whereas the husband has recourse to a get zikkui when the woman is unwilling to cooperate, the wife cannot resort to this device when the husband is recalcitrant. There is no procedure in Jewish law that permits a wife to use the get zikkui against an unwilling husband. Furthermore, as pointed out, the husband's remarriage without giving a get to his first wife would involve him only in the ban against polygamy. According to the traditional law, however, the woman who remarries without obtaining the explicit consent of the husband to a get would in effect be guilty of adultery, a much more serious charge under Jewish law. More on this shortly.

traditional law she has no recourse. Again we come up against a vexing situation in which the application of the traditional norms imposes extreme difficulties upon the woman.

When the woman is mentally incompetent, with no periods of lucidity, the situation is different. In this case it is necessary somehow to remove the penalties of Rabbenu Gershom's ban against the husband's having two wives. The procedure, which is used only in cases of mental incompetence, involves having a document drawn up by the bet din. The following is the text of the document (taken from material prepared by Rabbi Isaac Klein):

We the undersigned have consulted together regarding the judgment concerning *So-and-so the son of So-and-so* in order to free him from the herem of Rabbenu Gershom in order that he be permitted to marry an additional wife to his present one, *So-and-so the daughter of So-and-so*.

These were the facts in the case. In the year ____ *So-and-so* married *So-and-so the daughter of So-and-so* in the city of ____. In the year ____ she became insane so that it was necessary to hospitalize her in a mental hospital and she is still there. In the year ____ the husband received a civil divorce based on the expert testimony of physicians that his wife was hopelessly insane. The husband took upon himself to provide financial assistance for the care of his wife. The truth of these facts has been verified by us through the examination of the civil divorce and through consultation with the physicians who are attending the wife.

After much investigation we have agreed to permit *So-and-so the son of So-and-so* to marry another wife according to the facts and conditions which are before us. In the *Shulhan Arukh*, Even ha-Ezer, paragraph 1, subparagraph 10, Rabbi Moses Isserles rules that where the woman is insane it is proper to permit the husband to marry another wife. The author of the *Kol Bo* wrote that this permission be granted only with the concurrence of one hundred rabbis from three communities and three nations. Many decisors (poskim) have concurred in this ruling. Rabbi Joel Sirkes wrote: "I have a tradition from our master and rabbi, Rabbi Shachna, may his memory be for a blessing, who permitted a man to marry another wife in addition to the one he already had, since where the man has the duty to fulfill the mitzvah of 'be fruitful and multiply,' Rabbi Gershom did not enact his ordinance (against polygamy)." All the learned men of Germany and Russia have concurred. This only on condition that a get be written and placed in the possession of a shaliah, who will deliver it to her when she becomes well. As long as she is not well, he must see to her proper lodging and support so that she not be forsaken.

Therefore we have agreed to permit the man to marry without any doubt with the concurrence of one hundred rabbis on the condition that he give her a get when she becomes well and the agreement to provide support for her.

The rabbi who draws up the document then circularizes other rabbis (by mail, if necessary) to get them to sign the heter. The rabbis signing should be of three countries or provinces. It is generally accepted that here in the United States rabbis from three states are sufficient (or from three provinces in Canada).

Righting an injustice

Much of what we've discussed has pointed up one critical fact: there are many instances where the application of the traditional norms results in an injustice to the woman. This is especially true when the husband refuses to consent to a get, a situation that happens, unfortunately, frequently enough to be a serious issue. Sometimes there are cases of outright extortion: the husband will agree to give his wife a get only if he receives a certain amount of money. Other times it is difficult, even impossible, to locate the husband because he has disappeared or lives in isolation. In addition, there are also times where the husband seems to have perished, though there is no definite proof of his death. A fascinating novel called *The Aguna*, by Chaim Grade, tells of the tragic consequences of such a situation. There are also corollary cases, which can occur in situations calling for yibbum—Levirate marriages.

These are marriages where a man must marry his brother's childless widow. When practice of yibbum was abandoned, it became necessary for the brother-in-law to formally release the widow from the obligation. This ceremony is called halitzah. In cases where the brother-in-law cannot be located, where he is a minor, or where he refuses to go through with the ceremony, the woman is left an aguna—an "anchored-down" woman.

When the husband cannot locate his wife, or if she is insane or recalcitrant, traditional Jewish law provides relief options for him in the forms of a get zikkui or a heter meah rabbanim. The tragedy is that for the wife in these situations, traditional law supplies no such option. In the United States and Canada a Reform rabbi who does not accept the authority of halakhah will often be sought out when an aguna wishes to remarry. In Israel, where the law of the land is the law of the rabbis, the only recourse a woman has is to leave the country and marry elsewhere.

The entire situation is further complicated by the fact that traditional law does not permit a divorcée to marry a kohen—i.e., a member of the priestly families. This prohibition is based on a statement in Leviticus that reflects the special status a kohen enjoyed because he served in the Temple and that a divorcée was somehow considered flawed and therefore not a fit mate for a kohen. The enforcement of this norm in our society—which does not accept the notion that a divorcée is different from any other woman and where the functions and prerogatives of the kohanim are largely symbolic anyway—also results in situations that seem to be unfair and unjust. All these situations cry out for remedies.

Contemporary Orthodox authorities have so far not been able to do anything to help the aguna whose husband refuses to give her a get; whose brother-in-law (in the case of a childless widowhood) cannot be located, is recalcitrant, or is a minor; or whose husband becomes insane or disappears and therefore cannot authorize a get.

In the Conservative movement, however, there have been some very interesting developments in this area. Some remedies that have been instituted:

1. The "Lieberman ketubbah." In 1958 the Rabbinical Assembly began to include the following tenai—clause—written by Professor Saul Lieberman, in the marriage contract:

And both together agreed that if this marriage shall be dissolved under civil law, then either husband or wife may invoke the authority of the bet din of the Rabbinical Assembly and the Jewish Theological Seminary of America or its duly authorized representatives, to decide what action by either spouse is then appropriate under Jewish matrimonial law, and if either spouse shall fail to honor the demand of the other or to carry out the decision of the bet din or its representatives, then the other spouse may invoke any and all remedies available in civil law and equity to enforce compliance with the bet din's decision and this solemn obligation.

This addition was designed to bring a remedy when the husband refused authorization of the get out of pique or for purposes of extortion. The

When brothers dwell together and one of them dies and leaves no son, the wife of the deceased shall not be married to a stranger, outside the family. Her husband's brother shall unite with her: take her as his wife and perform the levir's duty (Deuteronomy 25:5).

Levirite marriage and halitzah

Levirite marriage is the marriage between a widow and the brother of the deceased. It takes place only if there were no children from the first marriage, and is done so that the deceased's name shall be carried on by the firstborn of the second marriage. If the brother does not wish to marry the widow, the halitzah ceremony takes place, during which the brother is rebuked and disgraced for refusing to carry out his responsibility. During the ceremony a special shoe is worn by the brother and is removed by the widow (hence the name halitzah = removal). For a full description of the ceremony, see Deuteronomy 25:5ff. and the *Encyclopaedia Judaica* article on levirite marriage.

Over the years there has been a growing trend to place priority on halitzah rather than on levirite marriage. This trend was accelerated by Rabbenu Gershom's ban on polygamy (see above), since a levirite marriage could lead to polygamy. In the state of Israel, levirite marriage has been prohibited and steps taken against recalcitrant men who try to extort money from the widow. The Reform movement has done away with the whole practice. The Conservative movement has not officially abolished halitzah, but the necessity for this ceremony is widely ignored. Halitzah is still practiced by Orthodox Jews.

Editors' note: This *Catalog* is committed to presenting many viewpoints without making value judgments in favor of any one position. However, in certain areas we feel that we risk betraying our own value system by following this policy. Divorce is one such area. While Orthodoxy may feel that there are certain situations which, no matter how much pain they create for people, cannot be changed because of demands of halakhah, we find it inexcusable that they have not dealt with the aguna problem—whether or not their solution would match ours. The problem is far too unjust, far too pain-provoking to far too many women for Orthodoxy to take refuge behind a wall of "the sacredness of unchanging halakhah." Because of our feelings, the tone of this article is perhaps slanted toward a more equitable solution of the aguna problem. In fact, we hold a position more radical than the one maintained by the Conservative movement, that is, that a provision should be made for a woman to give a get to a man just as a man gives one to a woman.

theory was that if he did so he would be assessed a fine, to be enforced by the civil courts, besides suffering the inconvenience of a defense against a law suit. It was thought that rather than go through these difficulties, the husband would authorize the execution of a get. This remedy was obviously not an effective solution when the husband had disappeared or was insane, or when he was so angry with his wife that he would rather pay the fine than give the get. The effectiveness of the procedure would also depend on the readiness of the civil authorities to enforce an agreement made under religious auspices.

The Orthodox community both here and in Israel refused to accept this tenai, and declared a ban against participating in any wedding ceremony where the "Lieberman ketubbah" was used. Most Conservative rabbis use the amended ketubbah for their wedding ceremonies. The usefulness of the tenai has been severely limited, since legal experts have concluded that it would not be enforceable in the civil courts.

2. A later suggestion was adopted by the Rabbinical Assembly (the organization of Conservative rabbis) which involved an antenuptial agreement signed by the bride and the groom. The text of the agreement is:

On the ____ day of ____, 19 , corresponding to ____ 57 , in ____, the groom, Mr. ____, and the bride, Ms. ____, of their own free will and accord entered into the following agreement with respect to their intended marriage. The groom made the following declaration to the bride:

I WILL BETROTH AND MARRY YOU ACCORDING TO THE LAWS OF MOSES AND ISRAEL, SUBJECT TO THE FOLLOWING CONDITIONS:

a. IF OUR MARRIAGE BE TERMINATED BY DECREE OF THE CIVIL COURTS AND IF BY EXPIRATION OF SIX MONTHS AFTER SUCH A DECREE I GIVE YOU A DIVORCE ACCORDING TO THE LAWS OF MOSES AND ISRAEL (A GET) THEN OUR BETROTHAL (KIDDUSHIN) AND MARRIAGE (NISSUIN) WILL HAVE REMAINED VALID AND BINDING.

b. BUT IF OUR MARRIAGE BE TERMINATED BY DECREE OF CIVIL COURT AND IF BY EXPIRATION OF SIX MONTHS AFTER SUCH A DECREE I DO NOT GIVE YOU A DIVORCE ACCORDING TO THE LAWS OF MOSES AND ISRAEL (A GET) THEN OUR BETROTHAL (KIDDUSHIN) AND MARRIAGE (NISSUIN) WILL HAVE BEEN NULL AND VOID.

The bride replied to the groom:
I CONSENT TO THE CONDITION YOU HAVE MADE.
(signed) ____ groom ____ bride

We the undersigned, acting as a bet din, witnessed the oral statements and signature of the groom and the bride.
____ Rabbi ____ witness ____ witness

This tenai gave authority to the bet din to annul the marriage ab initio if there was a refusal to authorize a get. This proposal, while providing a remedy for most cases of aguna, of course did not cover those marriages where this instrument had not been signed.

3. In a later action the Rabbinical Assembly invoked the power that the talmudic rabbis had to annul marriages. This is based on the formula pronounced during all Jewish marriage ceremonies: "You are betrothed unto me with this ring, according to the law of Moses and Israel." This is interpreted by the rabbis in the Talmud to mean that every bride and groom contract a marriage subject to the approval of the rabbinical authorities. Should the rabbinical authorities remove their approval, then the marriage would be null and void ab initio. This power was invoked by the rabbinic authorities in ancient times when the husband acted in an unjust way. It was suggested in later times that the power should be invoked again to solve the aguna situation. The Orthodox felt that though this power of annulment did operate during the talmudic period, it was never invoked in

posttalmudic times and therefore is not operable now. The Rabbinical Assembly did decide to invoke this ancient power to annul. Since, according to Jewish law, children born out of wedlock (to two unmarried people) are not in any way tainted and their status is not impugned, annulment of the marriage ab initio—meaning that technically the couple were really never married—would in no way affect the status of their children.

The remedy of annulment effectively solves the aguna problem, at least for the Conservative movement, and makes it possible for a wife to remarry even when her husband has refused to give her a get or has disappeared.

None of these actions by the Conservative rabbis have been accepted by Orthodox authorities; nor are they acceptable in Israel, where the chief rabbinate is the supreme authority in matters of marriage and divorce.

Getting a get: some experiences

It took a long time to make the decision to get a divorce. Very soon after my husband and I separated it became clear to both of us that we would not get back together. But the reality and finality of divorce scared me, and it was hard to decide to make a definite end to our four-year marriage.

When we were ready to go ahead with the divorce, I attempted to locate a rabbi to do the get. I discovered that there are very few rabbis who do gittin, and in fact I found only one in the San Francisco Bay area—I believe he is the only one in northern California—who does.

I spoke to the rabbi to find out what was involved in getting the get. He told me briefly what it would be like and what I would have to do. Among the things he told me was that both my husband and I would have to be there (unless we appointed shelihim); that he would provide the witnesses and did not want me to bring my own; and that it would cost $150.

I talked with many of my friends about my feelings about the divorce. I especially wanted to talk with people who had gone through the experience of a traditional Jewish divorce. Rabbis vary in how they carry out the procedure, so it was particularly helpful for me to talk with people who had been divorced by the rabbi who was going to do my get. I learned that the procedure would take several hours, during which I would be in the rabbi's study with nothing to do but wait. I knew I would not want to be alone during that time, so I asked the rabbi in advance if I could bring a friend with me. Since the procedure ended up taking four hours, I was very glad I had my friend there.

The divorce took place on a Sunday morning at the home of the rabbi. It was a fairly long drive from the city where my husband and I live, so, being on reasonably good terms, we decided to drive over together. As soon as we arrived at the rabbi's house, the rabbi took my husband downstairs to his study. My husband and I were never in the same room from then on until four hours later, when my husband presented me with the get.

Upstairs in the living room (where I was sitting with my friend) were two men who I presumed were the witnesses. I did not know for sure until I asked, because we were not introduced. This kind of impersonal atmosphere was typical of the entire get procedure. The witnesses were friendly when I talked with them, but the whole thing seemed very routine to them, as it probably was.

After about ten minutes the rabbi took me to his study, where he asked me, as he had asked my husband, if I was certain I wanted a get and if I felt

A Final Word
Jewish procedures concerning divorce reflect the sanctity of the marriage bond. A relationship begun with solemnity, ritual, and meaningful symbolism should be terminated with equal seriousness. In addition, Judaism makes every effort to render the divorce procedure as free from pain and intrusion into the privacy of the individuals as possible. Perhaps, though, there is a certain wisdom in a system whose ritual for terminating a relationship involves the face-to-face confrontation of both parties and the symbolic acting out of the separation. In any case, we urge those of you who are getting divorced to obtain a get or, if you're a divorce lawyer, that you encourage your Jewish clients to obtain one; and we urge those already divorced to go through a Jewish divorce ceremony in addition to a civil one. To all such people we pray that you find love, fulfillment, and peace.

Miriam Oles, who recently had a Jewish divorce, writes of her experiences: The idea of writing about the experience of getting a traditional Jewish divorce first occurred to me the night before I got my get. I was home alone, feeling sad, a bit lonely, and apprehensive about what was going to happen the next day. I looked for something to read to help me prepare for my divorce the next morning. I wanted something to tell me more about what to expect. I wanted to read about Jewish thoughts, customs, history, or clever sayings pertaining to the get. I searched for something to hold on to from the Jewish tradition to help me through that difficult time. Among the books I looked through was *Catalog 1*, which, like other books, had much to say about Jewish marriage but nothing about divorce. I hope by writing this piece to give some support and encouragement to others who may go through the same experience.

there was any chance of our getting back together. I talked to him a little about the circumstances of our divorce and about my feelings. I asked the rabbi if any couples had ever changed their minds when he asked them that question. He told me that one couple had decided at that point not to go ahead with the divorce, but they finally divorced six months later.

For the next three and a half hours I sat in the rabbi's study with my friend. During this time the rabbi was carefully writing the get document with a quill pen. He wrote most of it in the study and from time to time would go upstairs where my husband was sitting with the witnesses.

Those hours of waiting were long and difficult for me. I remember being very nervous. I dreaded the moment when the actual divorce would take place, and I was anxious for it to be over. I spent the time talking with my friend, crying from time to time.

The rabbi finally said that the get was ready and the time had come. Before we joined my husband and the witnesses in the other room, the rabbi instructed me about how to accept the get from my husband. I was to stand with my arms held out in front of me and the palms of my hands together. When my husband put the get into my hands I was to close my hands over it, then put it under my arm (to indicate that I was taking possession of it), and walk away.

We went upstairs to where my husband was standing with the two witnesses. From this point everything seemed to go very fast. The rabbi told my husband and me to stand facing each other. The rabbi asked me if I accepted the divorce of my own free will, and I said I did. He said that the actual moment of divorce would be when my husband put the get into my hands. My husband then repeated after the rabbi a statement in Hebrew and English saying that he released me from our marriage and that I was free to marry someone else. My husband put the get into my hands, and I took it as the rabbi had told me to and walked away. It was a very sad moment for me, and I was relieved when it was over.

A few minutes later the rabbi took the get from me and gave it to my now ex-husband in the other room. While my ex-husband held the get, the rabbi made two cuts in it with scissors. He repeated the procedure with me holding the get. The rabbi kept the get and gave each of us a certificate, signed by the witnesses, saying that we were divorced.

It felt strange for us to drive home together after that, and I wished we had come in separate cars.

When I got home several of my friends called me to wish me well. One person came over and brought me a gift, and the support and concern of my friends during the time of my divorce meant a lot to me.

Some Practical Advice Based on Experience

1. The woman is apt to be bored during the preparation of the get and much of the formal procedure, since her part is quite small. For that reason, bringing along a friend or a book to occupy you can be helpful.

2. There was an old custom for the participating rabbi to try to prolong the divorce proceedings as much as possible in the hope that the couple might have a change of heart and decide to reconcile. Nowadays, when virtually all couples obtaining a get have already had a civil divorce for some time, most rabbis do not do this. It can be a wise precaution, however, to discuss your feelings about this with the rabbi beforehand.

3. A priority might be to have one of your friends who is qualified to do so act as a witness. Approach the rabbi beforehand and try to arrange this, since frequently the witnesses otherwise chosen may not make you feel comfortable. If this cannot be done, try to arrange for someone supportive to be there with you.

4. Generally, you might talk to the rabbi beforehand about the entire process. The civil divorce is often very cold, legalistic, and emotionally difficult, and the objective should be for the Jewish divorce to be as warm, human, and emotionally involving as possible.

For general advice on divorce, the best resource around is *Women in Transition: A Feminist Handbook on Separation and Divorce*, Charles Scribners, 1975; $6.95 in paperback. This was put out by a Philadelphia women's collective called Women in Transition, which offers free legal counseling and referrals as well as general advice.

Bibliography

Amram, David Werner. *The Jewish Law of Divorce*. Boston: Herman, 1968.

"Divorce." *Encyclopaedia Judaica*, vol. 6. Jerusalem: Keter, 1972.

Falk, Ze'ev W. *Jewish Matrimonial Law in the Middle Ages*. New York: Oxford University, 1966.

Fried, Jacob. *Jews and Divorce*. New York: Ktav, 1968.

Israel, Stan. ed. *A Bibliography on Divorce*. New York: Bloch, 1974. Non-Jewish material.

Kohler, Kaufmann. *The Harmonization of the Jewish and Civil Laws of Marriage and Divorce*. New York: Central Conference of American Rabbis, 1915.

Medicine

Introduction

The relationship between Judaism and medicine has been a long and cordial one. Good health was prized in the Jewish tradition above almost all other considerations. In fact, according to the *Shulhan Arukh*, "regulations concerning health must be observed more stringently than ritual laws" (Jakobovits, *Jewish Medical Ethics*, p. 7—full references are included in the Bibliography at the end of this chapter). There are at least two reasons for this attitude:

1. Ill health blunts spiritual sensitivity:

Since when the body is healthy and sound [one treads in] the ways of the Lord, it being impossible to understand or know anything of the knowledge of the Creator when one is sick, it is obligatory upon man to avoid things which are detrimental to the body and acclimate himself to things which heal and fortify it (Maimonides, *Mishneh Torah*, Hilkhot Deot 4:1).

2. Furthermore, people are created in the image of God. Disease, particularly if caused by inattention to basic hygiene, diminishes that image. A story is told about Hillel:

When he had finished the lesson with his pupils, he accompanied them part of the way. They said to him: "Master, where are you going?" "To perform a religious duty." "Which religious duty?" "To bathe in the bath house." "Is that a religious duty?" He answered them: "If somebody is appointed to scrape and clean the statues of the king that are set up in the theaters and circuses, is paid to do the work, and furthermore associates with the nobility, how much more so should I, who am created in the divine image and likeness, take care of my body!" (*Leviticus Rabbah* 34:3).

Thus preventive medicine, the attempt to forestall disease by taking appropriate measures for personal and communal hygiene became the norm in Judaism. In keeping with this, deliberate misuse of one's body was regarded as abhorrent. People were expected to treat their bodies with the reverence that the image of God demanded.

You MAY be created in God's image, Mr. Levi, but if you are, God needs to go on a diet.

Whoever is overzealous in fasting should be regarded as a sinner (Taanit 11a).

Medical attention

The Lord has created medicines out of the earth, and a sensible man will not refuse them. ... My child, do not be negligent when you are sick ... leave room for the physician ... for you need him (Ecclesiasticus 38:1–12).

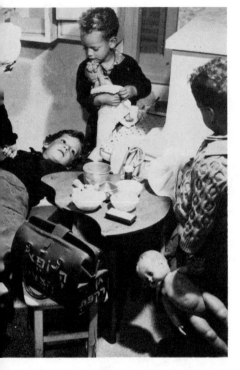

Despite the best precautions, people still get sick. The same reverence for life that prompted Jewish scholars to introduce so many rules of hygiene also led them to realize the importance of seeking prompt medical attention for illness. In fact the rabbis maintain that it is forbidden to live in a city where there is no physician (Kiddushin 66a).

They deduce the obligation to seek medical care directly from the Bible. For example, Exodus 21:18–19 states that the obligation of one who injures another is to "pay for his idleness and his cure." According to the Targum and other sources, the phrase means that he shall pay the doctor's bill. Thus there is biblical sanction for the requirement that a person seek medical care.

The Jewish view of pain tends to reinforce these positive feelings about medicine. The use of appropriate painkilling medications for terminally ill patients and women during delivery—which we take for granted in modern society—was sanctioned by Judaism long before their general acceptance in Western civilization. Concern for pain and suffering also serves as the basis for rabbinical opinions approving contraception, sterilization, and abortion—in some cases, to spare a woman recurrent anguish after a painful birth.

These attitudes also resulted in the more humane treatment of criminals. In order to spare the victim prolonged or undue pain, the Talmud (Sanhedrin 35a; Semahot 2:8) ruled that a death sentence must be implemented within one day. Furthermore, the condemned criminal must be drugged prior to execution. These laws show sensitivity to suffering that I have often found lacking in our own society. It was logical to look upon medicine as the means to relieve suffering: "Whoever is in pain let him go to the physician," advises the Talmud (Bava Kama 46b).

Origin of the my-son-the-doctor syndrome

The Torah gave permission to the physician to heal; moreover, this is a religious precept and it is involved in the category of saving life (Berakhot 60a; *Shulhan Arukh*, Yoreh Deah 336:1).

The concept of saving life—pikuah nefesh—is of paramount importance in Judaism. In cases of a threat to life almost every law of the Torah is suspended. In many ways this is the guiding principle in determining Jewish attitudes toward medicine.

With such unqualified approval in Jewish sources, it is not surprising that medicine ranked with the rabbinate as a vocational choice for Jews and that, in fact, it was common to pursue both these careers simultaneously. Fully half of the best-known rabbis in the Middle Ages were also physicians (Jakobovits, *Jewish Medical Ethics*, p. 205).

Communal approval, however, wasn't the only factor that stimulated Jews to enter medicine. Many Jews became physicians because practicing medicine enabled them to circumvent the barriers that shut the Jew out of the surrounding culture. In medieval Europe their command of languages and general cosmopolitanism provided Jews with the tools to transmit Greek and Arabic medicine to Christian Europe—a pattern that was repeated in different settings up to modern times. In fact, the ubiquity of Jews as physicians was not without its ironies. During the same time that

Jews were held in high esteem as physicians to several popes, their compatriots outside Rome were suffering under the Inquisition and other church-approved persecutions.

Despite Judaism's enthusiasm for medicine, however, its attitude toward doctors and their motives at times expressed ambivalence (to put it mildly). What could possibly make a medieval Jew skeptical of such a pillar of society as a Jewish doctor? The same thing that makes a modern Jew skeptical: his fees! The Talmud expresses the ambivalence well. In one place (Taanit 21b) it heaps glowing praises on a local doctor, Abba the Bleeder, who left a box outside his office for the deposit of fees so the poor wouldn't be embarrassed by their inability to pay. In another place a more cynical sage questions the quality of care the poor would get if they were dependent only on the goodwill of the physician: "A doctor for nothing is worth nothing" (Bava Kama 85a). This sentiment was echoed over a thousand years later, in 1666, when a congregation in Hamburg decided not to accept the offer of a physician to give free medical care to the poor because "it is not fitting to engage someone without salary; for the payment will force the doctor to be in time when called in by a patient" (Jakobovits, *Jewish Medical Ethics*, p. 225).

But not every community was wealthy enough to pay a physician to attend the poor; nor were physicians always so magnanimous as the doctor of Hamburg in offering their services. Therefore, in order to ensure that those without money received some type of medical care, communal authorities sometimes had to intervene. A nineteenth-century rabbi, Eleazer Fleckeles of Prague, ruled that the religious court could compel a recalcitrant physician to attend a patient without charge if the doctor had refused to visit because the patient was unable to pay. All these examples certainly give us pause when we blithely assume that the tradition viewed doctors with simple naive pride!

Communal responsibility for the sick

Communal involvement in the care of the sick has a long history in Judaism. The earliest provisions for the care of sick Jews that we know of were the houses set aside for lepers in biblical times. In the talmudic period and early Middle Ages special sections of the houses set aside for visiting strangers were apparently also used for the sick. By the eleventh century such a house had a specific name: the hekdesh, or bet hekdesh ha-aniim—the house consecrated to the needy. Found mostly in Germany, they served as a combination home for the poor and wayfarers and hospital for those too poor to afford medical care in the home. In other communities the care of the sick was entrusted to the members of the Hevra Kadisha— the Burial Society.

Such arrangements were sporadic at best. It wasn't until the time of the shtetl that a satisfactory system of medical care was established. For over two hundred years, beginning in the seventeenth century, Jewish communities in Eastern Europe maintained remarkably comprehensive medical care programs.

Medical care in the shtetl was designed to provide the sick with spiritual, social, and religious support, as well as medicine and care by a physician. Among the essential components of this health care system were communal

Flesh of fat chickens and broth made therefrom are the most valuable foods with which sufferers from hemorrhoids should be nourished (Maimonides, *Treatise on Hemorrhoids*).

Obesity is harmful to the body and makes it sluggish.... Therefore extremely obese individuals should travel to the seashore, do much walking in the sun, and especially bathe in the sea air in order to lose weight, since the sea air causes dissolution of liquids. ...Stay away from hot water... except... steam baths (Maimonides).

For anal worms, take acacia, aloes, white lead, silver dross, a charm containing phyllon, and the excrement of doves and apply them wrapped in linen rags in summer and in cotton in winter (Gittin 69b).

As a remedy for eye inflammation, apply the white of the bile of an ox thirty-four times to your eye (Bet David 36a).

physicians, surgeons, apothecaries, hospitals, nurses, and sick visitation societies....

Arrangements between the community and the physician varied. In some communities, the physician was provided with a house. He was often exempt from local taxation, but was only occasionally given an actual salary. In Frankfurt the communal physician was forbidden to accept anything from the poor, could accept from the middle class amounts they were able to pay, and was paid a set fee by the rich.

In some communities, the community council reimbursed the physician on a fee-for-service basis when he cared for the poor to ensure that the poor received good care. Other communities specified in his contract that there was to be no difference in treatment and conduct between the rich and the poor. Occasionally, it was specified how often the sick were to be visited, as well as what arrangements would be made for coverage....

One of the more important components of communal medical care in the shtetl was the sick visitation society. Everyone in the community was expected to serve as a visitor, and a small committee usually took responsibility for scheduling.

The visitors were to watch over the sick, to see that they ate what their physician recommended, and to ensure that they received the proper medicine. Often the visitors acted to help supervise the communal nurses, but occasionally they carried out nursing functions. Their presence was intended to provide the sick with psychological and spiritual support as well as medical care (Copans, pp. 3–4).

The warmth and comprehensiveness of the shtetl system certainly contrasts with the cold impersonality of our modern high-powered medical establishment (and by and large, despite Jewish-establishment claims to the contrary, modern "Jewish" hospitals are not better in this regard than any other hospitals). In the past ten years community-based medical clinics have begun to appear in the United States, and home care programs for the elderly are starting to take hold. Community health workers are going into homes to explore the social bases of disease. Let's hope that the movement back to greater communal responsibility continues to flourish and grow.

Ethical roots

With medicine so prominent in the life of the Jewish community and with the large overlap at various periods between the medical and religious professions, it is natural that medical ethics has received a good deal of attention in Judaism. Although each particular issue has its own special features, two general characteristics are of interest because of their uniqueness to Judaism:

1. Ethical discussions are never simply abstract, philosophical matters. Most often they arise almost indirectly as a consequence of legal discussions about concrete problems.

For example, the rabbinical definition of death, crucial to discussions of euthanasia, comes out in the context of a discussion of how deeply we may dig to extricate someone from a building that has collapsed on the Shabbat. Digging is ordinarily forbidden on Shabbat, but since pikuah nefesh takes precedence over the laws of Shabbat, one does attempt to free the person from the rubble. Once s/he is found to be dead, however, further digging is forbidden. The crucial question, then, is how do you determine that someone has died.

One talmudic scholar asserts (Yoma 85a) that the presence or absence of breathing is the key feature in assessing life, and therefore one stops digging at the level of the nose. This is the view generally accepted by most later scholars. Another opinion (ibid.) is that one must dig further—to the level of the heart, because the heart is the key. One clairvoyant scholar even suggested that the navel is the true indication!

Lungs, heart, navel—the interesting feature about this discussion, for our present purpose, is not so much the question of where you look to see the signs of life, but rather that there is no abstract ethical principle being debated. The underlying stimulus for the whole discussion is the practical question of violating the laws of Shabbat.

2. The second characteristic is related in certain ways to the first and is really more of a constantly recurrent problem than a characteristic: how do you decide what is a legitimate Jewish ethical position? The question seems a bit irrelevant at first. If a scholar states an ethical position then that's his position, and you take it or leave it on its own merits. That may seem logical to us, but that's not the way it works in Judaism. Almost all organized Jewish thinking on matters of medical ethics was done within the framework of the halakhah, a comprehensive system of legal ordinances affecting every aspect of a Jew's life. The range of halakhic concern is enormous and all-encompassing. It tells the traditional Jew what foods to eat and what kinds of pots to use for cooking them. It tells how to slaughter a chicken ritually and how to give charity sensitively. Finally, and certainly not incidentally, it also tells the traditional Jew how to behave ethically.

To find out what the halakhah has to say on a given topic, you go to your local traditional scholars or rabbis. They know the answer to your question or they consult another rabbi or a standard textual authority for the answer. In theory the Bible is the ultimate authority, but for all practical purposes the Talmud fills that role. If the Talmud doesn't give a direct answer, then subsequent codes may do so. The last authoritative code is the *Shulhan Arukh*. It was published in 1565. If the *Shulhan Arukh* doesn't answer the question directly, one turns to the commentators on the *Shulhan Arukh*, and the commentators to the commentators . . . on up to the twentieth century. In theory there is one and only one correct answer to any given question, and when it is arrived at, it is as binding as the Bible (in effect a divine injunction) or the Talmud. Looked at on paper, the whole process seems very dispassionate and orderly. In practice, there are a lot of problems; two of these are pertinent to our situation:

1. How are halakhic decisions affected by medical and scientific advances?

2. How dispassionate are the processes that go into a halakhic decision?

In addition to being a compendium of legal debates and decisions, the Talmud is filled with anecdotes, folktales, and a variety of other materials, including health rules, remedies, and medicoreligious laws: "Circumcisions should not be performed on cloudy days or days when a southerly wind blows" (Yevamot 72a); "Rabba ben Shmuel also said in the name of R. Hiyya: After every food eat salt and after every beverage drink water and you will come to no harm. One who doesn't do this by day is liable to be troubled with an evil smelling mouth, and by night with croup" (Berakhot 40a).

It soon became apparent to later scholars that these talmudic remedies and rules not only didn't work but in some cases could be dangerous. Rabbi Jakobovits mentions a number of situations when talmudic rules were abrogated:

Ethical imperatives are . . . at one with the directives of halakhah; it is halakhah which determines that which is permitted and that which is forbidden in the realm of ethics (Bleich, "Abortion in Halakhic Literature," p. 73).

For a chronic heat stroke, take a black hen, cut it open lengthwise, shave the crown of the patient, put the bird on it, and leave it there until it sticks. The patient should go to a river and stand up to his neck in water until he feels faint, after that he should swim out and sit down (Gittin 67b).

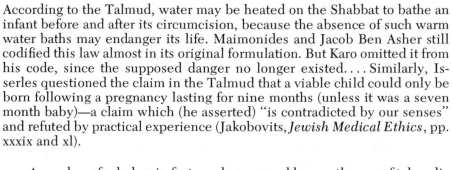

According to the Talmud, water may be heated on the Shabbat to bathe an infant before and after its circumcision, because the absence of such warm water baths may endanger its life. Maimonides and Jacob Ben Asher still codified this law almost in its original formulation. But Karo omitted it from his code, since the supposed danger no longer existed.... Similarly, Isserles questioned the claim in the Talmud that a viable child could only be born following a pregnancy lasting for nine months (unless it was a seven month baby)—a claim which (he asserted) "is contradicted by our senses" and refuted by practical experience (Jakobovits, *Jewish Medical Ethics*, pp. xxxix and xl).

A number of scholars in fact, made a general ban on the use of talmudic remedies. "We must tell you," wrote Sherira Gaon in the tenth century, "that our sages were no physicians.... You must not, therefore, rely on medicines mentioned in the Talmud" (see ibid., p. xxxviii).

The fact that it was necessary to refute so much of talmudic medicine was of great concern to later scholars, since the Talmud is the cornerstone of rabbinic scholarship.

Several sources mention that it was, in fact, forbidden to put the application of talmudic remedies and medicines to the test, since their failure might be attributed, not to the changed conditions of time and place, but (possibly without justification) to the limited or erroneous knowledge of the talmudic sages. This consideration, it was suggested, explains the exclusion of these recommendations by Maimonides and in the later codes; for the operation of such cures and treatments might lead people "to disparage our rabbis, of blessed memory" (ibid., p. xxxiv).

Since it was unacceptable to admit possible fallibility on the part of the rabbis, other reasons had to be sought. Three major explanations arose:

1. One of the most common was that the nature of humans had changed since talmudic times. For example, in referring to the discrepancy noted above between the talmudic and later perceptions of the length of pregnancy, Rabbi Solomon Duran (c. 1400–67) declared: "The duration of pregnancy is in our days—owing to the change of nature—different from talmudic times" (Zimmels, p. 60).

2. Another view is that any discrepancies between talmudic scholarship and later science is due to the special nature of the case:

According to the Talmud the embryo has no definite shape until 40 days after conception; scholars, however, maintain that they found it already shaped after 30 days, sometimes after 45 days. This does not refute the view of the sages, since they dealt only with ordinary cases (Jacob Emden, seventeenth century, quoted in Zimmels, p. 62).

3. A third explanation for the inapplicability of talmudic dicta in later periods is that later generations have lost the competency of earlier ones. There was a general belief among the rabbis that a gradual deterioration of the physical and mental faculties of man was taking place over time, e.g., a decline in longevity since the time of the biblical giants who lived eight hundred or nine hundred years. Its application to the Talmud goes like this: the rabbis indicate that if a woman dies in labor on Shabbat a knife could be carried through a public domain (ordinarily forbidden on the Shabbat) to open her abdomen and remove the fetus, which might be alive. But, according to the sixteenth-century commentator R. Moses Isserles, "this is no longer done even on weekdays, because 'we are no more competent' to recognize the moment of the mother's death with sufficient accuracy to enable the child to live and to prevent hastening the mother's death by a premature incision" (Jakobovits, *Jewish Medical Ethics*, p. xlii). Thus,

the Talmud is not wrong. People's faculties of perception have simply deteriorated.

The point of all this is that however unusual their explanations may seem by our standards, many of the later rabbis recognized that new scientific information has a clear impact on the way we approach medicoreligious law. The problem is that contemporary scholars don't seem to agree with this approach. For example, we have noted above that the rabbis defined death as the cessation of respiration. In the intervening years, particularly the last ten, the concept of brain death has replaced earlier definitions (for reasons that are explained in detail further on). What we have seen above leads us to believe that earlier scholars would have been open to such advances. But in the writings of one of the most prolific contemporary scholars writing in English the sense of openness diminishes:

> It must be emphasized that in all these questions involving the very heart of a physician's obligations with regard to the preservation of human life, halakhic Judaism demands of him that he govern himself by the norms of Jewish law, whether or not these determinations coincide with the mores of contemporary society. Brain death and irreversible coma are not acceptable definitions of death insofar as halakhah is concerned. The sole criterion of death accepted by halakhah is total cessation of both cardiac and respiratory activity (Bleich, "Establishing Criteria of Death," p. 107).

If we accept the norm stated earlier—that you find answers to halakhic (i.e., ethical for our purposes) questions by going to your local traditional rabbi—then we'll end up with potentially problematic answers like these. Any sense we ourselves have of what the historical development of Jewish sensitivities was in a given area is irrelevant. The most recent answer is The Answer. I believe that this is too limiting for our purposes, so I choose to take a historical, not a strictly halakhic, approach in presenting these questions.

There's a second reason why I prefer a historical approach. It has to do with the problem I mentioned earlier: how dispassionate are the processes that go into a halakhic decision? The whole thing seems very cut-and-dried. For example, in discussing abortion in another article, Rabbi Bleich makes the case for the detached approach to ethics:

> There can be no doubt that a pregnancy contraindicated by considerations of social desiderata and personal welfare poses grave and tragic problems. We are, indeed, keenly aware of the anguishing emotional ramifications of such problems and are acutely sensitive to their moral implications. Yet when we are confronted by these and similar dilemmas, our response cannot simply echo humanistic principles and values, but must be governed by the dictates of halakhah (Bleich, "Abortion in Halakhic Literature," p. 73).

Fine. Let's not get emotions mixed up with decisions about abortion. There's only one problem with such a noble ideal. The seventeenth-century author of the responsum that has served as the model for almost all subsequent rabbinic decisions on abortion, Rabbi Yair Bacharach, doesn't adhere to it. Rabbi Bacharach was asked by a physician whether an abortion could be performed upon a woman who became pregnant through adultery. His disdainful reply to the physician's question certainly cannot be faulted for echoing "humanistic principles and values," nor is it the model of rational detachment:

> You have asked a difficult question; a woman who performed adultery while under her husband [i.e., married], and she should have the brazenness to ask this type of question from a rabbi! And I think that the format of the question—referring to a married woman—is a fabrication. It never was

Most ass drivers are wicked, most camel drivers are honest, most sailors are pious, the best of physicians is destined for Gehinnom [Hell] (Kiddushin 4:14).

It is forbidden to live in a city in which there is no physician (TJ Kiddushin 66d).

Uncleanliness of the head leads to blindness, uncleanliness of garments leads to insanity, uncleanliness of the body leads to ulcers and sores; so beware of uncleanliness (Nedarim 81a).

Do not sit too much because it is bad for piles; do not stand too much because it is bad for the heart; do not walk too much because it is bad for the eyes; but spend a third of the time sitting, a third standing, and a third walking (Ketubbot 111a).

and never was created [i.e., it never could have happened that way]! (*Havat Yair*, Frankfurt edition, 1699, responsum no. 33).

And if there is any doubt left about his attitude, he concludes: "There is no more to be said about this. And please, my brother, don't bother me with questions such as these because with difficulty have I answered you this time!" (ibid.).

What Rabbi Bacharach's comments reveal rather clearly is the degree to which rabbinic decisions are affected by factors other than strict logic or halakhic principles of interpretation. The rabbis are human beings like the rest of us. They often have special insights into the nature of people and God, insights that at times have the spark of the divine in them, insights that can provide standards for a community of Jews to live by. But they can be inconsistent, swayed by emotion, even wrong at times. And at those times, we must judge for ourselves what to do.

Let's take a look at some of the areas that give cause for concern in Jewish attitudes toward medicine.

The definition of death

One curious side issued raised by modern respirators is that for chronic use they are attached directly to the trachea at a point low in the neck—not at the nose. Is a person then who is otherwise perfectly alert considered dead by the criteria of those who regard the passage of air through the nose as paramount?

Beginning with a case mentioned earlier, we realize that in order to be able to deal with such questions as euthanasia and organ transplantation, it is important first to have an understanding of what constitutes death. As noted before, the basic talmudic definition is that death occurs when respiration ceases. The Talmud bases this distinction on Genesis 7:22: ". . . in whose nostrils was the merest breath of life."

This notion that life entered and departed from the nose was very widespread in Jewish thinking. The Midrash speaks of the death of Aaron's sons (who offered "alien fire" at the altar and were instantly killed—Leviticus 10:1–2) as occurring through the nose: "From the holy of holies issued two flames of fire, as thin as threads, then parted into four, and two each pierced the nostrils of Nadab and Abihu, whose souls were burnt, although no external injury was visible" (Louis Ginzberg, *Legends of the Bible* [Philadelphia: Jewish Publication Society, 1966], p. 419). And similarly, traditional legend has it that the ancients died by sneezing (Joshua Trachtenberg, *Jewish Magic and Superstition* [Philadelphia: Jewish Publication Society, 1966], p. 211).

Whatever its etiology, the basic Jewish instinct in determining death was to look at the nose. Absence of a heartbeat was also regarded by many rabbis as a useful ancillary criterion.

Until recently these two features were the only two that seemed necessary in defining death. However, terminally ill patients can now be kept breathing indefinitely on respirators and the heart can be stopped for hours while corrective cardiac surgery is done.

Current medical thinking on death has therefore focused elsewhere: on the function of the brain and the central nervous system. When the brain is so severely damaged that a patient is totally unresponsive to external stimuli, has no spontaneous movements or breathing, has no measure of brain activity, and fulfills certain other criteria, most neurologists declare that death has occurred ("Report of the Ad Hoc Committee of the Harvard Medical School to Examine the Definition of Brain Death," *Journal of the AMA* 205 [1968]:337–40). Does this make all Jewish definitions obsolete?

In view of what we have seen so far, the answer would have to be yes.

But remarkably, there is another much less known Jewish definition, propounded over eight hundred years ago by Maimonides, that has a surprisingly modern ring: death can be said to have occurred "when the power of locomotion that is spread throughout the limbs does not originate in one center but is independently spread throughout the body" (commentary on Mishnah Oholot, 1:6, quoted in Rabinovitch, p. 24). This definition focuses on the nervous system but it also focuses on death as a process. Nowadays ethical thinkers are pointing out how difficult it is to formulate a definition of death. Maimonides recognized this point long before respirators forced us to confront the issue.

Euthanasia

If we are not sure exactly what death is anymore, preparing for it has been even more perplexing. When medicine was more art than science, life-saving measures were soon exhausted and there was little left to do but comfort the patient and pray. Today a person can be so seriously injured in an accident or by a stroke that s/he will never recover the ability to perceive and communicate, yet modern devices enable the lungs to continue to exchange oxygenated blood to keep the body tissues alive for months or years. But despite the fact that the tissues have oxygen, we are left with a number of questions:

1. Is the person, in fact, alive?
2. What does it mean to turn off the machinery that prolongs this vegetative state?

We can get clues to all the answers by starting with the last. A person whose death is imminent from natural causes is called a goses, the term deriving from the rattling of secretions in the throat that indicates a person is near death. The Talmud (Semahot 1) lists six rules regarding a goses:

Rule 1. A dying man is regarded as a living entity in respect to all matters in the world.

Rules 2, 3. We do not make any postmortem preparations while he is still alive.

Rule 4. We may not close the eyes of a dying man. Anyone who touches him is a murderer. For Rabbi Meir used to say: He can be compared to a lamp that is dripping (going out); should a man touch it, he extinguishes it. Similarly, anyone who closes the eyes of a dying man is considered as one who has taken his life.

Rules 5, 6. We do not prematurely mourn or eulogize him.

These formulations, which are repeated in all subsequent codes, effectively deem any form of active euthanasia to be a capital crime. Other sources indicate that a dying person should not even be informed of his status until the very end, lest his will to live be removed:

Even when the physician realizes that his patient approaches death, he should still order him to eat this and not to eat that, to drink this and not to drink that; but he should not tell him that the end is near (Midrash Rabbah on Ecclesiastes, quoted in Jakobovits, "The Dying and Their Treatment in Jewish Law," p. 121).

All these discussions seem to presuppose a person lying quietly in a room, gradually sinking away. Very few people would argue that this poses

Another problem
A person suffers from an incurable cancer that produces excruciating pain. Death will not come for weeks. What moral judgment do we pass on someone who ends this person's agony with an overdose of morphine?

a profound ethical problem. The problem arises when we consider the person who is dying in severe pain.

One of the reasons that the rabbis may not have dealt with such a problem is that until recently most people could not be kept alive long enough to suffer for weeks or months from their terminal illnesses. A few years ago someone with cancer simply stopped eating because it was too uncomfortable and soon died. Nowadays, s/he has intravenous feedings while various treatments are tried. Although many new treatments for cancer have been found, there are still varieties of cancer in which most people are not helped by treatment once the cancer has spread too far to be removed by surgery. The last days or months of such a terminally ill patient are an agony for him and for those who share them with him. What is it possible to do in circumstances like these?

We have already seen that Judaism sees the alleviation of pain as a virtue. There is therefore no restriction as to the amount of pain-relieving medication that may be given to a person. However, deliberate administration of a lethal dose is not condoned by Jewish tradition. Such an act is seen to bear a close resemblance to being an accessory to a suicide, and intentional suicide is forbidden in Jewish law. Although extenuating circumstances such as emotional instability and martyrdom were taken into account by some scholars, deliberate termination of one's life to avoid the pain of disease does not appear to be such a circumstance.

On the other hand, while it is forbidden to actively hasten the death of a dying person, the removal of artificial impediments to death is permissible. The authoritative commentator on the *Shulhan Arukh*, Rabbi Moses Isserles, states that

if there is anything which causes a hindrance to the departure of the soul such as the presence near the patient's house of a knocking noise such as wood-chopping or if there is salt on the patient's tongue, and these hinder the soul's departure, then it is permissible to remove them from there because there is no act involved in this at all, but only the removal of an impediment (*Shulhan Arukh*, Yoreh Deah, 339:1).

What constitutes an impediment then becomes the issue. A seventeenth-century scholar, R. Jacob ben Samuel, suggests that "it is forbidden to hinder the departure of the soul by the use of medicines" (*Beit Yaakov* 59, quoted in Rosner, p. 120). There is no unanimity about this, however; Rabbi Jakobovits says that technically the discussion applies only to the last three days of life (Jakobovits, "The Dying and Their Treatment in Jewish Law," p. 248).

The problem today is that modern technology has extended the state of goses far beyond what naturally would have occurred. Patients with massive strokes, cancer refractory to medication, and other terminal conditions often spend their last days or months vegetating, essentially unresponsive to any stimulus except overwhelming pain from bedsores, irritating intravenous or stomach feeding tubes, and the pain of the illness itself. In these cases, the removal of feeding tubes and other impediments to dying would seem perfectly consistent with Jewish tradition as expressed by Rabbi Isserles.

Having found a positive attitude in Judaism for the removal of "impediments," we may be in a better position to answer the first question posed earlier: what about the person in "irreversible coma," whose body is maintained by a respirator because his/her brain is so damaged that the respiratory center no longer stimulates. Unless the coma is due to a drug overdose, if certain criteria (noted in "Definition of Death") are satisfied, we can say with certainty that the person never will wake up. Is such a

When you are in need of a physician you esteem him a god;
When he has brought you out of danger, you consider him a king;
When you have been cured, he becomes a human like yourself;
When he sends his bill, you think him a devil (Jedaiah b. Abraham, 13th century).

person alive in any Jewish sense? According to the criteria of spontaneous respiration and Maimonides's definition of central control, the answer has to be no. The substance of life has departed such a body, leaving behind only the barest wisp as a reminder of what once was. Rabbi Isserles's injunction applies even more in this case than the earlier one, because it is so clear that we are simply holding up a process that nature would have long ago completed except for our intervention.

Thus we see that in certain circumstances at the end of life, euthanasia is consistent with Jewish attitudes. What about euthanasia at the opposite time of life—infancy? There has been a good deal of publicity about recent instances in which mongoloid or seriously deformed babies were simply allowed to die by the withholding of necessary surgery or medications. This kind of euthanasia would be difficult to justify in Jewish tradition. Such a baby is not in the process of dying. It has barely been born. The criteria applied to people dying of terminal disease simply don't pertain here.

Organ transplantation

There is another side to all this concern with death: the matter of organ transplantation. In any organ transplant, the donor organ must be alive and healthy. This poses no problem when there is a kidney transplant from a living relative, since the kidney is functioning normally in the donor until it is removed. But when the organ to be transplanted comes from someone who is dead, the matter becomes more complicated. Often organs are taken from a young, otherwise healthy person who has been in a serious accident and suffers such severe brain damage that his/her chances of recovering are nil, although his/her kidneys or heart may be fine.

A number of questions arise here:

1. Is the concept of organ transplantation acceptable in Jewish tradition?

The answer here is pretty generally yes. Again, the principle of pikuah nefesh is overriding. In the case of cadaver donors, pikuah nefesh takes precedence over such otherwise controversial considerations as deriving benefit from the dead or delaying burial of the dead (both of which are frowned upon [Avodah Zarah 29b; Sanhedrin 46b]).

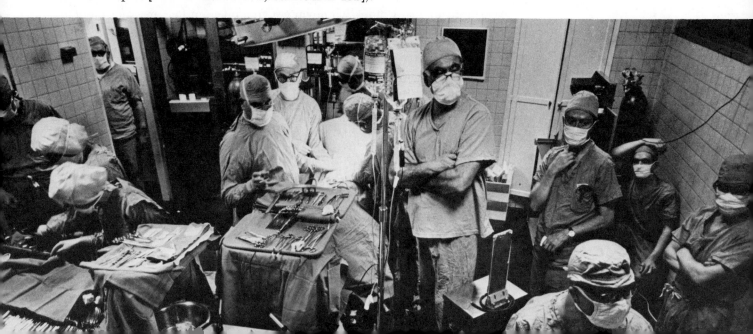

2. When can organs be removed from a cadaver donor?

This question really amounts to asking when a person can be declared dead, since no one would suggest plundering the organs of a comatose patient if s/he stood a chance of recovery (although taking a kidney from an irreversibly comatose patient who was to be maintained indefinitely on a respirator has been considered at various times by modern physicians). In the case of someone in irreversible coma, this is presumably just after the respirator is turned off and the patient shows no signs of spontaneous respiration. This criterion would apply no matter what organ was involved in the transplant.

3. A third problem that applies only to living donors is the question of whether someone is allowed to put himself in danger to benefit another person. While the incidence admittedly is very low, there is a risk of death from any general anesthetic procedure. Nonetheless, Rabbi Jakobovits (quoted by Rosner, p. 167) feels that as long as the probability of saving the recipient's life is substantially greater than the risk to the donor's, Judaism sees no bar to donating a kidney for transplant.

Experimentation

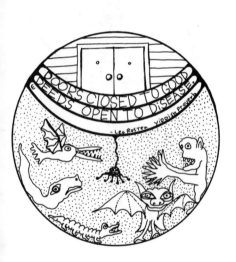

The final question regarding transplantation arose in the context of early unsuccessful heart transplants; such procedures were, by nature, a kind of experimentation, since the techniques were clearly imperfect at the time. Is a person permitted to submit to such experimentation if there is a good chance that it will fail? Before answering the question, a brief survey of the recent status of human experimentation is in order.

Thousands of physically normal prisoners, mental patients, and others are entered every year into research projects that they often don't understand and the consequences of which often remain for many years. Until very recently, when the Department of Health, Education, and Welfare issued guidelines prohibiting the practice, many experiments contained exculpatory language regarding negligent injuries in their consent forms. Extensive publicity was given recently to a study in which a group of southern blacks with syphilis were followed for years without treatment to observe the natural course of the disease. But for every well-publicized case there are many more that never get general attention: an experiment to test a new drug for treating asthma that involved deliberate provocation of asthmatic attacks in children, some of them severe; a test in South America (with U.S. money) of a new contraceptive device that resulted in forty-eight unwanted pregnancies among 262 women (see The *Hastings Center Report*, vol. 3, June 1973).

When stricter standards have been promulgated, the researchers have simply moved away from the U.S., to countries where there is less control over their activities.

The simplest way to prevent such excesses would be to eliminate medical research completely, but this is really not a satisfactory solution. Unfortunately, it is very clear that there is no substitute for the human being as the model for illness after animal experimentation has been carried out. The alternative to scientific experimentation is trial and error medicine, which is probably more hazardous in the long run. What we need are adequate guidelines to protect everyone concerned. Rabbi

Jakobovits ("Survey of Recent Halakhic Periodical Literature," *Tradition*, Winter 1966) lists some criteria based on Jewish sources which serve as a very useful and very sensitive starting point. The first four:

1. Possibly hazardous experiments on humans may be performed only if they may be potentially helpful to the subject himself, however remote the chances of success are.
2. Even untried or uncertain cures should be applied in attempts to ward off certain death later, if no safe treatment is available.
3. In all other cases, it is as wrong to volunteer for such experiments as it is unethical to submit persons to them with or without their consent, whether they are normal people, criminals, prisoners, cripples, idiots, or patients on their deathbeds.
4. If the experiment involves no serious hazard to life or health, the obligation to volunteer for it devolves on anyone who may thereby help promote the health of others.

By these criteria a heart transplant would be perfectly justifiable in someone who stands no chance of survival by any other approach. So would other less hazardous experiments—trials of medications, for example, if the benefits outweigh the hazards or if the hazard is not serious. One of the major ethical advances is guideline four, which removes medical experimentation from the prisons, mental hospitals, and indigent wards and places it in the general community, where it belongs.

Plastic surgery

A curious side issue of this discussion is whether plastic surgery is permitted by Jewish law. One of the halakhic principles underlying Rabbi Jakobovits's criteria is Maimonides's injunction (Hilkhot Rotzeiah 1:4) that one is forbidden to "wound one's body except for therapeutic purposes." Since plastic surgery is simply cosmetic, shouldn't it be forbidden? Apparently not, argue two contemporary rabbis, Yehiel Berish and Menashe Klein (quoted in Jakobovits, "Survey of Recent Halakhic Periodical Literature," *Tradition*, Fall 1974), who cite as proof a standard talmudic commentary (*Tosafot*, Shabbat 50b), which maintains

that a state of mind which prevents a person from mingling with people constitutes pain within the halakhic definition of that term. . . . Therefore, if such an individual shuns normal social intercourse as a result of deformity or other disfigurement, the condition causing distress may be corrected by means of plastic surgery.

Autopsy

Theological perceptions of the nature of the body and soul may vary, but we cannot escape the fact that the time immediately following death is suffused with the memories and perceptions of life. This rush of memories and nostalgic recollections is, at the same time, accompanied by a sense of finality. Everything is over now, for our loved one—and for us in our relationship with that person. When the doctor comes and interrupts this bereaved state by saying that an autopsy would be beneficial, trying to decide what to do becomes just one more trying experience on top of what has already been a difficult ordeal.

The autopsy itself is essentially a medical operation performed after death. An incision is made with a scalpel, just as in any operation. The internal organs are examined visually and tiny samples are taken for examination under the microscope. Then the incision is sewn closed. All incisions are carefully made so that no disfigurement is produced in places like the face.

Jewish attitudes

What I'd like to do in this section is to try to provide some information to help in making that decision if it becomes necessary: (1) a description of what's involved in an autopsy; (2) a few words about Jewish attitudes regarding autopsy.

According to all evidence the process of embalming as practiced by the ancient Egyptians consisted of disemboweling the body and filling the cavity with certain unguents (*Encyclopaedia Judaica*, 3:931).

The earliest Jewish references to dissection of a body are in the Bible—in Genesis 50:2, 26, where the embalming of Jacob and Joseph are mentioned. This apparently involved the opening of the body.

However, there is no record of anatomical studies for medical purposes until the time of the Talmud. R. Yishmael (Jerusalem Talmud, Niddah 4:7) recounts, without negative judgment, Queen Cleopatra's practice of giving the king the bodies of condemned female slaves for dissection. The Talmud (Berakhot 45a) also notes that R. Yishmael's disciples boiled the body of a condemned prostitute to determine the number of bones in human beings.

Based on these and other references, Rabbi Jakobovits states:

It is noteworthy that no voice of protest was raised against these practices or their description in the Talmud. [In fact] the allegation of Jewish religious opposition to dissection [cannot] be sustained by any direct reference to the subject on the part of a single Jewish physician or rabbi before the 18th century. On the contrary, there is some evidence to suggest that a few Jewish physicians did in fact carry out postmortem examinations very occasionally (Jakobovits, "Survey of Recent Halakhic Periodical Literature," *Tradition*, Winter 1964–65, pp. 135, 143).

Nonetheless, when a formal inquiry to rabbis was finally made in the eighteenth century regarding the permissibility of autopsy, the answer was quite clearly no.

For a nosebleed, take a kohen whose name is Levi and write Levi backwards, or take any man and write: "I Papi Shila bar Sumki" backwards (Gittin 69a).

שוברנ
ANCIENT HEBREW
REMEDY
Cures ✡
Biliousness
Colic
Dyspepsia
And Sour Stomach

Do not get in the habit of drinking medicine, and do not have your teeth extracted (Pesahim 113a).

The first opinion was given by Rabbi Jacob Emden in response to a medical student's question regarding dissection for medical education. Rabbi Emden declared that such dissection is forbidden on the grounds that it is deriving benefit from the dead, which is forbidden by the Talmud (Sheilat Yaavetz 1, no. 41—see Jakobovits, ibid., p. 145). The second opinion was given by Rabbi Ezekiel Landau of Prague. The question was asked whether an autopsy could be performed on a patient who had died after surgery for a bladder stone, to ascertain what therapy would be proper for such stones in the future. Rabbi Landau forbade the autopsy as a desecration of the dead. Only if there was a patient immediately available who would benefit from the knowledge could the autopsy be permitted (Rosner, p. 136). Until very recently almost all rabbinic thinkers subsequent to Rabbi Landau used his opinion as the cornerstone for their decisions.

This all appears very straightforward until one looks at the reasons behind these views. Three texts are quoted to justify a prohibition against autopsy. The first is Deuteronomy 21:22–23, which states: "If a man is guilty of a capital offense and is put to death, and you impale [hang] him on a stake, you must not let his corpse remain on the stake overnight, but must bury him the same day." This is carried a bit further in the second source,

Sanhedrin 47a: "Just as hanging all night is a desecration, anything else which amounts to a disgrace is also prohibited." This still pertains only to criminals. The final source mentioned is Maimonides, who extends the prohibition to all the dead (Hilkhot Sanhedrin 15:8, quoted in Rosner, p. 140). But this is as far as the sources go. Do they justify the kind of blanket condemnation against autopsy that Rabbi Landau enunciates?

It is clear from what we've seen that Judaism regards the dead body of even a criminal with a substantial measure of respect. This attitude shows up elsewhere in Jewish sources. One good example is found in the Talmud (Hullin 11b), which carefully limits the amount of postmortem dissection that may be done in criminal cases:

Why do we not fear that the victim may have been afflicted with a fatal organic disease, for whose killing a person is not punishable as a murderer? Is it not because we follow the majority, and most victims of murderers are not so afflicted? And should you say that we can examine the body—this is not allowed because it would thereby be mutilated. And should you say that since a man's life is at stake, we should mutilate the body, there one could answer that there is always the possibility that the murderer may have killed the victim by striking him in a place where he was suffering from a fatal wound, thus removing all traces of the wound. In such a case, it is clear that no amount of postmortem examination should show that the victim was afflicted with a fatal illness (Hullin 11b, quoted in Rosner, p. 139).

This example wasn't used by the rabbis to justify their position on strictly medical dissection, but it is instructive all the same. In fact, the point is not so different from the point made by modern physicians—an autopsy is useful only when the benefits to be gained are clearly defined and the person doing the examination is competent. As an editorial in the *Journal of the American Medical Association* put it:

It is a pernicious misconception that the mere performance of postmortem examination leads to progress in medical science or the discovery of new diseases, or the advancement of medical frontiers. We lose sight of the fact that progress depends not on the autopsy but on the person who is examining the material (*Journal of the AMA* 191 [1965]:1078–79).

The author of this editorial is not arguing that autopsies should be stopped—simply that we must be clear in our own minds about what the benefits are in a given situation. These feelings are quite similar to those expressed in the recent writings of Rabbi Jakobovits. In something of a departure from the scholars who strictly follow Rabbi Landau, Rabbi Jakobovits declares:

Autopsies now bear a relationship to the saving of life not only in the hope they hold out for finding new cures for obscure diseases, but also in testing the effects and safety of new medications and in demonstrating errors of diagnosis and treatment ("Survey of Recent Halakhic Periodical Literature," *Tradition*, Winter 1964-65).

However, he notes that autopsies are not to be done routinely, and when they are done, they should be performed with appropriate respect:

Any permission for an autopsy is to be given only on condition that the operation is reduced to a minimum, carried out with the greatest dispatch, in the presence of a rabbi or religious supervisor if requested by the family, and performed with the utmost reverence and with assurance that all parts of the body are returned for burial (ibid.).

These seem like eminently sensible criteria.

The rabbis tell us that when a funeral cortege meets a bridal procession, the former allows the latter to pass first. The needs of the living take precedence over the rights of the dead. Carried out with respect and dispatch, autopsies play a significant role in enhancing the health of the living. They have an honorable place in Jewish tradition.

Contraception, sterilization, and artificial insemination

The biblical injunction to "be fertile and increase" is regarded by Jewish tradition as one of the fundamental commandments incumbent upon Jews. A man was considered by early sources to have fulfilled his duty to procreate if he had two children. Maimonides, however, suggests that even this could be improved upon: "Although a man has fulfilled the mitzvah of procreation, he is commanded by the rabbis not to desist from procreation while he yet has strength" (quoted by Feldman, p. 50).

Procreation clearly holds an important place in the Jewish scale of values. However, the scale could be said to be missing about half its balance weights: all these references indicate that the commandment is incumbent only upon men, not women. In fact, most of the legal rulings regarding contraception and sterilization reflect this situation. The only types of contraception permitted by traditional Jewish law are those that the woman uses—birth control pills or a diaphragm. (Intrauterine devices are forbidden because they work by preventing implantation of the fertilized ovum—in effect inducing an abortion.) Similarly, sterilization is generally frowned upon but is permitted by the most traditional authorities when a woman fears the pain of subsequent pregnancies—she is permitted to drink a sterilizing potion. (Later scholars realized that sterilizing potions, in fact, had a minimal effect in preventing pregnancies.)

Sterilization of a male is absolutely forbidden. Anything that interferes with normal completion of the sex act by the male is also forbidden, e.g., condoms and coitus interruptus, although these are permitted when semen is to be obtained for artificial insemination (which is permitted by rabbinic law as long as the donor is the recipient's husband; artificial insemination by anyone else is considered to constitute adultery).

If all these strictures surrounding the sexual act sound a bit foreign to modern ears, it is perhaps because the principles underlying them may no longer ring so true today. For example, one of the major concepts underlying the traditional attitude is the prohibition against onanism—frustration of the sexual act by letting the seed go to waste. This prohibition is derived from the Bible. Genesis 38 describes the case of Onan, whose brother had died childless, leaving Onan bound by biblical law to marry his brother's wife:

Then Judah said to Onan, "Join with your brother's wife and do your duty by her as a brother-in-law, and provide offspring for your brother." But Onan, knowing that the seed would not count as his, let it go to waste whenever he joined with his brother's wife, so as not to provide offspring for his brother. What he did was displeasing to the Lord (Genesis 38:8-10).

The question here is what exactly was "displeasing to the Lord"? If one looks at the passage straightforwardly, it would appear that the problem was Onan's refusal to fulfill his conjugal obligation to his brother's wife. Letting his seed go to waste was strictly secondary. However, the early rabbis indicated that this was not the way they chose to read the passage. The Talmud (Niddah 13a) quotes the teaching of R. Yohanan who suggested: "Whoever emits semen in vain is deserving of death; as it is written: What Onan did displeased the Lord, and He slew him" (quoted in Feldman, p. 111).

While the later rabbis did not incorporate the death penalty into their

IT will be as if you prevented me from committing murder

He who does not engage in procreation is as if he committed murder (Talmud, Yevamot 636).

legal decisions on the spilling of seed, R. Yohanan's tone sets the moral standard for later legal opinions. Thus Maimonides writes:

It is forbidden to expend semen to no purpose. Consequently, a man should not thresh within and ejaculate without. . . . As for masturbators, not only do they commit a strictly forbidden act, but they are also excommunicated. Concerning them it is written, Your hands are full of blood (Isaiah 1:15) and it is regarded as equivalent to killing a human being (quoted in Rosner, p. 45).

Why did the rabbis recoil in such horror at the nonprocreative spilling of seed? There are no certain answers to this question, but it is possible that two factors may have played a role. First, the climate at the time of the Talmud's development was one of substantial intellectual and religious ferment. Numerous Jewish sects, one of which later became Christianity, made their appearance. Preoccupation with bodily purification, de-emphasis of the role of the body, and a general asceticism pervaded such sects. Christianity considered total abstinence to be the ideal. While normative Judaism specifically repudiates abstinence and deplores the restriction of sexuality to strictly procreative purposes (a man is expected to "give happiness to the woman he has married" (Deuteronomy 24:5) and is required to be attentive to her sexual needs—again, this is addressed only to the man), it is possible that we see in the recoiling from onanism the subtle influence of a more ascetic tradition.

Another factor that may have influenced rabbinic attitudes concerns the nature of the physiological aspects of conception. The respective contributions of the man and woman to the production of a child have been debated since antiquity. Feldman documents the wide variations in opinion among Jewish scholars about the matter. Here is one view, found in the Talmud (Niddah 31a) and quoted by later scholars:

There are three partners in man . . . his father supplies the semen of the white substance, out of which are formed the child's bones, sinews, nails, brain, and the white in his eye. His mother supplies the semen of the red substance, out of which is formed his skin, flesh, hair, and the black of his eye. God gives him the soul and breath, beauty of features, eyesight, hearing, speech, understanding, and discernment. When his time comes to depart this world, God takes His share and leaves the shares of his mother and father with them (Feldman, pp. 132-33).

The "semen of the red substance" presumably refers to menstrual blood, as the following midrashic passage indicates:

Job said, "Hast Thou not poured me out like milk and curdled me like cheese?" (Job 10:10-12). A mother's womb is full of standing blood, which flows therefrom in menstruation. But, at God's will, a drop of whiteness enters and falls into its midst and behold a child is formed. This is likened unto a bowl of milk: when a drop of rennet falls into it, it congeals and stands; if not, it continues as liquid (Leviticus Rabbah 14:9, quoted in Feldman, p. 133).

Later scholars were even more specific in their sense of what the sperm was all about. One view, which has its precursors in earlier thought but flowered most explicitly in the Middle Ages and later, was the idea that the sperm contained a small man (homunculus), complete in all its parts, waiting to develop in the fertile environment of the woman. Such a sperm was thought by some medieval mystics to develop in the brain, then pass down the spinal cord, acquiring its various human characteristics along the way, and finally emerge as a fully developed potential human being. The implication of this is clearly noted:

This drop comes from a holy place, the abode of the soul, the brain. . . . Therefore we are forbidden to destroy seed, because to do so is verily to commit an act of destruction, of stunting (R. Joshua ibn Shuaib, an early fourteenth-century preacher, quoted in Feldman, p. 116).

This attitude presumably underlies the view of the *Zohar* that spilling seed unnecessarily is a sin more serious than all the sins of the Torah (Feldman, p. 114). This perception of the sperm as homunculus had a strong effect until surprisingly late. When the invention of the microscope in the late seventeenth century permitted men to see the sperm for the first time, one of the disciples of Leeuwenhoek claimed to have seen a complete miniature human figure inside the sperm. Rabbi Feldman quotes the response of R. Jacob Emden to this development:

Now it has been seen through the viewing instrument that magnifies, which is called a microscope, that a drop of man's sperm, while yet in its original temperature, contains small creatures in man's image and likeness. They live and move to and fro within the sperm. Now you can understand how right the sages were and how all their words are true and just, even in matters hard to know or imagine. You will also understand why the *Zohar* found this evil to be so severe . . . and why repentance is so difficult, etc. How strange the talmudic idea that spilling seed is "like murder" seemed to the "philosophizers" among us before the microscope was invented. They thought that destroying seed is like destroying wood which has not yet been made into a chair, not knowing that seed is potentially the "chair" itself, the end product in miniature (Feldman, p. 121).

Whether these historical points in fact explain the basis of the Jewish attitude toward contraception, sterilization, and artificial insemination is difficult to say. What we can say is:

1. It is clear that the sperm was felt to be invested with much of the potential for a new human life. Therefore the rabbis felt it appropriate to impose certain constraints on sexual activity. What is interesting is that their constraints were limited. Given the harshness of some of the views we have quoted, one might expect them to have expressed an opinion much closer to that of the Catholic Church. The rabbis never permitted themselves to go so far in their legal decisions, however.

2. Limited or not, any restrictions based upon a perception of the distinction between male and female roles do not sit well with modern sensitivities. Therefore, traditional approaches to contraception may have limited receptivity today.

3. Be that as it may, the rabbinic sense of the positive nature of marriage and marital sex remains with us today.

Abortion

[The fetus is] the artifice of the Holy One, blessed be He, and His workmanship (*Zohar*, Shemot 3b).

Despite recent technical advances that have made abortions safer and easier, the ethical problems involved are no less vexing. Many of the problems are old ones, highlighted by changing modern sensitivities, improved scientific understanding, and technical expertise. What is the status of the fetus? Is it simply "the thigh of its mother," as the Talmud (Hullin 58a) suggests at one point. Or is it something more ethereal, as the *Zohar* contends?

What are the grounds for abortion? Should it be performed simply for the mother's "need," as one seventeenth-century rabbi (R. Joseph Trani) suggests; or is it an "appurtenance to murder" that should be performed only in the face of life-threatening circumstances, as asserted by former Israeli chief rabbi Unterman?

These wide variations of opinion reflect a curious ambivalence in Jewish tradition regarding abortion. A rather permissive attitude emerges from a number of early sources. Exodus 21:22-23 states that

when men fight, and one of them pushes a pregnant woman and a miscarriage results, but no other damage ensues, the one responsible shall be fined according as the woman's husband may exact from him. . . . But if other damage [i.e., the death of the woman] ensues, the penalty shall be life for life.

The Bible assigns a value to human beings; see, e.g., Leviticus 27:1–8.

Thus the legal status of the fetus falls into a wholly different category from that of the mother. Its accidental destruction is punishable simply by a fine—of an amount equivalent to its property value, according to later sources (Rashi, Sanhedrin 57b, 72b; Maimonides, Hilkhot Hovel Umazik 4:1). This perception of the fetus is consistent with most of the opinions given in the Talmud. In the case of a difficult labor where the mother's life is threatened, permission is granted to extract the embryo "limb by limb, because her life takes precedence over its life; once the greater part is already born, it may not be touched, for we do not set aside one life [nefesh] for another" (Oholot 7:6). A fetus, then, does not acquire the rights of a nefesh—a human being—until it has passed more than halfway out of the birth canal. This distinction between a fetus and a human being is reiterated by later commentators, who specifically exclude the killing of a fetus as a crime under the laws of homicide (Feldman, pp. 254-55).

Two other talmudic references emphasize the secondary status of the fetus. Both discuss the treatment of a condemned woman who is pregnant. The first (Arakhin 7a) states that one does not delay the execution of a pregnant woman until she gives birth unless she is actually in labor at the time. Why? Because the fetus is an organic part of the mother. In fact, one is permitted to go even further, according to the second reference (Arakhin 32a): "If the pregnant woman is about to be executed, one strikes against her womb so that the fruit may die first, in order to avoid her disgrace."

Rashi explains "disgrace" to mean that the mother might have vaginal bleeding following the execution. To avoid this potential embarrassment, an abortion is permissible.

Elective abortion

None of this early material deals with purely elective abortion at the mother's request. However, with this material alone as a basis, we should not be surprised that a relatively permissive attitude might emerge. In fact, the very first responsum on elective abortion reflected precisely this tradition.

The specific question raised was whether a Jew might assist a gentile who desired an abortion. It was addressed to Rabbi Joseph Trani, the chief rabbi of Turkey in the early seventeenth century. In his reply Rabbi Trani devotes very little attention to the question of performing an abortion on a gentile before turning his concern to what is permitted for a Jew:

There is not destruction of life here; even with regard to Jews a fetus is not considered a person. It is only money that the Merciful One obligated the

man to pay to the husband, as it is written, "according to what the husband shall assess him" (Maharit responsum no. 99, Furth, Germany).

Then, taking note of most of the biblical and talmudic references we have quoted, he concludes:

We see that to avoid the mother's disgrace you actively kill the fetus and we don't worry about the possibility of homicide. Therefore with a Jewish woman because of the mother's need, it would seem it is permissible to take part with them (i.e., assist) that she should abort, since it is for the healing of the mother (ibid.).

Rabbi Trani's sanction for abortion in the interests of the mother's health in certain ways seems a rather unremarkable extension of the permissive tradition developed earlier. However, it is interesting in two respects. First, it points out that Jewish thinkers took a remarkably long time to come to grips with the question of elective abortion. The reasons for this silence are not entirely clear. It was not caused by rabbinic ignorance regarding the practice of abortion in the general society. Rather, as Rabbi Jakobovits suggests, "the explanation seems to be . . . that feticide was virtually nonexistent in Jewish society at any time" (ibid.).

Given this long delay in consideration of the matter of elective abortion and given the pattern of the early permissive tradition, which it follows so directly, there is a second reason why Rabbi Trani's responsum should be of more than passing interest. Surprisingly enough, the next responsum on the subject—almost a century later—reaches precisely the opposite conclusion! This is the responsum of Rabbi Yair Bacharach, which we alluded to earlier. (Remember that the problem involves a woman who has become pregnant through adultery and is now very remorseful.)

After the deed was done she regretted it, and she gave her voice in cry day and night, she let her tears come down like a stream, and she knocked her head against the wall until blood flowed; she told her husband and also requested from a wise man that he should set a penance for her to do (*Havat Yair,* responsum no. 33).

Rabbi Bacharach's reply is the perfect embodiment of the ambivalent Jewish attitude toward abortion that we mentioned earlier. His intemperate introduction regarding the woman's motives—for which, by the way, he is taken to task by a later commentator, Rabbi Jacob Emden ("let's not raise doubts about the format of the question," Sheilat Yaavetz, no. 43)—rather pointedly highlights his sense of discomfort with the matter. After this shaky start, he proceeds to cover much of the material with which we are already familiar. He quotes the section from Oholot and suggests that it may be permissible to dismember a fetus, even if it is not for the purpose of saving the mother, as long as labor has not begun. He then quotes the portion of Arakhin that one may beat on the abdomen of a condemned woman to induce abortion, with the notation: "therefore you don't wait for her to give birth because it's not called nefesh at all."

Several other references are quoted with inconclusive results. He then tentatively reaches the same conclusion as Rabbi Trani: "If so, according to what I've written, your question would be completely permissible from the legal standpoint of the Torah . . . " But in the rest of the sentence he immediately backs off: " . . . were it not for the custom which is widespread among us and among them [gentiles] because of the fence against immorality and licentiousness."

With this aboutface a restrictive attitude toward abortion begins that, with few exceptions, has lasted into the twentieth century. Rabbi

There is no reference to the subject [of abortion] in the codes and even the responsa do not mention it until the 17th century (Jakobovits, "Review of Recent Halakhic Periodical Literature," *Tradition*, Spring 1963, p. 73).

Bacharach uses the last half of his responsum to build the case against abortion that is used as a model by almost all subsequent commentators.

1. Jewish tradition enumerates seven laws incumbent upon the "sons of Noah" (gentiles). One of these is capital punishment for murder: "Whoever sheds the blood of man,/ By man shall his blood be shed" (Genesis 9:6). But according to one talmudic commentary, if you read the phrase in Hebrew, you get: "Whoever sheds the blood of a man *in* a man. . . ." Who is a man in a man? A fetus. Therefore abortion is a capital crime for gentiles, and, concludes R. Bacharach, "although it's true a Jew isn't culpable, it still isn't permitted."

2. The section from Arakhin that indicates that one does not delay executing a pregnant woman actually can be interpreted to mean that in any other circumstances, abortion is forbidden: "Were it not for the fact that we don't want to hold up her execution, we would save the fetus. Certainly you shouldn't cause its death, which is forbidden" (ibid.).

3. Abortion constitutes a form of onanism—wasting seed for naught—which is forbidden by Jewish law. It is open to question whether this law applies to women, but nonetheless:

Whether or not the issue of spilling seed is relevant, once fertilization has occurred, it certainly should not be permitted. Therefore anyone who helps in this is an accessory to a crime. Whoever involves himself in this and causes this to happen, I suspect him to have sinned (ibid.).

4. Finally, as almost an afterthought following the formal conclusion of the responsum, R. Bacharach notes the discrepancy between the formulation of the Talmud and that of Maimonides regarding the permission to extract a fetus "limb by limb" in situations where the mother's life is threatened. The Talmud (Sanhedrin 72a) suggests a reason why extraction of the fetus "limb by limb" is permitted. Isn't the fetus a "pursuer," a legal connotation describing someone who is chasing after someone else to kill him? Since one is permitted to kill a "pursuer," the suggestion goes, feticide could be permitted in cases where the fetus constitutes a threat to the mother's life. The reasoning sounds good but is rejected by the Talmud a few lines further on, on the grounds that the mother is being pursued by Heaven, not by the fetus. Unfortunately, in his *Mishneh Torah*, Maimonides states as truth what the Talmud has specifically rejected:

Therefore the sages ruled that when a woman has difficulty in giving birth, one may dismember the child in her womb—either with drugs or by surgery—because he is like a pursuer seeking to kill her. Once his head has emerged, he may not be touched, for we do not set aside one life for another (Hilkhot Rotzeiah u-Shmirat Nefesh 1:9, quoted in Feldman, p. 276).

Rabbi Bacharach and most later commentators seize upon this discrepancy to restrict the indications for an abortion by declaring that Maimonides's formulation has a hidden meaning, which we have to ferret out. What Maimonides means to do, they assert, is to limit the indications for abortion to those situations in which the mother's life is directly threatened, i.e., in which the fetus acts like a "pursuer." Without some other reason, such as saving the mother, it would be forbidden to kill the fetus (*Havat Yair*).

Looking at these and similar arguments in the light of the earlier sources, it is clear that Rabbi Bacharach is reaching pretty far to find a legal basis for his point of view. The first argument flies in the face of all other talmudic opinion about the nonhuman status of a fetus. The second seems internally weak. The third, based on onanism, is as problematic as the

Thirteen things were said concerning bread eaten in the morning: it is an antidote against heat, cold, winds, and demons; it makes the simple wise, and it causes one to triumph in a lawsuit, assists one to learn and teach Torah, causes one's words to be heeded, and helps retain one's scholarship; one's flesh does not exhale a bad odor; one is attached to one's wife and does not lust after another; it destroys tapeworms, and, some say, it drives forth envy and causes love to enter (Bava Metzia 107b).

Rabbi Papa said: Hence no circumcision may be performed on a cloudy day or on a day on which the south wind blows, nor may one be bled on such a day. At the present time, however, many people are in the habit of disregarding these precautions. "The Lord preserves the simple" (Yevamot 72a, quoting Ps. 116:6).

whole concept of onanism itself (see "Contraception, Sterilization, and Artificial Insemination").

The fourth argument is equally difficult. Maimonides may simply be stating that the fetus is "*like* a pursuer" to give a philosophical rationale for the permission to abort a woman who is in danger (the Talmud's "pursuer"), but whatever his rationale it would be no more logical to deduce that Maimonides's discussion refers to a time earlier than the onset of labor than it would be to assume that the talmudic discussion itself has implications for the time before the onset of labor.

It is tempting simply to dismiss much of his case as an aberration on the basis that his introduction reveals a hopeless initial bias. There is only one difficulty in doing that: when the next responsum on abortion appeared some fifty years later, precisely the same ambivalence was present. This is the responsum of Rabbi Jacob Emden, one of the most renowned scholars of the eighteenth century. Rabbi Emden is regarded by modern scholars (like Rabbis Feldman and Bleich) as one of the pillars of the liberal tradition regarding abortion:

The most permissive ruling with regard to therapeutic abortion, one to which later authorities take strong exception, is that of R. Jacob Emden, who permits performance of an abortion not only when the mother's health is compromised but also in cases of "grave necessity," such as when continuation of the pregnancy would subject the mother to great pain (Bleich, "Abortion in Halakhic Literature," p. 94).

Yet elsewhere in the same responsum R. Emden notes: "According to what we have said, generally speaking with a kosher [i.e., legitimate] fetus, there is a prohibition against destroying the fetus except in a case of adultery, where it is permissible and may in fact be a mitzvah" (Sheilat Yaavetz).

In fact, even his permissive opinion is stated with some ambiguity:

Even if the fetus is kosher, there would be a point of view to be lenient for a great need as long as the birth process has not begun, even if it is not to save the life of the mother, just to save her from a great pain. But this requires further investigation (ibid.).

So what's going on here? Are the rabbis for or against abortion and why are they having so much difficulty deciding?

To understand what's happening, we first have to be aware that even in early sources there coexisted with the permissive tradition another tradition that recognized that the fetus's potential for humanity puts it into a very different category from that of simply being an undifferentiated organ of the mother. The Talmud speaks of a fetus as the "thigh of its mother" in the context of a conversion, not abortion, to indicate that the conversion of the mother includes the fetus. Based on this talmudic sentiment, Shabbat laws may be violated to save a fetus: "Violate for him this Shabbat so that he may keep many Shabbatot" (see Feldman, p. 264). Specific ritual behavior is prescribed after an abortion, although mourning per se does not occur. A fetus is, if not fully human, at least a "potential human being" (Rabbi Unterman's phrase).

The halakhic and human dilemma

The rabbis recognized this tradition. Rabbi Bacharach mentions the issue of Shabbat laws in his responsum but found them to be an inconclusive basis for a legal decision. Therefore we ignore them. But, in fact, we don't ignore them. This is the dilemma of the halakhah. There may be terribly important sentiments within Jewish tradition that clearly have a bearing on our decision-making processes. The problem is that if they originate outside the legal tradition or cannot be derived from principles of halakhic interpretation, they cannot be incorporated into the conscious decision-making process. The result is a subconscious tension that finds its outlet either in the ambivalence that we see in the responsa or in an attempt to extract conscious legal decisions consistent with our subconscious goals by introducing what appear to be extraneous matters like onanism.

Most of us are not comfortable with the circumlocutions that result from the latter approach. Open ambivalence rings truer to our ears. Admittedly, the ring can be a bit hollow at times, but in this case I think we can extract something of value. What Judaism seems to be saying is that the legal bars to abortion are, in fact, very few. On the other hand, our moral sensitivities, expressed most poignantly in the *Zohar*, dictate that the fetus's unique potentiality must be considered as well. The question then is not *whether* abortion may be done but, rather, *when* the potentiality for humanity becomes "sufficiently compelling" (in the words of the U.S. Supreme Court in January 1973) to make an abortion morally inappropriate.

Decisions affecting abortion

For the Supreme Court, the compelling feature was the ability of a fetus to survive on its own, even if only for a few seconds. In 1975 that seemed to be at about twenty-four weeks of pregnancy. The problem with twenty-four weeks is evident to anyone who has seen a twenty-four-week-old fetus. At twenty-four weeks a fetus has spontaneous movements in the uterus and looks very much like a small child. In many ways, twenty-four weeks is too late. The commitment to humanity is too compelling. Furthermore, scientific assessments of the point at which a fetus is viable are not entirely helpful. It is clear that advancing technology will push this date back further and further, as test-tube babies become a reality. Since the decision to have an abortion is ultimately a human one, we need more human criteria.

Judaism suggests two other times that we might consider. The first is forty days, during which time the embryo is said by the Talmud (Yevamot 69b) to be merely a "bag of waters." All but the strictest scholars permit abortion during this period. There are problems with this time, though. Most pregnancies are not detected until after this time. Potential considerations such as the presence of Tay-Sachs disease in the fetus are not apparent until much later (see Jewish Genetic Diseases). Thus forty days is simply too soon.

Perhaps a more suitable time is about three months (thirteen weeks). The Talmud (Niddah 17a) speaks of three months as the time when pregnancy is noticeable and fetal movements are about to be perceptible to the mother (see Feldman, p. 266). In Western parlance the latter are known as "quickening," and it usually occurs at sixteen or seventeen weeks. (Perhaps our inability to detect quickening as early as the women in talmudic times is another example of the decline in human sensitivities that we mentioned earlier.) English common law held that an abortion before quickening was not indictable. Tay-Sachs and several other inherited Jewish diseases can usually be detected by fifteen or sixteen weeks (although no earlier). Rabbi Feldman (p. 226) quotes a responsum that permitted an abortion in the first three months on the "grounds that we are not yet dealing with an embryo and the danger to the woman is less now than it would be with an abortion later on."

The importance of quickening in our scale of values lies in the fact that it is the most human of values—the time when a woman detects the presence within her of a living entity. This sensitivity will not change with scientific advances, and if we assume that the talmudic "three months" is, in fact, more like fifteen to seventeen weeks, it is in many ways a very suitable guide to the question, When does the potentiality of a fetus become "sufficiently compelling"?

There are other factors besides time that may play a role in affecting the decision to have an abortion. One of these is the state of health, or potential state of health, of the fetus. It's been obvious that Jewish tradition places little emphasis on the health of the fetus. The mother's health is the primary concern. However, in a situation where the child would be born with Tay-Sachs disease or a similar degenerative condition, there is another factor that must be considered. Such a fetus has already begun, in utero, to accumulate the abnormal fats that will lead to its inexorable death within four or five years. It is, in effect, dying from the moment of conception. The Talmud (Berakhot 43b) indicates that such an abnormal fetus "is not regarded as an offspring" and that if a woman aborts, the ritual laws concerning an ordinary fetus are not observed (see Rosner, p. 75—the specific example in the Talmud was a creature with a double spine; Tay-Sachs disease was not identified until recently). Under the circumstances, an abortion performed at any time before the onset of labor would be in harmony with both the legal and moral tradition. ("Prior to the onset of labor" for practical purposes really means up to twenty-four weeks, since any fetus that can breathe spontaneously after an abortion must be kept alive.)

There is controversy regarding situations of *possible* malformations, e.g., a woman who is exposed to rubella. A child will not inevitably die under such circumstances, and the technology is not currently available to discern in utero what abnormalities might be present. Rabbi Unterman sees no distinction between a normal fetus and a fetus that is potentially abnormal because of the mother's exposure to rubella. He forbids the abortion of either under any circumstances except those threatening the life of the mother. However, another contemporary thinker, Rabbi Eliezer Waldenberg, head of the Jerusalem bet din—religious court

indicates that the difficulties engendered by the birth of an abnormal child may render abortion a "grave necessity" and therefore permissible according to the previously cited view of R. Emden. R. Waldenberg permits such termination of pregnancy within the first three months following conception, provided there is as yet no fetal movement (Bleich, "Abortion in Halakhic Literature," p. 105).

There are other considerations that may play a role in affecting decisions about abortion. Do we as Jews have a special responsibility to bear children since the Holocaust (as some modern thinkers have suggested)? No one can make that choice for any other Jew, and the answer to this question depends on your own sensitivity. However, this responsibility should certainly fall no more heavily on a Jew contemplating abortion than on any Jew considering limiting his/her family.

There is a second consideration, however, that may be more cogent for some. There are many childless Jewish couples who would welcome a child. A pregnant woman might find that her sense of potential life is sufficiently compelling to keep her from having an abortion, yet she feels that her life would be intolerably burdened by the presence of a child. Under such conditions, allowing the child to be born and adopted would not only be satisfying to her but immeasurably enriching to the recipient family (see Adoption).

This is the appropriate point, it seems, to summarize where we are with regard to abortion, but I want to add one very important proviso. The purpose of this chapter is to present options, not dogmas. There is a wealth of material here, and a person desiring an abortion must decide for herself what speaks to her particular sensitivities. For those who are interested in my readings of the tradition, here it is:

Judaism views the fetus as an entity that is an organic part of the mother and at the same time as a potential human being, with all the creative possibilities this implies. Abortion is no substitute for adequate birth control measures. It is appropriate when continuation of a pregnancy would harm the physical or mental health of the mother. The mother should be the primary person to decide what impairs her mental health. (A pregnant mother may disregard her husband's objection to her eating food for which she craves, even if it may harm the child she carries—Jakobovits, "The Consideration of Human Pain in Jewish Law," *Harofe Haivri*, 1959, no. 1, p. 165.) An additional factor that should enter into consideration is the length of the pregnancy. After fifteen to seventeen weeks, when fetal movements can be felt and it is apparent that the fetus is very well developed, the claim of the fetus to human status becomes greatly strengthened. Except in the case of a life-threatening illness, Tay-Sachs disease, or other degenerative disorders, Jewish tradition provides little sanction for an abortion after this period.

Bibliography

A few general remarks. All the references listed here are secondary sources. There is a wealth of information collected within them, but since the primary sources they have to draw on are so voluminous, some selectivity is inevitable. Furthermore, as we saw in dealing with the responsa on abortion, the original sources can at times lend themselves to different interpretations, depending on which sections are quoted. This is usually not a major problem, but if you really want as balanced a view as possible, consult several of the references. Ideally, look at the original Hebrew or Aramaic sources.

GENERAL

There are three general references that provide a comprehensive overview:

1. Jakobovits, Immanuel. *Jewish Medical Ethics*. New York: Bloch 1975.

This is by far the best work on the subject of Jewish medical ethics. Rabbi Jakobovits is thorough and tries to take a balanced point of view within the tradition of Orthodox scholarship. Don't skip the footnotes. They are as valuable as the text. The newest edition takes up recent issues, i.e. organ transplantation.

2. Rosner, Fred. *Modern Medicine and Jewish Law.* New York: Yeshiva University, 1972.

CONCLUSION

Why do we continue to treat seriously the ethical positions developed by the rabbis? We know that technological progress creates new dilemmas for medical ethics; and we are also aware that there are those who say that it is these very technological advances that should provide the key to ethical development. However, events in the past thirty years suggest that technological advances do not necessarily enhance ethical sensitivities. Under the circumstances, it seems valuable to consider the insights of Jewish scholarship.

While the rabbis may have been limited by an inferior technology, the problems they dealt with are as old as humanity itself: birth, pain, death. They were immersed in the problems of people. They sometimes brought their own biases, which we have to take into account. But they also brought a great deal of sensitivity to human needs. The life-giving nature of this sensitivity stems from early Jewish traditions: "You shall keep My laws and My rules, by the pursuit of which man shall live: I am the Lord" (Leviticus 18:5). This is affirmed in the thinking of those scholars who permitted the violation of some of the most sacred laws of the Torah to save life or relieve suffering. In an age where we are bound by little, being bound by their sensitivities is a good start toward ethical behavior.

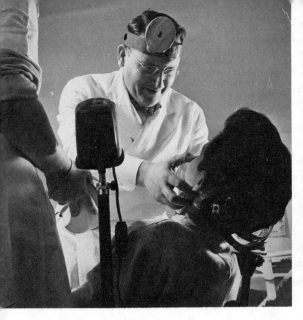
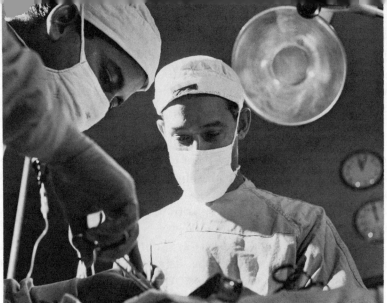

Dr. Rosner's work is not as comprehensive as Rabbi Jakobovits's, but he presents a great deal of information on the subjects he does cover. He discusses most of the newer issues, e.g., organ transplantation and modern concepts of the definition of death. A major virtue of the book is its extensive quotation of critical sources. At times he is less balanced than Rabbi Jakobovits, e.g., a rather hortatory chapter on "The Morality of Abortion."

3. Zimmels, H. J. *Magicians, Theologians and Doctors.* New York: Philip Feldheim, 1952.

A wonderful book, filled with material on talmudic and medieval medicine: theories of disease, remedies, notes on different medical specialties. In addition, it contains a substantial amount of information on purely ethical questions, randomly sandwiched into various sections of the book. Anyone interested in Jewish medicine should have it. The book is still in print.

Although it is not, strictly speaking, a single reference, there is a fourth source worth mentioning:

4. *Tradition*, a journal of Orthodox Jewish thought, published quarterly by:

Rabbinical Council of America
220 Park Ave. South
Suite 900
New York, N.Y. 10003

With few exceptions, the Orthodox are the only ones who care enough about Jewish medical ethics to deal with the subject systematically and in depth. Although I don't always share their point of view, they are the people to whom we frequently turn to find the best compendiums of Jewish sources on a particular subject. Almost every issue of *Tradition* contains topics relevant to questions of medical ethics. Much of the material in Dr. Rosner's book originally appeared there. In addition to articles in specific areas, it also has a section entitled "Survey of Recent Halakhic Periodical Literature," which contains valuable summaries of articles in Hebrew and English on all kinds of timely issues.

5. Articles on specific issues can be found in the *Encyclopaedia Judaica* (Jerusalem: Keter, 1972) and *The Jewish Encyclopedia* (New York: Funk & Wagnalls, 1904). They vary in thoroughness.

6. There is one other general source—the publications of the Hastings Institute of Society, Ethics, and the Life Sciences. They contain material of general interest in every conceivable area of medical ethics. Very little of it is specifically directed to Jewish medical ethics, although there have been recent articles by Rabbi J. David Bleich (whose work we quoted earlier) and Rabbi Seymour Siegel, professor of ethics at the Jewish Theological Seminary. Despite the lack of a specific Jewish orientation, these publications are a valuable resource from which every professional involved in the

social and life sciences would benefit. Associate membership at $15 per year entitles one to the bimonthly *Hastings Center Report* plus special publications, including a comprehensive bibliography in medical ethics that is updated each year:

> **Institute of Society, Ethics, and the Life Sciences**
> **623 Warburton Ave.**
> **Hastings-on-Hudson, N.Y. 10706**

Besides the above, additional references on specific topics are:

HISTORY OF MEDICINE, HYGIENE FOLK REMEDIES, FOLKLORE, DOCTORS

1. Friedenwald, Harry. *The Jews in Medicine.* Baltimore: John Hopkins, 1944. 2 vols.; recently reprinted, New York: Ktav Publishers.
Vol. 1 is the most interesting.
2. Cohen, A. *Everyman's Talmud.* New York: Dutton, 1949.
See especially chapter 8, "The Physical Life."
3. Rosner, Fred, and Munter, Suessman. *The Medical Aphorisms of Moses Maimonides.* 2 vols. New York: Yeshiva, 1970.
————. *Medical Writings of Moses Maimonides.* 4 vols. to date. Philadelphia: Lippincott, 1969–72.
Much of these works are Maimonides's compendiums of the works of Galen and other Greek and Arabic physicians, although he includes original material as well. They are noteworthy mostly for the ubiquity of chicken soup as a remedy for everything from asthma to hemorrhoids.
4. Pollack, Herman. *Jewish Folkways in Germanic Lands.* Cambridge, Mass.: M.I.T., 1969.
Superb chapters on Jewish folk medicine.
5. Trachtenberg, Joshua. *Jewish Magic and Superstition.* Philadelphia: Jewish Publication Society, 1966.
Fascinating; relevant material scattered throughout the book (paperback).
6. The Rephael Society, which is the medical and dental section of the Association of Jewish Scientists, has published a whole series of halakhic bulletins on topics of concern to Orthodox Jewish physicians and dentists. They represent a very conservative point of view but are worth looking at. Write to:

> **The Rephael Society**
> **84 Fifth Ave.**
> **New York, N.Y. 10011**

7. Copans, Stuart A. "Community-Based Medical Care Systems: An Unexplored Alternative" (unpublished). Copies may be requested from Stuart A. Copans, M.D., Thetford Center, Vermont 05075.

DEFINITION OF DEATH

1. Rabinovitch, Nahum. "What Is the Halakhah for Organ Transplants?" *Tradition.* Spring 1968.
2. Rosenfeld, Azriel. "Refrigeration, Resuscitation, and the Resurrection." *Tradition.* Winter 1964–65.
3. Bleich, J. David. "Establishing Criteria of Death." *Tradition.* Winter 1973.
4. Plumand, Posner. *Prognosis in Coma and the Diagnosis of Brain Death in Diagnosis of Stupor and Coma.* Philadelphia: F. A. Davis, 1972.
5. Jakobovits, Immanuel. "The Consideration of Human Pain in Jewish Law." *Harofe Haivri,* 1959, no. 1.
Harofe Haivri is a journal that was published in Hebrew and in English until 1962. It had a number of articles of interest on the history of medicine and medical ethics. Several were by Rabbi Jakobovits and contained mostly material found in his book—but the articles also contained some information not found in his book.

EUTHANASIA

Jakobovits, Immanuel. "The Dying and Their Treatment in Jewish Law." *Harofe Haivri* 2 (1961).

ORGAN TRANSPLANTATION

Rabinovich, Nahum. "What Is the Halakhah for Organ Transplants?" *Tradition.* Spring 1968.

HUMAN EXPERIMENTATION

1. Jakobovits, Immanuel. "Survey of Recent Halakhic Periodical Literature." *Tradition.* Winter 1966.
2. Siegel, Seymour. "A Bias for Life." *Hastings Center Report.* June 1975.

AUTOPSY

Jakobovits, Immanuel. "Survey of Recent Halakhic Periodical Literature." *Tradition.* Winter 1964–65.

ABORTION

1. Feldman, David. *Birth Control in Jewish Law.* New York: N.Y.U., 1968.

The most comprehensive study available of Jewish attitudes about contraception, this book also has about fifty pages on abortion. The first chapter is a superb introduction to the structure of Jewish law.

2. Bleich, J. David. "Abortion in Halakhic Literature." *Tradition.* Winter 1968.
3. Klein, Isaac. "Abortion and the Jewish Tradition." *Conservative Judaism.* Spring 1970.
4. Jakobovits, Immanuel. "Review of Recent Halakhic Periodical Literature." *Tradition.* Spring 1963.
5. *Roe et al.* v. *Wade.* United States Supreme Court decision of January 22, 1973.

CONTRACEPTION, ARTIFICIAL INSEMINATION, STERILIZATION

Feldman, David. *Birth Control in Jewish Law.* New York: N.Y.U., 1968.
See description above.

Some medicine does in a week

What no medicine does in seven days.

I think the drug companies paid him to say that.

Yiddish Proverb Trans. Leo Rosten

The Jewish Deaf Community

Tales

At first recollections came slowly to these people, many of whom grew up together, went to school together, and now share their adult life together as they try to remember how they first discovered their Jewishness. Before we continue, you, the reader, must understand that these memories are communicated in sign language, the language of many deaf people. The words written here can only approximate the gestures, eye movements, facial expressions, and signs that are the real language of these accounts. A sixty-year-old deaf woman walks to the center of the circle and begins signing her story:

My first Jewish memories. . . . Well, I became deaf at the age of seven. I had just started Hebrew lessons and naturally wanted to continue studying, even though I was now deaf. So I went to the rabbi and asked him if he himself would teach me, since the religious school had told my parents I could not attend regular classes—"too hard to teach a deaf child," they said. My protests that I could read lips were ignored by everyone. So, I approached the rabbi hoping for private lessons. I believed that he would never refuse me . . . but I was wrong. Deaf people do not have to learn Hebrew, he said; I would never be called to the Torah anyway, either as a deaf person or as a woman. My heart sank at this introduction to the hearing world's attitude to the deaf. But I was determined to learn Hebrew with or without his help.

In those days we spent long hot summers sitting on porches and playing in the streets of the city. My father owned a seltzer water factory, which he operated in the basement of our house. Each day I took a bottle of that cool seltzer water and sat on the front steps of our house in clear view of my girl friends (who had stopped coming to see me after I became deaf; I guess they were afraid of me). My girl friends looked at my bottle of cool seltzer water: it was so hot and they were thirsty. Finally, after several days of long-faced stares, they came over and asked me for a drink. I said, "If you teach me Hebrew I will give you a whole bottle of seltzer water every day." They agreed! So that summer I learned Hebrew by trading seltzer water from my father's factory for the alef-bet. I can still remember: alef, bet gimmel, dalet, heh, vav, zayin . . . [she continues until she reaches tav].

Others in the group start signaling for attention, demanding an audience for their experiences. One man quiets the group and begins:

Nod by Curtis Robbins

I wandered in a mood of
anguish, loneliness, and
aimlessness in one conclusion:
I am, as I was, an angry Jew
not at you, nor them, nor Thou
but me—who never understood;
they—who never taught,
and Thou—who made me seek.

I remember the first day my grandfather took me to temple. We entered. I sat among the beards [the sign for beard is a pun on the sign for Jew; both are made by pulling on a beard in front of one's face], those long free beards without end, swaying up and down, moving back and forth. I remember trying to find the lips and mouths covered by those beards but the beards moved too quickly and the mouths refused to stop between the words. I did not understand the purpose of the moving beards until much later.

"I was the only deaf Jew in Panama," signs another man. "The ONLY deaf Jew," he signs again. We wait . . . his silence continues . . . and every one here understands the meaning of his silence.

I used to go to a Catholic residential school for the deaf. One Christmas vacation I came home. Before going to sleep I knelt by my bed, folded my hands, bent my head, and began to pray the Lord's Prayer as we did in school every night. Suddenly I felt my mother's hands pulling me up by the hair. She shook my shoulders and with clear words she said: "Jews don't kneel." That is how I found out I was a Jew.

When I was little [continues another man] all my friends were Catholic; I too went to a Catholic school for the deaf, so I thought I was Catholic also. One day one of my friends came to school and told me that six million Jews were killed in World War II. I was shocked. Six million killed, killed, killed, I signed over and over. Then my friend said: "And you are also a Jew!" I was terrified. Six million Jews killed, and I am a Jew! Will I be killed? I raced home and asked my mother: Am I a Jew? Yes, she said. I started to protest. I am not a Jew. I am a Catholic, I am a Catholic. And for many years I denied my Jewishness because I was afraid to die like the six million. No one ever explained what it meant to be Jewish except for the story of the six million that I heard from my Catholic friend. Now I understand there is more, and I am proud to be a Jew.

The recollections continue: denying of Bar Mitzvah lessons; going to hearing services and having to sit quietly for hours, sometimes in the back row where lip reading is impossible; not understanding your own wedding or the funeral eulogy of someone you loved, because there is no interpreter; seeing candles, menorot, mezzuzot, Torahs, but never understanding what they mean, what they are used for; frustration, despair, boredom, and great courage—these themes recur again and again in the life stories of the Jewish deaf community. Yet these experiences are seldom known to the hearing world. I pray that this article opens up lives of Jewish deaf people to the hearing world, and encourages communication and understanding between hearing and deaf people.

The meaning of deafness: realities

1. There are approximately 2 million deaf and hard-of-hearing individuals in the United States (1 per 1,000); they tend to live close to urban areas, where jobs are more plentiful.

2. The majority of deaf people have hearing parents but marry a deaf spouse.

3. Deafness may be caused by a variety of diseases, such as rubella or spinal meningitis. Deafness can also be inherited (there are families with four or more generations of deafness). And deafness can be the result of physical injury caused by accidents.

4. A deaf person is either prelingually or postlingually deaf (i.e., his/her deafness occurred before or after the child acquired language) or else is hard of hearing, which means that the person has some hearing loss but can function as a "hearing" person.

5. Although many deaf people are difficult to understand because they do not always have tone control or good pronunciation, almost all deaf people have the use of their voices, since deafness does not affect the vocal cords. Therefore the phrase deaf and dumb should never be used. As a deaf friend of mine likes to say: "I may be deaf and dumb, but the dumbness has nothing to do with my deafness."

These are some of the facts of deafness, but what is the meaning of deafness to a deaf person? How does deafness affect one's life? To quote Helen Keller:

I am just as deaf as I am blind. The problems of deafness are deeper and more complex . . . deafness is a much worse misfortune. For it means the loss of the most vital stimulus—the sound of the voice that brings language, sets thoughts astir, and keeps us in the intellectual company of people.

Deafness means . . .

. . . fighting for understanding each day
. . . suffering job discrimination, underemployment, or unemployment
. . . being barred from jury duty, being effectively excluded from the legislative process, being constantly dependent on the hearing world for interpretation of events: in the courtroom, in a doctor's office, at public events, at lectures, in the schoolroom, at social service agencies
. . . never really being sure if agencies or people understand what you are saying/asking/needing and constantly being misunderstood
. . . relying on a lot of secondhand information, and therefore being denied spontaneous experiences and immediate response to those experiences
. . . (often) having no telephone service to the hearing world (some public buildings and essential services like police stations do have TTY's but many do not)
. . . never being able to make a telephone call from a public phone even in an emergency situation
. . . relying on the mail to make appointments far in advance, and not being able to cancel anything at the last minute
. . . experiencing a test of nerves everytime you step outside to shop, buy a pack of cigarettes, order at a restaurant, ask for directions
. . . almost never explaining that you are deaf and that others should please speak slowly
. . . hoping that you can read the person's lips
. . . being stared at as if you are crazy when you sign to your deaf friends
. . . living in a very close-knit community, where it is often hard to escape into anonymity or maintain a private life
. . . being tripped up by people who are unaware of your deafness (being paged in a public place over a loudspeaker, missing an announcement in a crowd, etc. etc.)
. . . helping one's hearing children overcome the embarrassment of bringing shy friends home to meet deaf parents, or helping your hearing parents accept the fact that you are deaf
. . . feeling isolation and terrible loneliness as you try to live in both the

TTY—Tele-typewriter machine that enables deaf people to use telephones. It functions like a teletype machine. The phone is plugged in to a special typewriter, which received voice impulses and translates them onto a receiving typewriter (you need a TTY on both ends to use the machine).

hearing and deaf world, while being marginal to both (perhaps the result of being sent to hearing school, which you don't really adjust to, and having a few deaf friends on the outside)

One could continue endlessly.

As Fred Schreiber puts it in his article entitled "The Meaning of Deafness": "The least crippling problem of a deaf person is the inability to hear." The situations we have presented often result from the hearing world's insensitivity to the deaf individual and not from the condition of deafness per se. The easing of the problems of deafness will only occur when hearing people understand the meaning of deafness and become sensitive and responsive to the problem.

The deaf Jewish community: institutions and leadership

Judging by the ratio of deaf to hearing in the general population, there are probably about five to six thousand Jewish deaf people in the United States. The main organizing factor in the Jewish deaf community is the shared experience of deafness, rather than the usual Reform, Reconstructionist, Conservative, or Orthodox identification.

In 1956 Jewish deaf people who felt the need to experience and live their Judaism in a supportive community where they could be active instead of passive participants, where they could articulate their own needs and work to realize their own vision within the Jewish way of life, joined together to form the National Congress of Jewish Deaf (NCJD). Since its establishment the NCJD has hosted a national convention every two years and draws the Jewish deaf community and interested hearing Jews from all over the United States and Israel. These conventions provide a chance for Jewish leaders and lay people to meet and discuss common problems and share successful programing ideas.

One main concern of the NCJD is to encourage rabbis to work with the deaf, to learn sign language, and to become familiar with deaf needs. To that end an endowment fund was set up in 1960 and actually did provide the funds for Alton Silver, a deaf graduate of Gallaudet College, to enter Hebrew Union College, the Reform movement's rabbinical school. (Tragically, Alton Silver died before completing his studies and the deaf community still mourns his loss. May his memory be a blessing.)

Gallaudet College—a fully accredited college for deaf people in Washington, D.C. All courses are conducted in sign language. Special courses in teaching deaf people are offered.

The NCJD also publishes a periodical called the *NCJD Quarterly*, which keeps the scattered Jewish deaf community in touch with events happening in the local organization.

There are twelve local chapters affiliated with the National Congress of Jewish Deaf. These include (for specific addresses, check list at end of article):

1. Hebrew Association of the Deaf of New York (HAD of New York), which claims a membership of about 750 (however, that number also includes people who are members of Temple Beth Or of the Deaf of New York, so the real number is smaller). HAD, which was organized in 1907, meets at the New York Society for the Deaf in Manhattan. Presently the group is composed of people over fifty-five, many of whom live in a housing project for elderly deaf called Tanya Towers on Fourteenth Street. The group meets formally once a week on Wednesdays for a social evening and

provides High Holiday services and a Passover Seder, in addition to own-
ing cemetery plots for its members. This year a prayer–lunch–adult-
education program met once a month on a Shabbat morning and attracted
close to seventy people. Both men and women wear tallitot and are called
to the Torah. The recollections of first Jewish memories came from discussions by this group during adult education.

2. Temple Beth Or of the Deaf (New York area) attracts a membership
of over 125 families and functions like a traditional congregation—with a
Sisterhood, rabbi, religious school, temple board, social activities, adult
education, and religious services on a fairly regular basis. Temple Beth Or
came into existence in 1960, when the younger members of HAD wanted to
become a separate congregation and also sought more leadership responsibility for themselves. Since that time they have been looking for a permanent location in which to build or buy a temple. Members live all over the
New York area: Brooklyn, the Bronx, Manhattan, Queens, and New Jersey,
which makes meeting together a real effort.

3. Brooklyn Hebrew Society of the Deaf, organized in 1928, now has a
membership of about eighty people, split between defined groups of parents and their children (ages 25 to 30, and 55 to 80). They meet once a
month on Sundays except during July and August. There are religious
services on holidays. Susan Greenberg, one of the hearing members, does
the interpreting, This year they are trying to start a Sisterhood. Because of
the distances people must travel, the group remains somewhat fragmented.

4. Hebrew Association of the Deaf of Philadelphia was founded in
1907. HAD of Philadelphia meets once a month and has a membership of
100 with no rabbi or teachers. When children are Bar/Bat Mitzvah age, they
must seek private tutors. The group holds religious services on holidays,
and sponsors social activities as well. Services are lead by a deaf woman
named Betty Kreiger Oshman, who has been my teacher in sign language
and is a beautiful signer. Before she moved to Philadelphia recently she
interpreted for the many hearing rabbis who worked with Temple Beth Or
in New York.

5. Jewish Society for the Deaf of Baltimore, with a membership of
seventy people, was organized in 1919. They meet once a month on a
Sunday and hold services on the major holidays, hiring a hearing rabbi and
an interpreter.

6. HAD of Cleveland claims a membership of eighty, and has about
twenty-five to thirty active couples, mostly over fifty-five years old. Organized in 1935, they are sponsored by the Jewish community center,
where they meet once a month on a Sunday. Recently Herb Schwartz, a
hearing rabbi who knows sign language and has worked with the deaf in
the past, moved to Cleveland. He now occasionally invites the deaf community to come to Friday night services at his own congregation and then
conducts the services in sign language. The deaf community is grateful, but
he feels this is "only a bandage measure until something more permanent
can be worked out."

7. HAD of Chicago, known since 1971 as Congregation Bene Shalom,

was organized in 1955. This group also functions like a congregation, with a full-time rabbi, Doug Goldhammer, who knows sign language and in fact does the morning news in sign language for the Chicago area deaf community. The congregation has many younger members (eighty active members altogether) and sponsors religious, educational, and social activities. They also boast a choir, where songs are sung in sign language, and their own prayer book.

8. HAD of Los Angeles has a membership of one hundred people. Organized in 1947, this group meets once a month and sponsors High Holiday services (again, a rabbi with an interpreter), as well as social and religious activities. HAD helped encourage the formation of Temple Beth Solomon of the Deaf in 1960, when the fragmented nature of the groups made it clear that two organizations were necessary.

9. Temple Beth Solomon of the Deaf, of Van Nuys, California is now the only deaf congregation with its own building. The membership is mostly elderly (no religious-school-age children or teenagers) and meets for religious services as well as for social activities with a hearing rabbi and an interpreter. They would like to hire a full-time rabbi to give continuity to the group's religious activities.

10. HAD of Boston, organized in 1961, has a membership of sixty people. They sponsor religious and social activities (their favorite is captioned films—regular films with captions for deaf audiences). Services are conducted by the members on High Holidays; otherwise they attend services among hearing congregations, with an occasional interpreter. They meet once a month on Saturday at Saint Andrew's Center of the Deaf.

11. Hillel of Gallaudet College has been in existence for over a decade and is sponsored by the Washington, D.C., Bnai Brith. Membership varies from year to year, depending on the number and interest of the Jewish students on campus. There is no Hillel rabbi, but they always meet for the major holidays and for scattered social activities and events. Alton Silver really helped crystallize the group. This group would also like a Hillel rabbi (one who knows sign language, of course!) on a permanent basis.

12. Washington Society of Jewish Deaf was formed only a few years ago and meets once a month for activities and services during the major holidays. When they can convince one of the few hearing rabbis who know sign language (like Laurence Hoffman of New York) to come down for the High Holidays, then Hillel and the Washington Society get together for services.

In summary, most of the groups meet only once a month—to

socialize—and around the major holidays, i.e., Rosh ha-Shanah, Yom Kippur, and Passover. Most do not have either part-time or full-time rabbis (except the Chicago and New York groups), and most rely either on their own membership or outside hearing rabbis with interpreters—which can be disastrous, since the English prayer books of both the Reform and Conservative movements are difficult to translate into sign language and don't make much sense when translated.

The groups are very isolated but nonetheless are self-motivated. Yet the problems of geographical fragmentation, scarcity of skilled religious school teachers, and lack of strong Jewish backgrounds force most of the groups to struggle to maintain their religious existence. They originally modeled their organizational structures on the deaf clubs, which are primarily social groups, adding such features as Sisterhood, Brotherhood, and High Holiday and Passover services. Gradually some also adopted the temple-building need, thus the search for "a building of our own" and the establishment of temple boards and building funds. Neither model has served the Jewish needs of the groups very well. And in a community where most knowledge is obtained visually, there is almost no effort to develop educational material, religious services, and skilled Jewish deaf professionals—any or all of which would help increase the commitments to an understanding of Jewish life. There are also almost no organized religious schools run by the deaf population, and the thirteen to thirty age group is not actively participating in the Jewish deaf community. This community feels a passion for its Jewish existence, but is denied the opportunity to build a rich and varied Jewish life.

The loss of this community would be tragic to everyone. The deaf community, despite its limited resources and the seriousness of its problems, has a deep abiding commitment to Judaism. And the hearing world has much to gain from the unique experience of the deaf community, both through the incredible contribution of sign language to religious experience and the personal life stories of these people.

Jewish religious and educational institutions serving the deaf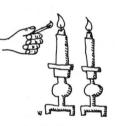

The Jewish deaf community is badly neglected. This is due more to lack of awareness that deaf people even exist than to a deliberate policy of neglect. Deaf people have a low visibility to the hearing world because of their own tight community structure and the fact that deafness is not an externally apparent affliction. A common remark by a hearing person (and one that reveals the total lack of awareness of the problem) is the one frequently made to me when I mention that I work with the deaf community: "Oh, you must know braille!" One says "deaf" and people immediately think "blind" because the deaf experience has not touched their lives (most people are not even aware of it when they pass a deaf person on the street). I am raising the issue of neglect to encourage Jewish institutions at least to examine the possibility of helping deaf communities achieve the same level of religious education and Jewish identity that they strive for in the Jewish hearing world. Excellent programs exist for the blind and other handicapped people in all three movements—why have we never reached out to the deaf?

The "movements"

Let's begin by taking a look at the rabbinic institutions, since the lack of qualified rabbis and teachers is the problem most often articulated by the deaf community itself. If I overlook any program or individual in my discussion, please let me know!

None of the rabbinic institutions offer courses in sign language—something that is essential in working with the deaf. Nor is the issue of deafness discussed in any of the pastoral psychology courses or special education courses. Even the minimal level of just being aware of the problem is absent; most rabbinic and education students finish their studies without once discussing deafness. Although Hebrew Union College did open its doors to Alton Silver, a deaf rabbinic student, instead of placing him at their school in New York, which has a large deaf community, they placed him in Cincinnati, so that he had to commute to New York to serve as the student rabbi of the Jewish deaf community. The school meant well but simply didn't consider the issue. Doug Goldhammer, a graduate of Hebrew Union College, conducted his ordination service in sign language, which, let us hope, raised some consciousness within the Reform movement.

But the point here is that at least one lecture in all the years of rabbinic or Masters students' education—whether Reform, Conservative, Orthodox, or Reconstructionist—should be devoted to the situation of the Jewish deaf community. Most rabbis will encounter at least one deaf person directly (although I suspect that the one or two deaf Jewish couples in each Jewish community scattered around the United States go unnoticed by the local Jewish institutions). We should know how to respond, and if we cannot respond ourselves we should certainly know whom/what to contact. By the omission of courses in sign language and deaf awareness, the rabbinic institutions are unintentionally preventing the training of qualified Jewish teachers of the deaf. The optimum situation would be an active encouraging of the Jewish deaf community to send interested deaf people to rabbinic professional schools, provide the expenses for costly interpreter service, and help these Jewish deaf people become skilled teachers in their own communities. This would provide the link between the Jewish deaf and hearing world—which are now separated by growing noncommunication.

The Reconstructionist, Reform, Conservative, and Orthodox national institutions are in similar positions of nonaction vis-à-vis the deaf community—with certain exceptions. The three deaf congregations in Los Angeles, Chicago, and New York are affiliated with the Reform movement, which has extended help when asked. The Federation of Reform Synagogues found Beth Or its present location and then invited me (I am the student rabbi there) to conduct services in sign language at the Thirty-third Annual Delegate Assembly of the New York Federation of Reform Synagogues, which gave an audience of over one hundred synagogues an introduction to the deaf world. They have indicated a willingness to offer funds for projects involving the Jewish deaf community—but here the initiative must come from the deaf community itself.

The Conservative movement has almost no contact with the deaf community, except in individual cases like the Miller family of New York, who helped found the Washington Society of Jewish Deaf, and Herb Schwartz, a graduate of the Jewish Theological Seminary, who published an article on deafness in the Winter 1974 issue of *Conservative Judaism*, entitled "To Open the Ears of the Deaf" (vol. 27, no. 2) and presently serves the Jewish

I should note that we lag far behind the Christian community, which has trained many deaf ministers, priests, and educators.

deaf community in Cleveland. Institutionally, however, there is no contact. The Tikvah program of Camp Ramah, for instance, which is devoted to the handicapped community, has many programs and sponsors a summer camp, but offers no programing for the deaf.

Within the Orthodox movement, the National Conference on Synagogue Youth (NCSY) publishes a monthly newsletter with stories and games about holidays geared to deaf children and teenagers. In addition, the Hebrew Institute for the Deaf, an Orthodox oralist day school in Brooklyn, offers the only Jewish day school program for deaf children in the country. NCSY in New York is trying to attract deaf Jewish teenagers by sponsoring Shabbat weekends and social events—but this is limited to the Brooklyn Jewish community.

oralist school—teaches the deaf to communicate through oral language rather than sign.

Social service agencies

In New York, the New York Society *for* the Deaf (NYSD) is a good example of a typical hearing agency that serves the deaf community. The society, which began specifically as a Jewish philanthropic organization in 1911, is still supported by the Federation of Jewish Philanthropies but has gradually expanded its base of service to include the needs of the non-Jewish deaf population. The society offers programs in vocational training, rehabilitation, family counseling, summer camping for the elderly, communication skills training, psychological testing, etc. Until recently, however, Jewish services were minimal, centering around their sponsorship of the Hebrew Association of the Deaf (which, as we have seen, is fairly independent of the society). A once-a-month sign language service and study group–lunch program that was initiated this year attracted over sixty people from the area. The society also subsidized a teachers' training program that trains Jewish deaf to be religious school teachers and educators; NYSD also pays a number of HAD members to teach Bar Mitzvah students privately when the need arises. However, the community is still not being served properly. The problem lies in the attitude of the agency's board members toward the ability of deaf people to run their own programs. "New York Society for the Deaf," commented one deaf man, "is just that: *for* the deaf, and not *of* the deaf." There is only one deaf board member on the NYSD board, which decides policy and programing: one deaf voice is heard in the decision making that affects all deaf lives. Ruth Brown Sturm, a deaf Jewish woman who lives and teaches in New York, comments: "We have educated ourselves now sufficiently so that a great many of us can communicate with our Jewish hearing peers. Therefore there no longer remains any reason why hearing impaired people should not be consulted in the making of Jewish 'laws' concerning them."

Communication controversy

There is another problem that prevents many Jewish deaf people from receiving an adequate Jewish education: the oral/sign language controversy. Approximately 90 percent of deaf children have hearing parents, which may mean that deaf children are not exposed to deaf adults until relatively late in life. Moreover, a war still rages within the deaf community itself, and between the hearing and deaf communities, over how to educate

OUR FINGERS BEND
STRETCH
PLEAD
QUESTION
AND HOPE.

OUR ARMS BEAT OUT THE
    RHYTHM OF OUR SOULS
EACH OWN THEIR OWN BEAT
BODIES DROWNING
GOING UNDER
INTO THE WATER
INTO THE DEEP WATERS
REACH OUT FOR A HAND
WAVE FOR A HAND
SIGN FOR A HAND
TO HELP PULL THEM OUT.
PULL US OUT OF THE WATER
GOD
WHEN WE FEEL LIKE WE ARE
    DROWNING
DURING THIS DAY OF PEACE
WE REACH OUT AS ONE FAMILY
SO THAT AS ONE FAMILY WE CAN
    FIND THE RIGHT WAY TO
    LIVE TOGETHER.
WE JOIN HANDS
AND THROUGH THE SQUEEZING
WE FEEL THE RHYTHM OF GOD.
WE SIGN
AMEN.

Shabbat sign language prayer
by Lynn Gottlieb

deaf children—by using the oral method (strict lipreading, no signing, emphasis on communication rather than total personality development) or total communication (an approach that encourages any method of communication, i.e., oral, sign language, finger spelling, gestures—whatever best suits the individual). The rationale behind the oral method is that deaf people should be encouraged to adapt to the norms of the general society, thereby making their own lives easier. Total communication recognizes that not all children can cope with only lipreading and oral education—so teachers of TC encourage methods that give the child language and allow the child to express him/herself naturally and totally.

The deaf community tends to support total communication, while many institutions in the hearing world that serve the deaf tend to support oral education. Hearing parents of deaf children are caught in the middle. Instead of objectively evaluating the child's individual needs, they maintain the goal of wanting their children to be as "normal" as possible—and hence many deaf children are denied an education and a childhood experience that would allow them to develop their full creative and human potential. Often hearing parents refuse to send their children to any place that uses sign language, thereby unconsciously encouraging the child to become negative toward other deaf people who do use sign. Frequently these kids develop a kind of self-hatred, since despite the fact that sign language is so natural to them, they must suppress it and act like hearing people. Many deaf people never overcome the deep frustration created by this conflict in their childhood. I believe that hearing parents who deny their deaf children a chance to explore the meaning of their deafness within the deaf community deny them positive deaf adult role models, and, worse, deny them an easy method of communication that would allow these children to share their problems, joys, and life experiences.

How their Jewish identities fit into the scheme is frequently not dealt with because they have not yet confronted the primary reality of their own deafness. The Jewish community must seek to reach out to hearing parents of deaf children and encourage their participation in Jewish life from a very early age, in using teaching methods that help the child develop his/her potential for living and at the same time encourage parent-child communication—real communication—within the family situation. Jewish schools and teachers presently using only the oral communication method must be encouraged to develop programs that meet the needs of all their children, and must help parents to be accepting of their children's deafness so they can also be accepting of their Jewishness.

Jewish sign language

I remember the first time Jerry Winston took me to Beth Or to witness a service in sign language. Betty Kreiger Oshman was signing the prayers, and I immediately fell in love with sign language. Words cannot begin to describe the effect of sign language on the prayers: you *must* see, *must* experience the power, the movement, the beauty of sign. The prayers dance their meaning, the whole body participates. You have a new understanding, a clearer vision. The language of our prayer books (the English translation) does not provide the simplicity and directness that sign language draws from the words in order to transmit them effectively.

Therefore we at Beth Or translated the prayer book to fit the needs of sign language. Words are not spelled out by finger spelling; rather, each word has a hand symbol to express that word. The following prayer from a sign language service also reflects the Jewish deaf experience. But to truly understand and appreciate these words, you must see them signed. Find a deaf person or an interpreter and get that person to sign the service.

The prayers are in capital letters to make the reading easier for deaf people (who must read and sign simultaneously).

WASHING OF THE HANDS IN PREPARATION FOR PRAYER

THIS MORNING WE WILL PRAY WITH OUR HANDS.
OUR HANDS WILL SIGN THE PRAYERS WHICH SING WITHIN US;
OUR HANDS WILL EXPRESS OUR HEART'S MEANING;
OUR HANDS WILL SIGN WHAT WORDS CANNOT SAY.
BEFORE WE BEGIN TO PRAY
WE NEED SPECIAL PREPARATION TO HELP US ENTER THE
    MOOD OF PRAYER.
THEREFORE WE WILL WASH OUR HANDS WITH WATER,
FOR WATER IS A SIGN OF NEW UNDERSTANDING.

We read in the Book of Psalms about the washing of hands (free translation).

WHO WILL GO UP TO THE PLACE OF GOD,
WHO WILL ENTER GOD'S HOLY PLACE?
THE PERSON WHO HAS CLEAN HANDS AND AN OPEN HEART,
WHO HAS NOT USED HIS HANDS TO HURT PEOPLE,
NOT TURNED HER HEAD AWAY FROM SOMEONE SIGNING.
THAT PERSON WILL RECEIVE A BLESSING FROM GOD.

(from Nishmat Kol Hai):

WITH ALL MY BODY AND ALL MY SOUL,
WITH MY HANDS,
WITH MY WHOLE BEING,
I WILL PRAISE YOU AND SIGN.
LORD, WHO IS LIKE YOU?
WHO CAN DO WHAT YOU DO?
O GREAT MIGHTY AND HONORED
GOD,
SUPREME GOD,
MOTHER OF HEAVEN AND EARTH.
LET US SING AS KING DAVID
SANG:
"BLESS THE LORD, O MY SOUL,
AND LET MY WHOLE BEING
PRAISE GOD'S HOLY NAME.
LET US SIGN: AMEN."

Shema

In sign language "God is One" can also mean "God is alone." The Shema is a prayer in which we remind ourselves of the aloneness of God. God created people in His/Her image and so we are also reflections of God. And so we too can feel terrible loneliness and separation from other people. That is why we pray the Shema together—to leave our aloneness and enter the human community. Only by seeing each other's signs can we learn to understand each other and thus break the walls of loneliness. Let us sign together:
HEAR O ISRAEL! THE LORD OUR GOD, THE LORD IS ONE.

ABRAHAM

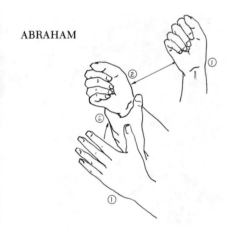

PEOPLE (OF TORAH)   JEW

PEOPLE

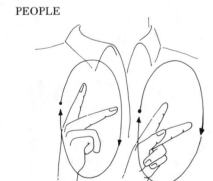

TORAH

A new interpretation of the Shema is based on a discussion that occurred during one Friday night service. We raised the question, What does the Shema say to us?

We usually think of the Shema as a prayer that tells all Israel to hear that God is One. The Shema is also a prayer that speaks of the frustration we feel in communicating with each other. How many times do we cry out to be seen or heard by another person? How many times have we felt the frustration of trying to explain our feelings to another person, failing, trying again, and failing again. And even worse, asking a person: "Do you understand me?" and receiving a nod of the head, yes, yes, knowing that the person is lying, that the person does not really understand—perhaps does not want to understand. At what point in our efforts to communicate do we give up and feel that trying is useless?

The Shema is a prayer that encourages us to keep trying to communicate. Jews have prayed the Shema for thousands of years. For thousands of years we keep trying to make ourselves understood, listened to, seen. We tell each other, and others in the world: SHEMA! Look at me! Understand us! The meaning of the Shema is to keep trying to communicate, to have faith that at some point we can break the walls that hold us back from understanding one another. Perhaps it is God who is signing the Shema to us, who is crying at us, whom we do not see or understand.

Language reveals the way of life of its people, and sign language is no exception. Unfortunately, however, signs have not yet been developed to express the Jewish experience, since most religious sign language used by the Jewish deaf has been developed by the Christian community. However, this situation is slowly changing as Jewish awareness grows among the deaf community. Here are a few Jewish signs, some of which have been used for generations in the American Jewish deaf community:

JEW: pulling a beard (male chauvinism is by no means limited to the hearing community!). This sign may be anti-Semitic, as the sign for a grabby person is also made by a pulling motion under the chin. Since sign language is ideological as well as representational, it should reflect the Jewish way of thinking—so, in an attempt to create a sign that includes *all* Jewish people, I have been using "people of Torah" while saying the word Jew. This is certainly not definitive, so please, if you have any suggestions for a sign for Jew, write to me!

TORAH: opening the scrolls. Because many Jewish deaf people have no Jewish educational opportunities, they do not know the word Torah and use instead the Christian sign for Bible: the sign for "Jesus book,"which show the hands of Jesus on the cross.

YOM KIPPUR: a sign I invented, taking my idea from the beating of the chest on this holiday. In Israel the sign is covering the mouth—no food on Yom Kippur. The Jewish concern for eating comes through in much Israeli sign language!

YOM

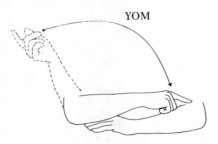

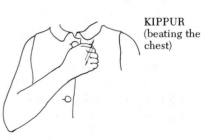

KIPPUR
(beating the chest)

PASSOVER: Martin Sternberg of the NYU Deafness Research Center relates the history of the old sign for Passover. In Scotland people drink beer and eat hard crackers, which, apparently, they break with their elbows. Some deaf Scottish orphans brought their sign for cracker, i.e., hitting the elbow, to America at the turn of the century. The American Jewish deaf community used it to represent matzah, and then Passover. This sign did not exactly convey the meaning of Passover. So at a sign language workshop at an NCJD convention in 1974, Celia Warshawsky, who helped publish an interreligious manual of sign language, and Alice Soll, an active member of Temple Beth Or, and I brainstormed together and came up with a sign that shows the Passing Over into freedom. This sign is slowly gaining acceptance within the community.

ABRAHAM: an old sign that shows God holding back the hand of Abraham at the sacrifice of Isaac.

PRAYER: first we used the Christian sign for prayer, which none of us were happy with. I asked some deaf Israeli Jews what their sign was. It's so beautifully obvious: shuckling—swaying.

A midrash on the Jewish sign for prayer: the Jewish deaf community's sign for prayer is swaying with a book. Why do we sway back and forth when we pray? Because each prayer has its own rhythms, its own way of breathing. We sway to help us feel the rhythm of the prayer. Many times the words that come from our mouths are separated from the way our bodies feel. During prayer we try to unite our bodies and our thoughts in the rhythm and the words of prayer. Sign language helps us come even closer to the true meaning of the prayers, because in signing, our words and feelings and rhythms are united in the sign.

Many deaf people can and do learn Hebrew. In fact, since I have been with Beth Or there have been three Bar Mitzvahs, all of whom read from the Torah and signed at the same time! We speak the Hebrew words while using English signs—sign language provides instantaneous translation!

PASSOVER (OLD SIGN)

PASSOVER (NEW SIGN)

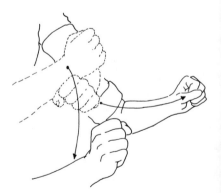

PRAY
(move whole body
back and forth)

Judaism's view of deafness: the reality and the need for change

I put this section at the end because I feel that the deaf experience must first be presented to the community and understood before we begin to see how Jewish law handled the situation. There is some material available on this subject, which can be found in the Bibliography. Here I would just like to comment that in the past the deaf community was not understood, and the rabbis, although showing some compassion, especially in the private lives of deaf individuals, did not understand the capabilities of deaf people. Today the situation is radically different from that in talmudic and post-talmudic times. Halakhah needs to be updated to meet the needs of the Jewish deaf community. We cannot continue to exclude them from our midst.

In Jewish law deaf people were grouped with minors and the insane, i.e., those people who could not be held responsible for their actions. In terms of ability to handle responsibilities, the rabbis considered deaf people to be more like children than like the insane. Therefore, while the deaf person was excluded from the public life of the Jewish community (i.e., could not serve as a witness, lead public prayer, be involved in property transactions, etc.), the validity of private life was recognized. For example, a person could be married and divorced in sign language if both parties understood sign language. A deaf person was also obligated to fulfill the mitzvot. For a detailed account of which mitzvot and how this took effect, see the article on deafness in either *The Jewish Encyclopedia* or the *Encyclopaedia Judaica*. From the folk myths and stories, however, we see that deaf people were considered highly emotional: for instance, the (deaf) person who kills Esau is called Hushim, meaning emotion; in the story he kills him very violently by beating him over the head with a stick until he crushes Esau's skull.

The rabbis operated on the assumption that deaf people did not have any language and therefore could not communicate (which in many cases was true in the ancient world, since deaf people were pretty much ignored and affliction was often seen as a kind of punishment from God). Today, however, we can understand deaf people: deaf people do have language and can communicate. In fact, as early as 1864 there was a school in Vienna that trained deaf children to speak Hebrew and read Jewish texts. That school raised a question to the general community: Since these people can function as "normal" individuals, shouldn't they be treated as hearing people? The question was answered negatively by the Jewish community.

We can no longer continue to answer negatively. Halakhah must reflect the existing situation and reality—and so the question of deafness must be reexamined by people who either understand deafness or are deaf themselves, as well as people involved in the halakhic process. Deaf people should be allowed to serve as witnesses, especially to events conducted in sign language, should be able to "chant" the Torah in sign language (according to a ruling of the bet din of London in 1963, they may be called up to the Torah to recite the blessing), should be counted in minyans, etc. We must be willing to use interpreters when a deaf person is not understood by hearing people. The halakhic world must begin to respond to the deaf world—so we can truly become one community of Jews.

Toward total communication

Bibliography: general books on deafness

1. Most materials on deafness are available through:

National Association of the Deaf
814 Thayer Ave.
Silver Spring, Md. 20910

If you are interested in sign language books, books on the deaf census, the psychology of deafness, or stories in sign language, write them and ask for a complete reading list. If you are just beginning to learn about the problems of deafness, I recommend *They Grow in Silence* by Vernon and Mindel.

2. The NYU Research Center on Deafness also puts out excellent materials on deafness, especially a book called *Readings on Deafness*, available for $3. Their address is:

Deafness Research and Training Center
New York University
New York, N.Y. 10003

3. A popular book, *In This Sign* by Joanne Greenberg, is readily available at any bookstore or library.

Jewish material

4. Check out the articles on deafness in *The Jewish Encyclopedia* and the *Encyclopaedia Judaica*.

5. For those of you who live in the New York area, the Jewish Theological Seminary library has a pamphlet, which may be available in other Jewish libraries—or ask them to send you a Xerox copy:

Jewish Theological Seminary
3080 Broadway
New York, N.Y. 10027

The Matter of Reading the Torah by a Deaf Person—A responsum of the bet din of London 1963, by Rabbi Lev Grosness. The library call number is BM 663 G75.

6. Look up "Deaf" and "Deafness" in the index (vol. 7) of Louis Ginzberg's *Legends of the Jews* (Philadelphia: Jewish Publication Society, 1954).

7. "To Open the Ears of the Deaf" by Herb Schwartz, in the Winter 1974 issue of *Conservative Judaism* (vol. 27, no. 2), deals with rabbinic and biblical attitudes toward deafness, contrasts them with Roman law, and makes suggestions for change.

8. Look up חרש in a concordance.

9. For a deaf child you may want to subscribe to:

Our Way
116 E. 27th St.
New York, N.Y. 10016

This is a magazine for children with Jewish holiday descriptions, games, legal guidance on kashrut, articles by deaf children.

10. "Workshop on Orientation of Jewish Religious Leaders and Lay People to Deafness and Vocational Rehabilitation," a booklet published by the U.S. Department of Health, Education, and Welfare, is obtainable from:

Rehabilitation Services Administration
Washington, D.C. 20201

11. Write to the National Congress of Jewish Deaf explaining your interest and request any material they might have. Write to either:

Gerald Burstein   or   **Alexander Fleischman**
6131 Claridge Dr.   **9102 Edmonston Ct.**
Riverside, Calif. 92506   **Greenbelt, Md. 20770**

12. Write to any of the congregations or associations and request a copy of their bulletins (see the list at the end of this section).

13. I have been involved in many programs for the deaf, and I would like to share some of my work with you. I have helped to organize:
   a. a prayer–luncheon–adult-education program
   b. a retreat for deaf Jewish teenagers
   c. discussion groups

For information on any of these programs or for materials on prayer or sign language write to me:

Lynn Gottlieb
407 Central Park West, Apt. 5C
New York, N.Y. 10025

14. Contact the closest person or organization on the NCJD list and explain that you would like to arrange a service in sign language for your congregation, so you can share a sign language experience. Ask the deaf congregation or group to participate in and conduct the service through an interpreter.

15. Arrange a dialogue between Jewish deaf and hearing people in your community—ask them to talk about their experiences growing up as Jewish deaf people, what it's like to be deaf in your community. Really try to have a small group discussion or presentation. Do not talk through the interpreter—talk to the deaf people directly (using the interpreter when necessary).

16. To find deaf people, look in the phone book's Yellow Pages under DEAF and see if there is a deaf club in your community; it may have Jewish members. Invite them to lunch or services with an interpreter. You can also call the Department of Education to see if there are any deaf schools in the area—that is a way of finding deaf children with hearing parents. Contact the parents of Jewish children and find out if their children are being served Jewishly.

17. Call up vocational rehabilitation for the deaf and find out if they have any Jewish clients.

18. Please—if you officiate at a wedding or funeral or any Jewish event where deaf people are involved, *GET AN INTERPRETER*. Many deaf

people are ashamed to admit they need an interpreter—don't make them sit in silence.

19. If there is a deaf church in your area, deaf Jews are probably attending it because of the lack of Jewish facilities. Ask the priest or minister if s/he is aware of any Jewish people in the congregation.

20. If you have found some Jewish deaf children and are looking for teachers who know sign language, check out the deaf institutions in the area for Jewish public school teachers who may be prepared to teach in a religious school; or ask Jews who work professionally with the deaf: social workers, rehabilitation counselors, psychologists, etc. Get them all together and develop an outreach program for your community.

21. Use visual material to teach: movies, videotape, slides, painting, books with clear print and pictures, captioned films, demonstrations using physical objects, any art material or media; or teach an idea through movement, pantomime, gestures. Abstract ideas are hard to grasp through sign language—try focusing on concrete experiential things.

22. For materials *by* deaf people contact:

Ruth Brown Sturm
31-27 32nd St.
Long Island City, N.Y. 11106

23. **The National Technical Institute for the Deaf**
Rochester, N.Y.

has a Hillel whose rabbi is Danny Grossman, a student at Reconstructionist College.

24. Do not be afraid to approach a deaf person. Even if you have trouble communicating, keep trying—we must work toward a diversified yet unified Jewish community.

 Resource people

Rabbis

There are other rabbis working with the deaf. The ones I've mentioned are:
Rabbi Douglas Goldhammer
  312 W. Dickens Ave.
  Chicago, Ill. 60614
Rabbi Herb Schwartz
  18506 Wewell Rd.
  Shaker Heights, Ohio 41422

General Resources (officers of the NCJD)
Gerald Burstein
  6131 Claridge Dr.
  Riverside, Calif. 92506
Emanuel Golden
  2308 Haddon Pl.
  Bowie, Md. 20715
Kenneth Rothschild
  25 Wagon Wheels Rd.
  Poughkeepsie, N.Y. 12601
Mark Corson
  18540 Plummer St.
  Northridge, Calif. 91324
Leonard Warshawsky
  5036 Conrad St.
  Skokie, Ill. 60076
Alexander Fleischman
  9102 Edmonston Ct.
  Greenbelt, Md. 20770
Roslyn Rosen
  9249 Limestone Pl.
  College Park, Md. 20740
  write her for NCJD publications

Celia Warshawsky, chairman
  5036 Conrad St.
  Skokie, Ill. 60076
  write her for information about religious development

National Congress of Jewish Deaf: constituent organizations

Baltimore JSD
Stephanie Julius
  3115 Shelburne Rd.
  Baltimore, Md. 21208
Boston HAD
Eva Rosenstein, Secy.
  154 Salisbury Rd.
  Brookline, Mass. 12146
Brooklyn HSD
Susan B. Greenberg, Secy.
  81-18 151st Ave.
  Howard Beach, N.Y. 11414
Chicago HAD
Barrett Galpern, Secy.
  5920 N. Kenmore Ave.
  Chicago, Ill. 60660
Congregation Bene Shalom of the Hebrew Association of the Deaf of Chicago
Barrett Galpern, Secy.
  5920 N. Kenmore Ave.
  Chicago, Ill. 60660
Cleveland HAD

Janice Brown
  4498 Raymont Blvd.
  University Heights, Ohio 44118
Gallaudet College Hillel Club
Bob Weinstein, Pres.
  Hillel Club, Gallaudet College
  Washington, D.C. 20002
Los Angeles HAD
Elliott Fromberg
  1029 N. Hayworth Ave.
  Los Angeles, Calif. 90046
New York HAD
Sam Becker, Secy.
  c/o New York Society for the Deaf
  344 E. 14th St.
  New York, N.Y. 10003
Philadelphia HAD
Ben Pollack, Secy.
  9801 Haldeman Ave., Apt. D204
  Philadelphia, Pa. 19115
Temple Beth Or of the Deaf (N.Y.)
c/o Mrs. Alice Soll
  195 Princeton Dr.
  River Edge, N.J. 07661
Temple Beth Solomon of the Deaf
Mrs. William Hoaglin
  13580 Osbourne St.
  Arleta, Calif. 91331
Washington Society of Jewish Deaf
Roslyn Rosen, Secy.
  9249 Limestone Pl.
  College Park, Md. 20740

The Jewish Blind

In tradition

There is a curious and unusual ambivalence that is apparent in biblical and rabbinic attitudes toward the blind. With our contemporary knowledge and sensitivities we would expect that, barring situations where full participation is *physically* impossible, the blind would be bound by the same tradition that binds every other Jew. This is not, however, necessarily the case. Let's look specifically at some biblical and talmudic examples.

A blind person who cannot ascertain the directions of the winds will turn his or her heart to the direction of heaven (Berakhot 30a).

The Torah warns us twice against any mistreatment of the blind: "You shall not insult the deaf, or place a stumbling block before the blind" (Leviticus 19:14); and "Cursed be he who misdirects a blind person on his way" (Deuteronomy 27:18). Yet the patriarch Isaac, having lost his sight in old age, is portrayed as easily deceived. Moreover, a blind priest is disqualified from sacrificing or approaching the altar: "No man of your offspring throughout the ages who has a defect shall be qualified to offer the food of his God . . . no man who is blind, or lame, or has a limb too short or too long . . . he shall not profane these places sacred to Me" (Leviticus 21: 17–23). (Despite the fact that a blind priest cannot offer "the food of his God," he is permitted to partake of it.) The fact is that the blind, together with cripples and lepers, were outcasts of society in biblical times and were kept quarantined outside the town limits; they became paupers and were a menace to passersby. (When King David besieged the Jebusites at Jerusalem, there were so many blind and crippled beggars that he was forced to take strict measures against them—2 Samuel 5:6.)

Rabbinic attitudes to the blind also betray similar ambivalences. On the one hand, unlike the deaf-mute, the blind person is not considered subnormal in Jewish law. For example, although Rabbi Judah exempted the blind from all religious obligations in the second century, later rulings eased that exemption. Similarly, the prohibition against the blind's reciting the first of the introductory blessings to the Shema—because they praise the daily renewal of light—was amended, since the blind enjoy the benefits of light even if they can't see. The law against a blind person being called up to the reading of the Torah was abolished with the institution of the baal koreh, who reads the Torah on behalf of everyone called up. Furthermore, the Mishnah permits a blind person to testify as a witness, and although a

Note: Euphemisms such as sagi nahor, meaning "with an excess of light," were used to refer to the blind.

totally blind person could not act as a judge, when actual cases arose, it was not forbidden (Sanhedrin 34b).

While there is no record of actual discrimination against the blind, there was derision just the same. The Talmud compares the blind, the leper, the childless, and the pauper to the dead (Nedarim 64b), quoting from Lamentations (3:6) "He has made me dwell in darkness, / Like those long dead." The blind were exempt from pilgrimage to Jerusalem on holidays even if the blindness was only in one eye, for Rabbi Yohanan said: "One must see as he is seen" (Mishnah Hagigah 1:1).

Because of these attitudes, the blind continued to be exempt from certain areas of ritual life, even if the areas did not require full sight for performance and even if the exemption had been lifted by law. For example, they were not allowed to shecht—butcher meat (*Shulhan Arukh*, (Yoreh Deah 1:9 and commentaries). Despite the fact that the blind were eventually permitted to be called up to read the Torah, as mentioned, Rabbi Moses Zacuto of the seventeenth century related that the rabbis of Poland did not allow a blind man to read the Scriptures. In Ferrara a blind man named Norzi was refused permission to read; an exception was made for the blind Rabbi Jacob Lianna only because of his superior biblical and talmudic learning (*Pahad Yitzhak*, letter Samek 24b).

In practice

Obviously, we are not allowed to mistreat any Jew. Why then do we urge less than total participation by the blind? The blind are singled out for special attention in the Torah because—like the widow and the orphan—they are more helpless than the rest of the community. Unlike the widow and orphan, however, the blind were exempted from full participation in Jewish ritual life.

The amazing fact is, however, that throughout history blind Jews *did* take upon themselves the obligation of fulfilling all the commandments. There were an unusual number of talmudic sages who were blind. Two of them, Rabbi Joseph and Rabbi Sheshet, held that the blind must perform all religious duties; they themselves recited the Haggadah on Passover before the assembled family (Pesahim 116b). (Indeed, about Rabbi Sheshet it was remarked that he was known for his remarkable discernment of the approaching Persian kings among many legions [Berakhot 58a].) These men participated in Jewish life despite contrary rulings by their contemporaries.

Among blind scholars after talmudic times were Rabbi Judah Gaon of Pumbedita, the accredited author of *Halakhot Gedolot*; Isaac Sagi Nahor ben David, "the father of the Kabbalah," who lived at the end of the twelfth century; Rabbi Abraham Judah Zafig, born blind in Tunis, who lived in Jerusalem and wrote *Einei Avraham* (The Eyes of Abraham); and Rabbi Joseph ben Azriel ha-Levi Schnitzler, the author of an illustrated commentary on the last nine chapters of Ezekiel, explaining the whole plan of the Temple—courts, gates, etc.—which he dictated to the reader of the Hamburg congregation in London in 1825.

The sad truth is, however, that although we know the stories of exceptional Jews who became prominent in these fields against overwhelming odds, we have almost no knowledge of the average blind person. There are no records of how the blind functioned in Jewish communities, what role they played economically, how they were treated socially. Until very recently there was so little understanding of physical handicaps that the blind, deaf, crippled, and mentally ill were in the same position—they were ostracized, either by members of their families or by themselves. From cases like that of the blind rabbi who was allowed to read the Torah publicly whereas a blind layman was not, we can surmise that a blind person had to be extraordinarily gifted in order to be treated as a normal human being. In other words, even after the official restrictions against the blind were relaxed, prejudice and fear prevented enlightened treatment.

How it changed

Until braille was invented in 1829, the blind had little access to the products of civilization: philosophy, literature—all learning expressed in the written word. Unless they were fortunate enough to be read to, most blind people remained uneducated and illiterate. After the Enlightenment in the eighteenth century, sighted Jews could overcome enough obstacles to integrate themselves into the Christian intellectual world; for the blind Jew such acceptance was virtually impossible. Even if blind Jews had access to works in braille, they had to read the products of an outside culture. That knowledge would only alienate them more from the Jewish community.

Thus the Jewish blind had to remain in intellectual darkness. The most significant advance in educating the blind Jewishly came much later, with the invention of Hebrew braille in the 1930s. The consequences of a Hebrew braille alphabet were enormous: for the first time the Jewish blind could really be "People of the Book." As a result, blind Jews can now read the Bible in Hebrew (in twenty encyclopedia-sized volumes); they can daven—pray—from the official Orthodox, Conservative, or Reform prayer books and be part of a congregation; and they can join their families on Passover in reading the Haggadah.

Today

The key to integrating the blind into society is our confidence in their ability to participate fully in the community. Dr. Jacob Fried, executive director of JBI, has said: "The greatest problem for the blind are the attitudes of the sighted world, which considers them either mendicants or incompetents." The higher unemployment rate among the blind stems solely from misconceptions and discrimination that have not been completely conquered—employers often do not want the "bother" of hiring a blind person.

Some Suggestions

1. If you know Hebrew well enough to read it, help teach a blind person the Hebrew braille alphabet (see the International Hebrew Braille Alphabet, printed at the end of the chapter). You can learn the braille yourself or just correct the blind person's mistakes in the Hebrew.

2. Alert the blind people you know, or parents of blind children, to the services of JBI. Treat them as equals in synagogues, classrooms, and youth groups.

3. Teach Hebrew songs to blind children, who can follow the words and music from braille song sheets.

4. When teaching crafts or folk dancing, adjust directions and simplify the tasks ONLY IF NECESSARY. In groups of both blind and sighted people, it might be helpful to assign buddies in order to facilitate learning.

6. To record books of all kinds, JBI and similar secular institutions welcome volunteers who are willing to give the time and energy as readers. This is a serious task that requires some training, but it is very worthwhile.

7. When you see a blind person crossing the street or getting on a bus, ask if help is wanted. If it is, *give* your arm (no one likes to be led), and warn as you approach curb or steps.

8. Never be embarrassed to use the phrase "you see." Even people with functioning eyes often don't.

9. Don't bend over backwards to accommodate a blind person, but don't ignore difficulties either. You can only learn the balance by talking and spending time with blind people. There are general pointers, but your behavior ultimately depends on the individual you're involved with, as in all human relationships. Be helpful when asked, and do your best to be sensitive.

10. As you defuse your misconceptions about the blind, fight discrimination in your community.

Senior citizens who were born blind are still illiterate for the most part. But they can have their world opened by records. Among those available from the Jewish Braille Institute, who pioneered in ending the isolation of blind Jews, are the High Holiday and Shabbat services; the Haggadah; and classics of Yiddish literature, such as the works of Sholem Aleichem, I. L. Peretz, Isaac Bashevis Singer, and others. The latter are especially cherished by elderly Jews who have never become fluent in English.

Because of the advances in technical innovations and—more important—in public awareness, a new generation of children and young adults can now take advantage of the same opportunities as their sighted peers. With the help of the Jewish Braille Institute, a religious school education is available to any blind Jewish child; JBI will provide all English and Hebrew books in braille as gifts. Blind children can attend Hebrew schools and Hebrew-speaking camps (as both campers and counselors). No blind child need be denied a Bar/Bat Mitzvah ceremony; the individual Bar/Bat Mitzvah portion is available in both English and Hebrew, as are materials for use by the teacher. JBI has recorded the first Hebrew conversation course, with accompanying Hebrew-English braille and large-type manuals.

Blind Jews can (and do) attend college, rabbinical and cantorial schools, and music schools—through the development of a music typewriter that enables a blind musician to write musical arrangements without having to pay a sighted arranger to do it.

In fact, the average blind person can function as well as the average sighted person, given the proper training. The sound of cars moving indicates traffic patterns the way green and red lights do; cooking is possible through smell, touch, and hearing, with the help of especially adapted measuring devices. There are blind people in every occupation where vision is not absolutely necessary.

Michael Levy, coauthor of this article, who is himself a blind person, is now studying at the Jewish Theological Seminary. He says: "I do not miss the visual aspects of the world, and I certainly derive much joy from those aspects that I can share. There are certainly enough bird songs, plants, and terrain changes on a hike, for example, to keep me occupied. While sightseeing, I like people to spontaneously describe colors, signs, and what they see in the distance. In general, descriptions and identification of the world around them are necessary for a blind persons, who can then describe and point to that world for sighted people. 'What does s/he want,' people often ask about the blind, treating us like children. We want the dignity and responsibility to which we are all entitled."

Jewish institutions

In America

Jewish Braille Institute
110 E. 30th St.
New York, N.Y. 10016

founded in 1931, provides braille, recorded and large-type materials of Jewish content to the blind. The JBI Free Circulating Library contains over fifty thousand books covering a wide range of interests: tradition, history, fiction, humor, Yiddish—among others. Upon request, JBI will send its books and tapes all over the country; whatever they don't have, they will either tape or braille, depending on the order and the needs of the person who is ordering. JBI also publishes a monthly literary magazine, *The Braille Review*, which features articles from the major intellectual magazines as well as original contributions. With the JBI, the *Review* sponsors an International Literary Braille Competition, which accepts entries from blind writers of all races, creeds, and nations. For children JBI will supply the necessary material for any school curriculum, as we have mentioned. The institute produces this material in its own recording studio.

Most important, JBI gives the blind an opportunity to celebrate communally. It holds gatherings at the institute for the holidays of Sukkot, Hanukkah, and Shavuot. On Sukkot, for example, a sukkah is built in their year-round fragrance garden, where the blind can smell and touch dozens of plants.

JBI serves an estimated six thousand out of the fourteen to sixteen thousand Jewish blind in the United States. (Exact numbers of the Jewish blind are difficult to ascertain, for even today many are self-ostracized from the greater community.) There are several reasons why less than half of the Jewish blind are serviced: parents are embarrassed by their child's blindness and turn to secular institutions so that their child won't have to make a "double" adjustment; some parents are not aware of the free services offered by JBI; the children themselves may pull out of Jewish schools and youth groups because of the difficulties. Senior citizens who lose their sight in later years—from diabetes or simply from age—are often unaware of JBI's existence.

Recently JBI and the Jewish Blind Society of England cosponsored the First Conference for the Jewish Blind, which took place in Jerusalem in August 1975. These and other issues of concern were discussed, and many suggestions and solutions were generated.

In Israel

One difference between Israeli and American attitudes to treatment is the legal definition of blindness: Israel more strictly defines it as 2.5 percent vision or less; in the U.S. it is 5 percent or less. Thus many more people are considered blind in the U.S. than in Israel. Another difference is that in Israel there are more institutions that segregate the blind from the general community, whereas JBI's policy is total integration with supplementary aid.

Israel has several institutions for the blind.

The Central Library for the Blind
4 Histadrut St.
Netanya, Israel

provides services similar to those of the JBI library. The two institutions complement each other, supplying texts and materials for each other's needs. Unlike the U.S., Israel has rehabilitation centers for the blind: in Haifa (Migdal Or), in Beersheba (George Simmons Rehabilitation Center), and in Tel Aviv (Center for the Blind of Israel). These centers offer casework reorientation and special training and courses.

The Jewish Institute for the Blind, founded in 1902, cares for the majority of blind children in the country. It has a kindergarten and elementary school, where subjects are taught in braille, as well as boarding facilities for pupils attending regular secondary school. It also has a vocational school, industrial training shop, braille printing press, and two houses for mentally or physically handicapped blind adults.

The Orah Weaving Workshop for the Blind was established by the Women's League for Israel in cooperation with Israel's Ministry of Social Welfare. The workshop provides employment opportunities for sightless young women (and a few men), enabling them to gain economic and social independence.

The National Council for the Blind—established in 1958—coordinates, researches, and plans assistance to the blind and is represented on the World Council for the Blind.

Secular institutions in America

Each state has an agency for the blind.

The Division for the Blind and Physically Handicapped
Library of Congress
Washington, D.C. 20542

has information on where to buy or borrow books and periodicals, including catalogs of braille music and appliances and scientific instruments adapted for use by blind people. Volunteers in studios throughout the country tape college-level material under the sponsorship of:

Recording for the Blind
215 E. 58th St.
New York, N.Y. 10022

Blind people are the best source of information on what it is like to be blind. The National Federation of the Blind "is not an organization speaking for the blind, it is the blind speaking for themselves." Information about NFB and its efforts to obtain complete equality and integration of the blind in society can be obtained by writing to its national offices:

National Federation of the Blind
218 Randolf Hotel Bldg.
Fourth and Court Sts.
Des Moines, Iowa 50309

Local affiliates can be contracted through the NFB.

The Jewish Guild for the Blind
15 W. 65th St.
New York, N.Y. 10023

is one of the largest multiservice agencies available. (The word Jewish refers only to the fact that most of the voluntary fund raising is done by the Jewish community. Like Jewish hospitals, the guild has a Jewish name but services the entire community.) The guild has an extensive circulating braille and cassette library and offers many programs for all age groups—from vocational and rehabilitation training to health services. Participants in their senior citizens' group work program and residents of the

Home for the Aged Blind
75 Stratton St. South
Yonkers, N.Y. 10701

are predominantly Jewish. Kosher food is available at the home upon request.

Rabbi Judah ha-Nasi and Rabbi Hiyya, while traveling, came to a certain town and inquired whether there were any learned men whom they could honor by a visit. The townspeople directed them to a blind scholar. Rabbi Hiyya said to Rabbi Judah: "Do not disgrace your excellence. Let me visit him," but Rabbi Judah insisted on accompanying him. When they were about to leave, the blind man acknowledged the visit by saying: "You have honored by your audience one who is seen but sees not. You shall be blessed and acceptable before One who sees but is invisible" (Hagigah 5b).

Rabbi Yossi could not understand an apparently illogical passage in Deuteronomy, "And you shall grope at noon as the blind gropes in darkness" (28:29), until he chanced to meet a blind man who was walking at night with a lantern in hand. When the rabbi inquired, the blind man explained that the lantern was of great service to him in enabling passersby to guide and protect him from obstacles and pitfalls (Megillah 24b).

THE INTERNATIONAL HEBREW BRAILLE ALPHABET

Hebrew Letter	Braille	How Pronounced
א aleph	⠁	silent
ב bet	⠃	B as in "boy"
ב vet	⠧	V as in "Victor"
ג gimel	⠛	G as in "good"
ד dalet	⠙	D as in "dog"
ה hay	⠓	H as in "her" but silent at the end of a word
ו vav	⠺	V as in "Victor"
ז zayin	⠵	Z as in "zoo"
ח het	⠭	"CH" as in the German word "doch"
ט tet	⠞	T as in "Tom"
י yod	⠚	Y as in "yes" or when it carries a vowel. Otherwise it prolongs the sound of the vowel carried by the preceding letter.
כ kaf	⠅	K as in "kind"
כ chaf	⠡	CH as in the German word "doch"
ל lamed	⠇	L as in "let"
מ mem	⠍	M as in "man"
נ nun	⠝	N as in "no"
ס samach	⠎	S as in "set"
ע ayin	⠷	silent
פ peh	⠏	P as in "pit"
פ	⠋	F as in "fit"
צ tsadi	⠮	TS as in "tsar"
ק kuf	⠟	K as in "kid"
ר resh	⠗	R as in "run" or a trilled R or a guttural R
ש shin	⠩	SH as in "ship"
ש sin	⠱	S as in "set"
ת taf	⠾	T as in "Tom"
ת saf	⠹	S as in "set" in the Ashkenazic / T as in "Tom" in the Sephardic

Vowel

Hebrew Letter	Braille	How Pronounced
ָ komets		O as in "for" in Ashkenazic / A as in "ah" in Sephardic
ֳ hataf komets		O as in "for" in Ashkenazic / A as in "ah" in Sephardic
ַ patah		A as in "ah"
ֲ hataf patah		A as in "ah"
ֶ segol		E as in "set"
ֱ hataf segol		E as in "set"
ִ hirik		EE as in "feel"
ִי hirik gadol		EE as in "feel"
ֵ tsere		A as in "take"
ֵי tsere gadol		A as in "take"
ֹ cholem		O as in "for"
וֹ cholem-vav		O as in "for"
וּ shuruk		U as in "zoo"
ֻ kubuts		U as in "zoo"
ְ sheva		Silent or almost so
ּ dagesh		silent
ה mappik-hay		When a dot is present in the "hay" at the end of a word, it indicates that the "hay" should be aspirated.

כט א מיי׳ פכ״א מהל׳
איסורי ביאה הלכה
כג ועש״ע אה״ע סימן ג
סעיף יד וטוש״ע א״ח
סימן כג סעיף ד :

ל ב מיי׳ פי״ה מהלכות
מלכים הלכה יב :

לא ג מיי׳ פי״ד מהלכות
דעות הלכה ב :

לב ד מיי׳ פי״ב מהל׳
שבת הלכה א ופכ״ג
הלכה ו סמ״ג לאוין סה
וטוש״ע או״ח סימן שיח
סעיף יב :

רבינו חננאל

הוא ומשום דשמעיה
מר׳ יוחנן הזכיר בעל
השמועה . ושנינן ג
לאפרושי מאיסורי שרי
כדעתיה דר׳ מאיר : תניא לא
ישטוף אדם בבריכה
מלאה מים ואפילו
זומרת בחול מפני
חזיית לר׳ אבהו
שהניח ידיו כנגד פניו
של מטה וכו׳ פי׳ ר׳
משום מוליאר הגרוף
שותין ממנו בשבת.
הגרוף שותין ממנו
בשבת. פי׳ בקונטרס

הסוגיא

מוליאר

לפי שאין מוסיף הבל אלא משמר
ומקיים חום שלו ואנטיכי אפי׳
גרופה אין שותין הימנה לפי שמוספת
הבל ואין נראה דלא שייך למיגזר
במוסיף הבל אלא בהטמנה גזירה שמא
יטמין ברמן ועוד דלחוק לומר
דמתני׳ איירי כשעתה האיסור ועוד
דלאנטיכי אוסר בכל ענין לשתות
אפילו בהטמנה ומי להחזיר
תנן משהין אפילו בחמו גרוף ועוד
אי משום תוספת הבל אמרה ליה
מתני׳ בשתיה תקשה לרבה ורב
יוסף דשרו לעיל (דף לח.) בשכח
קדרה ע״ג כירה ובשלה בשבת אפ״ג
דלא נתבשלה כמאכל בן דרוסאי ואפי׳
במזיד וגי׳אא כפי׳ ה״ר פורת מוליאר
הגרוף שותין הימנו בשבת שמזוגין
המים חמין בין כך שהמים אין כ״כ
חמין במוליאר שיתבשל היין מן המים
שמוזגין לתוכו אבל אנטיכי אע״פ
שגרופה אין שותין הימנה לפי שאנטיכי
יש בה הבל יותר ומתבשל היין מן
דמתיבת סבעת מעלית
הנהר אין לו פנאי
להתחמם כמו שאין
פנאי בלבשות לנסך
פנאי נגע דלא
חיישינן ליה והני מילי
דשרי להניח ידיו כנגד
פניו של מטה כשעולה
מן הנהר אבל כרב דאמר
כל המניח ידיו כנגד
פניו של מטה כאילו
כופר בבריתו של
אברהם אבינו וכרכנן
דבי רב אשי דכי נחתי
זקף כי סלקי שהו :
אמר רב הונא כל
העולה מבבל לא״י עובר
בעשה שנאמר בבלה
יובאו ושמה יהיו עד
יום פקדי [יהיו] עד
יום פקדי אבא ומצא
לר׳ יהודה במרחץ והי׳
אומר לשמשיו בלה״ק
הביאו לי נתר הביאו
לי.מסרק פתחו פומייכו
והסיקו הבלא ואשתו
מיא דבי באני למדתו
סמנו דבי באני למדתו
חול מותר לאומרו
בלה״ק . אמר
אילו לא [באתי] אלא
לשמוע דבר זה די לי :
מתני׳ מליאר תנא מים
מבפנים ונחלים מבפנים
הוא של חרם ואם
גרף נחלים שרי
אנטיכי א״ד נחמן בי
דודי רשל נחושת היא
תניא כרב נחמן אנטיכי
אע״פ שגרופה אין שותין

הגמרא

לעולם אמר אבי עשאוה כבוליעת דתנן
*בולשת שנכנסה לעיר בשעת שלום חביות
פתוחות אסורות סתומות מותרות בשעת
מלחמה אלו ואלו מותרות לפי שאין פנאי
לנסך אלמא כיון דבעיתי לא מנסכי ה״נ
כיון דבעיתי לא אתי להרהורי והכא מאי
ביעתותא ביעתותא דנהרא איני והאמר ר׳
אבא אמר רב הונא אמר רב כל המניח ידו
כנגד פניו של מטה כאילו כופר בבריתו של
אברהם אבינו לא קשיא הא כי נחית הא
כי סליק כי הא דרבא שחי ר׳ זירא זקיף
רבנן דבי רב אשי כי קא נחתי זקפי כי קא
סלקי שחו *ר׳ זירא הוה קא משתמיט מדרב
יהודה דבעי למיסק לארעא דישראל דאמר
רב יהודה כל העולה מבבל לא״י עובר
בעשה שנאמר °בבלה יובאו ושמה יהו
אמר איזיל ואשמע מיניה מילתא ואתי
ואיסק אזל אשכחיה דקאי בי באני וקאמר
ליה לשמעיה הביאו לי נתר הביאו לי
מסרק פתחו פומייכו ואפיקו הבלא ואשתו
מיא דבי באני אמר אילמא *(לא) באתי
אלא לשמוע דבר זה די בשלמא הביאו
נתר הביאו מסרק קמ״ל דברים של חול
מותר לאומרם בלשון קדש פתחו פומייכו ואפיקו הבלא נמי כדשמואל דאמר
שמואל הבלא מפיק הבלא אלא אשתו מיא דבי באני מאי מעליותא דתניא
יאכל ולא ישתה דם תחילת חולי מעיים *אבל ולא הלך ד׳ אמות
אבילתו מרקבת וזהו תחילת ריח רע הנצרך *לנקביו ואבל דומה לתנור
שהסיקוהו ע״ג אפרו וזהו תחילת ריח זוהמא רחין בהמין ולא ישתה מהן דומה
לתנור שהסיקוהו מבחוץ ולא הסיקוהו מבפנים רהין בהמין ולא נשתטף בצונן
דומה לברזל שהכניסוהו לאור ולא הבניסוהו לצונן רחין וכל ולא סך דומה למים
ע״ג חבית : מתני׳ מוליאר הגרוף שותין הימנו בשבת אנטיכי אע״פ שגרופה
אין שותין הימנה : גמ׳ היכי דמי מוליאר הגרוף תנא מים מבפנים ונחלים
מבחוץ אנטיכי רבה אמר בי כירי רב נחמן בר יצחק אמר בי דודי מאן
דאמר בי דודי כ״ש בי כירי ומאן דאמר בי כירי אבל בי דודי לא תניא כוותיה
דרב נחמן אע״פ שגרופה וקטומה אין שותין הימנה מפני שנחושתה שנרושתה
מחממתה : מתני׳ המיחם שפינהו לא יתן לתוכו צונן בשביל שיחמו
אבל נותן הוא לתוכו או לתוך הכוס כדי להפשירן : גמ׳ מאי קאמר אמר

[ברלשית ו] וגי׳ כבולשת עשאוה
להא דר׳ אבוה בולשת חילות גיים
הבא לעיר על שם שמחפשין ובולשין
את העיר קרי לה בולשת : בשעת
שלום . כגון שהוא של אותה מלכות
שאלו כופר . דנראה שהוא בוש
בדבר . כי נחית . לנהר פניו כלפי
הנהר ואין כאן משום לגיעות אסור
לכסותו : כי סליק . ופניו כלפי העם
מותר משום לגיעות : ר׳ זירא זקיף.
דחיים לדרב שלא יראה כסופר :
משתמיט . היה ירא לירא ות לו משום
דהוה בעי דבי זירא למיסק לא״עא
דישראל ורב יהודה לא סבירא ליה
וירא פן יגזור עליו מליך : בבלה
יובאו ושמה יהיו עד יום פקדי וגו׳.
ור׳ זירא אמר לך הא׳ קרא בכלי שרת
כתיב כדאמרינן בשני דייני גזירות
(כתובות קיא).:הביאו לי נתר.להוץ את
ראשי וקאמר לה בלשון הקודש: פתחו
פומייכו . וינגם הבל בית המרחץ
לתוך הגוף ויוליא הבל של זיעה :
ואשתו . מן מים חמין ואפי׳ לא הוחמו
אלא לרחיצה: מותר לאומרן: בבית
המרחק ואפי׳ בלשון קודש: הבלא.
דמרחק הנכנס דרך הפה : מפיק
הבלא . דזיעה : ולא הלך ד׳ אמות -
קודם שיפן : מרקבת . אוגה מתעכלת
לעשות זבל : ריח רע . ריח הפה :
ריח זוהמא . כל גופו מזוהם בזיעה
תמיד . ולא הסיקוהו מבפנים . שאיו
מעיב לכלוס : ולא הבניסוהו לצונן.
שכן מחזקין את הברזל : למיס פ״ג
חבית . על שולי ולדדיו שאינם נכנסים
לתובו : מתני׳ מוליאר הגרוף
מן הגחלים מבע״ט : שותין . ממימיו
בשבת ואע״פ שהוחמו קלת מחמת
הכלי לפי שאין מוסיף הבל אלא
משמר ומקיים חום שלהם שלא ילטנו
בגמרא מפרש מוליאר מים מבפנים
וגחלים מבחוץ כלי שים בו בית קיבול
קטן אלל דופנו מבחון מחובר לו וטוטן
שם גחלים והמים בקיבולו הגדול

ראשית קראתי אתכם · ראשית הבוצה (ירמיה ב) · פסקי ראשית · ראשית עריסתיכם (במדבר טו) · הריני נוטל נשמתכם ~
רביעית הדמים ויכבד ויכבד שם ויבטל שם ראשיתהם וסם נגטמו על כך כדאמרינן בברכות רבה היה איבדה חלקו של עולם ~
אד״ר שנעתרים בחלה ובכתה וכבתה גרו של עולם ושפכה דמו ועוד שגלרי הבית תלוין בה · לארכן שהוא
אומרים חדו לסביבא עד שלא יקום · ויהא עודא להשליכו כך הואיל ואיתרע מזלה מזומנת פורענוקה לבא · רי

ראשית קראתי אתכם על עסקן ראשית
הזהרתי אתכם נשמה שנתתי בכם קרויה
*על עסקן נר הזהרתי אתכם אם
מקיימים אותם מוטב ואם לאו הרי
נשמתכם ומ״ש בשעת לידתן אמ...
תורא הדד לסבינא אבי אמר
אמתא בחד מחטרא ליהו
שבקיה לרויא דמנפשיה
אמר רעיא חגרא ועיזי
מילי ואבי דרי חושבו...
חנואתא נפישי אהי ל...
מיבדקן אמר ריש ל...
גישר רב לא עבר
עליה ומתפיסנא נ
שטנא בתרי אימ
*דאמר תורא אמ
אילעולם אל יעמ...

study

Jewish Education

Introduction

"Jewish education"—in the last few years, this phrase has been applied to everything from the open classroom to intensive text study, from once-a-year retreats to twenty-four-hour-a-day live-in programs. Everyone has a different idea of what Jewish education is and where it should be going.

The difficulty of defining Jewish education is a reflection of the problems inherent in establishing goals and curricula for the Jewish school. At one time it was assumed that the purpose of the Jewish school was to transmit knowledge, skills, and values. How this was done depended, of course, on the branch of Judaism under whose aegis a school was established. Often it was felt that the transmission of knowledge would automatically result in moral and religious behavior. After all, "the ignorant man cannot be pious."

However, experience has shown that changes in people are not caused by textbooks alone, that human interactions have as much to do with the development of a child's personality as a school—perhaps more. In providing the setting for the acquisition of knowledge, the Jewish school expected parents to share in the task of "teaching their children diligently" how to live as Jews. In the decades that followed World War II many parents abdicated that responsibility. Giving acceptance by the secular world the top priority, they played down Judaism and called into question the place of Jewish learning in American society. The school tried to influence children to adhere to Jewish values that were openly rejected by their parents—but in vain.

The problem remains in the schools of the mid-1970s. Many parents still work against the school rather than with it. They discourage their children from practicing what they learn, yet blame the school if their child does not retain his/her Jewish identity. By now it is clear to all Jewish educators that parents are the real teachers of their children. The school should supplement and reinforce what is lived at home, and family education should be considered the most viable supplement to the traditional Jewish classroom.

Another difficulty of the Jewish school has been its isolation from other forms of Jewish learning. As an entity unto itself, the Hebrew school was concerned primarily with formal classroom experiences. Youth groups and

---

A *Note about education and the Jewish establishment*

Much criticism has been leveled at the federations (the major fund-raising bodies for the Jewish community) for not treating seriously the plight of Jewish education and for not providing enough funds to Jewish educational projects and programs. The federations in turn point to figures that indicate, for example, that the level of funding to Jewish education rose from 23.8 percent of the total federation allocation in 1969, to 24.3 percent in 1970, and continues to go higher (as of 1975, exact figures for federation allocations were only available up to 1970). Critics maintain that this is not happening fast enough and say the state of Jewish education is so critical that the community can no longer afford the luxury of Band-Aid tactics. In any case, it is true that federations now give more money to Jewish education, and it is equally true that what they give is not enough.

But the problems go deeper than funding. Unfortunately, internal political pressures and interagency disagreements sometimes prevent the national and local organizations from working together as a united front. What is needed is not solely greater funding for Jewish education (although this is important) but the encouragement of dedicated and talented people who are willing to join with others in working for the good of the *entire* Jewish community.

summer camps were not seen as "educational." Fortunately, within the last five years changes in Jewish education have taken place; informal education is beginning to be seen as vitally important to supplement, or in some cases to replace, the classroom. It is recognized that different kinds of learning are most effective at various developmental stages of the child, and we are beginning to experiment with serious alternatives to formal education.

We are also utilizing techniques from the secular world. Terms such as "confluent education," "values clarification," and "open classroom" have entered the Jewish school vocabulary. It is regrettable that many of these methods have been adopted wholesale, without any adequate study of their applicability to Jewish education and the goals of a Jewish school. But certainly well-researched experiments are necessary, and as long as the methods are adaptable to our goals, the results may warrant the experiments.

There remains a crucial point to discuss: our goals are not well thought out, consistent, or agreed upon by the general Jewish community. The end product of Jewish education has become a ceremony instead of a human being. We are not clear what we want from the school or, for that matter, from the camps and youth groups. We use words like "identity," "survival," "knowledge," "loyalty," "observance"—without really defining and clarifying what we mean. The same words are used by groups with differing educational philosophies, and the same texts and sources are used by many without adequate definition of function. If our goal is to create an "identified" Jew (whatever that may be), then perhaps nonclassroom activities are best suited to this purpose. If we want to create an "educated" Jew, then the classroom becomes an important tool.

Once realistic goals are established, suitable materials must be created and utilized. The goals, of course, will change as the program is planned and implemented. Teachers must therefore be given good in-service training and follow-up supervision; they should also be given the proper status and salary. Jewish education ought to be a viable career option for dedicated professionals.

The future of Jewish education lies in the ability of its professionals to create and carry out sensitive, well-structured goals and programs. Jewish education must be seen as a continuum from birth on, with each new life phase creating new possibilities for Jewish and human growth.

This chapter is an attempt to describe what's happening on the Jewish educational scene. In it you will find examples of the different kinds of programs available; "Resources" and the contact chart will help you locate your area of interest and tell you who to get in touch with; a Bibliography is also included, to provide a sampling of the literature in each area of Jewish education.

Exactly what Jewish education should be has been the subject of controversy for years. To examine the philosophical trends or to posit personal visions of Jewish education is not within the scope of this chapter. The material contained in these pages is necessarily limited and cannot even begin to cover the whole scope of the field. Truly, everything a Jew does may be considered educational, because it affects his/her life and is a response to his/her world. This *Catalog* itself is "Jewish education," in that any vehicle for exploring, explaining, discovering, and sharing Jewish life is nothing other than education.

I hope that some of you reading this will share your experiences with me. Perhaps together we can create new vistas and fulfill old dreams.

Note: Things change so quickly in the Jewish educational field that it is not only possible but probable that some of the information contained in this article will be incomplete. Feel free to contact me with new information, which will then be included in subsequent printings.

Early childhood education

If your child is between the ages of three and five, the chances are good that you can find a Jewish nursery program to meet your needs. There are some excellent schools throughout the country—schools that combine secular and Jewish studies to produce an experience within the Jewish tradition that is consistent with the principles of good early childhood education. Because of this, early childhood education has the potential to be one of the most successful areas of Jewish education.

This is not to say that there are no problems. While it is true that, more than in any other area of Jewish education, many Jewish early childhood teachers are well trained in the secular field and bring a competency in principles and methods to the classroom, it is also true that this skill is sometimes not coupled with adequate Jewish training. Because of this, schools frequently lack much Jewish content. Yet they can get away with calling themselves Jewish because their classes are held in a Jewish institution or because they are receiving funds from a Jewish organization. In addition, although there is a wealth of early childhood materials commercially available, there are very few Jewish toys and games that are suitable for the three- to five-year-old. Menorah cookie cutters and "read aloud" stories with Jewish content are inadequate for establishing an in-depth Jewish program.

The needs are clearly known. In terms of curriculum, teachers must be encouraged to produce such material and a publisher must be found (the Jewish publishers have been noticeably reticent) who will take a chance on producing Jewish materials for the young child. We must also encourage Jewish competency in teachers who have skills in early childhood education, so that there can be an integrated approach to Jewish life during these vitally important years of development.

There are a variety of early childhood programs, ranging from a Jewish Montessori school to developmentally oriented, discovery-based programs

One positive development is the increasing growth of early childhood programs in day schools. The child begins his/her higher Jewish education at the age of three or four in an all-encompassing Jewish environment, and continues in that same school through at least the elementary years.

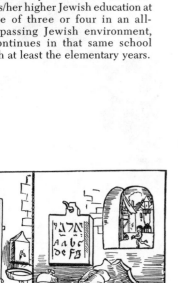

in the classrooms. For a complete description of your community's programs, check with your local Jewish board of education, the synagogues, and the community centers. Check also to find out which teachers have both Jewish and general early childhood training and skills.

To meet the need for child-care education, some communities have extended day nursery programs that run from 9 A.M. till 2 or 3 P.M. Few, if any, schools have total day care facilities for the full day. Check out such programs in your area. If you can't find one, get together with some friends and some Jewish early childhood teachers and lobby for them!

Day school education

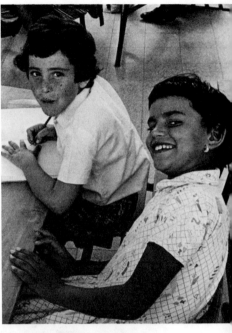

The day school form of education has earned increasing popularity recently. Advocates of the day school feel that it is the best way to teach Jewish values and knowledge. The framework of daily Jewish education coupled with a good general education is seen as an answer to the problems of an assimilationist society.

Yet there are some problems with day school education. The benefits of small classes, motivated children (who are able to maintain a dual study program), and Jewishly concerned families (who may or may not be committed to observance) must be weighed against the question of separation and isolation from the outside world.

The "integration" of religious and secular worlds, lauded by many of the day schools, rarely is successful. One type of learning is usually emphasized in the school. The Orthodox schools maintain a strict dichotomy be-

tween general and religious studies, and do not foster questioning of traditional Jewish values and behavior. In the most traditional of these schools, the general studies are seen as necessary in America but not intrinsically valuable. The ideal is still to study as much Torah as possible. Other Orthodox schools, however, do recognize and respond to the demands of a secularist world while providing daily experiences in Jewish living.

In the Conservative and Reform day schools, the general studies are sometimes stressed. Since parents are sending their children to a private as well as a Jewish school, the highest academic standards are maintained and encouraged. In Reform day schools more time is designated for general studies than for Hebrew studies; in Conservative schools "equal time" is a stated principle but is not always practiced.

Yet despite these problems we believe that the day school is still the best alternative for Jewish education in our present society. It is a setting in which Jewish identity is formed by daily living experiences, as well as through study; the level of knowledge and commitment to Judaism by day school students is high; the school has the potential to be highly effective and to become a major force for commitment. In addition, day school graduates frequently make Judaism and Jewish education their careers. In view of this, it becomes very important that these students be provided with a rich experience and as much knowledge as possible, so that the background they bring to their careers in the Jewish community is a positive one.

The major branches of Judaism operate day schools on both elementary and high school levels. Most Orthodox education takes place within the day school framework. Reform and Conservative day schools serve only a small fraction of their affiliates (five Reform schools and forty-seven Conservative ones are now in operation). The Orthodox organization of day schools, Torah Umesorah, tells us that there is a day school in every city with a Jewish population of over seventy-five hundred and that efforts are now being made to establish schools in districts that have between five thousand and seventy-five hundred Jews. There probably is, then, some kind of day school close to your home. Keep in mind that each school has its own philosophy. A number are experimenting with new methods, such as individualization, open classes, and integration of formal and informal learning. Check with the national organizations for lists of schools, addresses, and educational goals.

Afternoon school education

Afternoon school education, better known (not always affectionately either) as Talmud Torah or Hebrew school, has been the traditional vehicle of learning for the majority of Jews. Offering a course of study that has included a maximum of six hours of study per week (with many Reform and Conservative schools offering less!), the school has attempted to supplement the home and the public school and to prepare the child for participation in Jewish life. The emphasis in the school has often been on acquisition of skills and knowledge of texts.

Yet in spite of well-meaning efforts, the afternoon school has had a low level of academic achievement. The six-hour program is too short, the courses are too fragmented to allow for in-depth study. By the age of thirteen the average Hebrew school student is on a second-grade public school

level in terms of knowledge. Yet s/he is expected to have achieved a lifelong commitment to Jewish tradition and values. The student knows that afternoon school is not considered important to his/her parents, that they resent the incessant carpool trips and the demands of time, money, and commitment. Furthermore, experiencing secular and Jewish learning in different settings, the student cannot help comparing the two—with Hebrew school coming out a poor second. The late afternoon time slot encourages lack of respect for the school—the student is tired, the teacher (who has probably put in a full day's work already) is exhausted and impatient, the subject matter is "boring," and the parents are annoyed about impositions on their time.

Moreover, the teachers in the afternoon school are often embarrassingly underpaid—a fact that has certain consequences. The early grades remain largely female preserves, and in fact men who seriously entertain thoughts of entering the field of Jewish education professionally lose status in the community. Furthermore, scattered throughout the system are teachers who are poorly trained in general education and psychology and have a rigid view of their roles as teachers.

Finally, the subject matter taught in the afternoon school has long been a subject of controversy. The limited amount of time means that choices must be made and priorities set. Is Bible, history, laws, or Hebrew going to be emphasized? Should Hebrew be stressed as a conversational tool, since successful language acquisition requires frequent reinforcement and diligent study (which are not always possible in the afternoon school)? Or should we teach only enough Hebrew to enable our students to use the language in prayer and study, reserving teaching conversational skills until there is a trip to Israel in the foreseeable future?

Wherever children are learning, there dwells the Divine Presence.
yiddish proverb Trans. Leo Rosten

All these issues pose serious problems for the community. Since the afternoon school continues to be the form of education chosen by most Jewish parents, innovative leaders are desperately trying to create new structures and to provide new teaching methods.

Some innovations have already been made. New curricula are being prepared by all the major movements in Judaism, and new goals are being formulated. The new programs take into account the child's developmental level as well as his/her interests and abilities, and they attempt to provide social, moral, and emotional growth in addition to intellectual achievement. Some of these creative ventures are described in "Something Old . . . Something New" (see below). More information may be had by contacting the national organizations.

In some areas of the country, the congregational afternoon school has given way to an intercongregational school or a community school. The sharing of resources, students, and teachers can provide a unique and creative environment for Jewish learning.

**American Association for Jewish Education
114 Fifth Ave.
New York, N.Y. 10011**

has a great deal of information on school consolidation that it will be happy to share with you.

The typical afternoon school is under the auspices of one of the national organizations and has programs reflecting local and/or national concern. But there are a number of schools not affiliated with a specific group, which have formulated their own goals and curricula to meet the needs of their communities. Some of these programs are taking place within the havurah movement, which sees them as alternative frameworks for Jewish education. For more information, contact:

**New York Havurah
Jay Greenspan
299 Riverside Dr., #30
New York, N.Y. 10025**

**Farbrengen
c/o Art Waskow, IPS
1901 Q St. N.W.
Washington D.C. 20009**

High school education

There are also a number of independent secular and Yiddish schools. Check the contact chart for names and addresses (see pp. 188-89).

Jewish high school education is an expanding, exciting field in which more new projects are taking place than in any other branch of Jewish education. The range and variety of high school programs include study of texts and sources, minicourses, informal weekend and summer experiences, Israel programs, and community service projects. The possibilities for a teenager are vast. No longer is it an intolerable burden for the Bar/Bat Mitzvah to continue high school education in Hebrew school. The best programs and most exciting, creative projects are often not even available until the eighth grade! As s/he gets older the choices and opportunities become more varied, from trips to Israel to being teacher aides in the classroom, from free university-style classes to retreats and experiential learning.

More and more emphasis is being placed on the affective forms of education. The goal of many programs is to create a community—by moving beyond structure, by emphasizing the interpersonal, and by reaching out to adolescent needs. Without denigrating this approach, we need to recognize the legitimacy of cognitive learning for this age as well. The real danger of such creativity, and one we must constantly keep in mind, is that such styles of education can become "trendy," picking up on the newest fad whether applicable or not.

One specific high school concept that is unique is the "boarding

Four characters of those who sit before the Wise. A sponge, a funnel, a strainer, and a sieve. A sponge because it sucks up everything; a funnel because it receives at one end and lets out at the other; a strainer because it lets out the wine and keeps back the dregs, a sieve because it lets out the coarse meal and keeps the fine flour.
                                                    — Pirke Aboth

school" program. Two different approaches to the program are to be found in the Brandeis Institute's program and in the Maayan school created by the Chicago Reform movement. For details about goals, programing, and materials for each of the schools, write to:

Brandeis Institute
Brandeis, Calif. 93064

Rabbi Bernard Kaye
Maayan
100 W. Monroe St.
Chicago, Ill. 60603

There is an abundance of high school programs for Americans in Israel. Just about every synagogue, community center, and youth organization sponsors summer programs in Israel. Both local schools and national educational organizations also sponsor programs, which can range from a few months of study to four full years of high school in Israel. Most Israel-America secondary school programs are half- or full-year programs. See the contact chart for specifics.

One additional high school program should be mentioned; it is one of the more creative projects available for the teenager:

Jewish Educational Workshop
300 Welsh Rd.
Horsham, Pa. 19044

has revised the camping concept of creative living experiences and provides a year-round, ongoing weekend center for small groups of teenagers. The participants are involved in every aspect of the weekend, from the initial planning, research, and programing to the cooking and clean-up at the workshop's house. It has proved successful since its inception. Get in touch with Steve Stroiman, the workshop's director, to find out more about the how and why of the JEW.

For general information about high school programs, whether formal or informal, check with your local and national organizations (see "Resources").

Jewish studies in public schools

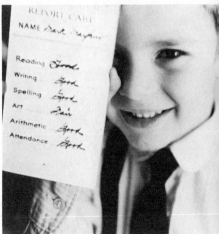

In the last few years there has been a growing interest in introducing Jewish ethnic studies into the public school curriculum, both as an educational vehicle and as a means of reaching unaffiliated Jewish youth. Hebrew has been a language elective in over eighty public high schools for many years, and now social studies programs that deal with Judaism, Soviet Jewry, Israel, and Jews in America are being introduced. The availability of these programs depends in large part on local demand and on the attitudes of the school principals and department heads.

Since this is a relatively new field, it is hard to evaluate the success of ethnic programs in public schools. Certainly we are all aware of the dangers of merging church and state and want a program that is noncoercive and informative. Besides, is it necessary? What, if anything, does it detract from the traditional role of the Hebrew school as supplier of knowledge about Judaism? Will it eventually replace the Hebrew school altogether? What influence will learning about other religions have on our children? Can it be a positive learning experience for them? Have the basic foundations of Judaism already been established and deeply implanted in our children by the time they reach public school? If not, what are we doing about it?

For general information about teaching religion and ethnic studies in the public school, contact:

Religious Education Association
545 W. 111th St.
New York, N.Y. 10025

You may also want to take a look at an article by David Washburn in *Social Education*, "Where to Find Ethnic Studies Materials" (1975).

Some programs you might want to look into:

1. The United Federation of Teachers of New York offers course material for Jewish ethnic studies. One of their units is *Topics in the Jewish American Heritage: Curriculum and Study Guide for Teachers*. They also have information on Soviet Jewry, Israel, and Judaism. Write to them at:

United Federation of Teachers of New York
260 Park Ave. South
New York, N.Y. 10010

2. The Anti-Defamation League of Bnai Brith has published a book by Jerome L. Ruderman, *Jews in American History: A Teacher's Guide*. It is available by writing to:

Anti-Defamation League
315 Lexington Ave.
New York, N.Y. 10016

3. The Board of Jewish Education of San Francisco, in cooperation with the San Francisco Jewish Community Relations Council, is developing a kindergarten through grade 6 curriculum for Jewish social studies to be used in the public schools. Their address is:

Board of Education of San Francisco
639 14th Ave.
San Francisco, Calif. 94118

4. **American Association for Jewish Education**
114 Fifth Ave.
New York, N.Y. 10011

has a Commission of Jewish Studies in Public Schools, the purpose of which is to help educators plan programs and to provide materials, faculty referrals, and evaluations of Jewish studies courses. Their publications include *Viewpoint* (ten study units on Israel), *The Holocaust, Jewish Protest in the Soviet Union, The Short Story in Jewish Literature, History of the Jews, Guidelines for Public School Teaching, The American Jewish Experience, Jews in Israel and Other Lands Abroad, World Jewish History*, and more. They will be happy to send you information concerning their programs, which can be used for all Jewish educational programs, both in and out of the public school.

Informal education–camping

Camping continues to be an area of creativity in informal Jewish education. Most Jewish camps offer some sort of education programing for campers and/or staff. The youth movement camps utilize their facilities to provide training in leadership as well as education. Jewish studies, intensive Hebrew courses, work study options, and movement philosophy make up some of the structure of youth organizations such as Young Judaea, Habonim, Bnei Akiva, and Hashomer Hatzair.

Of course the programing at any camp reflects the philosophy of its directing body. Camps also maintain their own standards for admission requirements as well. The Ramah camps, for example, require their campers to be currently enrolled in an accredited Jewish studies program. The Massad camps have strict admission requirements as well. (Both Ramah and Massad offer exceptionally fine Hebrew and religious educational programing for both campers and staff members.)

There are many camps sponsored by Jewish community centers, federations, and independent organizations, each with its own degree of Jewish commitment and programing. Federation camps often are Jewish in name only, while Jewish community center camps frequently commit themselves to Jewish programing. A new and growing trend in camping is for bureaus of Jewish education to establish their own camps, as extensions of the Hebrew school experience. In this way the summer camp becomes an integral part of the congregational school program, and has the potential to be a very exciting and major new force in Jewish education.

If you are thinking about a summer camp, check with the camps, movements, and national organizations for information concerning educational stance, religious orientation, admissions, procedures, etc. The contact chart contains a sampling of Jewish overnight camps. One of the most important things to look for is whether the camp you are interested in is accredited by a professional camping association.

There are some things to be aware of in choosing a camp. You should know that a good Jewish camp offers significant Jewish models to your child. The staff will have a variety of talents, and experimentation in informal and formal settings will be encouraged. Know, too, that a camp that does a good job of creating an intense two-month away-from-home environment will also be creating possible conflicts between parents and children when the summer is over. It is far easier to live Jewishly at camp than at home, and the camper may have difficulty adjusting to his/her old life-style (or the parents to a new one!).

Marilyn Sladowsky
808 West End Ave.
New York, N.Y. 10025

who has worked in different camp settings for a number of years, has a great deal of knowledge and experience working with Jewish camps, and will be happy to help you choose the right environment for your child. Also write to:

National Jewish Welfare Board
Dept. of Camping
Rosalyn Krigsfield, Director
15 E. 26th st.
New York, N.Y. 10010

for directories of Jewish day camps and resident summer camps.

In addition to the NJWB, the following agencies have camp facilities or lists of other facilities suitable for family institutes, retreats, and camp experiences:

National Ramah Commission
3080 Broadway
New York, N.Y. 10027

Union of American Hebrew Congregations
838 Fifth Ave.
New York, N.Y. 10021

Division of Community Services
Yeshiva University
186th and Amsterdam Ave.
New York, N.Y. 10033

Adult education

A number of Jewish community centers offer excellent programs for adults. Check with the center in your community for a description of what is offered. Keep in mind, though, that the quality of adult education is determined largely by the people teaching. So check out teachers as well as courses.

When a Teacher fights with his wife, its Tough on his students.
—Yiddish proverb
Trans. Leo Rosten

Many synagogues have established adult education programs to meet the needs of their congregants. Some communities have one large educational center in which the entire community is invited to participate. Other congregations prefer to create their own specific classes and lectures in their own building. These synagogues often receive prepared course outlines and curricular material from their national affiliate organizations. Some of the more popular trends in adult education, described in material available from these groups, include parent-child study programs, family education, and camping experiences.

An exciting program for adults is sponsored by Gratz College in Philadelphia. Known as PACE, it is a free outreach, on-campus program in which the individual needs of each adult are provided for. Once you decide what you are interested in, Gratz provides you with your own "mentor," who maps out a plan with you that can include anything from assisting the head of the Jewish federation to engaging in deep scholarship. For more information, contact:

> **Rabbi Howard Bogot**
> **Gratz College**
> **10th St. and Tabor Rd.**
> **Philadelphia, Pa. 19141**

Another outstanding program has been developed by Hadassah. It is well researched and designed to build leadership ability. For a catalog of study guides and learning units, write to:

> **Naomi Sarlin**
> **Hadassah Education Dept.**
> **65 E. 52nd St.**
> **New York, N.Y. 10022**

> **Bnai Brith Education Dept.**
> **1640 Rhode Island Ave. N.W.**
> **Washington, D.C. 20036**

with Lily Edelman at the head, also has compiled a large amount of excellent material, especially for conference and for Shabbat programing.

Colleges and universities in America and Canada offer a wide range of Judaica courses, often including complete Judaic studies departments. See

Catalog 1 for a full description of college programs. You may also want to take a look at a catalog called *Jewish Studies in American Colleges and Universities* published by the Bnai Brith Hillel Foundation.

Frequently Jewish teacher-training institutions and universities offer courses for the general community. Take a look at the list of teacher-training schools (see "Resources"). The University of Judaism in Los Angeles has one of the best adult education programs in the country. Perhaps schools in your own area have good programs as well.

Established by the American Jewish Committee in association with the University of Haifa, the Academy for Jewish Studies without Walls offers accredited courses in a variety of Jewish subjects. For a complete catalog and description of their program, write to:

Academy for Jewish Studies without Walls
165 E. 56th St.
New York, N.Y. 10022

And last but not least there are the many educational programs for Americans that take place in Israel. See the contact chart for a list of groups that sponsor such programs.

Special education

Recognizing the need in Jewish education for materials and programs to service special students with learning problems, a growing number of communities have established classes for the special Jewish child. Taught by professionals in special education who also have extensive training in Judaism and Jewish education, the ideal Jewish special class creates a stress-free, structured environment in which each child is individually taught to reach his/her potential. The goal is for the child to acquire knowledge and skills, to participate as fully as possible in the life of the Jewish community, and to develop a positive identification with Judaism.

Very few materials geared specifically to the requirements of the special child now exist. One excellent program that is available is *The Shabbat Kit*, by Barbara and Herbert Greenberg, both experts in special education for the Jewish child. The kit contains tactile and visual material for the child with learning and perceptual problems, and is also useful for the primary grades. The kit and a teacher's guide are available from:

United Synagogue Book Service
155 Fifth Ave.
New York, N.Y. 10010

The National Commission on Torah Education (Orthodox) has available on cassette tapes the proceedings of a conference on special education held in December 1974. They include a discussion of problems and programs in the afternoon, day, and yeshivah high schools. They are available from:

National Commission on Torah Education
500 W. 185th St.
New York, N.Y. 10033

NCTE is also preparing a hotline for referrals and a special education resource center. Plans now include the development of a modified yeshivah high school program for the nonacademically oriented student.

Movement	Early childhood	Day Schools	Afternoon Schools
Orthodox	National Commission on Torah Education (NACOTE) 500 W. 185th St. New York, N.Y. 10033 (212) 568-8400	Torah Umesorah 229 Park Ave. South New York, N.Y. 10003 (212) 674-6700 Rabbi Bernard Goldenberg Merkos L'Inyonei Chinuch (Hasidic) 770 Eastern Parkway Brooklyn, N.Y. 11213 (212) 493-9250	National Commission on Torah Education 500 W. 185th St. New York, N.Y. 10033 (212) 568-8400 Rabbi Robert Hirt
Conservative United Synagogue of America 155 Fifth Ave. New York, N.Y. 10010 (212) 260-8450	Dept. of Education	Solomon Schechter Day School Assn. Mr. Chanoch Shudofsky	Dept. of Education (elementary, secondary and adult) Dr. Morton Siegel
Reform Union of American Hebrew Congregations 838 Fifth Ave. New York, N.Y. 10021 (212) 249-0100	Dept. of Education	Dept. of Education Ms. Judy Paskind (six schools now in existence)	Dept. of Education Rabbi Daniel B. Syme
Reconstructionist Jewish Reconstructionist Foundation 15 W. 86th St. New York, N.Y. 10024 (212) 787-1500	Programing in individual congregations		Programing in individual congregations
Zionist 515 Park Ave. New York, N.Y. 10022 (212) PL2-0600			
Other	Local boards of Jewish education; especially good programing in boards of these cities: New York, Chicago, Los Angeles, Boston, Baltimore, Miami	Independent day schools in local communities—check with your local boards for lists of schools	

Jerusalem was destroyed because the children did not attend School.
Talmud: Shabbath

High Schools	Informal Education–Camping	Adult Education
Dept. of High School Education Community Service Division, Yeshiva University 500 W. 185th St. New York, N.Y. 10033 Classes, informal programs, Torah leadership seminars, summer-in-Israel programs, Bnai Hillel Honor Society, in-depth study programs at yeshivot National Conference of Synagogue Youth 116 E. 27th St. New York, N.Y. 10016	Camp Morasha Metropolitan N.Y. Commission on Torah Education 1277 E. 14th St. Brooklyn, N.Y. 11230 Bnei Akiva (Camp Moshava, Torah Vaavodah Institute 25 W. 26th St. New York, N.Y. 10010 (212) 673-2626	National Commission on Torah Education 500 W. 185th St. New York, N.Y. 10033 (212) 568-8400
Dept. of Education (elementary, secondary and adult) Classes, informal programs, United Synagogue Youth, leaders' training fellowship, summer-in-Israel programs, in-depth study at Jewish Theological Seminary Prozdor High School	Camp Ramah National Ramah Commission 3080 Broadway New York, N.Y. 10027 (212) RI9-8000	Dept. of Education (elementary, secondary and adult) Dr. Morton Siegel
Dept. of Education Rabbi Daniel B. Syme Classes, informal programs, Sinai Plan for concentrated Jewish Study, mitzvah corps, leaders' training institute, family and youth weekends, National Federation of Temple Youth, summer-in-Israel programs, in-depth study at Hebrew Union College–Jewish Institute of Religion Prozdor High School	Dept. of Camping, Union of American Hebrew Congregations Rabbi Allan Smith NOTE: There are many other good Jewish camps—check with the directory for a full listing	Dept. of Education Rabbi Daniel B. Syme *(illustration)*
Programing in individual congregations		Programing in individual congregations
Dept. of Education and Culture— High School in Israel programs: Kfar Blum, Kadourie, host program, kibbutz, youth village high school, semester programs for day school students, high school seniors and graduates, summer-in-Israel programs Dept. of Torah Education—Tochnit Yud Gimel (for seniors) Bnei Akiva programs, one-year programs with local schools, summer-in-Israel programs Zionist Organization of America 145 E. 32nd St. New York, N.Y. 10016 Mollie Goodman Academy at Kfar Silver Solomon Schechter Day School Association—one-year high school program at Givat Washington American Zionist Youth Foundation— summer-in-Israel programs	Tel Yehuda (Young Judea) Hadassah Zionist Youth Commission 817 Broadway New York, N.Y. 10003 (212) 260-4703 Hashomer Hatzair (Camp Shomria) 150 Fifth Ave. New York, N.Y. 10011 (212) 929-4956 Ichud Habonim Labor Zionist Youth 575 Sixth Ave. New York, N.Y. 10011 (212) 255-1796	American Zionist Youth Foundation— summer-in-Israel programs, ages 18-25 in kibbutz, folk dance, music, drama, archaeology and more. Long-term programs—Pardes Study Program, Sherut La'Am volunteer work in development towns, study on kibbutz and at universities, work with new Russian immigrants Dept. of Torah Education—summer-in-Israel programs for college and graduate students. Year-round study at Hartman College, Gold College for Women, and Jerusalem Torah College for Men Dept. of Education and Culture—Hayim Greenberg College in Israel, summer programs for college students, educators, and interested laypeople
Check also with the national youth movements for their summer/ year-in-Israel projects	Massad Camps, Inc. 426 W. 58th St. New York, N.Y. 10019 (212) 265-7240 Bnai Brith Camps 1640 Rhode Island Ave. N.W. Washington, D. C. 20036 (202) EX3-5284 Cejwin Camps, Inc. 1124 Broadway New York, N.Y. 10010 (212) 725-9440	Federation and YM/YWHA Camps—check with the *Directory of Jewish Resident Summer Camps* available from: National Jewish Welfare Board 15 E. 26th St. New York, N.Y. 10010 Camp Yavneh Hebrew College 43 Hawes St. Brookline, Mass. 02146 (617) 232-8710	Local federations, community centers, and Y's sponsor adult education programs. Check with organizations in your community For Israel study programs, check with national Zionist organizations and with universities in Israel and America

The Maimonides Institute for Exceptional Children is devoted to the care, education, and training of retarded, brain-damaged, and emotionally disturbed Jewish children. While they accept non-Jewish children at both their schools (one in Monticello, N.Y., one in Far Rockaway, N.Y.), the orientation of the school is toward traditional Judaism. There are both residential and nonresidential students, and the school operates summer camp programs. For information, write to:

Maimonides Institute for Exceptional Children
34-01 Mott Ave.
Far Rockaway, N.Y. 11691

The Tikvah program of the United Synagogue and National Ramah Commission is a summer camp program for learning-disabled teenagers. There are currently two camps—one in Palmer, Mass., and one in Conover, Wis.—which provide educational, social, and emotional programing for adolescents with learning and perceptual problems. The campers are integrated into the life of the total camp and participate in both their own division and in general camp activities. An extensive winter follow-up program exists. For more information, contact:

Tikvah
National Ramah Commission
3080 Broadway
New York, N.Y. 10027

Jewish Braille Institute
110 E. 30th St.
New York, N.Y., 10016

provides recordings, large-type books, and books in braille for the Jewish blind or partially sighted. Write to them for a complete catalog (see also The Jewish Blind).

New York Society for the Deaf
344 E. 14th St.
New York, N.Y. 10010

offers programs and help for the person who has difficulty hearing. Write to them for more information (see also The Jewish Deaf Community).

Some colleges offer courses in Jewish education for the special child. Among them are:

Teachers Institute
Jewish Theological Seminary
3080 Broadway
New York, N.Y. 10027

which offers a course in Educating the Child with Learning Disabilities, and

Ferkauf Graduate School of Yeshiva University
55 Fifth Ave.
New York, N.Y. 10003

which has a social learning curriculum for the mentally retarded.

Shalaym is an organization for the parents of exceptional children. Sponsored by:

United Synagogue Dept. of Education
155 Fifth Ave.
New York, N.Y. 10010

its purpose is to secure and promote programs, arrange funding, etc. for the welfare of Jewish exceptional children.

Some local bureaus of Jewish education and individual congregational

The world itself rests upon the breath of the children in our schools.
—Talmud: Shabbath

schools throughout the country offer programs for the special child. Check with your Jewish community organizations to see what's available in your area, as well as with

Bureau of Jewish Education
76 Dorrance St.
Providence, R.I. 02903

Something old . . . something new . . . something borrowed to teach a Jew

Creative things are happening in Jewish education. If you walk into any good Hebrew school, day school, or high school, you are likely to be shown materials prepared by the teaching staff to meet that particular school's needs; you may be taken on a tour of resource rooms and learning centers; you may well be asked to observe a master teacher who is demonstrating new ideas and techniques.

Unfortunately the creative teaching going on in one school is often not communicated to other schools and tends to get overlooked in the twisted jungle of structure and administrative details. No one ever hears about the new programs created by these scattered pockets of innovation. Lack of communication leads to duplication of ideas and efforts.

The American Association for Jewish Education has attempted to remedy this gap by preparing a yearly roundup of new programs in Jewish education, published in the AAJE's journal, *The Pedagogic Reporter.* While many innovations are described in the journal, only member organizations are solicited for ideas, and thus the many unaffiliated groups that are doing exciting projects are left out. In addition, the annual roundup describes the programs in fairly general terms, and there is no direct implementation available for the person who wants to create a similar program. S/he must contact the individual school for information on methodology. Regrettably, many of the programs described are one-shot deals, and are not followed through for continuing use. Still, the AAJE is the major unbrella organization for Jewish education in the U.S. We'd like to see it become a major force for unity, communication, and goodwill among Jewish educators.

How nice it would be to have a clearinghouse for all programing material, a resource of specific goals, plans, and evaluations for all educators! We understand that Gratz College is planning to start a computerized retrieval center for Jewish education—nu . . . we're waiting for what sounds like a terrific idea.

We've listed here some selected examples of creative work presently going on in Jewish education. Sorry to perpetuate the ills, but for details you'll have to contact the individual school or group initiating the program.

Organizations devoted to creativity in Jewish education

Alternatives in Religious Education
1110 Holly Oak Circle
San Jose, Calif. 95120
Audrey Friedman Marcus

is a group that produces materials in religious education for varied levels and subject matter. They provide workshops for teachers and create new curricular materials. Some of their materials include minicourses, games, tapes, the Rocky Mountain Curriculum Planning Workshops, and two publications, *The Inkling* and *Alternatives in Religious Education*.

Jewish Educational Workshop
300 Welsh Rd.
Horsham, Pa. 19044
Rabbi Steven Stroiman

provides informal programing for high school youth, ages fourteen to eighteen, and teacher training workshops for school personnel. Small groups of teenagers participate in the monthly weekends devoted to Jewish learning and living in an informal atmosphere reminiscent of good Jewish camp experiences.

Jewish Teacher Center—the Dolores Kohl Workshop
161 Greenbay Rd.
Wilmette, Ill. 60091

offers resources and an environment so that people can create their own materials. The staff provides excellent guidance and suggestions.

Melton Research Center
3080 Broadway
New York, N.Y. 10027
Rabbi Joel Roth

This research center for Jewish education, specializing in the inquiry-discovery method of teaching, provides curricular materials in Bible, prayer, and Hebrew language. Materials in history, holidays, and mitzvot are in preparation. An experimental biblical Hebrew language program is under way, and teacher training workshops in Bible, prayer, and biblical Hebrew are held throughout the country.

Recent educational trends

1. *Media*: See the chapter entitled Media.
2. *Confluent education*: This form of education stresses the learning of subject matter within personal, experiential, developmental situations. The institution predominantly responsible for developing this approach in Jewish education is:

Hebrew Union College–Jewish Institute of Religion
3077 University Mall
Los Angeles, Calif. 90007

A description of the project and teacher-training programs are available from the project director, Dr. William Cutter.

3. *Open education and individualization*: It has been difficult to transfer intact the principles of open education into the Jewish classroom. Reports of successful experiments utilizing open education techniques may be found in a booklet, *Opening the School and Individualizing Instruction*, by:

> **American Association for Jewish Education**
> **114 Fifth Ave.**
> **New York, N.Y. 10011**

Results of a conference on Open Schooling and Individualization, held in March 1975, are available from the AAJE in a booklet called *To Everything There Is a Time*.

Three schools that have developed programs of varying intensity in open education are:

> **Salanter Riverdale Academy** (an Orthodox day school)
> **655 W. 254th St.**
> **Bronx, N.Y. 10471**

> **Congregation Beth Yeshurun**
> **4525 Beechnut Blvd.**
> **Houston, Tex. 77035**

> **Poughkeepsie Community Hebrew School**
> **110 Grand Ave.**
> **Poughkeepsie, N.Y. 12603**

Write to these schools for information concerning the process of change from a traditional to an open environment, teacher training, and the development of resource centers and materials.

4. *Retreats and weekends*: The most recent trend in Jewish education has been away from the structure of the classroom to an informal, camplike environment in which Judaism can be experienced as well as studied. An entire issue of the AAJE's *Pedagogic Reporter* for Spring 1975 is devoted to new experiments in this field. The Conference Plan, created in 1967 by Audrey Friedman Marcus and Rabbi Joseph Goldman of Temple Micah, Denver, Colo., was the first weekend program in Jewish education. It is described and evaluated in the Spring 1975 *Pedagogic Reporter*. A booklet entitled *Serving Jewish Families in Camp Settings*, by Bernard Reisman, is available from:

> **Council of Jewish Federations and Welfare Funds**
> **Institute for Jewish Life**
> **315 Park Ave. South**
> **New York, N.Y. 10010**

5. *Family education—the "in" program of the future*: A number of congregations have instituted programs in family education, consisting of study sessions and activities geared to the whole family.

As an outgrowth of the Conference Plan, some congregations have bought campsites and have hired personnel to deal with informal camping programs in the schools.

> **Park Synagogue Religious School**
> **330 Mayfield Ave.**
> **Cleveland Heights, Ohio 44118**

has instituted a Family Mitzvah Program and has available a brochure describing the program.

> **United Synagogue of America**
> **155 Fifth Ave.**
> **New York, N.Y. 10010**

has a Family Kallah Program and in May 1975 held a Family Education Conference. Check also with your local board of Jewish education for a listing of family programs in your area.

6. *Outreach programs*: A number of projects have been created to reach the Jew who has not previously been involved in Jewish education. One such program, known as Operation Torah-SEED (Summer Educational Environmental Development), provides a yeshivah community in small towns where Jewish learning is usually not available. Run by Orthodox rabbinical students and some married couples, the yeshivah introduces local students, lay people, and community leaders to a "beis medrash" form of study—a Torah-based form of higher education—for six weeks. For further information, contact:

**Torah Umesorah
229 Park Ave. South
New York, N.Y. 10010**

A Drop-In Program is in effect in Chicago, Ill., sponsored by:

**Associated Talmud Torahs Consolidated Hebrew High Schools
2828 Pratt St.
Chicago, Ill. 60645**

in which any student is welcomed regardless of background or age.

An outreach program to extend classroom learning into the home has also been created by:

**National Commission on Torah Education
186th St. and Amsterdam Ave.
New York, N.Y. 10033**

Check with your local community groups to see if an outreach project is available in your area.

7. *Values education*: The Samuel A. Fryer Educational Research Foundation of Torah Umesorah has developed a Moral Sensitivity Training Program. The texts in English and Hebrew, teachers' guides, and taped model lessons can be obtained by contacting Torah Umesorah.

**Gratz College
10th St. and Tabor Rd.
Philadelphia, Pa. 19141**

has established a Youth Dialogue Program with unaffiliated teenagers.

The Bureau of Jewish Education of Rhode Island recently held a conference to train teachers in "moral sensitivity." Details can be obtained by writing to:

**Bureau of Jewish Education
76 Dorrance St.
Providence, R.I. 02903**

Value Clarification Programs are going on in both Conservative and Reform synagogues, and some resource materials are presently in preparation.

8. *Informal education*: Of course, the national and local youth groups throughout the country contribute a great deal to Jewish education. By providing a variety of creative informal experiences, the youth groups integrate the world of Judaism into the general life of their members, and respond Jewishly and sensitively to the needs and challenges of today's youth. *Catalog 1* has a listing of the major Jewish youth organizations, and it is well worth checking them out and finding a group in your community.

9. *Community involvement*: Many schools throughout the country have programs of service to the community wherein high school students serve as volunteers and aides in social action and social service projects. Check with local schools and boards to find out how to get involved.

A new concept of community and school cooperation is exemplified in a program initiated by Gratz College in Philadelphia. The college provides in-service courses for federation workers and conducts a college class led jointly by the staffs of the college and the Jewish Y's and centers. The goal is to maximize the resources of the school and the community, to produce dialogue and new ideas. For details write to:

Gratz College
10th St. and Tabor Rd.
Philadelphia, Pa. 19141

So you want to be a Jewish educator?

If you are thinking of making Jewish education your profession, be prepared for a rocky but fulfilling career. You will probably receive little pay, work long hours, create much of your own material, and meet with resistance by some segments of the community. On the other hand, you may be able to work together with students to bring about learning, growth, and mutually rewarding experiences. You will learn a lot about yourself and your Jewish tradition, and you can be an instrument for change in your community. You can be creative and explore untapped worlds. In short, you will be a pioneer and researcher of alternatives and new ideas in the Jewish field.

How to become a Jewish educator

It doesn't matter whether you are in high school, college, graduate school, whether you are a veteran teacher or layperson, there are courses available to prepare you to teach basic and new material, courses that augment your knowledge and challenge your creativity. We have listed steps in the process of educating the would-be educator, with possibilities at each educational level.

LEVEL 1: HIGH SCHOOL

1. Courses in Jewish studies at public schools (see "Jewish Studies in Public Schools")
2. Courses at community or congregational high schools (see "High School Education")
3. Courses at all-day high schools (see "Day School Education")
4. Teacher-training programs, teacher aid programs, teen leadership projects, community service and training, internship programs with teacher-training school. Check your local boards and congregations
5. Intensive study programs at teacher-training schools
6. Leadership programs sponsored by national youth organizations (see *Catalog 1* for list)
7. Summer in Israel leadership programs (see "Resources")

LEVEL 2: COLLEGE AND ADULT TRAINING

1. Courses in Jewish studies at universities (see *Catalog 1* for list)
2. Courses at teacher-training institutions (see "Resources")
3. Training programs in Israel. An excellent program exists at the Cen-

If dreams ever turn into reality, the structure of Jewish education in America will soon be changing, and the following list of career choices will become significantly viable:

Some Career Options
afternoon school teacher, day school teacher, informal éducation coordinator, youth activities worker, camp director (winter/summer), curriculum planner/coordinator, school administrator, university instructor, Hillel director, boarding school director/teacher, Israel program coordinator, historian, author/textbook writer/teachers' guides and curricular materials writer, media specialist, creative arts specialist (dance, drama, art, song, puppetry), special education teacher/coordinator, remedial specialist, language specialist, Bible specialist, prayer and synagogue skill specialist, social worker, counseling psychologist, federation specialist in Jewish education, promotional specialist (enrollment, recruitment), teacher resource specialist (coordinator of secular and religious materials)

ter for Jewish Education in the Diaspora. For more information, contact:

American Friends of the Hebrew University
11 E. 69th St.
New York, N.Y. 10021

Many other universities in Israel also sponsor programs in education. Check the catalogs of the schools you're interested in. The major national educational organizations also sponsor teacher-training programs. See "Adult Education" for a list of programs sponsored by American Zionist Youth Foundation, World Zionist Organization, National Commission on Torah Education, United Synagogue, and Union of American Hebrew Congregations.

4. Summer training programs in Israel and America (see "Adult Education"). Many of the colleges and teacher-training institutions conduct special summer programs—they're worth looking into!

LEVEL 3: SPECIFIC IN-SERVICE TEACHER-TRAINING PROGRAMS

1. In-service workshops and training sessions sponsored by local bureaus and boards

2. For college-age teachers:

Rocky Mountain Curriculum Planning Workshops
3945 S. Oneida St.
Denver, Colo. 80237

3. Jewish Educational Workshop—informal techniques for teachers and school personnel:

Jewish Educational Workshop
300 Welsh Rd.
Horsham, Pa. 19044

4. Training sessions for teachers of Bible, prayer, and biblical Hebrew, master teachers/supervisor program

Melton Research Center
3080 Broadway
New York, N.Y. 10027

5. Confluent Education Workshops

Hebrew Union College–Jewish Institute of Religion
3077 University Mall
Los Angeles, Calif. 90007

6. Exchange Teachers Program

American Association for Jewish Education
114 Fifth Ave.
New York, N.Y. 10011

7. Aish Dos Training Program for Teachers

Torah Umesorah
229 Park Ave. South
New York, N.Y. 10003

8. Early Childhood Education Workshops

Board of Jewish Education
426 W. 58th St.
New York, N.Y. 10019

9. College Internship and Graduate Residency Program in Jewish Education Stone–Sapirstein Center for Jewish Education

Yeshiva University
500 W. 185th St.
New York, N.Y. 10033

10. Teacher-Initiated Experimentation Program (proposals for new projects):

**Gratz College
10th St. and Tabor Rd.
Philadelphia, Pa. 19141**

11. Conferences and special meetings sponsored by national and local organizations on current issues in Jewish education

12. Internship Program in Jewish Education

**Teachers Institute
Jewish Theological Seminary
3080 Broadway
New York, N.Y. 10027**

13. Training for Day School Teachers

**McGill University
P.O. Box 6070
Montreal, Quebec
Canada**

14. Master Teacher Program

**Board of Jewish Education
426 W. 58th St.
New York, N.Y. 10019**

GRANTS AND SCHOLARSHIPS

There is a limited amount of money around for Jewish teacher training, special projects, in-service programs, etc. Each of the different organizations listed below has its own area of interest, its own set of requirements for funding. Write them for specific information and applications.

**Memorial Foundation for Jewish Culture
15 E. 26th St.
New York, N.Y. 10010**

**National Foundation for Jewish Culture
122 E. 42nd St.
New York, N.Y. 10017**

**Institute for Jewish Policy Planning and Research
1776 Massachusetts Ave. N.W.
Washington, D.C. 20036**

**Council of Jewish Federations and Welfare Funds
315 Park Ave. South
New York, N.Y. 10010**

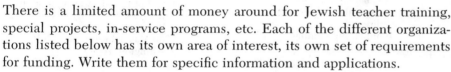

Note: Be sure to check with *Catalog 1* for a list of colleges and universities that offer programs in Jewish studies. See also the sections in this chapter, "Adult Education" and "So You Want To Be a Jewish Educator?"

Resources

National organizations

The following are national and local organizations that specialize in Jewish education:

American Association for Jewish Education
114 Fifth Ave.
New York, N.Y. 10011
Fradle Freidenreich will be most helpful. Coordination and support of community schools and organizations

Commission on Jewish Education of the Union of American Hebrew Congregations and the Central Conference of American Rabbis
838 Fifth Ave.
New York, N.Y. 10021
contact: Rabbi Daniel Syme
Reform objectives and educational practice

Department of Education and Culture—World Zionist Organization, American Section
515 Park Ave.
New York, N.Y. 10022
(212) PL2-0600
Furtherance of Hebrew language and Israel programs

Department of Torah Education and Culture–World Zionist Organization, American Section

515 Park Ave.
New York, N.Y. 10022
(212) PL2-0600
Furtherance of commitment to
Judaism and Israel

I.L. Peretz Workmen's Circle Schools
175 E. Broadway
New York, N.Y. 10002
(212) 889-6800
Yiddish schools

Merkos L'Inyonei Chinuch, Inc.
Central Organization for Jewish
Education
770 Eastern Parkway
Brooklyn, N.Y. 11213
(212) 493-9250
Hasidic educational programs

National Commission on Torah Education
Community Service Division, Rabbi
Isaac Elchanan Theological
Seminary,
Yeshiva University
500 W. 185th St.
New York, N.Y. 10033
(212) 568-8400
Orthodox objectives and educational
practices

National Council for Jewish Education
114 Fifth Ave.
New York, N.Y. 10011
(212) 675-5656
Council for educators

National Council for Torah Education
200 Park Ave. South
New York, N.Y. 10003
(212) 673-8100
Religious Zionists of America,
educational goals and programs

National Hebrew Culture Council
1776 Broadway
New York, N.Y. 10019
(212) 247-0741
Furtherance of Hebrew language and
culture programs

Sholem Aleichem Folk Institute
41 Union Sq.
New York, N.Y. 10003
(212) 255-7140
Yiddish schools and programs

Solomon Schechter Day School Assn.
155 Fifth Ave.
New York, N.Y. 10010
contact: Dr. Chanoch Shudofsky
Conservative day school education

Torah Umesorah
National Society for Hebrew Day
Schools
229 Park Ave. South
New York, N.Y. 10003
(212) 647-6700
contact: Rabbi Bernard Goldenberg
Day school education (Orthodox)

United Synagogue Commission on Jewish
Education
155 Fifth Ave.
New York, N.Y. 10010
(212) 260-8450
contact: Morton Siegel, director
Conservative objectives and
educational practices

Youth and Education Dept.
Jewish National Fund
42 E. 69th St.
New York, N.Y. 10021
(212) 879-9300
Israel programing

Other organizations involved in Jewish education

Alternatives in Religious Education
1110 Holly Oak Circle
San Jose, Calif. 95120
contact: Audrey Friedman Marcus,
who is always wonderfully helpful.
Innovative curricular materials and
workshops for teachers

American Jewish Committee—Education
Department
165 E. 56th St.
New York, N.Y. 10022

American Zionist Youth Foundation
515 Park Ave.
New York, N.Y. 10022
contact: Donald Adelman, director
Israel programs

Bnai Brith Education Department, Hillel
Foundation
1640 Rhode Island Ave. N.W.
Washington, D.C. 20036
contact Lily Edelman, director,
Education Dept.
Adult programing, college
programing

Brandeis Camp Institute
Brandeis, Calif. 93064
Informal programing for college and
adults; boarding school

Hadassah Education Dept.
65 E. 52nd St.
New York, N.Y. 10022
contact: Naomi Sarlin, director
Programing for adults

Jewish Educational Workshop
300 Welsh Rd.
Horsham, Pa. 19044
contact: Rabbi Steven Stroiman,
director
Informal programing

Jewish Reconstructionist
Foundation—Education Dept.
15 W. 86th St.
New York, N.Y. 10024
Reconstructionist objectives and
educational practices

Jewish Welfare Board
15 E. 26th St.
New York, N.Y. 10010
Camping and community center
programing

Melton Research Center
3080 Broadway
New York, N.Y. 10027
contact: Rabbi Joel Roth, director.
Inquiry-based methods, research, and
programs for Jewish education

Union of Orthodox Jewish Congregations
of America-Education Department
116 E. 27th St.
New York, N.Y. 10016
Adult education, youth groups

Local agencies

(Fed. refers to Federation Committees)

Alabama
Jewish Education Committee (Fed.)
3960 Montclaire Rd.
Birmingham, 35213

Arizona
Jewish Education Council (Fed.)
1718 W. Maryland Ave.
Phoenix, 85015

Jewish Education Committee (Fed.)
102 N. Plumer Ave.
Tucson, 85719

California
Bureau of Jewish Education of the
Jewish Federation Council of
Greater Los Angeles
590 N. Vermont Ave.
Los Angeles, 90004

Jewish Education Council for
Alameda and Contra Costa
Counties
3245 Sheffield Ave.
Oakland. 94602

Bureau of Jewish Education
4079 54th St.
San Diego, 92105

Bureau of Jewish Education of San
Francisco, Marin County, and the
Peninsula
639 14th St.
San Francisco, 94118

Colorado
Denver Jewish Education Committee
(Fed.)
100 Kittridge Bldg.
Denver, 80202

Connecticut
Bureau of Jewish Education
1184 Chapel St.
New Haven, 06511

Delaware
Wilmington Jewish Education
Committee (Fed.)
701 Shipley St.
Wilmington, 19801

District of Columbia
Board of Jewish Education of the
Jewish Community of Greater
Washington
1330 Massachusetts Ave. N.W.
Washington, 20005

Florida
Central Agency for Jewish Education
4200 Biscayne Blvd.
Miami, 33137
contact: Abraham Gittelson, associate
director

Georgia
Bureau of Jewish Education
1753 Peachtree Rd. N.E.
Atlanta, 30309

Bureau of Jewish Education
5111 Abercorn St.
Savannah, 31405

Illinois
Associated Talmud Torahs
2828 W. Pratt Blvd.
Chicago, 60645

Board of Jewish Education of
Metropolitan Chicago
72 E. 11th St.
Chicago, 60605

Indiana
Jewish Educational Assn.
6711 Hoover Rd.
Indianapolis, 46260

Iowa
Bureau of Jewish Education
924 Polk Blvd.
Des Moines, 50312

Jewish Federation of Sioux City
524 14th St.
Sioux City, 51105

Kentucky
Bureau of Jewish Education
3600 Dutchmans Lane
Louisville, 40205

Louisiana
Jewish Education Committee (Fed.)
211 Camp St.
New Orleans, 70130

Maine
Jewish Education Committee (Fed.)
341 Cumberland Ave.
Portland, 04101

Maryland
Board of Jewish Education
5800 Park Heights Ave.
Baltimore, 21215

Massachusetts
Bureau of Jewish Education
72 Franklin St.
Boston, 02110
contact: Louis Newman

United Hebrew Schools
979 Dickenson St.
Springfield, 01108

Michigan
United Hebrew Schools
21550 W. Twelve Mile Rd.
Southfield, 48076

Minnesota
Talmud Torah of Minneapolis
8200 W. 33rd St.
Minneapolis, 55426

Talmud Torah of Saint Paul
636 S. Mississippi River Blvd.
Saint Paul, 55116

Missouri
Jewish Education Council of Greater
Kansas City
7721 State Line, Suite 127
Kansas City, 64114

Central Agency for Jewish Education
225 S. Meramec, Suite 400
Saint Louis, 63105

Nebraska
Bureau of Jewish Education (Fed.)
101 N. 20th St.
Omaha, 68102

New Jersey
Jewish Education Committee of
Federation of Jewish Agencies
5321 Atlantic Ave.
Ventnor, 08406

Bureau of Jewish Education
2395 W. Marlton Pike
Cherry Hill, 08034

Jewish Education Association of
Metropolitan New Jersey
120 Halsted St.
East Orange, 07018

Board of Jewish Education
152 Van Houten St.
Paterson, 07505

New York
Bureau of Jewish Education
787 Delaware Ave.
Buffalo, 14209

Board of Jewish Education
426 W. 58th St.
New York, 10019

Bureau of Jewish Education
440 E. Main St.
Rochester, 14604

Ohio
Bureau of Jewish Education
1580 Summit Rd.
Cincinnati, 45237

Bureau of Jewish Education
2030 S. Taylor Rd.
Cleveland, 44118

Jewish Education Committee
United Jewish Fund and Council
1175 College Ave.
Columbus, 43209

Bureau of Jewish Education
184 Salem Ave.
Dayton, 45406

Board of Jewish Education
2727 Kenwood Blvd.
Toledo, 43606

Oklahoma
Jewish Education Committee (Fed.)
#200 Plaza Bldg.
8 E. 3rd St.
Tulsa, 74103

Oregon
Jewish Education Assn.
6651 S.W. Capitol Highway
Portland, 97219

Pennsylvania
Gratz College
10th St. and Tabor Rd.
Philadelphia, 19141
contact: Daniel Isaacman, President

Board of Jewish Education—Phila.
Branch, United Synagogue of
America
1701 Walnut St.
Philadelphia, 19103

United Hebrew Schools and Yeshivos
of Philadelphia
701 Byberry Rd.
Philadelphia, 19116

School of Advanced Jewish Studies
315 S. Bellefield Ave.
Pittsburgh, 15213

Hebrew Institute of Pittsburgh
6401-07 Forbes Ave.
Pittsburgh, 15217

Rhode Island
Bureau of Jewish Education
76 Dorrance St.
Providence, 02903

Tennessee
Jewish Education Study Committee
(Fed.)
5325 Lynnland Terr.
Chattanooga, 37411

Committee on Jewish Education
(Fed.)
81 Madison Bldg.
Suite 1200
Memphis, 38103

Jewish Education Services
3500 West End Ave.
Nashville, 37205

Texas
Commission for Jewish Education
5601 Braeswood
Houston, 77035

Utah
Jewish Education Committee (Fed.)
2416 E. 1700 South
Salt Lake City, 84108

Virginia
Bureau of Jewish Education (Fed.)
7300 Newport Ave.
Norfolk, 23505

Jewish Education Committee (Fed.)
5403 Monument Ave.
Richmond, 23226

Washington
Community Study Committee on
Jewish Education (Fed.)
Securities Bldg., Suite 606
Seattle, 98101

Jewish Education Committee (Fed.)
Box 8134 Manito Sta.
Spokane, 98103

Wisconsin
Board of Jewish Education
4515 West Good Hope Rd.
Milwaukee, 53223

Canada
Board of Jewish Education
22 Glen Park Ave.
Toronto, Ontario

Winnipeg Board of Jewish Education
370 Hargrave St., Room 200
Winnipeg, Manitoba

Teacher-Training Schools

California
University College of Jewish Studies
University of Judaism
6525 Sunset Blvd.
Los Angeles, 90028
Programs: BA, teacher certification,
teacher training for Jewish schools

Hebrew Union College–Jewish
Institute of Religion
3077 University Mall
Los Angeles, 90007
Teacher-training programs and
workshops in confluent education

Illinois
Spertus College of Judaica
618 S. Michigan Ave.
Chicago, 60625
Teacher-training programs combined
with Chicago universities, BHL,
BJS, BA degrees

Maryland
Baltimore Hebrew College
5800 Park Heights
Baltimore, 21215
Dual degree programs with
undergraduate and graduate
schools in the area, teacher
training, adult education center

Massachusetts
Hebrew College
43 Hawes St.
Brookline, 02146
Degree programs with local
universities, BHL, BJE, MHL,
MJE degrees, teacher training

Michigan
Midrasha–College of Jewish Studies
21550 W. Twelve Mile Rd.
Southfield, 48075
Hebrew and Judaic studies
departments, BHL, Hebrew
teachers certificate, BJE, associate
in Judaic studies programs with
local colleges

New York
Hebrew Union College–Jewish
Institute of Religion
School of Education
40 W. 68th St.
New York, 10023
MA in religious education for
principals, teacher-training courses
for BJE certification

Herzliah Hebrew Teachers Institute and Jewish Teachers Seminary and People's University
69 Bank St.
New York, 10014
BJL, DJL degrees, teachers diplomas, undergraduate and graduate programs in Yiddish, Hebrew, and Jewish social studies

Teachers Institute–Seminary College of Jewish Studies
Jewish Theological Seminary
3080 Broadway
New York 10027
contact: Sylvia Ettenberg, associate dean, Professor Joseph Lukinsky, Joe Reimer, Dr. Burton Cohen
Combined program with Columbia University, Teachers College, and other local schools, BA, BHL, teachers diploma, MA, MHL, DHL degree programs

Yeshiva University
500 W. 185th St.
New York, 10033

Schools

Erna Michael College of Hebraic Studies
Teacher training, BA, BS, Hebraic studies diploma, Hebrew teacher, diploma

Stern College for Women
253 Lexington Ave.
New York, 10016
BA, Hebrew teachers diploma, liberal arts college for women, Hebrew teacher-training program combined with Ferkauf Graduate School and Wurtzweiler Social Work School

Teachers Institute for Women
253 Lexington Ave.
New York, 10016
Training for intensive Hebraic-oriented Jewish schools, Hebrew teachers diploma, BS degree

Ferkauf Graduate School of Humanities and Social Sciences
Bernard Revel Graduate School
Dept. of Jewish Education
55 Fifth Ave.
New York, 10003
MS in Jewish elementary education, MS in Jewish secondary education, Ed.D degree in administration and supervision of Jewish education, BA, MA in Jewish studies, MA, MS, PhD in Jewish studies

Ohio

Cleveland College of Jewish Studies
2030 S. Taylor Rd.
Cleveland, 44118
Hebrew Department, Judaic Studies Department, combined programs with local colleges, BHL, MHL, Hebrew teachers diploma, BJS, Sunday school teacher degrees

Pennsylvania

Gratz College
10th St. and Tabor Rd.
Philadelphia, 19141
contact: Dr. Saul Wachs, Rabbi Howard Bogot
College, high school, adult education departments, teacher training, and advanced Jewish studies, BHL, MHL, BA degrees

Journals

The following is a list of some of the journals that can keep you informed about developments in Jewish education:

Adult Jewish Education
National Academy for Adult Jewish Studies
United Synagogue of America
155 Fifth Ave.
New York, N.Y. 10010

Alternatives in Religious Education
110 Holly Oak Circle
San Jose, Calif. 95120

Bitaon Chemed
Religious Zionists of America
200 Park Ave. South
New York, N.Y. 10008

Compass
Union of American Hebrew Congregations
838 Fifth Ave.
New York, N.Y. 10021

The Inkling
Alternatives in Religious Education
3945 S. Oneida St.
Denver, Colo. 80237

Jewish Education
National Council for Jewish Education and for Jewish Education
114 Fifth Ave.
New York, N.Y. 10011

Jewish Heritage
Bnai Brith Adult Education
1640 Rhode Island Ave. N.W.
Washington, D.C. 20036

The Jewish Parent
National Association of Hebrew Day Schools–Torah Umesorah
229 Park Ave. South
New York, N.Y. 10003

National Council for Torah Education Journal
Yeshiva University
500 W. 185th St.
New York, N.Y. 10033

The Pedagogic Reporter
American Association for Jewish Education
114 Fifth Ave.
New York, N.Y. 10011

Religious Education
Religious Education Association (interreligious association)
409 Prospect St.
New Haven, Conn. 16510

Sheviley Hahinukh
National Council for Jewish Education and American Association for Jewish Education
114 Fifth Ave.
New York, N.Y. 10011

Synagogue School
United Synagogue of America
155 Fifth Ave.
New York, N.Y. 10010

Your Child
United Synagogue of America
155 Fifth Ave.
New York, N.Y. 10010

Publishers

Glen Hoptman, of Ossining, N.Y. has compiled a list of some of the organizations and publishing houses that produce materials and books for Jewish education. One publisher, Behrman House, offers a wide variety of materials for all age groups. As part of its catalog, Behrman House includes a section on developmental levels and suggests a curriculum for the entire school. Many of the other publishing houses also offer school programs, based mostly on the material they themselves publish. With the knowledge that no one curriculum or approach is "God's law from Sinai," you will be able to carefully examine catalogs and choose materials appropriate to your needs.

Alternatives in Religious Education
1110 Holly Oak Circle
San Jose, Calif. 95120

American Association for Jewish Education
114 Fifth Ave.
New York, N.Y. 10011

American Zionist Youth Foundation
515 Park Ave.
New York, N.Y. 10022

Behrman House Inc.
1261 Broadway
New York, N.Y.10001

Board of Jewish Education (Jewish Education Press)
426 W. 58th St.
New York, N.Y. 10022

Bloch Publishing Co.
915 Broadway
New York, N.Y. 10010

Hebrew Publishing Co.
79 Delancey St.
New York, N.Y. 10002

Jewish Welfare Board
15 E. 26th St.
New York, N.Y. 10010

Keter Publishing House
P.O. Box 7145
Jerusalem, Israel
or
104 E. 40th St.
New York, N.Y. 10016

Ktav Publishing Co.
120 E. Broadway
New York, N.Y. 10002

Melton Research Center
3080 Broadway
New York, N.Y. 10027

Or and Kol
Government of Israel Trade Center
111 W. 40th St.
New York, N.Y. 10018

Media Judaica
1363 Fairfield Ave.
Bridgeport, Conn. 06605

Schocken Books
200 Madison Ave.
New York, N.Y. 10016

Union of American Hebrew Congregations
838 Fifth Ave.
New York, N.Y. 10021

United Synagogue Book Service
155 Fifth Ave.
New York, N.Y. 10010

Bibliography for the educated and educator

The following Bibliography, collected from a number of sources, consists of some of the books and articles available to the person interested in a specific area of Jewish education. I have also listed a few textbooks that I have enjoyed using. This list is by no means complete; it is only a sampling of the literature in each field. Although most of the books listed deal with Jewish education, much is to be gained from reading the secular literature in each area of interest as well.

Special education

American Association for Jewish Education. *Bibliography of Jewish Special Education Materials.* New York: American Association for Jewish Education, 1969.

Greenberg, Barbara. *Bibliography of Resources on Jewish Special Education.* New York: United Synagogue Commission on Jewish Education, 1973.

———, and Greenberg, Herbert. "The North Bellmore Experiment." *Synagogue School* 31 (June 1973).

Schwartz, Elliot. *A Manual for Organizing Classes for Jewish Special Children.* New York: United Synagogue Commission for Jewish Education, 1975.

———. "A Very Special Child." *Synagogue School* 31 (June 1973).

Stisken, Hershel M. *A Survey of Jewish Religious Programs for the Handicapped,* New York: American Association for Jewish Education, 1968.

Early childhood education

American Association for Jewish Education. "Jewish Education: The Early School Years." *Pedagogic Reporter* 24 (Fall 1972): 3.

Bessler, Helen. *Beresheet: A Kindergarten Guide.* New York: Union of American Hebrew Congregations, 1969.

Chanover, Hyman. *A Curriculum Guide for the Kindergarten.* New York: United Synagogue Book Service, 1960.

Chicago Board of Jewish Education. *Manual for the Nursery School and Kindergarten.* Chicago: Board of Jewish Education, n.d.

Feldman, Estelle, and Heckelman, Dvorah. *Learning Experiences in the Jewish Foundation Schools.* New York: Board of Jewish Education, 1971.

Galupkin, Esther. *A Kindergarten Curriculum for the Day School.* New York: Torah Umesorah, n.d.

Day school education

American Association for Jewish Education. "New Approaches in Day School Education." *Pedagogic Reporter* 23, no. 3 (March 1972).

Berman, S. J. et al. "The Jewish Day School: A Symposium." *Tradition* 13 (Summer 1972).

Beth Am Synagogue. *The Beth Am Experiment.* Miami: Beth Am Synagogue, n.d.

Dessler, N. W. *Suggested Curriculum for the Day School.* New York: Torah Umesorah, n.d.

Gordis, Robert. *The Day School and the Public School: A Strategy for Jewish Survival Today.* New York: American Jewish Congress, n.d.

Malzberg, Amy. *Jewish Day Schools in the United States.* New York: American Jewish Committee, n.d.

Singer, David. "The Growth of the Day School Movement." *Commentary* 56 (August 1973).

Torah Umesorah. *Directory of Day Schools in the United States and Canada.* New York: Torah Umesorah, n.d.

Afternoon school education

Ackerman, Walter. *An Analysis of Selected Courses of Study of Conservative Congregational Schools.* New York: Melton Research Center, 1969.

Eisenberg, Azriel. *A Curriculum for the Small Jewish Religious School.* New York: United Synagogue of America, n.d.

Lieber, David. "The Conservative Congregational School." *Conservative Judaism* 27 (Summer 1973).

Ruffman, Louis L. *Curriculum Outline for the Congregational School.* New York: United Synagogue of America, 1959.

Spiro, Jack. "Toward a Conceptual Framework for Reform Jewish Education." *Compass*, January-February 1971.

Stern, Jay. "The Afternoon Jewish School." *Jewish Spectator,* Spring 1975.

High school education

Kurzband, Toby K. *The Senior High School in Reform Jewish Religious Schools.* New York: Union of American Hebrew Congregations, 1962.

United Synagogue Commission on Jewish Education. *Manual for a Comprehensive Jewish High School.* New York: United Synagogue of America, 1973.

Jewish studies in public schools

Anti-Defamation League. *Teaching about Jews and Judaism: Bibliographic and Audio-Visual Aids.* New York: Anti-Defamation League, 1974.

Ecumenical Study Commission on Religion in Public Schools. "Religion and the Public School Curriculum." *Religious Education*, no. 68, pt. 2, July/August 1972.

Hochhauser, J. "Teaching Jewish Literature in a Public High School." *Jewish Digest*, no. 18, July 1973.

Scult, Melvin. "Jewish Studies in the Public School: Opportunity or Danger?" *Reconstructionist*, no. 38, October 1972.

Soloff, Emily. "Jewish Education in Secular Schools." *Israel*, September 1972.

Adult education

Beckerman, Marvin. "Adult Jewish Education: Present and Future Directions." *Religious Education* 8 (January/February 1973).

Bnai Brith Hillel Foundations. *Jewish Studies in American Colleges and Universities.* Washington, D.C.: Bnai Brith Hillel Foundations, 1972.

Greenberg, S. "Lifetime Education as Conceived and Practiced in the Jewish Tradition." *Religious Education*, June 1973.

National Council on Adult Jewish Education. *Guide to Select Adult Jewish Educational Materials.* New York: American Association for Jewish Education, 1969.

Neusner, Jacob. "Departments of Religious Studies and Contemporary Jewish Studies." *American Jewish Historical Quarterly* 63 (June 1974).

———. "Graduate Jewish Studies." *Jewish Spectator* 39 (Spring 1974).

Schwartzman, Sylvan D. "Parent Education: The Critical Dimensions." *Journal of the Central Conference of American Rabbis* 19 (Autumn 1972).

Sklare, Marshall. "Problems in the Teaching of Contemporary Jewish Studies." *American Jewish Historical Quarterly* 63 (June 1974).

Teacher training

Dushkin, A. M. *A Comprehensive Study of the Jewish Teacher Training Schools in the Diaspora.* Jerusalem: Hebrew University, 1971.

Gorr, Alan. "Simulations for the Training of Jewish Educators." *Synagogue School* 32, no. 1-2 (Winter 1973–74).

Janowsky, Oscar. *The Education of American Jewish Teachers.* Boston: Beacon Press, 1967.

Schiff, Alvin et al. "New Models in Preparing Personnel for Jewish Education." *Jewish Education* 43, no. 3 (Fall 1974).

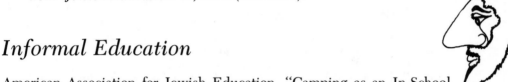

Informal Education

American Association for Jewish Education. "Camping as an In-School Experience." *Pedagogic Reporter* 26, no. 3 (Spring 1975).

Fein, Leonard; Reisman, Bernard; et al. *Reform Is a Verb.* New York: Union of American Hebrew Congregations, n.d.

Friedman (Marcus), Audrey. *The Temple Micah Conference Plan.* New York: Union of American Hebrew Congregations, 1969.

Gerard, Bert S. *The Junior High School Youth Group.* New York: Union of American Hebrew Congregations, n.d.

Jewish Welfare Board. *Directory of Jewish Resident Summer Camps.* New York, National Jewish Welfare Board, 1973–74.

Novak, William. "Notes on Summer Camp: Some Reflections on the Ramah Dream." *Response*, Winter 1971–72.

Reisman, Bernard. *Serving Jewish Families in Camp Settings.* New York: Institute for Jewish Life, 1973.

Schoolman, Leonard. *Religious School Camp Weekend Manual.* New York: Union of American Hebrew Congregations, 1970.

United Synagogue Youth Commission. *Summer Activities Manual.* New York: United Synagogue Youth, 1972.

Warshaw, E. "The School as Community." *Synagogue School* 30, no. 3–4 (Summer 1972).

Weber, Eli. *Program Guide for the Jewish Camp.* New York: American Zionist Youth Foundation, n.d.

Israel

Chazan, Barry. "Out of Zion, Part 3: Teaching Israel in the 70's." *Journal of the Central Conference of American Rabbis* 20 (Winter 1973).

Greenberg, S. "The Role of Israel in American Jewish Education." *Jewish Education* 42 (Spring 1973).

Landress, Sylvia. *Selected Books on Israel.* New York: American Zionist Youth Foundation, n.d.

Levin, Schlomo. "Israel and Jewish Education in America." *Jewish Education* 43, no. 3 (Fall 1974).

Romirowsky, Leah. *Unit on Israel.* Chicago: Board of Jewish Education, 1969.

Sachuk, Levi. *Ten Lesson Plans on Israel.* New York: Department of Edu-

cation and Culture, World Zionist Organization, 1973.

Spotts, L. H. "Instructional Materials about and from Israel." *Jewish Education* 42 (Spring 1973).

Torah Education Department. *Curriculum on Israel for Day Schools.* New York: Torah Education Department, World Zionist Organization, n.d.

Union of American Hebrew Congregations. *Israel: Course Syllabus for Teachers and Adults.* New York: Union of American Hebrew Congregations, n.d.

Open education and individualization

American Association for Jewish Education. *To Everything There Is a Time.* New York: American Association for Jewish Education, 1975.

————. *Opening the Schools and Individualizing Instruction.* New York: American Association for Jewish Education, 1973.

Koller, Cherie. "A Time for Joy." *Response* 5, no. 3 (Winter 1971–72).

Creativity

Congregation Beth Yeshurun. *Competency-Based Instruction in Jewish Education.* Houston: Beth Yeshurun, n.d.

Cutter, William, and Dauber, Jack. *Confluent Education in the Jewish Setting.* Los Angeles: Hebrew Union College–Jewish Institute of Religion, 1971.

Gerard, Bert. "Religious Institutions II—The Hidden Agenda in Religious Education." *Religious Education* 69 (March/April 1974).

Lister, L. "Encounter, Inquiry, and Discovery in Jewish Education." *Religious Education* 67 (November/December 1972).

Ravitch, Diane. "Moral Education and the Schools." *Commentary* 56 (September 1973).

Rephun, Schlomo. *Grouping for Instruction.* New York: Torah Umesorah, 1969.

Wachs, Saul. "Affective Learning and the Jewish Tradition." *Jewish Education* 43 (Spring 1974).

History

Axelroth, Dorothy G. *A Course Syllabus on Ancient Jewish History.* New York: Union of American Hebrew Congregations, 1971.

Butwin, Frances, and Blecher, Arthur. *The Jews of America.* New York: Behrman House, 1973.

Chazan, Robert, and Raphael, Marc Lee. *Modern Jewish History: A Source Reader.* New York: Schocken Books, 1974.

Efron, Benjamin, and Chanover, Hyman. *Jewish Civics Source Book.* New York: American Association for Jewish Education, 1975.

Eisenberg, Azriel, and Segal, Abraham. *Readings in the Teaching of Jewish History.* New York: Jewish Education Committee, 1956.

Feldman, E. "Jewish History and American Education." *Judaism* 21 (Fall 1972).

Fishbein, Irwin H. *Basic Themes in Jewish History.* New York: Union of American Hebrew Congregations, 1968.

Lubetski, Meir, and Lubetski, Edith. *Writings on Jewish History.* New York: American Jewish Committee, 1974.

Marcus, Jacob R. *An Index to Scientific Articles on American Jewish History.* Cincinnati: American Jewish Archives, 1971.

Ruderman, Jerome. *Jews in American History,* New York: Ktav, 1974.

Prayer

Eisenberg, Azriel. *Readings in the Teaching of Prayer and Siddur.* New York: Jewish Education Committee, 1964.

Fahs, Sophie L. *Worshipping Together with Questioning Minds.* Boston: Beacon Press, 1965.

Grishaver, Joel Lurie. *Shema Is for Real—Teacher's Guide.* Chicago: Olin-Sang-Ruby-Union Institute of the U.A.H.C., n.d.

Jacobson, Burt. *The Teaching of the Traditional Liturgy.* New York: Melton Research Center, 1971.

Matt, H. J. "The Goals of Teaching Jewish Prayer." *Synagogue School* 31 (Summer 1973).

Rabinowitz, C. D. *A Teacher's Guide for the Teaching of Prayer* (in Hebrew). New York: Torah Umesorah, n.d.

Rossel, Seymour. *When a Jew Prays* (plus teacher's guide). New York: Behrman House, 1973.

Wachs, Saul. *An Application of Inquiry-Teaching to the Siddur.* New York: Melton Research Center, n.d.

Bible

Bial, Morrison, and Simon, Solomon. *The Rabbi's Bible.* New York: Behrman House, 1966.

Greenberg, Moshe. "On Teaching the Bible in Religious Schools." In *Modern Jewish Educational Thought,* Weinstein and Yizhar, eds. Chicago: College of Jewish Studies, 1964.

———. *Understanding Exodus.* New York: Behrman House, 1969.

Hadassah Education Department. Leaders' guides (for the books of the Bible). New York: Hadassah Education Department.

Jacobs, Louis. *Jewish Biblical Exegesis.* New York: Behrman House, 1973.

Leibowitz, Nehama. *Studies in the Weekly Sidrah.* Jerusalem: Torah Education Department, World Zionist Organization, 1954–61.

Miller, Donald E.; Snyder, Grayden F.; and Neff, Robert W. *Using Biblical Simulations.* Valley Forge, Pa.: Judson Press, n.d.

Newman, Louis. *Genesis: The Student's Guide* (plus teacher's guide). New York: United Synagogue Commission on Jewish Education, 1967.

Newman, Shirley. *A Child's Introduction to the Torah.* New York: Behrman House, 1972. (Teacher's guide also available.)

———. *A Child's Introduction to the Early Prophets.* New York: Behrman House, 1975. (Teacher's guide also available.)

Rabinowitz, C. D. *A Teacher's Guide and Syllabus for the Teaching of the Weekly Haftarah* (in Hebrew). New York: Torah Umesorah, n.d.

———. *A Teacher's Guide for the Teaching of Tanach* (in Hebrew). New York: Torah Umesorah, n.d.

————. *A Teacher's Guide to Difficult Areas in Chumash and Rashi* (in Hebrew). New York: Torah Umesorah, n.d.

Sarna, Nahum. *Understanding Genesis*. New York: Schocken, 1970.

Spotts, Leon H. *The Wisdom Literature of the Bible*. New York: Union of American Hebrew Congregations, 1967.

Hebrew

Dorph, Sheldon. *Hebrew Language Program for the High School*. Los Angeles: Board of Jewish Education, 1975.

Ducoff, Helen. *How to Read Hebrew (and Love It!)*. San Francisco: Jewish Education Society, 1973.

Educational Materials Corporation. *Biyad Halashon Language Program*. Saint Paul: Educational Materials Corporation, n.d.

Eisenberg, Azriel. *Readings in the Teaching of Hebrew*. New York: Board of Jewish Education, 1961.

Kohn, Rebekah J. *A Practical Guide for Teaching Hebrew*. New York: Board of Jewish Education, 1967.

Melton Research Center. *Experimental Biblical Hebrew Language Program*. New York: Melton Research Center, 1975.

Holidays

American Zionist Youth Foundation. Manuals for Sukkot, Hanukkah, Tu Bishvat, Purim, Pesah, Yom Haatzmaut, Tisha B'Av, Shabbat. New York: American Zionist Youth Foundation, 1974.

Goodman, Philip. *Sabbath—Program Material for the Jewish Community Centers*. New York: Jewish Welfare Board, 1975.

Goodman, Robert. *A Guide to the Teaching of Holidays and Festivals*. Milwaukee: Board of Jewish Education, n.d.

Mayanoth: Jewish Teachers Companion—The Festivals, General Jewish Subjects, Shavuoth, Yom Haatzmaut (in Hebrew). New York: World Zionist Organization, n.d.

Rocky Mountain Curriculum Project No. III: *There Is a Season: A Values Approach to Jewish Holidays*. Denver: Alternatives in Religious Education, n.d.

General readings in Jewish education

Ackerman, Walter. "Jewish Education—For What?" *American Jewish Yearbook*, vol. 70. Philadelphia: Jewish Publication Society, 1969.

————. "The Present Moment in Jewish Education." *Midstream*, December 1972.

American Jewish Committee. *Colloquium for Jewish Education*. New York: American Jewish Committee, 1971.

American Jewish Year Books, published annually by the American Jewish Committee and the Jewish Publication Society.

Arian, Shraga. "An Agenda of Questions for Jewish Education." *Synagogue School* 30, no. 1–2 (Fall 1971).

Birnbaum, Philip. *A Book of Jewish Concepts*. New York: Hebrew Publishing Co., 1975.

Brickman, W. W. "Selected Bibliography of Jewish Education in Historical and International Perspective." *Jewish Education* 41 (Fall 1972).

Brodie, Deborah. *Selected Jewish Books*. New York: Jewish Welfare Board, 1975.

Chazan, Barry. " 'Indoctrination' and Religious Education." *Religious Education* 67 (July/August 1972).

Cohen, Jack. *Jewish Education in Democratic Society*. New York: Reconstructionist Press, 1964.

Fox, Seymour. "A Prolegomenon to a Philosophy of Jewish Education." Available from the Department of Education, Hebrew University, Jerusalem, Israel.

Goldman, Ronald. *Religious Thinking from Childhood to Adolescence.* New York, Seabury Press, n.d.

Goodman, Hannah. *Aspects of Jewish Life.* New York, National Jewish Welfare Board, 1974.

Jewish Book Council of America. *A Book List for the Jewish Child.* New York: National Jewish Welfare Board, 1971.

Jewish Education Directory. New York: American Association for Jewish Education, 1974.

Kaunfer, Marcia. *An Annotated Bibliography of Jewish Textbooks.* New York: Melton Research Center, 1975.

National Commission on Torah Education. *The Jewish Educational Scene—A Critical Appraisal.* New York: National Commission on Torah Education, 1972.

Pilch, Judah, and Ben-Horin, Meir. *Judaism and the Jewish School.* New York: Bloch, 1966.

Schiff, Alvin. "Funding Jewish Education—Whose Responsibility?" *Jewish Education* 42 (Summer 1973).

Segal, Judith. *An Annotated Bibliography of General Juvenile Literature to Be Used within the Jewish Educational Curriculum.* New York: Melton Research Center, n.d.

United Synagogue Commission on Jewish Education. *Bibliography of Reference and Methodological Materials for the Jewish Teacher.* New York: United Synagogue, 1973.

Weinstein, David, and Yizhar, Michael, eds. *Modern Jewish Educational Thought.* Chicago: College of Jewish Studies, 1964.

World Zionist Organization. *Jewish Education in the Diaspora.* Jerusalem: World Zionist Organization, 1971.

Zibbell, Charles. "Federations, Synagogues and Jewish Education in the 70's." *Jewish Education* 43, no. 3 (Fall 1974).

Catalogs and programing materials

The following boards, organizations, etc. have a wealth of material available. It is well worth writing to them for their catalogs. Check also throughout this chapter for additional places to contact for material.

American Association for Jewish Education. Annual roundups of new programs in Jewish education. New York: American Association for Jewish Education.

American Zionist Organization Youth Foundation. Catalogs of Israel, youth, and holiday programs. New York: American Zionist Youth Foundation.

Bnai Brith. Sabbath and holiday programing material. Washington: Bnai Brith Education Department.

Board of Jewish Education. Early Childhood Education Library—books on holidays, simple stories in Hebrew. New York: Board of Jewish Education.

National Conference of Synagogue Youth. Holiday programing material for youth groups. New York: National Conference of Synagogue Youth.

Rocky Mountain Curriculum Planning Workshops. Catalog of programs and materials for the teacher and the classroom. Denver: Alternatives for Religious Education.

Union of American Hebrew Congregations. Programing material for schools and youth groups; many excellent textbooks. New York: Union of American Hebrew Congregations.

United Synagogue of America. Programing material for adult education, youth groups (Atid, United Synagogue Youth, Leaders Training Fellowship), and schools. New York: United Synagogue of America.

World Zionist Organization. Books on Israel and Hebrew textbooks for all ages, as well as programing material. New York: World Zionist Organization.

"It seems to me . . . that the East European yeshivah is in many ways a more profound example of an open type of education, one that is more appropriate for our purpose, than those which have been uncritically adopted from the general field" (Joseph Lukinsky).

"What is needed is the possiblity of truly joint efforts by scholars, educators, and students" (Joseph Lukinsky).

"That future [of a people] cannot be sacrificed to fads and fashions, to that which is inauthentic" (Joseph Lukinsky).

"We must always remember the basic imperative of education: the obligation to be humane" (Morris Sorin).

"The problem is that we test children in subjects thay haven't necessarily studied fully, and don't evaluate properly the areas which they have worked in" (Fradle Freidenreich).

"The 'grand questions' of Jewish education are indeed important concerns of contemporary Jewish educational thought. But the real contribution of contemporary philosophy of Jewish education lies not in the answering of the grand questions, but in enabling us to ask and understand them better" (Barry Chazan).

"We must try to give new validity to ethnic attachment, meaning to Jewish peoplehood. . . . We must be able to convince our children that we hold these commitments not because we have simply accepted them from our past, or because they serve our interests, but because they do indeed provide the best pattern to organize our lives on earth" (Nathan Glazer, quoted by Edward T. Sandrow).

"Too often our cognitive materials do not reflect our concern to develop morally viable human beings" (Sidney Selig and Rabbi Gerald Teller).

"It is almost as though Jewish education and Jewish educators have forgotten the problem of ends or goals. Or possibly they have assumed that the ends are given and therefore need not be reexamined. . . . There have been many people who have documented the extent to which Jewish education is aimless" (Seymour Fox).

if dreams came true there'd be . . .

a unified Jewish community . . . enough money to provide for expert professional materials . . . one central resource for secular and Jewish educational materials . . . Jewish boarding schools . . . havurot instead of classrooms . . . havurot instead of synagogues . . . public schools coordinated with Jewish studies programs . . . a well-worked-out philosophy of Jewish education . . .

Hebrew schools that kids want to come to . . . year-round family education in every community . . . carpools as classrooms — cassettes in every car . . . Jewish theater as an educational tool . . . camping as part of an overall program . . . evaluations of programs and sharing of resources . . .

"Jewish education is an unrewarding profession financially and in terms of status. It is also part-time work. The result of this is that only the very dedicated or the very incompetent would choose to enter the field" (Neal Kaunfer).

"But I don't want to go to Hebrew school! Why do I have to be in the dumb class?"
   "Because I can only carpool on Mondays and Wednesdays."

"The trouble with too much education is that it is all compromise oriented and based on someone else's experience—not the learner's" (Ephraim Warshaw).

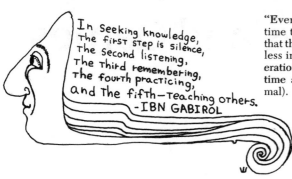

In Seeking knowledge,
The first step is silence,
The second listening,
The third remembering,
The fourth practicing,
and the fifth—Teaching others.
—IBN GABIROL

"Even if a method were found at one time to be fruitful, it is quite possible that this same method would be worthless in teaching the members of a generation far removed from that age in time and character" (Nahman Krochmal).

"The actual effect of a Jewish education as it is conducted at present is to leave the child in a state of mental confusion. Either he intuitively realizes that he is not being taught what the teacher actually believes, or he inwardly revolts at the demand upon his credulity" (Mordecai Kaplan).

"Judaism and Jewish education never had, nor do they now have, the sharp distinction between religion and ethnicity implicit in contemporary American language and life" (Barry Chazan).

Learning
requires a talent for sitting.
—Yiddish Proverb—Leo Rosten

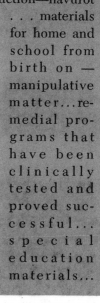

no politics or jealousy influencing Jewish education... harmony between synagogue and school... harmony between school and home... non-indoctrination of Judaism — room for freedom of thought, feeling, and action... Jewish day care centers... good people in the field...

curricular material coordinated from nursery school through adult education... goals that are created with the child's developmental level in mind... peer group instruction—havurot psychological services in all Jewish schools... self-study programs... schools on wheels... cooperation with Christian educators... toys, books, games for every developmental level...

... materials for home and school from birth on — manipulative matter... remedial programs that have been clinically tested and proved successful... special education materials...

"When judged by even the least demanding standard of what it means to be an educated Jew, it is hard to avoid the feeling that the academic aspirations of the one-day-a-week school are either a colossal joke or an act of cynical pretentiousness" (Walter Ackerman).

"At each level educational activity has an integrity of its own, but its full meaning is achieved only when it has an integral relationship to what came before and what will come after" (Walter Ackerman).

"Who runs the school is less important than how it is run" (Walter Ackerman).

"The belief that the Jewish school must be unique may be chimerical, but the development of this quality surely is worth a try!" (Walter Ackerman).

"Schools are in the knowledge business and it is by this alone that they should be judged" (Jay Stern).

"The average Hebrew afternoon school pupils, by Bar/Bat Mitzvah, have spent—if they attended a good Jewish school—the same number of hours in Hebrew school as in the first grade of public school" (Jay Stern).

"Only rarely does a tradition specify its ideal of the educated man explicitly enough for educational purposes. Instead, it is implied in stated ideals and approved conditions of the state, the society, the family, the hero, the person, and the relations of men to each other and to God" (Joseph Schwab).

"No matter what its structure or orientation, the Jewish school conceives its primary function to be the transmission of knowledge of the sacred texts" (Walter Ackerman).

Jewish Toys and Games

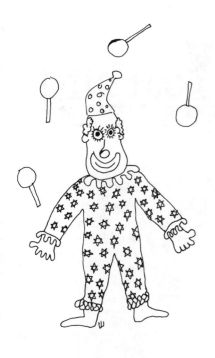

It is important that Jewish parents give their children toys that will help them form positive, realistic, exciting images about their Jewish heritage. It is not necessary for the children to be hit over the head with these concepts, nor do they have to be particularly religious. It is only necessary that the ideas be clear, simple, and relevant.

In a world of slick advertising, an awakening sense of aesthetics should prompt Jewish parents to pay attention to the aesthetic and tactile qualities of the toys they buy for their children. It is extremely important that Jewish children have good Jewish toys to play with. We are a philosophical island in an alien culture, constantly inundated with images, traditions, sights, sounds, smells, and concepts that have nothing whatever to do with our own heritage. Or with our philosophies. Our children are particularly vulnerable to these outside images, because they are in the process of formulating their own perception of reality. They are forming a collection of images in their subconscious minds that will have a profound effect on their assimilation of future knowledge. The images they absorb as children form the foundation of the attitudes they will have as adults.

In particular, children develop attitudes toward the things around them through sight, sound, touch, smell, and taste. These sense perceptions are far more persuasive and far more memorable than anything their parents or teachers tell them. This is why playtime is really a very powerful source of learning.

Making toys yourself

All you have to provide is the Jewish concepts. You can even get help in coming up with Jewish ideas from your own rabbi.

The more you can involve your children in the process of planning and making their own toys, the more they'll get out of them. If you can show them how to do it and then turn them loose, they will not only get profound satisfaction from their accomplishment, they will also develop a rewarding attachment to the toy. They will love the toy because it is theirs—in the fullest sense possible, that of creation. And if you help them just the right amount, they will develop a very keen understanding of the concept embodied in the object.

Use wood, Plexiglas, Masonite, metal, leather, or anything else that looks exactly like what it is. Avoid anything that isn't what it looks like.

Children detect phoniness very quickly. An illusion, after all, is only an illusion. And when we're talking about Jewish toys and Jewish concepts, we're talking about the real thing. So use real materials. Use your imagination. And try to incorporate some information into the process. (See "Other Game Sources" for books on toy making.)

As an example of what's possible, you can simply cut out a picture of an important Jewish event, glue it to a piece of wood, and then cut it into pieces with a jigsaw to make a simple puzzle. You should sand the edges smooth after cutting, give each piece a thin coat of polyurethane varnish, and let it dry thoroughly before reassembling the pieces. It will be practically indestructible. Be sure you explain the story to your children when you present the puzzle.

You can also make simple models of things like Noah's ark, the Tabernacle, etc. The important thing is that you use good materials and keep the design simple. Always tell the story and explain what it means.

Very effective and very easy techniques for making toys and educational materials already exist. Ideas from the secular market can be adapted directly to the making of Jewish toys and Jewish educational materials. Here's a sample list of some very good books on the subject:

1. *How to Parent* by Dr. Fitzhugh Dodson (Los Angeles: Nash Publishing). Get this book at the library and read Appendix A, "Toys and Play Equipment for Children of Different Ages and Stages." Also see Appendix B, "Free and Inexpensive Children's Toys from A to Z."

2. *Teaching Montessori in the Home* by Elizabeth G. Hainstock. There are two of these books—"The Pre-School Years" and "The School Years." They are loaded with ideas for toys, games, and learning materials that can be transformed instantly into *Jewish* toys, games, and learning materials.

3. *I Saw a Purple Cow and 100 Other Recipes for Learning* by Ann Cole (Boston: Little, Brown). This book has a good resource list as well as ideas for toys and games.

4. *The Hanukkah Book* by Mae Shafter Rockland (New York: Schocken, 1975). Shows you how to make toys for Hanukkah.

This is just an idea of what's available. Any major bookstore will have shelves overflowing with do-it-yourself books on toys, games, and educational materials.

materials
3/16" holes (made with 3/16 drill)
5/32" hard braided cotton cord
3/8" thick hardwood

directions
help elijah climb to heaven. Pull alternately on one cord then the other

1. LET THERE BE LIGHT
2.
3.
4.
5.
6.
7. ...AND HE RESTED.

Torah Toys: *a new resource*

In 1975 a group of us who had been trying to find creative Jewish toys for our kids became very concerned about the lack of high quality resources. The typical Jewish toy in America looked to us as if it had been designed on the back of a paper napkin by a Jewish shmattah merchant and then sublet to a factory in Hong Kong. So we got together out of mutual desperation and began to develop toys that would communicate Jewish concepts to children by using simple bold graphics, the best available materials, and the most up-to-date design techniques. By combining our various talents, we gradually began to create toys that we felt were successful in bringing Jewish ideas to our children in ways that were alive, honest, and true.

In the good old American tradition, we decided to create a company so that others who shared our needs could benefit from our projects. And so Torah Toys, Inc., was born.

Below are some examples of the kinds of toys we've been producing. (If you drop us a line at:

Torah Toys
1570 E. Edinger Ave.
Santa Ana, Calif. 92705

Incidentally, we include an explanation of the design with everything we make. We urge you too to write out an explanation of every toy you make for your children. Hand print it, using simple words, and include only the major issues—just enough so that the child will understand what s/he's looking at and have some idea of what the visual image means.

we'll send you a complete catalog of our work.) We believe that many of the types of things we do are replicable if you take a good look at how they're put together.

1. *Puzzles:* There's no doubt about it, children like to do puzzles. So the first group of designs that we worked out were all puzzles that could easily be done by the preschool child. The Symbolic Shabbat Puzzle, the Mother and Children Shabbat Puzzle, and the Days of Creation Puzzle all link up with basic Jewish concepts in designs that children find colorful and appealing.

The two Shabbat design puzzles are 12″ x 12″ and made of ⅜″ wood fiberboard backed with Masonite. They are replicable quite easily by using the directions we included earlier for creating a puzzle from a picture. Instead of pasting on the picture, however, you would cut a piece of fiberboard or other stable material to the proper size, sand and prime the surface, and paint a picture over the primer. Jigsaw out the pieces in simple shapes, trying not to create sharp corners or long, thin pieces. You can either stop here or go one step further. If you want to back the puzzle with Masonite or other thin, hard material, you have to leave a border around the puzzle when you jigsaw out the pieces. Glue the border to the backing and then the pieces will fit inside. The advantage of the backing is that the puzzle does not require a flat surface; it can be worked on the child's lap—or anyplace else.

The Days of Creation Puzzle is a 9″ x 12″ puzzle die-cut from hardwood laminate. The design is preprinted on paper and laminated to the wood. To make this yourself you would use the directions for creating a puzzle out of a picture.

2. *Place mats:* We took one of our puzzle design ideas—the Daily Blessings Puzzle—made it available as a place mat as well as a puzzle. We've found this design ideal for beginning to teach children about the holiness of food and the blessings to be said over various foods—and keeping the place mat available on the table reinforces the learning process.

To make your own Jewish place mats, laminate any design printed on paper between two pieces of 5-mil plastic sheets. Any hobby shop can tell you where to get the plastic laminating material.

3. *Shabbat in a sack:* We also designed detailed miniatures of the basic Shabbat objects, handlathed out of natural birch. This is not easy to do—unless you're really good with a lathe, you're better off buying these ready-made. We recommend that you get each child his/her own set. Stanley made the mistake of giving his two girls one set to share and regretted it instantly. Everybody wants to play the leading role.

Other game sources

Games are a bit harder to create yourself, yet here again there are very few Jewish games around that are interesting and inexpensive. The following are some of the possibilities we've turned up:

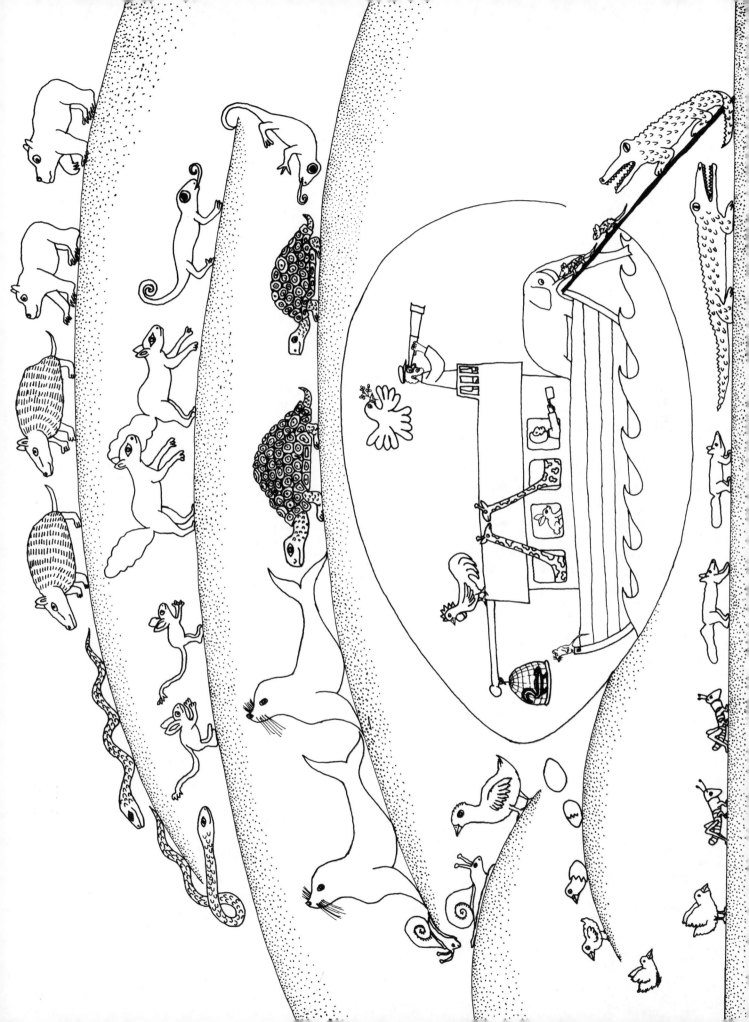

Directions
① Trace plan for cutting
② cut page out – color
③ paste to ¼ plywood
        or masonite
④ paste cutting plan to back
        of wood c̄ Rubber cement
⑤ cut puzzle apart

1. The Scrabble people make a complete Scrabble set in Hebrew, which sells for about $5. If you have trouble finding it, you can write directly to the manufacturer:

Selchow & Righter Co.
Bay Shore, N.J. 11706

2. Marcia Kaunfer has been designing games for years. Some of her games have been produced by

American Association for Jewish Education
114 Fifth Ave.
New York, N.Y. 10010

Pull the string to make him Daven

and can be purchased from them. These include Proposal—a simulation game about the issues of boundaries and Arab refugees in the Arab-Israeli conflict. The game is being revised in light of Israel's withdrawal from the Suez Canal. It is available with a student's guide and a teacher's guide— they are 50¢ each.

She has also developed a Jerusalem game that deals with the internationalization of Jerusalem and a game about Arab propaganda in America. Neither of these games has been published as yet but should be available from the American Association for Jewish Education by the time this *Catalog* is out.

3. Another Marcia Kaunfer game, called Dilemma, has been produced by Behrman House. It deals with the problems of allocation of funds to local agencies and has been mistakenly called the "Establishment Game." The catch with the game is the price—$25, although it is occasionally put on sale for $9.95. It's available from

Behrman House
1261 Broadway
New York 10002

4. **The Board of Jewish Education of New York**
426 W. 58th St.
New York, N.Y. 10019

has published a Hebrew card game called Kartison le-Shabbat. Simple Hebrew is used and it is suitable for elementary age students. It costs $2.95.

5. Alternatives in Religious Education has published a game called the Holocaust Game, which uses a game format to teach children about the Holocaust. It costs $8 and is available from

Alternatives in Religious Education
1110 Holly Oak Circle
San Jose, Calif. 95120

6. **The Israel Educational Materials and Games Center**
c/o Israel Trade Center
111 W. 40th St.
New York, N.Y. 10018

is the largest distributor of Israeli games in America. They have hundreds of games, some of which are really delightful.

7. **Ktav Publishing Co.**
120 E. Broadway
New York, N.Y. 10002

is the largest American publisher of Jewish toys. These range from puzzles and games to masks and toys. The quality varies greatly from poor Jewish adaptations of secular toys to toys of some ingenuity and interest. Catalogs available.

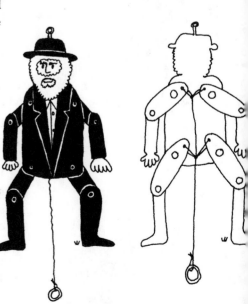

The dancing Hasid

Teaching the Holocaust to Children

Judaism is a religion that stresses remembrance—zakhor. We are admonished in the Bible to "remember Amalek," and along with Amalek goes Haman, Titus, and all those who persecuted and murdered Jews. If for no other reason, the Holocaust should be taught—because we are a people of memory and because the Holocaust is an event so mythic in proportion that it will be many generations before we can assimilate and merge it into our Jewish soul consciousness. The danger will be, of course, that those younger Jews who have no direct or indirect line to the event will not allow themselves to be touched by it. We *must*—we have the obligation to—make them understand, to make them remember. The Holocaust is something that did happen—it happened in our lifetime, so to speak, and in the lifetime of the children, because there are still parents and grandparents who can talk about it. It is a catastrophic event that has no parallel. Many writers have said: "We are all survivors." This could well be a beginning for you: "What does that mean, 'We are all survivors'? We weren't even born—and yet . . ."

I'm not even sure if the term teaching should be used in connection with the Holocaust. Perhaps children should be "exposed," since the subject is not like mathematics, where one plus one equals two; or physics, where there are certain positive laws; or historical events, which we can evaluate from the safety of time; or even literature, where we can put words in the author's mouth and ideas into his/her work—even ideas of which s/he had no notion. No matter how much you put together and how many times you go over it, conclusions are not—*cannot*—be reached about the Holocaust. Let us say, then, that we will expose the children—expose them to facts, to resources, visual, oral, and written, and hope that their conclusions, if there are conclusions, will activate them now and in the future on crucial issues that may threaten them as Jews, their freedom, the existence of Israel, or the human race. And we can hope that their study will lead them closer to the heart of the issue—what *does* it mean, after all, to be a Jew? What does the Holocaust have to say to us about ourselves?

We simply cannot do justice to the subject in one day or any short period of time, for we would then only be appealing to the students on a purely emotional level rather than on an intellectual one that seeks to

understand the history, culture, and psychology of the event. It must be a subject incorporated into the curriculum of every school and taught to every student on his/her own level: third- and fourth-graders can absorb some of what happened, fifth- and sixth-graders certainly can understand and respond. With the older children it is easier to get the information across, but sometimes their attitudes and skepticism are hard for the teacher to cope with. But I believe that if it is handled with patience and honesty, students will learn about the subject and become absorbed in it. A good way to begin with the junior high and high school age youth is to have them write an essay on "Why is it important to remember the Holocaust?" or, "What do I know about the Holocaust?" This will give the teacher an idea of just how much the children know and where s/he must begin.

Priorities

The priorities in teaching this subject ought to be:

1. *Knowledge of the period*: You can begin before 1933 if you have time. If not, start briefly with 1933, with Hitler's life, with the Nuremberg Laws, then go on to Kristallnacht, the attack on Poland, etc. A day school in Cleveland, Ohio, began with a theme they had just studied in Bialik, "We are the last generation of slaves and the first generation of free men." It fit in beautifully with Passover, the Holocaust, Yom Haatzmaut—Israeli Independence Day, and the holiday of Shavuot.

The Nuremberg Laws become an excellent springboard for studying the enslavement of people by attrition of their civil liberties, a subject that can also be explored in social studies, in history, and in the Bible. Hebrew students can study Hebrew material relating to the subject, but they have to have a pretty fair knowledge of the language because there is little or nothing on the subject in very simple Hebrew.

Knowledge is essential. You can create an emotional climate in the classroom, but if the child has no background knowledge it will be a subject that will soon be forgotten and relegated to ancient history. Yet a typical comment from all the students that I "exposed" to the Holocaust (and this was merely a matter of eight 45-minute sessions) was, "It is history about *today*, not like Joseph in B.C.E." (These were ten-year-olds!)

If in the course of your teaching something comes up to which you have no answer, it is important to tell the children you don't know. Assign the questioner the task of ferreting out the answer, or promise to find it out for them before the next session; but don't try to bluff your way through.

2. *Emotion*: Empathy for the survivors and the victims is the second priority. There is really nothing wrong with kids crying. Parents, teachers, principals are always afraid of this, yet I believe you have won a victory if a child can be moved to tears for fellow human beings. In the retelling of what happened in ghettos, concentration camps, and forests, the kids will understand and react, especially if you focus on individuals.

Once I gave a lengthy talk to students about the Holocaust. The next week a mother told me this story: In their household, each Friday evening after supper the parents would ask the children what they had learned that week. The youngsters could talk out things that puzzled, bothered, or astonished them. Their youngest daughter—the one who had heard my "speech"—had never had anything to contribute, a circumstance that had

Two very crucial areas in teaching or discussing the Holocaust are (1) the problem of resistance, and (2) the behavior of the Judenrat. Your unit can be a six-week unit for 45 minutes a week or a semester unit for an hour a day, depending on whether it is a Sunday school, Hebrew afternoon school, or day school. But no matter how long the unit is, if you can impart to the children the insurmountable difficulties in trying to resist and make them aware of the terrible burden of choice in the selections by the Judenrat, you will have made a great contribution.

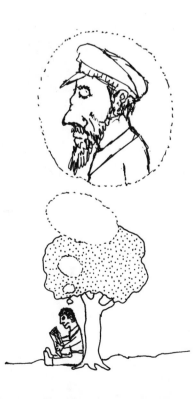

bothered her parents. This Friday, however, she came home and, having taken copious notes, told everyone what she had learned. Her mother was overjoyed that she had been motivated enough to remember and to recount the lecture as she had heard it.

3. *Action*: We can hope that the combination of knowledge and emotional impact will lead the students to take some kind of action, not only now but throughout their lives. At present the Arab boycott can be discussed—including its implications—and a comparison made to the boycott that Hitler placed on Jewish goods, Jewish firms, Jewish establishments, Jewish doctors, etc. Ask: "What can we do about it?" They can be alerted to take up the cause where there is any attrition of civil liberties, because even the most insignificant curtailment can erode the rights of Jews and non-Jews alike.

4. *Values*: There are many values that can be discussed within the framework of the Holocaust: case studies about "just following orders," defining personal involvement, making life-and-death choices, deciding what constitutes heroism.

Resources

Wherever possible avoid fiction when you use or assign reading material, because children tend to doubt the "truth" of the account behind the fiction and are apt to believe the whole thing was made up. Recently I spoke to about fifty children at a day school and told them that instead of talking about a million and a half children who perished at the hands of the Nazis, I was going to talk about only three. After I related three episodes from three diaries in the Yad Vashem bulletins, the children said over and over: "Did it really happen? Is it really true?"

In order to impart the facts, the facts must be known by the imparter, the teacher. At the end of this chapter there is a syllabus, which can be used with older children or pared down for younger children—using more detail for the day school, less detail for the Sunday school.

True, there are a number of very good books that are fictionalized accounts of real happenings, e.g., *The Upstairs Room* (by Johanna Reiss), *I Am Rosemarie* (by Marietta Moskin), *Uncle Misha's Partisans* (by Yuri Suhl), and *Night* (by Elie Wiesel); and two good nonfiction accounts, *Young Moshe's Diary* (by Moshe Flinker), and of course *The Diary of Anne Frank*. However, too many teachers think that *The Diary of Anne Frank* is the beginning and end of Holocaust literature. It is all right to have the children read it, but not as a be-all and end-all—perhaps, rather, as a beginning. One good assignment, in fact, might be to have a good reader read and compare for the class the two personalities of Anne Frank and young Moshe Flinker, the former coming from an uninformed and uncommitted Jewish family and the latter an Orthodox Jew. Another moving account of an Orthodox young man is *The Yellow Star* by Unsdorfer. My own book, *The Holocaust: A History of Courage and Resistance*, covers the entire period and includes in it "things to think about," which can evoke from the children all kinds of discussions and responses.

There are movies, film strips, cassettes, and records available on the subject. Perhaps one of the best movies to start off with would be "The Hangman." A lively and stimulating discussion should follow on man's responsibility for his fellowman. A new filmstrip has been issued by the Jewish Labor Committee in New York: "The Warsaw Ghetto: Holocaust and Resistance," but it may be a little too rough for the younger children; it probably should not be used until at least the seventh grade. It is narrated by Theodore Bikel and Vladka Meed, a survivor.

Tools for translating reality

There are a number of aspects that are especially difficult to convey to children (and grownups too). How large was the Warsaw ghetto? To say that it was 840 acres means nothing. But if you take the trouble to locate an area in your city that is 840 acres and learn that one square mile is 640 acres, then you realize that the size of the Warsaw ghetto was 1⅓ square miles. Find out how many people live in this area—it should be an area that is close to where most of the children live. Explain that into this area where about 10,000 people usually live, between 330,000 and 500,000 people were jammed, about thirty-five times as many people as are living there now (use the statistics in your neighborhood). Ask the children: "How would you like to have thirty-five more people living in your house?" This brings the reality within the realm of the child's understanding.

Try to visualize 6 million. We pointed out the stadium in Cleveland—it seats 80,000—and told the kids to "empty it out seventy-five times." Still, it doesn't mean much. X times the population of your city may be used as a yardstick, but it too means little. One United Synagogue Youth leader had his kids sit in a circle and count. By the time they reached a couple of thousand they were weary of it. Another technique that has been used during Holocaust programs is that of calling out the names of some of the victims throughout the program in an undertone.

Finally, the best device in exposing the children to this subject is to invite into the classroom speakers who are themselves survivors. The children respond amazingly well and begin to understand in ways that movies, books, and tapes cannot achieve. One fine secular high school teacher who teaches the literature of the Holocaust followed my advice and began using this technique, which has proved remarkably successful for her too.

In addition, the children should be asked whether they know of anyone in their family who was involved in the Holocaust. If so, perhaps they could interview that person or invite him/her to appear before the class. The American Jewish Committee is now compiling (from many cities) an oral history library of interviews of Holocaust survivors. Possibly these

Perhaps the best technique is to mention the number constantly but emphasize individual stories or the lives of specific children, who will, even in death, come to life for our students.

tapes could be obtained. If not, certainly the AJCommittee would share with you the names of the people interviewed. As long as we have survivors they are our best resource, but even these people should have a briefing from the teacher about what approach to take when speaking to children.

I went out into the hinterland—to Burton, Ohio, where there is no Jew for miles around—with a survivor friend of mine who is an excellent speaker. On the way, I suggested that she stress certain things that she might not stress to a Jewish audience, e.g. the humanity of the girls in her room in the concentration camp and their attempts to help each other; the fact that after liberation when they caught the female head of the camp who had beaten, tortured, and killed them—caught her trying to escape with a suitcase full of the victims' gold and other belongings—the only thing they did to her was cut off her hair. This in addition to her own personal story was very moving.

Other methods can be used in teaching the Holocaust. One teacher crowded her class into a too-small cloakroom and made them sit there quietly for forty-five minutes. At one camp the counselor woke the children in the morning, did not allow them to eat breakfast or go to the bathroom, and herded them down to the beach, where they were fenced in with a rope; he would not let them leave for a couple of hours. At a day school the children had a yellow star pinned on them, which they wore all day and then wore home. I really do not like to use any of these gimmicks. I believe the only thing that goes through the students' minds is: "Boy, when I'm done with this, I'll eat plenty!" or "I'll run around like crazy!" Since they know that soon there will be an end to it, attempts to create physical deprivation frequently seem to backfire.

What might be more valuable is for the teacher to propose an imaginary fallout shelter—or indeed even create one. A child is picked to be the "owner," and s/he has to choose only six out of all the children to be in the shelter with her/him. How does s/he choose? This child because of being a friend, that child because s/he has a swimming pool? A child with a defect over one who is perfectly healthy?

Another idea might be to have a debate. One side, for example, could argue that "the Judenrat was responsible for the death of thousands—perhaps millions—of Jews. If they had refused to comply with Nazi demands after they became aware of death camps, many Jews would have been saved," versus the proposition that "many Judenrat members chosen by the Nazis quit and/or committed suicide. Others refused Nazi favors and most—not all, but most—tried to do the best they could for the ghetto people. That Jews were to be murdered was a Nazi decision. Which Jews were to go first was a Judenrat decision." Care must be exercised in the wording of these debate topics, because there is a danger that the one who is really "wrong" will be so convincing that the children will go away thinking he was really "right." On the other hand, this too could serve as a good lesson: no matter how right you are, if the other fellow is more glib he can win—in politics, in getting a job, and in a fight for life.

The student response

We have mentioned what we hope would be gained by the child as a result of these studies: knowledge, empathy, and possible action. The sessions always ought to be ended with creative expressions from the children. If the course is short, you can wait until the end to suggest writing, painting, or composing music; if it lasts a semester, it is best not to wait that long. A very moving and effective way to introduce your creative period is to have the kids sit quietly at their desks or on the floor. Supply them with paper, paints, crayons, Magic Markers, and maybe even clay. Pull the blinds, at least partially; turn off the lights; light a Yahrzeit candle (telling them what this candle means); and let them produce their creative works in this quiet and solemn atmosphere. It was Shraga Arian's idea to put the written and artistic works together on a scroll (it can be wrapping paper or shelf paper) so that it becomes a kind of megillah—a megillat ha-Shoah—a scroll of the Holocaust. A service can be composed by students or by the teacher using biblical quotes or quotes from various things they have read. This service can also be conducted by the light of six candles or six Yahrzeit candles. I have made a candelabrum from a styrofoam block spray-painted black, in which I inserted six long white tapers. The service was read by the students by the light of these tapers. Another effective program was done by teenage United Synagogue members in our synagogue, who read their parts from various stations in the synagogue, including the balcony. The voices coming from all over were eery, haunting, and very effective.

Finally

Teachers will probably get a lot of flack from supervisors, parents, and sometimes from rabbis about teaching this sensitive subject. Unless you are confronted by an actual "I refuse to allow you to do this in my school," go ahead with it. I think ultimately everyone will gain from the results. I had an experience with the parents of a ten-year-old youngster who refused to allow their child in my class while I taught this subject. I agreed and suggested that he go to the other fifth-grade class for the duration of the six-week "experiment." The next week the child was back in my room and insisted on staying through all the sessions, and even participating in the final program.

The most difficult question you will be asked is, "Why did it happen?" This is a theological "why?" (There are a number of books on the subject, including Richard Rubenstein's *After Auschwitz* and Eliezer Berkovits's *Faith after the Holocaust*. Perhaps you may want to invite rabbis into your school to discuss this subject; it might be interesting to explore the different points of view on the Holocaust—Reform, Reconstructionist, Conservative, and Orthodox—if indeed they have different points of view.)

Shraga Arian ל״ז, who was one of our finest educators, said in answer to this question: "To me the Holocaust is not a dilemma of God, but a dilemma of man. The Holocaust proved not that God was dead, but that man's humanity to man was dead. Man is given the freedom to choose: the Germans chose to exercise unbridled evil; the world Jewish community chose to exercise silence; the world chose to exercise indifference."

Syllabus and bibliography for teaching the Holocaust

Goals

1. *Knowledge*: of a short history of European anti-Semitism; of prewar Jewry—how and where they lived and attitudes of non-Jews toward them; of how a man like Hitler could attain the power that he did; of the atrocities committed under his aegis and by him; of the Final Solution; of the re-

sponses of the victims; and finally of the attitudes toward Jews in postwar Europe and America.

2. *Emotion:* to develop in the student a strong personal sense of identification with individuals who suffered and resisted and who were victims of man's inhumanity to man.

3. *Theology*: to begin the student thinking about the theological questions resulting from the Holocaust and about some of the answers that have been offered.

4. *Action*: through knowledge and understanding of the event, students should be able to relate it to modern society, develop an awareness of the concepts and dimensions of genocide, and work together with the larger community to prevent such happenings in the future. Perhaps they will want to teach others, to arrange programs about this catastrophe for the community and for other schools.

Students will be alerted to signs of aberrations in their political leaders and will stand up in protest against inequitable laws, laws prompted by discrimination and hatred, so that such a state of affairs does not arise again.

I. ORIGINS OF THE HOLOCAUST

    A. Political and racial anti-Semitism
    B. Religious, political, and racial role of the church historically in our time

RESOURCES

Students will be on the lookout for anti-Semitism in today's society; will understand the importance of the existence of the state of Israel and do whatever they can to ensure its existence, including writing letters, picketing, boycotting, contributing financially.

Books
Talmon, J. L. *European History as the Seedbed of the Holocaust* (pamphlet).
Flannery, Edward. *The Anguish of the Jews*. New York: Macmillan, 1965.
Isaac, Jules. *The Teaching of Contempt*. London: Elek Books, 1966.
Poliakov, Léon. *History of Anti-Semitism*. 3 vols. London: Elek Books, 1966.
Parkes, James. *Conflict between Church and Synagogue*. London: Soncino Press, 1934.

II. EUROPEAN JEWRY BEFORE THE HOLOCAUST

    A. The shtetl Jews in Poland, Russia, and other East European countries
    B. The Haskalah
    C. Emancipated Jews in Western Europe
        1. Jewish life in Germany
        2. Rate of assimilation of German Jews
        3. Intellectual Jewish life in Germany
        4. Importance of Jews in German economy—their fate regardless of their importance

RESOURCES

Books
Zborowski, Mark, and Herzog, Elizabeth. *Life Is with People*. New York: Schocken, 1953.
Liptzin, Solomon. *Germany's Stepchildren*. Philadelphia: Jewish Publication Society, 1944; paperback, Philadelphia: Jewish Publication Society, 1961.
Meyer, Michael A. *Origins of the Modern Jew*. Detroit: Wayne State University, 1967.
Roskies, David. *The Shtetl Book*. New York: Ktav, 1975.

Filmstrip
"The Vanished World." New Jewish Media Project, 35 mm., 20 minutes, slides with sound tape on reels.

Slide
"The Life That Disappeared." Scholastic Magazines Inc., sound, 1974.

Films
"L'Chaim" (ORT).
"Let's Rejoice." Wombat Productions, 16 mm., 10 minutes, color and sound.
"Man's Inhumanity." Center for Cassette Studies #6473, distributed by Xerox, Inc., 56 minutes.
"The Last Chapter—History of 1000 Years of Polish Jewry." Ben Lev Productions, Inc. (22 E. 17th St., New York, N.Y. 10003), 35 mm., 90 minutes.

III. BACKGROUND OF CONDITIONS BETWEEN END OF WORLD WAR I AND THE RISE OF HITLER, 1918–1933

    A. Defeat of Germany—humiliation
    B. *Deutschland-über-alles* syndrome—minibiography of Hitler
    C. Establishment of German Workers party—1919
    D. Writing of *Mein Kampf*
        1. Under what circumstances?
        2. What did it contain?
        3. Public reaction
    E. Deepening crises of East European Jewry

RESOURCES

Books
Hitler, Adolf. *Mein Kampf* (selections). New York: Simon and Schuster, 1940.
Shirer, William L. *The Rise and Fall of the Third Reich*. New York: Simon and Schuster, 1960.
———. *The Rise and Fall of Adolf Hitler*. New York: Random House, 1961.
———. *Berlin Diary*. New York: Alfred A. Knopf, 1941.

IV. HOW HITLER CAME TO POWER

    A. Political approach
    B. Economic factors—country's problems blamed on Jews, Communists, and Freemasons
    C. Psychological factors—the "big lie"
    D. Hitler's actions
        1. Brownshirts and force
        2. Reichstag fire
        3. Abolition of civil liberties
    E. Opposition to Hitler
        1. How much?
        2. How handled?

RESOURCES

Books
Boldt, Gerhard. *Hitler: The Last Ten Days*. New York: Coward McCann & Geoghan, 1973.
Speer, Albert. *Inside the Third Reich*. New York: Macmillan, 1970.
Gilfond, Henry. *The Reichstag Fire, Feb. 1933*. New York: Watts, 1973.
Raab, Earl. *Anatomy of Nazism* (pamphlet). New York: Anti-Defamation League of Bnai Brith, 1961.
Allen, William S. *The Nazi Seizure of Power*. Chicago: Quadrangle, 1965.

Movies
"The Hangman." Contemporary Films, 12 minutes, color, 1964.
"The Twisted Cross." Kent State University Audio-Visual Services (Kent, Ohio 44242), 55 minutes, black and white.

V. WHEN AND HOW JEWS BECAME SCAPEGOATS AND HOW HITLER IMPLEMENTED HIS INITIAL PERSECUTION OF THEM

    A. Nuremberg Laws—1935

1. Reich Citizen's Law
2. Law for protection of Germans
3. Other discriminatory laws

B. Kristallnacht
   1. What?
   2. When?
   3. Why?
   4. Where?
   5. How?

C. German Jews who left Europe for Palestine, America, and other countries
   1. When could they leave and how did they leave?
   2. Which Jews left?
   3. Those who remained—why did they stay?
      a. Economics
      b. Old age and infirmity
      c. Confidence that old order would be restored
      d. It-can't-happen-here syndrome

RESOURCES

Books

Dawidowicz, Lucy S. *The War against the Jews, 1933–1945*. New York: Holt, Rinehart and Winston; Philadelphia: Jewish Publication Society, 1975.

Hilberg, Raoul. *The Destruction of European Jewry*. Chicago: Quadrangle, 1967.

———. *Documents of Destruction*. Chicago: Quadrangle, 1971.

Movie

"The Rise of Hitler." Kent State University Audio-Visual Services (Kent, Ohio 44242), 26 minutes, black and white.

Filmstrip

"Anatomy of Nazism." 55 textual frames in color, distributed by Anti-Defamation League of Bnai Brith (315 Lexington Ave., New York, N.Y. 10016).

VI. **CONQUEST OF EUROPE BY THE NAZIS**

A. Austria—*Anschluss*, 1938, political
   Czechoslovakia—sold at Munich, 1938–39, political
   Poland—1939, military
   Holland, Belgium, France, Norway, Denmark—1940, military

B. What to do with the Jews?
   1. How to make Europe *Judenrein*
   2. Evian Conference in France
   3. Wansee Conference
   4. Madagascar Plan

C. Dehumanizing Jews
   1. Yellow star
   2. Ghettos
   3. Lack of food, medicine, and sanitary facilities
   4. Contradictory orders
   5. Brutality
   6. Use of Jews as police and leadership

D. Invasion of Russia and beginning of mass killing operation—Final Solution/genocide

RESOURCES

Books

Reitlinger, Gerald. *The Final Solution*. New York: A. S. Barnes, 1961.

Schoenberger, Gerhard. *The Yellow Star*. New York: Bantam, 1973.

Eban, Abba. "The Holocaust," in *My People*. New York: Board of Jewish Education, 1973.

Filmstrip
"The Holocaust." ARE (3206 S. Paul St., Denver, Colo. 80210).

Movies
"The Legacy of Anne Frank." Script by Virginia Mazer, "Eternal Light" kinescopes, color, 1967.
"I Never Saw Another Butterfly." Script by Virginia Mazer, 16 mm., 30 minutes, produced by the Jewish Theological Seminary in cooperation with NBC, 1966; distributed by the National Academy for Adult Jewish Studies of the United Synagogue of America (218 E. 70th St., New York, N.Y. 10021).

Record
"I Never Saw Another Butterfly" (available from above source).

VII. FINAL SOLUTION CARRIED OUT

    A. Establishment of ghettos
        1. Lodz, Warsaw, Vilna, Shrodula, Riga, etc.; Terezin
        2. Work ghettos
        3. Transit stops
    B. Establishment of concentration camps
        1. Work camps—conditions, kinds of work
            a. Oranianburg
            b. Birkenau
            c. Others
        2. Death camps—why most in Poland?
            a. Belzec
            b. Sobibor
            c. Treblinka
            d. Auschwitz
            e. Maidanek
            f. Others

RESOURCES

Books
Birnbaum, Halina. *Hope Is the Last to Die*. New York: Twayne, 1971.
Glatstein, Jacob; Knox, Israel; Margoshes, Samuel, eds. *Anthology of Holocaust Literature*. Philadelphia: Jewish Publication Society, 1968.
Meed, Vladka. *On Both Sides of the Wall.* Tel Aviv: Ghetto Fighters House and Hakibbutz Hameuchad Publishing House, 1972.
Flinker, Moshe. *Young Moshe's Diary*, Jerusalem: Yad Vashem, 1965; New York: Board of Jewish Education, 1971.
Ringelblum, Emanuel. *Notes from the Warsaw Ghetto*. New York: McGraw-Hill, 1958.
Levi, Primo. *Survival in Auschwitz*.
Nyeszli, Miklos. *Auschwitz*. New York: Frederick Fell, 1968.
Isaac, Jules. *The Teaching of Contempt: Teaching Roots of Anti-Semitism*. Translated by H. Weaver. New York: Holt, Rinehart and Winston, 1964.

Record
"Readings from Elie Wiesel." Jewish Heritage Series. Spoken Arts, Inc. (New Rochelle, N.Y. 10801).

Films
"Warsaw Ghetto." Time-Life Films, 16 mm., black and white, 51 minutes.
"Night and Fog." Directed by Alain Resnais, Contemporary Films, McGraw-Hill (330 W. 42nd St., New York, N.Y. 10036), 16 mm., color, 31 minutes.
"Distant Journey." Screenplay by Radok. Czech dialogue, English subtitles. 95 minutes. Can be ordered from Audio Brandon Films, Inc. (34 MacQueston Pkwy. South, Mt. Vernon, N.Y. 10550).
"Sighet, Sighet." Contemporary Films, McGraw-Hill, 27 minutes.
"Memorandum." National Film Board of Canada, distributed by Contemporary Films, McGraw-Hill, 16 mm., 58 minutes, 1966.

A letter to Halina Birnbaum, author of *Hope Is the Last to Die*, from a young student:

Dearest Halina,
  I read your book. I couldn't sleep at night after reading from it. But I still read on. I'd cry sometimes, and I wasn't surprised. I lost most of my father's family during the Holocaust. But that's really nothing.
  I've been thinking about Dina lately. You sure have a nice friend there. How did you meet her? My father was born in Luck, Poland (pronounced "Lutsk"). Have you heard of that town before? When he was six, the war broke out. Him, his brother and parents ran away. They had a friend who had an ambulance truck. The friend let them on, along with about 10 others. My father's aunt Paula and her baby (Fagela) was running after the truck. . . . She was shot down and her baby was killed.
  I was named after Paula (Karen Paula). I am really glad I have a father like I have, and I thank God he's alive.
  Who do you live with? Do people feel sorry for you because of what happened? I don't feel sorry. I am sorry. It will never happen again. If Jews heard about the extermination beforehand, could they convert?
  I hate to say your book is good. . . .
  I guess it's not what it's about. It's how you wrote it.
  I hope the rest of your life is wonderful—

        Sent with much love,
            Karen
  I'd appreciate a note.

Karen Zinker
Cleveland, Ohio

VIII. QUALITY OF LEADERSHIP

A. In the ghettos
  1. Warsaw—Czerniakow
  2. Lodz—Rumkowski
  3. Vilna—Gens
  4. Sosnowitz—Merin
B. Rabbinical leaders
  1. Germany—Leo Baeck
  2. Denmark—Rabbi Melchior
  3. Italy—Rabbi Zolli
  4. Greece—Rabbi Koretz
C. Is suicide the answer?
  1. Zeigleboim
  2. Czerniakow
D. Who can judge them?

RESOURCES

Books
Trunk, Isaiah. *Judenrat*. New York: Macmillan, 1972.
Tushnet, Leonard. *The Pavements of Hell*. New York: St. Martin's, 1973.
Korman, Gerd. *Hunter and Hunted*. New York: Viking, 1973; Delta, 1974.

Films
"Games of Angels." Janus New Cinema/Walerian Browczyk, color, 13 minutes.
"Denmark '43." Learning Corporation of America (711 Fifth Ave., New York, N.Y. 10022), 16 mm., 22 minutes.

IX. RESISTANCE—WHAT IS RESISTANCE?

A. Active resistance—in the ghetto
  1. Vilna
    a. Wittenberg
    b. Madesker
    c. Kowalski—underground press
    d. Kovner
  2. Warsaw
    a. Anilewitz
    b. Zuckerman
    c. Lubetkin
  3. Kovno—Elkanan Elkes
  4. Holland—Abraham Asscher and David Cohen
  5. Others—some forty ghettos in Eastern Europe
B. Active resistance—in the forests
  1. Uncle Misha—Mottele
  2. Dr. Atlas

3. Dov Ven Yaakov
4. Yehiel Grynszpan
5. Vitka Kempner and others

C. Active resistance—in the camps
1. Sobibor—Pechersky
2. Treblinka
3. Auschwitz
4. Krusyna
5. Krychow

D. Passive resistance
1. Celebrating holidays in camps, forests, ghettos
2. Observing mitzvot—even on the brink of death
3. Music—Theresienstadt and other places
4. Underground education and cultural events
5. Diaries—Ringelblum, Flinker, Kaplan, and others
6. Art
7. Individuals—J. Korczak, V. Frankel, and others

RESOURCES

Books

Syrkin, Marie. *Blessed Is the Match*. Philadelphia: Jewish Publication Society, 1976 (reissue).

Goldstein, Charles. *The Bunker*. Philadelphia: Jewish Publication Society, 1970.

The Book of Alfred Kantor. New York: McGraw-Hill, 1971.

Klein, Gerda. *All but My Life*. New York: Hill and Wang, 1971.

Gray, Martin. *For Those I Loved*. Boston: Little, Brown, 1972.

Rosen, Donia. *The Forest, My Friend*. New York: Bergen-Belsen Memorial Press, 1971.

Shabbatai, K. *As Sheep to Slaughter?* New York: World Association of Bergen-Belsen Survivors, 1963.

Bauer, Yehuda. *They Chose Life* (pamphlet). New York: American Jewish Committee, 1973.

Ainsztein, Reuben. *Jewish Resistance in Nazi-Occupied Eastern Europe*. London: Paul Elek, 1974.

Stadtler, Bea. *The Holocaust: A History of Courage and Resistance*. New York: Behrman House, 1974.

I Never Saw Another Butterfly. New York: McGraw-Hill, 1964.

Terezin. Prague: Council of Jewish Community in Czech lands, 1965.

The Holocaust and Resistance. Jerusalem: Yad Vashem, 1970.

Barkai, Meyer. *Fighting Ghettos*. Philadelphia: Lippincott, 1962.

Suhl, Yuri. *Uncle Misha's Partisans*. New York: Four Winds Press, 1973.

Hyams, Joseph. *A Field of Buttercups*. Englewood-Cliffs, N.J.: Prentice Hall, 1968.

Films

"A Tear in the Ocean." By Henri Glaser, distributed by Levitt-Pickman Film Corp., color, 86 minutes.

"Warsaw Ghetto," by the Jewish Media Project, 35 mm. slides with sound tapes on reel, 20 minutes.

Filmstrip

"The Warsaw Ghetto: Holocaust and Resistance." Narrated by Theodore Bikel and Vladka Meed, Jewish Labor Committee (25 E. 78th St., New York, N.Y. 10021).

X. YOUTH ALIYAH

A. Purpose of project
B. People involved
1. Recha Freier
2. Henrietta Szold
3. Joop Westerwill
4. Joachim Simon (Shushu)

5. Carl Netter
6. Israel Belkind
7. Siegfried Lehmann
8. Hans Beyth
9. Others
C. How did youth escape?
D. What happened to those who came to Israel on Youth Aliyah?

RESOURCES

Books

Pincus, Chasia. *Come from the Four Winds*. New York: Herzl Press, 1970.

Freier, Recha. *Let the Children Come*. London: Weidenfeld and Nicolson, 1961.

Kol, Moshe. *Youth Aliya* (booklet, Document #1). Jerusalem: UNESCO, 1957.

XI. ALIYAH BET

A. What was it?
B. Purpose of operation
C. People involved
    1. Yehuda Arazi
    2. Eliyahu Golomb
    3. Saul Avigur
    4. Israel Galili
    5. David Ha-Cohen and others
D. How did the organization develop?
    1. During the war
    2. After the war—what happened to Jews who tried to return to their homes in Eastern Europe?
    3. Purchase of ships
        a. How?
        b. From whom?
        c. Recruitment of crews
        d. Financing
    4. Roundup of refugees
        a. From where?
        b. How accomplished?
    5. Problems with British
    6. Experiences with some ships
        a. *Pentcho*
        b. *St. Louis*
        c. *Af Al Pi Chen*
        d. *Ulua*
        e. *Enzo Sereni*
        f. *Patria*
        g. *Struma*
        h. *Exodus*
    7. Was project successful?

RESOURCES

Books

Bauer, Yehuda. *Bricha: Flight and Rescue*. New York: Random House, 1970.

Eliav, Arie. *Voyage of the Ulua*. New York: Funk & Wagnalls, 1969.

Thomas, Gordon. *Voyage of the Damned*. New York: Stein and Day, 1974.

Hasler, Alfred A. *The Lifeboat Is Full*. New York: Funk & Wagnalls, 1969.

Kluger, Ruth, and Mann, Peggy. *The Last Escape*. New York: Doubleday, 1973.

Vida, George. *From Doom to Dawn*. New York: Jonathan David, 1967.

Cassette tapes

"Voices of History." Board of Jewish Education, New York.

"After Liberation." By Judah Naditch.

A. Palestine Jewry's efforts
   1. Joining the enemy (Britain) to fight the common enemy (Nazis)
   2. Jewish Brigade
   3. Parachutists
      a. Enzo Sereni
      b. Hannah Senesh
      c. Haviva Reich
      d. Abba Bereditchev
B. Danish rescue
   1. Why was Denmark different?
   2. Who was involved in rescue in Denmark?
      a. How?
      b. Why?
C. What happened in Holland?
   1. Collaborators
   2. Those who helped
      a. How?
      b. Why?
D. Joint Distribution Committee—what did they do?
E. Red Cross
   1. Did they help?
   2. If not, what was their excuse?
   3. Were they consistent in their reasons or was it plainly anti-Semitism?
F. Non-Jews
   1. Civilians in various countries?
   2. Church and church officials?
   3. The righteous gentiles
G. America
   1. Before the war
   2. During the war
   3. After the war—immigration quotas

RESOURCES

Books

Yahil, Leni. *Rescue of Danish Jewry*. Philadelphia: Jewish Publication Society, 1969.

Werstein, Irving. *That Denmark Might Live*. Philadelphia: Macrae Smith, 1967.

Agar, Herbert. *The Saving Remnant*. New York: Viking, 1962.

Waagenaar, Sam. *The Pope's Jews*. LaSalle, Ill.: Open Court, 1973.

Presser, Jacob. *The Destruction of the Dutch Jews*. New York: Dutton, 1969.

Morse, Arthur A. *While Six Million Died*. New York: Random House, 1969.

Feingold, Henry. *The Politics of Rescue: The Roosevelt Administration and the Holocaust*. New Brunswick, N.J.: Rutgers, 1970.

Senesh, Hannah. *Her Life and Diary*. New York: Schocken, 1972.

Masters, Anthony. *The Summer That Bled*. New York: St. Martin's Press, 1972.

Bar Adon, Dorothy and Pesach. *Seven Who Fell*. Tel Aviv: Tia, Zionist Youth Organization, 1947.

Lapide, Pinhas. *Three Popes and the Jews*. New York: Hawthorn Books, 1967.

Filmstrip

"Rescue in Denmark." Union of American Hebrew Congregations (Eyes Front Series), distributed by the American Jewish Joint Distribution Committee, 1972.

Dramatization

Peter Weiss. "The Investigation."
Rolf Hochhuth. "The Deputy."

Film
"An Act of Faith" (in two parts). Produced by the New York Board of
    Rabbis in cooperation with CBS (10 E. 72nd St., New York 10016), 30
    minutes each, 1961.

Cassettes
Voices of History: "Danish Rescue" and "The Parachutists." Available
    from Friends of the Jewish Theater for Children (426 W. 58th St., New
    York, N.Y. 10019).

XIII.   SPIRITUAL CONDITION OF JEWS AFTER THE HOLOCAUST

A. After Auschwitz
    1. What are the theological implications of the Holocaust?
    2. What are the theological responses?
    3. Is God dead?
    4. Were there instances of faith in the face of despair?
        a. Did prayer help some victims?
        b. Was fighting back as much an answer of faith as accepting
            fate with dignity?
    5. The true story of the ninety-three maidens
    6. Yossel Rakover—fiction or fact?

RESOURCES

Books
Rubenstein, Richard. *After Auschwitz*. Indianapolis: Bobbs-Merrill, 1966.
Prager, Moshe. *Sparks of Glory*. New York: Shengold, 1974.
Berkovits, Eliezer. *Faith after the Holocaust*. New York: Ktav, 1973.
Frankl, Victor. *Man's Search for Meaning*. Boston: Beacon, 1965.

Record
"Yizkor." By Sholom Secunda. Ethnic Music Publishing Co. (Carlstadt,
    N.J. 07072).

XIV.   FACING UP TO THE HOLOCAUST

A. Nazi-hunters
    1. Reaction to them
    2. Cooperation
    3. Capture of Eichmann
        a. By whom?
        b. How?
        c. His trial
    4. Nuremberg trials
        a. How conducted
        b. Meaning of site

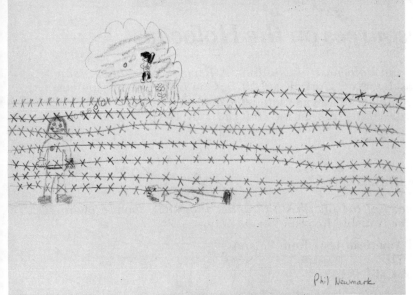

Phil Newmark

c. Who were tried?
d. Conclusions
   5. Is "only-following-orders" reason legitimate?
      a. Any value to this?
      b. What is invalid about it?
B. How do people react to the Holocaust?
   1. How do we react to Germans?
   2. How about individual reparations?
   3. How about reparations to Israel?
   4. Economic ties between Germany and Israel
C. Establishment of the state of Israel
   1. Result of the Holocaust
   2. How do Israelis react and commemorate?
D. Yom ha-Shoah in the Diaspora
   1. Is there value in remembering?
E. Is there value in teaching the subject in public schools? In religious schools?
   1. Is it mentioned in textbooks?
   2. If not, what can we do about it?
   3. At what age can children be exposed to this?
F. Should we forgive and forget?

RESOURCES

Books

Friedman, Tuviah. *We Shall Never Forget* (album of photographs). Haifa Documentation Center, n.d.

Wiesel, Elie. *One Generation After*. New York: Random House, 1970.

Hausener, Gideon. *Justice in Jerusalem*. New York: Harper & Row, 1966.

Wiesenthal, Simon. *The Murderers among Us*. New York: McGraw-Hill, 1967.

Korman, Gerd. *Hunter and Hunted*. New York: Viking, 1973; Delta, 1974.

Heydecker, Joe J., and Leeb, Johannes. *The Nuremberg Trials*. Cleveland: World, 1962.

Cassette

"The Holocaust: A Study in Values" (includes case histories). Teacher guide, student manual, and cassette available from:

Alternatives in Religious Education
1110 Holly Oak Circle
San Jose, Calif. 95120

Movie

"Trial at Nuremberg," Kent State University Audio-Visual Services (Kent, Ohio 44242), 26 minutes, black and white.

Other resources on the Holocaust

1. *Teaching the Holocaust to Children: A Review and Bibliography* by Diane K. Roskies, New York: Ktav, 1975. One of the best resources around, with a complete review of methodological approaches.

2. *Nightwords: A Midrash on the Holocaust* by David Roskies, published by

**Bnai Brith
1640 Rhode Island Ave. N.W.
Washington, D.C. 20036**

3. *The Tragedy of the Jewish Child under the Nazis,* mobile photographic exhibition available from the

**Congress of American Jews from Poland
6534 Moore Dr.
Los Angeles, Calif. 90048**

4. *Warsaw Ghetto,* mobile photographic exhibition available from Bnai Brith (same address as no. 2 above).

5. *The Holocaust and the Resistance,* mobile photographic exhibition available from

**American Federation of Jewish Fighters
505 Fifth Ave.
New York, N.Y. 10017**

6. *Replica of One of the Smaller Labor Camp Barracks,* full-scale exhibit, transportable, available from

**Vivienne Herman
1793 Cornelius Ave.
Wantagh, N.Y. 11793**

7. *Holocaust and Heroism,* picture set, 36 minutes, available from

**Ministry of Education and Culture
Center for Fostering Jewish Consciousness
Jerusalem, Israel**

8. *Resistance,* 36-picture set, available from the same place as no. 7.

9. *Guide to Memorials and Monuments Honoring the Six Million,* available from

**American Jewish Congress
15 E. 84th St.
New York, N.Y. 10028**

10. *The Holocaust: A Case Study of Genocide,* 70-page guide for teaching the Holocaust as a minicourse, published by the American Association for Jewish Education.

11. *The Jewish Catastrophe in Europe,* textbook published by the American Association for Jewish Education, with teacher's guide.

12. *The Holocaust,* multimedia presentation by Jay Bender, 45 minutes, available from

**Network
36 W. 37th St.
New York, N.Y. 10016**

13. *The Rise and Fall of Eastern European Jewry,* a multimedia presentation by David Roskies, available from same source as no. 12 above.

14. Finally, Gert Jacobson has executed a series of paintings called "Holocaust." A film of the series is now available. Contact her at:

**Lafayette Pl., #229
7500 Callaghan Rd.
San Antonio, Tex. 78229**

Talmud Torah Lishmah: Study of Torah for Its Own Sake

An introduction and a sample

"If you follow My laws [decrees] and faithfully observe My commandments [I will grant your rains in their season]" (Leviticus 26:3).

"If you follow My laws"—we can perhaps take this to mean "if we observe the commandments"; however, this creates a redundancy with the second half of the verse, which says explicitly "observe My commandments." How then shall we explain "if you follow My laws?" Rashi says it means that "you shall always be working hard in Torah."

I have heard my holy master and teacher, Rabbi Zalman Halevi (Shelita—may he live a long life), give this explanation of Rashi's comment:

"We may ask what does 'working hard in Torah' mean? Some say this means that upon encountering a difficulty one does not give up until solving it. If in business or secular science one encounters a problem (however difficult) yet does not leave it without solution, how much more ought we to struggle toward a solution with a difficult problem in Torah?

"But if this is the explanation, why then did the Torah use the word 'decrees'—which (as we know) means the laws that have no rational explanation. We must say, therefore, that talmud Torah—the study of Torah— itself is a decree. The verse means, then, that even if one knows the law, even if one is a talmid haham—scholar—he must still struggle and strive with Torah. There is no rational explanation for this. It is built into the soul of the Jewish people. It is a decree."

My teacher Rabbi David (Shelita) adds (and he is a man of the world) that no work of the human spirit—whether it be by Homer, Beethoven, or Rembrandt—has the power to transport him like the confrontation with a piece of Talmud.

What is this power that the Torah has over Jews? What is the source of this thing we say is "built into the soul of the Jewish people"? It is a mystery indeed, but not so hidden that we cannot glimpse it occasionally—much like the beautiful princess in the castle that the holy *Zohar* talks about. She shows herself but briefly and partially at a window.

In a word, it is the *eternity* of the Torah—a word much abused and metamorphosed into something cold and forbidding. To the lovers of Torah, however, it is a word filled with joy and song, meaning many things. For example:

The following chapter is both an explanation and a sample. Some parts will have to be gone over not once but two or three times to understand the principle. The beginning half of the chapter is the prelude to the text at the end, which is itself only a prelude to your beginning to study for yourself.

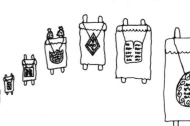

Tannaim are scholars from the mishnaic period (up to 200 C.E.); amoraim are scholars from the talmudic period (200–500 C.E.).

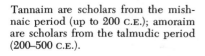

1. Time stops in the world of talmud Torah. The Talmud doesn't tell us what Rav and Shmuel thought, said, and did. Rav and Shmuel *themselves* think, say, and do it before our very eyes. After learning for a time, we find the tannaim and amoraim becoming so real to us that they are our living teachers. We know them as people and as saints—know them better, sometimes, than we know our contemporary friends and teachers.

Within the context of all of this, there is a strange custom among Jews that requires explanation. Rabbis who have died in recent times are mentioned with the phrase זצ״ל—זכר צדיק לברכה, "The memory of the righteous is a blessing," but those who died earlier are just mentioned by name, without this phrase. Is the memory of Rabbi Akiva or Rav Ashi (first and fourth centuries respectively) less a blessing than that of Rav Kook זצ״ל? The answer is that the teachers of the past become part of the living consciousness of the people. They become alive again and continue to live eternally. Scripture says (Proverbs 14:3): "The lips of the wise protect them," which means: "One who says Torah in the name of its originator causes his lips to speak in the grave" (i.e., as if the dead him-/herself still lives). A personal note, to demonstrate the psychological reality of this assertion: after learning Torah for a year or so I came on the passage that tells of Rav's funeral, and I burst into tears. While I know that people—even saints—do not live two thousand years, somehow Rav had become so alive for me that I reacted to his death as I would have to personal loss.

2. Time ceases to have real meaning in the world of talmud Torah. A question asked in the third century is answered in the thirteenth—or perhaps in the twenty-third.

3. Similarly, space ceases to have meaning in the world of talmud Torah. A question asked in Germany is answered in Fez, an interpretation given in Sura is contested in Troyes.

If the Talmud juxtaposes two opinions on the interpretation of the Mishnah, i.e., "Rava said so-and-so," but "Ulla said such-and-such," one might assume that Rava and Ulla were contemporaries. They weren't in time, but they are in Torah. Most amazing, an argument can take place in reverse order of history. A problem of the sixteenth century can be answered two hundred years earlier! An answer given in the seventeenth century can be challenged in the fourteenth. This has, of course, a rational explanation. The later answer was anticipated by the earlier scholar and was challenged—the later sage, unaware of this, made his statement anyway. But this is not the explanation in the consciousness of the Jewish people. Torah is metahistory. All is extant at any given time.

An example: In the Talmud, Baba Metzia 47b, we learn that Rav defined the word asimon as "(not valid) coin given as a token to the bathhouse keeper." An objection is raised to Rav's definition because of the statement in another mishnah: "We do not redeem the second tithe with an asimon *or with coins given as tokens* in the bathhouse"; we see from this statement that an asimon is *not* a coin given as a token. The two are mentioned separately. And if you say that the second phrase is meant as an explanation of the word asimon (i.e., an asimon is defined as a coin given as a token), I will counter and say that we have a baraita—an extracanonical mishnah—which states: "We *may* redeem second tithe with an asimon, says R. Dosa, but the sages say nay: and they all agree that we may not (redeem second tithe) with the coins given as tokens to the bathhouse." Therefore they *must* be different, and Rav's original definition is disproved. But such examples can be disillusioning. If there is explicit proof from tannaitic sources that an asimon and a token are two different things, how did a great sage like Rav err? Do we assume that he didn't know the mishnah and baraita?

A Turkish rabbi answered that "this is not difficult—Rav didn't know this baraita, but he knew the mishnah and believed that the phrase "or a coin given as a token" was an explanation of asimon (*Ein Yehosef*). A Spanish sage counters: "Whether or not Rav knew this baraita, he certainly knew the mishnah, and the end of the mishnah itself—not quoted here—proves that the two are different, so there still remains a difficulty." A perfectly logical and acceptable dialectic. Except that the Turkish rabbi, Rav Yosef Hazzan, lived in the seventeenth century and the Spanish Rav Yitzhak Abuhav in the fifteenth! Diachrony has become synchrony. The Torah is one building, all planned at once but built over many centuries—each generation placing its stones, its buttresses, and its decorations, yet creating one unified structure whose parts all harmonize with each other. Always new but unchanging. It is written: "Anything that a veteran talmid [student of the Torah] will say was already revealed to Moses at Sinai."

Thus West European post-Renaissance ideas of achievement are reversed. The greatest accomplishment is not to say what has never been said before but to arrive independently at an idea that has been said by the great. This is the logic of the berakhah, "Blessed is He who has directed me to think like the great ones."

To give a new interpretation—lehadesh—does not mean to produce something original, but rather to make new something old, not to innovate but to renovate. The Hebrew word has both meanings. I have heard my friend Rabbi Moshe Dreisinger quote the name of our holy teacher Rabbi Moshe Feinstein (Shelita) who often said: "What is hiddush, what is true

If you have followed the Rav versus the baraita and the R. Yosef versus R. Yitzhak Abuhav disagreements, you are beginning to get the hang of the thing.

Those that give up the yoke of Torah, take on the yoke of worldly cares.

Upon Three Things The World Stands Upon Torah Upon Worship and Upon the showing of Kindness.

—Pirke Aboth

Every single day a voice goes out from Sinai because Sinai is forever; it is always Now in Torah.

May the enlightened understand. המבין יבין

hiddush? To say what was said to Moshe Rabbenu [Moses our Teacher] at Sinai."

4. The Torah is eternal in another sense as well. It is the place where God meets wo/man. The center of the world. Where the temporal becomes nontemporal. We had two such places; the holy of holies was once this center, but "since the Holy Temple has been destroyed, all that is left us is the four cubits of the halakhah."

When God gave us the Torah, He didn't open a window, hand something through it, and close it again. He simply opened a window. For me, the Torah is that window. When we study and keep, teach and establish, we are in contact with God; as it is said: "To learn, to teach, to observe, to practice." We need only begin to realize it, for it is certainly so.

Nu! Lomir lernen a shtikl Torah: so let's learn a little Torah

Remember, we are not learning here in order to do (that's another part of our daily learning!), even though R. Yisrael Salanter held that learning for the sake of doing is the true talmud Torah lishmah. I think we do not deny that aspect in any way if we find another, an abstract or perhaps mystical, understanding of talmud Torah lishmah—that of study for its own sake. We are not learning in order to teach (although of course that is also essential); we are not even learning in order to know (although knowing has holiness too); we are learning . . . just to learn. For the sake of the mitzvah and for the joy (simha shel mitzvah) of learning itself. There are some physical ways to get into the rhythm of learning:

1. If you can chant a little—like the chant you learned for the four questions—do.

2. If you can loosen your body and shuckle—sway—as you chant, do.

3. If you can punctuate with your thumbs—thumbs up for a question, down for an answer (like your voice)—do. All the "choreography," surprisingly, helps a lot.

We are learning in Talmud, Baba Metzia 78a. The Mishnah teaches: If one leases a donkey from his fellow and the donkey is seized by the government for unpaid labor, or corvée [Aramaic: אנגריא —forced labor, service], the owner may say to the lessee: "The donkey that you leased is before you." (I.e., it is a misfortune to the lessee; since he had already rented and paid for the donkey, it is immaterial that it was seized.)

Gemara: Rav says that this mishnah only applies to temporary seizure; however, if the donkey is seized permanently, the owner must provide another donkey to the lessee. Shmuel says that, whether permanent or not, if it was taken on the way, the owner may say: "The donkey that I leased to you is before you"; if the donkey was not seized on the way, the owner must provide another.

At this point we think to ourselves: All right. Rav's distinction I understand. If it's temporary, the lessee's work is only interrupted; it is not ended entirely. But what does Shmuel mean? Specifically, what does "on the way" mean? Rashi anticipated us and answered that if it was taken on the way, i.e., if the government led the donkey (loaded with government goods) along the same route that the lessee wished to travel, the owner may say: "The donkey which you leased is before you." Why can he say this?

A PAGE FROM THE BABYLONIAN TALMUD
Treatise Sanhedrin, 29a
Romm edition, Vilna, 1895

A discussion of methods of examining witnesses and ascertaining the validity of their evidence

Because it is the method of the angaros (royal courier) to take a donkey and travel with it until meeting another donkey and then commandeer the second and return the first. Since it was simply the bad luck of the lessee that he met an angaros who wanted to travel in the same direction, he, the lessee, loses out and must rent another animal until he and the angaros meet someone else with a donkey and his is returned.

All of this is a pretty complicated explanation. Fortunately the Tosafot (glossators on Rashi) have a simpler one. They maintain that if the angaros and the lessee were traveling the same route, then the lessee is out of luck because it was by his own volition that the donkey was out in public where the angaros could normally commandeer them. However, if the donkey was still in the owner's stable (even though the lessee had already contracted to rent it), then the donkey would have been seized in any case. Therefore it is the owner's misfortune.

Go back now and remind yourself of Rav and Shmuel's views, because the Talmud objects. We learn in a baraita that if one rents a donkey and it is taken for the angaros, the lessor must provide another. This contradicts the mishnah. (Thumbs and voice up.) No problem for Rav. He says that the one talks about being permanently taken and the other talks about a temporary seizure. (Down.)

But what can Shmuel say? (Up.) If you maintain that for Shmuel there is also no difficulty because one is "on the way" and one is not—you will find the end of that baraita proves that this is not so: Rabbi Shimon ben Elazar says, "If on the way he may say, 'Your donkey is before you,' if it was not seized on the way, he must supply another donkey. Therefore we say that the first authority holds that there is no difference"! (Up.) "So!" says Shmuel. "But Rabbi Shimon ben Elazar holds as I do, and I am in accordance with him." (Down.)

All right, it's interesting dialectic, but what has it to do with holiness? What do donkeys have to do with eternity? Rabbi David (Shelita) says that the Kedushah—the sacred liturgical "Holy, Holy, Holy is the Lord of hosts"—is the heart of religious experience. Cleaving to God—to God's demands on us—acknowledges His holiness. The lifeblood of holiness is present even in the farthest reaches of learning; and so a sugya—portion—about donkeys pumps blood even to the fingernails.

Hasidic teachings place learning, however important, lower than prayer. I am a Litvak (Lithuanian, a non-Hasid); I must use an explanation that places learning and prayer at least on the same level. If prayer is the "service of the heart," as our holy rabbis maintain, then learning is the "service of the mind." The rational faculty of people must also be turned to God through the utilitarian and, more especially, the nonutilitarian study of Torah. Our intellect should not be wasted on nonsense, or worse, turned toward untruth. And so perhaps the most seemingly secular in Torah is the holiest, perhaps the least practical is the most relevant.

These are truths that must be believed—like all religious truths. How to begin? With a teacher. And a friend. Or better yet, a friend who can teach you. The Talmud is a difficult, but by no means impossible, sea to swim in. Many have begun as adults and learned how to learn. Many rabbis and students will be happy to help. Get a group together. Make sure your teachers are good: "If the teacher seems to you like an angel (authentic and passionately committed)—learn!"

Use Adin Steinsaltz's Talmud if you know Hebrew, El Am if you don't. But if you don't know Hebrew, learn it. Don't use the Soncino English translation—you'll lose the flavor.

Upon asking his teacher if he should study the laws of conscientious objection in Torah, a friend of mine received this response: "No, study the laws of the sacrifices—that is more relevant."

To begin, go to the Jewish Theological Seminary for a Summer Institute, or take Talmud at a university. But remember that it is Torah. Go to Lubavitch. (See *Catalog I*, "Hasidic Communities.") Go to Israel. Pardes Institute, Hartman College, or Mount Zion Yeshivah are good for Americans (see As the Jew Turns: Baal Teshuvah). In Far Rockaway, N.Y. Rabbi Freifeld has a wonderful yeshivah for beginners; but be prepared for full commitment.

Begin any way you can. Talmud Torah is the essence of Judaism.

Giving a Devar Torah

I think of how many times I have gone to meetings, dinners, and programs sponsored by or concerned with the Jewish community—to find that the only authentically Jewish thing was that we met at all, that we were concerned with the community. There is always an invocation, it is true, but an invocation is *not* a devar Torah. An invocation is usually a plea for God's blessing on the gathering. I have ceased listening to most of them. But a devar Torah . . . that's a whole other thing! A devar Torah is simply one Jew sharing with the rest of the community of Jews something s/he has learned, thought about, toyed with, confronted, or worked through. It is not preaching; preaching goes against the very grain of the thing. It is a sharing, an invitation to others to join you, perhaps to respond to the issues you raise. It can be very short; it need not divert you from your purpose in meeting, but should imbue you with a transcendent sense that you are bound in other ways than simply this time and this place.

So . . . the plot. It behooves all of us who share this concern to mediate with every Jewish organization or community that we belong to, *whether these organizations are ostensibly "religious" in nature or not*, to renew this tradition of exchanging a devar Torah when we meet. Be loving—but firm. I have done it at times and found almost invariably that people respond so positively, so enthusiastically, are so challenged and challenging intellectually to me, that I wonder why we never did it before and when we can do it again. It is a joy to behold—and a joy to celebrate—when Jews spend the first five or ten minutes of a fundraising or social planning meeting reestablishing the fact that they are Jews. As it is written: "If you do thus, you shall be happy and all will be well with you" (*Pirkei Avot* 6:4).

It is written: "If two sit together and exchange no divrei Torah, they are a meeting of scoffers . . . but when two sit together and do exchange divrei Torah, the Divine Presence abides with them."

It is further written: "If three have eaten together at a table and have spoken no divrei Torah, it is as if they had eaten of sacrifices to dead idols . . . but if three have eaten together at a table and have spoken there divrei Torah, it is as if they had eaten at the table of the Lord."

What is this meant to tell us? Quite simply that when Jews gather for any purpose under heaven, they must act as Jews—and imbue their meeting with a recognition of the divine by speaking words of Torah to each other. While in most cases a community of Jews is reckoned to be ten people—the quorum referred to as a minyan, necessary for all communal prayer—in the case of divrei Torah the presence of two Jews constitutes sufficient recognition of their community to require them to meet over, or perhaps through, words of Torah. Whatever the reason that we meet, we acknowledge that there is something binding us that transcends and soars above all other concerns—our community, our sense of the divine, our commitment to a Jewish way. In a sense this is the foundation upon which we ought to conduct our business.

Traditional and not-so-traditional methods for interpreting Torah

Introduction

Rabbi Akiva died a dreadful death. It is said that his flesh was pulled apart with hooks, but that during this final agony the sage appeared blissful in the presence of his Roman captors:

And he prepared himself to take upon himself the yoke of the Kingdom of Heaven in love (by reciting the Shema) and his students said to him:

"Rabbi! Haven't you done enough?" He replied to them: "All my life, I worried about this verse 'Hear O Israel, the Lord our God, the Lord is One. And you shall love the Lord your God with all your heart, with all your soul, and *with all your might*.' And even though He would take my soul, I have said: 'O, when will the time come that I might fulfill it!' And now, the opportunity has come into my hands—and should I not fulfill it?" (Berakhot 61b).

He was, to the end, a martyr for the right to interpret. Earlier, when he had decided to join the revolt of Bar Kokhba against the power of Rome, he made interpretation—that right, that duty, that destiny—the crucial issue:

One time, the authorities decreed that Israel should not occupy itself with Torah. Papus ben Yehuda came upon Rabbi Akiva assembling groups in public and engaging in the study of Torah. Rabbi Akiva said to him: "You, Papus, whom they call wise, you are but a fool! I'll give you an analogy. The matter is like that of a fox who walks up and down a riverbank, watching the fish jump about here and there. He says to them: 'Why are you fleeing?' They reply: 'Because of the nets and hooks that human beings bring upon us.' He says to them: 'Why don't you come ashore, and we can live together, just as your parents used to live?' They reply: 'You are one who's famous for being shrewd—you are but a fool! If we're afraid here where we live safely, should we not be even more afraid in a place of mortal danger?' With us, it is similar: if we are afraid when we study Torah, which is called 'our life and strength of days,' then if we should leave off from words of Torah, how much the more so!" (Berakhot 61b).

Rabbinic method and language

Not a word of Scripture was allowed to pass the rabbis without being toyed with, turned against itself, paired with a contradictory word or with exactly the same word used in another context. The rabbis, therefore, understood that the Torah is in itself an interpretation of itself.

The method of rabbinic literature is the method of quotation. One sage states an opinion, and it is weighed against another, or against the majority of the sages. In this way it is emphasized that no opinion, no utterance, no interpretation is privileged, even where it is declared to prevail.

Jewish literature remains haunted by the minority opinion, much in the same way that the Jews as a whole remain a minority that haunts the majority. The dialectical method of pilpul—literally, "pepper" (the rabbis' felicitous term for hairsplitting interpretation, for restless discovery of ever more new facets, new dimensions to an argument)—remained a revolutionary method, even where revolutionary impulses lay dormant. It guaranteed that no language should be accepted as sacred. The rabbis understood that most imitations of the Bible's language fell flat, that imitation usually devolved into attempts to clothe oneself in the costumes of the past, to yearn nostalgically for something that could never be repeated, to abandon the responsibility to find authentic language for the *present* time. So the rabbis, despite their apparent conservatism, were the true revolutionaries, for they recognized that revolution reaches into language. The superficial "flatness" of rabbinic style, in contrast to the apparent "poetry" of biblical language, conceals a revolutionary revival of the power of common speech.

It is for this reason that the Talmud and Midrash, because of their own critical spirit, paradoxically became "sacred" literature *as soon as new, succeeding critical languages were invented*: philosophy, commentary, codes, and mystical speculation. The true sacredness of a text, then, rests in its power to generate interpretation.

Becoming a darshan: speaking words of wisdom

It is said in the tradition that every one of us must, sometime in our life, write a Sefer Torah. The custom refers to a literal act of writing; that is, each of us must become a scribe. (The tradition leaves a loophole: if one does not possess the skills of a scribe, one may commission another to perform this labor.) But I choose to read this injunction in a more fundamental sense— that each of us must, in effect, write the Torah from scratch, write it in our hearts and in our lives, *live* the many sides of the Torah in our own experience, and strive all our lives to unify them. This means, then, that all of us must become darshanim—interpreters.

I first learned how to "do" midrash (literally, a "searching out," i.e., interpretation) when I was a member of Havurat Shalom in Boston from 1969 to 1971. Before that I knew how to do scholarship on the Bible and how to do preaching, but not both as one act. Stimulated by the presence of people who were deeply committed to *both* scholarship and spiritual search, I began to experiment with a new idea; namely, that the devar Torah—the spiritual teaching of Torah on Shabbat and other occasions, when Jews meet—could also incorporate scholarship and historical understanding. I began to read biblical history, anthropology, sociology, etc., on the one hand, and Midrash and Kabbalah, on the other. I was determined that the insights derived from the former could enrich the latter, and that the latter could flow organically from the former.

In truth, however, the idea is not new. The rabbis of old—for example, Maimonides, Ibn Ezra and Abarbanel—did not shrink from the scientific scholarship of their own day. They could not afford to. It is only in our own time, when science and the spiritual world appear to have broken irrevocably with each other, that we imagine that we must live only in one or the other. But in truth we can afford to do so even *less* than our ancestors. It is a fatal luxury. Doing midrash is precisely an effort to bridge these worlds.

So, to give a devar Torah one must study. One must read the so-called scientific study of the Bible, and one must read what the rabbis and mystics have done with the same insights. One must learn that interpretations of the Torah exist on multiple levels, precisely because reality is multiple. Obviously, one cannot learn this in one jump. It is a lifetime of work, and it is a delight to see how one's insights about the Torah change from year to year. But think of it: your entire life engaged in the study of a single text! The world around us tries to divide us, from each other and against ourselves. Only by centering our lives on a single book—and for some of us it may even be a single story, a single verse, a single word!—can we ever aim at unity of thought, discourse, and action. The study of a single book does not close us off from other books; quite the opposite. Only thus can we perceive the other books as standing in some kind of relation *to each other*; only thus do the other books come alive, become coherent, produce insight. The study of a single book helps to organize the other books; the study of the other books helps to deepen our understanding of the single book.

The following are some points I follow for doing midrash. They have no particular order; I write them as they occur to me. Feel free to pick and choose among them for those that speak to you. It is not necessary to do all of them—treat all of this like a smorgasbord:

1. Take the act of giving divrei Torah very seriously. Regard it as a quest for self-understanding, understanding of others, and understanding of existence itself. Consider it as a form of spiritual exercise, a type of yoga, if you will. Consider it as a something that does not come to an end as soon as one has delivered a talk, but rather as something which begins at that point to open new stages of comprehension, to establish new tasks, and to create new priorities. After I have engaged in Torah discussion with friends, I find us saying, for days, weeks, months, and in a few cases years afterward: "I keep thinking about what we said about such-and-such." The devar Torah is like a stone dropped into a pool. The waves ripple infinitely.

2. Do not be afraid to take liberties with the tradition, but at the same

time, recognize your responsibility to the tradition. We are not forbidden to come up with new ideas (the *Zohar* says: "With each and every *new* interpretation of the Torah, a new heaven is created"). But to a certain extent we are obliged to try to relate our new ideas to the *whole* of tradition. In this situation, of course, we cannot expect to command a knowledge of the whole tradition; rather, we must relate a new idea to the whole tradition *that is known to us*, even if it is very little. In the early stages it is better to err on the side of scandalous creativity. The deeper we go in our labor of interpretation, the more of the tradition do we *appropriate* for ourselves, and therefore the more confidence we will have to speak, without fear that we are doing violence to the tradition. The more we study, the more we realize the immense strength and wisdom of the tradition, and therefore the more we realize that it's really almost impossible to do violence to it: the tradition is stronger than any one interpretation, even an interpretation that is made to prevail.

3. On the other hand, we can do violence to each other. The devar Torah must always be an effort to speak with real, flesh-and-blood people, whose sensibilities must be respected. The devar Torah can only take people where they are willing and ready to move. The darshan—interpreter—must not lay a trip on people. The darshan's job is to try to bring out the interpretation that is potentially present in the group as a whole—a task which in the short run may be painful or difficult, but in the long run must heal, revive, and repair. The darshan must therefore consider carefully his/her audience, even if that audience is only oneself. One must, moreover, be prepared to learn from one's audience. In fact, when I present a devar Torah to a group, it is usually in the form of a question that I believe the group can help me solve. This must not merely be a questioning to manipulate a group into giving what I regard, in a preconceived way, as *the* answer. I genuinely have questions. Rabbi Abraham Joshua Heschel may have had something like this in mind when he said that we—our generation—have forgotten how to ask the right questions. Always let your devar Torah arise from the deepest questions within you.

4. Keep a journal devoted exclusively to interpretation. This journal must be separate from one's diary or other notebooks or workbooks. It need not be restricted to Torah literature—it may include other literature from Jewish tradition or literature outside of Jewish tradition that we believe will deepen our understanding of the Torah. Before writing our own interpretations, we should write out *in full* the excerpt we have chosen to interpret. Sometimes all that is required is the act of writing it out. Sometimes the juxtaposition of quotations is *itself* an interpretation, one that requires very few words, very little effort on our part, to "explain." But once we have written out quotations or juxtaposed quotations, then we should go back and try to explain, even if we find the act redundant. Many times the connection between juxtaposed interpretations is clearer in our own heads than it will be for other people. Therefore we must retrace our own steps and try to discover what led us to find one idea, or combination of ideas, significant. This effort will, in turn, lead to new ideas, new insights.

5. In giving a devar Torah to a group, keep it simple. Do not expect to discuss the entire parashah—or even more than a paragraph, a few verses, a single verse, or a single word. The parashah (plural, parshiyot), literally, "division" (also called the sidra), is the weekly division of the synagogue Torah reading, arranged according to an annual cycle, beginning and ending on Simhat Torah. Every parashah contains an accompanying haftarah (literally, "conclusion"), a reading from the prophetic books of the Hebrew Bible (including the historical books Judges through Kings). The fact is that

To give a devar Torah, one must not be in a hurry. One must be ready to experiment and make mistakes. One must not be afraid of one's own capacity to interpret. One must recognize that each interpretation is a preparation for the one that follows. Therefore one must write down these interpretations, save them, and compare them from one year to the next. A good idea is to keep a journal.

complexity will arise of its own accord, and therefore it is essential that the material dealt with be of a manageable scope. To teach yourself or a group the endless possibilities that inhere in the smallest unit, you should practice at first with the smallest units, then work outward. Find the one verse or word that you can present as "pivotal" to the whole parashah. This means, of course, that you may have to study the whole parashah, but don't expect to tell all that you learn. Otherwise, the Torah discussion becomes a lecture, an academic report.

6. In seeking in your private study to arrive at an understanding of the parashah as a whole, try—even before you consult extrabiblical sources—to comprehend the way the parashah itself is structured. Why did the rabbis divide up the Torah text in the particular way that they did? How does the parashah begin, through what trajectory does it travel, where does it end and why? How—considered only within its boundaries—does it form a complete story or argument? Then think of the parashah in relation to the remainder of the Torah, and then in relation to the haftarah (the prophetic selection that is read with the parashah in the synagogue). Let the haftarah comment on the parashah (sometimes the reason for juxtaposing the two will appear trivial—a single repeated word or motif—but more often the connection will be profound and subtle).

7. Recognize the multiple levels of interpretation of the Torah—literary, historical, moral, mystical, etc.—and learn to make distinctions for yourself, in your journal and in private study, and for groups in Torah discussions between the various levels. Always try to announce, to yourself and to others: "Now we shall try this approach; now we shall try that approach." This helps to clarify the discussion and pinpoint the issues at stake in the text. If we want to learn about, let us say, the political and demographic history as presented in the stories of Abraham, we do not go—at least not at first—to the symbolic meaning of "Abraham" among the Kabbalists! Eventually that might be useful to us, but not at first. In the early stages of our study we should line up a series of reference works (there is a Bibliography at the end of this chapter) appropriate to each level of interpretation; and in presenting a discussion we should be careful to indicate clearly what world we're in at each stage of the discussion: biblical, rabbinic, kabbalistic, Hasidic, philosophical, or historicocritical. Eventually, of course, we will want to unify those realms. But we cannot do it easily. And we must remember that people usually want insights that help them arrive at self-understanding—so that while a complete survey of the multiple levels of interpretation might be useful to us privately, it will be less so to the group as a whole.

8. Do not be afraid to bring in a non-Jewish perspective to a devar Torah (provided, of course, that you clearly announce it as such in your

public discussion). This may include scientific scholarship, philosophy, poetry, fiction, literary criticism, world history, or current events. Remember, however, we are appropriating that material for Jewish tradition, rather than the other way around. Exodus 12:35-36 says that the Israelites, before their exodus from Egypt, "borrowed" from the Egyptians various valuables and household goods, and thereby "stripped the Egyptians." This may serve as a model of our relationship to the non-Jewish intellectual world in our interpretation of the Torah: we borrow ideas from the world around us, but precisely so that we may make our commanded journey.

The chances are, however, that many of the insights we would expect to appropriate from the non-Jewish world are already present, in one form or another, in Jewish tradition itself. So we should ask first if we can make the point from Jewish literature; only afterward, and only if the point is important and compelling, should we borrow from others.

9. Sometimes, of course, it becomes very important to know what Jewish interpreters and non-Jewish interpreters did with the same material. Unfortunately, such discussions usually take the form of "Rah, rah for our side!" Please remember that the differences between Jews and Christians, or Jews and Moslems, important as they seem to be, are still an in-house dispute, a discussion between members of the same human family. Remember, as well, that it is harder than it may first appear to discover "the Jewish point of view" on this or that issue. We eventually find that Jewish tradition, even the narrowest definition of Jewish tradition, contains ideas that are quite heterodox in implication. We also find that Jewish tradition is not, in all respects, more "enlightened" than non-Jewish traditions.

10. The best non-Jewish material that will aid us in the study of the Torah is not the material that *proclaims*—for example, poetry, philosophy, or theology (although not all such literature proclaims)—but rather material that engages in *critique*, especially literary criticism. Much of what passes for "literary criticism" in biblical scholarship really falls into the first category, subtly disguised as "scientific" scholarship. So one must go to literary criticism about works of literature other than the Bible, because the Bible is still too much of a sacred text in both the Jewish and the non-Jewish world to be evaluated creatively.

Literary criticism, especially of fiction, generally knows how to ask the kind of questions that will sharpen our understanding of the Torah: What is happening in the plot? What is happening to the characters? What sort of characters are we dealing with? What kinds of paradoxes and contradictions are being established? What is the style of the language and diction, and why is this style important in this particular place? Who is the narrator? What tone of voice is the narrator speaking in? Is the narrator being straightforward and earnest, or is s/he being devious and subversive? Do any key words or phrases recur, and if so, why? What is the "musical" design of the text, irrespective of what is being reported? And so forth; these questions are limitless.

11. In other words, don't be alarmed at the prospect of treating the Torah as *fiction*. This does not reduce its reality or its religious meaning. The fact is, long before modern literary criticism came to be the rabbis were asking the same sorts of questions about the text, and it is to their literature—the Talmud and the Midrash—that we should go first. (Only *after* reading modern literary criticism, however, can we fully appreciate the sophistication of the rabbis in their literary understanding of the Torah.) On one level, of course, the rabbis were attempting to combat subversion of the Torah by skeptics and maligners. But in doing so they knew

There is still a great deal in the Torah that we may legitimately feel has not been heeded by the nations of the world. There is also much that has not been heeded by Jews. We must learn to make these distinctions.

exactly what were the most subversive questions to ask, and they unhesitatingly proceeded to ask them. A standard rabbinic discussion of a verse or passage reads something like this: "One might ask, does not A contradict B? But there is no contradiction here, because A refers to such-and-such a situation, and B to such-and-such." The answer, by making logical distinctions or attempting to, is usually not as subversive as the question. But once the question is asked it cannot be erased, even by an answer, and it serves as a guide to deeper understanding. The rabbis and the mystics, however, probably knew this from the start.

12. In seeking insights and interpretations, *dig for the less obvious.* Everyone knows that the Bible frowns on slavery, unwarranted wars, mistreatment of paupers, widows, and orphans, idolatry, blasphemy, profanation of Shabbat, and dishonor to one's parents. What *else* can be said about these things? What sorts of psychology and philosophy can you find beneath a legal stipulation? Where we are dealing with laws, what relationship does the particular legal material have to the surrounding narrative? (The interplay of law and story are carefully modulated in the Torah.)

13. Cultivate a special relationship to a single story or event or personality. Let that portion serve as a guide to self-understanding for a period of time—say, a few weeks or months or a year. Then go on to another. Record your impressions in your journal. Let the portion you have chosen serve as the key for the interpretation of other stories, events, and personalities. If you have the same name as a biblical character (and if you have a Hebrew name at all, the chances are most likely that you do), study that character— or any other character you are particularly drawn to or troubled by. Compare the biblical treatment of that character to the rabbinic legends about him/her. Imagine yourself in a dialogue with that character (write it out). Experiment with several of these special relationships for quite some time (perhaps years or even decades).

14. In order to get a clear sense of the multiple ways to treat the Torah text, sometime in your private study pick a *small* unit and trace its treatment by postbiblical, medieval, and modern tradition and scholarship. For example, take the short narrative that describes the seduction of Eve, or the Tower of Babel, or the sacrifice of Isaac, etc. and read (1) the midrashic material on the passage, (2) Rashi and other medieval commentators, (3) a modern historicocritical commentary, (4) a Christian theological commentary, (5) a modern Jewish theological or philosophical treatment, (6) a literary study, etc. (see the Bibliography at the end of this chapter).

Certain contemporary writers, most notably Franz Kafka in his book *Parables and Paradoxes* (New York: Schocken, 1961) and Leszek Kolakowski in his book *The Key to Heaven* (New York: Grove Press, 1973), have written—from a more or less secular perspective—what we might call modern "midrashim" based on biblical stories. I would include selections from these and other writers as examples of what can be done creatively in interpretation.

15. Groups that engage in regular study and discussion of the Torah should begin to cultivate a certain group consciousness with regard to their Torah study. Divrei Torah can either be delivered extemporaneously or read, depending on the mood and occasion—but those that are written (and any extemporaneous talks that are written down afterward) should be collected and kept in a communal notebook. Just as the individual members keep journals, so this communal notebook will serve as a record, from one year to the next, of the growing depth and awareness of the community in their interpretation of the Torah. Individuals, furthermore, could comment

Groups might even consider selecting the best or most representative divrei Torah and publishing them. We are the makers of Jewish folklore and Jewish wisdom, and therefore it is not pretentious or overambitious to say that this material has permanent value.

on each other's commentaries and interpretations, and these "supercommentaries" could be arranged on a page in surrounding columns, similar to traditional Hebrew commentary.

16. You might consider breaking out of the written form of commentary and interpretation, and include in your delivery one or more *pictures* (famous painting or engravings, your own sketches, news photos, etc.) which you feel comment on or illustrate some aspect of the Torah text. Likewise, you might include a passage of music or song that you feel expresses something relevant to the text (unless your group frowns on recorded music on Shabbat, if that is when you meet).

17. Consider the Torah text, and our interpretation thereof, as a nexus bringing together the following great themes:

    a. the interpretation of the rise, decay, and crisis of civilized life

    b. the study of the close and complex dialectical interrelationship of Israel and the nations

    c. the exploration of personal spiritual qualities and of personality types

    d. the study of the family and family relationships

    e. the record of the growth and changes in Israel's self-concept as a nation

    f. a reflection of social and political issues relevant to contemporary life

    g. a changing and often contradictory portrait of God, and of the relationship between God and humanity, God and Israel

    h. a study of religious leadership and aspects of religious community

    i. an exploration of problems of language and communication

    j. a reflection on the cycles of time and seasons, and the contrast between cyclic time and forward-moving historical time

    k. reflections on the nature of religious ritual and celebration, of sacrifice, prayer, and penitence, or priesthood and prophecy.

It is up to you each time to select the issue that you wish to emphasize or to discover how these various themes interact in the same text. Obviously, you cannot treat all of them together in the same talk, but in preparing, try to note as many of them as you can and then *select*.

18. There is no order of priority regarding your consultation of commentaries and reference works (see the Bibliography), but if you happen to be in a hurry, the most useful works to consult are the commentary of Rashi (Rabbi Solomon ben Isaac, who lived in the eleventh century in France, whose commentaries on both Bible and Talmud remain the most lucid and indispensable guide to the normative Jewish point of view on the text); Louis Ginzberg's *Legends of the Jews*; Nehamah Liebowitz's *Studies in the Weekly Sidra*; the *Midrash Rabbah* (available in both Hebrew and English); and (in Hebrew) Bialik and Ravnitsky's *Sefer ha-Aggadah*. But then . . . you should not be in a hurry. Even these reference works, handy as they are, should be studied slowly and reflectively.

Interpretation is invariably subversive. It is a political act. It is violent with its own words and signs: it shatters them and rearranges them in exhilarating new combinations. Interpretation recognizes the double nature of language, the double potential of all utterances that seek to move people to action. And, too, interpretation is preoccupied with itself. It chases its own shadow. Even in the dullest language and most lifeless meters, interpretation is a bit mad, a bit poetic. Its meters rise silently from its oscillating chase of its readers, itself, its readers, itself, its readers, itself. . . .

You are interpreters; you are poets; you are mad. Only gradually will you learn to know it. Only gradually, because your lifetime is to be a preparation for interpreting. Every lifetime well spent is a life of study—wherever that study may be applied: in the streets, in the household, in the law courts, in the laboratory, in the labor unions, in the prisons, in the parliaments, in the marketplace, in the house of prayer, in the solitude of oneself. But all of this is dangerous.

The maggid once said to his disciples: "I shall teach you the best way to say Torah. You must cease to be aware of yourselves. You must be nothing but an ear which hears what the universe of the word is constantly saying within you. The moment you start hearing what you yourself are saying, you must stop" (*Tales of the Hasidim*, Martin Buber).

Selected annotated bibliography

The following list is not intended to be exhaustive. I have included the books that would be of most use to the beginner in the study and interpretation of the Torah, both modern scholarly works and traditional Jewish commentaries and midrash collections, but have radically simplified the list on the assumption that the reader is either unacquainted with, or is a beginner in, the Hebrew language.

Scholarly commentaries

1. *The International Critical Commentary.* Edinburgh: 1895 on; many volumes, various editors.
2. A. S. Peake, ed. *A Commentary on the Bible.* London: Thomas Nelson and Sons, 1919, 1960.
3. W. Lock and D. C. Simpson. *Westminster Commentaries.* London: Methuen, 1904 on.
4. W. R. Nicoll. *The Expositor's Bible.* London: Hodder and Stoughton, 1887 on.
5. F. C. Eiselen et al., eds. *The Abingdon Bible Commentary.* New York: 1929.

The above books represent scholarship along the lines of the classical "documentary hypothesis," first formulated definitively in Germany by Julius Wellhausen in the nineteenth century. Many of the insights of these commentators have become dated by more recent research, but biblical scholarship in general adheres even today to the lines established by this older scholarship. Some more recent scholarly commentaries include the following:

6. *The Interpreter's Bible.* New York and Nashville: Abingdon, 1953—a collation of the King James and the Revised Standard versions, together with two commentaries, one historicocritical, the other Christian-theological.
7. G. Ernest Wright et al., eds. *The Old Testament Library,* several volumes. Philadelphia: Westminster, 1962 on—commentaries on individual books of the Bible, oriented toward "form criticism" and "tradition history" (those schools of biblical research concerned with the oral tradition behind individual units of narrative and law, as distinguished from the literary compositions of larger units; more recent volumes have stressed "redaction history," i.e., study of the way that smaller units coalesced into their final assemblage).
8. W. F. Albright and D. N. Freedman, eds. *The Anchor Bible.* New York: Doubleday, 1966 on—new and sometimes unconventional translations of individual books of the Bible, together with detailed commentaries based on archaeological research and comparative Semitic philology. This series is excellent but must be used with care; a knowledge of Hebrew is helpful. Of the Torah books, only E. A. Speiser's translation and commentary on Genesis is available at present.

Two commentaries by critical scholars of Jewish origin are especially interesting and useful because of the challenges they represent to the classical "documentary hypothesis":

9. Benno Jacob. *The First Book of the Torah: Genesis.* New York: Ktav, 1974—this work is an abridged English translation of a work originally published in German (Berlin, 1934).
10. Umberto Cassuto. *A Commentary on the Book of Genesis,* 2 vols. Jerusalem: Magnes Press, 1961; orig. published in Hebrew, 1944.

——. *A Commentary on the Book of Exodus.* Jerusalem: Magnes Press, 1967—cf. Cassuto's interesting and provocative work, *The Documentary Hypothesis and the Composition of the Pentateuch.* Jerusalem: Magnes Press, 1961; orig. published in Hebrew, 1941.

Please note that these scholars do not represent an Orthodox-fundamentalist view. They are firmly grounded in modern critical scholarship. Their insights into the literary problems of the Torah books are extremely perceptive and useful, although here again a knowledge of Hebrew is helpful.

Critical introductions to the Bible and Bible dictionaries

1. S. R. Driver. *Introduction to the Literature of the Old Testament*. New York: Scribners, 1909.
2. Otto Eissfeldt. *Introduction to the Old Testament*. New York, 1965.
3. R. H. Pfeiffer. *Introduction to the Old Testament*. New York, 1956.
4. J. Hastings. *A Dictionary of the Bible*, 5 vols. Edinburgh, 1898–1904; one-volume ed., New York, 1909.
5. J. D. Davis. *The Westminster Dictionary of the Bible*, revised and rewritten by H. S. Gehman. Philadelphia: Westminster, 1944.
6. G. A. Buttrick et al., eds. *The Interpreter's Dictionary of the Bible*, 4 vols. New York and Nashville: Abingdon, 1962—an excellent work and perhaps the best all-around reference work on the Bible to date.

Histories of ancient Israel

1. John Bright. *A History of Israel*. Philadelphia, 1959—a standard work, representing the classical critical outlook combined with an orientation toward more recent research in archaeology and comparative Semitics.
2. Martin Noth. *History of Israel*. New York, 1958—the best work to read in comparison to Bright, because it advances certain radically skeptical ideas concerning the authenticity of biblical traditions.
3. W. F. Albright. *The Biblical Period from Abraham to Ezra*. New York, 1963—an excellent short summary of biblical history, available in paperback.
4. Yehezkel Kaufmann. *The Religion of Israel*. Chicago, 1960—not a history of Israel per se, but a history of Israelite religion; an absorbing and interesting work that challenges the established theories of the "documentary hypothesis." Kaufmann's work is generally respected by historicocritical scholars, but not accepted as normative. His principal thesis is that the so-called priestly material of the Torah books ("P") is the earliest, rather than the latest, stratum of composition.

The following works by Jewish historians might usefully be read and compared to the above works:
5. Salo W. Baron. *A Social and Religious History of the Jews*. Vol. 1: *To the Beginning of the Christian Era*. Philadelphia: Jewish Publication Society, 1952.
6. Simon Dubnow. *A History of the Jews*. Vol. 1: *From the Beginning to the Early Christian Era*. London: Thomas Yoseloff, 1962.
7. Yehezkel Kaufmann. "The Biblical Period." In *Great Ages and Ideas of the Jewish People*, Leo W. Schwarz, ed. New York: Modern Library, 1956, pp. 3-92.

Archaeological studies and works on the ancient Near East

1. W. F. Albright. *From the Stone Age to Christianity*. Garden City, N.Y., 1957—an excellent and standard introduction to biblical history from the archaeologist's perspective.
2. ———. *Archaeology and the Religion of Israel*. Baltimore, 1953—a supplement to the above work.
3. D. N. Freedman and G. E. Wright, eds. *The Biblical Archaeologist Reader*, vol. 1 (Garden City, 1961), vol. 2 (ed. D. N. Freedman and E. F. Campbell, Jr., Garden City, 1964), vol. 3 (ed. E. F. Campbell, Jr., and D. N. Freedman, Garden City, 1970)—anthologies of some of the most important articles appearing in the journal *The Biblical Archaeologist* in recent decades.

Giving a Devar Torah

The God of Abraham, the God of Isaac
An Aramean fugitive, my father Abraham, an atheist, refused to serve the gods. "The gods," he'd say, "are merely an excuse for people to enslave each other—they are a lie, bad faith, false consciousness." And so he sought a nonreligion, a precise refusal of servitude to god or man, and picked up followers among the alienated in Haran. In debt up to his neck to Eliezer of Damascus, he gleaned the other debt-slaves, the pickpockets, the sharecroppers, the unemployed—some blacks, rebellious women, poets, hipsters, clowns—and ran. They took to the hills together, formed a band, and learned to fight and, intermittently, to wheel and deal. They entertained and rented themselves out as soldiers, tinkers, busboys, builders, midwives, and popular musicians. Here and there they managed to grab up a little land.

Meanwhile, they gave their non-religion an unpronounceable and secret name. Some of the gang would joke about it and say the name meant simply "Let it be"—a private joke they shared, since "god" to them meant slavery, and they were relatively free. But the nearby townsfolk didn't understand the joke and thought the strangers, too, like themselves, were worshiping a god. Abraham's people sometimes played along, and at times took on the local languages and ways.

Their women they would call their sisters, an excuse they gave at first to city folk, because they knew the townspeople would be enraged to find them treating wives as equals, and would murder them for their subversion. But then, as such things go, the name caught on, and it became an appellation of affection: "How beautiful your breasts, my sister-bride!" one of their racy private songs would go, and among themselves they used to say: "Our women? They are queens, they laugh at gods, and we are kings; our kingdom's everywhere, north, south, east, west—and all the nations of the world are blessed in us, but we, we let them think they have it their way."

But Abraham foresaw, as well, the need for discipline. He taught, and acted out as parables, the paradoxes of their way, teaching them to think in dialectics, to interpret cryptic stories, meditate, and engage in peppery arguments for fun. And he devised a harrowing initiation to teach the kids what they were up against. A child would be bound up like a ram and would watch his father raise a knife to slaughter him—but then back away, release him, and sacrifice a ram instead. Then the father would embrace the child, welcome him anew to life, and say: "Death is everywhere, my child. Today, you learned to feel its presence. You will have death with you everywhere you go, and you will see the cities of the world where people worship death, revere him as their god.

Today I placed before you life and death, and just as I have *chosen* here to let you live, so may you *choose* life, and nevermore forget that only choice can vanquish death. Death is your friend—he lets you know the stakes are high—but he is not your god."

From then on the child was called a "chosen one," for he learned what choice meant and how to choose.

On the day that Abraham led his own son through this ritual, on a mountain at high noon, they sat a long while afterward and talked. The father told the boy about his own childhood and talked about the idols in Haran; involuntarily, he raised his hand for emphasis above his head, as if to smash them once again, but caught himself, embarrassed—for he realized suddenly that he still held the knife above his son. Then he flung it out with all his strength and watched it disappear, whirring softly, across the spacious valley lying below. And Isaac laughed, and said: "I see." Abraham, his eyes aflame, turned back to him and kissed him, clasped him to his breast, and wept: "Thank you. Now you've earned yourself a name. Now you understand."

And Isaac, his voice now changed into a man's voice, said: "Tell me, Abba . . . you have left your father's house. Will I do the same? And will my child?" "You have done so already," Abraham replied. "More than this is not given you to know." And Isaac squinted. Suddenly his vision dimmed a bit. Looking at the ground, he said: "Abba, I'm afraid!"

And Abraham, grown a bit afraid himself but not altering his voice, held his son to him again and said: "Hush, my child. There are those who even now are worshiping the fear of Isaac."

(Joel Rosenberg)

Abraham

Abraham's spiritual poverty and the inertia of this poverty are an asset; they make concentration easier for him, or, even more, they are concentration already—by this, however, he loses the advantage that lies in applying the powers of concentration.

Abraham falls victim to the following illusion: he cannot stand the uniformity of this world. Now the world is known, however, to be uncommonly various, which can be verified at any time by taking a handful of world and looking at it closely. Thus this complaint at the uniformity of the world is really a complaint at not having been mixed profoundly enough with the diversity of the world.

I could conceive of another Abraham for myself—he certainly would have never gotten to be a patriarch or even an old-clothes dealer—who was prepared to satisfy the demand for a sacrifice immediately, with the promptness of a waiter, but was unable to bring it off because he could not get away, being indispensable; the household needed him, there was perpetually something or other to put in order,

4. George E. Mendenhall. *The Tenth Generation: The Origins of the Biblical Tradition.* Baltimore and London, 1974—while some of the chapters are of a somewhat technical nature, this book is an excellent and persuasive study representing more recent insights into the history of ancient Israel; many of the ideas of this book are summarized in less technical form in three articles by Mendenhall appearing in *The Biblical Archaeologist Reader*, vol. 3.

5. H. Frankfort et al. *Before Philosophy: The Intellectual Adventure of Ancient Man.* Baltimore and London, 1946, 1966—excellent essays by various scholars, addressed to the lay reader, on the life and thought of the ancient Near East, including a chapter on biblical thought.

6. James B. Pritchard, ed. *Ancient Near Eastern Texts Relating to the Old Testament.* Princeton, 1955—a thorough one-volume anthology of the literature of the ancient Near East exclusive of the Bible, including mythological, historical, ethical, theological, and legal writings.

7. Cyrus H. Gordon. *The Ancient Near East.* New York, 1953—a concise and well-written survey of the civilization of the ancient Near East.

Books of special interest by Jewish theologians grounded in historicocritical scholarship

1. Martin Buber. *The Prophetic Faith.* New York, 1965—a concise and well-written study of the idea of prophecy in ancient Israel.

2. ——. *Moses: The Revelation and the Covenant.* New York, 1958—a philosophically and theologically oriented study of the biblical traditions about Moses and the Sinai covenant.

3. ——. *The Kingship of God.* New York, 1967—a somewhat difficult book exploring the concept of the kingship of God.

4. Abraham J. Heschel. *The Prophets.* Philadelphia, 1962—Heschel's beautifully written classic study of the ideas and personalities of biblical prophecy.

5. Franz Rosenzweig. *The Star of Redemption.* New York, 1971—Rosenzweig's monumental work of Jewish philosophy is extremely difficult reading, but contains some beautiful insights on biblical categories of thought, as reinterpreted by later Jewish tradition and by Rosenzweig's own existential outlook.

Linguistic and other critical aids for those who know Hebrew

1. Rudolf Kittel. *Biblia Hebraica.* Stuttgart, 1945—a critically edited text of the Hebrew Bible, with variorum notes.

2. S. Mandelkern. *Konkordentzia la-Tanakh* or *Veteris Testamenti Concordantiae.* Jerusalem: Schocken, 1967—a listing of every word in the Hebrew Bible and where it occurs. Extremely useful for those who wish to study the comparative usages of biblical words and grammatical forms according to their context.

3. E. Katz. *A Classified Concordance to the Torah.* Jerusalem and New York, 1964—a concordance arranged according to topics and concepts; can be used by those who do not know Hebrew.

4. F. Brown, S. R. Driver, and C. A. Briggs. *A Hebrew and English Lexicon of the Old Testament.* Oxford, 1907, 1966—a standard and thorough lexicon, but now somewhat dated.

5. W. Baumgartner. *Lexicon in Veteris Testamenti Libros.* Leiden, 1948–53—a more up-to-date lexicon than that of Brown, Driver, and Briggs.

6. J. W. Weingreen. *A Practical Grammar for Classical Hebrew*, 2d ed. London, 1959—the standard introduction to biblical Hebrew, for the beginner.

7. W. Gesenius. *Hebrew Grammar*. Trans. Benjamin Davies, rev. E. Kautzsch and E. Mitchell. Andover, 1883; more recent editions available—a standard older study of biblical Hebrew, somewhat out of date. This is *not* a textbook, like Weingreen's, but a linguistic study.

8. George Landes. *A Student's Vocabulary of Biblical Hebrew Listed According to Frequency and Cognate*. New York, 1961—an important reference work and learning tool.

Hebrew commentaries translated into English and other Jewish commentaries

1. J. H. Hertz. *The Pentateuch and Haftorahs*. London: Soncino Press, 1950—a standard but somewhat stuffy commentary on the Torah from a modern Orthodox perspective, by the late chief rabbi of England. Based on the 1917 Jewish Publication Society translation of the Bible.

2. A. Cohen. *The Soncino Chumash*. London: Soncino Press, 1945—the old JPS translation, plus a digest of the most important commentaries by medieval commentators, including Rashi, Ibn Ezra, and Nahmanides.

3. Nehamah Liebowitz. *Studies in the Weekly Sidra*, numerous series, New York: World Zionist Organization Department for Torah Education and Culture in the Diaspora, 1958 on—perhaps the best single guide for preparation on individual parshiyot, containing much valuable rabbinic discussion and a lucid modern commentary from a religious perspective.

4. Abraham ben Isaiah and Benjamin Sharfman. *The Pentateuch and Rashi's Commentary*, 5 vols. Brooklyn, N.Y.: S. S. and R. Publishing Co., 1949—an interlinear translation of both the Torah text and Rashi's commentary.

5. M. Rosenbaum and A. M. Silbermann. *Pentateuch with Targum Onkelos, Haftaroth and Rashi's Commentary*, 5 vols. New York: Hebrew Publishing Company, 1935—another translation of Rashi, not interlinear, but containing some useful notes in the back of the book.

6. Charles B. Chavel. *Ramban* [Rabbi Moses ben Nahman]: *Commentary on the Torah: Genesis–Numbers*. New York: Shilo, 1972–75. More volumes in preparation.

Modern Jewish translations of the Bible

1. *The Holy Scriptures according to the Masoretic Text*. Philadelphia, Jewish Publication Society, 1917—the older Jewish translation, similar in style and spirit to the King James and Revised Standard versions.

2. *The Torah: The Five Books of Moses*. Philadelphia: Jewish Publication Society, 1962—a lucid and fluent translation of the Torah, executed with the aid of modern critical scholarship; very useful for groups that meet regularly for study and prayer. In recent years JPS has also issued other translations of biblical books, including Isaiah, Jeremiah, Psalms, the Five Megillot (Esther, Song of Songs, Lamentations, Ecclesiastes, and Ruth), and Jonah.

3. Everett Fox. "In the Beginning: A New English Rendition of Genesis." *Response* 14, Summer 1972—a poetic and eminently readable translation of Genesis, based on the Buber-Rosenzweig German translation.

Midrash collections and midrash digests in English

The Midrash is not a single book, but a genre of Jewish literature devoted to commentary and exposition of the Hebrew Bible. Unlike the commen-

the house was never ready; for without having his house ready, without having something to fall back on, he could not leave—this the Bible also realized, for it says: "He set his house in order." And, in fact, Abraham possessed everything in plenty to start with; if he had not had a house, where would he have raised his son, and in which rafter would he have stuck the sacrificial knife?

This Abraham—but it's all an old story not worth discussing any longer. Especially not the real Abraham; he had everything to start with, was brought up to it from childhood—and I can't see the leap. If he already had everything, and yet was to be raised still higher, then something had to be taken away from him, at least in appearance: this would be logical and no leap. It was different for the other Abrahams, who stood in the houses they were building and suddenly had to go up on Mount Moriah; it is possible that they did not even have a son, yet already had to sacrifice him. These are impossibilities, and Sarah was right to laugh. Thus only the suspicion remains that it was by intention that these men did not ready their houses, and—to select a very great example—hid their faces in magic trilogies in order not to have to lift them and see the mountain standing in the distance.

But take another Abraham. One who wanted to perform the sacrifice altogether in the right way and had a correct sense in general of the whole affair, but could not believe that he was the one meant, he, an ugly old man, and the dirty youngster that was his child. True faith is not lacking to him, he has this faith; he would make the sacrifice in the right spirit if only he could believe he was the one meant. He is afraid that after starting out as Abraham with his son he would change on the way into Don Quixote. The world would have been enraged at Abraham could it have beheld him at the time, but this one is afraid that the world would laugh itself to death at the sight of him. However, it is not the ridiculousness as such that he is afraid of—though he is, of course, afraid of that too and, above all, of his joining in the laughter—but in the main he is afraid that this ridiculousness will make him even older and uglier, his son even dirtier, even more unworthy of being really called. An Abraham who should come unsummoned! It is as if, at the end of the year, when the best student was solemnly about to receive a prize, the worst student rose in the expectant stillness and came forward from his dirty desk in the last row because he had made a mistake of hearing, and the whole class burst out laughing. And perhaps he had made no mistake at all, his name really was called, it having been the teacher's intention to make the rewarding of the best student at the same time a punishment for the worst one.

(Franz Kafka, *Parables and Paradoxes* New York: Schocken, 1961)

Abraham, or Lofty Grief

The story of Abraham and Isaac was philosophically interpreted by Sören Kierkegaard and his successors as the problem of fear: Abraham was to sacrifice his son at God's command. But whence came his certainty that he had rightly understood the command? In other words, the interpretation of the Isaac affair from an existentialist point of view starts out from the assumption that the final decision lay with Abraham, that Abraham had no way of obtaining full certainty as to the source or the content of the command, and that he was seized with fear and trembling at the thought that he might be sacrificing his son's life in vain. Abraham, therefore, is a personification of fear in a situation in which a choice must perforce be made between great values and in which there are no external reasons on which to ground the choice.

I confess that I'm inclined to solve this problem in a considerably more simple way, namely, that has some bearing on Abraham's past. I am assuming that Abraham could not doubt the divine origin of the command. Absolutely reliable means were at his disposal for concluding an agreement with his Creator, means unknown to us today. He saw a good deal of Him and even enjoyed a certain familiarity with his superior. I also take into account the famous promise that the Lord had made to him, the promise to make of him the progenitor of a great, of an especially blessed, people, which would eventually assume an extraordinary position in the world. He attached only one condition thereto: absolute obedience vis-à-vis authority. If Abraham had not been sure that God really had spoken to him, God's intention would have been senseless. He wanted, in fact, to test the loyalty of His subject so He had to find a means to awaken in Abraham the unshakable conviction that he had received precisely such an order from his superior. Otherwise, the aim of the undertaking would not be achieved—instead of reflecting on whether he should carry out the order, Abraham would perforce have reflected on whether he had actually received a command. In other words, Abraham is responsible for the notion of the state's supreme claims. The future fate of the people and the greatness of the state depend upon the loyal execution of superior orders. But the superior authority demanded from him that he sacrifice his own child. Abraham had the nature of a lance corporal and was used to sticking exactly

tary literature, which consists of books published in the name of a single commentator, midrash collections contain interpretations by many sages, including anonymous sages, brought together usually in a verse-by-verse format. There were many midrash collections edited throughout the Middle Ages and into modern times. The following titles are those midrash collections available in English:

1. *Midrash Rabbah*, 10 vols. London: Soncino, 1948—the main midrashic collection, actually composed of numerous smaller collections, each of a different nature, but arranged in a book-by-book and verse-by-verse format, covering the Torah and numerous other books of the Bible.

2. *The Babylonian Talmud.* London: Soncino, 1948—contains many aggadot (Jewish legends, anecdotes, and homilies) based on Scripture; to use as a reference work for a given chapter and verse of the Hebrew Bible, the reader should consult the scriptural reference index in the index volume of this set.

3. *Ein Jacob.* Translated by S. Glick. New York, 1920—a collection of the aggadic material of the Talmud without the legal material.

4. Gerald Friedlander. *Pirke de Rabbi Eliezer.* London, 1916—an interesting and important midrash collection, dealing mostly with the stories in Genesis, containing much material of a mythological and mystical nature.

5. W. Braude. *Pesikta Rabbati*, 2 vols., Yale Judaica Series. New Haven: Yale, 1968—rabbinic discourses for feasts, fasts, and special Sabbaths.

6. ———. *Midrash on Psalms*, Yale Judaica Series. New Haven: Yale, 1959.

7. ———. *Pesikta de-Rav Kahana.* Philadelphia: Jewish Publication Society, 1975—another collection of rabbinic discourses for special occasions.

8. Louis Ginzberg. *Legends of the Jews*, 7 vols. Philadelphia: Jewish Publication Society, 1956—the most indispensable companion to Torah study, containing a digest of midrashim on all of the narrative, and some of the legal, material of the Torah. The midrashim are arranged to read as a single, connected work, which is somewhat misleading if one is more interested in the original midrashic sources, but an invaluable and eminently readable guide for the beginning student. Actually, this is one of those rare works that is equally valuable for scholars and lay readers. The fifth and sixth volumes contain Ginzberg's prodigious scholarly notes, and the seventh volume is an exhaustive index of ideas, motifs, and names.

9. ———. *Legends of the Bible.* Philadelphia: Jewish Publication Society, 1956—an inexpensive one-volume abridgment of the above work, minus notes and index.

10. J. Z. Lauterbach. *Mekilta de-Rabbi Ishmael*, 3 vols. Philadelphia: Jewish Publication Society, 1933-35; paperback, 1976—a critical edition and translation of one of the earliest midrash collections, containing commentary on Exodus (chs. 12 and following).

11. M. Simon and H. Sperling. *The Zohar*, 5 vols. London: Soncino, 1934, 1970—the *Zohar*, though arranged like a verse-by-verse midrash on the Torah, is actually a work of a quite different character from midrash. It is the classic text of Jewish mysticism, purportedly composed by Rabbi Shimeon bar Yohai in the second century C.E., but actually composed by Moses of Leon, a thirteenth-century Spanish Jew; it contains many delightful stories of Rabbi Shimeon and his circle. As an aid in the study of the Torah this is heady stuff and should be used with care, and only after rabbinic works have been consulted. This collection poses enormous difficulties to the uninitiated reader; a more useful digest of *Zohar* material, also arranged according to the order of the Torah books, is Gershom G. Scholem's *The Zohar: The Book of Splendor* (New York: Schocken, 1949 and later; available in paperback), which is oriented to the lay reader.

12. M. Kasher. *The Encyclopedia of Biblical Interpretation.* New York: American Biblical Encyclopedia Society, 1953—a partial English translation of Kasher's monumental *Torah Shelemah*, a compendium of every major midrash and commentary on each verse of the Bible. Only about ten volumes are available in English at present; the work is in progress.

Commentaries and midrash collections and digests in Hebrew

For an exhaustive bibliography of rabbinic literature in Hebrew, and commentaries thereto, the reader should consult:

1. John T. Townsend. "Rabbinic Sources." In *The Study of Judaism: Bibliographical Essays*, R. Bavier et al. New York: Anti-Defamation League of Bnai Brith, 1972, pp. 37-80.

2. Hermann Strack. *Introduction to the Talmud and Midrash*. Philadelphia: Jewish Publication Society, 1945; New York: Harper & Row, 1965—the standard reference work on Talmud and Midrash, somewhat out of date but containing literally hundreds of titles, together with a useful classification and description of the major rabbinic works.

OTHER USEFUL COLLECTIONS AND REFERENCE WORKS

1. A. Hayman. *Sefer Torah Haketuvah ve-ha-mesurah al Torah, Nev-i'im u-Ketuvim*. 3 vols. Tel Aviv: Dvir, 1964-65 (a reproduction of the 1936-39 ed.)—an exhaustive index to every midrashic source on a given verse of the Hebrew Bible, including the *Zohar*.

2. M. D. Gross. *Otzar ha-Aggadah*. 3 vols. Jerusalem: Mosad ha-Rav Kook, 1954—a collection of rabbinic legends and sayings, arranged alphabetically according to idea or motif.

3. H. N. Bialik and Y. H. Ravnitsky. *Sefer ha-Aggadah*. Tel Aviv: Dvir, 1960—the indispensable reference work for those who know Hebrew, containing rabbinic aggadot arranged both according to the order of biblical narrative, and topically, by concept or motif; also contains biographical material on the sages, culled from rabbinic literature, and two indexes, one of proverbs and sayings, the other topical.

Modern literary approaches to the Bible and form criticism

1. Hermann Gunkel. *The Legends of Genesis*. New York, 1970—an introductory work by the father of Old Testament form criticism. This book

to instructions from above—nevertheless, he was not without sympathy for the fate of his family. When God ordered him to sacrifice his son in the fire He did not deem it necessary to justify the order. Superiors are not in the habit of explaining orders to subordinates. The essence of an order is that it must be executed because it is an order and not because it is reasonable, promising of success, or well thought out. It is by no means required that the executant understand its meaning; were it so, it would inevitably lead to anarchy and chaos. A subordinate who asks about the meaning of an order is a sower of disorder, a sterile argumentative person. At bottom, he is a smart aleck, an enemy of authority, of the social order, and of the establishment.

But what if the order demands that you slay your own son?

Abraham's conflict is the actual conflict of the soldier. Abraham knew that he found himself in an unnatural situation. A proof of this is furnished by the fact that as he neared the sacrifice site he ordered the servants to remain behind on the pretext that he and his son wanted to pray. Actually, he wanted to carry out this hideous assignment all by himself. He did not betray the aim of the outing even to his son. He wanted to prevent Isaac from perceiving that he was being victimized by his own father.

Upon arriving at the spot, Abraham, without further ado, began to lay the logs in an orderly pile. This required some adroitness because the logs kept rolling off the pile and Abraham had to begin to rebuild the pyre several times from scratch. Isaac did not lend a hand in these preparations, but kept fearfully watching his father and timidly asking some questions, to which he received only peevish and grudging replies.

Finally the matter at hand could no longer be delayed. Abraham did not want to enlighten Isaac about his fate; such an instruction was not included in the command. Therefore he could spare the child its horror. He wanted to kill him with a lightninglike blow from behind, with an expert blow that would give the boy no time to think of the fate in store for him.

But his plan miscarried. Isaac clambered up on the pile where his father had ordered him to rectify a minor detail in the construction. At this moment Abraham raised the heavy bronze sword which ordinarily he used to slaughter oxen. At this self-same moment, however, the cry of the angel resounded in the air: "Stop!" This cry was immediately followed by a cry of horror. Isaac had turned around and had caught sight of his father standing there, as if frozen, with the raised weapon, lips pursed and a look of brutal determination on his face. Isaac fell to the ground in a faint.

God smiled good-naturedly and patted Abraham on the shoulder.

"You act just as you are supposed to," He said appreciatively. "Now I know that at My command you would not even spare your own son!" Thereupon He repeated the old promise to increase and multiply Abraham's people and to help them destroy their enemies: "Because you have hearkened to My voice."

The story ends on this note. It could, of course, also have ended differently. Had Isaac not turned his head at the last moment, he would have known nothing whatsoever of what was transpiring behind his back. He would have made his way down from the pile a moment later and seen his father standing there calmly, with the sword on the ground beside him. Thus the whole story would have unfolded outside Isaac's consciousness and only between Abraham and God. It would have served to exemplify a particular kind of upbringing. But Isaac saw, and Abraham was content because he had earned God's recognition, had received His confirmation that a great state would arise in the future, and, finally, had not offered up his son as a burnt offering. Everything had a happy ending and there was much merriment in the family. Isaac, of course, never got over his shock. From this time on he was wobbly on his legs and the mere sight of his father made him feel queasy. But he lived long and enjoyed a great success.

Moral: Some effete intellectuals and hysterical, whining milksops may say from the standpoint of morality it makes no difference whether Abraham slew his son or merely raised his sword with this purpose in view and then was restrained by somebody at the last moment. We, the real men, along with Abraham are of the opposite opinion. We consider the result and know that it matters not whether he wanted to kill or not. The point is that he did not kill. So we all laugh uproariously over God's splendid joke. You can see for yourselves, finally, that He is indeed a capital fellow.

(Leszek Kolakowski, *The Key to Heaven* New York: Grove, 1973)

is terribly dated, but it is still an important guide to literary study of the Bible, written from a scholarly perspective.

2. Claus Koch. *The Growth of Biblical Tradition*. New York, 1969—an up-to-date introduction to the perspectives and methods of form criticism, together with some sample analyses of biblical passages.

3. K. R. R. Gros Louis, J. S. Ackerman, and T. Warshaw. *Literary Interpretations of Biblical Narratives*. New York and Nashville, 1974—a valuable collection of essays presenting literary studies of selected biblical narratives.

4. Nahum M. Sarna. *Understanding Genesis*. New York: Schocken, 1970—a modern study of Genesis by an author sensitive to literary values in the text. Contains a valuable bibliography.

5. Moshe Greenberg. *Understanding Exodus*. New York, 1974—together with Sarna's work, this book forms part of a series of biblical studies for the lay reader published by the Melton Institute. The Melton books also contain teacher's and student's guides.

6. Everett Fox. "The Buber-Rosenzweig Translation of the Bible." *Response*, no. 12 (Winter 1971–72), pp. 29-42—a valuable discussion of the problems of translating the Bible, containing much material of interest to the literary study of the Torah.

7. Eric I. Lowenthal. *The Joseph Narrative in Genesis*. New York: Ktav, 1973—a well-written and useful extended study of a single story cycle; a useful model of the kind of insights that are possible from literary study.

8. George Steiner. "Schönberg's *Moses and Aaron*," in Steiner's book *Language and Silence*. New York: Atheneum, 1969—a beautifully written article on a modern opera based on the story of the Exodus, in which many important literary insights about the Torah narrative are educed.

The following works are so-called structuralist studies of certain parts of the Bible and are very useful to a literary understanding:

9. Edmund Leach. "Lévi-Strauss in the Garden of Eden." *Transactions of the New York Academy of Sciences* 23-24 (1961): 386–96.

10. ———. "Genesis as Myth." *Discovery* 23 (1962): 3-35.

11. ———. "The Legitimacy of Solomon: Some Structural Aspects of Old Testament History." Reprinted in M. Lane, ed. *Introduction to Structuralism*. New York, 1970, pp. 248-92.

12. Mary Douglas. "Deciphering a Meal." *Daedalus*, Winter 1972, pp. 68-81.

13. ———. "The Abominations of Leviticus," in her *Purity and Danger: An Analysis of the Concepts of Pollution and Taboo*. Baltimore, 1966, pp. 54-72.

Other useful literary and/or scholarly approaches to the Bible from a modern Jewish perspective:

1. Samuel Sandmel. *The Enjoyment of Scripture*. New York: Oxford, 1972.

2. Maurice Samuel. *Certain People of the Book*. New York: Knopf, 1955—intriguing, very well written personality studies of biblical characters.

3. Bernard J. Bamberger. *The Bible: A Modern Jewish Approach*, 2d ed. New York: Schocken, 1963.

4. W. Gunther Plaut. *A Commentary on Genesis*. New York: Union of American Hebrew Congregations, 1975.

Discussions of biblical commandments from a religious perspective

1. S. R. Hirsch. *Horeb*, 2 vols. London: Soncino, 1962.

2. Moses Maimonides. *The Commandments*, 2 vols. London: Soncino, 1967.

As the Jew Turns: A Guide to Baalei Teshuvah

In the classical interpretations, teshuvah is seen as a mitzvah involving a psychological technique of self-rehabilitation. It is a process to be worked through and achieved. One *does* teshuvah, the doing being a step beyond its mere contemplation.

Jewish tradition places an emphasis on the role of actions (mitzvot) over precisely formulated creeds of belief and allegiance. Thus the baal teshuvah—master of repentance; one who turns—often begins his/her trek back to an effective and gratifying Jewish consciousness through the renewed acceptance of neglected observances and symbols.

It is important to keep in mind that turning to God is not reserved for the so-called sinner—a concept foreign to authentic Jewish thinking—but is an obligation of all Jews at all times. Thus the term baal or baalat teshuvah—the possessor of teshuvah—is a misleading one that has entered the vocabulary of traditional Jews in recent years. It suggests that the Jew from a nonobservant background is the prime target of the teshuvah process. It tends to equate the acceptance of ritual practices with teshuvah itself. It often fails to generate the more accurate concept that repentance is the property of all, that observant Jews may be as much in need of teshuvah as the nonobservant Jew.

One of our most erudite sages, Rabbi Moshe ben Maimon (the Rambam or Maimonides), codified the laws of teshuvah in ten chapters of his massive twelfth-century code, the *Mishneh Torah*. These chapters were based upon his formulation of the single positive mitzvah: "Sheyashuv ha-hoteh mei-heto lifnei ha-Shem ve-yitvadeh—the transgressor shall return from his transgression before God and shall confess."

The Rambam begins with an understanding of a person's capacity for self-examination—rather than self-depreciation or self-mortification. This understanding is the primary step in the process of return. The process continues with the human faculty to confront an issue. Verbalization (confession) and the arriving at a state of confidence that the misdeed will not be repeated complete the process of teshuvah. Furthermore, the only test of a successful "return" is that one refrains from repeating the transgression when similar circumstances arise. Teshuvah, then, for the Rambam, is rooted entirely in a well-defined concept of the freedom of human action, an idea that permeates all rabbinic thinking.

Every Jew is obligated to do teshuvah, to return. Teshuvah—turning; repentance; response—is an essential component of both Jewish law and lore. Its theological implications are momentous and its spiritual uplifting is unparalleled. Teshuvah occupies a central position in all discussions of the Jew's relations to other human beings.

Great is repentance, for it brings healing to the world. —Talmud

A TALE OF TESHUVA

Rabbi Abraham Isaac ha-Kohen Kook (1868–1935) also considered teshuvah and, in an amalgam of both the rabbinic and mystic traditions, states in his highly venerated *Lights of Teshuvah* that

repentance is the healthiest experience of the soul. A healthy soul and a healthy body must inevitably attain the great happiness of teshuvah, and in this state the soul will feel the greatest natural pleasure.

He continues:

Repentance exalts man above all the degradations to be found in the world; nonetheless, man does not become alien to the world; rather, he uplifts with himself the world and life (ch. 12).

Rav Kook also introduces the juxtaposition of individual and general teshuvah, the former

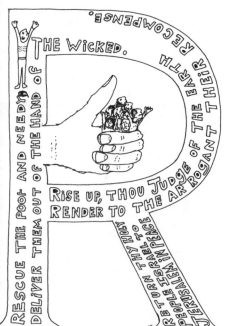

corresponding to specific sins as well as to many sins. Man places his sin "before his face," and is remorseful for it. He is pained because of his having been snared in sin; he senses within himself the sacred freedom, so pleasant to his weary soul and is progressively cured. The radiant lights of the sun of mercy, transcendental mercy, cast their rays upon him, and he becomes joyful.

The latter, general teshuvah,

comes to one who, though no specific sin or sins of the past come to his mind . . . is greatly pained . . . that the light of God does not shine upon him. . . . He is embittered at himself and finds no escape from the trap of his pursuers, which has no specific nature. . . . From amidst this spiritual bitterness teshuvah emerges as healing by means of a skillful physician.

This is clearly a description of the paranoia and self-deprecation that result from the general malaise of alienation from God and/or self. It is to be treated by the "skillful physician," who might either be the spiritual mentor, the Tzaddik ha-dor (the Righteous One of the generation; the rebbe to his followers), or, from another vantage point, the psychiatrist, who will help release the pained individual from his/her feelings of worthlessness.

Teshuvah for Rav Kook, as well as for the Rambam, is based on a highly developed sense of selfhood:

When one forgets the essential nature of the soul, when one averts his thought from the quality of introspection, everything becomes confused and in doubt. The principal teshuvah, which illumines the dark places, is the return of man to his self [sheyashuv adam l'atzmo], to the source [shoresh] of his soul, and immediately he will return to God, the soul of all souls and will progress higher. . . . Therefore through the great truth of return to self shall there be a return of man, the nations, the world and all worlds, existence in its entirety, to its Maker to be illumined by the light of life (*Lights of Teshuvah*, ch. 15).

In a penetrating comment on how teshuvah in Jewish tradition varies from the secular prescription for human success, Alan Mintz suggests that "through teshuvah, the Jew experiences reconciliation. . . . The secular vision of growth, on the other hand, is based on a fantasy of breakthrough rather than reconciliation" (*Response*, no. 13, p. 36). Teshuvah, then, does not share in secular power and control over human experience. It becomes, rather, a vehicle for the psyche to diminish the feelings of competition and tortured inadequacy in the light of realistic existential situations.

Teshuvah allows for the admission of frailty but denies fatalism or defeat. Its proclivities are such as to force Jews out of a cumbersome routine of self-denial. As the Rambam masterfully concludes in his *Laws of Teshuvah*:

One who serves God out of a feeling of love, who is involved in doing good deeds, and walks in the paths of wisdom [does so] for no utilitarian reason: not out of fear of pernicious consequences, and not out of desire to be an heir to bounteous goods. But [he who] acts truthfully [does so] for the sake of truth and for the ultimate good that will flow from that truth. As it is written in the Torah, "And you shall love the Lord your God" (Deuteronomy 6:5). And when it shall pass that man will love God in a worthy fashion, he will perform all of his duties with ahava [love], rather than out of yira [fear].

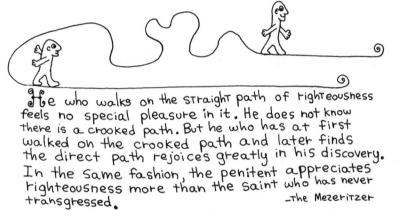

He who walks on the straight path of righteousness feels no special pleasure in it. He does not know there is a crooked path. But he who has at first walked on the crooked path and later finds the direct path rejoices greatly in his discovery. In the same fashion, the penitent appreciates righteousness more than the saint who has never transgressed.
—The Mezeritzer

The process of teshuvah has given rise to many customs and traditions. Here are some of them:

1. Teshuvah for ritual misdeeds seeks the acceptance and compassion of God. Social misdeeds, however, even where they do involve ritual transgressions, demand not only the divine compassion but the human as well. The individual must confront the victim and rectify his/her actions to that person and seek the victim's forgiveness.

2. Self-examination, verbalization, and commitment to refrain from repetition of these misdeeds must also be addressed to the victim of the violation. The victim's teshuvah is also deemed a righteous act.

3. Tradition does not view human frailty and imperfection as impenetrable or unsurpassable obstacles to righteousness. The Rambam, in a terse and majestic statement of faith, invokes his optimism that all people can return.

4. Special days in the calendar are set aside for teshuvah. While these days are seen as expecially effective for entering the mood of return, they do not preclude teshuvah throughout the year. These ten days of teshuvah (Aseret Yemai Teshuvah—Days of Awe) cap a month of preparation for the High Holidays. They are the intermediate days between the Jewish New Year (Rosh ha-Shanah) and the Day of Atonement (Yom Kippur)—a season that traditionally offers a period of self-examination and a return to unity (at-one-ment) of people, the world, and God. This individual teshuvah (cloaked in the liturgy of community) is a prelude to a year in which it must join force in a larger and more general return.

5. The emphasis on return and renewal is linked in Jewish mystical lore with the attempt at the repair (tikkun) of the cosmic rip in the world order. There is no concept of original sin in Jewish thought; however, a theme that does run through midrashic (homiletic) and kabbalistic writing is the fall of people and people's subsequent fervor and frustration in setting straight a world gone astray. The individual enters the world with a clean slate and only his/her subsequent actions can sully this slate. The

cosmos, however, is a living and breathing organism that has the flaw of degeneration and decay, the glory of rebirth and realization. Through tikkun and teshuvah the individual acquires the ability to magnify his/her mundane actions to a cosmic scale. The objectively viewed deed has little semblance to the world-repairing reverberations it produces.

6. Teshuvah demands more of the inner self of the Jew than his/her pocketbook, temple affiliation, or commitment to the Jewish gastronomic heritage. Teshuvah asks that the periphery be moved to the center, that *Judaism* become the main axis of your life—replacing whatever else bound you before. It maintains that Judaism is no more than the sum of the Jewishness of its members.

How to get in touch with others to get in touch with yourself

As mentioned, any discussion of teshuvah in Jewish tradition must take into account the reality of the nonhalakhic nature of modern Jewish life. Thus in recent years the "return" has manifested itself in the appearance of many institutions, some traditional, others innovative, that gear themselves to the needs of returners: Jews who have lost touch with the classical texts and modes of thought of Jewish life.

Nonetheless, if a common characteristic had to be formulated for all of Jewish life through the centuries, it would be the study of Torah. We begin, therefore, by believing that the returner of today will find a commitment to the study of Torah—in its broadest definition—to be a first step toward a return to the Jewish people and to the unique history and ideals they represent.

To avoid making a mistake that might leave you dissatisfied and unhappy, try to consult as many of the institutions as possible, whether here or in Israel, before making a choice—and remember that you can always change. Since these particular institutions were set up to cater to your needs, you must make sure that the institution you choose can reflect those needs rather than obliterate them.

The following guide will mention and evaluate some of the institutions of Jewish learning that offer courses of studies for beginners. It is important to keep in mind that every institution has carved for itself a particular area of competence in which it and its students feel they are best able to operate. This needs to be reiterated to every would-be student. Experience shows that it is all too easy to get into an institution that is inappropriate for your particular needs. For example, the balance between freedom and authority differs in each place. The positive point to make here is that, taking these institutions as a whole, they *do* represent a wide range of choices, whatever your particular preference.

In the U.S.

The eastern seaboard still offers the primary sources for a prospective returner. Various centers of Jewish learning operate in the metropolitan New York area. These include institutions of almost every kind, ranging from establishment rabbinical seminaries to small esoteric groups in the caverns of the traditional community. This guide will not devote itself to the general overview of availability of Jewish studies in the U.S.; rather, it will present the yeshivot that cater to the returner.

1. **Lubavitch**
770 Eastern Parkway
Brooklyn, N. Y. 11213

Main headquarters for the worldwide Habad (Lubavitch) movement. It offers an address to all Jews wishing to experience this brand of Hasidic life. Lubavitch offers the returner a chance of seeing an organic Jewish community in an unusual setting. Two weekends a year are specifically set apart for participation of college-age students. Its yeshivah for male returners is:

2. **Hadar Hatorah**
824 Eastern Parkway
Brooklyn, N. Y. 11213

Hadar Hatorah is rapidly becoming one of the successful institutions for beginners. In recent years there has been a reemphasis on talmudic studies. The Hasidic content of the learning obviously permeates the seder ha-yom (study sessions). Dorm facilities are available.
The yeshivah for women:

3. **Bais Chana**
15 Montcalm Ct.
Saint Paul, Minn. 55116

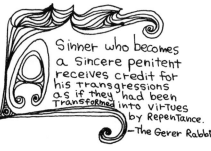

Sinner who becomes a sincere penitent receives credit for his transgressions as if they had been transformed into virtues by repentance.
—The Gerer Rabbi

has a summer institute as well as a year-round program. Travel subsidies from New York headquarters are available. Many of the women return to New York after study and join the community. Learning emphasis is on Tanach (Hebrew Bible), commentaries, and, of course, the Hasidic masters. Dorm facilities are available. (For Lubavitch centers in Israel, see the guide to New Yeshivot below.)

A note on Lubavitch: The Hasidic and mystical tradition as interpreted by Lubavitch sees teshuvah as obligatory for all Jews. Their goal of offering each Jew the opportunity to participate in the mystical struggle to bring on the redemption has made them the most outreaching Jewish religious group in the last decade. Lubavitcher Hasidim are successful in breaking the contemporary taboo against fundamentalist God-talk in so-called sophisticated circles. The American Jewish milieu, a cradle of conceptualizations and demythologizations of Jewish belief, has offered little opportunity for either temple-affiliated or non-temple-affiliated Jews to enhance their personal lives with the recognition of a personal God.

Habad, in spite of its modern publicity methods, offers little compromise with modern life. It is precisely this noncompromise that is its most successful drawing card. The initiate to Habad seeks total immersion in an ethical-cultural atmosphere that presupposes a critical stance toward American life. While Lubavitch does not oppose the ideals of freedom propounded in the American creed, they do criticize the "wantonness" condoned in a free society. Hasidism offers a viable alternative for Jews disappointed within the Emancipation and its ideals (i.e., the introduction of the Jew into Western society as an equal). In many ways Lubavitch shares with Zionism this ideological rejection of the Emancipation and assimilation into Western culture.

Lubavitcher Hasidim have a double standard. Returning Jews are encouraged to make use of their secular achievements, whereas "homegrown" Hasidim are not encouraged to expose themselves to the outside world. The returning Jew often feels this dichotomy; and in a group like the Lubavitchers, where punctilious observance and spiritual ecstasy are precariously linked, there is a heightened disparity between the intellectual seeking and the intellectual openness of the group.

The presence of a rebbe, in the dynamic figure of Rabbi Menachem Schneerson, gives Habad an aura of majesty that merely joining a study circle cannot parallel. The ethos of rebbe-worship is beyond the scope of this account; however, this factor is an important psychological underpinning for both the avid interest in Lubavitch and for defections from the community.

1. **Michel Abehsera**
1852 E. 7th St.
Brooklyn, N.Y. 11223

is himself a Lubavitcher who is surrounded with a group of returners at various stages of commitment to Lubavitch. Michel is the world renowned macrobiotic who has written numerous books on this style of eating. Many of his followers combine this way of eating/thinking with a commitment to

Judaism, and an interesting mixture of the contemporary-traditional sometimes results. There is no formal program of study but lots of activities.

2. **Shar Yashuv Yeshiva**
Rabbi Freifeld
1284 Central Ave.
Far Rockaway, N.Y. 11691

is an eclectic type of yeshivah, appealing to both mystically and rationally inclined returners. There are separate programs for men and women. Dorm facilities are available.

3. **New England Torah Institute**
Rabbi Levi Horowitz
1710 Beacon St.
Brookline, Mass. 02146

is under the auspices of the Bostoner Rebbe at the New England Hasidic Center and has both part- and full-time courses. Emphasis is on Talmud, properly imbued with the Hasidic spirit. There is a summer program as well. Its program for women is called the Lionel Goldman Seminary of Jewish Studies and is run on the same premises as the men's, with an emphasis on traditional women's roles.

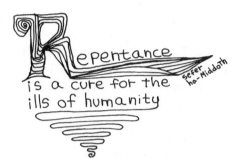
Repentance is a cure for the ills of humanity
Sefer ha-Middoth

4. **Lincoln Square Synagogue**
Rabbi Shlomo Riskin
200 Amsterdam Ave.
New York, N.Y. 10023

under the dynamic leadership of Rabbi Riskin, has an enormously popular adult study program that reaches out to the returner and nonreturner alike. The program has continued to grow in popularity, and currently attracts hundreds of people from all over the New York–New Jersey area. Men and women study together.

5. **Yeshiva University's James Striar School**
Amsterdam Ave. and 186th St.
New York, N.Y. 10033

has an excellent program for males wanting to combine college with returning. Teachers are generally of high quality. Dorm facilities are provided.

The New Yeshivot have all proved themselves to be of a high standard. Nevertheless, the style of teaching varies from yeshivah to yeshivah, and, again, you must be careful to choose the right one. More information is available in the booklet *Learning to Learn: A Guide to the New Yeshivot in Israel* by Mordechai Beck (published by the World Union of Jewish Students, cost $1). For copies, please inquire either at your local WUJS office or contact:

Mordechai Beck
Yohanan ben Zakai 103/15
Gonen, Jerusalem, Israel

In Israel

There are at present a number of institutions in Israel that run programs in Judaism for the mature beginner. These institutions frequently cater specifically to the needs of returners, although in almost every yeshivah there are at least some students who have had a basic Jewish education. These yeshivot are striking out in new directions, making adjustments for returners that have never been made before, and hence we call them the New Yeshivot.

1. **Kfar Habad**   **Shimon Naftalis**   **any local branch**
Rabbi Gafni Ad   **Bet Habad**   **of Lubavitch**
Kfar Habad, Israel   **53 Rechov Habad**
                        Old City, Jerusalem, Israel

Kfar Habad is the oldest yeshivah in Israel that accepts beginners. Its peculiarities are twofold. Its course for beginners is designed to link up with the studies in the main yeshivah and ultimately with the Lubavitch movement as a whole, with its headquarters and rebbe in Brooklyn, N.Y. Thus the changeover from beginning to main course can be fairly rapid and will include a trip to the New York headquarters. The second unique feature of the Kfar is its special brand of intellectual hassidut, known as Habad (an acrostic of hochmah, wisdom—binah, discernment—daas, practical knowledge). The Habad system is considered capable of answering all intellectual, emotional, practical questions that a student might have. For those that find their niche in Habad, this is more than probably true.

> 2. **Diaspora Yeshivah**
> **Rabbi Mordechai Goldstein**
> **P.O. Box 6426**
> **Old City, Jerusalem, Israel**

provides a full-time program for both men and women—no background necessary. Rabbi Mordechai Goldstein is the primary teacher and his charismatic personality influences the nature of the school. When it started in 1967 it attracted a wild assortment of kids, and many legends grew up—not all of them pretty or, for that matter, deserved. In time it has cooled down considerably, though it is still a place in which "wilder" elements might find a home. It retains its original ruggedness of character, and both its program and environment demand a certain toughness. Incidentally, it is the only New Yeshivah that has begun to build an on-going community of its students and graduates.

> 3. **Magen Avraham**
> **Rabbi Rabinovitz**
> **Hatam Sofer 8**
> **Bnei Brak, Israel**

was started as an adjunct to the other more traditional yeshivot in Bnei Brak. It nevertheless retains its independence of—or at least its interdependence with—its immediate environment. It is small—both physically and in numbers of students. Its program is straight learning for absolute beginners in an environment described by the dean as "yeshiverish." It does indeed seem to have created the atmosphere of a traditional yeshivah, yet its students exude a marvelous air of well-being and write glowingly of their life there. Kfar Habad and Ohr Samayach send their absolute beginners there.

> 4. **Ohr Samayach**
> **Rabbis Schiller, Weinbach, Rosenberg**
> **3 Tidhar St.**
> **Jerusalem, Israel**

is a straight place for straight guys, concerned with bringing out the best in its students by attempting to push them carefully to their limits. It runs a very intensive beginner's program, reviewing as much basic material as possible in the shortest possible time. This includes Talmud for beginners —which might mean Talmud without even using a text. The yeshivah is very interested in using the media to get across traditional Orthodoxy to a wider audience. It hopes to form a group of students and graduates to work on projects such as their glossy magazine *Shma Yisrael*, music, and films.

> 5. **Eysh Hatorah**
> **Rabbi Weinberg**
> **Misgav Ledach 52**
> **Old City, Jerusalem, Israel**

is the brainchild of Reb Noach Weinberg—his fourth yeshivah for beginners. He's probably the one man with the most comprehensive idea of what a beginner's program should consist of. His ideas stem from a no-nonsense approach to basics. His program includes memorization of the 613 mitzvot, a crash course in Bible and prayer, and a review of the forty-eight ways of learning Torah according to the Mishnah. It also means working through the basics of the self—what you are, what you want and why, and—with this knowledge—becoming a good human being. Some will be stimulated by this approach; others will find it too open too soon; and some might find it a bit too comprehensive.

6. Dvar Yerushalayim
Rabbi Horovitz
Rehov Harav Blau 18
Sanhedria, Jerusalem, Israel

is, by its own admission, a potpourri yeshivah. Started by two English rabbis, it now has a largely non-English clientele. Its year-long course includes a variety of Jewish subjects—philosophy, musar, hassidut—plus a slower introduction than most to Talmud and other texts. The student is given a "grocer's guide" of Judaism without necessarily being fed on any one product. Its course is flexible, but some might find it initially frustrating.

7. Shapell College
Rabbi Bravender
2 Sederot Hameiri
Jerusalem, Israel

GUILT is not so bad as the road to it.
Yiddish proverb   Trans. Leo Rosten

commonly known as Hartman College (its original name), emphasizes the acquiring of skills needed to study the Talmud. It is unique in that its women's division (located at 2 Haor St., Jerusalem) is the most intellectually oriented of all the yeshivot.

8. Nvei Yerushalayim
Rabbi Refson
P.O. Box 16020
Jerusalem, Israel

is the only women's yeshivah totally on its own. Its style tends toward the older type of women's seminary—not that this makes its learning program any less effective. Far from it. But its emphasis is on normalcy—the normalcy of its students, the normalcy of its teachings. It does not indulge in too much speculation, preferring the practical approach, which is to be found in its teacher-training program and in the reinforcement given its students to take up a career in teaching or communal work. Its discipline is fairly tight, but it does not disguise its intentions to its students.

9. Pardes
Rabbi Berkovitz
Rehov Gad 10
Baka, Jerusalem, Israel

interestingly, describes itself as the "un-yeshivahlike yeshivah," and certainly it is radically different from the other New Yeshivot in that it teaches men and women together. This, plus its insistence that the students live away from the yeshivah and the general encouragement it gives to learning and speaking in Hebrew and relating to the Israeli surroundings, does make it more like college and less "yeshiverish."

Most of the yeshivot have accommodations on the premises or nearby. The exception is Pardes, as explained above. Some other yeshivot also allow a student who is not quite prepared to accept certain commitments as far as observances are concerned to live off the premises, at least for a while.

Great is the power of teshuvah, for it brings healing to the world, and even if one individual does teshuvah, both he and the entire world are forgiven (Babylonian Talmud, Yoma 86a).

The yeshivot all have official fees, but normally they ask for only what a student can afford. No one is ever turned away for lack of money.

SYNAGOGUE AND PRAYER

The Geography of the Synagogue

At the Upper West Side Minyan in New York, the custom has arisen to pass the Torah from person to person after it is removed from the ark, amid great celebration and joy. This is done in accordance with the verse, "They all accept the rule of the kingdom of heaven—one from the other; and with love they all grant permission—one to the other—to make holy their Creator."

One Shabbat a visitor who had never seen the custom before broke down and wept as he received the Torah and passed it on. He explained later that, on the infrequent occasions he had been to synagogue since his Bar Mitzvah, he had refused all honors offered him because he had forgotten many of the rituals and was afraid to shame himself by making mistakes.

This chapter is written to honor a man who once joined us in prayer and taught us to treasure our familiarity with our synagogue and its rituals.

Introduction

Jews pray in community because prayer is seen as a communal activity. And while it is true that "the Lord resides in every place," it is nonetheless true that we reserve a special place, a communal place, for our prayer and we use a special vehicle, a siddur, to pray.

Many rituals have grown up around the synagogue. Some are directly descended from the Temple; others grew up throughout Jewish history; still others are modern-day innovations. The following is an attempt to explain the "geography" of the synagogue, the structure of the service, the roles you may be asked to play and what these entail. This will be a how-to, what, when, and where chapter—no philosophy or theology. For more information about some of the issues contained herein see Prayer, Prayer Books, and the Pray-er.

Some general rules of behavior

1. When you enter a traditional synagogue, put on a kippah if you are a male (supplies are kept in almost every shul), and keep it on—even during the Kiddush and/or meal that follows the service.

2. In traditional synagogues it is forbidden, even after the service, to smoke on Shabbat (*ask* if you're not aware of synagogue policy).

3. On some occasions, following the Kiddush there will be a lunch to which guests of the Bar/Bat Mitzvah are invited. Don't automatically assume that if you've been to services, you are invited to the lunch. However, you are usually invited for Kiddush.

4. It is bad form to take a Bar/Bat Mitzvah gift with you when you go to a traditional synagogue on Shabbat. Carrying is prohibited on Shabbat, and most traditional synagogues treat this prohibition seriously. Taking a monetary gift with you even in envelopes is especially offensive, since this not only ignores the prohibition against carrying, it also ignores the prohibition against handling money (and things representing money, such as checks, bonds, etc.) on Shabbat. See the *Catalog 1* chapter on Shabbat for full explanations.

5. The no-carry principle in a traditional synagogue on Shabbat is also, by extension, the don't-bring-a-pocketbook (handbag, suitcase, briefcase, etc.) dictum.

6. An extension of the no-money principle is the don't-jangle-the change-in-your-pocket-if-you're-bored rule.

7. In traditional synagogues, women commonly cover their hair during the service. Frequently lace nets are provided for women who forget to wear a hat or scarf.

8. In traditional Judaism, writing is prohibited on Shabbat and holidays, so needless to say, don't go to synagogue with your Bic sticking out of your breast pocket (or with cigars sticking out either—see no. 2 above).

9. While there is no problem in the Reconstructionist, Conservative, and Reform movements about riding to synagogue in a car on Shabbat, Orthodox synagogues do not condone driving. Accordingly, try to be sensitive to such feelings when confronted with the situation. There is no reason to park your car in the synagogue parking lot or right in front of the building when you could park a block away and offend no one.

10. In many synagogues men wear tallitot during the Morning Service (both Shabbat and weekdays). On weekdays men wear tefillin for the Morning Service. If you own these articles bring them to the appropriate services. If you don't own a tallit, almost any synagogue will provide you with one; if you don't own tefillin, some synagogues will be able to provide and some won't. In any case, in some shuls it is not a social solecism to pray without tefillin. (See the *Catalog 1* chapters Tefillin and Tallit for guidance on how to put them on.) Women should use their own sensitivity and discretion to guide them in the matter of wearing tefillin and tallitot.

11. For all occasions when you enter a synagogue, you should dress appropriately. Perhaps it is not fitting to approach God when you are not carefully attired; certainly it shows no respect to a community to ignore its standards of dress. In traditional synagogues women should wear dresses with sleeves and men should wear clean, pressed slacks and shirts. Most synagogues prefer jacket and tie. Some synagogues are tolerant of women in slack suits; others are not. Check the local policy before sallying forth.

12. Except for nos. 1, 3, 7, 10, and 11 above, these rules do not apply during a normal weekday service.

Roles of the synagogue functionaries

A synagogue may have none, all, or some of the following functionaries, who perform differing roles during a service:

1. *Rabbi*: gives sermons, explains service, announces pages, gives benediction; s/he also counsels, teaches, mediates, organizes, visits the sick and bereaved, etc.

2. *Hazzan*: chants and sings prayers, using traditional and new melodies (see "Hazzanut").

3. *Gabbai* or *shammash*: coordinates activities during a service; gives out honors, e.g., aliyot (explanation later); assists Torah reader; may teach Bar/Bat Mitzvah, as may the hazzan; will organize holiday festivities, etc.

4. *Torah reader*: reads from the Torah on Shabbat, holidays, Monday and Thursday morning (often the same as one of the above functionaries).

5. *Ushers*: will sometimes provide you with a siddur—prayer book—and a Humash—Bible (from which you can follow the Torah service); will sometimes escort you to your seat.

It is common practice for non-Jews to wear a kippah (as a mark of respect) but not a tallit or tefillin for the service.

Entering the synagogue

As you enter the synagogue/sanctuary/prayer room, you should have the following (women are not required to don the first three; some synagogues may even frown on a woman wearing these articles, so let your own sensitivities decide):

kippah (except in many Reform temples)
tallit (ditto)
tefillin (ditto—also, you need them *only* on weekdays)
siddur
Humash (only on Shabbat, holidays, Monday and Thursday)

The last two items can usually be found in bookcases either right before you enter the room or right after. In some shuls the siddurim (plural of siddur) are placed on each seat, and the Bibles are given out by the ushers just before the Torah service begins. In some traditional shuls you don't take a Humash from the bookcase until the time for the Torah reading. In such shuls you simply amble over to the bookcase at that time (along with everyone else) and pick one up.

The tallit (and/or tefillin) can be put on either before entering the room or when you get to your seat (the latter is usually the case with tefillin). The kippah is put on before entering the room.

Where to sit

In most synagogues you can sit wherever you like. If you are there for a simha—joyous occasion—such as a Bar/Bat Mitzvah, an usher may show you to the area where the family and relations are sitting. If it is an Orthodox synagogue, remember that men and women sit in separate areas. In a few synagogues the regular members have customary seats. Sometimes there are seat plaques to indicate such seats; at other times you just have to step (sit) carefully. Often you will be told which areas are open territory. The eastern wall (the wall with the ark) is a place of honor in old-style synagogues, and in general you shouldn't just wander over and sit yourself down there. In non-Orthodox synagogues you can always get a seat in the front row. People in general tend to sit toward the back (in fact, a mark of a good synagogue is one where people sit up front).

Geography

Looking around the synagogue you will see the eastern wall, where the aron ha-kodesh (the holy ark) is located. The ark is the repository for the Torah scrolls when they are not in use. It also serves as the focus for one's prayers. Above the ark is located the ner tamid—the eternal light—recalling the eternal light in the Temple (Exodus 27:20–21).

Arks can be decorated in innumerable ways and come in many different sizes, shapes, and materials. The central part of the ark is a cabinet that contains the Torah scrolls. This usually has a parokhet—curtain—covering it. (Many Sephardic shuls do not have a parokhet.) The parokhet is often elaborately designed with many embellishments; some shuls have a special white parokhet used only for the High Holidays. Because the parokhet is considered holy, it is treated like any holy object—e.g., books, Torah scrolls, etc.—and is never discarded.

When the parokhet is drawn aside, you will see (in most shuls) the doors to the ark, which are, again, often elaborately decorated. Opening the doors, you will see a cabinet usually lined in velvet where the Sifrei Torah—the Torah scrolls—rest. Many shuls have large numbers of scrolls donated by people to commemorate an event or to memorialize or honor a person, so to accommodate all the Sifrei Torah, the ark will sometimes have more than one "shelf."

The scrolls themselves are covered by cloth mantles (covers) elaborately designed on the front. These mantles are open at the bottom and closed at the top except for the two openings that enclose the rollers. This and the other objects described below are considered holy and, once again, are never discarded when worn out. Often there are a number of other objects decorating the Torah. These can include:

1. *keter or atarah*: crown of silver on top of the Torah; this emphasizes that the "Torah is a crown for Israel."

2. *rimmonim*: finials—separate decorative objects adorning the tops of the rollers.

3. *tas*: breastplate or silver shield hanging over the front of the Torah (reminiscent of the breastplate of the high priest in the Temple).

4. *yad*: a metal or wooden pointer used by the Torah reader to help him/her keep the place as s/he reads from the scroll (it is not permissible to touch the Torah—i.e., the parchment—itself with one's hand).

These objects can be very ornate and come in many different styles. Since Sephardic Jews keep their Torah inside a wooden case, often covered with silver, they do not use a cloth cover. Interestingly enough, they also read from the Torah without removing it from this case.

If all these decorative coverings were removed, we would find the sash or buckle that keeps the Torah rollers clasped together tightly. It, too, is often decorated with elaborate care. (See "The Wimpel" under Birth.) If this sash were removed, we could unroll the Torah scroll.

The Torah is handwritten by a trained scribe on parchment made from a kosher animal (see Scribal Arts in *Catalog 1*). The Torah has to be written with no mistakes; the letters must be clear, the writing must not be faded. If there is something wrong with the Torah it cannot be used until it is repaired by a scribe.

The Sefer Torah is the holiest of holy Jewish objects. Jews have often risked their lives to save a Sefer Torah from fire or desecration. When it is old—beyond use—it cannot be improperly treated or discarded, but must be reverentially buried (as are the covers, parokhet, etc.). So holy is a Sefer Torah that almost the only purpose for which it is permitted to be sold is to ransom a human being. Only life itself has more holiness to us than the words of Torah.

The Torah is also above the standard Jewish categories of pure and impure. It can therefore never be made impure (so all this nonsense about women touching a Sefer Torah and rendering it impure is based on mistaken custom).

If we look closely at an unrolled scroll, we can see that the words are written in aligned columns. There are spaces similar to paragraphs every once in a while. Every few columns a seam will be evident where two pieces of parchment have been joined together. If the Torah were unrolled to one end, we'd see that the parchment is attached to rollers. These wooden rollers are called etzei hayyim—trees of life—a name taken from the verse, "She [the Torah] is a tree of life to them that lay hold upon her" (Proverbs 3:18). These rollers extend below and above the parchment so that the Torah can be unwrapped as it is being read and so that the scroll itself can be carried easily.

In old-style traditional shuls the ark is not set on a stage, though in most of the newer shuls it is. Similarly in some traditional shuls the amud —where the hazzan davens—is flat on the ground (or even below ground). This is based on the verse, "Out of the depths I call You" (Psalms 130:1)— and the feeling that the hazzan should speak from a humble position. However, in many shuls today there is a stage in the front of the room on which there is the ark, the desk from which the hazzan prays (often facing the congregation), the place from where the Torah is read (often the same as the hazzan's desk), chairs for the rabbi, president, other shul officers, and a stand from which the rabbi speaks. (It is customary for the Bar/Bat Mitzvah to sit up front also.) In more traditional shuls there is a stage which holds the ark, a stand from which the rabbi speaks, chairs for the rabbi, etc. Somewhere at the base of the stage is an amud, which faces the ark.

In the middle of these traditional shuls there is a bimah—a raised platform holding a reader's table facing the ark. This table is used for reading the Torah and provides a central place from which the hazzan can occasionally pray. Wherever the reading table is, whether in front or in the middle, it is covered by a mappah—embroidered cloth—so the Torah does not rest on plain wood while being read.

The bimah might also have holders for the Torah and crown ornaments, etc. In the less traditional shuls similar objects will be near the reader's desk on the podium. There are all sorts of in-between geographic positions, based on the traditionalism of the shul. At one time the Torah was read from the middle of the shul so that people could hear it wherever they were seated. The hazzan would pray at the front to be near the Torah

AND This is our new synagogue. The Triangular supports represent The spiritual strivings of American Judaism; the randomly placed stained glass windows represent The contact between The american Jewish community and The outside culture; and The crown on top represents The crown of The Torah!

Very impressive! was The architect Jewish?

OF course not! we wanted a famous architect.

He must Have charged a lot!

Actually we got a bargain. The design was left over from a chain of swiss cheese shops THAT Failed.

ark—the symbol of God's presence in the synagogue. Recent innovations such as the microphone have changed the way some synagogues are built. Also, some synagogues have turned the hazzan and/or Torah reader around to face the congregation rather than the ark.

After entering the synagogue and sitting down, the next step (assuming you've come late—a common enough occurrence!) is to find out where the congregation is in the prayer book. The best way to do this is to crane your neck and peer into someone else's siddur; however, you can listen to the leader and try to figure out the probable place s/he is up to in the siddur.

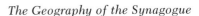

A guide to the structure of the service

Different synagogues will have different services. What follows is an outline of the traditional service, although obviously the spectrum of Orthodox to Reform offers a great deal of variance from this structure. Thus it is a good idea to take a look at the introduction to the siddur, which will probably state the philosophy of the editor with regard to tradition. Despite changes, however, the basic outline of the traditional service is usually still there and can be expected to proceed along the following lines:

1. *Birkhot ha-Shahar*: Morning Blessings. This is the introductory part of the service and consists mainly of a series of blessings that deal with the body, freedom and bounty, and gratitude for waking up to a new day. This section is designed to help people move from the physical waking up each morning to a spiritual reawakening. It tries to ease you into the prayer service. Sometimes the hazzan reads many of the blessings out loud and the congregation answers, "Amen." This section, most of which is said sitting down, was one of the last added to the service; in fact, originally many of these blessings were said individually at home. Sometimes there are one or two Kaddishes said at the end of this section. (See "Kaddish" below.)

The following sample is taken from the Conservative prayer book. Other prayer books have slightly different versions:

בָּרוּךְ אַתָּה יְיָ אֱלֹהֵינוּ מֶלֶךְ הָעוֹלָם אֲשֶׁר נָתַן לַשֶּׂכְוִי בִינָה לְהַבְחִין בֵּין יוֹם וּבֵין לָיְלָה.

בָּרוּךְ אַתָּה יְיָ אֱלֹהֵינוּ מֶלֶךְ הָעוֹלָם שֶׁעָשַׂנִי בְּצַלְמוֹ.

בָּרוּךְ אַתָּה יְיָ אֱלֹהֵינוּ מֶלֶךְ הָעוֹלָם שֶׁעָשַׂנִי בֶּן חוֹרִין.

בָּרוּךְ אַתָּה יְיָ אֱלֹהֵינוּ מֶלֶךְ הָעוֹלָם שֶׁעָשַׂנִי יִשְׂרָאֵל.

בָּרוּךְ אַתָּה יְיָ אֱלֹהֵינוּ מֶלֶךְ הָעוֹלָם פּוֹקֵחַ עִוְרִים.

בָּרוּךְ אַתָּה יְיָ אֱלֹהֵינוּ מֶלֶךְ הָעוֹלָם מַלְבִּישׁ עֲרֻמִּים.

בָּרוּךְ אַתָּה יְיָ אֱלֹהֵינוּ מֶלֶךְ הָעוֹלָם מַתִּיר אֲסוּרִים.

בָּרוּךְ אַתָּה יְיָ אֱלֹהֵינוּ מֶלֶךְ הָעוֹלָם זוֹקֵף כְּפוּפִים.

בָּרוּךְ אַתָּה יְיָ אֱלֹהֵינוּ מֶלֶךְ הָעוֹלָם רוֹקַע הָאָרֶץ עַל הַמָּיִם.

בָּרוּךְ אַתָּה יְיָ אֱלֹהֵינוּ מֶלֶךְ הָעוֹלָם שֶׁעָשָׂה לִי כָּל־צָרְכִּי.

בָּרוּךְ אַתָּה יְיָ אֱלֹהֵינוּ מֶלֶךְ הָעוֹלָם אֲשֶׁר הֵכִין מִצְעֲדֵי גָבֶר.

בָּרוּךְ אַתָּה יְיָ אֱלֹהֵינוּ מֶלֶךְ הָעוֹלָם אוֹזֵר יִשְׂרָאֵל בִּגְבוּרָה.

בָּרוּךְ אַתָּה יְיָ אֱלֹהֵינוּ מֶלֶךְ הָעוֹלָם עוֹטֵר יִשְׂרָאֵל בְּתִפְאָרָה.

בָּרוּךְ אַתָּה יְיָ אֱלֹהֵינוּ מֶלֶךְ הָעוֹלָם הַנּוֹתֵן לַיָּעֵף כֹּחַ.

"Blessed art Thou, O Lord our God, King of the Universe, who hast given the mind understanding to distinguish between day and night.

Blessed art Thou, O Lord our God, King of the Universe, who hast made me in Thine image.

Blessed art Thou, O Lord our God, King of the Universe, who hast made me free.

Blessed art Thou, O Lord our God, King of the Universe, who hast made me an Israelite.

Blessed art Thou, O Lord our God, King of the Universe, who openest the eyes of the blind.

Blessed art Thou, O Lord our God, King of the Universe, who clothest the naked.

Blessed art Thou, O Lord our God, King of the Universe, who releasest the bound.

Blessed art Thou, O Lord our God, King of the Universe, who raisest up them that are bowed down.

Blessed art Thou, O Lord our God, King of the Universe, who stretchest out the earth over the waters.

Blessed art Thou, O Lord our God, King of the Universe, who hast provided for all my needs.

Blessed art Thou, O Lord our God, King of the Universe, who guidest the steps of man.

Blessed art Thou, O Lord our God, King of the Universe, who girdest Israel with strength.

Blessed art Thou, O Lord our God, King of the Universe, who crownest Israel with glory.

Blessed art Thou, O Lord our God, King of the Universe, who givest strength to the weary."

2. *Pesukei de-Zimra*: Verses of Praise/Song. To understand Pesukei de-Zimra we'll have to make a brief excursion into the world of berakhot—blessings.

Berakhot

These are the basic structural units of the service. There are three kinds of berakhot (described in the chapter Berakhot in *Catalog 1*), but we are concerned here with only one kind: the Birkhot Hodaah—the blessings of praise and gratitude (to God). These come in brief forms (blessings said before eating food) and lengthy forms (the type found in prayers). We are concerned here only with the lengthy berakhot.

The form of the long blessing is:

1. introductory berakhah
2. middle part of praise
3. closing berakhah.

There is a theme (though it is sometimes loosely constructed) throughout a berakhah. The summation/quintessence of the theme can be found in the beginning or ending berakhah.

The form of the beginning berakhah is:

"Barukh attah, Adonai Eloheinu, Melekh ha-Olam . . . Blessed are You, Lord our God, King of the Universe. . . ."

בָּרוּךְ אַתָּה יְיָ אֱלֹהֵינוּ מֶלֶךְ הָעוֹלָם . . .

The form of the ending berakhah is shorter:

"Barukh attah, Adonai . . . Blessed are You, Lord. . . ."

בָּרוּךְ אַתָּה יְיָ . . .

As an example, look at Barukh She-amar at the beginning of Pesukei de-Zimra. This is a very typical blessing of thanksgiving. However, it is somewhat misleading. The first part is really only an addition to the berakhah: though it begins with the word Barukh (she-amar, etc.) the rest of the formula is not there. Therefore they are just phrases of praise and not blessings. If you look into the middle of this prayer you will see a line beginning "Barukh attah, Adonai." This is the beginning of the real blessing. Now skip to the last line and you'll see the formula of the closing blessing: "Barukh attah, Adonai, Melekh Mehullal ba-Tishbahot." The theme, as can be easily seen, is the praise of God, our King, and this theme is carried out throughout the blessing—from beginning to end.

BARUKH SHE-AMAR

"Blessed be He who spoke, and the world came into being; blessed be He. Blessed be He who created the universe. Blessed be He who says and performs. Blessed be He who decrees and fulfills. Blessed be He who has mercy on the world. Blessed be He who has mercy on all creatures. Blessed be He who grants a goodly reward to those who revere Him. Blessed be He who lives forever and exists eternally. Blessed be He who redeems and saves; blessed be His Name. Blessed art Thou, Lord our God, King of the Universe, O God, merciful Father, who art praised by the mouth of Thy people, lauded and glorified by the tongue of Thy faithful servants. With the songs of Thy servant David will we praise Thee, Lord our God; with his hymns and psalms will we exalt, extol, and glorify Thee. We will call upon Thy Name and proclaim Thee King, our King, our God. Thou who art One, the life of the universe, O King, praised and glorified be Thy great Name forever and ever. Blessed art Thou, O Lord, King extolled with hymns of praise."

בָּרוּךְ שֶׁאָמַר וְהָיָה הָעוֹלָם, בָּרוּךְ הוּא. בָּרוּךְ עוֹשֶׂה בְרֵאשִׁית, בָּרוּךְ אוֹמֵר וְעוֹשֶׂה, בָּרוּךְ גּוֹזֵר וּמְקַיֵּם, בָּרוּךְ מְרַחֵם עַל הָאָרֶץ, בָּרוּךְ מְרַחֵם עַל הַבְּרִיּוֹת, בָּרוּךְ מְשַׁלֵּם שָׂכָר טוֹב לִירֵאָיו, בָּרוּךְ חַי לָעַד וְקַיָּם לָנֶצַח, בָּרוּךְ פּוֹדֶה וּמַצִּיל, בָּרוּךְ שְׁמוֹ. בָּרוּךְ אַתָּה, יְיָ אֱלֹהֵינוּ, מֶלֶךְ הָעוֹלָם, הָאֵל, הָאָב הָרַחֲמָן, הַמְהֻלָּל בְּפִי עַמּוֹ, מְשֻׁבָּח וּמְפֹאָר בִּלְשׁוֹן חֲסִידָיו וַעֲבָדָיו. וּבְשִׁירֵי דָוִד עַבְדְּךָ נְהַלֶּלְךָ, יְיָ אֱלֹהֵינוּ; בִּשְׁבָחוֹת וּבִזְמִרוֹת נְגַדֶּלְךָ, וּנְשַׁבֵּחֲךָ וּנְפָאֶרְךָ וְנַזְכִּיר שִׁמְךָ וְנַמְלִיכְךָ, מַלְכֵּנוּ אֱלֹהֵינוּ. יָחִיד, חַי הָעוֹלָמִים, מֶלֶךְ, מְשֻׁבָּח וּמְפֹאָר עֲדֵי עַד שְׁמוֹ הַגָּדוֹל. בָּרוּךְ אַתָּה, יְיָ, מֶלֶךְ מְהֻלָּל בַּתִּשְׁבָּחוֹת.

Berakhot serve as literary sandwiches, on both large and small scales. The beginning and ending blessing enclose the middle parts. Similarly, two long berakhot can enclose a whole section between them. In fact, you just looked at one half of the best example of this. The long blessing Barukh She-amar is the opening unit, and if you skip a lot of pages (say twenty to twenty-five or so) you will find a paragraph beginning with the word Yishtabah. This is the closing unit. Again, the theme is praise and the last line has the closing blessing, "El Melekh Gadol ba-Tishbahot... ha-Olamin" (notice the use of some of the same words as in the blessings of Barukh She-amar).

YISHTABAH

"Praised be Thy Name forever, our King, great and holy God and King, in heaven and on earth; for to Thee, Lord our God and God of our fathers, pertain song and praise, hymn and psalm, power and dominion, victory, greatness and might, renown and glory, holiness and kingship, blessings and thanks, henceforth and forever. Blessed art Thou, O Lord, most exalted God and King, Lord of wonders, who art pleased with hymns, thou God and King, the life of the universe."

יִשְׁתַּבַּח שִׁמְךָ לָעַד, מַלְכֵּנוּ, הָאֵל הַמֶּלֶךְ הַגָּדוֹל וְהַקָּדוֹשׁ בַּשָּׁמַיִם וּבָאָרֶץ. כִּי לְךָ נָאֶה, יְיָ אֱלֹהֵינוּ וֵאלֹהֵי אֲבוֹתֵינוּ, שִׁיר וּשְׁבָחָה, הַלֵּל וְזִמְרָה, עֹז וּמֶמְשָׁלָה, נֶצַח, גְּדֻלָּה וּגְבוּרָה, תְּהִלָּה וְתִפְאֶרֶת, קְדֻשָּׁה וּמַלְכוּת, בְּרָכוֹת וְהוֹדָאוֹת, מֵעַתָּה וְעַד עוֹלָם. בָּרוּךְ אַתָּה, יְיָ, אֵל מֶלֶךְ גָּדוֹל בַּתִּשְׁבָּחוֹת, אֵל הַהוֹדָאוֹת, אֲדוֹן הַנִּפְלָאוֹת, הַבּוֹחֵר בְּשִׁירֵי זִמְרָה, מֶלֶךְ, אֵל, חֵי הָעוֹלָמִים.

"OK, I can see the middle part and closing blessing, but where is the opening blessing of Yishtabah?" you ask. Good question. Because now you know that there is another blessing form: the Berakhot Semukhot le-hevratam—one berakhah linked to another. In a single prayer unit (remember, we are talking still about one unit—the Pesukei de-Zimra) the berakhot are linked together to form one large unit. They serve as the sandwiches or the boundaries of that unit; thus, Pesukei de-Zimra begins with the berakhah of Barukh She-amar and ends with the berakhah of Yishtabah. In such a case the second berakhah does not have a separate opening blessing since it has already had one. It is as though this opening blessing is good for all subsequent blessings within one large unit. When we get to the next section, the Shema, we will see a similar situation. The first berakhah will have an opening blessing, a middle, and a closing blessing, but the next two blessings will have only the middle sections (of praise) and closing blessings. One of the best-known examples of this is the Amidah (discussed later in detail). The first berakhah begins: "Barukh attah Adonai Eloheinu ve-Elohei avoteinu" (most scholars say that this is a variant of Melekh ha-Olam) and ends with "Barukh attah Adonai, Magen Avraham" (the theme deals with the merit of the patriarchs).

"Praised art Thou, O Lord our God and God of our fathers, God of Abraham, God of Isaac, and God of Jacob, mighty revered, and exalted God. Thou bestowest loving-kindness and possessest all things. Mindful of the patriarch's love for Thee, Thou wilt in Thy love bring a redeemer to their children's children for the sake of Thy Name."

On the Sabbath of Repentance add:
"Remember us unto life, O King who delightest in life, and inscribe us in the Book of Life so that we may live worthily for Thy sake, O Lord of life."
"O King, Thou Helper, Redeemer, and Shield, be Thou praised, O Lord, Shield of Abraham."
The next berakhah begins simply "Attah gibbor..." and goes to "Mehayyeh ha-meitim."
"Thou, O Lord, art mighty forever. Thou callest the dead to immortal life for Thou art mighty in deliverance."

From Shemini Azeret until Pesah add:
"Thou causest the wind to blow and the rain to fall."

בָּרוּךְ אַתָּה יְיָ אֱלֹהֵינוּ וֵאלֹהֵי אֲבוֹתֵינוּ. אֱלֹהֵי אַבְרָהָם אֱלֹהֵי יִצְחָק וֵאלֹהֵי יַעֲקֹב. הָאֵל הַגָּדוֹל הַגִּבּוֹר וְהַנּוֹרָא אֵל עֶלְיוֹן. גּוֹמֵל חֲסָדִים טוֹבִים וְקֹנֵה הַכֹּל. וְזוֹכֵר חַסְדֵי אָבוֹת וּמֵבִיא גוֹאֵל לִבְנֵי בְנֵיהֶם לְמַעַן שְׁמוֹ בְּאַהֲבָה.

On Shabbat Shuvah add:

זָכְרֵנוּ לַחַיִּים. מֶלֶךְ חָפֵץ בַּחַיִּים. וְכָתְבֵנוּ בְּסֵפֶר הַחַיִּים. לְמַעַנְךָ אֱלֹהִים חַיִּים.

מֶלֶךְ עוֹזֵר וּמוֹשִׁיעַ וּמָגֵן. בָּרוּךְ אַתָּה יְיָ מָגֵן אַבְרָהָם.

אַתָּה גִבּוֹר לְעוֹלָם אֲדֹנָי מְחַיֵּה מֵתִים אַתָּה. רַב לְהוֹשִׁיעַ.

From Shemini Azeret until Pesah add:

מַשִּׁיב הָרוּחַ וּמוֹרִיד הַגָּשֶׁם.

"Thou sustainest the living with loving-kindness, and in great mercy callest the departed to everlasting life. Thou upholdest the falling, healest the sick, settest free those in bondage, and keepest faith with those that sleep in the dust. Who is like unto Thee, almighty King, who decreest death and life and bringest forth salvation?"

מְכַלְכֵּל חַיִּים בְּחֶסֶד. מְחַיֵּה מֵתִים בְּרַחֲמִים רַבִּים. סוֹמֵךְ נוֹפְלִים וְרוֹפֵא חוֹלִים וּמַתִּיר אֲסוּרִים וּמְקַיֵּם אֱמוּנָתוֹ לִישֵׁנֵי עָפָר. מִי כָמוֹךָ בַּעַל גְּבוּרוֹת וּמִי דוֹמֶה לָּךְ. מֶלֶךְ מֵמִית וּמְחַיֶּה וּמַצְמִיחַ יְשׁוּעָה.

On the Sabbath of Repentance add:

"Who may be compared to Thee, Father of mercy, who in love rememberest Thy creatures unto life?"

"Faithful art Thou to grant eternal life to the departed. Blessed art Thou, O Lord, who callest the dead to life everlasting."

On Shabbat Shuvah add:

מִי כָמוֹךָ אַב הָרַחֲמִים. זוֹכֵר יְצוּרָיו לְחַיִּים בְּרַחֲמִים.

וְנֶאֱמָן אַתָּה לְהַחֲיוֹת מֵתִים. בָּרוּךְ אַתָּה יְיָ מְחַיֵּה הַמֵּתִים.

The next berakhah is the "Attah kadosh" and after that is "Attah honen," etc.

"Holy art Thou and holy is Thy Name and unto Thee holy beings render praise daily. Blessed art Thou, O Lord, the holy God.

אַתָּה קָדוֹשׁ וְשִׁמְךָ קָדוֹשׁ וּקְדוֹשִׁים בְּכָל-יוֹם יְהַלְלוּךָ סֶּלָה. בָּרוּךְ אַתָּה יְיָ הָאֵל הַקָּדוֹשׁ.

"You favor man with knowledge, and teach understanding. O favor us with knowledge, understanding, and discernment from You. Blessed art Thou, O Lord, gracious Giver of knowledge."

אַתָּה חוֹנֵן לְאָדָם דַּעַת וּמְלַמֵּד לֶאֱנוֹשׁ בִּינָה. חָנֵּנוּ מֵאִתְּךָ דֵּעָה בִּינָה וְהַשְׂכֵּל. בָּרוּךְ אַתָּה יְיָ. חוֹנֵן הַדָּעַת.

If you add them all up you'll find there are nineteen blessings, hence the name Shemoneh Esrei—meaning Eighteen Blessings (that little problem will be explained later). Again, the Amidah is one large unit and therefore the "Barukh attah Adonai-Eloheinu Melekh ha-Olam" (or its equivalent) is not repeated over and over again at the beginning of each berakhah.

The blessings also divide the service into parts 2, 3, and 4 (they are not really found after part 4). In part 1—Birkhot ha-Shahar—the structure is more complicated and nearly every berakhah stands as a unit by itself, presumably since they were once said individually at home. In this section there are two separate cases of berakhot that are linked with others. See if you can find them (answers are on page 290).

To go back to the second section, Pesukei de-Zimra: let's turn again to Barukh She-amar. If you look at the text of the berakhah, you'll see that it mentions "using the words of King David to praise God." This is what the rest of the Pesukei de-Zimra is about: the praise of God with the words of David—i.e., the Psalms. As you turn the pages between Barukh She-amar and Yishtabah, you'll see that almost without exception the prayers are psalms or collections of verses from different psalms; e.g., right after Barukh She-amar is such a collection: Hodu le-Adonai. Toward the end of the section (which concludes with Yishtabah), there is some material taken from other parts of the Bible, notably the Song of the Sea from Exodus.

Now that you understand blessings, keep your eye out for them as you make your way through the siddur, since they are the key unit for understanding prayer.

Kaddish

Among the best-known prayers, the Kaddish is written in a mixture of Aramaic and Hebrew. It is an old prayer that has become known as the "prayer of mourners," and since the practice of "saying Kaddish" for relatives who have died is widely practiced, it is well-known to many Jews. Its use as a mourners' prayer comes from the Middle Ages, although both then and today the Kaddish has a number of functions besides that for mourners. The functions are distinguished by the different types of Kaddish.

The purpose of this section is to prepare one for the central parts of the service that come next. On Shabbat (and holidays) additional psalms are said, as well as the strikingly beautiful hymn Nishmat Kol Hai (which is made up of a number of paragraphs and is added before Yishtabah). Immediately after that is a Kaddish. So . . . a word (or rather, two hundred words) about Kaddish.

1. *Hatzi Kaddish*: Half Kaddish. This shortened form is said by the hazzan after sections of the service have been completed. Ergo, the hazzan says it after Yishtabah, which finishes the Pesukei de-Zimra section. It thus serves as another sign that a section of the service is complete. Accordingly, it is said after the Torah is returned to the ark and before Musaf (again, the dividing line between two different services: that of Shaharit—the morning prayer—and Musaf—the additional prayer said on Shabbat and holidays (see Prayer, Prayer Books, and the Pray-er).

"Magnified and sanctified be the Name of God throughout the world which He hath created according to His will. May He establish His kingdom during the days of your life and during the life of all the house of Israel, speedily, yea, soon; and say ye, Amen."

Congregation and reader

"May His great Name be blessed forever and ever."

Reader

"Exalted and honored be the name of the Holy One, blessed be He, whose glory transcends, yea, is beyond all praises, hymns, and blessings that man can render unto Him; and say ye, Amen."

יִתְגַּדַּל וְיִתְקַדַּשׁ שְׁמֵהּ רַבָּא. בְּעָלְמָא דִּי בְרָא כִרְעוּתֵהּ. וְיַמְלִיךְ מַלְכוּתֵהּ בְּחַיֵּיכוֹן וּבְיוֹמֵיכוֹן וּבְחַיֵּי דְכָל בֵּית יִשְׂרָאֵל בַּעֲגָלָא וּבִזְמַן קָרִיב. וְאִמְרוּ אָמֵן.

Congregation and Reader

יְהֵא שְׁמֵהּ רַבָּא מְבָרַךְ לְעָלַם וּלְעָלְמֵי עָלְמַיָּא.

Reader

יִתְבָּרַךְ וְיִשְׁתַּבַּח וְיִתְפָּאַר וְיִתְרֹמַם וְיִתְנַשֵּׂא וְיִתְהַדָּר וְיִתְעַלֶּה וְיִתְהַלָּל שְׁמֵהּ דְּקֻדְשָׁא. בְּרִיךְ הוּא. לְעֵלָּא מִן כָּל בִּרְכָתָא וְשִׁירָתָא תֻּשְׁבְּחָתָא וְנֶחֱמָתָא דַּאֲמִירָן בְּעָלְמָא. וְאִמְרוּ אָמֵן.

2. *Kaddish Shalem*: Full Kaddish. This is the long form and signifies the absolute end of the service. It is thus said after the Amidah of Shaharit and the Amidah of Musaf (seen as two completely separate services, even though they are said on the same morning) to show that the service is essentially over. However, since additional readings have been added after the Amidah, this effect of showing the end of the service has been somewhat obscured. Similarly, you will find this Kaddish at the end of Shaharit, Minhah, and Maariv during the week, to indicate a conclusion. It is said by the hazzan.

Reader

"Magnified and sanctified be the Name of God throughout the world which He hath created according to His will. May He establish His kingdom during the days of your life and during the life of all the house of Israel, speedily, yea, soon; and say ye, Amen."

Congregation and reader

"May His Name be blessed forever and ever."

Reader

"Exalted and honored be the Name of the Holy One, blessed be He, whose glory transcends, yea, is beyond all praises, hymns and blessings that man can render unto Him; and say ye, Amen.

May the prayers and supplications of the house of Israel be acceptable unto their Father in heaven; and say ye, Amen.

May there be abundant peace from heaven, and life for us and for all Israel; and say ye, Amen.

May He who establisheth peace in the heavens, grant peace unto us and unto all Israel; and say ye, Amen."

Reader

יִתְגַּדַּל וְיִתְקַדַּשׁ שְׁמֵהּ רַבָּא. בְּעָלְמָא דִּי בְרָא כִרְעוּתֵהּ. וְיַמְלִיךְ מַלְכוּתֵהּ בְּחַיֵּיכוֹן וּבְיוֹמֵיכוֹן וּבְחַיֵּי דְכָל בֵּית יִשְׂרָאֵל בַּעֲגָלָא וּבִזְמַן קָרִיב. וְאִמְרוּ אָמֵן:

Congregation and Reader

יְהֵא שְׁמֵהּ רַבָּא מְבָרַךְ לְעָלַם וּלְעָלְמֵי עָלְמַיָּא.

Reader

יִתְבָּרַךְ וְיִשְׁתַּבַּח וְיִתְפָּאַר וְיִתְרֹמַם וְיִתְנַשֵּׂא וְיִתְהַדָּר וְיִתְעַלֶּה וְיִתְהַלָּל שְׁמֵהּ דְּקֻדְשָׁא. בְּרִיךְ הוּא. לְעֵלָּא מִן כָּל בִּרְכָתָא וְשִׁירָתָא תֻּשְׁבְּחָתָא וְנֶחֱמָתָא דַּאֲמִירָן בְּעָלְמָא. וְאִמְרוּ אָמֵן.

תִּתְקַבֵּל צְלוֹתְהוֹן וּבָעוּתְהוֹן דְּכָל יִשְׂרָאֵל קֳדָם אֲבוּהוֹן דִּי בִשְׁמַיָּא. וְאִמְרוּ אָמֵן.

יְהֵא שְׁלָמָא רַבָּא מִן שְׁמַיָּא וְחַיִּים עָלֵינוּ וְעַל כָּל־יִשְׂרָאֵל. וְאִמְרוּ אָמֵן.

עֹשֶׂה שָׁלוֹם בִּמְרוֹמָיו הוּא יַעֲשֶׂה שָׁלוֹם עָלֵינוּ וְעַל כָּל־יִשְׂרָאֵל. וְאִמְרוּ אָמֵן.

ISAIAH 5,18

3. *Mourners' Kaddish*: This is said at the end of the weekday and Shabbat services, after each of the "finishing touches" of the service (in the forms of the Alenu, psalm of the day, etc.) which have been added as endings to the service (which means that the Kaddish Shalem has already been said). It differs from the Kaddish Shalem in that it omits the line beginning "Tiska bale. . . ." The Mourners' Kaddish, unlike the Kaddish Shalem, is said by those in mourning (see Death and Burial in *Catalog 1*). It is said a number of times during the service. In some traditional synagogues it is said once before Barukh She-amar. (It is also said between Kabbalat Shabbat and Maariv on Friday nights.)

MOURNERS' KADDISH

"Glorified and sanctified be God's great Name throughout the world which He has created according to His will. May He establish His kingdom, hastening His salvation and the coming of His Messiah, in your lifetime and during your days, and within the life of the entire house of Israel, speedily and soon; and say, Amen.

יִתְגַּדַּל וְיִתְקַדַּשׁ שְׁמֵהּ רַבָּא בְּעָלְמָא דִּי בְרָא כִרְעוּתֵהּ; וְיַמְלִיךְ מַלְכוּתֵהּ, וְיַצְמַח פֻּרְקָנֵהּ וִיקָרֵב מְשִׁיחֵהּ, בְּחַיֵּיכוֹן וּבְיוֹמֵיכוֹן וּבְחַיֵּי דְכָל בֵּית יִשְׂרָאֵל, בַּעֲגָלָא וּבִזְמַן קָרִיב, וְאִמְרוּ אָמֵן.

May His great Name be blessed forever and to all eternity.

יְהֵא שְׁמֵהּ רַבָּא מְבָרַךְ לְעָלַם וּלְעָלְמֵי עָלְמַיָּא.

Blessed and praised, glorified and exalted, extolled and honored, adored and lauded be the Name of the Holy One, blessed be He beyond all the blessings and hymns, praises and consolations that are ever spoken in the world; and say, Amen.

יִתְבָּרַךְ וְיִשְׁתַּבַּח, וְיִתְפָּאַר וְיִתְרוֹמַם, וְיִתְנַשֵּׂא וְיִתְהַדָּר, וְיִתְעַלֶּה וְיִתְהַלָּל שְׁמֵהּ דְּקֻדְשָׁא, בְּרִיךְ הוּא, לְעֵלָּא (לְעֵלָּא) מִן כָּל בִּרְכָתָא וְשִׁירָתָא, תֻּשְׁבְּחָתָא וְנֶחֱמָתָא, דַּאֲמִירָן בְּעָלְמָא, וְאִמְרוּ אָמֵן.

May there be abundant peace from heaven, and a good life, for us and for all Israel; and say, Amen.

יְהֵא שְׁלָמָא רַבָּא מִן שְׁמַיָּא, וְחַיִּים טוֹבִים, עָלֵינוּ וְעַל כָּל יִשְׂרָאֵל, וְאִמְרוּ אָמֵן.

He who creates peace in His celestial heights, may He create peace for us and for all Israel; and say, Amen."

עֹשֶׂה שָׁלוֹם בִּמְרוֹמָיו, הוּא יַעֲשֶׂה שָׁלוֹם עָלֵינוּ וְעַל כָּל יִשְׂרָאֵל, וְאִמְרוּ אָמֵן.

4. *Kaddish de-Rabbanan*: The Rabbis' Kaddish. This Kaddish, which is said after studying, appears three times in the siddur—once toward the end of the Birkhot ha-Shahar, once during the Friday night service, and once toward the end of Shabbat morning service—always after passages of a legalistic nature. It is considered that saying prayers of a halakhic nature engages the congregation in study—a meritorious act. It is said by the hazzan and the mourners (mourners should practice saying it beforehand since it contains additional wording of a tongue-twisting variety).

A PRAYER FOR SCHOLARS

קַדִּישׁ דְּרַבָּנָן

"Magnified and sanctified be the Name of God throughout the world which He hath created according to His will. May He establish His kingdom during the days of your life and during the life of all the house of Israel, speedily, yea, soon; and say ye, Amen.

יִתְגַּדַּל וְיִתְקַדַּשׁ שְׁמֵהּ רַבָּא. בְּעָלְמָא דִּי בְרָא כִרְעוּתֵהּ. וְיַמְלִיךְ מַלְכוּתֵהּ. בְּחַיֵּיכוֹן וּבְיוֹמֵיכוֹן וּבְחַיֵּי דְכָל בֵּית יִשְׂרָאֵל. בַּעֲגָלָא וּבִזְמַן קָרִיב. וְאִמְרוּ אָמֵן.

May His great Name be blessed forever and ever.

יְהֵא שְׁמֵהּ רַבָּא מְבָרַךְ לְעָלַם וּלְעָלְמֵי עָלְמַיָּא.

Exalted and honored be the Name of the Holy One, blessed be He, whose glory transcends, yea, is beyond all praises, hymns, and blessings that man can render unto Him; and say ye, Amen.

יִתְבָּרַךְ וְיִשְׁתַּבַּח. וְיִתְפָּאַר וְיִתְרֹמַם. וְיִתְנַשֵּׂא וְיִתְהַדָּר. וְיִתְעַלֶּה וְיִתְהַלָּל שְׁמֵהּ דְּקֻדְשָׁא. בְּרִיךְ הוּא. לְעֵלָּא (וּלְעֵלָּא) מִן כָּל בִּרְכָתָא וְשִׁירָתָא. תֻּשְׁבְּחָתָא וְנֶחֱמָתָא. דַּאֲמִירָן בְּעָלְמָא. וְאִמְרוּ אָמֵן.

Unto Israel and unto our scholars, unto their disciples and pupils, and unto all who engage in the study of the Torah, here and everywhere, unto them and unto you, may there be abundant peace, grace, loving-kindness, mercy, long life, sustenance, and salvation from their Father in heaven; and say ye, Amen.

May there be abundant peace from heaven, and a happy life for us, and for all Israel; and say ye, Amen.

May He who establisheth peace in the heavens, in His mercy grant peace unto us and unto all Israel; and say ye, Amen.

עַל יִשְׂרָאֵל וְעַל רַבָּנָן. וְעַל תַּלְמִידֵיהוֹן וְעַל כָּל תַּלְמִידֵי תַלְמִידֵיהוֹן. וְעַל כָּל מָאן דִּי עָסְקִין בְּאוֹרַיְתָא. דִּי בְאַתְרָא הָדֵין וְדִי בְכָל אֲתַר וַאֲתַר. יְהֵא לְהוֹן וּלְכוֹן שְׁלָמָא רַבָּא. חִנָּא וְחִסְדָּא וְרַחֲמִין. וְחַיִּין אֲרִיכִין. וּמְזוֹנָא רְוִיחֵי. וּפֻרְקָנָא מִן קֳדָם אֲבוּהוֹן דִּי בִשְׁמַיָּא וְאַרְעָא. וְאִמְרוּ אָמֵן.

יְהֵא שְׁלָמָא רַבָּא מִן שְׁמַיָּא. וְחַיִּים טוֹבִים עָלֵינוּ וְעַל כָּל יִשְׂרָאֵל. וְאִמְרוּ אָמֵן.

עֹשֶׂה שָׁלוֹם בִּמְרוֹמָיו הוּא בְּרַחֲמָיו יַעֲשֶׂה שָׁלוֹם עָלֵינוּ וְעַל כָּל יִשְׂרָאֵל. וְאִמְרוּ אָמֵן.

With these four types of Kaddishes and an understanding of their differences, you'll be able to discern the flow of the service quite easily.

Minyan

Rabbi Yohanan said: When the Holy One, blessed be He, came to the synagogue and did not find there ten people, He became angered and said: "Why have I come to find no one who calls upon Me and no one to whom I can respond?" (Berakhot 6b).

A number of sections of the service are considered to have a special kedushah—holiness—and so can only be said "in community." Therefore it is required that they be said in the presence of ten Jews—the community gives these parts of the service the importance and dignity they deserve. Based on the verse, "God stands in the divine assembly [congregation of God]" (Psalms 82:1), it is said that God is present in a community of ten. The parts for which a community is required include Kaddish (of any variety), the Borkhu, the Kedushah and repetition of the Amidah, and the reading from the Torah. If you were praying alone (or with less than ten), you would skip those parts of the service. This is one reason why praying with a minyan is considered preferable to praying alone.

Some of our Hillel students taught it to him as a tenth for a minyan, but now our Rabbi can't decide if it's an obligation or a sin.

Borkhu

So we've just finished the Pesukei de-Zimra section and the hazzan has said a Hatzi Kaddish. The hazzan now says Borkhu: "Bless the Lord who is to be praised," and the congregation responds, "Praised be the Lord who is blessed for all eternity." This line is repeated by the hazzan.

Reader
"Bless the Lord who is to be praised."

Congregation and reader
"Praised be the Lord who is blessed for all eternity."

Reader
בָּרְכוּ אֶת יְיָ הַמְבֹרָךְ.

Congregation and Reader
בָּרוּךְ יְיָ הַמְבֹרָךְ לְעוֹלָם וָעֶד.

As is obvious from the words, this is a call to prayer by the hazzan, to which the congregation responds by saying: "Let us pray!" It serves as an introduction and a focusing of attention before the next section—the Shema and its berakhot. Borkhu also marks the beginning of the major part of the

service, since Pesukei de-Zimra is really an introductory portion that pre- 277
pares us for the coming attractions.

The Geography of the Synagogue

Shema and its berakhot

This section includes the oldest parts of the service and at one time was basically the whole service. Since the period of the Second Temple, the service has expanded in both directions from this central portion:

Berakhot—Pesukei de-Zimra—Borkhu—SHEMA—Amidah—(Torah service)—(Musaf)—Alenu

Even today the phrase Shema Yisrael is the most powerfully dramatic, most universally known of all phrases from Jewish worship. Because this part of the service is so old, it is regarded as a total fixed unit and one is not allowed to interrupt it with talking. Its importance is shown by the fact that if you come late, you should skip the first part in order to say this part with the rest of the congregation (only afterwards do you go back and say the psalms of Pesukei de-zimra). This entire section is structured around the Shema.

"Hear, O Israel! The Lord our God, the Lord is One."

שְׁמַע יִשְׂרָאֵל יְהֹוָה אֱלֹהֵינוּ יְהֹוָה אֶחָד.

The Shema is followed by the phrase:
"Blessed be His glorious kingdom forever and ever"

בָּרוּךְ שֵׁם כְּבוֹד מַלְכוּתוֹ לְעוֹלָם וָעֶד.

דברים ו' ד'—ט'

and three paragraphs from the Bible:

You shall love the Lord your God with all your heart and with all your soul and with all your might. Take to heart these instructions with which I charge you this day. Impress them upon your children. Recite them when you stay at home and when you are away, when you lie down and when you get up. Bind them as a sign on your hand and let them serve as a symbol on your forehead; inscribe them on the doorposts of your house and on your gates (Deuteronomy 6:5–9).

וְאָהַבְתָּ אֵת יְהֹוָה אֱלֹהֶיךָ בְּכָל־לְבָבְךָ וּבְכָל־נַפְשְׁךָ וּבְכָל־מְאֹדֶךָ. וְהָיוּ הַדְּבָרִים הָאֵלֶּה אֲשֶׁר אָנֹכִי מְצַוְּךָ הַיּוֹם עַל־לְבָבֶךָ. וְשִׁנַּנְתָּם לְבָנֶיךָ וְדִבַּרְתָּ בָּם בְּשִׁבְתְּךָ בְּבֵיתֶךָ וּבְלֶכְתְּךָ בַדֶּרֶךְ וּבְשָׁכְבְּךָ וּבְקוּמֶךָ. וּקְשַׁרְתָּם לְאוֹת עַל־יָדֶךָ וְהָיוּ לְטֹטָפֹת בֵּין עֵינֶיךָ. וּכְתַבְתָּם עַל־מְזֻזוֹת בֵּיתֶךָ וּבִשְׁעָרֶיךָ.

דברים י"א י"ג—כ"א

If, then, you obey the commandments that I enjoin upon you this day, loving the Lord your God and serving Him with all your heart and soul, I will grant the rain for your land in season, the early rain and the late. You shall gather in your new grain and wine and oil—I will also provide grass in the fields for your cattle—and thus you shall eat your fill. Take care not to be lured away to serve other gods and bow to them. For the Lord's anger will flare up against you, and He will shut up the skies so that there will be no rain and the ground will not yield its produce; and you will soon perish from the good land that the Lord is giving you.

Therefore impress these My words upon your very heart: bind them as a sign on your hand and let them serve as a symbol on your forehead, and teach them to your children—reciting them when you stay at home and when you are away, when you lie down and when you get up; and inscribe them on the doorposts of your house and on your gates—to the end that you and your children may endure, in the land that the Lord swore to your fathers to give to them, as long as there is a heaven over the earth (Deuteronomy 11:13–21).

וְהָיָה אִם־שָׁמֹעַ תִּשְׁמְעוּ אֶל־מִצְוֹתַי אֲשֶׁר אָנֹכִי מְצַוֶּה אֶתְכֶם הַיּוֹם לְאַהֲבָה אֶת־יְהֹוָה אֱלֹהֵיכֶם וּלְעָבְדוֹ בְּכָל־לְבַבְכֶם וּבְכָל־נַפְשְׁכֶם. וְנָתַתִּי מְטַר־אַרְצְכֶם בְּעִתּוֹ יוֹרֶה וּמַלְקוֹשׁ וְאָסַפְתָּ דְגָנֶךָ וְתִירֹשְׁךָ וְיִצְהָרֶךָ. וְנָתַתִּי עֵשֶׂב בְּשָׂדְךָ לִבְהֶמְתֶּךָ וְאָכַלְתָּ וְשָׂבָעְתָּ. הִשָּׁמְרוּ לָכֶם פֶּן יִפְתֶּה לְבַבְכֶם וְסַרְתֶּם וַעֲבַדְתֶּם אֱלֹהִים אֲחֵרִים וְהִשְׁתַּחֲוִיתֶם לָהֶם. וְחָרָה אַף־יְהֹוָה בָּכֶם וְעָצַר אֶת־הַשָּׁמַיִם וְלֹא־יִהְיֶה מָטָר וְהָאֲדָמָה לֹא תִתֵּן אֶת־יְבוּלָהּ וַאֲבַדְתֶּם מְהֵרָה מֵעַל הָאָרֶץ הַטֹּבָה אֲשֶׁר יְהֹוָה נֹתֵן לָכֶם. וְשַׂמְתֶּם אֶת־דְּבָרַי אֵלֶּה עַל־לְבַבְכֶם וְעַל־נַפְשְׁכֶם וּקְשַׁרְתֶּם אֹתָם לְאוֹת עַל־יֶדְכֶם וְהָיוּ לְטוֹטָפֹת בֵּין עֵינֵיכֶם. וְלִמַּדְתֶּם אֹתָם אֶת־בְּנֵיכֶם לְדַבֵּר בָּם בְּשִׁבְתְּךָ בְּבֵיתֶךָ וּבְלֶכְתְּךָ בַדֶּרֶךְ וּבְשָׁכְבְּךָ וּבְקוּמֶךָ. וּכְתַבְתָּם עַל־מְזוּזוֹת בֵּיתֶךָ וּבִשְׁעָרֶיךָ: לְמַעַן יִרְבּוּ יְמֵיכֶם וִימֵי בְנֵיכֶם עַל הָאֲדָמָה אֲשֶׁר נִשְׁבַּע יְהֹוָה לַאֲבֹתֵיכֶם לָתֵת לָהֶם כִּימֵי הַשָּׁמַיִם עַל־הָאָרֶץ.

The Lord said to Moses as follows: Speak to the Israelite people and instruct them to make for themselves fringes on the corners of their garments throughout the ages; let them attach a cord of blue to the fringe of each corner. That shall be your fringe; look at it and recall all the commandments of the Lord and observe them, so that you do not follow your heart and eyes in your lustful urge. Thus you shall be reminded to observe My commandments and to be holy to your God. I the Lord am your God, who brought you out of the land of Egypt to be your God: I, the Lord your God (Numbers 15:37–41).

וַיֹּאמֶר יְהוָה אֶל־מֹשֶׁה לֵּאמֹר. דַּבֵּר אֶל־בְּנֵי יִשְׂרָאֵל וְאָמַרְתָּ אֲלֵהֶם וְעָשׂוּ לָהֶם צִיצִת עַל־כַּנְפֵי בִגְדֵיהֶם לְדֹרֹתָם וְנָתְנוּ עַל־צִיצִת הַכָּנָף פְּתִיל תְּכֵלֶת. וְהָיָה לָכֶם לְצִיצִת וּרְאִיתֶם אֹתוֹ וּזְכַרְתֶּם אֶת־כָּל־מִצְוֹת יְהוָה וַעֲשִׂיתֶם אֹתָם וְלֹא תָתוּרוּ אַחֲרֵי לְבַבְכֶם וְאַחֲרֵי עֵינֵיכֶם אֲשֶׁר־אַתֶּם זֹנִים אַחֲרֵיהֶם. לְמַעַן תִּזְכְּרוּ וַעֲשִׂיתֶם אֶת־כָּל־מִצְוֹתָי וִהְיִיתֶם קְדֹשִׁים לֵאלֹהֵיכֶם. אֲנִי יְהוָה אֱלֹהֵיכֶם אֲשֶׁר הוֹצֵאתִי אֶתְכֶם מֵאֶרֶץ מִצְרַיִם לִהְיוֹת לָכֶם לֵאלֹהִים אֲנִי יְהוָה אֱלֹהֵיכֶם.

Both before and after the Shema (and the three paragraphs we will subsume under the general term Shema) there are long berakhot. In Shaharit there are two before the Shema and one after: (1) Yotzer Or—Light and Darkness; (2) Ahavah Rabbah—the Love of God and Israel; and (3) Emet ve-Yatziv—Redemption. In Maariv—the evening prayer—the Shema is preceded by two berakhot and followed by two. (In Minhah—the Afternoon Service—Shema is not said.) The first three berakhot in Maariv have similar themes to those of Shaharit. The fourth berakhah is Hashkiveinu—a prayer for peace and general well-being.

Just by looking through the Shema section you'll be able to pick out the various themes as well as the beginning and end of each berakhah. (Note: the first one is *very* long. Also note: the third berakhah begins with the word "Emet" after the end of the third paragraph of Shema.) The Shema section in Shaharit ends with "Barukh attah Adonai gaal Yisrael":

"O Rock of Israel, arise to help Thy scattered folk; Deliver all who are crushed beneath oppression's heel.
Thou art our Savior; the Lord of Hosts is Thy Name; Blessed art Thou, O Lord, Redeemer of Israel."

צוּר יִשְׂרָאֵל קוּמָה בְּעֶזְרַת יִשְׂרָאֵל. וּפְדֵה כִנְאֻמֶךָ יְהוּדָה וְיִשְׂרָאֵל. גֹּאֲלֵנוּ יְיָ צְבָאוֹת שְׁמוֹ קְדוֹשׁ יִשְׂרָאֵל. בָּרוּךְ אַתָּה יְיָ גָּאַל יִשְׂרָאֵל.

Unlike other sections, however, the Shema section does not have a Kaddish or any other sign of separation between it and the next section—the Amidah. In fact, traditionally the one was supposed to immediately follow the other, with no interruption. Therefore some people do not respond with "Amen" to the blessing Gaal Yisrael (as is the normal procedure when the hazzan recites a blessing). In fact, in some places the hazzan doesn't even say the last two words aloud to "avoid" the problem of people saying "Amen." Scholars surmise that this interconnectedness between the Shema and Amidah sections is to stress their unity. Some maintain that the Amidah was an addition to the Shema service, but that to stress its equal importance no interruption was permitted. If this *was* what the rabbis were after then they succeeded quite well, since both the Shema and Amidah are today treated with equal sanctity (in fact sometimes the Amidah is considered the more important of the two prayers).

Let me warn you, Rabinowits. Don't sit near Rabinowits. He Hums "Home on the range" during the Amidah.

The Amidah

This section is a series of berakhot that is found in every service—weekday, Shabbat, or holiday; morning, afternoon, or evening. It is called either Amidah (meaning "standing"—since it is customary to stand while saying it) or Shemoneh Esrei—the Eighteen Blessings—because at one time it contained . . . eighteen blessings.

The Amidah has three parts:
1. the first three berakhot
2. the middle section
3. the last three berakhot.

PART 1

This is found in every Amidah. The section is basically one of praise of God and deals with:
   a. the merit of the patriarchs
   b. the greatness of God who can resurrect the dead
   c. the holiness of God.

PART 2

The middle section is different for weekdays and for Shabbat. On weekdays it consists of thirteen berakhot of petition asking for wisdom, health, the rebuilding of Jerusalem, etc. On Shabbat and holidays it has only one central berakhah, reflecting, appropriately enough, either the Shabbat or the holiday themes. (The one exception is the Rosh ha-Shanah Musaf service, which has three central berakhot rather than one.) It is felt that one should rejoice with unadulterated celebration on Shabbat and holidays and should therefore not engage in petitionary prayers. Therefore there are only seven blessings on Shabbat and holidays (3-1-3), not nineteen (3-13-3).

PART 3

The last three berakhot are also found in every service and serve to express our gratitude for what God has given us. The three themes are:
   a. the acceptance of our prayers
   b. gratitude
   c. peace.

Following the last berakhah is a prayer called Elohai Nitzor, which was composed in talmudic times. It is in the first-person singular (most Jewish prayer is in the plural) and is customarily said as soon as one completes the Amidah.

THE REPETITION

It is probably most accurate to say that there are really two Amidahs:
   a. the silent one
   b. the repetition by the hazzan.

In many synagogues the Amidah is first said silently by each person. Afterwards the hazzan repeats the entire Amidah out loud. When the hazzan finishes the second berakhah, the congregation stands (during the rest of the repetition most congregations remain seated) to recite the Kedushah, which is never said by an individual during the silent prayer.

Kedushah

Not to be confused with the Kaddish (which we spoke about earlier) or Kiddush (the blessing over wine, which we'll mention later)—although of

Okay, so there are supposed to be eighteen blessings. But with typical Jewish arithmetic, if you count them there are nineteen. Strange. But not so strange. Here in operation is how the siddur functions as a kind of historical autobiography of the Jews. Many Jews joined the early Christian movement, both in order to escape Roman persecutions and because they supported the new sect. Some even turned traitor and informed against the Jews to the Romans. The difficulty was in determining who these traitors were because they continued to come to the synagogue and take part in Jewish life. In order to weed out such traitors, Rabbi Gamaliel dreamed up an ingenious strategy. He added to the Shemoneh Esrei another section, which contained a malediction against the Judeo-Christians. Any person who did not respond with a resounding "Amen" at the end of that section was immediately suspect. Abraham Millgram points out in his book *Jewish Worship* that the benediction "used to read somewhat as follows: 'For apostates may there be no hope, and may the *Minim* [Judeo-Christians] and heretics speedily perish'" (p. 105). The blessing was somewhat changed later on but never entirely done away with, for a similar problem of traitorous apostates arose again in the Middle Ages. The section now reads: "And for slanderers [informers] let there be no hope, and let all wickedness perish." P.S.: Naturally some scholars maintain a different blessing was the nineteenth—the one concerning David.

the same root derivation. The Kedushah is one of the prayers for which a minyan is needed. The term means "holiness" and is probably taken from the phrase "Holy Holy Holy," which is in the middle of the Kedushah (it is also the theme of the third blessing). It consists of a series of verses, which are chanted responsively by the hazzan and the congregation. (There are variations between weekday, Shabbat, Shaharit, and Musaf Kedushahs.)

SHABBAT AND HOLIDAY SHAHARIT KEDUSHAH (ASHKENAZIC) קדושה

When the reader chants the Amidah, the Kedushah is added:

"We sanctify Thy Name on earth even as it is sanctified in the heavens above, as described in the vision of Thy prophet:

And the seraphim called one unto another saying:

Holy, holy, holy is the Lord of hosts,
The whole earth is full of His glory.

Whereupon the angels in stirring and mighty chorus rise toward the seraphim and with resounding acclaim declare:

Blessed be the glory of God from His heavenly abode.

From Thy heavenly abode, reveal Thyself, O our King, and reign over us, for we wait for Thee. O when wilt Thou reign in Zion? Speedily, even in our days, do Thou establish Thy dwelling there forever. Mayest Thou be exalted and sanctified in Jerusalem, Thy city, throughout all generations and to all eternity. O let our eyes behold the establishment of Thy kingdom, according to the word that was spoken in the inspired psalms of David, Thy righteous anointed:

The Lord shall reign forever. Thy God, O Zion, shall be Sovereign unto all generations. Hallelujah!

Unto all generations we will declare Thy greatness and to all eternity we will proclaim Thy holiness. Our mouth shall ever speak Thy praise, O our God, for Thou art a great and holy God and King. *Blessed art Thou, O Lord, the holy God."

On the Sabbath of Repentance, conclude thus:
"Blessed art Thou, O Lord, the holy King."

When the Reader chants the Amidah, the Kedushah is added:

נְקַדֵּשׁ אֶת־שִׁמְךָ בָּעוֹלָם כְּשֵׁם שֶׁמַּקְדִּישִׁים אוֹתוֹ בִּשְׁמֵי מָרוֹם. כַּכָּתוּב עַל־יַד נְבִיאֶךָ. וְקָרָא זֶה אֶל־זֶה וְאָמַר.

קָדוֹשׁ קָדוֹשׁ קָדוֹשׁ יְיָ צְבָאוֹת, מְלֹא כָל־הָאָרֶץ כְּבוֹדוֹ.

אָז בְּקוֹל רַעַשׁ גָּדוֹל אַדִּיר וְחָזָק מַשְׁמִיעִים קוֹל מִתְנַשְּׂאִים לְעֻמַּת שְׂרָפִים לְעֻמָּתָם בָּרוּךְ יֹאמֵרוּ.

בָּרוּךְ כְּבוֹד־יְיָ מִמְּקוֹמוֹ.

מִמְּקוֹמְךָ מַלְכֵּנוּ תוֹפִיעַ וְתִמְלוֹךְ עָלֵינוּ כִּי מְחַכִּים אֲנַחְנוּ לָךְ. מָתַי תִּמְלוֹךְ בְּצִיּוֹן. בְּקָרוֹב בְּיָמֵינוּ לְעוֹלָם וָעֶד תִּשְׁכּוֹן. תִּתְגַּדַּל וְתִתְקַדַּשׁ בְּתוֹךְ יְרוּשָׁלַיִם עִירְךָ לְדוֹר וָדוֹר וּלְנֵצַח נְצָחִים. וְעֵינֵינוּ תִרְאֶינָה מַלְכוּתֶךָ כַּדָּבָר הָאָמוּר בְּשִׁירֵי עֻזֶּךָ עַל־יְדֵי דָוִד מְשִׁיחַ צִדְקֶךָ.

יִמְלֹךְ יְיָ לְעוֹלָם. אֱלֹהַיִךְ צִיּוֹן לְדֹר וָדֹר. הַלְלוּיָהּ.

לְדוֹר וָדוֹר נַגִּיד גָּדְלֶךָ. וּלְנֵצַח נְצָחִים קְדֻשָּׁתְךָ נַקְדִּישׁ. וְשִׁבְחֲךָ אֱלֹהֵינוּ מִפִּינוּ לֹא יָמוּשׁ לְעוֹלָם וָעֶד. כִּי אֵל מֶלֶךְ גָּדוֹל וְקָדוֹשׁ אָתָּה. * בָּרוּךְ אַתָּה יְיָ הָאֵל הַקָּדוֹשׁ.

On Shabbat Shuvah conclude thus:
בָּרוּךְ אַתָּה יְיָ הַמֶּלֶךְ הַקָּדוֹשׁ.

After the Kedushah, the hazzan concludes the third blessing and continues with the repetition of the Amidah. The Kedushah is, in fact, really the middle part of the third blessing, which deals with the holiness of God.

The congregation responds at one other time during the repetition. In the next to the last blessing Modim, there is a paragraph that the congregation says while the hazzan chants out loud the regular Modim prayed earlier in silence.

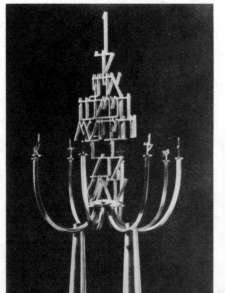

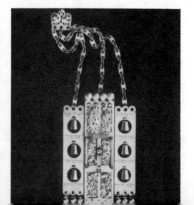

When the reader repeats the Amidah, the congregation responds here by saying:

"May our eyes behold Thy return in mercy to Zion. Blessed art Thou, O Lord, who restorest Thy Divine presence to Zion."

"We ever thank Thee, who art the Lord our God and the God of our fathers. Thou art the strength of our life and our saving Shield. In every generation we will thank Thee and recount Thy praise—for our lives which are in Thy charge, for our souls which are in Thy care, for Thy miracles which are daily with us, and for Thy continual wonders and favors—evening, morning, and noon. Beneficent One, whose mercies never fail, Merciful One, whose kindnesses never cease, Thou hast always been our hope."

When the reader repeats the Amidah, the congregation responds here by saying:

"We thank Thee, who art the Lord our God and the God of our fathers. God of all mankind, our Creator and Creator of the universe, blessings and thanks are due to Thy great and holy Name, because Thou hast kept us alive and sustained us; mayest Thou ever grant us life and sustenance. O gather our exiles to Thy holy courts to observe Thy laws, to do Thy will, and to serve Thee with a perfect heart. For this we thank Thee. Blessed be God, to whom all thanks are due."

When the Reader repeats the Amidah, the Congregation responds here by saying:

וְתֶחֱזֶינָה עֵינֵינוּ בְּשׁוּבְךָ לְצִיּוֹן בְּרַחֲמִים. בָּרוּךְ אַתָּה, יְיָ, הַמַּחֲזִיר שְׁכִינָתוֹ לְצִיּוֹן.

מוֹדִים אֲנַחְנוּ לָךְ, שָׁאַתָּה הוּא יְיָ אֱלֹהֵינוּ וֵאלֹהֵי אֲבוֹתֵינוּ לְעוֹלָם וָעֶד. צוּר חַיֵּינוּ, מָגֵן יִשְׁעֵנוּ אַתָּה הוּא. לְדוֹר וָדוֹר נוֹדֶה לְּךָ, וּנְסַפֵּר תְּהִלָּתֶךָ, עַל חַיֵּינוּ הַמְּסוּרִים בְּיָדֶךָ, וְעַל נִשְׁמוֹתֵינוּ הַפְּקוּדוֹת לָךְ, וְעַל נִסֶּיךָ שֶׁבְּכָל יוֹם עִמָּנוּ, וְעַל נִפְלְאוֹתֶיךָ וְטוֹבוֹתֶיךָ שֶׁבְּכָל עֵת, עֶרֶב וָבֹקֶר וְצָהֳרָיִם. הַטּוֹב כִּי לֹא כָלוּ רַחֲמֶיךָ, וְהַמְרַחֵם כִּי לֹא תַמּוּ חֲסָדֶיךָ, כִּי מֵעוֹלָם קִוִּינוּ לָךְ.

When the Reader repeats the Amidah, the Congregation responds here by saying:

(מוֹדִים אֲנַחְנוּ לָךְ, שָׁאַתָּה הוּא יְיָ אֱלֹהֵינוּ וֵאלֹהֵי אֲבוֹתֵינוּ. אֱלֹהֵי כָל בָּשָׂר, יוֹצְרֵנוּ, יוֹצֵר בְּרֵאשִׁית, בְּרָכוֹת וְהוֹדָאוֹת לְשִׁמְךָ הַגָּדוֹל וְהַקָּדוֹשׁ עַל שֶׁהֶחֱיִיתָנוּ וְקִיַּמְתָּנוּ. כֵּן תְּחַיֵּנוּ וּתְקַיְּמֵנוּ, וְתֶאֱסוֹף גָּלֻיּוֹתֵינוּ לְחַצְרוֹת קָדְשֶׁךָ לִשְׁמוֹר חֻקֶּיךָ וְלַעֲשׂוֹת רְצוֹנֶךָ, וּלְעָבְדְּךָ בְּלֵבָב שָׁלֵם, עַל שֶׁאֲנַחְנוּ מוֹדִים לָךְ. בָּרוּךְ אֵל הַהוֹדָאוֹת.)

In some congregations the entire repetition of the Amidah is not done. Instead, three customs have arisen:

1. After the berakhah Gaal Yisrael, the hazzan begins to chant aloud the first two berakhot of the Amidah and the congregation says it along with the hazzan. Then the Kedushah is said (out loud, of course). When the third blessing is over, the rest of the Amidah is said silently.

2. Basically the same as the above except the hazzan alone says the first two berakhot—the congregation only listens. Then the Kedushah is said by the hazzan and the congregation. After it is finished, the congregation then starts the silent Amidah from the beginning.

3. The silent Amidah is done first in a regular fashion. Then the hazzan does the repetition in its regular fashion until the conclusion of the Kedushah. However, after ending the third blessing, the hazzan does not continue with the repetition but skips to the next portion of the service (which varies, depending on whether it's a weekday, Shabbat, holiday, etc.).

All three methods are meant to save time and to avoid the custom of repetition, which arose during a period when there frequently were not enough prayer books for all the congregants, so people had to rely on *hearing* the repetition of the Amidah to fulfill the precept to pray. Since this is obviously not the case today, and since it can be quite boring to hear chanted back at you what you just finished praying yourself, these three methods for avoiding the repetition are frequently used.

The next part of the service varies, depending on a number of factors:

1. On weekdays traditional congregations say Tahanun, which is a section of petitionary prayers asking especially for forgiveness and mercy. On Mondays and Thursdays after Tahanun, there is a Torah service.

2. On Shabbat the Amidah section is followed immediately by the Torah service.

3. On holidays the section called Hallel—which is a collection of psalms of praise—is recited (it begins and ends with a berakhah) before the Torah service.

Thus after the Kaddish on Mondays, Thursdays, Shabbat, and holidays the Torah is read. (On weekdays following Tahanun there is a Hatzi Kaddish; on Shabbat and most holidays after Hallel, there is a Kaddish Shalem.) This, then, is the next part of the siddur.

The Torah service

The Torah service is the third major part of the service. While studying is certainly not the same as praying, study of Torah is of such central concern to the Jew that it is important that it be included with prayer (see Talmud Torah Lishmah). Accordingly, so that we will not go three days without Torah, a Torah service is included in the services on Mondays, Thursdays, Shabbat, and holidays.

The Torah service consists of three parts:
    Part 1: taking the Torah out of the ark
    Part 2: the actual reading from the Torah (and Prophets)
    Part 3: returning the Torah to the ark.
This part of the service contains a number of roles; you may be honored by being asked to perform one of them.

PART 1: TAKING THE TORAH OUT OF THE ARK

Opening the ark: The ark is opened as the verse "And it came to pass that when the ark moved forward . . ." is said by the congregation (which is standing to honor the Torah).

The ark is opened.

"And it came to pass that when the Ark moved forward, Moses said: Rise up, O Lord, and let Thine enemies be scattered; and let them that hate Thee flee before Thee.

For out of Zion shall go forth the Torah, and the word of the Lord from Jerusalem.

Blessed be He who, in His holiness, gave the Torah to His people Israel."

The Ark is opened.

וַיְהִי בִּנְסֹעַ הָאָרֹן וַיֹּאמֶר מֹשֶׁה קוּמָה יְיָ וְיָפֻצוּ אֹיְבֶיךָ
וְיָנֻסוּ מְשַׂנְאֶיךָ מִפָּנֶיךָ. כִּי מִצִּיּוֹן תֵּצֵא תוֹרָה וּדְבַר־יְיָ מִירוּשָׁלָיִם:
בָּרוּךְ שֶׁנָּתַן תּוֹרָה לְעַמּוֹ יִשְׂרָאֵל בִּקְדֻשָׁתוֹ.

As we have said, most arks have a parokhet—curtain—in front, which covers the doors. The parokhet can be drawn aside either by the pull of a cord (like drapes) or simply being pulled aside by hand. The cord is usually on the right side of the ark. Then there are the ark doors, which either slide apart to each side or open outward toward you (in some synagogues the doors are on the outside and the parokhet is on the inside).

The person honored with opening the ark is usually not formally called up to perform the task, as is the case with an aliyah (see below), though some synagogues have the custom of announcing that So-and-so is honored with opening the ark (especially at Bar/Bat Mitzvahs, etc.). Usually the gabbai of the shul will come over to you and ask you to open the ark (s/he will also give out the other honors). If you don't want to do it, you can decline politely (however, if it's a Bar/Bat Mitzvah, you may be inadvertently insulting someone). But before you decline, keep in mind that it is truly a great honor to be allowed to perform such a holy task. Feel free to ask the gabbai any questions you might have. S/he will be close by to give you a signal when it is time to open the ark if you are unsure about details.

After the ark is open and the appropriate verses are chanted, either the person honored with opening the ark or a person separately honored will carefully take the Sefer Torah out of the ark and hand it to the hazzan. On some holidays, various and separate portions of the Torah will be read, and so more than one scroll is used. Then a third person will be honored with holding the second Sefer Torah. This person should follow behind the hazzan in the "processional" described below. The same is true for a third Sefer Torah holder.

Lifting the Torah out of the ark: The simplest way is to place your stronger hand underneath the Torah, slide your other hand around the middle of the scroll to hold the back, lift, and turn toward the hazzan (who will then have received the Torah with the front side facing the congregation—that is, away from his body). Imagine yourself lifting a baby from a carriage (only in an upright position).

Carrying the Torah: It should be held upright resting against your right shoulder. One hand should hold the bottom roller, the other can do the same as long as it supports the Torah sufficiently so that there is no danger of its falling (God forbid). The Torah is not supposed to be held like a baby—cradled in your arms; it should be held upright against your shoulder.

The Torah is always carried with the rolled part in front—facing outward. And, incidentally, you can always tell which is the front of a Sefer Torah because the front of the Sefer Torah cover is always elaborately decorated and the back is not.

Remember: Lift the Torah up and out; then turn and hand it to the hazzan. (*You* turn—not the Torah.)

When the hazzan has the Torah, the ark should be closed. The cord for closing the parokhet is sometimes on the left side of the ark. On Shabbat the hazzan will chant two phrases facing the congregation, beginning with Shema Yisrael. Then the hazzan turns to the ark and bows, saying: "Gadlu la-Adonai..." (this phrase is also said on weekdays when the Torah is read).

The reader takes the scroll of the Torah.
Reader and congregation

"Hear, O Israel! The Lord our God, the Lord is One."

Reader and congregation

"One is our God; great is our Lord; holy is His Name."

Reader

"Extol the Lord with me, and together let us exalt His Name."

The Reader takes the Scroll of the Torah
Reader and Congregation

שְׁמַע יִשְׂרָאֵל יְהוָֹה אֱלֹהֵינוּ יְהוָֹה אֶחָד.

Reader and Congregation

אֶחָד אֱלֹהֵינוּ גָּדוֹל אֲדוֹנֵינוּ קָדוֹשׁ שְׁמוֹ.

Reader

גַּדְּלוּ לַיָי אִתִּי וּנְרוֹמְמָה שְׁמוֹ יַחְדָּו.

Following this, a procession is formed as these verses are chanted:

"Thine, O Lord, is the greatness and the power, the glory, the victory and the majesty; for all that is in the heaven and on the earth is Thine. Thine is the kingdom, O Lord, and Thou art exalted supreme above all. Exalt the Lord our God, and worship at His footstool; holy is He. Exalt the Lord our God, and worship at His holy mountain; for the Lord our God is holy."

לְךָ יְיָ הַגְּדֻלָּה וְהַגְּבוּרָה וְהַתִּפְאֶרֶת וְהַנֵּצַח וְהַהוֹד. כִּי־
כֹל בַּשָּׁמַיִם וּבָאָרֶץ לְךָ יְיָ הַמַּמְלָכָה וְהַמִּתְנַשֵּׂא לְכֹל לְרֹאשׁ.
רוֹמְמוּ יְיָ אֱלֹהֵינוּ וְהִשְׁתַּחֲווּ לַהֲדֹם רַגְלָיו קָדוֹשׁ הוּא. רוֹמְמוּ
יְיָ אֱלֹהֵינוּ וְהִשְׁתַּחֲווּ לְהַר קָדְשׁוֹ כִּי־קָדוֹשׁ יְיָ אֱלֹהֵינוּ.

The hazzan leads, carrying the Torah (followed, if applicable, by the other people carrying the other Torahs) followed by the ark-opener, etc. In some places the rabbi also joins the procession. The ark-opener should follow in the procession until s/he reaches his/her seat or the place where the Torah is read. Not to return immediately to your seat is considered a mark of honor to the Torah. If you are not honored, as the Torah comes by you in the procession it is customary to touch it with your tallit or siddur (in some places, just with your hand) and then bring the tallit or siddur to your lips and kiss it.

The procession wends its way through the shul until it reaches the bimah. The hazzan places the Torah (face up) on the reading table—gently lowering it, never allowing it to drop, never treating the Torah roughly. The other Torot (if any) are placed in holders, or someone (often a child) is honored with being allowed to hold them. At this point the congregation is seated.

In some shuls the ushers will now give out Bibles; if not, people should go over and pick them up, after which the page or at least the portion for that week will be announced. (Each week a different section of the Torah is read in succession, so that between each Simhat Torah the entire Bible has been completed.)

PART 2: READING THE TORAH

The Torah is read from a reading desk located either in the front or middle of the shul. In more traditional congregations the reader faces the ark. In others the reader faces the congregation. The person who reads from the Torah is called the baal koreh. This person reads the Torah on behalf of everyone who is called up (indeed, on behalf of everyone who is present), except if a Bar/Bat Mitzvah reads for him/herself. There will, in addition, be one person standing on either side of the reading table: the gabbaim. Sometimes you may be honored by being given the role of gabbai. Your job is to stand by the scroll, doing any or all of the following:

1. holding the top roller of the Torah so it doesn't roll inward;

2. helping to unroll the Torah as the reader finishes one column and goes on to the next;

3. looking in a Humash—Bible—to correct any mistakes the reader might make while reading;

4. shaking hands and saying "Yasher koah—May your strength increase"—to someone who has just received an aliyah;

5. assisting the person doing hagbah (explained later) by carrying over to him/her the sash, Torah cover, etc.;

6. placing the cover over the Torah when it is not being read from, e.g., during a mi-she-berakh;

7. generally being useful.

Incidentally, Kabbalists see this entire scene as a dramatic reenactment of the Revelation at Sinai. Thus the Torah reader would represent God, the person called for an aliyah would represent the people Israel, and the gabbai who does the calling up of the aliyot would represent Moses.

A gabbai may also be needed to help "undress" the Torah (which is now lying on the reading table) in order to prepare it to be read. If the Torah has breastplates, pointers, etc., they are usually removed before the Torah is laid on the reading platform, but if this was not done, they are, of course, removed before the Torah cover is taken off. These are not used during the Torah service and can be carefully placed out of the way.

One person then presses down on the bottom rollers while another pulls the Torah cover off the top of the Torah. Then the sash should be untied (or unbuckled) and slipped out from underneath the Torah. Both should be carefully placed to one side.

Aliyot: It is a great honor to be "called" to the Torah. This is called an aliyah (plural aliyot) and means literally "going up"—which is usually true, since the reading stand is frequently elevated. It is also a term of spiritual significance, as it is written in Deuteronomy 5:28: "But you remain [stand] here with Me."

The number of aliyot depends upon the sanctity of the day. Thus:
1. a weekday (and also Saturday afternoon) = 3 aliyot
2. New Moon and intermediate days = 4
3. holidays = 5
4. Yom Kippur = 6
5. Shabbat = 7

Sometimes the number of aliyot are added to in order to be able to honor more people. This is especially true at Bar/Bat Mitzvahs, aufrufs (when a bridegroom is called to the Torah), etc. (See Weddings in *Catalog 1*.) Traditionally the first aliyah is given to a kohen, the second to a Levite, the rest to Israelites (plain Jews). The terms kohen and Levite refer to people descended from the priestly families who serviced the Temple in Jerusalem. They are still considered to have special status, and this is one of the (few) ways it is acknowledged.

If there is no kohen or Levite present, anyone can be called for the aliyot (some places will call a Levite for the first aliyah and an Israelite for the second if there is no kohen present; some will call two kohanim for the first two aliyot if there is no Levite). A kohen or Levite cannot receive any of the other prescribed aliyot, e.g., 3–7 on Shabbat. S/he can be given maftir or an additional aliyah can be made. SO a word about maftir. . . .

On days when the haftarah is read (holidays and Shabbat) there is an additional aliyah called a maftir. On Shabbat this is usually the last few verses of the portion, which are read over again (having already been read as part of the seventh aliyah). On holidays this is often a separate section (sometimes from the second scroll) dealing with the holiday. The person who has the aliyah for maftir also reads the haftarah (see below).

If you are honored with an aliyah (you are usually asked by the gabbai/usher), you should put on a tallit if you're not already wearing one. In many traditional synagogues you will be called up by your Hebrew name, e.g., Pinchas ben (son of) Meir (see "Names" in Birth). Some of the more scientifically aware synagogues will acknowledge the existence of your mother and call you up as Pinchas ben Meir u-ben Ruth (Pinchas the son of Meir and Ruth). Be prepared for such radicalism.

In other synagogues they will just announce the number of the aliyah. Regardless of whether number or name is called, you are summoned either by the words "Ya-amod (masculine form of "Stand"), David ben . . ." ("Ta-amod" is the feminine form) or "Ya-amod hamishi" (the fifth aliyah). You will be called to the aliyah after the person before you has made his/her concluding berakhah. When called, you should go up to the reading table

If you're not sure whether you are a kohen or a Levite, check with your parents, grandparents, etc. If your name is Cohen or Katz you are probably a kohen. If you're not sure and can't find out, welcome to the plebian class!

and stand to the right of the Torah reader. In some synagogues a mi-she-berakh ("May He who blessed our fathers . . . also bless . . .") is said for each person who has an aliyah. This is said for the previous person while you come up for your aliyah. At the conclusion of the mi-she-berakh, or after you have come to the reading table, the reader will point out the place in the Torah. Take the end of your tallit in your right hand, touch the place in the Torah, bring the tallit to your lips, and kiss it. Then:

The person called to the Torah recites:
"Bless the Lord, who is blessed."

The congregation responds:
"Blessed be the Lord, who is blessed forever and ever."

S/He repeats the response and continues:
"Blessed art Thou, Lord our God, King of the Universe, who hast chosen us from all peoples, and hast given us Thy Torah. Blessed art Thou, O Lord, Giver of the Torah."

After the Torah is read, you say:
"Blessed art Thou, Lord our God, King of the Universe, who hast given us the Torah of truth, and hast planted everlasting life in our midst. Blessed art Thou, O Lord, Giver of the Torah."

The person called to the Torah recites:

בָּרְכוּ אֶת יְיָ הַמְבֹרָךְ.

The Congregation responds:

בָּרוּךְ יְיָ הַמְבֹרָךְ לְעוֹלָם וָעֶד.

He repeats the response and continues:

בָּרוּךְ אַתָּה, יְיָ אֱלֹהֵינוּ, מֶלֶךְ הָעוֹלָם, אֲשֶׁר בָּחַר בָּנוּ מִכָּל הָעַמִּים וְנָתַן לָנוּ אֶת תּוֹרָתוֹ. בָּרוּךְ אַתָּה, יְיָ, נוֹתֵן הַתּוֹרָה.

בָּרוּךְ אַתָּה, יְיָ אֱלֹהֵינוּ, מֶלֶךְ הָעוֹלָם, אֲשֶׁר נָתַן לָנוּ תּוֹרַת אֱמֶת וְחַיֵּי עוֹלָם נָטַע בְּתוֹכֵנוּ. בָּרוּךְ אַתָּה, יְיָ, נוֹתֵן הַתּוֹרָה.

(You should try following the reader in the Torah as best you can during the aliyah.)

After the aliyah is finished and you have said the appropriate berakhah, move over to the right side of the bimah. If it is the shul's custom to say the mi-she-berakh, they will say it for you now, so be prepared to repeat your name. Continue to stand there while the person gets his/her aliyah. During the next aliyah, follow the reading in the scroll or with the gabbai in his/her Humash. Your remaining there is to show reluctance to leave the Torah quickly. After the next person has said the closing berakhah, you should shake hands with the reader, gabbaim, rabbi, president, whoever else is on the podium (especially in nontraditional shuls) and even with people you pass on the way back to your seat (especially in traditional shuls). This is done so people can congratulate you on your honor. In some shuls it is customary to take a longer way back to your seat than the one you took to get to your aliyah—again, to show your reluctance to leave the Torah.

When there is a maftir, that aliyah is preceded by a Hatzi Kaddish to indicate the difference between it and a regular reading.

Following the completion of the Torah reading, there is a hagbah (lifting up) and gelilah (rolling) of the Torah. This consists of someone's lifting the Torah and turning it around so the congregants can see the actual writing on the parchment while they say Ve-zot ha-Torah:

"This is the Torah which Moses placed before the children of Israel. It is in accordance with the Lord's command through Moses."

וְזֹאת הַתּוֹרָה אֲשֶׁר שָׂם מֹשֶׁה לִפְנֵי בְּנֵי יִשְׂרָאֵל, עַל פִּי יְיָ בְּיַד מֹשֶׁה.

Then the Torah is "dressed" once again in its stately coverings and made ready to be returned to the ark. If more than one Torah has been used, the same procedure is followed with each.

How to do hagbah and gelilah: Torah scrolls can be fairly heavy, but hagbah need not be restricted only to the muscular. The average reasonably healthy person should be able to do hagbah. However, when the reading is from the beginning of Genesis or the end of Deuteronomy, the weight will be largely on one side of the Torah (left and right side respectively). Keep this in mind if you are asked to do hagbah.

Gelilah, in contrast, is very easy and is often given to children under Bar/Bat Mitzvah age (who aren't old enough for an aliyah).

To do hagbah, you should:

1. unroll the Torah until about three columns are showing;

2. try to get a seam in the middle, so that in case (God forbid) the scroll should start to rip, it will rip along the seam;

3. slide the scroll toward you so that the bottom rollers are off the reading table;

4. grasp each roller firmly;

5. using the table to get leverage, bend your knees and push down on your ends of the scroll;

6. when the upper ends of the scroll are in the air, lift the scroll so it is upright. Your arms should be about mid-chest height as you bring yourself to an upright position. Be careful not to catch the edge of the rollers under the reading table;

7. turn around so the inside of the scroll—i.e., the writing—is visible to the congregation;

8. after the congregation has finished chanting Ve-zot ha-Torah (or even during the chanting in some congregations), sit down in the chair provided for you.

Now the gelilah person will take over, and all you have to do at this point is to help roll up the Torah and keep the Torah steady as the gelilah person performs his/her task.

To do gelilah:

1. As soon as the hagbah person has sat down you should grasp the tops of the rollers and roll the Sefer Torah rollers together (with the aid of the hagbah person).

2. It is customary to roll the Genesis side of the scroll (your left side) on top of the other side. Therefore put the roller in your left hand above the roller in your right as you roll the two halves together.

3. Then take the sash or buckle and fasten it around the Torah with the clasp or tie side facing the front of the scroll (i.e., the hagbah person). If you have a sash, wind it around as many times as necessary, making sure you have enough to tie a bow at the end (a bow tie is used because traditional law prohibits tying permanent knots on Shabbat, but bow ties, which are easily opened, are not considered permanent and are therefore permitted). Some congregations have a wimpel (see Birth), which is wrapped many times around the Torah and is tucked in rather than tied.

4. Next, take the Torah cover and fit it over the scrolls with the decoration side facing the hagbah person. Make sure the holes at the top of the cover fit over the rollers and the cover is pulled all the way down.

5. If it is the custom of the shul at this point to put the pointers and breastplates over the Torah (pointer usually is put over one roller, breastplate over both rollers), do so. In some shuls the pointer, etc. are put on only after the haftarah is chanted, not before.

After this is completed, the Torah is either (a) given to the hazzan to return to the ark, or (b) if there is a haftarah, it continues to be held by the hagbah person (or someone else) or it is placed in special wooden holders.

To hold a Torah while you are sitting is very simple: hold it upright in your lap, putting one of your hands on the bottom rollers and curving your other arm around the middle of the Torah to prevent it from slipping. If you can, rest the rollers on the edge of the seat or your legs. Once the hagbah

Note: The important thing for hagbah is to keep the Torah scroll steady during the entire procedure. If you can do that, you should have no problems at all. It really is much easier than you think (or than we can explain).

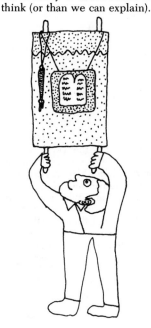

and gelilah people are finished, they should shake hands with everyone, as described above with the aliyot.

Haftarah: As mentioned, the haftarah is chanted by the person who had the maftir aliyah. The haftarah consists of a selection from the Prophets or the Writings. In nearly all congregations it is read from a printed Bible rather than from a scroll. In general, this is the section (sometimes also the maftir in the Torah) that the Bar/Bat Mitzvah person struggles through. (In some traditional shuls, the Bar/Bat Mitzvah reads the whole portion from the Torah.) This is preceded and followed by blessings, which conclude this section of the Torah service.

PART 3: RETURNING THE TORAH

On weekdays this is a fairly simple procedure. The hazzan picks up the Torah and does a reverse procession through the shul. Usually the same people will carry the other Torahs, if any, and the same person will open the ark and return the scroll. Then the ark is closed and the Torah service is completed.

On Shabbat and holidays the basic pattern is similar, though some preliminary prayers may be added, i.e., Yekum Purkan, Ashrei, the announcement of the New Moon, etc., depending on the synagogue custom and the time of the month. On weekdays we would now have the last portion of the service, which consists of a series of prayers beginning with Ashrei and going through U-va le-Tzion—dealing with many different themes, such as praise of God, God's holiness, redemption, etc. At the conclusion of U-va le-Tzion, a Kaddish Shalem is recited, marking the end of the service. However, this is followed by a number of additional prayers, usually the Alenu and psalm of the day. Each of these is followed by Mourners' Kaddish. And that's the end.

Musaf

On Shabbat and holidays there is a Hatzi Kaddish after the Torah service to divide the Torah service from the next major portion—Musaf. However, before the Kaddish and Musaf many rabbis give sermons, which will vary in length, quality, and subject matter. The general rule of thumb is that the less traditional the synagogue, the more important the role of the sermon.

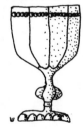

The Musaf—additional—prayer is said only on Shabbat and holidays. It consists basically of an Amidah similar to the Shaharit Amidah, except that it has a different middle berakhah section dealing with sacrifices and other themes. It, too, has a silent Amidah and a repetition (or one of the variants described above). The Amidah is followed by a Kaddish Shalem, signifying the end of the service. After this, some additions (which are of a legalistic nature) are included. Again, the recitation of these legalistic passages is considered to be the same as your studying them, so they are followed by the Rabbis' Kaddish (see "Kaddish" above). This is followed by Alenu, in most shuls by the psalm of the day, the Mourners' Kaddish and sometimes a few hymns such as "Anim Zemirot." The service usually concludes with the singing of "Adon Olam" or "Yigdal."

In some congregations a benediction or announcements are made at the end of the service. Some have the Bar/Bat Mitzvahs make Kiddush (the blessing over wine) and ha-Motzi (the blessing over bread) so that people can immediately eat the refreshments after the service.

The term Kiddush has taken on an additional reference—including as it now does the cake, hors d'oeuvre-y type food, etc. served after services. Most shuls have a Kiddush at the end of all Shabbat and holiday morning services (and sometimes after other services). These vary in elaborateness, usually being more lavish for a simha—joyous occasion—e.g., anniversary, wedding, Bar/Bat Mitzvah, etc. However, before rushing off to gorge on the goodies, remove your tallit (and fold it if necessary), and, if it belongs to the shul, return it to where you got it. Do likewise with the prayer books and Bibles, unless they are meant to be left at the seats. It is customary to shake hands with the people around you and to say: "Gut Shabbes" or "Shabbat Shalom," i.e., a good/peaceful Shabbat. Similar greetings for holidays are "Gut Yontev—Good Holiday" and "Hag Sameah—Happy Festival."

Minhah and Maariv

Whether on weekdays or holidays, these services usually take place fairly close together (around sundown). These are much shorter services than the one already described but follow patterns similar to those of the morning service.

MINHAH

Ashrei (psalm) preparation

Amidah (repetition with Kedushah) central portion of prayer

Tahanun petitionary (traditional shuls)

Kaddish Shalem end of service

Alenu conclusion

Mourners' Kaddish

Maariv has a slightly different character because at one time it had no Amidah and wasn't obligatory; therefore it has no repetition or Kedushah. For the same reason there is a Hatzi Kaddish between the Shema section and the Amidah (unlike Shaharit, when no interruption is permitted).

Ve-hu Rahum verse of introduction

Borkhu call to prayer

Shema and its verses central portion

some verses and Hatzi Kaddish separate the two parts

Amidah central portion

Kaddish Shalem end of service

Alenu, Mourners' Kaddish, psalm for the day, etc. conclusion

MOURNERS' KADDISH

On Shabbat and on holidays there are slight changes. On Friday night additional psalms and hymns are added to greet the Shabbat. These are called Kabbalat Shabbat and are recited before the Maariv Service.

It is impossible to describe all the different variations in the services for special occasions, holidays, and the combination of holidays and Shabbat. But we've given the basic pattern, and this should enable you to get by on most occasions. If you are interested in the order of services on holidays, see:

1. the Festivals in *Catalog 1*;
2. a shul luach—a ritual synagogue calendar. For this you'll have to know Hebrew.

Even the High Holiday service follows this pattern. It only seems to be quite different because the Amidah repetition is much longer and contains much additional liturgical poetry, e.g., Unetaneh Tokef, the martyrology, as well as the blowing of the shofar. Essentially, however, the structure of the liturgy is similar. To negotiate the differences confidently, it is always advisable to spend some time looking through the mahzor to get some idea of the order of the service.

Some points about the Reform service

While Reform Judaism follows the basic pattern of the service we have described, it also makes some major changes in that service. It should be noted that a typical Reform service is difficult to describe, since such services vary greatly from synagogue to synagogue. The Reform movement has recently published a new prayer book containing significant changes from the standard *Union Prayerbook*. The move toward tradition and more Hebrew in Reform prayer is very marked. Also, both the old and the new prayer books have alternate services (up to half a dozen for Friday night in the new prayer book): Reform congregations can either do all six in rotation or else focus on one as their basic choice. These services run the gamut from marked similarity to the traditional service to vast differences from it.

The major changes in services by the Reform movement include:
1. extensive use of English
2. abbreviation of the service
3. emphasized roles of the rabbi and cantor

This last needs some explaining. It means that the rabbi's sermon plays an important role in the service, e.g., twenty to twenty-five minutes out of an hour-long service are devoted to it. It also means that nearly all the roles in the service are filled by the rabbi and a cantor, so it is unlikely that you will be asked to do anything in a Reform service. There are no aliyot, hagbah, ark-openers, etc. The basic service follows the pattern, preparation—Shema—Amidah—conclusion, but in a much abbreviated version. The first two sections of a traditional service, i.e., Birkhot ha-Shahar and Pesukei de-Zimra, are quite abbreviated and often are just a paragraph or two of introductory thoughts. However, even the Shema and Amidah are much shortened. The Torah service in many synagogues does

not have a procession with the Torah after it has been taken from the ark. Unless there is a Bar/Bat Mitzvah, the reading is done by the cantor, who reads from the Torah scroll with trope (the traditional melody) or from a Bible (only done in some places). The portion is translated into English, either verse by verse or at the end. The service ends with the Adoration (similar to Alenu) and the Mourners' Kaddish. Prayer books usually indicate when one should stand and sit at services, but there are certain places to watch out for:

1. Most Reform congregations stand for the Shema Yisrael. The Shema is viewed as the central creed of Jews, and to emphasize its importance these congregations recite it while standing.

2. In some congregations everyone (not just the mourners) stands while the Mourners' Kaddish is said.

Some other points:

3. The Friday night service usually begins with candlelighting by a woman.

4. The evening services on Shabbat and holidays are often more important than the morning services (some congregations don't have morning services). Therefore, the Torah is read in some shuls on Friday night. Check with the local congregation about their service schedule. (Similarly, many Reform congregations do not have services during the week.)

5. Responsive readings play an important part in the service.

6. Reform observes only one day of yom tov for all Jewish holidays (see Festivals in *Catalog 1*).

7. No bowing is done at Borkhu, Amidah, Alenu, etc.

8. In many Reform congregations one is not required to wear a kippah or tallit; in some, wearing them is frowned upon.

9. Bar/Bat Mitzvah was long opposed by Reform. Instead, Reform instituted a collective ceremony done at the age of sixteen called Confirmation (see Confirmation). Despite this opposition, most Reform congregations do have Bar/Bat Mitzvahs.

A word about Reconstructionism

The Reconstructionist prayer book, used in only a few synagogues, is similar to the Conservative prayer books. Look at the introduction to learn where changes have been made for ideological reasons. Sometimes these changes involve only a word or two or the dropping of one line; it often appears at a quick glance that nothing was changed. The most apparent change is the Musaf Service, which has been significantly altered for ideological reasons. In most ways, however, Reconstructionist custom is similar to Conservative custom.

God says: "Who has ever come into a synagogue and has not found My glory there?" "And not only that," said R. Abu, "but if you are in a synagogue, God stands by you" (*Deuteronomy Rabbah*, Ki Tavvo 7:2).

Bibliography

1. The best book on prayer and the service is Abraham Millgram's *Jewish Worship* (Philadelphia: Jewish Publication Society, 1971). It's lucid, complete, and very readable.

2. Take a look at the *Encyclopaedia Judaica* (Jerusalem: Keter, 1972) articles on the Synagogue and Liturgy and Prayer. They're all good.

3. Finally, look at the Bibliography under "Prayer" in *Catalog 1* (in the chapter on Creating a Jewish Library).

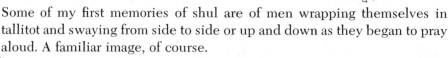

Movement of prayer

by Shulamit Saltzman

Some of my first memories of shul are of men wrapping themselves in tallitot and swaying from side to side or up and down as they began to pray aloud. A familiar image, of course.

In our prayers we bow, we lift our heels, we cover our eyes, we sway with the lulav, we encircle the synagogue with the Torah, and on Simhat Torah we dance.

But haven't we been dancing all along? The intricate choreography of a Jewish prayer service is so familiar to us all that we take it for granted. Only when a child or a visitor asks, "Why do you take three steps back there, why do you bow here?" do we notice that we have been dancing a prayer choreography for years without thinking about it.

What if, for once, we look at that choreography, analyze it, perform it intentionally, and expand its scope—and therefore its expressive powers!

We might begin a prayer service with individual enfoldment in the tallit. Lovingly we shape our bodies to its folds, we become one with it. It is both a garment and an extension of ourselves. It bounds us singly and apart from the others in the service, yet the simple fact of the shared experience creates a unity among us.

The praying begins imperceptibly, with each of us. There is a time of preparation. Perhaps we sway with eyes closed or we might sit very still, creating a meditative mood; some may chant a niggun—a simple tune with all the complexity of a thousand creations hidden within it. Each chooses his/her own way. We improvise to express our immediate individual responses.

Gradually the praying happens; the words are formed; the ritual proceeds as it has for countless years before. This time, though, we are aware of the past, of the others who have spoken the same words, danced the same dance. This time, we move consciously—our bodies responding rhythmically to the mood of the psalms, our gestures punctuating, deliberately, the lines of verse. Our bodies and our mouths speak simultaneously.

Borkhu becomes an event of major significance. A simple bow, choreographed and then offered to each worshiper/dancer for his/her own interpretive expression.

In the Shema we may not merely cover our eyes, but perhaps we will create wholeness in the room—shutting off the outside collectively rather than individually. And perhaps our Shema dance will go on for several moments before we will once again be willing to welcome the outside and include it in our prayers.

Then the Amidah will burst out, everyone's individual personal dance/prayer to God. "God, open my lips that my mouth may speak Thy praises," we say. And today we add, "God, open my soul, that my body may speak Thy glory."

Feel the circle of the Torah. It draws limits for us in our lives and in our prayers. As it passes round, encompassing us, we kiss it. As it draws us with it in its spiral, we cling to it, and to show it how we love it, we dance with it and before it. It need not be Simhat Torah. Any day full of prayer will do.

Such a service can be choreographed and directed, but its truth lies in the creative effort of each person involved in prayer. The remnants of Jewish choreography are so clear in our ritual. They await our rediscovery, they await our need to dance them once again.

A *chart lover's dream*

The Society of Chart Lovers has put together two charts—one to illustrate the types of movement commonly found during the service, and one to illustrate the places where one normally stands during the service.

TYPES OF MOVEMENT

WHEN	WHAT	HOW	WHY
In general	shuckling	sway your body gently or quickly (back and forth)	to involve our whole bodies in prayer: "All my limbs will speak to You"
During the silent Amidah and Kaddish	placing both feet together		to aid in concentration—kavannah; to be like the angels (spiritual), who stand only on one foot
Borkhu	bowing	bow from the waist as the hazzan says "Borkhu" and as you respond "Barukh..."	to bow before the King
Shema	closing or covering your eyes with your hand		to aid in kavannah—intention—so nothing will distract us
Shema	kissing tzitzit during the third paragraph of the Shema	gather four tzitzit and bring them together to the lips to be kissed at each mention of tzitzit in the third paragraph and on the first word ("Emet...") of the following paragraph. Some also kiss the tefillin—touch each box and bring fingers to lips— each time it is mentioned in Shema	to remind us of the tzitzit; for more about symbolism and direction, see *Catalog 1*, pp. 54-55
AMIDAH the verse before Amidah, "Adonai sifatai..."	approaching God	there are several customs: (a) walk three steps forward; or (b) walk back three steps and then forward three steps; start on your right foot	to approach God (alone); begin with your right foot—"the normal one"— to show your eagerness
"Barukh attah Adonai, Elo-heinu ve-Elohei Avoteinu..."	bowing	bend your knees at "Barukh," bend over from your waist at "attah," straighten at "Adonai"	symbolically to approach the King— God—as one enters His presence
"Barukh attah Adonai, Magen Avraham"	bowing	same as above	same as above
KEDUSHAH "Kadosh, Kadosh, Kadosh..."	rising on tiptoes	rise on your tiptoes three times (at each "Kadosh")	"to fly on your feet" heavenward
Birkhot Hodaah: "Modim anahnu lakh"	bowing	same as for the first berakhah of the Amidah	same as for other bowing
"Barukh attah Adonai hatov shimkha..."	bowing	same as above	same as above

WHEN	WHAT	HOW	WHY
"Oseh shalom bimromav . . ."	taking leave of God	take three steps backward, beginning with the left foot. At "Shalom bimromav" incline your head and shoulders to the right; at "Hu yaaseh shalom" incline your head and shoulders to the left; at "Alenu ve-al kol Yisrael" incline your head and shoulders forward; at "Ve-imru, Amen" stand upright	to take leave of God; this is the reverse of the approach to God: you step away facing the ark, using your left foot to show reluctance; you then bow in all directions (actually only three) to acknowledge God's presence everywhere and as a final leavetaking.
Tahanun	petitioning God	beginning with the verse "Rahum ve-hanun hatasi lifanekha," prostrate yourself by resting your head on your arm (your non-tefillin arm in the morning, your "weak" arm at Minhah)	to petition—similar to the falling posture done in the Temple; we do it in a sitting position rather than a full prostration; for weekdays only
TORAH SERVICE "Gadlu l'Adonai iti . . ."	bowing	bow from the waist as the hazzan says this verse	
Torah procession	kissing the Torah	see section in this chapter	to show respect and love for the Torah
KADDISH "Oseh shalom bimromav"	taking leave of God	see direction for the same verse at the end of the Amidah	to praise God and acknowledge His presence throughout the whole world
ALENU "Ve-anahnu khorim"	acknowledging God's Kingship over the world	bend knees at "Ve-anahnu khorim," bow at "U-mishtahavim," stand straight at "U-modim"	to bow before the King of the world as we say: "We bend the knee and bow . . ."

STAND UP CHART

WHEN	WHO
SHAHARIT Barukh She-amar . . .	in some shuls you stand
Mizmor le-Todah . . . (weekdays only)	in some shuls you stand
Hodu le-Adonai Ki Tov . . . (Shabbat and festivals)	in some shuls you stand
Barukh Adonai le-Olam Amen ve-Amen Va-Yevarekh David . . . be-mayim azim Ve-Yosha Adonai Bayom . . . Az Yashir Moshe u-vne Yisrael . . . . . . ehad u-shmo ehad.	in some shuls, you stand through the end of "ehad u-shmo ehad."
Yishtabah Shimkha La-ad . . .	in some shuls you stand
Kaddish	in very traditional shuls many people stand
Borkhu . . . le-olam va-ed	you stand
Shema Yisrael . . .	in Reform shuls you stand
Silent Amidah	you stand
Repetition of Amidah up to Kedushah	in some shuls you stand
Kedushah	you stand
Rest of repetition	in very traditional shuls many people stand
Modim de-Rabbanan (in repetition)	in a few shuls you stand
Hallel (festivals only)	you stand

WHEN	WHO
Torah Service: Va-yehi binsoa . . . Berikh Shemai . . . Shema . . . Gadlu . . . Lekha Adonai ha-gedulah . . .	you stand when the ark is opened and remain standing while ark is opened *and* while Torah is carried around shul, until it is laid flat on the reader's table
During time Torah (not haftarah) is read (or when people say the berakhot for their aliyot)	in very traditional shuls some people stand
When someone gets an aliyah from your family	in Sephardic shuls you stand
When either the portions of the Song of the Sea or the Ten Commandments are read; or when one of the Five Books of Moses are completed ("Hazak, hazak ve-nithazaik" is said after the last verse)	in some shuls you stand
During hagbah	you stand
During gelilah	in some shuls you stand until the Torah is put in its holder or held by someone in his/her lap
Prayer for the new moon	in some shuls you stand
Torah Returning Service: Yehallelu et shem Adonai . . . Mizmor le-David (Shabbat) . . . Le-David Mizmor (weekdays) . . . U-venuhoh yomar . . .	you stand while Torah is carried back to the ark, it is placed inside, and the doors are closed
Musaf (festivals treated like Shaharit Amidah—both silent and repetition—as outlined above)	you stand (see above)
Alenu . . . mitahat ain od Al kein nekaveh lekha . . . ushmo ehad	you stand in Orthodox and some Conservative shuls you stand
Mourners' Kaddish	mourners stand; in some very traditional shuls and in some Reform shuls everyone stands
Kaddish de-Rabbanan	mourners stand; in some very traditional shuls many people stand
Anim Zemirot	you stand, ark is open (only some shuls say Anim Zemirot)
MINHAH Amidah (silent and repetition) Alenu (Al kein nekaveh) Mourners' Kaddish	treated the same as for Shaharit
MAARIV Borkhu Amidah (silent, no repetition) Alenu (Al kein nekaveh) Mourners' Kaddish	treated the same as for Shaharit
KABBALAT SHABBAT–Friday night Borkhu Amidah (silent) Alenu (Al kein nekaveh) Mourners' Kaddish	same as regular Maariv
Special Elements: Mizmor le-David havu le-Adonai	in some shuls you stand
L'Kha Dodi	in some shuls you stand for all the stanzas, in others, you stand only for the last stanza: "Boee ve-Shalom Ateret . . ."
Veyekhulu . . . Barukh attah . . . Magen Avot . . . Eloheinu ve-Elohai . . . mekadesh ha-Shabbat	in some shuls you stand until the end of "Eloheinu ve-Elohai . . . mekadesh Shabbat"; in others you sit

Prayer, Prayer Books, and the Pray-er

Introduction

And if one knows of no deeper meanings than that we pray to God (may He be blessed) because God commanded us to pray to Him, our prayer breaks through and ascends to heaven, for the words of Torah and prayer possess such sublime holiness that, emerging from the prayer's heart in sincerity, they are capable of reuniting spiritual entities in the upper worlds (*Or Yesharim* in the name of Magen Avraham in the name of the Baal Shem Tov—S. Y. Agnon, *Days of Awe*).

Jews have no patent on prayer, which is as old and as universal as humanity itself. Prayer embraces all beings, forming links and bonds that we might never suspect existed. Still, the religious-psychological explanations for why people need to pray are as varied as the people themselves:

1. Compulsion—prayer as an uncontrollable human activity, a sort of law of nature: "I pray because I cannot *not* pray."

2. Loneliness—"I pray not to *get* something but to *be* with someone."

3. Hope—"I am in trouble—in dire need—and I hope to be saved by seeking the intervention of the Power above."

4. Guilt—"I feel I did something wrong and I must ask forgiveness."

5. Fear—the popular anthropological explanation of the caveman, etc.

6. Amazement—the sense of cosmos and history, of wonder—"How magnificent are Your works, O Lord!"

7. Thankfulness—"It is good to give thanks unto the Lord."

8. Dependence—the philosophy that the essence of religion is a person's search for a dependence on something (Schleiermacher).

9. Creatureliness—the philosophy that the created must relate to its Creator (Rudolf Otto).

10. Nearness of God—"As for me, nearness to God is good" (Psalms 73:28); this is a peculiarly Jewish concept.

11. Social pressures—when you go to shul or temple (depending on the neighborhood).

12. Imitation of other people.

The list goes on and on. Interestingly, there are perhaps just as many factors driving people *away* from prayer. Foremost among these are doubt, anger, despair, arrogance, and humility.

1. How do I know there is a God? What tells me He is capable of hearing me?

2. Why of all His myriads of creatures should He make Himself free to listen to me? After all, who am I, what am I in such a tremendous universe?

3. On the other hand, I am managing quite well without Him. I am master of my own fate. I pursue positive scientism and do not need crutches. As Bertrand Russell put it, aren't there more religious people in sailboats than there are on steamships?

4. Perhaps, most troubling of all, I am angry with God. He is not, as far as I am concerned, all that benevolent, compassionate, or righteous. I am haunted by the Holocaust and I ask whether I must be more pious than Rabbi Levi Yitzhak, the great Hasidic master who excelled both in love of God and love of Israel. I ask how *he* would have reacted after the Holocaust?

Reb Levi Yitzhak in tallit and tefillin
Stands motionless at his stall
His siddur lies open before him
But his lips utter nothing at all.

In his vision he sees scenes from the ghetto
The death, the agony of his mocked fold.
He stands there stubbornly silent
He is angry with his God of old.

Itzik Manger, translated from Yiddish by Pnina Peli

And yet it is true, despite all this, that each time I am able to truly say my prayer—to caress the words, absorb them, and by uttering them transform them into *my* prayer, *my* creation, I proclaim that I am aware, that I do not let God's world, God's creation, pass by unnoticed. That I react. That I am alive! And this for me is the true prayer—the real essence of tefillah.

Let's get acquainted with the word tefillah. It's a word that connotes prayer but means something quite different from the English word. It is a totally unique view of prayer and has introduced to the world an entirely new set of assumptions and requirements about the act of prayer. Tefillah, as Judaism sees it, is an act that involves three partners: there is *God*, to whom tefillah is directed; there is the prayer *person*, who, besides being obligated to pray, seeks, yearns for that personal dialogue with God; and there is *the prayer* itself—verbal, fixed, yet leaving space for additions, deletions, one-to-One discourse.

The relationship between the pray-er and the One who listens is epitomized for me in Reb Nahman of Bratslav's parable of the shepherd and the sheep. The shepherd sits with his flute while the sheep spread all around to graze and seek water. As long as the sheep hear the voice of the shepherd's flute they are safe. And as long as the shepherd can hear the baaing of the sheep, he can rush to their help if they get into any trouble. When the sheep, however, stray so far away that they can no longer hear the flute and the shepherd cannot hear their baaing—then are they truly lost.

As long as we hear the Voice that surrounds us, protects us, we can be assured that our voice is heard as well. And it is this hearing the Voice that justifies prayer. In fact, the very nature of Jewish prayer as it emerges from the siddur is just that—a response.

The siddur (the pray-er's book)

By siddur—literally "order" or "arrangement"—we mean the traditional Jewish prayer book. As a book it is peculiar in more ways than one. For one thing, it has no author, no editor; no date or locale can be affixed to it—it is a book that grew in many places over many generations, and is still growing. And it is this fact that is the real secret of the siddur. Because it is attributable to no one it belongs to *everyone*. Because no single person, group of people, community, or place controlled our siddur, it has the ability to reach out and touch each one of us, deeply responding to our own needs and our own emotional-psychological possibilities. There is a cosmic reality to it because it has the ability to transcend any one time, any one place,

any one person's thoughts or needs. A rare and profoundly beautiful gift to each of us.

But the siddur never was a wild or haphazard kind of collection. From all the historical research in the various components that make up the siddur, and from study of the theological, psychological, and anthropological aspects of the siddur, we *must* come away convinced that what seems like a loose compilation of texts is actually one of the most deeply rooted expressions of Jewish beliefs and experiences. It reflects, in a way, a well-balanced spiritual and in a real sense historical autobiography of the Jewish people throughout the ages. And yet this "unauthored" and "unedited" book has been through the strictest (though not always conscious) critical editing and process of selectivity by scores of generations of Jews. As Maimonides notes: "The number of prayers has not been prescribed by the Torah, nor has the wording of this prayer been fixed by the Torah, nor has any time been determined for it by the Torah" (Mishneh Torah, Hilkhot Tefillah 1:1).

Later the prayers were codified, and yet adding and dropping certain prayers and even changing others were not only to a certain extent legitimate—i.e., within the bounds of the halakhah—but such innovations and changes can only be seen as a part of the very nature of Jewish prayer. It was natural that the changing situation of the Jewish people, which was reflected in the development of the halakhah, was likewise reflected in the development of the siddur. But this was never undertaken lightly or frivolously, and certainly such changes were instituted to highlight the siddur rather than to obscure it. Because of this, the attempts that were begun some two hundred years ago with much revolutionary zest and enthusiasm to create a "new, modern, up-to-date, and acceptable" Jewish prayer book, seem now, in historical perspective, to be a vehicle for *getting away from* rather than *getting into* the very special character of Jewish prayer.

Keva and kavannah

The problem of three-times-a-day prayer arises when we try to be truly immersed in our prayer as often as we daven—pray. At what point, then, does our tefillah cease being prayer and become a meaningless recital of words? If "prayer is either poetry or blasphemy" (George Santayana), how does one put oneself into the mood for poetry three times a day? And what if one is so far removed that one does not hear even the echo of the music of the flute?

The real clash is between keva—the fixed verbal order of prayer—and kavannah—the inner participation of the total personality of the pray-er—which are both simultaneously equal requirements in tefillah. Is it inevitable that one must be lost for the other to be gained?

The talmudic rabbis, who laid the foundations for the siddur, were very much aware of this problem, as were, consciously or unconsciously, all those throughout the subsequent generations who added layer upon layer to the siddur. These people formulated the structure of the siddur to help us react to the totality of life as well as to its most minute details. Perhaps, then, the keva, the fixed order of prayer, is there to remind us of what we *should* be looking for, and the kavannah, the personal inspiration, is our own wholesome inner identification with all that emerges from the text.

Some suggestions will follow about how to help create the balance between keva and kavannah. But we must keep in mind that the rabbis felt that "a person should always see himself as if the Shekhinah is confronting him" (Sanhedrin 22a). The key words in this statement are "as if." We cannot come to prayer only after we have come to terms with every problem—theological, substantive, practical. We must start with the assumption of "as if"; only as we go on from there are we assured of meeting the Shekhinah.

Hasidic prayer

Hasidism is one movement that has had to take seriously the tension between keva and kavannah, since it sees prayer as absolutely central to the spiritual life of a Jew. In Hasidic terms, prayer is the vehicle that enables the beloved to come closer to the Loved One. As such, the pray-er must strive at all times to make the prayer pure, intentioned, and joyous. Each person, whether ignorant or learned, has the power to infuse such kavannah—intentions—into prayer, so that one's own consciousness becomes submerged in the Other Consciousness to which one strains.

A Hasid asked Rav Pinhas of Koretz why he prayed without using motions of his body and without making a single sound, when other tzaddikim often prayed with many gestures of enthusiasm and in a loud tone of voice.

The Koretzer answered: "When a tzaddik prays, he cleaves in truth to God and loses all sense of corporeality, as if his very soul had departed from his body. The Talmud tells us that in some people the soul leaves the body only after great agonies and convulsions, whereas in others it departs as quietly as one draws a hair out of milk or offers a kiss."

In addition to his concern, there is an emphasis on joy as a spiritual path. The feeling is that it is a privilege to perform God's will, and this knowledge creates joy. As such, spontaneous song and dance became a central part of Hasidic prayer—not as an art form but as a reaction against passivity and a straining toward arousing the entire body and soul toward prayer. As Abraham Millgram has written in his book *Jewish Worship*:

The Hasidim have dispensed with formality and decorum during their services. Loud chanting and shouting have been the rule. Frantic movements of the body and constant agitation are the normal accompaniments of prayer. Clapping of hands, gesticulating, and crying out periodically are not simply acceptable expressions of one's rapture; they are necessary adjuncts of true prayer. Each Hasid concentrates on his own prayer and expresses his ardor in his own way. Each one sings with ecstasy his own chant. As he chants or shouts, he sways and see-saws, lurches and leaps, shakes his body and claps his hands. . . . To the outsider, it all adds up to pandemonium. Not so to the Hasid. He is so immersed in his own prayers that he is completely unaware of the commotion about him. He has disciplined himself to concentrate on his own prayers so completely that he is oblivious to any chant or noise except his own. And he is convinced that God hears him individually, even as He hears everyone else individually, provided he prays with his whole heart.

R. Eliezer said: "If a person makes prayer a fixed task (keva) his prayer is *not* a supplication." The Gemara asks: "What is meant by keva?"

R. Jacob ben Idi said in the name of R. Oshaya: "Anyone whose prayer seems to him a burden." The rabbis say: "Anyone who does not recite it in the language of supplication." Rabbah and Rav Joseph both said: "Anyone who is not able to add something new to it" (Berakhot 29b).

R. Aha said: "A new prayer should be said every day" (Jerusalem Talmud, Berakhot 4:3).

Iyyun tefillah: a rediscovery of the radical

Iyyun tefillah means taking the siddur as a whole or taking each part of it and trying to look beyond the surface of the words. By the use of iyyun tefillah we cease to look upon prayer as a duty to be discharged with maximum speed and minimum attention, or, conversely, to be stretched out like an opera concert or a singalong session. Davening not only with

kavannah—the concentrated intention of every word—but also with kavannot—finding more than is offered by the surface—was the way those who were yodei tefillah—intimately acquainted with prayer—did their davening. We can do the same.

The Mishnah (Berakhot 5:1) tells us about the Hasidim Rishonim, the Jewish pietists of the early centuries (credited with setting up the body of the siddur) who would dwell on every prayer a full hour before and after its recitation. The Mishnah does not tell us how long the prayer itself took or what exactly the pietists did in this time—but simply that it took two full hours to "digest" tefillah.

A radical thought. It is clear that "dwelling on prayer," not just "doing it to get it over," is the ideal of Jewish prayer. For those who are still unconvinced, it is important to note that ONLY with regard to prayer is such a radical principle formulated in the halakhah (Tur Orah Hayim 1:1), i.e., that it is *how* one prays that counts . . . *and not how much*! Despite the obligation to pray the full fixed prayer, this classic book of Jewish law declares: "Tov meat bekavvannah meharbe shelo bekavannah—Better a little done with the proper intention than a lot without the intention."

So let's treat the Tur seriously. Find a prayer each day and really try to discover it—to make it your own. It may take you an hour to digest what it is you and it are saying to each other, to God. So be it. The Tur opens a door for us and we must take advantage of it. Choose a prayer and *pray* it. Renew it for yourself. Devour the words until they devour you—until you can truly say that it has become *your* prayer. That *you* have written it anew.

Personal prayers: some models

The dispute among the tannaim (mainly between Rabban Gamaliel and Rabbi Eliezer the Great toward the end of the first century) over whether one should adhere to fixed prayer or only spontaneous prayer, was carried over for several generations (see *Pirkei Avot* 2:18; Mishnah, Berakhot 29a). It resulted in the acceptance of the fixed order of prayer, with the added stipulation that this fixed order must be subject to constant renewal; and so this "constant renewal" itself became part of the Jewish tradition of prayer. This explains the existence of piyyutim (religious poems often composed by medieval cantors—see "Hazzanut" for an explanation) and of the niggunim of modern Hasidim, who would renew an old tefillah with a new niggun every so often to reawaken awe for the words.

It also explains Tahanun, the section that was added as a response to the need for personal prayers. In fact, however, personal additions were always privately instituted: indeed, some of these have come down to us:

1. Prayer of Rabbi Elazar (as found in Berakhot 16b)

May it be Thy will,
O Lord, our God,
to establish in our lot
love, fraternity, peace, and friendship,
to extend our domain with disciples,
to make happy our latter days with an
    expected end,
to give us a share in paradise,
to support us with a good companion,
and good inclination, in Thy world.
Let us find, on rising in the morning,
    the desire of our heart,
so that we may fear Thy Name,
and may the pleasure of our soul come
    favorably before Thee.

יְהִי רָצוֹן מִלְּפָנֶיךָ

יהוה אֱלֹהֵינוּ

שֶׁתַּשְׁכֵּן בְּפוּרֵנוּ

אַהֲבָה וְאַחֲוָה וְשָׁלוֹם וְרֵעוּת

וְתַרְבֶּה גְבוּלֵנוּ בְּתַלְמִידִים

וְתַצְלִיחַ סוֹפֵנוּ אַחֲרִית וְתִקְוָה

וְתָשִׂים חֶלְקֵנוּ בְּגַן עֵדֶן

וְתַקְּנֵנוּ בְּחָבֵר טוֹב

וְיֵצֶר טוֹב בְּעוֹלָמָךְ

וְנַשְׁכִּים וְנִמְצָא יְחוּל לְבָבֵנוּ

לְיִרְאָה אֶת־שְׁמָךְ

וְתָבֹא לְפָנֶיךָ קוֹרַת נַפְשֵׁנוּ לְטוֹבָה.

2. Prayer of Rabbi Elazar (Berakhot 4:2)

May it be Thy will,
O Lord, our God and God of our fathers,
that hatred toward us shall not arise in
    anybody's heart
and that hatred toward anybody shall not
    arise in our heart
and that jealousy toward us shall not arise
    in anybody's heart
and that jealousy toward anybody shall not
    arise in our heart.
May Thy Torah be our trade, all our living
    days,
and may our speech be entreaty before Thee.

יְהִי רָצוֹן מִלְּפָנֶיךָ

יהוה אֱלֹהֵינוּ וֵאלֹהֵי אֲבוֹתֵינוּ

שֶׁלֹּא תַעֲלֶה שִׂנְאָתֵנוּ עַל־לֵב אָדָם

וְלֹא שִׂנְאַת אָדָם תַּעֲלֶה עַל־לִבֵּנוּ

וְלֹא תַעֲלֶה קִנְאָתֵנוּ עַל־לֵב אָדָם

וְלֹא קִנְאַת אָדָם תַּעֲלֶה עַל־לִבֵּנוּ

וּתְהֵא תוֹרָתְךָ מְלַאכְתֵּנוּ כָּל־יְמֵי חַיֵּינוּ

וְיִהְיוּ דְבָרֵינוּ תַּחֲנוּנִים לְפָנֶיךָ.

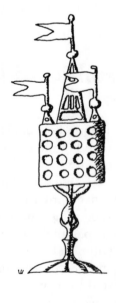

3. Prayer of Rabbi Alexandri (Berakhot 17a)

Master of the worlds,
it is revealed and known before Thee
that it is our will to do Thy will.
But what prevents this?
The leaven in the dough and the oppression
    by the kingdoms.
May it be Thy will,
O Lord, our God,
to subdue these, fore and aft,
that we may again abide by the laws of
    Thy will, with all our heart.

רִבּוֹן הָעוֹלָמִים

גָּלוּי וְיָדוּעַ לְפָנֶיךָ

שֶׁרְצוֹנֵנוּ לַעֲשׂוֹת רְצוֹנָךְ

וּמִי מְעַכֵּב?

שְׂאֹר שֶׁבָּעִסָּה וְשִׁעְבּוּד מַלְכֻיּוֹת

יְהִי רָצוֹן מִלְּפָנֶיךָ

יהוה אֱלֹהֵינוּ

שֶׁתַּכְנִיעֵם מִלְּפָנֵינוּ וּמֵאַחֲרֵינוּ

וְנָשׁוּב לַעֲשׂוֹת חֻקֵּי רְצוֹנָךְ בְּלֵבָב שָׁלֵם.

4. Prayer of Rabbi Yehudah ha-Nasi (the Prince) (Berakhot 16b)

יְהִי רָצוֹן מִלְּפָנֶיךָ
יהוה אֱלֹהֵינוּ
וֵאלֹהֵי אֲבוֹתֵינוּ
שֶׁתַּצִּילֵנוּ מֵעַזֵּי פָנִים
וּמֵעַזּוּת פָּנִים
מֵאָדָם רַע וּמִפֶּגַע רַע
מִיֵּצֶר הָרָע מֵחָבֵר רַע מִשָּׁכֵן רַע
וּמִשָּׂטָן הַמַּשְׁחִית
וּמִדִּין קָשֶׁה וּמִבַּעַל־דִּין קָשֶׁה
בֵּין שֶׁהוּא בֶּן־בְּרִית
וּבֵין שֶׁאֵינוֹ בֶּן־בְּרִית.

May it be Thy will,
O Lord, our God
and God of our fathers,
to deliver us from arrogant folk
and from arrogance,
from an evil person and from an evil encounter,
from the evil inclination, from an evil
    companion, from an evil neighbor
and from Satan the Destructive;
from a hard judgment and from a hard adversary,
whether he be a son of the covenant
or whether he be not a son of the covenant.

5. Prayer of Rabbi Saphra (Berakhot 16b and 17a)

יְהִי רָצוֹן מִלְּפָנֶיךָ
יהוה אֱלֹהֵינוּ
שֶׁתָּשִׂים שָׁלוֹם בְּפָמַלְיָא שֶׁל־מַעֲלָה
וּבְפָמַלְיָא שֶׁל־מַטָּה
וּבֵין הַתַּלְמִידִים הָעוֹסְקִים בְּתוֹרָתֶךָ
בֵּין עוֹסְקִין לִשְׁמָהּ
בֵּין עוֹסְקִין שֶׁלֹּא לִשְׁמָהּ
וְכָל־הָעוֹסְקִין שֶׁלֹּא לִשְׁמָהּ
יְהִי רָצוֹן שֶׁיִּהוּ עוֹסְקִין לִשְׁמָהּ.

May it be Thy will,
O Lord, our God,
to implement peace in the celestial court
as well in the earthly court,
and among the disciples who study Thy Torah,
whether they study it for its own sake
or whether they study it not for its own sake;
and all those who study it not for its own sake
may they study it for its own sake.

Renewal

At different times, different tactics were used in the fierce struggle for kavannah. Washing the hands, studying, reciting selected psalms or, for that matter, modern poetry as "preparation" for prayer all became part of the attempt at renewal. In fact, the preparation for prayer became, for some renowned pray-ers in the Jewish tradition, as important as the prayer itself. Prayers arose petitioning for the ability to pray, and a story is told of how the first of such prayers was written:

One day Rebbe Elimelech announced to his Hasidim that he was expecting two very important guests and said he was even then anxiously awaiting their arrival. Sure enough, in a short time two strangers appeared and Rebbe Elimelech greeted them warmly and took them to his study. To the amazement of the Hasidim, they were together in the study for many hours, and when they emerged the strangers thanked R. Elimelech and departed.

His Hasidim were consumed with curiosity about the two guests—non-Hasidim—whom the rebbe had greeted so warmly; and so they posed their questions to him.

He answered them saying that these men had been sent to him by the anshei Knesset ha-Gedolah—men of the Great Assembly (to whom the basic structure of the siddur is attributed). They had discovered that Rebbe Elimelech, finding the old prayers outdated and irrelevant, had made plans to write a new siddur. The representatives had begged to meet with him to argue against such an undertaking. They had convinced him that, despite all the criticisms leveled against it, the siddur was still valid and important to Jews everywhere. "But," he added, "we have come to an agreement that

Make every effort to pray from the heart. Even if you do not succeed, the effort is precious in the eyes of the Lord (Reb Nahman of Bratslav).

what is needed is a tefillah lifnei ha-tefillah—a prayer *before* praying." And so that is what R. Elimelech wrote.

Tefillah lifnei ha-tefillah, the desire to put oneself into the mood of prayer, is the reason that the siddur has grown to its present size. Most of it consists of various elements added to the original body of tefillah (the Shema and the Shemoneh Esrei) mentioned earlier. Such additions include psalms, portions of the Torah and Prophets, quotes from the Talmud, and many creative personal prayers and poems. Those were added both *before* and *after* prayer in order to make the precious moment of prayer itself sink into the life of the pray-er.

Here are a few examples:

1. The following prayer was written by our teacher Rabbi Abraham Joshua Heschel (may his memory be for a blessing):

Our yearning to You, answer, God!
Break Your silence, Master of all words!
Tortured millennia beseech you,
Reveal Yourself!
We want no maze of riddles!

Show us goodness in place of wisdom,
Joy instead of wonder.
Why do You tease us with our trust?
Are You mocking our pride in You?
True, You keep Yourself concealed
To arouse our desire for You.
Oh, see! Our suffering is disguised yearning for You,
Our sins—a tonic for our thirst for You.
Your silence is hell on earth—
I sense Your ear close to my pleasing lips and know:
Your sternness is more compassionate than my pity.
Yet often, out of revulsion,
Gall spurts out of a thousand mouths
And cries: God Himself is our prosecutor!
And at such times I can tell no one my mute word,
For more powerful than my faith
Is the doubt of a world
I would forgo all achievements and Your gifts to me
For but one enlightening word from You!
                    Translated from Yiddish by Pnina Peli

2. The following prayer is written by Leah Goldberg, a "nonreligious" Israeli:

Teach me, my God, a blessing, a prayer
On the mystery of a withered leaf,
On ripened fruit so fair,
On the freedom to see, to sense,
To breathe, to know, to hope, to despair.

Teach my lips a blessing, a hymn of praise,
As each morning and night
You renew Your days,
Lest my day be as the one before,
Lest routine set my ways.
        Translated from Hebrew by Pnina Peli

לַמְּדֵנִי אֱלֹהַי בָּרֵךְ וְהִתְפַּלֵּל

עַל סוֹד עָלֶה קָמֵל עַל נֹגַהּ פְּרִי בָּשֵׁל

עַל הַחֵרוּת הַזֹּאת, לִרְאוֹת, לָחוּש,

לִנְשֹׁם, לָדַעַת, לְיַחֵל, לְהִכָּשֵׁל.

לַמֵּד אֶת שְׂפָתוֹתַי בְּרָכָה וְשִׁיר הַלֵּל

בְּהִתְחַדֵּשׁ זְמַנְּךָ עִם בֹּקֶר וְעִם לֵיל,

לְבַל יִהְיֶה יוֹמִי כִּתְמוֹל שִׁלְשׁוֹם,

לְבַל יִהְיֶה עָלַי יוֹמִי הָרְגֵּל.

3. And this beautifully moving poem by Hannah Senesh, a young kibbutznik who volunteered during World War II to parachute behind enemy lines in Hungary and was later executed by the Nazis:

Better prayer without synagogue than synagogue without prayer.

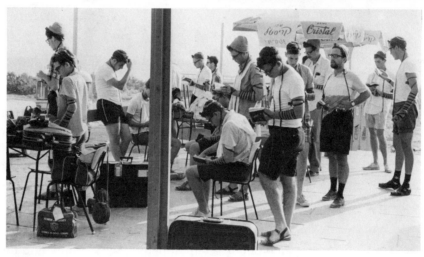

O God, my God,
May there ne'er cease to be
the sand and the sea,
the murmuring stream,
the heaven's bright gleam,
our prayer to Thee.

Translated from Hebrew by Pnina Peli

אֵלִי אֵלִי,
שֶׁלֹּא יִגָּמֵר לְעוֹלָם –
הַחוֹל וְהַיָּם,
רִשְׁרוּשׁ שֶׁל הַמַּיִם,
בְּרַק הַשָּׁמַיִם,
תְּפִלַּת הָאָדָם.

All this is the beginning, a preparation for the entry into God's chamber. I have, though, one last precious word to tell you—a secret I have learned. It is true what I had once been taught—and I have come to learn it for myself: we do not have to hold back from tefillah until we have settled all our theological struggles about the Being or definition of God. Jewish prayer does not even bother defining God, knows it as a very personal and individual confrontation. Our real secret is that Jewish prayer is hearing God's flute and being moved to answer it. And in that response is the beginning of our prayer.

There are also other ways besides tefillah lifnei ha-tefillah for achieving renewal. Music and singing can lead us onto the path. Silence, too, can be valuable in prayer—it gives us a chance to listen to the inner voice and also serves as a creative withdrawal to absorb the moment of prayer.

There are also the movements of the body and the entire choreography of prayer itself to help the pray-er get into prayer (see Movement of Prayer).

And there is the setting. One may, of course, offer prayers in any house or in any room. In fact, almost anywhere can become "the house of God." The Talmud tells us, though, that a room with windows open to the beauty of the world is preferable (Berakhot 17a). So, too, is prayer preferable at sunrise or in sunshine, when nature manifests God's glory and so moves the pray-er to understand the majesty, the wholeness of God's creation. Indeed, if we see the siddur as God's calling to us through creation, revelation, and history, and prayer as our response to Him, then praying surrounded by God's creation comes closest to the Jewish ideal: to "worship the Lord in the beauty of holiness" (1 Chronicles 16:29).

Every word of your prayer is like a rose which you pick from its bush. You continue until you have formed a bouquet of blessings, until you have pleated a wreath of glory for the Lord (Reb Nahman of Bratslav).

How to Survive Your Synagogue

Let all who are employed with the congregation act with them for heaven's sake (*Pirkei Avot* 2:2).

Some Jews don't belong in synagogues. I actually know a lovely man who fainted every time he went inside one. On the other hand, some Jews are quite pleased with things just as they are. They see the synagogue as a place of community. In it they experience friendship, support, and the good feeling that comes from worshiping in a style that feels right.

But there is a third group that finds it as difficult to live *with* the synagogue as to live *without* it. It is for them that this chapter was written.

There are two groups of these people. One is composed of people who are looking for a place to make Jewish religious discoveries. The other is a more amorphous group of people who simply find themselves dissatisfied with some or all of the following: the style of the services, the rabbi, the other congregants, the decorum, the lack of decorum, the liturgy. At many points these groups merge by their vague longings for something different. If you belong to either group, you probably want to glow a little when you leave the synagogue. You want to be lightly touched by something you don't quite understand but know is very powerful. You want some sense of the aliveness of Torah. You may be flirting with Jewish observance, though it doesn't quite make sense to you yet. Or it makes a little sense, but you would like it to make a lot more sense for all the trouble it causes you. You need the synagogue to help you along. How are you going to grow in a synagogue full of good people with slightly shriveled souls who seem to love responsive readings?

If you are in the first group, know that it can be hard to make serious Jewish religious discoveries in a synagogue today. That is because most of the regulars in the synagogue near where you live have settled into comfortable patterns of behavior. They are married people looking for areas of stability in a too-complicated world. They want the relationships between themselves to be relatively predictable. That is not an evil wish. It only means that your average synagogue goers are not likely to be engaged in the Grand Quest. They are not searching for what is Absolutely True, at least not anymore. Maybe they did once, but by now they have either decided that they are not ever going to get answers to big questions, which they have accordingly stopped asking, or (more probably) they have forgotten what the questions were. Now they are doing something else, something equally hard or maybe even harder. They are trying to raise children, make a living, keep up with the mortgage payments, and somehow remain reliable, committed members of the Jewish community. They are much more heavily committed to concreteness than to spirituality. It is a good thing for all of us that they are there, too, or there wouldn't *be* a synagogue for the religious adventurers to want to improve.

If you are one of the searchers from either group, the rabbi is probably puzzled by what to do about your needs. The desire may not be immediately accessible to him/her, but at some level of his/her soul, s/he wants the same things that you want for the synagogue. What you are talking about, though, is so remote and messianic that it is hard to take seriously. S/He wants Jews to be more Jewishly learned, more committed to the rhythms of the Jewish year, more faithful in their participation in the life of the synagogue, more devoted to Israel, to Soviet Jewry, and to righting the injustices of our society. His/her congregants are very far from these goals—and here you are pushing for spirituality and even asking to institutionalize this interest.

If you are only an occasional attender who expects the synagogue to launch your prayers heavenward, then forgive me but I have to give you a brief lecture. It is reasonable to want the synagogue to provide you with an environment in which true prayer is possible. It is not reasonable to expect the synagogue to provide you with a spiritual iron lung, to do for you what you cannot do for yourself. The essential work must be done by you. All that you can hope the synagogue will do is give you a small boost, help you along, provide you with a few people who are trying to accomplish what you are. You couldn't swim the English Channel as a three-times-a-year swimmer, and you are not very likely to get high in the synagogue if you only appear *there* three times a year.

But what if you *are* a serious religious searcher who has tried often and long; what if you are *not* just a passing kvetch? How then can the synagogue help you find what you are looking for?

First of all, you have got to understand the acoustic principles of synagogues. Formal synagogues are very quiet—usually *too* quiet for my taste—but less formal synagogues, which are usually the more traditional ones, are zoned for sound. Knowing that, you should locate yourself to suit your mood. People who want to talk sit in the back rows. People who really want to daven sit forward. If you sit very far back you will probably only hear talk about the stock market or the ball games. Midway along you may pick up some comments about the sermon or hear a discussion of an issue raised by the Torah reading. But if you really want to worship in a serious way, then go forward as far as you dare, hoping that you will not be too conspicuous.

Getting some private space in which to daven is immensely easier if you are a male and your synagogue is one in which a large tallit can be worn without giving an usher a heart attack. With your head covered by a large tallit, you can have all the aloneness you need right there in the presence of a community of Jews. And if the buzz of davening in your vicinity is right, you may really be able to pray. (It is in the tension between privacy and community that Jewish prayer is located.) A note of caution, however: if you sit there wrapped up in a big tallit and if that is not the convention of your synagogue, people are going to assume that you are superpious, and you are going to have to learn to live with those assumptions. A compromise is to hide in your tallit only on special occasions, like Yom Kippur. That will be less freaky; besides, that is a time when, given the crowds, you will need your privacy a lot more.

Hillel said: Do not separate yourself from the congregation (*Pirkei Avot* 2:5).

Some of the larger congregations are plagued with really tough ushers who are made extraordinarily anxious by asymmetry. They are determined to put you where *they* want you to sit. Take heart. After they get to know you, a brief conversation before services may help get you a bit more freedom than is normally accorded the Bar Mitzvah crowd.

What I don't like about the responsive reading is that the Rabbi gets all the good lines.

Because the tallit is very useful in helping men to pray, some brave women have taken to wearing them as well. But that occasionally provokes so much reaction that in your self-consciousness you can get about as much davening done as if you were sitting there naked. Some women have tried to wear a shawl instead—the more adventurous, a shawl with fringes. But male or female, you are not going to be able to worship successfully in a tallit or its equivalent until you are able to do so unself-consciously. Perhaps you should try wearing it at home first, for practice. If your synagogue is altogether the wrong setting for a tallit, try closing your eyes. Also consider sitting in the unused chapel for part of the service.

One of the characteristics of many synagogues is that the worship moves along rapidly. Just when you want to dive in and really work through an issue that the prayer book has suggested, the congregation is already moving on. Don't be intimidated. If you aren't ready to move on, don't. Stay as long as you need to, whenever you wish. Try limiting yourself to a verse or two and really work at them in order to rediscover life in words that have died. You may want to stand and sit with the rest of the congregation, at least if people do those things all at the same time in your synagogue, but don't be hurried through the text. As a matter of fact, you can decide beforehand that you are not even going to try to keep up, that it is going to take you six months to go through the entire service, and that you are not going to go through more than two or three prayers on any given week. You may find that you want to join in with the congregation on some of the more familiar refrains, but you don't need to decide about that until you see how it feels.

By the way, humming to yourself melodies of your choice can add much to your davening. However, doing this while the congregation sings another melody is next to impossible. Remember, much of the prayer book was committed to writing only to help the people who couldn't manage to formulate their own prayers (see "Hazzanut"). Use it as a springboard, not an anchor. If you can function well on your own, you do not need to be limited to the text.

At the same time, recognize that the traditional siddur contains a lot more than just prayers in the ordinary sense of the word. It is a veritable liturgical anthology. You can learn from it, fight with it, be infuriated by it. It is variously meditative, didactic, polemical, philosophical, poetic, historical; but whatever it is, it is always exceedingly busy. It can argue with you, offer consolation, raise questions, and offer answers. It has a lot of material that can keep you going if the creativity of your own head or soul has dried up.

There are other solutions to the problem of what to do:

a. when you seem to dry up inside;

b. if there is too much sermonizing that doesn't help you; or, worse yet,

c. if the service or sermon makes you angry.

There is other literature that you can appropriately read in a synagogue setting. One of the more obvious choices is the Hertz Torah. It, and its notes, are chock-full of information, pieties, neat little sermons, and, most important, the text of the Torah. Many synagogues will have it immediately available for you, but even if yours doesn't, having one with you is not likely to upset the people who are sitting near you. You shouldn't have to be a Marrano, but once again the problem is that if they get too upset, you are going to have difficulty concentrating.

There are other books that are serviceable in this context as well. High on the list should be the Hertz prayer book, because of its rich content. It, like the Humash mentioned before, has another advantage: they both have a Hebrew and an English text. If you are sitting with a Hebrew book in your hands, whoever is sitting next to you will conclude that you can't be all bad. When you become more daring, you can bring texts without any Hebrew. This is easier to do on the High Holidays, when you will be in the synagogue for a long time at a stretch. Then whoever is sitting near you will reconcile her/himself to the fact that s/he is sitting near an eccentric and will soon be borrowing your books. I would recommend texts like:

1. *Hammer on the Rock: A Midrash Reader*, edited by Nahum Glatzer (New York: Schocken, 1957).
2. *Tales of the Hasidim*, collected by Martin Buber (New York: Schocken, 1947).
For the High Holidays in particular consider:
3. *Days of Awe*, by S. Y. Agnon (New York: Schocken, 1959).
4. *Justice and Mercy*, by Max Arzt (New York: Holt, Rinehart, 1936)—a commentary on the traditional liturgy.
5. *The Rosh Hashanah Anthology* and *The Yom Kippur Anthology* by Philip Goodman (Jewish Publication Society, 1970 and 1971).

Once you begin to see what works for you, a few hours of browsing in your local Jewish bookstore may provide you with a lot of material.

You should know in advance that you are not going to have the same degree of spiritual earnestness whenever you go to the synagogue. Some of the time, perhaps more often than you think, you will be quite content— maybe even refreshed—just to visit with someone you haven't seen for a while. Who knows? Once or twice you might even want to talk about the stock market! If that happens, don't be too hard on yourself. You are not a religious failure. You will merely have made an important discovery—that a good synagogue should be designed to absorb many moods. It should have a place for you along with all of your fellow congregants at your best and at your most trivial as well. Just hope that you don't have to feel guilty for having been too judgmental when you were feeling high-minded. Relax, sit in the back row, and have a good Shabbosdik shmoose with a friend. Maybe you'll be back in the front row next week.

As a final piece of advice, consider trying to find a subgroup of people with concerns like yours, people who would find congenial the same style of worship that you do. The congregation may even welcome the formation of such an additional minyan, since the idea of a pluralistic synagogue has gained some acceptance lately. It can also be true that the idea will meet with congregational resistance. If that happens, you may wish to meet with your little subgroup on a once-a-month basis. Try not to stray too far from your synagogue. You need each other more than you may think. There are occasions when one has to break and formally organize something new, but that should only be a last resort. Before you do that, you should be quite convinced that what you are leaving is hopeless and that what you are forming will be better.

An Israelite in his relationship to the synagogue may be likened to a branch growing on a tree. As long as the branch is still attached to the tree, there is hope it may renew its vigor under favorable conditions, no matter how withered it may have become. But once the living branch falls away, all hope is lost (*Or Yesharim*, p. 96).

Keep in mind that if you come to the synagogue with young children, you should certainly provide them with Jewish stories that are appropriate to their age level. Fair is fair. (See "Children's Books" in *Catalog 1* for suggestions.)

Incidentally, all these remarks have been directed primarily to the experiences you are likely to have at Shabbat services. Daily services are likely to provide an easier atmosphere in which to express your own peculiar interests, but since in most synagogues these days they are designed primarily for people who want to say Kaddish, the service itself moves at an absolutely alarming rate. Before you catch your breath, the service may be over. Try it though. You may be lucky enough to find some good daily services.

Rabbi Yohanan the sandal maker said: "Every assembly which is the name of heaven will, in the end, endure" (*Pirkei Avot* 4:14).

Choosing a Rabbi

So, you want to survive in the Jewish community? Like-minded friends are crucial, whether you choose to live in a havurah or elect to throw your Jewish fate in with a synagogue community. However, for those who opt for the more traditional (small "t") form of community organization, the presence of a good synagogue rabbi is more than crucial, even more than a matter of life or death; it can be likened to the resurrection of the dead. How does one go about finding a good rabbi? And what constitutes a "good" rabbi?

A rabbi is only suitable if s/he is able to meet the needs of a particular congregation. If you are one of the people responsible for selecting a rabbinical leader, ask yourself: Why do I need a rabbi? There are several possible roles for today's rabbi. Which role do you most want to see filled—that of teacher? pastoral leader? synagogue administrator? No candidate who will act in only one of these roles is acceptable, but your chances of finding a suitable rabbi are highest when your priorities match the rabbi's.

Your move

If you are moving to a new city, whether to attend a school or start a new job, or if you are buying a home in your own town, you are in an enviable position. You can actively search for a suitable Jewish community—including, of course, a sympathetic synagogue rabbi. The consequences of finding such a community and rabbi can be more far-reaching than the location of good shopping areas, convenient bus routes, or adequate recreational facilities. Some families will gauge the distance they can comfortably walk on a Shabbat, taking into consideration children—present or potential—and will draw the appropriate-sized circle around the synagogue of their choice; they will then proceed to apartment- or house-hunt only within that designated area. Families have been known to sell their home and buy a new one in order to be within the "parish" of a particular rabbi.

Rabbi's move

Rabbis have been known to retire, die, be fired, or transfer, and you will find yourself in the position of having to look for a new rabbi. When this happens synagogues have found it efficient to appoint a selection committee, whose task it is to learn of possible candidates, interview them, and make recommendations to the synagogue's board. Such a committee must reflect the needs of your synagogue community. I suggest that it be composed of different age groups and include men and women. While few synagogues will think of including women on a rabbi selection committee, their participation in the selection is necessary if the rabbi is to serve the total community. Devoting considerable thought to the formation of this committee is well worth the time it takes; much depends on the idiosyncrasies of its constituents.

The rabbi as teacher

Until Jews settled in North America the term rabbi was synonymous with "teacher." A rabbi taught; his entire training was geared to the transmission of knowledge. Although the American rabbi may no longer be seen primarily as a teacher, there is no doubt that it is still an important role. Depending on your congregation's needs, a rabbi may have to teach anything from Hebrew reading to Talmud. And, of course, the rabbi as a sermon giver is part of this role as teacher. Less important than what a rabbi teaches is whether s/he sees the role of teacher as primary. If your congregation wants a rabbi because they want a teacher, your committee must look for a candidate who defines him/herself that way.

The rabbi as pastoral leader

Are you looking for a rabbi who will help you through the Jewish rites of passage—birth, puberty, marriage, and death? Should your rabbi's prime role be to guide you in the appropriate ritual demands, personally sharing in the joy and sorrow of your experience? While this role may be a throwback to Mosaic imagery and even an imitation of Christian clerical tasks, nevertheless the rabbi has been—and will continue to be—a community figure to whom people turn for support of all kinds. (Many rabbis can attest to an overwhelming case load during counseling hours.) For many Jews, the desirable rabbi is one who can movingly address the bride and groom under the huppah or be with you in a time of personal crisis. If the consensus of your congregation is that their needs will be best served by a pastoral leader, you must look for someone who can function that way.

The rabbi as synagogue administrator

Perhaps your synagogue is seen as the social center of your community. The words Jewish Center may even appear in its name, if the founders of the congregation felt that the fundamental purpose of the institution was to fulfill the social and recreational needs of the community. In this case your search for a rabbi will send you to a candidate who can knowledgeably and efficiently direct a social and recreational program. The scholarship and spirituality needed in a teacher or pastoral leader are less important than the leadership, imagination, and personality needed here.

A note of caution

The procedures and ethics of hiring any professional employee are standard: the courtesy, tact, and honesty that are necessary in every hiring situation are equally important in hiring a rabbi. However, certain aspects of the rabbinical selection process differ from the selection of other professionals. Choosing a rabbi can become very complicated because few lay people really know what a rabbi's job description ought to be, and fewer still will admit what they really want from their rabbi. Most people are too sophisticated to admit, for instance, that they are looking for a father figure.

Reread this note now, putting *yourself* in the position of the rabbi, and perhaps you will understand a little better the complex maze of conflicting needs, desires, and concerns that a rabbi must continually face.

Almost too obvious to mention are the graduating classes of the various rabbinical seminaries. If your congregation is young and willing to experiment, there are distinct advantages in choosing a recent rabbinical graduate.

Others will never own up to wanting a rabbi who can make them feel good inside (the Comfortable Pew Syndrome). Some lay people secretly hope that their rabbi will add a measure of excitement and controversy; others pray that their rabbi will create a large congregation, build a large building, and raise large sums of money. And don't overlook those who want a rabbi so that there be one more community figure whom they can control. All these needs spring from deep emotional sources but are rarely expressed. Expressed or not, they confuse and disrupt the selection and hiring process. At some point you may find a candidate, perfectly acceptable in your eyes, who is rejected by members of your committee for reasons totally incomprehensible to you; on some level that candidate may not be satisfying an emotional need that no one is prepared to spell out.

The search is on

Once it becomes public knowledge that you are in the market for a rabbi, letters will begin to arrive at the synagogue's office. Most will come from rabbis who want a change from their current position and thus, understandably, will request that their inquiries be kept confidential. While some of the letters may look inviting and may even lead to a serious prospect, it has been our experience that the most suitable candidates are already happily employed. It is possible, however, that your congregation may represent a move up—in terms of prestige or salary; besides, just as congregations are dissatisfied, so can rabbis be dissatisfied, and s/he could be looking for a new pulpit better suited to his/her needs.

Kidnaping is frowned upon in Judaism, and seduction fares no better, but there are ways of letting a rabbi know that a move to your congregation would benefit all concerned. Of course, approaching an assistant rabbi is a less heinous crime. Keep in mind that some of the best candidates are not to

be found in pulpits. Many Hillel directors are rabbis, and there is always the possibility that the change a Hillel director is looking for might be in the direction of a congregation. Consider, too, the many rabbis currently working in Jewish communal institutions like the American Jewish Congress, UJA, and Bnai Brith.

The Jewish studies programs developing in North American universities are gold mines for finding rabbis. Many rabbis teach because they have already opted out of the synagogue scene, but do not rule out the possibility of enticing an academician back into the pulpit. Such rabbis would be especially suitable for congregations who are interested in a teacher. Similarly, there are principals of day schools who might be attracted to the challenge of a congregation.

Every rabbinical seminary has its own placement bureau; their names and locations can be found at the end of the chapter. Before trying to circumvent them on the assumption that a successful rabbi doesn't require their services, remember that members of Conservative and Reform rabbinical organizations may not negotiate directly or indirectly with a congregation—or even recommend a colleague for a position—without consulting their respective placement committees.

Women rabbis have special problems finding jobs. Your congregation should think twice before refusing a woman candidate; any woman who has chosen to be a rabbi is probably used to working even harder than her male counterpart, and may be more compassionate as a result of the hostility she has encountered. If your congregation has already instituted the changes necessary for ritual equality between men and women, revising your image of the rabbi-as-father may be the next step.

The Reform and Reconstructionist movements are the only ones to have accepted women candidates in their rabbinical programs, and both concede the placement difficulty. Perhaps your congregation can help.

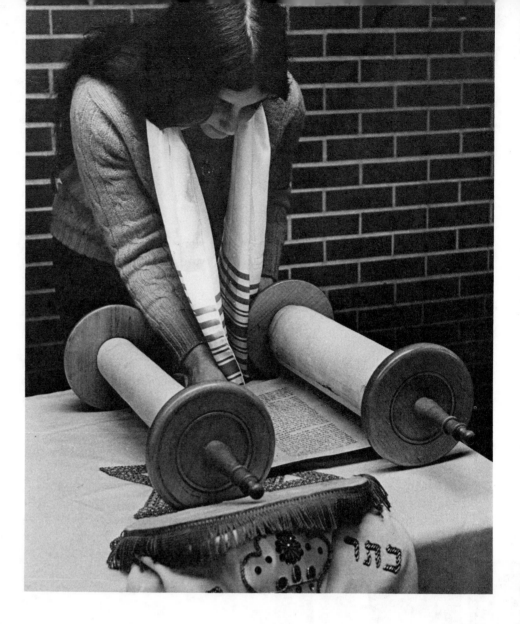

Another note of caution

The sectarian nature of North American Judaism divides the rabbinical seminaries roughly into Orthodox, Conservative, Reconstructionist, and Reform; most congregations belong to corresponding lay organizations. Before wasting the selection committee's time, it would be well worth your while to check out your synagogue's bylaws regarding what rabbinical ordination is "kosher" for your synagogue.

It was hard for Satan alone to mislead the whole world, so he appointed Rabbis in different localities.
—Nachman of Bratslav

Judgment day

Once your selection committee has zeroed in on a few suitable candidates, the interviewing process begins. Good interviewing procedures allow the rabbi to be exposed to the community in a variety of ways (and such procedures equally expose the congregation to the rabbi!).

Sermons

If the Shabbat morning services with their sermons are the focus of your synagogue's weekly calendar, it will be necessary to invite your candidate to spend a Shabbat in your community in order to preach. Bear in mind, however, that although a candidate will try to put his/her best foot forward, lack of familiarity with the congregation and nervousness may be a handicap. As best you can, try to give the rabbi an idea of what kind of sermons are especially enjoyable to the congregation, e.g., portion of the week, latest novel, political analysis, etc. Conversely, one excellent sermon is no guarantee of the quality of sermons to come.

The feedback from those congregants who attend the lecture, class, or sermon can be most helpful to the selection committee, which should seek out their opinions.

Teaching

If the educational program is a crucial part of your synagogue life, the candidate ought to deliver a public lecture; if small-group learning, such as a Shabbat afternoon shiur is your regular practice, you might ask the rabbi to conduct such a class, either on the ongoing topic or on a topic of the candidate's interest.

Good character

The quality hardest to assess in a candidate but undoubtedly the most necessary one is good character, otherwise known as menschlichkeit. No class or sermon can be as important as a rabbi's inner strengths, resources, and principles. It is not easy to judge character, but do persist in your attempt to discover what makes a candidate tick. Are issues that bother you also his/her concerns: halakhic inequities, synagogue decorum, aliyah? Will the candidate answer questions or does s/he like to avoid controversy? Is s/he "straight" when discussing financial matters? Does s/he listen as well as talk? Can s/he laugh? The moral tone of a congregation can be set by its rabbi, and no single step in choosing one can be as critical as that which draws a clearer picture of a candidate's character.

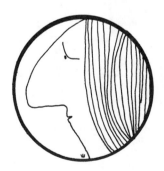

When feasible, an excellent way of acquiring information on a candidate's character is to visit the rabbi's previous congregation or setting. An astute observer can learn a lot at a yom tov service or a Bible class. Needless to say, when the candidacy is confidential, such a visit has to be arranged with utmost discretion.

From right to left

A True Story: A rabbi in a New York suburb was visited by a delegation of five Baptist lay people from a town in southern New Jersey. Convinced that he was to be subjected to yet another missionary attempt, he leaned back in his desk chair to await impatiently the expected rhetoric. None was forthcoming. His five visitors were, in fact, members of their church's minister selection committee, in the process of interviewing a candidate currently ministering to the Baptist congregation in the rabbi's New York suburb. Their own New Jersey church community prided itself on a tradition of brotherhood with its local Jews, and they wanted assurance that their candidate had maintained good relations with the suburban rabbi. The rabbi assured them of the good character of their candidate and then went on to express his pleasant surprise that so large a group would travel such a distance just to speak to him. "Oh no, rabbi," they replied, "we didn't travel this far to see you alone. From here we leave to meet with the local druggist, bank manager, public school principal, and social welfare bureau."

Such is thoroughness! While it may not always be feasible, there is a lot to be gained from visiting candidates on their home territory.

A final note of caution: Unlike other matchmaking procedures, no honeymoon follows the hiring of a new rabbi. Each rabbi has a particular style, and your congregation must be prepared to allow the new one a chance to adjust. There exists an unfortunate tendency to remember the strengths of the former rabbi and compare them to the weaker aspects of the new one. Be patient. The Messiah may not have arrived, but if you have chosen carefully, there is still a chance for partial redemption!

Just as it is important to match your congregation's needs to your candidate's strengths and interests, it is also important to assure a religious compatibility between congregation and candidate. Within each of the major religious camps there is a wide variance in observance and belief. If your Conservative congregation has organ music on Shabbat, your prospective rabbi has to be comfortable with it. If your Orthodox synagogue has maintained good relations with the local Reform and Conservative synagogues, is your candidate prepared to continue to work together with their rabbis? If your Reform temple has been introducing more Hebrew into its services, will your candidate support this trend? The place of women, the suitability of guest lecturers, even the height of the mehitzah—the partition between men and women—have been controversial synagogue issues, and it is advisable that in your discussions with candidates a meeting of the minds be arrived at.

Your responsibility

Hiring a rabbi demands scrupulous behavior, as much on your part as on the candidate's. Despite your natural inclination to sing the praises of your community, realize that the more honest you are about problems, the more likely you are to hire someone capable of handling them. By all means woo the candidate with your virtues, but remember that just as you'd prefer to know your rabbi's weaknesses *before* hiring, the person you're considering wants to take on the position with all possible awareness of its challenges. Financial difficulties, changing constituency, divided lay leadership—these issues should be discussed openly. There are enough adjustments ahead for both of you without your having to defuse the resentment of a rabbi who's been misinformed.

After interviewing many people over a long period of time, you can lose sight of the individual humanness of each candidate. Although you may be eager to expose the candidate to as many congregational situations as possible, be sure to leave enough time for rest and preparation (in addition to the more obvious courtesy of providing comfortable transportation and lodging). As soon as you have decided not to hire a candidate, inform him/her immediately; s/he is more insecure than you are.

In hiring as well as in firing a rabbi, it is important to keep in mind that the livelihood of a person and his/her dependents is in your hands. Even beginning negotiation is a serious responsibility: if you persuade a rabbi who has served elsewhere for a long period of time to join your community—only to decide after two years that you are dissatisfied—you may be destroying that person's prospect of ending a life of service in dignity. The rabbinate is a precarious occupation—a rabbi who has not been successful can't simply move to another city and try again.

Similarly, when members of another congregation ask your opinion of your former rabbi, be honest but aware that a person's material and emotional well-being can be shattered by a few careless comments. *No matter how demystified the rabbinic profession has become, it is still a sacred calling in Jewish tradition, and worthy of respect.*

Rabbinical placement service

Conservative Judaism

**Joint Placement Committee of the Rabbinical Assembly,
Jewish Theological Seminary, and the United Synagogue
of America
3080 Broadway
New York, N.Y. 10027**

Note: While you are free to approach any member of the Rabbinical Assembly, currently employed or not, that member is obliged to conduct all negotiations under the auspices of the Joint Placement Committee if he wishes to retain his membership in the Rabbinical Assembly.

Orthodox Judaism

**Yeshiva University's Rabbi Isaac Elchanan Theological Seminary
2540 Amsterdam Ave.
New York, N.Y. 10033**

**Hebrew Theological College
7135 N. Carpenter Rd.
Skokie, Ill. 60076**

**Mesivta Yeshiva Rabbi Chaim Berlin Rabbinical Academy
1593 Coney Island Ave.
Brooklyn, N.Y. 11230**

**Yeshivah Torah Vadaat
425 E. 9th St.
Brooklyn, N.Y. 11218**

DECIDING ON THE NEW RABBI

Note: While there are many other rabbinical yeshivot granting semikhah—Orthodox ordination—the graduates of the four at left are most likely to be interested in pulpit positions.

Reconstructionist Judaism

**Jewish Reconstructionist Foundation's Rabbinical College
2308 N. Broad St.
Philadelphia, Pa. 19132**

Reform Judaism

Note: Here, too, ethics dictate that you conduct all negotiations through the movement's placement service.

**Central Conference of American Rabbis' Placement Commission
790 Madison Ave.
New York, N.Y. 10021**

the arts

4

Crafts and Folk Art

Jewish folk art

There is endless debate about what a Jew is, what a Jew is meant to be, what Jews might become in the future. But for as long as our history has been transcribed we have always considered ourselves a people, a sometimes mystical mixture of religion, nationalism, folkways, and culture. We may be urban, sophisticated, and learned, but we're still a people—a folk. And as folk we have lived in many different countries, breathed in and absorbed many different cultures, and yet managed to develop a culture that reflected who we were.

Because of this very fact of Jewish life, there has been more "folk" than "fine" art in Jewish tradition. Even during those rare periods in our history when we have had the security and wealth necessary for the production of grand buildings and artifacts, it has always seemed to us to be more important to spend money for education and to help the hungry and poor. Since the physical world was seen as a place where one awaited the coming of the Messiah, it was considered more worthwhile to "invest" one's wealth in procuring a place in the world to come through the mitzvah of charity or other communal responsibilities. This is not to say that substantial buildings and costly ceremonial objects were *never* made, but only that fewer were made than might have been, even when the political climate allowed for them.

Throughout our history, however, the Jewish cycle of life and holidays has been enhanced by simple objects made of humble materials imbued with sanctity. These objects represent Jewish folk art.

What is folk art?

Although there have been paintings and sculpture that are considered to be folkloric, usually we are speaking about utilitarian objects when we discuss folk art. If ordinary people, even those who do not live in quaint villages, make something for their daily lives (or holidays and special events), using the best skills they have in order to make their creation as functional and as beautiful as they can, that is folk art. Certain aesthetes may tremble at that, but while I am ready to admit that some such objects may be more beautiful than others, I would hesitate to exclude from the realm of folk art any honest craft attempt that attains even minimal mastery. For me, folk art does not refer to the sublime artistic expression of a folk, but to the unpretentious art and craft of "The Folk." It is the art of the common people, made by them and intended for their use and enjoyment. The appeal of folk art is its ability to appeal to people directly and intimately, even to those totally uninitiated in the fine arts. The lack of academic mastery that we often see in folk art, which contributes to its charm, might perhaps limit its ability to describe, but never to express. When this expressive quality of folk art is infused with genius or inspiration, the results can be impressively beautiful.

Characteristically, folk art is an outgrowth of the artisan tradition rather than of the art academy. It feeds on craft and the desire of people to use their hands to work with satisfying materials. Although the folk artist uses whatever simple skills and talents s/he has, technical proficiency will usually be shown in the finished object because of familiarity with the materials.

Folk art has a sense of time built into it. Things are made for use; they're made as beautifully as they can be, the decorative qualities closely interwoven with the utility of the object; but above all, they are made to be used. Unlike art works made for public display, such as murals, huge paintings, sculpture, these objects are made of humble materials: paper, cloth, wood—all inexpensive, very accessible, and easily worked even by people with limited experience; hence they do deteriorate quickly. This is why most Jewish art objects perished along with the people who made them. Objects made of precious metals were often melted down or found their way to various non-Jewish treasuries; objects made of paper, wood, cloth, and clay rarely survived at all.

American folk art

The three waves of Jewish immigration to the United States—Sephardim, German Jews, and East European Jews—each brought with them some artifacts for domestic and synagogue use. To the degree that they were able to, they maintained contact with people in their countries of origin, from whom they were able to import additional artifacts as they were needed. Objects made in the United States were often very similar to those brought by the immigrants to this country, because they were made by people who were carrying on traditional crafts as they had learned them in various European countries. It is not surprising to find that an American style did not manifest itself in Jewish folk art during the early days of settlement. Artisans who made things for Jewish use were not concerned with expressing themselves in the American idiom; they simply wanted to make useful and necessary objects that would be as acceptable as the European prototypes with which they were familiar. Until World War II most Jewish artifacts were imported from Europe, both because of the links people had maintained with the Old World and because many of the craftsmen who immigrated to the United States found that other jobs were more lucrative than their traditional folk art work.

By the end of World War II, Jewish popular culture in America meant newspapers covering the floor and plastic covers on the furniture. We were a generation trying to make the transition from the rich traditions of the now-vanished shtetl to an American life-style—precisely at a time when

Jews have only been in America as a significant entity for about seventy years, and so we must be a little patient with ourselves as we wait for an identifiable "American Jewish style" to appear. If we work hard and produce as much as we can, in about two hundred years we should see results. When the archaeologists dig us up, they will find things that say the Jewish community was alive and well in the United States in the 1970s and 1980s. Now it is up to you.

those American arts and crafts were in a decline. American Jews flocked to the suburbs, where their diminished need for Jewish articles was met by synagogue gift shop Israeli imports and Lower East Side reproductions of nineteenth-century reproductions of seventeenth-century Judaica.

But times were changing. The art world turned its attention from Paris to New York, serious Jewish artists/craftspeople in the United States began to make beautiful contemporary ceremonial objects. These, however, were the work of professional artists, destined for a few collections among the wealthy. What of "The Folk" and their art? Unfortunately, with a few exceptions, very little Jewish handwork was done at first. This was true among the rest of the population as well; many crafts had grown into industries, and the efforts of individual artisans were lost in the depersonalization of mechanization.

In recent years, however, there has been a renaissance of interest and activity in the crafts. Not only have the number of professional craftspeople grown, but in just about every household across the country someone is making something. Whether it is clothes, candles, furniture, or jewelry, Americans are doing for themselves again and finding it both rewarding and fun. Now is an ideal time to use the skills we have all been learning in our other craft classes and begin to make our own American Jewish folk art objects. We cheat ourselves if we don't invest something of ourselves in making beautiful things for everyday use. We lose the opportunity to elevate the ordinary to the spiritual.

What to make and how to make it look Jewish

Make something you or your family need, using skills you already have. You might begin by making things for the holidays. In a sense holiday crafts will be easier because we have a great deal of knowledge about what things for the holidays look like, and the very nature of their function makes them Jewish. The biggest problem you may encounter is how to avoid clichés.

We live in a very secular society and not much of our time is spent in "religious" activity. How can we make the ordinary things of our daily lives look Jewish? I have been grappling with this problem for years, and the most important piece of advice I have for you is to become familiar with Jewish lore. Develop a body of Jewish knowledge; find out where you fit into this long chain of history. The more you read and look at, the more symbols will become available to you, the more ideas you will then have.

Symbols

1. The menorah is the oldest Jewish symbol.
2. The magen david—Jewish star—is a more recent Jewish symbol.
3. The combination of blue and white has a long and honorable tradition in Jewish lore.

The problem is to renew these powerful symbols. Starting with a magen david is like a drop in an ocean. Anything can be made Jewish, including hearts, trees, and peace signs. Reclaim symbols that have slipped away, such as:

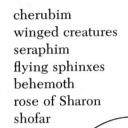

bells   cherubim   Leviathan

angels   winged creatures   lion

snakes   seraphim   deer

doves   flying sphinxes   pillars

fish   behemoth   pomegranates

candles   rose of Sharon   grapes

elephants   shofar

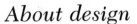

About design

Once you have decided what to make and which symbols you would like to use, the problem is how to design and make it. People often ask me how I come up with design ideas, how I get something down on paper, fabric, clay, or wood. Whatever talent I might possibly possess would be worth nothing at all if I didn't put in many hours of work on the basic design or composition of a project. If you conscientiously set out to design a pillow using your Hebrew name, for example, and you spend four hours every day for five days just working out the design, playing with the shapes of the letters, by the end of that twenty-hour period you will certainly have *something*. Maybe it won't represent true art, but you will have enough to work with. And the second time will be better. By the fifth or sixth design, you will see the beginnings of your own style emerging.

It is beautiful to think of crafts, art, music, or writing as gliding effortlessly from the moment of inspiration to the full realization of the finished work, of riding a crescendo of emotion that takes one easily and directly from idea to finished object. When it does happen that the original concept flows painlessly through the work stages and results almost miraculously in the finished product, the feeling of elation is enormous. But it rarely happens that way. Usually one has an idea—which brings with it that great burst of enthusiasm: "Wow, what a great idea!" Then come the hours of painstaking work to somehow give birth to the object called forth by the initial inspiration. The work can be rewarding, but must be recognized for what it is: work. You want what you are making to be around for a while, so allow plenty of time. It often takes days to develop a design. Once you have something you like, repeat it over and over again; it will change every time you use it and eventually you will have your own style. Style comes from endlessly plagiarizing yourself. If you make a doodle you particularly like, a very handsome menorah form perhaps, repeat that over and over and over again in order to build a pattern. Remember as you repeat it that repetition is the skeleton of a design and variation is its intelligence. So if you make a checkerboard effect out of your stylized menorah design in black and white, maybe do one in red, just to give it a little pizzazz.

If you can't draw, or think you can't, cut or tear paper shapes. Self-confidence comes with self-knowledge. Nothing is categorically *right*. Colors you like are the colors to use. If you panic about picking colors, simply look at the colors of your clothes, or those of the room around you, and you will see that you've already made many selections—you definitely have a preference for greens and blues or browns and yellows. Use what you like and what you are most familiar with.

About technique

Understand the basic process involved in the particular craft you are about to undertake, e.g., that batik is a wax-resist stencil method of colorfully designing fabric or paper. Then approach it in the easiest possible way. By simplifying wherever you can and using tools and techniques you are already familiar with from other types of craft work, you may in fact improve upon the "standard" way of doing something. The perniciously available kits often perpetuate the fear that things are impossibly difficult to do and that absolute precision and mastery of almost magical techniques are necessary in order to make the simplest things. If you have hemmed a skirt or sewn a button you can do embroidery. If you can cut and paste paper you can do wood applique. Remember, you are a folk artist, not Michelangelo.

The craft projects given here are not meant to be slavishly imitated, but rather to inspire you to make up your own version of Jewish Americana. Enjoy yourself. If you are committed to carrying out the work with intensity and a fresh approach, the results will show it. Just as scribes wash their hands and say a special prayer when they set out to write Torah scrolls, we too should begin our projects with a similar sense of dedication.

Paper cutting

The origin of most of the crafts is shrouded in the veils of prehistory. Every group uses variants of the same universal crafts to make objects that satisfy both its physical needs and the requirements of its emotional and cultural life. Because of its internal value system and its immediate life circumstances, a group develops preferences for and expertise in particular crafts at different times. At one time or another Jews have worked at just about every craft imaginable. Since ancient times, however, the most typical Jewish crafts have been calligraphy and textiles. For the past few centuries, paper cutting has been a popular Jewish folk craft.

Decorative designs have been cut from bark, parchment, fabric, and paper for thousands of years in many cultures throughout the world. In the Jewish communities of Holland and Italy, from the seventeenth to the early nineteenth century, paper and parchment cut work was a very popular way of decorating the borders of the Megillah—the scroll of Esther—and ketubbot—marriage contracts. Some of these marriage contracts became so elaborate that the local rabbis issued statements discouraging the commissioning of ketubbot that were exceedingly costly to execute. By the nineteenth century paper was easily accessible, and the popularity of paper cutting as a folk art grew, particularly among the Jews of North Africa and throughout the Pale of Settlement. In Eastern Europe paper-cuts were frequently used to make mizrahim—wall hangings on the eastern wall of the home—and shivvitim—votive wall hangings that were often painted with watercolors. Paper-cut Simhat Torah flags were popular, although few survive today. Many paper-cut amulets were made, particularly those that hung in the rooms of a new mother to protect her and the infant against Lilith and other possible evil spirits (see Birth). In the shtetls of Russia and Poland during the nineteenth century and until World War II, small, round, flower-shaped paper-cuts (called royselekh) were made to decorate the windows for Shavuot.

Usually our introduction to the craft of paper cutting is either a chain of paper dolls or folded paper snowflakes and doilies. Unfortunately most of us rarely go on to anything more ambitious. The revival of interest in so many traditional crafts offers an opportune moment to see if we cannot take up, revitalize, and even americanize the shtetl paper-cuts. Even the simplest paper-cuts are fun and satisfying to do, and with practice and experience, the range of possible uses for your paper-cuts multiplies. They can be used as decorative objects in themselves. Because they reproduce very well they are excellent ways of designing posters and greeting cards.

MATERIALS AND TOOLS

1. *Paper*: Anything that is thin, firm, and strong is fine. Typing paper and shelf lining paper are excellent. Construction paper is a little coarse, but if the design is not too finely detailed and you want a color or black, it is usable. Rice paper can be used for certain special effects, but some types have a tendency to curl. Coated colored paper, such as that used for Japanese origami, can be very attractive, but it is sometimes difficult to eliminate the fold marks from the finished work.

Paper-cuts can also be used effectively as stencils and patterns for work in other media.

2. *You will also need*:
   a. contrasting paper or cardboard to mount the completed design;
   b. rubber cement;
   c. pencils;
   d. assorted cutting tools, including pinking shears, manicure and embroidery scissors, utility hobby knife;
   e. an iron.

TO BEGIN

Begin at the end. Let's assume that you want to make a mizrah or amulet and plan to give it as a gift or to hang it proudly in a conspicuous place. In either case it will need a frame. Custom framing is incredibly expensive, so before you begin your paper-cut, find, beg for, or buy the frame. Used, odd-sized, and unusual frames are available at rummage and garage sales, antique and junk shops. Frame shops and galleries often have frames that have come off reframed work or were ordered and then not claimed. These will cost a fraction of what you would have to pay if you ordered a frame to fit your work. Once you have the frame, the outside dimensions and possibly the color of the paper and backing are already decided for you; so that's one more problem out of the way.

PROCEDURE

1. For your first paper-cut, pick symbols that are easily shown in silhouette: a crown, bird, magen david, hand, etc. Later you can go on to rampant or laughing lions, imaginary beasts, intertwined menorot, and complicated thematic material.

2. For a symmetrical two-part design (the hamsa—an amulet in the shape of a hand—and wedding announcements), fold the paper in half; in quarters for a design that will be repeated four times (the story frame).

3. Lightly sketch the desired shapes on the reverse of one half (or one quarter) of the paper. Make certain that parts of each figure touch each other. The trick is to have them touch just enough to keep the design from falling apart, but not so much that the individual shapes are lost. Don't go into too much detail in the drawing; just indicate the basic shapes and the points at which they will remain joined. When the work is partially cut out, you will be able to see those places where you can cut away more detail. If

you want a central image, a crown for example, draw only half of the crown along the center fold line. Paper-cuts lend themselves very well to distortion, so feel free to exaggerate the sizes and forms you are using. Scrolls, small geometric shapes, bars, and foliage can be used to hold your principal motifs together.

4. If you do not want the design to be totally symmetrical, cut out as much as possible, unfold the paper, and then on the right side of the paper (especially if it is lettering) lightly draw the shapes you will need.

5. Cut out the remaining parts of the design with the paper unfolded. Do not be distressed if you sometimes cut through a point you had intended as a link. When the work is glued to the background, it will hold together.

6. When the cutting is finished to your satisfaction (expect it to take longer than you think), unfold it and iron it with a warm iron to get the fold lines out.

7. Use rubber cement to glue it to a contrasting background. Use only enough glue to hold it at the corners and a few crucial points. Extra rubber cement is easily rubbed away with your finger.

The amulet shown was made for a friend when she had a studio-warming party. I used a standard good luck hamsa-style hand (hamsa, incidentally, is Arabic for "five") but doubled it, so that it looks like hands of blessing as well. (My own hand, now forever immortalized, served as the pattern.) The eyes represent the "evil eye" which the amulet is protection against, while the Hebrew letters say MAZEL TOV, which means both "congratulations" and "good luck." Mazel is the Hebrew word for "constellation"; the expression we use so familiarly has its origins in astrological beliefs, so that we are in reality wishing someone a "good constellation."

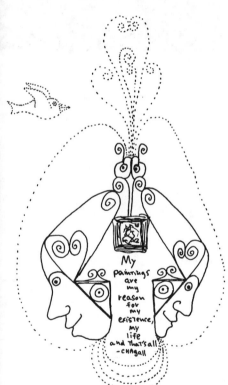
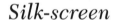

Silk-screen

A variation of the same design was used for the silk-screen prints and T-shirts. Using a paper-cut for silk printing is one of the easiest ways of getting effective designs with this medium. You can buy the basic silk-screen equipment at most hobby or art supply shops, or you can build your own. In either case I would suggest a trip to the craft books section of your library if you have never done silk screening before. It's simple, fun, and fast, and if you become addicted, the possibilities will be endless; but you can still have a good time and produce commendable work with the simple basic procedures.

PAPER-CUTS AS STENCILS

To use a paper-cut as a silk-screen stencil, cut your design from a strong, thin paper that is very slightly porous. Draftsmen's visualizing layout paper is excellent. It is like tracing paper but slightly softer. Good prints can be made using newspaper, though a newsprint stencil won't hold up as long as visualizing paper. The shapes of the paper-cut prevent the ink from passing through the silk to the paper or fabric below. It is the negative spaces around the shapes that will print in color; the shapes themselves will not print. Keep that in mind when you plan your design. Notice that the hands, which are dark in the original paper-cut, remain white in the silk-screen version.

Once you begin, the process goes very quickly, so prepare all your paper, T-shirts, or fabric in advance. It's frustrating to be looking for more paper the right size when your hands are dirty and the ink is drying in the screen.

1. Place a sheet under the silk-screen and put your paper-cut face up on it.

2. Gently lower the screen on top of it, being careful to keep it centered in the position you want it.

3. Put several spoonfuls of ink (use silk-screen ink, artist oil paints, or a mixture; experimentation and experience will help you develop individual preferences) along the top edge of the screen. You can often use silk-screen ink just as it comes from the can. Colors can be modified by mixing or adding artist's oil colors. A thick creamlike ink consistency is usually best. If the consistency is not suited to the particular stencil, you might lose some detail or clog the screen. Either problem is easily rectifiable by changing the amount of paint thinner in the ink.

4. Pull the squeegee across the screen toward yourself firmly and evenly. The paper-cut will be held against the screen by the paint.

5. Lift the screen and remove the first print.

6. Put a fresh sheet of paper in place and repeat. It is a good idea to have another person as a helper or "printer's devil." Someone should have clean hands to place and remove the prints and hang them up to dry. Most of us don't have the elaborate drying racks used in professional print shops, and you will soon run out of floor and table space. A clothesline or two strung temporarily across a room will accommodate a surprising number of prints hung back to back by their corners.

Cleanup is the part I hate. It seems to go on forever, so besides paint thinner, rags, and newspapers, I recommend some good music and company.

Paper-cuts can be used as patterns for other craft projects. It is especially useful for needlework. The design for the needlepoint cushion was first done as a very simple paper-cut. Transferring paper-cut designs to needlepoint is extremely easy.

1. Tape the paper-cut to a window and tape the needlepoint canvas over it.

2. Trace the outlines of the design onto the canvas with waterproof felt-tip pens.

3. After taking the canvas off the window, fill the shapes in with the felt-tip pen and with acrylic paints.

How to make soft-drink-can Hanukkiah

To make this Hanukkiah you will need:
1. an aluminum soft drink or beer can;
2. metal shears or heavy-duty scissors;
3. needlenosed pliers;
4. gloves. It is a good idea to wear thin cotton gloves while working with metal to avoid cuts.

To make a Hanukkiah like the one shown, you will need an aluminum soft drink or beer can. Unfortunately, no-deposit, no-return materials are very easily found all around us. I spent a very enjoyable day canoeing up and down the Delaware-Raritan Canal fishing out all the cans I found until I realized I would soon have enough to provide cans for all the readers of this *Catalog*. Here is a chance to put some of the debris of affluence to use. Pick cans with good colors on the outside because as you roll the metal, these will show on the front.

Using metal shears or heavy-duty scissors, cut off the top third of the can. Then cut away almost half the can vertically. To make the legs, cut four long narrow strips from the top edge down to the base. These should be about ¼″ wide and evenly spaced. Use the needlenosed pliers to pull the metal down and to curl it as shown in the photograph and diagrams. Cut the top edges of the three panels into fringes and curl them with the pliers as shown, using one of the fringes to form the shammash holder. If you use a large enough can (such as a coffee can or one from Pesah macaroons) and are careful, you might be able to cut and curl the candle holders from the otherwise unused base of the can. If not, just affix the candle in place with a little melted wax. There are directions and a pattern for making a tin-can Hanukkiah large enough to hold standard Hanukkah candles in *The Hanukkah Book* (New York: Schocken, 1975).

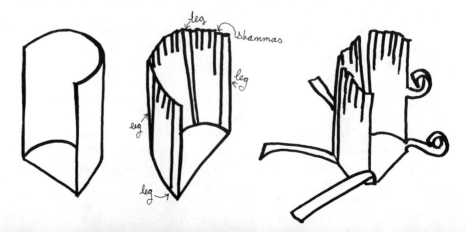

Other craft suggestions

Dona Rosenblatt has some other suggestions for projects using different kinds of crafts media. She especially urges anyone interested in doing serious craft work to become acquainted with the myriad craft books available in every library, and to investigate the many craft courses and minisessions that abound in every community.

Ceramics

Clay is an extremely versatile medium in which to work. It can be obtained in many forms for relatively little money.

The best way to obtain knowledge of techniques and some skill and self-confidence is to take a course at your local Jewish community center or at an adult education center. Such a course is inexpensive, and all materials are available and are usually included in the course fee. It is quite important to learn with someone to guide you and to point out what can be expected from the various clay bodies (porcelain is beautiful and delicate but very hard to work with; stoneware is very sturdy and can be used for bowls and goblets, as it is nonporous when glazed; earthenware is the easiest to obtain and can be fired in your oven, but remains porous even when glazed). Also, a good instructor will teach you the best ways to handle the clay and how to avoid errors that can cause breakage during drying and firing.

Once you have learned the techniques, there are a variety of objects you can create for use in Jewish ceremonies in your home.

Hints: Be sure to find out from the instructor the type of clay being used, the amount of expected shrinkage (7–15 percent), the types of glazes used in the studio. Under no circumstances should you use leaded glazes on objects that will hold food or drink. (Glazes containing iron are safe.)

SLAB-BUILDING

Creating objects using flat pieces of clay and coils will allow you to make:
1. a mezuzah
2. a seder plate
3. a menorah
4. Shabbat candlesticks

Creating cylindrical objects on a potter's wheel will allow you to create:

1. Shabbat candlesticks
2. a Kiddush cup

Since clay is a material that is formed as a direct result of the hand of the craftsperson, children as well as adults can work with great success in this medium.

Wood carving

Anyone who has been a scout knows something about wood carving. You can learn this craft by reading about it if there is no one to teach you. Tools are inexpensive, and wood for small projects is readily available. A piece of pine with a nice grain is quite suitable, as it is soft and easy to work with. Later you can stain it to give the appearance of teak, rosewood, walnut, or whatever.

Projects to consider in this medium include:

1. a mezuzah
2. Shabbat candlesticks
3. a Kiddush cup (Kos Eliyahu) with glass inside to hold wine
4. a hallah tray for Shabbat
5. a matzah tray for Pesah

This craft is one that older children (ten and older) might like to try.

Block printing

I can't think of anything nicer than having a child design and print his/her own New Year's card to send to friends and relatives.

The agent for printing may be wood, clay, or a potato. Basically, anything that you can cut into that maintains its shape is appropriate. Wood has the advantage of a long life, while potatoes just don't hold up (also, they smell funny after you work with them for a while).

Whatever you choose as the printing agent, remember that areas cut away will be white, the uncut areas will print.

Projects to consider:

1. New Year's cards
2. Bar/Bat Mitzvah invitations
3. cloths used as hallah or matzah covers

This is another craft in which children can participate at their own level.

Bread sculpture

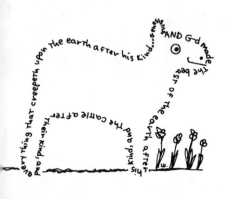

This is an idea that lends itself to hallah baking. What could be better than freshly baked bread formed into an attractive shape? Children will enjoy trying it, too.

Choose a simple yeast bread recipe (substitute honey for sugar—it tastes better and is more healthful). Make the dough as the recipe directs. The last rising before baking is the time to try your hand at creating a masterpiece. There need be no boundaries . . . just enjoy . . . and enjoy again when you sit down to eat.

With a little supervision from an adult, even preschoolers can make things they will be proud of.

1. *Paper plate grager for Purim*
   materials: 2 small paper plates
   tongue depressor
   dried beans
   crayons, paper and material scraps, yarn
   stapler
   a. Let the child decorate the backs of the two plates with the various materials.
   b. Place the beans on the inside of one of the plates, and put the other plate on top (with the decorated side up); staple all around.
   c. Insert the tongue depressor (one quarter of the length) between the two plates and staple in place.

2. *Paper plate puppets for Purim*
   Made with the same materials in the same way, except that the decorations should express the child's idea of a character from the Purim story.

3. *Paper chains to decorate your Sukkah*

4. *Paper flags for Simhat Torah*
   materials: triangular sheet of paper or poster board
   18″ dowel rod
   crayons, paints, paper scraps
   stapler
   a. Let child decorate the triangular paper with the crayons, paints, paper scraps.
   b. Staple the paper to the dowel rod.

Quilting, appliqué, embroidery, and needlepoint

These are cloth fiber techniques that can be used individually or in combination. There are many books available on these craft subjects. Also, since almost everyone knows how to do one or more of these crafts, you can learn from a friend.

QUILTING

Quilting is, basically, the art of sewing small pieces of material together. Traditionally, tiny scraps of cloth were put together to form geometric shapes, flowers, or colonial scenes. There is no reason why this technique cannot be adapted to Jewish motifs.

There are several ways of sewing the material. You may go traditional and use a quilting frame. Or you can sew the pieces by machine. My own method is to sew the pieces together by hand, using either the cross stitch or the satin stitch.

Once you have finished the piece you will need a backing. Choose a solid piece of cloth the same size as the quilted piece. It may be sewn directly to the quilted piece, or you can place a layer of quilt lining (polyester batting, available at fabric stores) between the two.

APPLIQUÉ

This is another method of piecing material. It too can be done either by machine or by hand.

The basic difference between quilting and appliqué is that in quilting you place small scraps of cloth side by side, while in appliqué you place specially cut shapes of cloth on a solid background.

QUILTING AND APPLIQUÉ TECHNIQUES

fold edges to be sewn together

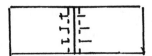

pin edges and sew by hand or by machine

Idea for Hallah Cover

cut 2 pieces to make a star

pin to finished cloth of desired size

add embroidered letters or designs around edges

EMBROIDERY

There are at least as many excellent books on this subject as there are embroidery stitches. Beautiful and delicate designs will be yours if you plan and work carefully.

NEEDLEPOINT

This craft is highly visible today. Kits abound, including those that show Hasidim at the Western Wall. Most of these are ugly and unimaginatively conceived. All are expensive. For ideas, check out older pieces (those done in the 1940s and earlier), books on the subject, and pictorials on Israel.

There are many stitches besides the traditional tent stich used in kits. There are a variety of cross-stitches, flower types, and vertical stitches.

GLOSSARY OF NEEDLEPOINT STITCHES

*Tent Stitch
diagonal*

Cross-stitch

Diagonal Florentine Stitch

Algerian Eye Stitch

*Reversible Tent Stitch
diagonal-2 down, 1 across
1 down, 2 across*

Upright Cross

Smyrna Cross

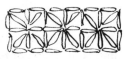

Gobelin and Variation

Rice Stitch

Buying materials instead of a kit can actually cost you less. It requires a lot of thinking before buying, but the results will be original—a statement about yourself. Canvas, in a variety of sizes (measured by squares per inch), is available by the yard. Yarns come in great varieties: there is no one kind of yarn for needlepoint. The only two things to consider when choosing yarns are that the yarn should be able to pass through the opening in the canvas, and that it be strong. Experiment with wools, synthetics, cottons, and blends.

When you have decided what you want to do (and have checked various yarn stores to see what yarns are available), make a full-color sketch, with some notation on special stitches you wish to incorporate. Map out the various areas on the canvas with a Magic Marker (outline only). Then you're off. When you have completed the piece, you can block it yourself (more savings): place a towel on the ironing board; put the needlepoint on top face down and add another towel on top; steam heavily several times and allow to dry before removing from the board.

PROJECTS TO CONSIDER FOR THESE CRAFTS

1. a hallah cover
2. a matzah cover
3. a head covering for candlelighting
4. holiday tablecloths
5. a tallit bag
6. bedspreads

THEMES FOR CONSIDERATION

1. rainbow after the flood
2. doves of peace
3. Garden of Eden (as imagined by yourself)
4. creation story—sun, moon, and stars; grass, flowers, and trees
5. firstfruits (Shavuot)
6. Jonah in the belly of the whale (child's coverlet)
7. alef-bet

Weaving

Weaving is done in all cultures in one form or another. Handweaving on large, complicated looms has been done in Europe for centuries. The craft was actually smuggled into this country when the states were still colonies. (The British forbade the colonists to weave their own fabrics so that they would be dependent on England for textiles.) Primitive cultures have developed their own types of simple looms, which have formed the basis for what we call primitive looms.

The following are directions for making, threading, and weaving on your own primitive loom. There are also many books available on how to weave without benefit of a complicated loom. Don't be put off by the phrase primitive loom, for you can weave in several techniques on such a loom. Besides, it is a good way to get acquainted with some of the techniques used by weavers. Remember, though, that this is only one type of loom, and the weaving instructions here will be for only one type of weave.

FRAME LOOM

As the name suggests, the basis of this loom is a frame. The best way to construct this frame is to get two pairs of stretcher strips (these are special wood strips notched at the ends so that they interlock), which can be purchased at an art supply store (they are generally used by painters to stretch canvas). They are measured by the inch: 18″ x 24″ is a good size for a loom.

STEPS FOR CONSTRUCTING AND DRESSING

Construction and dressing (putting the vertical threads on the loom) are done together to make the loom ready for weaving.

1. Put the strips together by interlocking the corners. No nails are necessary. Square the corners by placing each corner of the frame at the junction of a wall and the floor. Then tap the corner above. Do this to each corner in turn. This assures that each corner will have a true 90° angle.

2. Next you will need nails, a hammer, a pen, and a ruler. Measure off ½″ from each inside corner of one of the 18″ strips. Now, mark off each ¼″ interval from the first mark to the second. Hammer one nail at each ¼″ mark, and make each 1″ a diagonal from the top of the strip to the bottom (see #1 on the diagram).

3. Now you are ready to begin to dress the loom. The vertical threads you will be winding on the loom are the warp threads. The warp must be very strong, as it will be pulled in several directions many times before you are finished weaving. Cotton wrapping twine is excellent for the first project. (Later you can try other things.) To dress the loom, tie one end of the twine to the first nail on the left, using a square knot. Wrap the twine up and over the top, to the back of the loom. Then bring the twine down to the end of the loom with the nails, and wrap the twine around the next nail. Continue the process: up, over, down, and around, until every nail has a strand of twine around it. Tie off the end of the twine, with a square knot, at the back end of the loom. Before you tie this final knot, pull the warp as tight as possible (see #2).

4. The next step is to thread the warp. On a conventional loom you would actually pull the warp threads through the neddles (eye-shaped devices to separate the threads). Neddles ride on harnesses. The harness lifts a certain series of warp threads. So you will have to make a pair of unconventional harnesses—each to lift half of the warp.

For the first harness, to lift odd-numbered threads, us a flat piece of plywood, about 2″ wide by 1″ longer than the inside dimension of the loom. Drill a hole at each end of the stick. Slide the stick under the warp strands that are above the frame. Secure the stick to the side of the loom with a very loosely tied string (see #3 and #4).

For the second harness, you'll need a dowel rod the same length as the stick and a length of contrasting cord. You'll also need a cylindrical object with a slightly larger diameter than the dowel. Tie the string around the object with a square knot. Measure two inches, and tie around the object again. Repeat the process until you have as many loops, plus one, as there are threads under the stick. Push the stick as far to the back of the loom as possible. Place the dowel above the warp, and slip the first loop onto it. Take the entire strand of loops and slide it under the first warp thread under the stick, and up between that thread and its neighbor resting on the stick. Put the next loop on the dowel. Continue this process until each even-numbered warp thread is looped to the dowel. Be sure that the threads running to and from the dowel also fall between strands, one up and one down. When all the loops are on the dowel, spread them out evenly and secure each end loop to the dowel with rubber bands (see #5–8).

The loom is now threaded. When the stick is turned on its side, it will lift half the threads, and when the stick is returned to the resting position, the dowel when raised will lift the other half of the warp.

HELP! HELP!

I think its warp is worse than its woof!

3. warp stick

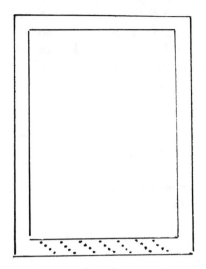

1. frame with nails set at ¼″ intervals

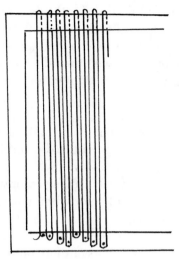

*2. threading the warp
(1st step of dressing the loom)*

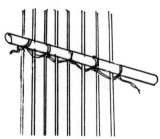

*4. warp stick secured in place—
alternate threads above it*

5. dowel rod

*6. string with loops at
equal intervals*

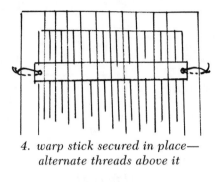

*7. dowel rod with string under
alternate warp threads—
loops on dowel*

WEAVING TECHNIQUE

The technique of weaving to be described is tapestry weaving. This is a weft-faced weave (the weft being the horizontal threads). That means that the warp is completely covered. You can make any kind of shape (circular shapes are very difficult though) by using different colors for each shape desired. You can also make vertical and horizontal stripes in this technique.

1. Before you actually start weaving there is one more thing to do. To help keep the warp spaced evenly, you will have to twine a piece of yarn around the warp threads. The yarn should be 2½ times longer than the width of the warp. Double the yarn and loop it over the first warp thread (half above and half below). Now pull the lower half up and over the next warp thread, while pulling the upper half under the same warp thread. Twist the yarn after each warp thread, and continue to put half the yarn over, and half under each warp thread. Try to keep these twists evenly spaced. When complete, tie the ends of the yarn with a square knot (see #9).

2. Have ready a full-sized full-color sketch of the project (remember to leave 2″–3″ at each end of the total length of the frame). Also, have ready the yarns you intend to use. Knitting yarns, especially bulky ones, are a good choice.

3. Shuttles are flat wooden implements used to hold yarn while weaving. It is not necessary to use shuttles, although they make weaving much easier. Shuttles are obtainable at some yarn stores, but if you cannot find any, you can make them. Use a 2″ wide strip of plywood, about 6″ long. Cut a semicircle at each end. Sand down all rough areas. Wrap as much yarn around the shuttle as you can (see #10).

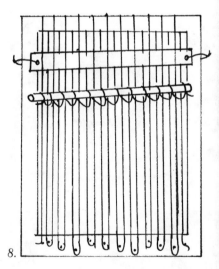

8.

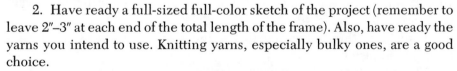

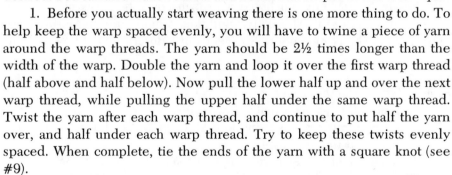

*9. double thread
used to space warp*

10. shuttle—with yarn

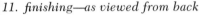

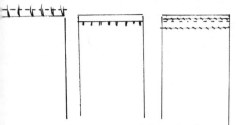

11. *finishing—as viewed from back*

4. Weaving is done by locking in the weft. To weave across the entire width of the warp, lift the dowel so that the threads looped to it rise above the others. Slide the shuttle through (leave a small length of yarn at the starting edge and tuck back to prevent unraveling). Put the dowel down. Turn the stick on its side and slide the shuttle back. Use a wide-toothed comb to push the weft thread down so that it completely covers the warp. Never pull the weft tightly, for this causes the width of the piece to diminish.

    a. Stripes

        horizontal: use one color all the way across the warp until the stripe is the desired height, then use the next color in the same way.

        vertical: use one color when you raise the dowel, and the second color when you raise the stick.

    b. Shapes

        the easiest way to weave shapes, or pictures, is to weave several shots (a shot=once across the warp) with one color in area you desire, and then weave the same number of shots of all the other colors that you wish in the same horizontal area.

5. Finishing is the final touch for your weaving. When you have finished weaving, cut the warp threads at the back of the loom. Slide the stick and the dowel out. Tie the warp threads (two together) as close to the body of the weaving as possible. Then slip the warp threads off the front of the loom and remove the double yarn at the base. Tie the warp threads together as before. You can leave the warp threads showing, as fringe, or cut them back, fold them over, and cover with seam binding (see #11). Projects for consideration:

    1. a hallah or matzah cover
    2. place mats for holidays meals
    3. a tallit bag

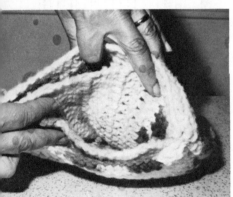

Crotcheted matzah cover

Last Pesah, Lesley Fox crocheted a matzah cover that was used at the communal Seder of the Alternative Religious Community in Marblehead, Mass. (where she is a member). She sends us a description of how she did it:

How I Made a Matzah Cover

    It's a matzah cover—for matzah, what else?

    I crocheted four squares using four kinds of multicolor yarn (because that was all I had in the house).

    I took a piece of matzah to decide on the size of the cover (some matzot are different sizes, you know), and I made each square a little bigger than the piece I used to measure.

    I crocheted three edges together so there would be places in between for three pieces of matzah.

    We put matzah in it and used it for Passover.

    I don't know how long it took to make because I wasn't counting.

    Things to remember: to measure, use matzah not bread.

        Lesley Fox
        ARC
        Age 9

Dance

Introduction

One of the ways Jews have expressed themselves throughout the ages has been through dance. It is perhaps the best-known way that we express our Jewish joy physically. (According to the *Encyclopaedia Judaica*, the high level of interest and development in choreography can be noted by the fact that the Bible has eleven verb forms to describe dancing.)

The spirit of dance is deeply imbedded in tradition. Miriam led the women of the escaping tribes in a victory dance after crossing the Red Sea. The Book of Samuel informs us that dance was an integral part of prophecy. Bands of people followed the prophet and together they joined in dance to work themselves up to heightened states of religious and prophetic consciousness. Psalms 149:3 proclaims: "Let them praise [God's] name in dance." And so we should.

Dance is a beautiful way to focus feelings and show emotions that words alone might strangle. It is a wordless pathway to a mystic union in special moments of ecstacy—a method of opening up to yourself and to other people. It is a participation in universal rhythm, a cosmic mystery.

Dance is a very human expression that combines the body and spirit of the dancer.

In the two millennia that the Jews have wandered over the face of the earth, exiles from their homeland, the dances mentioned in the Bible and Talmud were lost. Since the Jewish tradition prohibits the making of a "sculptured image," there are no pictorial records of how Jews danced. At the turn of the century, however, the seed of a new flowering of folk dance was sown by the exiles returning to Palestine. From many countries in Europe they brought with them the dances of the exile, which they adapted to their new life. The Hora, the national dance of reborn Israel, came originally from Romania, the Krakowiak from Poland, and the Tcherkessia from Russia.

In 1944 a folk dance festival held in Palestine at Kibbutz Dalia gave the country a dramatic realization of the wealth of ethnic material within its own borders. For the first time the many different ethnic groups, including Jews from oriental countries, performed their own authentic dances. Stimulated by this experience, a group of folk dance leaders and teachers began to choreograph and create new dances.

News was brought to Rabbi Moshe Leib that his friend the Rabbi of Berditchev had fallen ill. On the Shabbat he said his name over and over and prayed for his recovery. Then he put on new shoes made of morocco leather, laced them up tight, and danced. A tzaddik who was present said: "Power flowed forth from his dancing. Every step was a powerful mystery. An unfamiliar light suffused the house, and everyone watching saw the heavenly hosts join in his dance" (Martin Buber, *Tales of the Hasidim*).

you should see The Lubavitcher Rebbe and Rabbi Soloveitchik do a pas de deux.

Martin Buber wrote: "To divulge the mystery is called, in the speech of the ancient Greeks as in that of some other primitive peoples, 'to dance it out.'"

In Israel, the two groups preserving a real, authentic Jewish dance style are the Yemenites and the Hasidim. Even though they lived thousands of miles apart, their dancing can be referred to as something specifically Jewish.

The Yemenites

Yemen, which lies at the southern tip of the Arabian Peninsula, became the home of a handful of Jews who fled there after the destruction of the Second Temple. They lived for two thousand years in the heart of a Muslim world, cut off from contact with Western civilization and the mainstream of Jewish life. The Jews of Yemen preserved their fine cultural heritage: from the Arab world they took outward coloration, design, and art forms, but their religion remained authentically Jewish.

After Israel became a state, a prophecy came to pass: "I bore you on eagles' wings and brought you to Me," Exodus 19:4 had foretold. Airplanes became the eagle's wings as the Yemenites were flown to Israel en masse. Bringing with them their richly colorful tradition and folklore, they made a great contribution to the cultural life of Israel, especially in the field of dance. Many of their beautiful movements, steps, and hand gestures were incorporated into the repertory of Israeli folk dance.

Hasidim & other East European Jews

Hasidism, which arose in Eastern Europe in the eighteenth century, used the dance as a religious emotional outlet for the masses. Its spectacular spread made dancing a part of the everyday life of the people. The Hasidic dance, especially in the synagogue, assumed the character of a religious ritual similar to the ecstatic dances of the early prophets.

The founder of Hasidism, Israel ben Eliezer—Baal Shem Tov (Master of the Good Name, 1700–60)—believed that one could reach God not only through prayer but through singing and dancing as well. The Hasidim developed songs and dances that are uniquely Jewish and can be seen and heard to this day wherever Hasidim live. Israeli choreographers used some of their melodies to create dances based on the improvisational movements of the Hasidim.

Other East European Jews, who were not members of the Hasidic sect, also brought their dances with them during the great pre–World War I migration to America. Even though these dances did not play as important a part in their lives as dancing to wordless niggunim did in the life of the Hasidim, they were, and still are, performed at weddings and some holiday celebrations—usually in family surroundings.

Whole segments of the American Jewish community who had been unaware of the richness and depth of their heritage obtained new understanding and appreciation of their culture when, in 1926, the Moscow Habima visited New York with its production of *The Dybbuk*. Although presented in Hebrew, the play, through its magnificent use of gesture and line, created a sensation in the theatrical and dance world. It was the first

The Bible, the Yemenites, and the Hasidim are only some of the sources for the new dances of Israel. The dance steps of other ethnic groups such as the Circassians, Arabs, Druzes, Moroccans, and others are also included in some of these newly created dances.

time that Hasidic movement and dance steps were successfully included in a play in order to emphasize its action. The Beggars' Dance became a famous theater piece.

A second important event occurred shortly afterward, when Maurice Schwartz, in his production of *Yoshe Kalb*, portrayed the renewal that Jewish spiritual life experienced with the advent of Hasidism. This play, too, was outstanding for its dancing, which was choreographed by an American dancer, Lillian Shapero, who was very active in the Jewish theater and also gave her own dance concerts.

For the next thirty years, Jewish theater dance in America thrived in the hands of such pioneers as Benjamin Zemach, Dvora Lapson, Nathan Vizonsky (who organized his own Jewish Ballet Company), Corinne Chochem, Vyts Beliajus, Ruth Zahava, as well as teams like Delakova and Berk and Fibich and Berg.

Gradually interest in Jewish dance faded. In 1974, however, a revival seemed to take place. "A Day of Jewish Dance" was arranged at the 92nd Street YMHA in New York City for the Y's centennial celebration. It included folk dancing, lectures, films, and a concert entitled "Dances on Jewish Themes," choreographed by American dancers Sophie Maslow and Anna Sokolow, and Israeli dancers Zeeva Cohen, Hadassah Badouch, and Hava Kohav.

In addition, Jewish themes began to be introduced into the ballet world. Jerome Robbins created for the City Center Ballet a ballet based on Ansky's play *The Dybbuk*; it was called *Dybbuk Variations*, with music by Leonard Bernstein. Another piece choreographed by Pearl Lang around this time was called *The Possessed* and was also based on Ansky's play. And Eliot Feld, another contemporary Jewish choreographer, created two major Jewish pieces called *Sephardic Song* and *Tzaddik*.

All of these people reflect the growing new interest in utilizing Jewish themes in choreography.

Folk dance in America

In the early days of the Zionist movement in America, dance played a very important part in the youth education program. American Zionist youth

danced the same European dances then popular in Palestine, but they also used Hebrew songs to create dances with a uniquely American flavor, incorporating the swing and zest of American square dancing. The Double Hora, the Dundai, Paam Achat Bachur Yatza, and many more were among the Palestinian dances, as they were called, that had their origins in this country.

After the founding of the state of Israel, Palestinian folk dances gave way to the newly created Israeli folk dances. Mayim, Hine Ma Tov, Kuma Echa, Harmonica, etc. were adopted by the international folk dance circles in America. Y's, community centers, camps, and schools included Israeli folk dancing in their programs.

In addition to all this, dance groups coming from Israel inspired and enriched the American Jewish dance scene. Inbal, the Yemenite dance theater, brought to the United States in 1957, was a smashing success. The Music Hall of Israel visited America, frequently performing Israeli folk dances with a very exciting technique.

Because of all this, interest in Israeli folk dance has spread tremendously all over the United States in the last ten years.

Ironically, Israeli folk dance enjoys greater popularity in America than in Israel. Among American folk dancers its popularity ranks high, exceeded only by Yugoslavian and Greek dances. In colleges where international folk dance is taught, Israeli dances are always included. On some campuses Israeli folk dance is offered as a separate, accredited course. As enthusiasm for folk dance burgeons across the country, Israeli dance is becoming increasingly well known.

What accounts for the popularity of these dances? It is, of course, impossible to offer one definite answer. The dances, created in our lifetime, accommodate our way of expressing feelings through movement. The melodies and rhythms are very catchy, some of the basic steps are easy to learn and to remember. This, however, is only part of the answer. More important, it seems to me, is the strong identification of American youth with Israel; it is this feeling of closeness that gives these dances their special appeal.

The enthusiasm for Israeli folk dance in America has given rise to a novel phenomenon. Israeli folk dance teachers, living in the United States, are choreographing, recording, and teaching new dances all over the country. One can hardly keep up with the rapidly expanding repertory. While all of these new creations are called "folk dance," time alone will tell which ones will ripen into real folk dances. In any case, we are presently witnessing something unique—the accelerated, consciously nurtured development of a folk culture within our own generation.

Performing groups and styles

Dona Rosenblatt, who has been studying, teaching, and performing Israeli dance for years, offers the following comments about styles and performing groups.

Israeli dance, like other kinds of created dance, is a form of expression: self-expression for the choreographer, and an emotional and physical outlet for the dancers. More than that, at its best it preserves parts of the cultures in which Jews have lived. In this way Israeli dance is a record of things that would otherwise be lost in a melting-pot culture.

Here is a list of the various types of Israeli dance:

1. *Sabra dances*: These are exemplified by the Karmon troupe from Israel. Dances of this style are vibrant, free, and fast. These dances are the dances done most by recreational groups and are associated with the free spirit of the Israeli people. There is no special way to dance these dances—except to enjoy them.

Choreographers: Choreographers associated with this style of dance are Ashriel, Karmon, and Rivka Sturman, among others.

Examples: Examples of this style are Harmonica, Kuma Echa, Korim Lanu Lalechet, Hora Nirkoda, and Al Tira. Harvest and shepherd dances also fall into this group: Hacormim, Ez Vakeves, Haroa Haktana, and Shibolet Basadeh.

2. *Romantic dances:* These were created to fulfill a need for ballroom dances and are loosely based on the tango. These dances should be done with grace and a smooth style.

Example: The best example of this type of dance is Dodi Li.

3. *Hasidic dances:* These dances have the feel of the East European shtetl and, contrary to popular belief, are not "shleppy" or silly. When Hasidim danced, it was to express a spirituality, a closeness to God. In the best of these dances the music is joyous (though not boisterous) and the steps and movements are small and concise, with a great deal of inner feeling that radiates outward.

Examples: Examples of this style of dances include Nigun Bialik, Bechatzar Harabbi, and Yeverechecha.

4. *Debkas:* These are the dances of Israel's neighbors, the Arabs, and the style is developed directly from Arab culture. Many of the debkas of Israel, the best of them, are pure Arab dances. The movements are quick, sure, and sharp; the technique is to step on the feet, and then bounce, thus shaking the whole body. A dramatic visual effect is created.

Examples: Examples of this style include Debka Druz, Debka Halel, Hein Yerunan, Hahelech, and Mishal.

Choreographers: The finest Arab dances have been created by Moshiko Halevy. He has spent quite a bit of time among the Arabs, studying their dances.

Note: Not all dances titled Debka are debkas (example: Debka Dayagim) and, conversely, not all debkas have that word in their title.

5. *Yemenite dances:* These are probably the most misunderstood dances in the whole repertoire of Israeli dance. Many people believe that all slow dances are Yemenite-style dances. While it is true that almost all slow dances have Yemenite elements in them, that alone is not enough. The Yemenite step, as it is often taught, is without feeling; that is, the configuration is correct, but the spirit is missing. The Yemenite style, more than any other in Israeli dance, uses the whole body. In slow dances the mood is similar to that of restrained belly dancing—quite soft and undulating—while the faster dances bring to mind the dances of Africa. Words are really not adequate to describe the Yemenite style, although much of the movement was summed up by Moshiko when he said that the Yemenites danced as they did because they did not love the land in which they lived and so danced as if the earth were on fire.

Examples: Examples of the style include Ahavat Hadassah, Et Dodim Kala, and Hashachar (slow) and Ki Hivshiloo (fast).

Dance

These are not for everyone. When they are run seriously and conscientiously they are very challenging. But there is more to performing than simply enjoying the dances. If you like Israeli dancing for fun only, it is best to stay away from performing groups. If you are more serious and committed, then by all means consider joining such a group. Here are a few things you should know.

1. As a member of a performing group, you must be prepared to go to rehearsals on a regular basis.

2. You must always be punctual for rehearsals as well as performances.

3. You and your costumes should always be neat and clean.

4. Most important, you must be ready to do as the director of the group wishes. It is well to remember that the main function of such a group is to perform with precision and as a unit. This means that eleven group members must work together, and that each person will probably have to learn to do some things differently from his/her usual dances. The challenge and excitement come in learning special choreographies and working with other people to create something that audiences will take pleasure in watching.

Forming and directing a group: If you are an accomplished dancer and wish to form a group, there are many things to keep in mind. Most important is that the main function of the group is to perform: to bring the best of Israeli dance to the public in the most aesthetic way possible. In order for the group to perform there must be choreographies. It will be your job to create them and teach them to the dancers. When making a choreography, keep in mind the level of your dancers. Keep things interesting but don't overreach the dancers. You must also choose the music, make tapes that are of good quality, know a bit about sound systems and stage lighting. You should also be something of an amateur psychologist—you will be teaching and correcting people, and it is important not to hurt their feelings if it can be avoided. It is true that you will have a lot on your mind when teaching a choreography, but so will the dancers while they are learning it. Don't be impatient.

Here is my formula for running a rehearsal:

1. *Warmup:*

a. stretching exercises to loosen everyone up;

b. skill building—teaching various elements to give the dancers a chance to learn: jumps, mayim steps, Yemenite steps, turns, etc.;

c. style building—how you want the steps and other movements done; running, leaping, turns, Yemenite steps.

This can take from fifteen minutes to half an hour. The more you can teach in the warmup, the less you have to do later on. For instance, by

teaching the Yemenite steps as you wish to use it in the warmup, you don't have to stop in the middle of teaching the dance to teach that step.

Besides teaching skills during the warmup, you can also give people the opportunity to learn how it feels to do things as a unit (have groups of two or three run, hop, or leap across the room).

2. *Choreographies*: It is important for you, as choreographer, to know exactly what you want. You should devise some system of notation to show both position and movement of the dancers at all times, plus special notes about any body movements that occur. In teaching the choreography:

a. don't try to teach it all in one session;

b. start with the actual dances to be used. Introduce any changes in the steps at this time. If there is more than one dance in the choreography, teach only the one you will working on during that rehearsal;

c. after you have taught the steps and style, begin the choreography. Work on small sections, a phrase at a time, constantly reviewing the parts already learned.

3. After you have spent an hour on a choreography, it is time to move on to something else. I have found that after the warmup, followed by forty-five to sixty minutes' work on a lively choreography, it is a good idea to change the pace. Work for thirty minutes on a slow dance for women, then thirty minutes on a slow dance for men. This makes a good break and gives everyone a rest.

4. End the rehearsal by reviewing everything. The total time of the rehearsal should be two and half to three hours. If it has gone well, everyone will be satisfactorily tired, mentally and physically: the dancers from learning and you from teaching.

Choreography: When creating your sets, it is important to consider what you want. People will not sit thirty minutes watching your dancers doing circle dances. On the other hand, it is best to start simply. The goal is to create a design that moves and changes in interesting and unexpected ways, and with precision. I have found it best to use dances in "families" of style.

1. *Sabra dances*: These should be no longer that three minutes. If longer, the dancers may tire. Also the audience will get restless. Let the dances you choose work for you. Formations can easily be derived from the movements in the dances.

2. *Slow dances*: These can be very effective as a change of pace. A minute and a half or two minutes are about the limit for this type of dance.

3. *Debkas*: Men's dances of this type also provide a change in mood. They should be no longer than two and a half minutes.

4. *Ethnic dances*: These choreographies can be extended to from four

343

Dance

A wall of mirrors in the rehearsal hall is invaluable. The dancers can see how they look and correct themselves, and then internalize the feel of the steps, so that they will always do those steps correctly.

Here's a tip about performance length: when you are hired for a thirty minute show, make it a twenty minute show. People don't realize how long thirty minutes is, and the audience usually gets restless after about twenty minutes. Have an encore ready—just in case I'm wrong.

A word about modern dance
In modern dance, Dona suggests that other criteria operate than do in folk dance. Students of modern dance are taught how to feel the various parts of their bodies from the inside out. There is a great deal of importance attached to the ability to look inside oneself; but this very concern gives rise to various problems. The mystique of great introspection can produce cerebral, disconnected choreography with a dissonant stream-of-consciousness approach that is jarring to the audience and difficult for the dancer. She suggests that the modern dance choreographer choose a theme which can then be interpreted within the context of the dance. She also adds the following suggestions:

1. There is a great deal of material available for themes: something as simple as candlelighting for Shabbat; broad holiday themes—the harvest theme of Sukkot, the Purim story, the rededication of the Temple at Hanukkah; biblical characters and situations—Ruth, Cain and Abel, Jacob and Esau, the golden calf, etc.

2. Look also at midrash for ideas (see Bibliography for Giving a Devar Torah).

3. Choose the music after you have a very basic idea of what you want the total choreography to be. Then work out the piece in detail. Some of the Jewish music available is liturgical—both traditional and modern, Yiddish, Ladino and Yemenite, as well as new modern Hasidic or Israeli folk songs.

4. Again, costumes can be very important. Choose costumes of the period. Ancient Middle Eastern clothing lends itself especially well to modern dance: long flowing and slitted dresses, cloaks and capes, abas and kaffiyehs.

to eight minutes. Hasidic sets are extremely successful. You can add props to set a scene or tell a story. Yemenite sets can be very exciting, provided they are done with finesse and with attention to style points.

It is important to have a clear idea of what the total performance will look like. One thing to remember is that, unless you are very fortunate, most of your performances will not be on a stage. Most groups belong to a community center, a Hillel, or other social service agency. That means that you will be performing in schools, old age homes, temples, churches, and other places of that nature. It also means that your choreographies will have to be interesting up close as well as at a distance. Of course there will be opportunities for you to dance on the stage, too.

Building a repertoire is something that must be done all the time. Ideally, after two years the group should have about fifteen or so choreographies at its disposal.

Music: In order to have the music as you want it, it is necessary to make tapes. Be sure to get the best sound that you can. By using an adjustable turntable you can get the tempo exactly as you want it (most recordings are too slow to perform to).

Once you have a quality recording, copy it on to a reel-to-reel recorder, and keep that tape as your source. Use the original recording for rehearsals. When you put your performance together, record all choreographies on a new cassette in the order that they will be performed.

Start using the rehearsal tape as soon as possible. It gives the dancers a real lift to dance to the music they will use during their performances. It also will help the dancers get accustomed to the sound and the speed of the music.

Costumes: This can be an expensive proposition. Try to find someone in the fabric business who can give you a discount. To figure what you need, allow one and a half to two yards of fabric for each man's shirt, and three to four yards for each dress, plus an average of eight yards of trim per costume. Use a medium-weight material. That way the costumes will hang well and will also be comfortable. Buy wash and wear or no-iron fabric if at all possible. Men's shirts should be long enough to hit the hip bones, and girl's dresses should be mid-knee. Men's slacks must be bought on an individual basis. The dresses, however, can be made in a loose style with a separate belt. That way they can be passed along as some members of the group leave and others join. Build your costume wardrobe slowly: Sabra costumes the first year, then ethnic costumes at the rate of one set per year. Research the ethnic costumes carefully, so that they look authentic (take a look at the *Encyclopaedia Judaica* under "Dress," as well as *A History of Jewish Costume* by Alfred Rubens [New York: Funk & Wagnalls, 1967], $10; also see *Costumes in Patterns and Designs* by W. Tilke [New York: Random House, 1965]). For each set of costumes always try to get enough extra material to be able to make three to five extra—as insurance.

When to perform: It is all-important not to perform before the group is ready. In the first year that may mean taking six months to work up enough numbers and develop enough self-confidence. In each succeeding year you will be able to start performing earlier in the year. You'll have an existing repertoire and a core of returning dancers.

Do as many performances as you feel you can. At peak times of the year that averages about one performance every seven to ten days. Always make sure that you have enough dancers to do a particular performance. Give your dancers as much notice as possible for each performance.

Resources

The two main centers of Israeli folk dance in the United States are in New York and California. On the West Coast folk dance is even more popular and better organized than in the East.

Teachers active in New York City

Fred Berk is the founder and director of the Jewish Dance Division of the 92nd Street YM-YWHA, and also of the Israel Folk Dance Institute of the American Zionist Youth Foundation. Since 1950 he has directed their annual folk dance festival. He has also established leadership training seminars, a record distribution center, *Hora* (a folk dance publication), and an extensive summer program for Americans to study Israeli folk dance in Israel. Among his credentials are many recordings on the Tikva label and a book on Jewish dance entitled *Harikud*.

Fred Berk, Director
Israel Folk Dance Institute
515 Park Ave.
New York, N.Y. 10022

Dvora Lapson was one of the pioneers of Jewish and Israeli folk dance. She recorded many dances under the Israel Music Foundation label. She has published books containing music and instructions for dances in celebration of the Jewish holidays. She also lectures and leads workshops for teachers. Annually, she presents an Israeli folk dance festival for children.

Dvora Lapson
Jewish Education Committee
426 W. 58th St.
New York, N.Y. 10019

Moshe Eskayo, an Israeli dance teacher and choreographer, performs with his own company. He teaches at his studio and has recorded many dances on his own IFC label.

Moshe Eskayo
Café Eucalyptus
746 Broadway
New York, N.Y. 10018

Moshe Itzhak Halevy, known as Moshiko, was for a number of years a member of Inbal, choreographing folk dances which became very popular in Israel and America. Now residing in New York City, he records his dances on his own MIH Records label.

Moshiko
250 W. 15th St.
New York, N.Y. 10011

Teachers active in Los Angeles

Dani Dassa made Israeli folk dance popular on the West Coast. He also created many dances which he recorded on his own label. For many years he has been teaching at Brandeis Camp Institute and is now the owner of an Israeli nightclub.

ARNIE really gets into the dancing, doesn't he.

Dani Dassa
10618 Blythe Ave.
Los Angeles, Calif. 90064

Shlomo Bachar is also very active on the West Coast, creating and recording his own dances on his own label, Hadarim. He also teaches weekly sessions at his folk dance café, Hadarim.

Shlomo Bachar
Café Hadarim
1204 N. Fairfax
Los Angeles, Calif. 90046

The above-mentioned teachers are available for individual workshop weekends. For further information, write to the given addresses.

Where to dance Israeli folk dance

The following lists are necessarily incomplete. We have listed those centers where it is a safe bet that dancing will almost always be going on. Other programs meet less regularly and so have been omitted.

IN NEW YORK

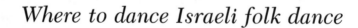

Monday
7:00 to 10:30 P.M.

Columbia University, Earl Hall
117th St. and Broadway, Manhattan
Leaders: Ruth Goodman and Paul Shapiro

Tuesday
8:00 to 10:30 P.M.

Queens College, Student Union Bldg.
Kissena Blvd., Queens
Leaders: Tsufit Baldor and Vicky Bogart

Wednesday
8:00 to 11:00 P.M.

92nd Street YM-YWHA
Lexington Ave., Manhattan
Leader: Fred Berk

Wednesday
8:30 to 10:30 P.M.

Queens Boro Hill Jewish Center
156-03 Horace Harding Expressway
Leader: Shulamit Kivel

Sunday 8:00 to 11:00 P.M.	Daniel Webster Jr. High School 11330 Graham Pl., W. Los Angeles *Leaders*: Jim Kahan, Gary Fox, and Larry Marks
Monday 7:30 P.M.	Intersection 2735 W. Temple *Leader*: Israel Yakovee
Tuesday 8:00 to 11:00 P.M.	Hadarim 1204 N. Fairfax *Leader*: Shlomo Bachar
Wednesday 7:30 to 11:00 P.M.	UCLA Hillel 900 Hilgard Ave. *Leader*: David Katz
Tuesday *Thursday* *Saturday*	Café Danssa 11533 Pico Blvd. *Leaders*: Israel Yakovee and David Pelletz

IN SAN FRANCISCO

Sunday 8:00 to 11:00 P.M.	Ashkenaz 1317 San Pablo Ave., Berkeley *Leader*: Ruth Browns
Tuesday 8:00 to 11:00 P.M.	Hillel Foundation 2736 Bancroft Way, Berkeley *Leader*: Judy Alter
Wednesday 7:30 to 10:30 P.M.	Ner Tamid Congregation 1250 Quintera at 24th Ave. *Leader*: Ruth Browns
Saturday 9:00 P.M. to 1:00 A.M.	Café Shalom JCC at 3200 California St. *Leader*: Ruth Browns

There is dancing going on in many other cities of the United States. The places are too numerous to list, and the places, time, and leaders are constantly changing. Almost every Hillel Foundation has an Israeli folk dance group, as do many Jewish community centers. The Israel Folk Dance Institute has a list of dance leaders in many parts of the country. For this information, as well as any other questions relating to Israeli folk dance, write to:

Israel Folk Dance Institute
515 Park Ave.
New York, N.Y. 10022

Workshops

Two one-week Israeli folk dance workshops are held every June. For details about both write to:

Camp Blue Star
Hendersonville, N.C. 28739

Also in June there is an annual Israeli folk dance weekend in the San Francisco area. For information write to:

Israeli Folk Dance Institute
6273 Chabot Rd.
Oakland, Calif. 94618

Israeli folk dance records are available at:

Louis Stavsky Co.
147 Essex St.
New York, N.Y. 10002

Worldtone, Inc.
56-40 187th St.
Flushing, N.Y. 11365

Zionist Youth Foundation
515 Park Ave.
New York, N.Y. 10022

Books

Berk, Fred. *Ha-Rikud: The Jewish Dance*. New York: American Zionist Youth Foundation and Union of American Hebrew Congregations, 1972.
Includes articles on dance in the Bible as well as on Yemenite and Hasidic dance.
———. *Hasidic Dance*. New York: American Zionist Youth Foundation and Union of American Hebrew Congregations, 1967.
History of Hasidic dance and dance instructions of Hasidic folk dances.
Brin-Ingber, Judith. *Shorashim*. New York: Dance Perspectives, 1970. Describes the development of Israeli folk dance and contains interviews with folk dance choreographers.
All the above books can be ordered from:

American Zionist Youth Foundation
515 Park Ave.
New York, N.Y. 10022

Also of note are two books by Dvora Lapson—both very difficult to obtain:
Folk Dances for Jewish Festivals. New York: 1961. Available from:

Jewish Education Committee
426 W. 58th St.
New York, N.Y. 10019

Dances of the Jewish People. New York: 1954. Available from:

Board of Jewish Education
426 W. 58th St.
New York, N.Y. 10019

Both these books are directed to teachers of children, although certainly some of the dances are suitable for adults.

Bulletins and pamphlets

Hora. Reports on Israeli folk dance activities in Israel and America; free; published by the American Zionist Youth Foundation.

Theater dance in Israel

Israel has four dance companies performing at the present time. The oldest and best-established is Inbal, the Yemenite Dance Theater, which makes frequent appearances in the United States and is always received enthusiastically here.

Batsheva is a modern dance company that was founded about ten years ago by Batsheva de Rothschild, one of the original benefactors of the Martha Graham Dance Foundation. Batsheva is well known in many parts of the world and is considered one of the best existing dance companies. It is now sponsored in part by the Israeli government.

Bat-Dor, also under the sponsorship of Batsheva de Rothschild, was created six years ago. They perform in their own amphitheater, which seats about three hundred people. Amazingly, the members of this company are almost all Israeli-born and -trained. Batsheva and Bat-Dor work with choreographers of international reputation and maintain a very high artistic level.

Classical Ballet is the fourth group. This is the first ballet company to be formed in Israel (1968), although ballet studios have existed there for a number of years. The dancers are Americans and perform on a very high technical level. The Panovs, recent Soviet emigrants, have joined this new ballet company.

These four groups exemplify the high standards that modern and classical dance have attained during the last fifteen years in Israel.

Buber on hitlahavut—rapture

At times it expresses itself in an action that it consecrates and fills with holy meaning. The purest form—that in which the whole body serves the aroused soul and in which each of the soul's risings and bendings creates a visible symbol corresponding to it, allowing one image of enraptured meaning to emerge out of a thousand waves of movement—is the dance. It is told of the dancing of one tzaddik: His foot was as light as that of a four-year-old child, and among all who saw his holy dancing there was not one in whom the holy turning was not accomplished, for in the hearts of all who saw he worked both weeping and rapture in one.

Israeli folk dance records in America

All records include instruction booklets unless otherwise noted.

Israel (folk dances) Label: Israel LP 7
Conducted by Neeman-Elyakum with Theodore Bikel, Rachel Hadass, Martha Schlamme, Mort Freeman. Dance consultant: Dvora Lapson.

Side One:		*Side Two:*	
Leor Chiyuchech		Mezarei Yisrael	
Mehol Hanoar		Vehay Ketz Shatul	
Bat Yiftach		Bat Harim	
Hanava Babanot		Mechol Hagat	
Sherele		Tcherkessia	

Hora Label: Elektra LP 186
With the Oranim Zabar Troupe. Soloist, Geula Gill. Arrangements by Dov Seltzer. Dance supervision: Fred Berk (no instruction).

Side One:	*Side Two:*
Mayim	Hora Mechona
Hine Ma Tov	Dodi Li
Im Hashachar	Bat Hareem
Harmonica	Mechol Ovadya
Iti Milvanon	El Ginat Egoz
Krakowiak	Vedavid

Israel (folk dances) Label: LP 5/6
Conducted by Elyakum Shapiro with Martha Schlamme and Mort Freeman. Dance consultant: Dvora Lapson.

Side One:	*Side Two:*
Mayim	Ken Yovdu
Hanoded	Lech Lamidbar
Hora Agadati	Bo Dodi
Im Hoopalnu	Sovevuni
Malu Asamenu Bar	Hava Netze
	Bmahol

Folk dances of Israel Label: Menorah 204
Music arranged by Dov Seltzer. Singer, Geula Gill. Dance consultant: Rivka Sturman.

Side One:	*Side Two:*
Kol Dodi	Vedavid
Hine Matov	Zemer Lach
Ahavat Hadassah	Kuma Echa
Dodi Tsach	Im Baarazim
Veadom	Hava Netze
Beer Basadeh	Bmachol
Or Chavatsalot	Megadim Lrei

Folk dance in Israel today Label: Collectors Guild CG-638
Israeli and European folk dances. Music by Effy Netzer. Singer, Regina Zarai (no instruction).

Side One:	*Side Two:*
Kuma Eha	Horah Nurim
Hineh Ma Tov	Mazurka
Nigun Atik	Ez Vakevez
Horah Nirkoda	Erev Ba
Bat Hacarmel	Debka Halel
Alexandrovah	Korovushakah
Cherkessia Kfulah	Hamahol Hayvani
Merkavah	Krakoviyak

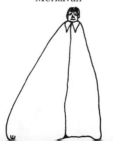

Dance along with Sabras   Label: Tikva LP 69
Arrangements by Ami Gilad. Dance supervision: Fred Berk.

Side One: Hava Netze   *Side Two:*   Al Tira
              Hanokdim   Likrat Shabat
              Hora Neurim   Haroa Haktana
              Taam Haman   Mechol Halahat
              Ez Vakeves   Roe Veroa
              Horat Hasor   Hora Mamtera
              Debkat Habir   Hora—Hava
                                            Nagila

Israel folk dance festival   Label: Tikva LP 80
Arrangements by Ami Gilad with Geula Zohar. Dance supervision: Fred Berk.

Side One: Dayagim   *Side Two:*   Bat Arad
              At Vaani   Ki Tinan
              Al Tiruni   Debka Gilboa
              El Hatal   Nad Ilan
              Yesh Et Laamol   Eretz Zavat Chalav
                                             Debka Rafiach
                                             Scotch

Dance with Rivka   Label: Tikva 98
Music arranged and directed by Shai Burstyn. Dance consultant: Rivka Sturman.

Side One: Erev Ba   *Side Two:*   Hashual
              Lean Noshevet   Hava Netze
                Haruach   Bmachol
              Syn-Co-Pe   Israeli Mixer
              Israeli Mazurka   Debka Leadama
              Hora Simchat   Ani Ledodi
                Heamel   Nearez Bhol
              Jonati   Mishlat

Debka   Label: Tikva LP 100
Arrangements by Ami Gilad. Dance supervision: Fred Berk.

Side One: Debka Halel   *Side Two:*   Zemer Atik
              Debka Debka   Ma Navu
              Debka Daluna   Hora Nirkoda
              Hein Yerunan   Kalu Raglayim
              Debka Dayagim   Eten Bamidbar
              Debka Druz   Niguno Shel Yossi

Dance for fun   Label: Tikva 104
Music arranged and conducted by Shai Burstyn. Singer, Geula Zohar. Dance consultant: Ayalah Goren.

Side One: Mi Yivne Bayit *Side Two:*   Hora Eylat
              Hamekholelet   Et Dodim Kala
              Bona Habanot   Uvanu Batim
              Debka Knan   Rikud Hakad
              Kaagadat Rivka   Debka Hakatsir
              Nitsaney Shalom   Debka Hakhamor
              Hoppa Hey

Dances for children   Label: Tikva 106
Music arranged and directed by Shai Burstyn. Singer, Ahuva Zadok. Dance consultant: Fred Berk.

Side One: Hora Medley   *Side Two:*   Hora Medura
              Simi Yadech   Havu Lanu Yayin
              El Harahat   Mechol Hagat
              Kuma Echa   Patch Dance
              Tcherkessia   Mayim
              Yemina, Yemina   Shibolet Basadeh
              Vedavid Yefei   Vehaya Keeitz
                Eynayim   Shatul

Potpourri   Label: Tikva 117
Music arranged by Ami Gilad. Dance consultant: Fred Berk.

Side One: Machar   *Side Two:*   Hacormim
              Shiru Hashir   Debka Dalia
              Bat Hacarmel   Bat Tsurim
              Debka Kurdit   Mi Yitheini Ohf
              Ana Halach   Vaynikehu
                Dodech   Inbalim
              Frelach
              Keshoshana

Panorama   Label: Tikva 140
Musical arrangements: Ami Gilad. Dance supervision: Fred Berk.

Side One: Shiboley Paz   *Side Two:*   Hadoodaim
              Nitzanim   Uri Zion
              Hora Bialik   Vayiven Uziyahu
              Tfillat Hashachar   Adarim
              Hagavia   Hora Chassidit
              Kumi Ori   Te Veorez

Rikudey-Am   Label: Tikva 138
Music arranged by Ami Gilad. Dance consultant: Fred Berk. This record is recommended for the teacher. Side One: Dances for children; Side Two: Basic popular dances.

Side One: Mechol Hagat   *Side Two:*   Harmonica
              El Harahat   Zemer Atik
              Shibolet Basadeh   Mechol Ovadya
              Patch Dance   Vedavid
              Hora Medura   Kuma Echa
              Yemina, Yemina   Dodi-Li
              Tcherkessia   Hine Ma Tov

New folk dances of Israel   Label: Tikva 142
Musical arrangements: Uri Hodorov. Dance supervision: Moshe Eskayo.

Side One: Shiboley Paz   *Side Two:*   Shetey Yonim
              Haeer Beafor   Simchu-Na
              Hacormim   Ma Avarech
              Befat Hakfar   Dror Yikra
              Debka Skayo   Salach
              Orcha Midbar   Baer Basadeh

Israeli folk dance party   Label: Tikva 145
Musical arrangements: Shai Burstyn. Dance supervision: Fred Berk.

Side One:		Side Two:	
Ki Hivshiloo			Dror Yikra
Im Bearazim			Yibanei
Mechol Hadvash			Hamikdash
Bechazar Harabbi			Debka Bedouit
Kissufim			Shimu-Shimu
Rav Brachot			Debka Chag
			Shuv Yotze
			Hazemer

Hasidic dances   Label: Tikva 147
Musical arrangements: Ami Gilad, Shai Burstyn, and Yossi Shlomer. Dance consultant: Fred Berk.

Side One:	Side Two:	
Bechazar Harabbi		Likrat Shabbat
Frelach		Niguno Shel Yossi
Chassene Tanz		Hora Chassidit
Tzadik Katamar		Patch Dance
Zemer Atik		Nigun
Hora Bialik		Mitzvah Tanz

Souvenir   Label: Tikva 148
Musical arrangements: Shai Burstyn. Dance consultant: Fred Berk.

Side One:	Side Two:	
Gozi-Li		Mitzva Tanz
Tslil Zugim		Hora Chemed
Lamnatseach		Pashtu Kvasim
Bein Nhar Prat		Mishal
Ronne Bat Tsion		Yarad Dodi Legano
Harimon		Tzadik Katamar

Israeli folk dances   Label: Hadarim LP 1
Presented by the Hadarim. Dance supervised by Sholomo Bachar. Musical arrangements: Eldad Peery (no instruction).

Side One:	Side Two:	
Hashachar		Erev Shel
Hoppa Hey		Shoshanim
Erev Ba		Lean Noshevet
Larokdim Heidad		Haruach
Hora Medura		Bat Yiftach
Ma Navu		Debka Rafiach
		Shibolet Basadeh
		Hora Eylat

Back from Israel   Label: Hadarim 3
Musical arrangements: Toby David, Eldad Peery. Dance consultant: Shlomo Bachar.

Side One:	Side Two:	
Hashachar		Hadarim
Hora Chemed		Sham Hareh Golan
Dror Yikra		Hora Or
Hora Chefer		Tzadik Katamar
Bein Nehar Prat		Ahavat Hadassa
Mishal		Kissufim

I remember   Label: Hadarim LP 4
Music arrangements: Toby David. Dance consultant: Shlomo Bachar.

Side One:	Side Two:	
Korim Lanu		Tzama Tzama
Lalechet		Tzur Mishelo
Yeverechecha		Debka Magen
Ahavat Hadassah		Mama Lo Raiti
No. 2		Israel, Israel
Nigun Nigunim		Shecharchoret
Misgav		
Hinach Yaffa		

Carmit   Label: Hadarim 6
Musical arrangements: Toby David. Dance consultant: Shlomo Bachar.

Side One:	Side Two:	
Sisu Vsimcha		Ronu Tzadikim
Hashkediot		Sulam Yaakov
Debka Oz		Debka Tzlil
Yira Ami		Kol Rina
Ki Ashamerah		Shir Hagalil
Haktana Hismika		Ein Adir
Hora Hadera		

Naarah   Label: IFC 1
Musical arrangements: Shlomo Shai. Dance consultant: Moshe Eskayo.

Side One:	Side Two:	
Naarah		Debka Bnot Hakfar
Livavteenee		Ad Or Haboker
Debka Skayo		Al Gemali
Ma Avarech		Nitzanim
Sapari		Elem Vesusato
Uzi		Zemer Ikarim

Kadima   Label: IFC 2
Musical arrangements: Shlomo Shai. Dance consultant: Moshe Eskayo.

Side One:	Side Two:	
Reiach Tapuach		Debka Oud
Hashir Sheli		El Ginat Egoz
Simchu Na		Sisu Et
Harishut		Yerushalayim
Shtu Adarim		Bein Nahar Prat
Yamin Usmol		Shibolim

Folkdances of Israel   Label: IFC 3
Musical arrangements: Toby David. Dance consultant: Moshe Eskayo.

Side One:	Side Two:	
Shir-Hachatuna		Debka Irit
Yedid Nefesh		Haeer Beafor
Befat Hakfar		Shalom
Simchat Heamel		Mi Emek Legivah
Orcha Bamidbar		Salach
Ad Or Haboker		Simcha

Dance with Moshiko (a double record)   Label: MIH-1
Musical arrangements: Albert Piamenta. Dances by Moshiko.

RECORD 1

Side One:	Side Two:	
Debka Uriya		Debka Bedouit
Et Dodim Kala		Lemaana
Ki Hivshiloo		Et Kashet Li
Eshkolot		Beabaya
Tfillat Hashachar		Hareshut
Hamecholelet		Hahelech

RECORD 2

Side One:	Side Two:	
Mechol Hadvash		Mishal
En Adir		Kissufim
Debka Knaan		Gaaguim
Hora Chemed		Dror Yikra
Debka Kurdit		Smadar

Dance with Moshiko   Label: MIH-3
Musical arrangements: Albert Piamenta. Dances by Moshiko.

Side One:	Side Two:	
Betof Utzlil		Al Yadil
Tama Temima		See Yona
Vesamahta		Marhaba
Behagecha		Ylelat Haruach
Eshal Elohay		Tinten Banat
Hamavdil		Debka Rafiyach
Ya Abud		

Plays for the Jewish audience

Jewish groups looking for appropriate material for amateur theater productions face special problems. Until the first Yiddish plays emerged in the last quarter of the nineteenth century, there was virtually no such thing as a Jewish play. Although dating from the sixteenth century, the Purim spiel—generally a comic group performance given at the Megillah reading or at the Purim meal—never gave rise to any other dramatic form in Jewish life. Yiddish plays emerged independently of the Purim spiel, developing out of modern Yiddish culture rather than from any ritual celebration. The cloyingly sentimental or melodramatic plays spawned by the Yiddish theater have, with a few exceptions, worn badly with time. Only in the twentieth century have plays of Jewish relevance figured in the non-Yiddish-speaking theater—and the number of these is still limited.

There is also the special problem of appropriateness in dramatic material, even among the Jewish-content plays that do exist. Amateur performances, often the work of synagogues or other Jewish community organizations, are likely to serve more as a communal celebratory function than as an artistic one. The point is to create a cultural event that is, essentially, a general affirmation of Jewish identity. Groups therefore seek material that is pleasing, or at least comfortable, rather than provocative and disturbing. This desire for a communal Jewish affirmation is completely understandable, but it does lead the group away from a play chosen for artistic considerations. Thus a synagogue group would probably shy away from *The Man in the Glass Booth*, which conjectures about the potential in all of us for becoming an Eichmann, in favor of something like *The Diary of Anne Frank*, an artistically less interesting play in which our status as the "good guys" is never in doubt.

Fees

Performance of professional plays entails payment of royalty fees to the agency representing the playwright. Plays in considerable demand, like *Fiddler on the Roof*, will cost more than less familiar ones, and you pay according to the number of performances you intend to give. An amateur group interested in a certain play usually begins by obtaining a book copy. The printed version probably will include the name and address of the agency necessary to contact in order to get permission to perform. Some of the plays discussed here are available in what are called acting editions. These are published by the agency holding the rights to the play and include staging information from the original professional production, which can sometimes be useful to an amateur group. Acting editions are usually stocked only in stores specializing in dramatic material such as:

> **Drama Book Shop**
> **150 W. 52nd. St.**
> **New York, N.Y. 10022**

Some agencies will send out script copies as a service covered by the cost of the performing rights. Another practice is to send what are known as *sides* instead of complete scripts. A book of sides includes all the words spoken by a single character, together with all that character's line cues. Thus an actor holding sides has only his own lines and cues but lacks the rest of the play. Amateurs, particularly children, may find sides difficult to work with. Frequently, an agency will send only one copy of a script, in which case the performing group has to provide copies for its actors and staff, using Xerox, mimeograph, or ditto machines.

Available plays

What follows is a brief and necessarily superficial survey of significant plays of Jewish interest. I deal only with plays available in English and, with a few exceptions, obtainable in book form. (Bibliographic information on all the plays I mention is presented at the end of the chapter.)

Holocaust

I have already touched on one of the major genres of modern Jewish drama, the Holocaust. *The Diary of Anne Frank*, by Frances Goodrich and Albert Hackett, is a stage version of the famous diary. Its advantages for amateur production include its single unit set and the accessibility of its characters to actors of amateur talent. The *Anne Frank* type of play is in a sense an act of theatrical memorial, and laudable for that reason; nonetheless, it is less than outstanding art. Yet that very aspect of it makes it excellently suited for a certain type of amateur theatrics.

A play of comparable merit is Arthur Miller's *Incident at Vichy*, which is about an assemblage of prisoners waiting to be interrogated by the Nazis in occupied France. Again, the play occurs within a single setting and the technical demands are minimal. There is an abundance of good roles but no parts for women (a frequent problem in picking material). The play demands skilled actors who can play scenes of extreme emotion and compensate for the occasional stiltedness of Miller's dialogue. Although it aspires to an examination of the nature of moral responsibility, the play's depth is limited to coming down squarely in favor of personal sacrifice for the good of others. Nevertheless, its affirmation of traditional verities recommends it, like *Anne Frank*, for certain amateur situations.

A drama of a very different order, *The Man in the Glass Booth*, by Robert Shaw, imagines an atrocities trial similar to the Eichmann proceedings in which evidence mounts that the man in the defendant's seat isn't the accused at all but a Jewish refugee impersonating the Nazi officer for reasons of his own. A nonprofessional group interested in this play should carefully consider the sort of audience it wishes to draw and the nature of the theatrical experience it intends to offer. *The Man in the Glass Booth* is a play of intriguing ideas written with great intelligence and wit, but one that will prove distressing to some audiences. While it is, I think, an expression of horror at mankind's capacity for cruelty, it suggests that one can only really affirm moral responsibility after having confronted the fragility of one's own complacent constructs of good and evil. The play's dramatic strategy depends largely on blasphemous humor and a genuinely disturbing irony. It is also dramatically difficult, with a central role that demands a virtuoso performance. The fifteen or so other parts, including roles for three women, remain very much in the shadow of the main role. This is not a work that can celebrate the positive and unified identity of a Jewish audience. Instead, it ends by throwing each audience member back on his/her own resources.

One of the best pieces of Holocaust drama for amateur performance does not, in fact, come from the professional theater. David Roskies's *Nightwords* is not a play in the conventional sense but a dramatic collage, drawing on sources ranging from traditional Jewish texts to secular Western literature and organized in the form of a memorial service. Although mostly in English, the work contains excerpts in Hebrew and Yiddish, accompanied in the printed text by transliteration and translation. The piece works either as an actual service, with parts divided among the participants, or as a staged dramatic performance. Its abstract format allows amateurs to forgo elaborate sets and production facilities and creatively incorporate dance, pantomime, and music according to their own desires and resources. A nonprofessional group can, with *Nightwords*, seek a level of achievement suitable to its ability without being forced to mimic a professional production that may be out of its range. For $1 per single copy (cheaper in bulk), *Nightwords* is available from:

Bnai Brith Hillel
1640 Rhode Island Ave. N.W.
Washington, D.C. 20036

A recent work growing out of the tradition of the Holocaust play is Elie Wiesel's *Zalman, or The Madness of God*, a drama about modern Soviet Jewry. *Zalman* is an untidy, occasionally awkward play which, through sheer passion, achieves a memorable power despite its flaws. The roles of the rabbi who disobeys the Russian authorities by refusing to keep his agony a secret, and Zalman, his seemingly crazed shammash, require actors of uncommon ability. *Zalman* is, so far, the only significant work in a fictional mode about Soviet Jewry.

Class plays

Jewish theater, like Jewish fiction, has its proletarian genre, the chief American practitioner of which was Clifford Odets. *Awake and Sing*, the play for which Odets is probably best remembered, has lost its force as a socialist call-to-arms, but still works as a very pleasant comedy-drama about the dreams for a better life of a Bronx Jewish family. The Jewishness of this play is implicit, the characters clearly a product of their ethnic culture but never raising it as an issue. Although *Awake and Sing* was written for the Stanislavsky-oriented actors of the Group Theatre in the thirties, its transformation with time from a realistic drama to a romantic nostalgia piece makes it accessible to the talents of untrained performers.

Much more bitter, complex, and difficult for Americans to perform than Odets's work are the Jewish "kitchen-sink" dramas of British playwright Arnold Wesker. Wesker, who in his *Wesker Trilogy* writes about English families of socialist, proletarian Jews, has his characters grow from the innocent idealism of the thirties into the disillusionment of the late fifties. Wesker is a saddened idealist-turned-realist, and his work suggests the pain of his metamorphosis. Like the people of Odets's play, Wesker's characters project an implicit Jewishness, not only in their occasional Yiddishisms but also in their moral obsessions. They seem to take their ethnicity for granted, apparently seeing it as a fact of life neither to be fought for nor denied. Because of their realistic lower-class British setting, the plays of *The Wesker Trilogy (Chicken Soup with Barley, Roots,* and *I'm Talking about Jerusalem)*, call for the most proficient American amateurs who can convincingly create an exotic milieu.

Yiddish plays

Another significant body of Jewish drama is either the product of the Yiddish theater or is based on Yiddish literary material. Virtually all Yiddish plays of substance that have been translated into English are included in Joseph C. Landis's anthology *The Great Jewish Plays* (New York: Horizon Press, 1966). The volume contains *The Dybbuk, God of Vengeance, Green Fields, King David and His Wives,* and *The Golem*.

The Dybbuk by S. Anski is probably the best-known play of the Yiddish theater. It remains a play of major stature, a challenging but feasible project for talented amateurs. Anski relates the story of the exorcism of a young man's tormented spirit from the body of the bride denied him in life.

A group undertaking *The Dybbuk* should consider the play's potential for spectacle and visual impact: choreography, music, and special effects that can enhance its somber and sometimes grotesque pageantry. Actors in *The Dybbuk* require considerable emotional range, but character motivation is generally straightforward and accessible.

God of Vengeance by Sholem Asch is a melodrama about a Jewish pimp who tries to insulate his virginal daughter from the sordidness of his life. Unaccustomed as we are to the notion of Yiddish pimps and prostitutes, the play now seems something of a curio, especially when it tosses in a dash of lesbianism for good measure. Still, Asch's writing has emotional substance and *God of Vengeance* may be worth reviving as a sort of museum piece. The cast consists of four men and seven women, with the role of the pimp making particular demands on an actor's emotional depth.

Green Fields, a sentimental light drama by Peretz Hirschbein, also survives primarily as a curiosity. Its story of young love in a pastoral world of almost universal goodwill may for some be a welcome relief from the less comforting perspectives of our own lives, but many will find it sentimentally cloying or unendurably bland. Actors of charm and vitality in the five male and five female roles may be able to infuse *Green Fields* with sufficient appeal to make it worthwhile.

I find *King David and His Wives* by David Pinski to be the biggest surprise in the Landis volume, a highly ironic usage of the King David legends as a springboard for an examination of the tensions between love, sex, and moral responsibility. The play is divided into five episodes, each involving a separate romantic or sexual encounter. Purists seeking a traditional telling of the David legends will be disappointed. Pinski takes liberties with the stories for his own purposes, setting up sexual aspiration as a metaphor for the striving necessary to all great achievement. Actors doing this play must be verbally adept enough to overcome the weight of the formal and biblical phrasing that characterizes much of the dialogue. Like *The Man in the Glass Booth*, this is not a play for all audiences, but worth doing under the right circumstances.

The last play in Landis's volume is the most difficult, both dramatically and literarily. *The Golem* by H. Leivick is a long, overwritten play in verse, fascinating nonetheless for its richness and depth. This version of the famous legend of a Prague rabbi and the clay man he brings to life juggles a host of themes, particularly various aspects of moral accountability, private, political, and spiritual. *The Golem* stands on its own as a literary work, but its length necessitates radical editing when done in performance. Stemming, like *The Dybbuk*, from the tradition of expressionistic theater, Leivick's play begs for a visually impressive production. A large cast of skilled actors could do a service both to theater and to Jewish culture by bringing *The Golem* to life again.

Two of the best pieces around for Jewish amateur production—*The Theater of Peretz*, by Isaiah Sheffer, and *The World of Sholem Aleichem* (which consists of three one-act plays: *A Tale of Chelm, Bontsche the Silent,* and *The High School*)—are entertaining and don't make excessive demands on the performers. *The Theater of Peretz* is a collection of short pieces by I. L. Peretz. While it was written for three actors, who play different roles in each segment, there is no reason not to involve more actors as desired. The simple storytelling format of the play (no sets are called for) makes it possible to include pantomime, dance, and music, and provides an outlet for whatever ingenuity the director can draw upon. Both the Peretz and Sholem Aleichem plays are excellent for high school or youth group dramatics.

Sholem Aleichem's stories are, of course, also the basis for *Fiddler on the Roof. Fiddler* has the disadvantage of overexposure and at the moment not too many people are eager to run another production of it. It is also unfortunate that so many tend to view it as the height of Jewish culture (Sholem Aleichem, after all) and as a realistic embodiment of Sholem Aleichem's world. It is an affable enough piece of theater, but its heart is closer to Broadway than to the shtetl. Still, it is a perfectly suitable play for an amateur group with musical resources that wants a safe and familiar commodity.

A much less known musical is *The Education of Hyman Kaplan* by Benjamin Zavin, which is based on the short stories of Leo Rosten about a Jewish immigrant learning English in night school. The show's humor is gentle and affectionate, and the play itself entirely pleasant, if not grippingly memorable.

A very amusing musical, *The Wise Men of Chelm* by Susan Nanus, is not in print as a book but can be obtained from the author's agent. This short play (it takes about an hour to perform), based on the traditional Jewish folktales about a town of fools, is excellent for young actors and serves nicely for adults too.

Still another musical, *Joseph and His Amazing Technicolor Dream Coat*, has been given frequent amateur performances. This mod-rock rendition of the Joseph story is the early work of Tim Rice and Andrew Webber, who later created *Jesus Christ Superstar. Joseph* has christological overtones of its own. But the work offers an excellent framework for theatrical inventiveness if a group is willing to ignore the hint that the coat of many colors is a metaphor for the coming of Christ. Although *Joseph* was performed in its original British production as a full evening, complete with dialogue, only the music and lyrics are available in the U.S. These are written in cantata form, constituting a self-sufficient piece even without dialogue, but the performing time is only about forty-five minutes. There is no need to leave it as simply a choral presentation; an inventive director or choreographer can give the piece an effective dramatic and musical stag-

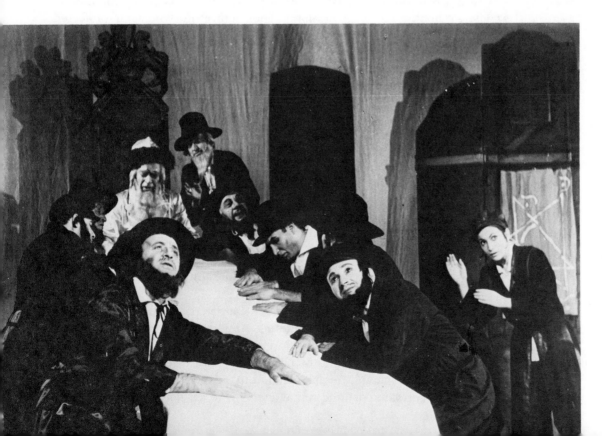

ing. Some find the unsophisticated level of the rock score irritating (those who like it best are people who don't generally like rock at all), but the music is fun enough if you don't ask too much of it.

Playwright Paddy Chayefsky also has a play based on biblical material, *Gideon*. The play purports to make a statement about humanism and theology but cannot really bear the weight of its own philosophical pretensions. Chayefsky's technique is largely parodic, turning God's emissary into a rambling bore and making Gideon a bit of a ninny. *Gideon* requires a large cast, the principal roles being male, plus male and female supernumeraries; the part of the angel calls for an excellent actor of verbal skill. Chayefsky is a good enough theater craftsman to keep things fairly entertaining, even though the play's intellectual aspirations run into trouble.

A more satisfying play by Chayefsky is *The Tenth Man*, his turn on the dybbuk myth. Unlike *Gideon*, this play succeeds quite nicely on its own terms, which are those of comedy and light drama. The setting is an Orthodox synagogue in Long Island, the characters familiar but colorful, and the style accessible to amateur performers. The role of the girl who appears to be possessed is the only female role in the play but probably the most difficult. *The Tenth Man* can be charming entertainment.

Some general advice for getting an amateur group together

If you are interested in drama and want to begin an amateur group, the task is not as difficult as you might think.

Get together with one or two friends who share your interest (preferably some with talent) and then figure out if you want to team up with any existing institution—e.g., Hillel, local synagogue or havurah, community center, school, etc.—or go it alone. Then figure out who your projected audience is and scale your ambitions accordingly (if you think you'll need money, apply to the institution that you team up with, if any). Then:

1. Choose a script.

2. Find a director. Frequently you can find a good amateur who has a sense of the role of the director and will volunteer time. Try borrowing or spiriting someone away from a college dramatic group or a community theater organization.

3. Round up a production staff based on the director's designated needs. Probably the director will want:

    a. a stage manager, who takes care of administration matters, acts as a liaison between the director and production staff, and takes staging notes at rehearsals;

    b. set builders—try to hunt up people with talent in painting and carpentry;

    c. lighting and sound people, who should have skill in electronics.

4. Procure the necessary equipment. Large cities usually have rental agencies that specialize in stage-lighting equipment. Local schools or colleges sometimes have equipment they are willing to lend.

5. Use the clothes owned by cast members or else try to borrow costumes from a synagogue, Jewish community center, or other organization. Otherwise, there are costume rental agencies to service your needs.

One or two other things: don't try to rush a play through. Make sure you have had enough rehearsal before you venture before an audience. And if you're looking around for audiences (and even if you're not) don't neglect your local old age or nursing home if the play is appropriate. The audience is sure to respond positively—and anyway it's a mitzvah.

Bibliography

Chayefsky, Paddy. *Gideon.* Dramatists Play Service Acting Edition, 1961.
———. *The Tenth Man.* New York: Samuel French Acting Edition, 1960.
Goodrich, Frances, and Hackett, Albert. *The Diary of Anne Frank.* New York: Samuel French Acting Edition, 1958.
Landis, Joseph C. *The Great Jewish Plays.* New York: Horizon Press, 1966. Includes *The Dybbuk, God of Vengeance, Green Fields, King David and His Wives,* and *The Golem.*
Miller, Arthur. *Incident at Vichy.* New York: Samuel French Acting Edition, 1966.
Nanus, Susan. *The Wise Men of Chelm.* Music by Wayne Alpert. Available from Sterling Lord Agency, 660 Madison Ave., New York, N.Y. 10016.
Odets, Clifford. *Awake and Sing.* Included in *Great American Plays of the 1930's.* New York: Dell paperback.
Perl, Arnold. *The World of Sholom Aleichem.* New York: Samuel French Acting Edition, 1953.
Rice, Tim and Webber, Andrew. *Joseph and His Amazing Technicolor Dream Coat.* Available only on recording, with lyrics included in the album. Specter Records.
Roskies, David. *Nightwords.* Published by Bnai Brith Hillel, 1640 Rhode Island Ave. N.W., Washington, D.C. 20036.
Shaw, Robert. *The Man in the Glass Booth.* New York: Grove Press, 1968. Also in Samuel French Acting Edition.
Sheffer, Isaiah. *The Theater of Peretz.* New York: Samuel French Acting Edition. 1964.
Stein, Joseph. *Fiddler on the Roof.* Music by Jerry Bock, lyrics by Sheldon Harnick. Pocket Books, 1965.
Wesker, Arnold. *The Wesker Trilogy.* Includes *Chicken Soup with Barley, Roots,* and *I'm Talking about Jerusalem.* New York: Penguin paperback, 1964.
Wiesel, Elie. *Zalman, or the Madness of God.* New York: Random House, 1974.
Zavin, Benjamin Bernard. *The Education of Hyman Kaplan.* Music and lyrics by Paul Nassan and Oscar Brand. Chicago: Dramatic Publishing Co., 1968.

Catalogs of plays

1. Scripts of the "Eternal Light" programs can be obtained for 50¢ apiece. There are two free catalogs one of the radio scripts and one of the TV scripts. Both are annotated. Write to:

Dept. of Radio & TV
Jewish Theological Seminary of America
3080 Broadway
New York, N.Y. 10027

2. YIVO Institute for Jewish Research has lists of Yiddish plays. Write to them (in English or Yiddish) at:

YIVO
1048 Fifth Ave.
New York, N.Y. 10028

3. The National Jewish Welfare Board has an Israel Program Resource with suggestions for plays. This is obtainable for $2 (prepaid) from:

The Publication Service
National Jewish Welfare Board
15 E. 26th St.
New York, N.Y. 10010

Note: The "Eternal Light" scripts range from bad to good. In general, stay away from scripts dealing with biographies, especially "heroes of the Conservative movement"-type scripts. Some of the better scripts are adaptations of stories by Peretz, etc.

Choral Music: How to Organize a Jewish Choir

Singers

 The first step is to gather singers. Although four people are technically enough to sing a large percentage of the choral repertoire, they will hardly produce a choral sound. Unlike a pop singing group, a choir consists of more than one voice per part. Two, three, and four voices singing each part will begin to sound like a choir, but only very accomplished singers can manage to sustain a beautiful *choral* sound with so few singers. The obvious alternative is to find as many people as possible: "The more the merrier" certainly holds true here; with many singers to call on you're not likely to be caught on a rainy night with no choir, as you might if there were only two people to a part.

Of course there are also some disadvantages to large groups. For one thing, a huge group can be physically unwieldy, as well as difficult to handle musically. It is hard to refine the sound of a large group, and an abundance of really good singers is rare—especially in a beginning group aimed at attracting interested amateurs. The notion that a few good singers will support a fledgling group is true up to a point, but in the end the poor singers will be heard, undermining the quality of the whole.

With the establishment of the state of Israel there has been an ever-increasing interest in all varieties of Jewish music. The natural love that all people have for singing has contributed to a special growth in the popularity of Jewish choral music; wherever there is a community of Jews there is likely to be an interest in organizing a Jewish choir. How does one go about it?

Recruitment

The individual imagination and resource of the choir's organizers will determine how singers are recruited. A likely base of operations is the local college, particularly the Hillel organizations (which may also be approached for rehearsal space—a necessity that can't be overlooked). Notices of rehearsal times can be announced in local newspapers and posted all over the campus and the city: in kosher butcher shops, restaurants, bookstores, synagogues—the possibilities are limitless. The best publicity, though, may be word of mouth. People who have friends in the group or who hear the group sing (once a nucleus has been gathered from other sources) make the likeliest candidates for new membership, and everyone associated with the group should be encouraged to bring in new people.

Classification

A new group eager to get going will be tempted to accept anyone who expresses the slightest interest in singing. At some point it may become necessary to institute a sort of audition, at least to root out the many nice people who simply can't sing! How rigorous the audition becomes will depend on how "professional" the group aims to be, but some way of classifying singers is always necessary.

The standard breakdown of vocal ranges for which most (though not all) choral music is written, is SATB from high to low—soprano, alto, tenor, bass. Assuming one's singers have reached puberty, the first two of these are women's voices, the last two men's (although there are many women who sing best in the tenor range). All scores for chorus will indicate the division of the parts, always from highest to lowest: thus a score labeled SSATBB calls for two soprano parts (the first, or higher, sopranos, and the second, or mezzo-sopranos, meaning "middle sopranos"), one part each of alto and tenor, and two bass parts (again, the first is the higher, or "baritone" part, the second, the lower bass part). A woman who sings higher than anyone she knows is not necessarily a soprano—she may have only low altos for friends. Similarly, the fellow who screeches may not really be a tenor, while the one who hides in the security of the low notes may not be a true bass. The only way to know is to check each singer's range.

The following are the various ranges that a singer should be able to handle:

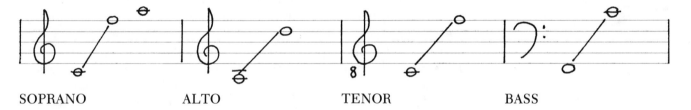

SOPRANO   ALTO   TENOR   BASS

(Note that the tenor part is written in the treble clef. The "8" under the clef means that the note sounds an octave below the one written.)

Of course there are parts calling for the singer to sing beyond either end of his/her range, but these are exceptional.

Musicality

While you're listening for range, you will also of course be listening for quality in your singers. A good voice does not always make a good musician—and you are also looking for some sign of musicality in your singers. A good way to check for musicality is to "test the ear" of your prospective chorister: play some groups of random pitches on any available instrument (a piano is suggested) and ask the auditionee to sing them back. The relative success or failure of this experiment will tell you a great deal about the innate abilities of this singer, all vocal considerations aside. (To be fair, be sure to play these random pitches within the singer's range.) A person who can't sing especially well but has a great ear may be an asset that a good but unmusical singer couldn't be.

The same is true of sight-readers. Sight-reading—the ability to sing on sight music that the singer doesn't know—is a skill that adds to the desirability of any singer; since few amateurs have really learned to sight-read,

Most people have difficulty singing their highest or lowest note on call; often that note isn't sung at all but simply "hit," and undesirably so. The easiest way to check true range is to have the singer sing scales up or down, going progressively higher or lower each time. By the way, remember to check the bottom of a soprano's range as well as the top of the bass's—you may both be surprised by what you discover.

however, lack of this ability shouldn't be of any particular concern if the singer has a good voice and ear.

Blending and balancing

Having put your singers into the proper categories and evaluated their musicality, you are faced with the problem of making them into a choir. The ideal of a choir is to produce *one* sound per vocal section, not many individual ones. This is a problem of blending, and some voices just don't mesh well with others. Choral singing means compromising the individuality of the singer to achieve one unified sound, and vocal quirks have to be kept under control or eliminated. Very thin, penetrating voices, or husky, almost hoarse-sounding qualities will stand out. People who have done extensive solo singing have often developed personal styles that include habits like "swooping" from one note to the next or "playing with" (changing) rhythms. None of these practices belong in a choir.

After finding the singers you feel will sound right in one section, you must be sure to balance each section so that one group won't overpower another. This is a very delicate task, and you can expect to be frustrated by the usually overwhelming difference between the numbers of men and women auditioning. Women will probably outnumber men by a ratio of at least two to one, and basses will outnumber tenors by about the same proportion. (Usually women are more interested in singing than men are, and there are more basses than tenors around.)

Numbers alone do not tell the whole tale, of course. One powerful tenor can drown out five weak altos, so that you must ultimately depend on the relative strengths and weaknesses of each singer, rather than on numbers. All is not lost even when numbers do bear out the worst expectations. There is much music written for SAB chorus, in which tenors can usually sing bass parts. In other cases altos can augment the tenor ranks. It is only when basses are at a premium that you are really in serious trouble, and then you might consider adding some cellos and/or string basses before giving up altogether!

Dedication

Once you've got the group you think will achieve the ideal sound, you're in business—assuming, of course, that everyone lives up to your expectations. Chances are you've evaluated your group correctly in musical teams, but being a good chorister implies more than being a competent musician; it means showing up regularly at rehearsals and really learning music. It's best to publicize your rehearsal schedule along with auditions so that prospective members can plan their schedules accordingly. It's also a good idea to make learning some music a part of the audition, thus making the audition a two-part procedure. This has the advantage of letting you hear the auditionee sing music, not just notes, which may shed new light on his/her capabilities. It also gives nervous singers a second chance to prove themselves after what might not have been a good first showing. Furthermore, it shows you how hard this person is willing to work. Someone who hasn't learned a part perfectly is probably not really concerned with getting in the chorus and wouldn't work very hard if accepted. Choral singing takes lots of effort for all concerned and must be approached with real sincerity and dedication.

The conductor

The conductor of the chorus should do the auditioning, or at least be one of the people on a committee (and auditions committees are a good idea, if possible, since they provide more diversity of opinion and less chance for error). For one thing, s/he is usually trained as a musician. The conductor is responsible for training the group and choosing its repertoire, and must therefore be familiar with all of the singers' capabilities.

But the conductor is not simply a musical figure. To train the group well, a conductor must also be a good teacher and, perhaps most important, a diplomat. Handling large groups is difficult at best, and the conductor must necessarily assume the role of benevolent dictator at times. The conductor sets musical standards for the group, and to achieve them must also set requirements for rehearsal attendance and discipline. S/he must be able to tell prima donna sopranos that they are not singing well and dull basses that they haven't learned their music—doing so firmly, but tactfully. It is a multifaceted and incredibly demanding role; the best musician in town is not necessarily the best candidate for the job. Choirs have been known to fall apart for want of good leadership, while other groups prospered under mediocre musicians.

Section leaders

To help the conductor on the musical side of things, it is useful to have people in the group who can act as accompanists and section leaders. It is sometimes wise to divide a chorus into its smaller component sections, to go over parts before everyone tries to read them together. For this a conductor needs assistants—section leaders whose job it is to learn the music before the rehearsal in order to help others in the section learn it. (Ideally these people should be sufficiently trained that they can help their sections even when last-minute plans keep them from previewing the music.) Section leaders can also discreetly help people during general rehearsals, so that the conductor doesn't have to stop for individual mistakes, interruptions that are time consuming and distracting.

Business

Often a fledgling chorus is organized by its prospective conductor. Under those circumstances the conductor becomes involved immediately in all sorts of extramusical considerations that prevent attending to his/her musical duties. It is a good idea to appoint or elect a committee to help with the many aspects of running a chorus.

We don't think of a choir as a business, but to a greater or lesser extent that's exactly what it is. Publicity is always a great concern—first for auditions, then for concerts—and a new chorus must be especially energetic in its quest for a forum in which to present its music. There is also a huge amount of correspondence involved—requests for information about the choir, ordering music, etc., all of which take time. Someone has to be responsible for maintaining a music library; making sure that all chorus members have copies of all the music and replacing lost scores is a never-ending job. There are also all kinds of money matters with which the conductor need not be concerned.

Costs

A word to the wise on that score: as in the case of all printed matter, there are music copyright laws which must be obeyed. Xeroxing music is a widespread but illegal procedure; more and more publishers are taking such violations to court. International copyrights on music printed in Israel are also binding. The proper fees should be paid for all music that will be performed in public.

Oh yes, money is what makes a chorus go round, and it takes quite a lot to get a chorus going and keep it that way. The initial costs of publicity and music for just the first season only begin to tell the tale. A well-organized choir will also want uniforms in which to perform, and official stationery on which to conduct business.

Then there are ongoing costs, which vary from choir to choir. Music costs are universally high—an obviously necessary evil.

It may be necessary to hire the accompanist, and the conductor also may ask for a salary; at the very least, his/her expenses should be reim-

bursed, and these can run the gamut from phone bills to parking fees to meals for potential contacts. You must remember that even if a conductor is helped in his/her business responsibilities by a committee or board of directors, s/he remains, to the public, the controlling figure. Incurring a variety of expenses is natural, not to mention the expenditure of time which often keeps the conductor from other more lucrative employment. A sensitive group, happy with its leader, would be wise to treat him/her well.

Funding

The problem of finding funds to sustain a chorus is always a serious one, but rarely impossible to handle. There are several ways to cut expenses and increase income if one takes the trouble to investigate them.

Once off the ground, a choir can incorporate as a nonprofit organization (which nearly all musical groups are). This relatively simple, inexpensive procedure, which can be handled by any friendly lawyer, carries with it many privileges. Most tangibly, it frees you from paying taxes on anything from music to phone bills—and we all know how those taxes add up! It also makes you a worthy subject of support by various magnanimous agencies whose sole purpose is to dispense their own seemingly boundless wealth. Private foundations delight in bestowing funds upon needy organizations, as do various city, state, and federal agencies created specifically for the purpose of furthering the arts. Once you are a nonprofit organization you are also a tax deduction for anyone who contributes to your well-being, and this fact should appear prominently in all your literature.

Do not neglect to appeal from the start to the various Jewish agencies in your area. Even if they cannot help you directly, they may be able to put you in touch with sources that can. It may also help your image to be associated with some Jewish organization or school, besides providing financial support.

You may decide to involve your chorus members in supporting their group. They may be asked to make or pay for their uniforms, thus cutting costs. It's a good idea to institute a music fee to cover the cost of the season's music. In that way members understand that they own, and are thus responsible for, their music. Then they are also free to mark their scores, which will help them learn the music. Some groups go so far as to charge a membership fee (which includes the music fee); revenues from it go toward the miscellaneous expenses that inevitably crop up, in addition to those already mentioned.

Concerts

By far the primary source of income for the chorus and its raison d'être are concerts. What to charge varies from chorus to chorus, depending on the size and quality of the group and the local standards. Always remember, though, that you are providing a unique service to a large group, and that many people's time is being invested. No matter how long your performance actually is, your chorus members must sacrifice an entire afternoon or evening for the event. While they are not directly reimbursed for their

You should decide on a fee and deviate from it as little as possible. Once you accept a lower fee, you will find it difficult to charge your normal price. The same considerations apply to requests for benefit performances from charities. As much as you may identify with their causes, be judicious in donating your services or you may find yourself with a bankrupt organization.

services, the fee they receive collectively as a choir should reflect these considerations.

The possibilities of where to give a concert are endless: synagogue groups are always interested in fund-raising events, and a concert of Jewish music is certainly appropriate; various groups will stage rallies at which you might appear; schools often want education programs, and youth groups enjoy being entertained at their gatherings; other nonprofit charitable organizations will approach you for your services as well. All of these will expose you to members of other prospective audiences, who, ideally, will be inspired to hire you for their own group.

One excellent way to accumulate funds is to sponsor your own concert, in your own behalf. You are responsible for renting a hall, publicizing the event, printing a program, and selling tickets—all of which are time consuming and expensive. The income to be gained, however, and the opportunity to appear before a large audience are probably worth the expenditure of time and energy.

Music

Once you have gone to the trouble of auditioning singers and organizing business aspects of the group, the problem (which you may have considered fleetingly when the idea of a Jewish choir first struck you) is what to sing. What is Jewish music, and what is available in the way of Jewish choral music? What makes a good concert?

Musicologists have long argued about what constitutes Jewish music, and there is no unanimity on the answer. All we can do here is suggest some kinds of music that, according to one opinion or another, fall into the category.

There is a great deal of music that can be considered "classical." Some of this is by Jewish composers: Salomone Rossi in the Renaissance and a myriad of cantor-composers, who set liturgical texts to music for chorus, from the nineteenth century (when choirs became important in the German Reform movement) to today. Other music has been translated into Hebrew by Israeli musicians, notably the oratorios of Handel and Mendelssohn, and shorter works by Renaissance and baroque composers. All of these are musically rewarding to sing and can be performed by inexperienced as well as professional singers.

Most audiences will appreciate music of this nature—in small doses. People who come to concerts of Jewish music are usually interested in more popular forms, and Israeli favorites of the "Hava Nagila" sort are plentiful. Gil Aldema has arranged many of Naomi Shemer's songs for choir, and these, as well as the arrangements of folk songs like those of Marc Lavry and Paul Ben-Haim (to name only a few of the many outstanding Israeli musicians), are always favorites. The Hasidic Song Festivals in Israel have also made that genre popular; selections from those annual festivals are available in choral versions. The folk songs and dances of the pioneer movement have been repeatedly arranged for chorus, as have Yiddish folk songs (which never fail to move an audience). You may also expand your repertoire by including settings of biblical texts in other languages—English is a popular choice (and may include spirituals), as is Latin, with its wealth of psalms settings.

Accompaniment

A question to ponder is whether to sing with accompaniment or without (a cappella). One factor to consider is the greater difficulty of singing without accompaniment, especially for an amateur group. Also remember that choral concerts are very difficult to endure. Despite the variety of music to be included in a program, there is a limit to the range of possibilities offered by the various combinations of human voices; instruments can break the monotony. Instruments also open up the repertoire to include rock pieces and larger orchestral works, which even an unskilled group can often manage.

Resources

Fortunately there is little difficulty in finding music. The following is only a partial listing of the resources available in the U.S. and Israel:

Jerusalem

Sofer
Ben Yehudah St.

Tel Aviv

Israel Music Institute
Shderot Chan #6

Israel Music Publications
Ben Yehudah St. #105

Mercaz Ltarbut U-lihinukh
Arlosoroff #93 (Histadrut Offices)

New York

Transcontinental Music Publications
1674 Broadway
New York 10023

Pennsylvania

Merion Music Co.
Bryn Mawr 19010

Organizing and running a successful Jewish choir are major undertakings. They involve loads of work, but are certainly not without rewards. The joy of singing is nearly indescribable. The following people involved with already existing choirs will be happy to try to explain more of what it's all about; they can provide you with additional advice, information, and encouragement:

Arbel Chorale

David Braverman, Music Director
5430 Woodbine Ave.
Philadelphia, Pa. 19131

Sharim Choir

Herman Goodman, Music Director
Spertus College of Judaica
618 S. Michigan Ave.
Chicago, Ill. 60605

Zamir Chorale of Boston

Josh Jacobson, Music Director
233 Bay State Rd.
Boston, Mass. 02215

Zamir Chorale of New York

Mati Lazar, Music Director
P.O. Box 422 Planetarium Station
New York, N.Y. 10024

Hazzanut

The primal hazzanut sound

Hazzanut (or chazzanus, as I learned to say it)—what is it (as they say in the Talmud)? For some it is an art form; for others a profession; for still others an unfamiliar bore. Ah, but for a few it is an indescribable way of experiencing the divine relationships between person and word, word and melody, melody and feeling, feeling and prayer, davener and God. Just as a beam of light hitting a crystal breaks into its component colors, so it is with the hearing or creation of the sounds of hazzanut—at least for a few of us. For us hazzanut is a passion, one we invite you to share.

Before getting into the familiar background of letters, words, and facts, let us start by understanding through personal experience. We recall that the Mishnah says that all of Torah is contained in the Ten Commandments; all of the ten in the first commandment; and all of the first commandment is contained in the first letter, the alef. Why? The alef has no sound of its own; rather, it is an opening. By uttering alef, God opened to us the powers of creation and blessing. By our repeating alef we let the divine flow in (remember the numerical value of alef is *one*—God is One).

Try the following

Now, let the breath
flow over the vocal
cords—that slight
tickling sensation
is a sign of life.
Push the breath
down into the gut—
let it rush through
your body.
Notice it comes
tumbling back—
let it come,
let it flow,
let the breath
become sound
and let the sound
become melody.

So,
the alef
breath—
that purest
opening which is
no-sound—becomes
translated to the
world-sound as nothing
more than the "still,
small *oy*." Now, let the
opening be heard, by
God, the One Who Hears
Opening—Sing . . . *Oy!*

To vocalize the letter alef,
momentarily close the glottis—
the fatty part hanging in
the back of your throat; then
let it spring open under the
pressure of your breath.
Do this three times. It
places you in an exposed,
open position. Do it
three more times.

Mazel tov! You have uttered one of the magical sounds of hazzanut—the oy. The more breath you took in, the deeper you brought it in, the more power you used to push it through your guts, and the wider your vocal cords and mouth opened to let it out—the more perfect the *oy* you produced. A not incidental by-product of this exercise will be an increased appreciation of the awesome potential beauty in hazzanut. Abraham Joshua Heschel once wrote:

On every sense, hazzanut is *histapkhut hanefesh* (outpouring of the soul) . . . . Indeed, a cantor standing before the ark reveals all his soul, utters all his secrets. The art of being a cantor involves the depth, richness, and integrity of personal experience . . . because wherever there is life, there is silent worship.

The gematria (numerical value) of shira (song) equals that of tefillah (prayer).

Historical development of hazzanut

In discussing the origin of Hallel (Psalms 113–118, recited on special occasions) the Talmud (Pesahim 117a) states that these psalms must have been known to Moses and the children of Israel at the time of the crossing of the Red Sea. The Talmud passage goes on to discuss the Hallel and suggests that it should be recited "at every important time and at every misfortune (may it not come upon them) and when they are redeemed." Underlying this discussion is a clear belief in the essential role played by song in facilitating human communication with God. It is written in the Haggadah: "Therefore we are obliged to praise, glorify, extol . . and to recite before Him a new song. Hallelujah." According to Mishnah Taanit 4:2-3, Mishnah Sotah 8:7-8, and Mishnah Arakhin 2:6, music played a major role in the sacrificial services performed at the Temple; in addition to using instruments, the Levites sang portions of the psalms and the Torah. In Talmud Sukkah 50b-51a we are told that the major value of the music was the singing. A. Z. Idelsohn wrote in *Jewish Music*: "The predominance of vocal music naturally grew out of the attitude toward music as a tool for the conveyance of ideas." Moreover, after the Temple was destroyed, it was the vocal music that was carried on in the synagogue; of the instruments used, only the shofar remains.

Many scholars, including Idelsohn, claim that the major modes of Jewish music extant today are directly traceable to the Temple tunes. They are present in their purest form in the chants used to recite the weekly Torah and haftarah selections. To understand the role of the hazzan we must understand how Jewish music developed; we must start with nusah.

All of us can be hazzanim singing of the glories and pains of the world; those with special talents can lead the rest of us when we daven—that is the role of the hazzan, to whom we now turn.

Make A joyful Noise Unto The Lord

Psalm 98   Psalm 100

The core of Jewish music: nusah

Nusah essentially refers to the "copied" or "accepted" way of chanting the service. It consists of a series of musical modes. A musical mode is composed of a number of tones motives (motives are groups of tones) within a certain scale. In simpler language, it represents a relatively fixed relationship of tones which can be placed together in numerous ways to produce a variety of tunes. The interrelationship of the *tones* creates the motives; the interrelationship of the *motives* creates the mode; the interrelationship of modes creates the tunes; and in particular the interrelationship of modes and tunes is a *nusah*.

In Jewish music the nusah is supreme—it is far more important than rhythm or harmony or theme. It is susceptible to improvisation and embellishment—in fact, it calls for them—but only within its fixed boundaries or relationships. Its raison d'être is to carry the meaning of a text of words, of ideas. However, it must convey the full meaning—not only the cognitive but also the deeper echoes of reality contained within the words. God makes things real through words ("God *said,* 'Let there be . . .' "); people make words real by deeds; song helps to make God real to people and (barukh ha-Shem—bless the Name) people to God.

The earliest nushaot (plural of nusah) were those used to chant various parts of the Bible. From the time of Ezra (c. 440 C.E.), public reading of selections from the Torah became a regular activity. In the course of time, the synagogue services incorporated not only weekly Torah readings but also selections from the Prophets (haftarah) and readings of certain books on particular occasions (e.g., Ruth on Shavuot, Song of Songs on Pesah, Ecclesiastes on Sukkot). Slightly different nushaot developed for each of these books, but all of them share an emphasis on use of the motives and close relationship to the meaning and syntax of the verses.

Most of the nushaot used in synagogues are derived from the aforementioned biblical modes. The major ones are:

1. Tefillah—or Adoshem Malakh—based on the Torah trope and used primarily for Shabbat services;

2. Selihah—based on the prophetic nusah and used for pleading in general and on the High Holidays in particular; and,

3. Magen Avot—a mixture of the modes and used as base for melodic pieces.

Another important mode, the Ahavah Rabbah, is the least related to ancient Jewish modes. Most scholars consider it to be of Mongolian Tartar origin. Its greatest use, therefore, was in southern Russia, Romania, and Hungary. However, almost all European Jewish communities made extensive use of it.

Davening revolves around singing or chanting, and this singing revolves around modes that express cultural understandings of not only texts but of people/God dialogues. These words in holy texts are alive with the living voice of God; nusah is one way of responding to the cries of our soul and to the soul itself. We have a different nusah for Friday evening, Shabbat morning, and especially Shabbat afternoon because each reflects different stages of the reality of Shabbat. Everyday, yom tov, Rosh ha-Shanah, Yom Kippur—all differ in meaning, in texture, and in nusah. Just as the Talmud represents the living oral Torah, so the nusah represents the living oral tefillah.

Not all the singing in synagogues, and certainly not all Jewish singing, is based solely on the modes described. In fact, many of the folk melodies of the peoples among whom Jews have dwelled have been adapted to Jewish songs, including major parts of the services. Many of the most famous Jewish prayer songs are adaptations of German and Gregorian melodies to Jewish texts, e.g., Kol Nidre, Alenu, Kaddish, Shema Yisrael, etc.

However, though related to and in some cases based on "foreign" melodies, those tunes were eventually accepted and considered traditional (ironically, they are often called the mi-Sinai—from Sinai—tunes) because they were similar to the motives contained in the traditional nusah. They added depth and character to the service by complementing and reinforcing the nusah. Helping maintain a balance between adherence to a binding tradition and openness to surrounding creative forces has been one of the major continuing roles of the hazzan, to whose history we can now return.

The role of the hazzan

Prayer as a regular element in Jewish worship existed alongside the system of sacrifices and grew in importance after the destruction of the Temple. A layperson known as a mitpallel led the people in prayer, whether at home, in a synagogue, or even in special sections of the Temple itself.

The mitpallel, acting in behalf of the people, composed most of the prayers as s/he went along, because the liturgy at that time was not fixed (Idelsohn, p. 102, claims that "sometimes . . . women were chosen to pray for the people"). The grammatical form of the word mitpallel itself tells us something very important. It is reflexive—to do something to oneself rather than to others. The mitpallel is "one who leads him/herself to pray" or, even more in keeping with the root meaning, "one who judges oneself." Prayer requires one to engage in self-judgment, to lay oneself open to a critical honesty. The person who leads public prayer must set the example for the kahal—the congregation.

As prayers developed and grew in importance, order and regularity began to be established. Moreover, as immediate contact with the Temple lessened, the problems of remembering the nusah grew. Therefore, the position of shaliah tzibbur developed.

A shaliah tzibbur—messenger of the congregation—was responsible for opening a service with the set prayers and for improvising other prayers that reflected needs or blessings.

In the early stages of synagogue worship the shaliah tzibbur was not filled by a professional functionary but was an honorary position. There *was* one professional functionary, however: the hazzan, a word derived from the root meaning "to oversee." The early hazzan was a shammash, one who kept the synagogue in physical order. Later he began to act as shaliah tzibbur for parts of the service.

The continuing growth in the complexity of the service, together with the dispersion of the Jews and a decline in general knowledge, combined to lessen the role of the honorary shaliah tzibbur and to increase that of the hazzan. Eventually many hazzanim also assumed the role of paytan—the one who composed piyyutim or religious poetry. After the destruction of the Temple, improvisational development of the major prayers ceased, and the piyyut became the major vehicle for expression of new feelings in response to changing conditions.

During the Middle Ages the hazzan began to play a number of major roles. He was the one who maintained the tradition of the nusah and the established prayers; he was the one who developed and put to music "modern" prayers in the form of poetry. The hazzan gradually became a major figure in Jewish life. Many rabbis of the Middle Ages were also hazzanim, skilled in singing and writing piyyutim. Some of the more famous among these rabbis were Moses ben Kalonymos (author of "Ein Kamocha"), Solomon ibn Gabirol ("Adon Olam"), Rabbi Judah he-Hasid of

These piyyutim are traditionally ascribed to these leading rabbis, though in recent years some of the authorships have been challenged by scholars.

Regensburg ("Anim Zemirot"), and Rabbi Amnon of Mainz ("Unetaneh Tokef").

As the services became more established and some piyyutim were incorporated into the order of the service, the emphasis on creativity shifted somewhat to the development of tunes. Many of the piyyutim were sung to the folk melodies of surrounding peoples; others were chanted according to nusah; and still others sung to a combination of these. Eventually the tunes used for the "songs" began to affect the nusah used for the established prayers and blessings; many battles were fought (some physical) over the use of the "foreign" tunes. As we've said, however, a few were so well accepted as to be considered from Sinai. Many rabbis tried to place restraints upon the hazzan. They developed a guideline: the beginning and end of each prayer had to be in accord with nusah, while the middle was open for improvisation. In addition, the Maharal inveighed against hazzanim who excessively showed off their talents by playing up to the masses and who appropriated "foreign" tunes indiscriminately.

Once the hazzan became a major religious functionary, serious questions arose as to his qualifications, his exact duties, and his remuneration. In the Talmud (Taanit 16a) we are told: "When they stand up for prayer . . . they send up one . . . who is modest and agreeable to the people, who knows how to chant and has a sweet voice; one who is well versed in Bible, in Mishnah, in Talmud, halakhot, and aggadot and in all the prayers." Those criteria—acceptable character; knowledge of nusah, the prayers, and Jewish learning; and a sweet voice—originally applied to a shaliah tzibbur and have always been the formal qualifications for a hazzan. Of course, since those criteria are largely subjective in nature, they have been applied differently and with varying emphases by different communities. The major conflict was between a sweet voice and a modest character; often the more beautiful and honored the voice, the less modest and agreeable the person.

As for the duties, these also varied. Some hazzanim were hired by the local Jewish community as a whole—the stadt (city) hazzan—and were only expected to lead the Additional Service on Shabbat and yom tov and the High Holidays. In smaller communities a hazzan was expected to act as a jack-of-all-trades—i.e. as the ritual slaughterer, the circumciser, and sometimes as the teacher of little children. Some hazzanim went from village to village, and from city to city, like traveling minstrels. Most, though, stayed in one locale and earned a modest income. Their salaries depended upon what they did. A not uncommon arrangement was for them to receive one-third of their income from parents of students, one-third from the community as a whole, and one-third from the wealthy members of the community. Many of them suffered great hardships because of their dependence upon the goodwill of the community, but they evidently considered such inconveniences minor in comparison with the honor of being a hazzan.

Beginning with the nineteenth century, we find two kinds of hazzanim. One, symbolized by Solomon Sulzer of Vienna (1804–91), undertook to cleanse the synagogue of its archaic orientalism and to infuse it with real music, i.e., music in keeping with the classical Western style that was then developing. The other was characterized by Nisson Spivak, known as "Nissi of Belzer" (1829–1906), who emphasized the orientalism, i.e., the adherence to modes, to motives, and to the use of emotional ornamentation. Sulzer and his followers adapted many of the existing Jewish melodies to classical forms. They wanted to evoke awe, majesty, order, solemnity, and harmony. Nissi of Belzer, from Eastern Europe, wanted to maintain the warmth, fire, and emotional feeling of the nusah. For the East European Jew, hazzanut was the way of crying out to God with a real "Yiddish kvetch."

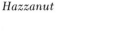

Those who could evoke such feelings in the people were felt to have a very special gift. The life story of one famous hazzan of the "old school," Yoel David Levinson (1813–50), is particularly revealing. At thirteen Yoel David was elected stadt hazzan of Vilna (succeeding his late father) and was married off to the daughter of a rich man. Receiving the title "Der Baal-Habayissil—the Little Master of the House," he embarked upon a career filled with adulation and adoration. However, a decade later he began to dabble in Western music and, according to legend, fell in love with a Polish woman. Realizing what had happened to him, Yoel David gave up hazzanut and became a wandering penitent who lived only to study Talmud and to pray. Once, near the end of his life, he was recognized and asked to lead Shabbat services. He agreed. A witness wrote:

His voice was a lyric tenor—rather weak, for he was greatly worn, and more spirit than body. . . . He seemed to stand before the pulpit entranced, oblivious of his environment, swaying in the higher spheres. His singing was without effort. He hardly even moved his lips. It was more an exhalation of soul than a sounding of voice.

The golden age of hazzanut

All this blossomed into the golden age of the hazzan at least in Eastern Europe and then in America before World War II. As both emancipation and persecutions began to spread seriously through East European Jewry in the last decades of the nineteenth century, many Jews abandoned their Jewish practices. America was no place for "superstition" and obsolete practices. Similarly, new winds of enlightenment were blowing in Eastern Europe; Jews could be "modern." Yet enlightened and nonenlightened alike shared one passion—listening to a great hazzan daven with awesome power and emotion.

During the golden age the great hazzanim occupied pulpits in large magnificent shuls in Warsaw, Vilna, Budapest, Prague, St. Petersburg, Kovno, Minsk, Odessa, Bialystok, Vienna, Berlin, and other great cities. They traveled throughout Europe. At first hesitantly and then in numbers, they began to come to America. New York shuls competed with each other in inviting a "star" hazzan to officiate on at least a few occasions and perhaps even to sign a contract for a few years. The arrival of a famous hazzan on the Lower East Side caused near riots as Jews flocked to listen to the voices of the golden hazzanim. Large new shuls were built primarily to house the spirited voices and their avid followers.

The most famous and the greatest hazzanim of the period began to come to America in the second decade of this century: Gershon Sirota, Zavel Kwartin, Mordechai Hershman, David Roitman, Pinchus Pinchik, Moishe Oysher, Benzion Kapov-Kagen, Berle Chagy, Joseph Schmidt, Joseph Shiskly, Aryeh Leib Rutman—there were all princes in their day. The king of the 1920s was Yossele—Yosef Rosenblatt, a small man with a powerful, beautifully controlled voice. Yossele, a hazzan who maintained adherence to a strict Orthodoxy throughout his life and had no formal music training, made the kvetch a tool of art and of prayer. Representative of a school of hazzanim famous for overpowering emotion, Yossele used a matchless falsetto to shock and challenge his listeners to open up. His life ended tragically. In his last years he was forced to perform cantorial pieces on the vaudeville stage in order to earn enough money to pay his debts.

In more recent times the list of great hazzanim is sadly short. Several, such as Richard Tucker and Jan Peerce, pursued careers at the Met and acted as hazzanim only for the High Holidays. However, there have been other greats, such as David Koussevitsky, Leib Glantz, Leibele Waldman, Sholom Katz, Samuel Malavsky, and the Hazzan Hador, Moshe Koussevitsky. The latter, who died in 1966, escaped from Warsaw in 1939 during the chanting of Neilah, the haunting prayer that concludes Yom Kippur; he returned to Warsaw in 1945 to recite Kel Maleh Rahamin, a prayer of mourning, and then left for England and the United States. For fifteen years he and his brother David led services in Brooklyn shuls only a few blocks away from each other. For a hazzan maven, Boro Park was heaven during those years.

I look forward to the development of a uniquely American nusah—one that reflects the milieu of Jews in America and draws upon the enriched elements of various folk cultures. Listening to and singing gospel, "soft country," and folk music feels a lot like singing nusah. Incorporating this music and even the words into davening adds depth and meaning for me. (Try whatever does the same for you, and then share your experience with the rest of us.)

Seedlings: toward an American nusah

Nusah, though it is based on and refers to tradition, has never been static. It grew best in times when Jews felt comfortable in their Jewishness and in their environment. We incorporated those parts of our cultural environment that reflected and reinforced our own living heritage (not incidentally, we have had a similar effect on the non-Jewish world, e.g., the Gregorian chant still used in Catholic Mass is based on Jewish nusah).

How to get into hazzanut

Hazzanut is a quintessential Jewish experience. It is authentically Jewish because it is built on and grows through a series of dichotomies/tensions/polarities that give meaning and force to Jewish life. For example, there is the pull between the new "foreign" music and the traditional nusah, as well as the tension between the role of the hazzan as egotistic artist and his role as shaliah tzibbur. There are tensions of the individual versus the community, of order versus spontaneity, of tune versus word and both versus thoughts and emotions. Above all, there is the unique pull on the hazzan: on the one hand, the hazzan is the representative of the people, a person making use of human skills to communicate with God; on the other hand, the hazzan is merely a vessel that God has shaped and is now filling with beauty in order to communicate with us. Our challenge is, if only for a few seconds, to share in the momentary shattering of the barrier between us and the Other. We all can become hazzanim because we all can dream (in Hebrew חזן = hazzan = same root as dream) and envision worlds of time, space, and being.

Some practical advice

The best way , of course, is to attend services at a shul where a good hazzan davens. This is very difficult because:

1. there are few good hazzanim;

2. the services in which they are involved are often stilted and not conducive to kavvannah—spiritual intensity;

3. most shuls do not appreciate their hazzanim, so they restrict their singing to a bare minimum; and

4. it takes a few visits to "know"the hazzan and begin to appreciate his nusah.

Nevertheless, here are a few personal suggestions: Boro Park (Brooklyn) is blessed with Moshe Stern, who succeeded Moshe Koussevitsky at Beth El, and an aging but still brilliant David Koussevitsky at Emanuel; Flatbush (also Brooklyn) has David Werdyger, a Gerer Hasid who sings with great passion; the Jewish Center in Hollis Hills, N. Y., has Sol Zim; in Boston, try Michael Hammerman at Kehillath Israel; in Pittsburgh, Moshe Taube at Congregation Beth Shalom; and in Baltimore, Saul Hammerman at Beth El (my home shul and the hazzan I have davened with for over twenty years). The best way to find a good hazzan is to ask around—especially among other hazzanim. If they think you are really interested, they might tell you where to go and what to listen for.

The worst way is to attend a "cantorial concert." These affairs often turn out to be Israel songfests or, even worse, cantorial caterings to the audience. Removed from its proper setting in shul, as part of davening, hazzanut can easily be tarnished by the vulgarities of our world. I remember one horrible concert where the hazzan asked the audience to choose between two songs for his encore—one, a tune jewel of hazzanishe music, "Sheyibaneh Bais Hamikdash" (a prayer for the rebuilding of the Temple), the other, "To Dream the Impossible Dream." The sitra achra (the demonic) won that round.

A somewhat less satisfying approach is to listen to records. First, the problems:

1. many of the recordings of the golden age are of very poor quality in terms of vocal fidelity and musical arrangements;

2. nearly all old and reissued recordings have defects, which you must learn to live with;

3. the same selections appear over and over on different records and different labels—you have to be careful;

4. a few jackets provide no help in identifying the "piece" being sung or the history of the hazzan;

5. prices are high;

6. many of the best or most renowned hazzanim have styles that are jarring to our ears—it takes a lot of patience to listen to, to absorb, to understand, and to experience the chanting, and a poor, unprofessional recording doesn't help. On the other hand, there are a number of fantastically captivating recordings, or at least fantastically captivating songs on some records.

Being able to appreciate and incorporate hazzanut requires an effort on your part—you have got to provide the kavvanah. Here are some personal suggestions for your preparation:

1. Hazzanut is definitely otherworldly at its best, so try to play the records only when you want to enter the other worlds.

2. Hazzanut is an esoteric art based on unique mixes of texts, nusah, sociohistorical styles, and personalized expressions; the more you move about all four, the easier will be your entrance into that world.

3. Just as hazzanut is highly personal and culturally rooted, so are its mavens and, even more, its critics; seek out the advice of people who err on the side of mercy.

4. Hazzanut demands participation; hidden between the notes, expressed in the phrasings, molding the melodies, hearing the oy, responding with joy—there is a bat kol, a heavenly voice, calling to the soul within us; only you can cry, sing, listen, respond.

The sounds of a hazzan are prayer derived from personal experiences and feelings, expressed in a collective manner, uttered with an oy, and fastened to a vision—reawakening the universe.

Recommended records

1. Leib Glantz—*Selihos Service*—Famous Records—FAM 1015. Recorded live, it captures the mystical, unique Glantz approach, which is a mixture of bare nusah and intensely personalized expressions.

2. Moshe Koussevitsky—*Festivals, Volume 3*—Collectors Guild ALE 203. Any recording of Moshe Koussevitsky's is worth having; especially look for ones where he sings "Sheyibaneh," "Hateh," "Rahamo," and "Ribbono Shel Olam" (Yom Kippur Katan).

3. Pinchus Pinchik—*Best Works of Pinchus Pinchik*—Greater Recording Co.—GRC 234. It includes "Rozo de-Shabbos" (Mystery of Shabbat), which lives up to its name.

4. Yossele Rosenblatt—"The Incomparable J.R."—RCA—VIC 1685.

5. Sholom Katz—*Rebuild Thy House*—Elana—ER 101.

6. Ben Zion Shenker—*Modziter Festivals, Volume 3*—NRS 1205. Shenker's records are in between hazzanut and Hasidic—listen to "Proke Yos Onokh."

7. David Werdyger—*Hasidic Nigunim*—Aderet—LPW 306.

Collections

1. *Seven Great Cantors*—Collectors Guild—GC 600. A good introduction.

2. *Rare Cantorial Gems*—Shirim—S 100400. If you find it, hold on to it!

3. *Voices of the Temple*—CBS (Israel) S64148. Best recordings of Moishe Oysher I've heard.

4. *Art of the Cantor*—RCA. Three records with Koussevitsky, Rosenblatt, and Samuel Vigoda, the package is well done and certainly a good base to build on.

The living world comes to us with the fullness of love and we kiss it with overflowing affection (Rav Kook).

Behold the one poor in deed and in awe stands before You. . . . May it be Your will that comes from You and goes to You . . . that all the messengers which raise up prayers shall bring my prayer before the throne of Your glory (Hinenni—hazzan's prayer).

Note: A good place to get reissues of old hazzanut records is:

Barry Serotta
Musique Internationale
3111 W. Chase
Chicago, Ill. 60645

Lift up Thy voice like a horn, cry aloud, spare not, and declare unto My people their transgressions, and to the house of Jacob their sins.

Introduction

The impact of electronic media has reached almost every aspect of modern life. It would be impossible to envision our daily lives without the wondrous technological inventions of computers, televisions, calculators, and satellites. Yet somehow, inexplicably, we have not focused our attention or our resources on this obvious fact relative to our "Jewish lives." Community organizations have no idea how to utilize public access cable TV channels to improve the image of Israel. Old age homes show Yiddish films in such poor condition that the elderly cannot make out the dialogue. On wintry afternoons Jewish community centers show dated, irrelevant films on non-Jewish topics. Schools have no video equipment to train and supervise teachers. College student groups have no films to counteract Arab propaganda on the campuses. Educators have inadequate budgets to rent quality films that enhance curricula.

The paucity of quality media resources is most immediately and devastatingly evident in the political sphere. While the Arab world is busy mounting a vigorous media campaign to disseminate its propaganda message, the Jewish world finds itself with few resources and only the barest mechanisms for coordinating media exploitation in Israel's behalf. On the religious scene, most church groups have invested heavily in fantastic audiovisual resources for the education and reinforcement of their constituency, while we have practically none.

Probably of greatest significance in the long run is the lack of quality media resources for fostering the Jewish knowledge and identity needed to ensure the spiritual suvival of Diaspora Jewry. The deplorable lack of media resources takes on a new dimension with the recognition that the average North American child in the 1970s lives in an entirely different world from that of his parents. Most of today's youth no longer have any direct contact with the rich cultural and religious traditions of immigrant grandparents. The demise of the extended family has separated the young from the old. The Holocaust is a historical event learned about through textbooks, if at all. Israel is a foreign land six thousand miles away. Intermarriage is a common occurrence, and tradition is a song from a movie.

According to a recent study by Children's Television Workshop, the creators of *Sesame Street*, children watch television for more hours in a given year than they sit in a classroom. Even the adult population has been engulfed by this new technology. Visual images in living color have become the language of today. Unfortunately, however, the majority of Jewish institutions in this country are still in the Dark Ages, relying primarily on the printed word and contenting itself with antiquated, sepia-colored film-strips in their occasional foray into "modern" technology. While the world at large has moved on to multidimensional modes of transmitting oral tradition, the Jewish world remains bound to the page.

The need for resources to enhance the quality of Jewish life and foster Jewish identity is crucial. Learning resources are no longer mere teaching aids or supplementary materials. The modern media have become a crucial weapon—a vital priority in the effort to preserve and nurture Jewish life.

Two obvious problems: money and expertise

Lack of financial resources is generally cited as the reason that most Jewish institutions are so far behind in the media revolution. Money is indeed an important aspect of the problem. The new technology is expensive: 16 mm. color film costs about $1,500 per minute to produce professionally; a videotape port-a-pak outfit runs at least $2,000; a good 16 mm. film projector costs $500. In the past, each individual institution in a community could afford a modest stock of media equipment and materials, but the sums involved in the new media make individual ownership outmoded, impractical, and fiscally impossible. Many professionals who would like to make effective use of the available technology are thus frustrated by lack of money.

Besides cost, the new technology presents another objective problem: few Jewish professionals even know how to operate the sophisticated equipment of the electronic age. What equipment does exist is generally locked in closets except when a rare "medianik" happens on the scene. In the past, when the most complicated task was operating the simple film strip projector, every professional could make use of media. But the new technology calls for an expert, someone who really knows what s/he is doing, to ensure proper operation and maintenance.

More importantly, creative use of equipment requires full-time, trained media personnel. Anything that does not require large expenditures (the creation of a super 8 animated cartoon by schoolchildren, for example) does require creative, trained leadership. The non-Jewish world has long recognized the validity and importance of this specialty: the best universities in the country offer graduate degrees in media, and some academic disciplines even require courses in media. However, few individuals with this kind of training are found in the employ of the Jewish community.

THIS IS THE Beer-SHEBA CAMEL MARKET IN A SANDSTORM.

Two underlying problems:
community structure and the lack of understanding of the modern media

While money and expertise are obvious elements in the delayed development of media use in the Jewish world, there are two other key contributing factors. One is the very *structure* of the Jewish community. Both nationally and locally, Jewish institutions are rarely organized in such a way that central resources can service an entire community. Historically the American Jewish community has been fragmented into parallel structures. Each group has undertaken separately a full range of functions, including funding, public relations, programing, and the provision of resources. There is, in fact, little precedent for an agency to provide a service to all educational, communal, religious, and volunteer groups on a functional basis.

Although the pooling of resources is still something of a radical notion in the contemporary Jewish community, in recent years the non-Jewish world has embarked on an entirely new approach to community organizations that render human services and operate educational institutions. The traditional agencies have been replaced by interdisciplinary and interdepartmental approaches. One manifestation of this is the learning resource centers, combining print and audiovisual materials that have been developed in many communities. These centers serve the needs of educational institutions as well as other community agencies or organizations. Many high school media centers service local firemen and Audubon societies, health clinics and clubs for the elderly.

This kind of interagency cooperation is rare in Jewish life today, except for the ad hoc responses to extreme crises or special events. The Jewish world has only very recently begun to evolve new structural mechanisms to coordinate approaches to shared problems and goals. For example, in some communities where the rapid deterioration of inner-city neighborhoods has trapped a segment of elderly Jewish citizens, the communities have taken unprecedented steps to form new interagency bodies to meet this challenging need. In some small Jewish communities, where professionals serve dual roles and lay leadership overlaps, the rigid division between institutions has been bridged.

Still, for the majority of Jewish communities, the idea of establishing a special body, designed and created specifically to provide learning resources to *all* segments of the community, may seem like heresy. If a new understanding of the importance of modern media leads to an acceptance of the idea of establishing media centers, the communities will be forced to face, on an empirical level, the all-important question of community structure.

Even after the structural problems are faced, the second problem must be dealt with: the new media are seldom understood or given high priority within Jewish circles. Only the Jewish public relations and fund-raising professionals have begun to appreciate how vitally important the media are. As a result, 90 percent of all media work in the Jewish world today is geared to campaign objectives. Few of the operative educational or communal national agencies have a media professional on their staffs. The fact that public relations and media use are not synonymous is not even understood by many people.

In the past decade the new nonprint media have developed into an enormously important aspect of the work of every school, college, and social agency in the non-Jewish world. A gigantic commercial industry has developed to service the hardware and software (programing) needs of these institutions. The new technology has revolutionized educational methodology, both in the formal classrooms and communal activities. Marshall McLuhan has aptly observed: "We are entering the new age of education that is programed for discovery rather than instruction." Participatory learning rather than passive learning has become the norm. The new media play a prominent role in "learning by doing."

Doing media Jewishly

Before you attempt any project or production utilizing media hardware equipment, certain things should be clear to you. To begin with, media hardware (machinery) consists of precision instruments. As long as your equipment is in working condition, it will function properly—providing you know how to operate it. Do not be afraid to approach a machine, push buttons, turn knobs. Learn how to operate the equipment you are using. Don't get into the habit of blaming malfunctions on the machine. Equipment *does* wear down: when a bulb blows out during the showing of a film it is *your* responsibility to have another bulb on hand. To avoid such problems, you should check all media hardware before use. Make sure your camera is in perfect operating condition if you don't want the lab to return a roll of film with only blank pictures.

More importantly, there is nothing intrinsically "Jewish" about any piece of media equipment. Hardware is simply the tool to present the software—the movies, filmstrips, videotapes, photographs, recordings— you create or use. A 16 mm. projector is not Jewish; a film about Jewish immigration to the Lower East Side of New York is. So is a filmstrip about the Holocaust, a photographic exhibition about synagogue architecture, a videotape of a model Seder, a slide-tape presentation on how to bake hallah, an overhead transparency detailing the structure of the Morning Service on Shabbat. Jewish media are entirely in the hands of the user or creator. The human component determines the Jewish content of any media production or program.

Equipment

Leslie Kane of New York and Amy Kronish of Boston have some suggestions to make about equipment:

A prerequisite to becoming a Jewish medianik, either as a producer of materials or as a user or programer, is knowledge about and access to quality hardware equipment or materials. Quality does not imply the latest or most expensive, but rather equipment that is sturdy, reliable, and serviceable. Visit as many media equipment dealers as possible to price and compare various models and brands of media hardware. Ask dealers to demonstrate the uses of each machine in which you are interested. Ask directors of local media centers which pieces of machinery they prefer and WHY. Above all, make sure to consult *The Audio-Visual Equipment Directory*, available from:

> **National Audio-Visual Association, Inc.**
> **3150 Spring St.**
> **Fairfax, Va. 22030**

or your local library or media center. This directory is an invaluable guide to a large majority of hardware equipment available in North America. Not only does it picture a particular item, it gives specifications and pricing information as well. The directory lists information about trade and brand names, audiovisual equipment dealers by city and state, and dealers of miscellaneous accessories and materials. It is your best companion for comparative shopping.

To give you an idea of the range and type of media equipment that exists, the following list has been compiled. It is by no means exhaustive. Furthermore, one person cannot attempt to master the skills needed for each individual medium, let alone purchase every item on the list. I suggest that you choose one medium—such as super 8 film making or animation—and acquire the equipment and skill needed to become proficient before becoming involved in a second medium. The media and equipment from which you can choose are:

SCREENS

standing matte screen white, with keystone eliminator, 60″ x 60″

16 MM. FILM PROJECTION

16 mm. projector, manual load, with external speaker, extra take-up reels, Mylar (cement) splicer, lubricating oil

SUPER 8 FILM MAKING

super 8 projector
super 8 or 8 mm. movie camera, dual 8 movie editor
for animation: 8 mm. or super 8 movie camera with single frame capability and cable release, heavy duty tripod, close-up zoom lenses, copy stand with lights, sound equipment (tape recorder)
materials: Kodachrome film or Ektachrome EFB film for fast processing, art supplies, blank white leader, cleaning gloves

OVERHEAD TRANSPARENCIES

overhead projector with cornerpost, good focusing capability, and strong lamp
projection stand
transparency-making machine to produce transparencies, spirit masters, and mimeo masters from carbon-based printed materials
materials: thermal acetate, write-on acetate, grease pencils, permanent markers, cardboard frames.

AUDIO EQUIPMENT

cassette tape recorder with slide-synch pulse button reel-to-reel tape recorder
phonograph
cassette duplicating machine—a high-speed cassette copier to provide multiple copies of the same cassette
materials: cable for attaching cassette to slide projector, interconnecting cables for dubbing between cassette tape recorder, and from record to cassette or reel-to-reel tape recorders, endless loop cassette

VIDEO EQUIPMENT (½″ EIJA standard)

port-a-pak—a portable video tape camera and deck is an absolute necessity, your first piece of video equipment
black and white television monitors (2) for playback
video decks (2) (VTR—videotape recorder) to provide editing capability and playback
tripod, cables, battery and battery charge, lights
materials: blank videotape, half-hour and one-hour reels

single lens reflex camera
slide sorter, slide viewer
slide projector—Kodak Carousel with remote control and automatic focus
    copy stand and lights

FILMSTRIP

filmstrip projector
filmstrip viewer—for individual or small group viewing
materials: U-Film or write-on 35 mm. film to create your own filmstrips

DRAWING ON 16 MM. FILM

16 mm. clear leader, double perforated
materials: fine point felt-tip markers, permanent ink, ink for use on plastic,
    crow quill penholder and points
16 mm. black leader (with emulsion), double perforated, for scratching
materials: silk screen line cutter, metal hole punchers, sandpaper, clear
    and blank leader

Technical information on how to operate equipment is readily available. Make sure that your dealer demonstrates and familiarizes you with any item you purchase. Be sure that you obtain the manufacturer's operating instruction manual and guarantee. If equipment is purchased second-hand, write to the manufacturer for an instruction manual; they will supply it.

Do not hesitate to ask competent media technicians to demonstrate and help you learn to operate the equipment. Take advantage of any courses offered by high schools or local colleges in how to operate media equipment. These courses, which usually require simple projectors, offer "hands-on" instruction that will give you valuable experience.

PUBLICATIONS

Though our main concern is media hardware and software, the printed word cannot be ignored by medianiks. Make use of the various journals and magazines in the field, available at your local public or university library. Among the best are:

    1. **Audio-Visual Instruction**
    Association for Education, Communications and Technology
    1201 16th St. N.W.
    Washington, D.C. 20036

Monthly. $12 a year. Developments in education using audiovisual methods of instruction.

    2. **Film News**
    250 W. 57th St.
    New York, N.Y. 10019

Bimonthly. $6 a year. Discusses and reviews films, film conferences, and materials and equipment in the AV field.

    3. **Media and Methods**
    134 N. 13th St.
    Philadelphia, Pa. 19107

Monthly. $9 a year. Discusses the latest techniques, materials, and equipment in the AV field.

4. **Super 8 Filmaker**
10 Pelham Parkway
Pelham Manor, N.Y. 10036

Bimonthly. $6 a year. Home-movie making, animated film, and techniques for use with children.

The Jewish Media Service of the Institute of Jewish Life has designed five manuals to assist in the creative use of media in Jewish settings. For $1 each they are available from:

Jewish Media Service
65 Williams St.
Wellesley, Mass. 02181

1. *Jewish Programing: The Potential Videotape for Creative Utilization*, by Seymour Epstein.
2. *Using the Overhead Projector: A Guide*, by Nathaniel A. Entin.
3. *Super 8 Filmaking: An Exercise in Group Process*, by Amy Kronish.
4. *The Use of 16mm Film with Special Emphasis upon Jewish Schools and Community Centers: A Model Lesson Procedure*, by Nathaniel A. Entin.
5. *The Language Laboratory and the Teaching of the Hebrew Language*, by Nathaniel A. Entin.

People–resources

Besides these written sources, there is a small cadre of extremely capable people in the Jewish world who know how to use media creatively and are willing to share their skills and ideas:

Martin Cooper and Leslie Kane
Board of Jewish Education
426 W. 58th St.
New York, N.Y. 10019

Eric Goldman
New Jewish Media Project
Network
36 W. 37th St.
New York, N.Y. 10018

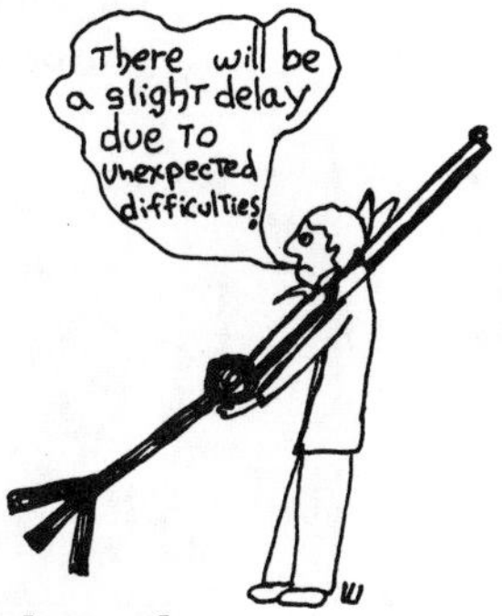

In an attempt to aid student film makers, Eric runs a filmfest for independent film makers. He is always looking for good films (distributed with a discount to college groups) and can be counted on for recommendation of topnotch material.

Nathaniel A. Entin
Gratz College
10th St. and Tabor Rd.
Philadelphia, Pa. 19141

Seymour Epstein
McGill University
Montreal, Quebec, Canada

Al Karbal
Congregation Shaarey Tzedek
27375 Bell Rd.
Southfield, Mich. 48075

Edmond Lipsitz
Canadian Jewish Congress
150 Beverly St.
Toronto, Ontario, Canada

Amy Kronish and Michael Swirsky
Jewish Media Service
Institute for Jewish Life
65 Williams St.
Wellesley, Mass. 02181

Evelyn Orbach
Jewish Community Relations Council
163 Madison Ave.
Detroit, Mich. 48226

Joseph Shoham
Board of Jewish Education
22 Glen Park Ave.
Toronto, Ontario, Canada

Shimshon Zeevi
Jewish Community Center
103 W. Rampart Dr.
San Antonio, Tex. 78216

Reuven Yalon and Earl Lefkowitz
Bureau of Jewish Education
2030 S. Taylor Rd.
Cleveland, Ohio 44118

Creating new media

The most important aspect of doing media is the participatory reward for those involved. The positive nature of the involvement is almost impossible to measure or describe aptly in writing. One needs to "do" and to "see" the results to fully appreciate the impact. Here are a few suggestions for productions you might attempt as a beginner—or as an old hand for that matter!

Overhead transparencies

Drawings by children to express their feelings about Shabbat
Song sheets for a kumsitz
Next year's budget requirements for the board of directors
Hebrew grammar assignment—conjugation of Hebrew verbs in their various binyanim with overlays
Enlarged printing for presentations to elderly persons who have sight difficulties

 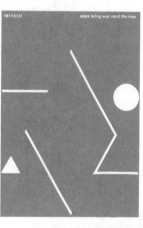 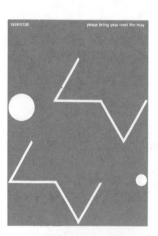 

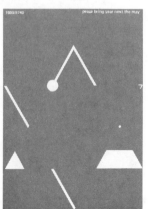   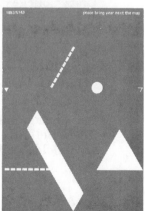

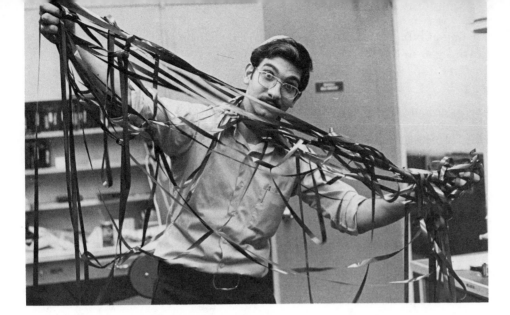

Super 8

Film on art in the synagogue
Animated film of the exodus story for a model Seder
How to prepare for Shabbat
Creative children's story for Purim with puppets
How to bake hallah

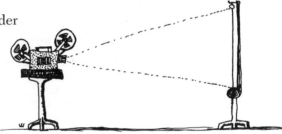

Videotape

Record of the activities in a Jewish neighborhood to learn about community
    structure
Tape of a school play rehearsal to improve presentation—tape of final ver-
    sion for parents
Tape of a teacher at work to help improve his/her technique
Record of a rally or historic event
Demonstration of how to build your own sukkah
Interview with your grandparents for an oral history project

Slide shows

Montage of Jewish immigration to America over two hundred years
History of your own Jewish community from memorabilia
History of Israel through Israeli stamps
The elements of a Jewish wedding ceremony
Preparation of the Seder table

Existing media materials

Besides the actual creation of new media materials, you can become involved with media in another way—by using existing media materials creatively in a variety of Jewish settings. The big problem is to know which
films or slides or tapes are good for your specific purposes. The following is

a listing of bibliographies and reviews of Jewish audiovisual materials that can aid you in the selection process:

1. Efron, Benjamin. *Multi-Media Resources on the Jewish Community.* 1973, $3.50.

American Association for Jewish Education
Commission on Jewish Civics
114 Fifth Ave.
New York, N.Y. 10003

A selected, annotated, and graded listing of materials for teaching Jewish civics. Nearly nine hundred multimedia resources in the fields of the American Jewish and world Jewish community are given.

2. *Guide to Feature and Documentary Films for the Hillel Program.* 1973, free.

Bnai Brith Hillel Foundations
1640 Rhode Island Ave. N.W.
Washington, D.C. 20036

Contains a topical listing of full-length and short films. Subjects covered are Israel, the Nazi period, the Holocaust, Soviet Jewry, Yiddish films, aspects of Jewish history, and Jewish artists. The *Guide* includes descriptive entries, and although some details are inaccurate, they are good at recommending films for campus programing.

3. *Jewish Audio-Visual Review.*

National Council on Jewish Audio-Visual Materials
American Association for Jewish Education
114 Fifth Ave.
New York, N.Y. 10003

Technical information, source, content, and critical review are given for each. Although this information is often dated and inaccurate, the evaluations of films and filmstrips are useful.

4. *Medium.* Free.

Jewish Media Service
Institute for Jewish Life
65 Williams St.
Wellesley, Mass. 02181

A Jewish media review including critical evaluations and detailed content analysis of existing media materials by subject area, information about technical developments, advance television program listings, and Jewish media news.

5. *Source Directory of Jewish Audio-Visual Materials.* 1975, $1. Available from Jewish Media Service. A comprehensive catalog of organizations, producers, and distributors of Jewish audiovisual materials with catalog descriptions. The *Directory* includes annotations, bibliographies, and reviews of Jewish materials.

6. *Soviet Jewry: A Catalog of Media Materials.* 1975, $1. A complete catalog of films and other media materials dealing with Soviet Jewry. Brief descriptions of each item and some recommendations are included. Available from Jewish Media Service.

7. Chayym Zeldis. *On Jews and Judaism: A Selected List of Films and Filmstrips.* 1969, 35¢.

American Jewish Committee
Institute of Human Relations
165 E. 56th St.
New York, N.Y. 10022

An annotated listing of films and filmstrips on the topics of religion and ethics, history, world Jewry, Israel and traditional practices, including some brief descriptions and recommendations.

Take a look also at the New Jewish Media Project column in:

Network
36 W. 37th St.
New York, N.Y. 10018

It reviews new acquisitions by the New Jewish Media Project and keeps up with developments in the media world. Monthly, $10 a year.

The following film reviews have been developed to make you aware of the types of materials available, and to guide you in developing a series of programs or courses:

THE CONFESSION
138 minutes, color, 1970, rental $150.

Subject: East European Jewry, Soviet Jewry
Distributor: Contemporary–McGraw-Hill, Princeton Rd., Hightstown, N.J. 08520

This is Costa-Gavras's savage, realistic dramatization of the horrors of a staged Stalinist purge trial in Communist Czechoslovakia. Based on the autobiography of Artur London, a Jew and former Czech undersecretary of foreign affairs, it describes the process of psychological and physical torture used to force London's confession to crimes he did not commit, a process now inflicted upon some Jewish activists in the Soviet Union.

THE DYBBUK
(original film version), 120 minutes, in Yiddish with English subtitles, black and white, 1937, rental $50.

Subject: East European Jewry
Distributor: Cinema Service Corp., 49 Joseph St., New Hyde Park, N.Y. 11040

Based on S. Anski's classic, it tells the story of two young lovers whose plan to marry is frustrated when the girl is betrothed by her father to another man. Her lover's desperate appeal to the intervention of mystical powers leads to his death, and his soul comes to possess the body of his beloved. The ambience of the film is that of the pious Polish shtetl of the premodern era. Its enduring value lies in the vivid, haunting inside view it provides of that spiritual world, as well as the testimony it bears to the cultural creativity of modern Polish Jewry.

THE DYBBUK
95 minutes, color, in Hebrew with English subtitles, 1970, rental scaled according to use.

Subject: East European Jewry
Distributor: Audio Brandon, 34 MacQuesten Pkwy., Mount Vernon, N.Y. 10550

Starring David Opatoshu, this is the new Israeli-made version of the classic Yiddish film. See film capsule above.

FIDDLER ON THE ROOF
178 minutes, color, 1971, rental $150.

Recommended for: age 12 up
Subject: East European Jewry, Jewish marriage
Distributor: JWB Lecture Bureau, 15 E. 26th St., New York, N.Y. 10010

This vigorous, beautifully photographed film adaptation of the successful Broadway musical, based in turn on Sholem Aleichem's play and novel *Tevye the Dairyman*, provides a colorful, sentimental, but finally moving portrait of Jewish village life in czarist Russia. The story concerns the breakdown of traditional patterns under threat from within (the desire of three of the hero's daughters to marry men of their own choosing) and without (pogrom and expulsion). But the old conditions of life, painted here in very broad, almost caricaturing brushstrokes, are still intact enough to be convincing. The film is superb as entertainment and may be useful as an adjunct to serious discussion.

THE FIXER
132 minutes, color, 1969, rental $75.

Subject: East European Jewry, Soviet Jewry
Distributor: JWB Lecture Bureau, 15 E. 26th St., New York, N.Y. 10010

Starring Alan Bates and Elizabeth Hartman, this is the story of a simple Jew—amoral, apolitical, and areligious—caught up in the wave of anti-Semitic persecution that swept czarist Russia in the late nineteenth century. Based on the true story of the Mendel Beiliss case and Bernard Malamud's award-winning retelling of it, this powerful film portrays the Jew's imprisonment and torture on the age-old charge—contrived by the authorities for political purposes—of the ritual use of a murdered Christian's blood. Beiliss's ultimate triumph, in managing to survive and winning the right of trial, turns him into a symbol of resistance to injustice.

JEWS IN RUSSIA
Two-part color filmstrip with accompanying cassettes, 1973, purchase $28.

Recommended for: ages 12-14
Subject: Soviet Jewry
Distributor: Jewish Education Press, 426 W. 58th St., New York, N.Y. 10019

An exhaustive history of Jewish life in Russia since the eighteenth century, divided into two parts, "Under the Czars" and "Under the Soviets." Touched on are social and economic conditions, cultural life, governmental and popular anti-Semitism, key personalities, the impact of particular movements and historical events, and the recent protest movement and emigration. The visuals—realistic drawing, and photographic collages—are often good, but the narration, while informative, is melodramatic, hard to follow, and amateurishly read.

L'CHAIM
90 minutes, color, 1973, rental scaled according to use.

Recommended for: age 14 up
Subject: East European Jewry
Distributor: Women's American ORT, 1250 Broadway, New York, N.Y. 10011

Made as a paean to ORT and a document of its history, this film provides us with much more: a colorful and often moving history of Russian Jewry over the last 150 years. A skillful montage of rare still photographs is combined with Jewish folk music and a fine narration by Eli Wallach to portray the culture of the Jews of the Pale, their emergence into modernity, and the great historical upheavals of which they were the victims.

THE LAST CHAPTER
90 minutes, black and white, 1965, rental $100.

Recommended for: age 16 up
Subject: East European Jewry
Distributor: Ben-Lar Productions, 311 W. 24th St., New York, N.Y. 10011

A lyrical but unsentimental record of the millennium of Jewish life in Poland, chronicling political, social, economic, and cultural achievements—and Polish Jewry's sudden demise in our own time. Narrated by Theodore Bikel, and compiled largely from historic documentary footage made on location, this epic film stands by itself as an evening program, though it could well be used in the context of a course or discussion or with a live speaker.

OUT OF BONDAGE

23 minutes, color, 1974, rental $10, including discussion guide and supplementary materials.

Recommended for: age 14 up
Subject: Soviet Jewry
Distributor: Jewish Media Service, Institute for Jewish Life, 65 Williams St., Wellesley, Mass. 02181

Scenes and interviews of recent Jewish emigrés from the Soviet Union, on their way across Europe to Israel, are interspersed with vivid flashbacks of the whole of Russian-Jewish history—in the form of drawings, still photographs, exceptional old film footage and music. A living connection is thus established between the present-day drama of Soviet Jewry and its rich, often somber past. Fine editing and a moving narration by Theodore Bikel make for a strong film experience, suited for use as the centerpiece of an evening program or as the introduction or summation of a course unit. But the film's call for response to "the challenge given our generation" might make it a bit too partisan for public school audiences and some non-Jewish audiences.

THE LIFE THAT DISAPPEARED

80 slides with accompanying cassette and teacher's guide, 16 minutes, black and white, rental $15.

Recommended for: high school, college, and adult audiences
Subject: Holocaust, East European Jewry
Distributor: Jewish Media Service, Institute for Jewish Life, 65 Williams St., Wellesley, Mass. 02181

This slide/tape program photographed and narrated by Roman Vishniac provides an intimate glimpse of everyday Jewish life in Poland's cities and villages in the years immediately preceding the Holocaust. Vishniac's eloquent, earthy photographs and quiet, wistful description of them have an authenticity and immediacy that make abstract generalization superfluous. The effectiveness of the program will be enhanced by thorough audience or class preparation; a superb teacher's guide, including a script, discussion questions, and glossary, is provided for this purpose.

THE SHOP ON MAIN STREET

128 minutes, black and white, 1965, rental $85.

Subject: Holocaust, East European Jewry
Distribution: JWB Lecture Bureau, 15 E. 26th St., New York, N.Y. 10010

Directed by Jan Kadar and Elmer Klos, this was the winner of an Academy Award for best foreign film. It is a haunting tragicomedy set in a small Czech town during the early days of the Nazi occupation. Ida Kaminska stars as a stubborn but lovable old Jewish widow who, in her innocence and deafness, is unable to comprehend the meaning of the grim events taking place around her. The ambivalent attempt of one of the gentile townspeople to save her from deportation and death highlights and personalizes the complex relations between Jews and non-Jews that obtained in that milieu over many centuries.

THE SONG AND THE SILENCE

80 minutes, 1969, rental $100.

Subject: Holocaust, East European Jewry
Distributor: JWB Lecture Bureau, 15 E. 26th St., New York, N.Y. 10010

The film takes place in a small Jewish community in Poland at the time of the Nazi occupation in 1939. Through Rabbi Shlomo and his family, we come to know the spirit of the common people, their joys and sorrows, their rich religious and communal life. As the world watches in silence, we see the vibrant tapestry of a thousand-year-old community disintegrate in the grip of Nazi brutality. We see too how the dream of Palestine and freedom gives hope and courage to the community as it fights for its survival.

SOVIET JEWS: CULTURE IN PERIL
27 minutes, black and white, 1970, rental $15.

Recommended for: age 16 up
Subject: Soviet Jewry
Distributor: Anti-Defamation League, 315 Lexington Ave., New York, N.Y. 10016

This hard-nosed CBS News documentary presents a lucid digest of the complex legal, political, and social issues surrounding the status of the Jewish minority in the Soviet Union. Though sympathetic to the Jewish plight, it takes pains to present the larger context of Soviet domestic and foreign policy. An extended interview with an articulate young emigré and some interesting footage of early twentieth-century Jewish village life provide points of human identification, but the overall studio format is talky and static, making the program suitable only for more serious-minded audiences. On the other hand, its "neutral" auspices and intelligent script will lend it and the cause of Soviet Jewry credibility in the eyes of critical viewers.

SOVIET JEWRY: HOPE, DESPAIR, AND STRUGGLE
69 slides with script, color, 1971, purchase $17.50.

Recommended for: age 16 up
Subject: Soviet Jewry
Distributor: Union of American Hebrew Congregations, 838 Fifth Ave., New York, N.Y. 10016

A well-done series of recent, slide-mounted color photographs, accompanied by a carefully researched factual script, portray the present-day people and places that are the remnants of the once-flourishing world of Jewish life in the Russian empire. The pictures serve as points of departure for a skeleton description of Soviet Jewry's history and present struggle. Made by UAHC, the program emphasizes restrictions on Jewish religious life, linking them to protest abroad and the process of emigration to Israel. The slide/script medium requires a good reader, but affords flexibility in the use of the material.

A TEAR IN THE OCEAN
86 minutes, 35 mm., color, 1972, rental scaled according to use.

Subject: Holocaust, East European Jewry
Distributor: Levitt-Pickman Film Corp., 505 Park Ave., New York, N.Y. 10022

Based on a story by Manes Sperber and directed by Henri Glaeser, the film is a moving exploration of Jewish responses to the Holocaust. The unprecedented torment and destruction brought by the Nazi invasion confront the hero with a choice between armed resistance and fidelity to the ancestral ways of his people. In the denouement, he joins a band of ghetto partisans in their fight to the death.

UNDER THIS SAME SKY
20 minutes, black and white, rental $12.

Recommended for: high school and adult audiences
Subject: Holocaust, East European Jewry
Distributor: Jewish Media Service, Institute for Jewish Life, 65 Williams St., Wellesley, Mass. 02181

This film tells the story of the Warsaw ghetto—its creation, the violent resistance it offered to Nazi oppression, and its demise—in counterpoint to scenes of life in the new Polish housing projects built after the war on its ruin. Made in the 1950s by the Polish State Film Company, this film is remarkable not only for its source, but for the crushingly ironic finale it provides to the whole history of Polish Jewry. Though marred by a melodramatic narration and some unimaginative postwar footage, the earlier films of ghetto life upon which it draws are superb.

Judaica Philately

Introduction

Philately is the art of collecting postage stamps, envelopes, postmarks, and other related postage items. Judaica philately is, of course, the collecting of items that have something of Jewish interest as their subject matter.

I've been collecting Judaica philately for the last five years. It's proved to be a fascinating and invaluable hobby for many different reasons. Almost every aspect of Jewish history becomes so much more real when you're collecting stamps from countries around the world. In addition, you can learn about farflung Jewish communities in countries such as Surinam and India, which released stamps depicting their own synagogues.

The political direction a country is heading in can sometimes become apparent through this hobby. For example, why did Czechoslovakia issue a set of six stamps commemorating the Jewish community and its history in 1967—and then withdraw the set after the start of the Six-Day War? Stamps can be a fascinating barometer of the official policy of the government of a country. Egypt, for example, issued a stamp depicting a map of Israel with a blood-drenched dagger stabbed into the middle of the map.

In addition, you can begin to confront some of the contemporary issues within the Jewish community around the world. If you collect stamps depicting Jewish people, you might become involved yourself in trying to determine "Who is a Jew?"

Stamps have intrinsic value. Any hobby that can provide a possibly profitable financial investment, a sense of Jewish history, an understanding of the world political situation, a new knowledge of distant Jewish communities, and a growing awareness of contemporary Jewish problems has got to be considered a valuable one. And besides all that, it's fascinating fun.

Ways of collecting

Although collecting Judaica stamps is a specialization in itself, there are many ways to be a Judaica philatelist. First, unless you have an unlimited budget, it is absolutely vital to limit yourself. There are many angles for you to consider:

1. *People:* Many collectors concentrate on collecting "Jews on stamps"; but even limiting yourself to this area involves making decisions:

a. Karl Marx is surely a Jew on stamps—hundreds of them! Do you want just one Marx or every Marx? Same with Einstein and other very prominent Jews.

b. Will your Jews on stamps be restricted to religious figures like Maimonides—of whom three countries have issued stamps?

c. Will you broaden the collection to include just any Jew? Several countries have Mark Spitz on stamps. Does he belong in your Judaica collection?

d. How about converts—both to and from? And is Jesus a "Jew on stamps"?

e. Do you want to limit it to Jews in the arts? Surely the Russian stamp of Sholem Aleichem is appropriate, but what about George Gershwin?

2. *Holocaust:* There have been very many stamps, postcards, postmarks, and envelopes that deal with the destruction of European Jewry, as well as other aspects of the Holocaust. This is in itself an entire area of collecting. You will no doubt be surprised to see which countries have stamps in this area. Some of these stamps are quite dramatic and moving. There is also the field of concentration camp mail. Prisoners in concentration camps were permitted at times to send a limited amount of mail to people outside the camps. The camps had special postal stationery for prisoners to use for this purpose. Many of these items still exist and are collected. It was especially interesting to me to learn that many people who otherwise might not have been found were located by means of this mail.

3. *General:* You can collect anything that appeals to you, remembering to stay within your budget. It is a must to establish a budget, for you will find that there is so much material, so much you will want to own, that you'll have to restrict yourself. By keeping within your budget, slowly but surely you will build a fine collection. Areas in which to build your collection include:

a. synagogues (there are a few dozen from all over the world);

b. the Bible;

c. Jews in certain fields (for example, Jewish Nobel Prize winners can be a field of its own);

d. Jewish art and artists (also a field of its own). You can collect anything, from the works of Jewish artists that appear on stamps, such as art by Chagall or Modigliani, to Jewish and biblical subjects in art that appear on stamps, such as "David and Goliath" by Caravaggio.

4. *Israel:* You will have to decide to what extent Israeli stamps will be a part of your collection. Obviously, Israel is an area of specialty all its own. But within the area of Judaica, your decisions on how you are to limit your collection will define the extent to which Israeli stamps may be appropriate. Some consider every Israeli stamp a Judaica stamp. Others will only take stamps that are specifically Jewish. You will have to decide if references to Israel by other countries' stamps are Judaica. For example, is the portrait of Zalman Shazar on a Brazilian stamp right for your collection? And what about anti-Israel stamps—of which there are some? And anti-Semitic stamps? Is an anti-Israel stamp anti-Semitic?

Judaica philately and the United States; or, let's hear it for some political action!

The United States Postal Service issues too few Judaica stamps. While some examples of Jews on stamps have been issued, such as Albert Einstein and George Gershwin, Judaica, nonetheless, does not seem to enjoy a priority for the United States. Particularly when compared to other countries, the U.S. does rather poorly.

In April 1975 the United States Postal Service issued a stamp commemorating Haym Salomon, a Jew famous for his activities during the American Revolution. The stamp reads: "Contributors to the cause . . . Haym Salomon, Financial Hero." Salomon's place in American history is not to be disputed; however, his contributions to the American Revolution were not just financial. And while Haym Salomon certainly deserves a stamp in his honor, this stamp is a reminder to the Judaica collector that the U.S. should have other Jewish individuals besides Jewish financiers to honor, and that in addition to people there are historic synagogues and other Jewish subjects which many nations commemorate on stamps but the U.S. has thus far neglected.

Moreover, I have always found it fascinating to examine the subjects of the stamps issued by different countries as a key to their internal conditions. It is curious (though not surprising) that the U.S. issues two stamps yearly in honor of Christmas. Each stamp indicates that it is a Christmas stamp, though one will have a more "secular" design than the other.

There is a procedure for suggesting certain subjects for U.S. stamps. According to the U.S. Postal Service, hundreds of organizations approach it with ideas. It often takes years to persuade them—if in fact you are successful. Decisions are made by appointed groups not affiliated with the postal system, although the final decision is up to the U.S. Postal Service. The office to contact is:

The Philatelic Stamp Division
U.S. Postal Service
L'Enfant Plaza
Washington, D.C. 20060

There are many ways to collect Judaica. However you decide to do it, remember:

1. Try to define your scope (although this will change as your interests change).

2. Try to collect systematically—even by country. Otherwise you can get lost very easily.

3. Give yourself a budget—and stick to it!

4. If you are a beginner, read up on general stamp collecting—including the care of stamps. In Judaica philately you will not be able to buy a stamp album and fill in the pages. Your job will be more difficult—but also more creative.

Organizations you should know about

One of the benefits of joining a philately organization is simply being able to share your collection with others. Sure, you can collect on your own and share with friends and family. But if you wish to display your collection publicly, share problems and solutions with others, share new discoveries in the field, obtain quick information about newly issued stamps, or just meet people with similar interests, then the following organizations will be helpful:

1. **Judaica Historical Philatelic Society (JHPS)**
P.O. Box 484 Cooper Sta.
New York, N.Y. 10003

Founded in 1963, the JHPS is devoted solely to Judaica philately. They hold monthly meetings at the Collector's Club, 22 E. 35th St., New York, N.Y. Meetings are every third Tuesday at 8 P.M. and guests are always

welcome. Besides publishing occasional monographs (works on specialized stamp topics), JHPS publishes a journal called *The Judaica Philatelic Journal*. For Judaica philately, this is THE organization.

2. Society of Israel Philatelists (SIP)
3619 Antisdale Ave.
Cleveland, Ohio 44118

Although members of SIP specialize in Israel rather than Judaica philately, this can be a valuable organization since Israel does produce some stamps of interest to many Judaica philatelists. Founded in 1948, SIP also publishes *The Israel Philatelist* bimonthly.

3. American Topical Association (ATA)
3306 N. 50th St.
Milwaukee, Wis. 53216

ATA is devoted to persons collecting stamps by subject rather than by country. You will find collectors of "chess," "nudes," "libraries," "women," and hundreds of other topics. ATA maintains a slide and lecture service, a translation service for thirty-three languages, and information on over two hundred topics (including Judaica); it also publishes a journal called *Topic Times*. ATA was founded in 1949.

4. Bnai Brith Philatelic Service
1640 Rhode Island Ave. N.W.
Washington, D.C. 20036

This service is devoted mainly to producing "covers" of Jewish interest (covers are envelopes, usually with an artistic design that corresponds to a stamp). For example, when the United States printed a stamp called "Rise of the Spirit of Independence," Bnai Brith published a series of covers, including one on Haym Salomon. You receive a fact sheet with each cover.

5. The Collector's Club
22 E. 35th St.
New York, N.Y. 10016

Founded in 1896, the Collector's Club maintains an extensive library devoted to philately. They also house the meetings of many stamp clubs, including the Judaica Historical Philatelic Society.

Bibliography

Books and monographs

While there are few books on the subject, the following will be of some interest to the collector of Judaica:

1. *Judaica on Postage Stamps*, by John Henry Richter. $10. Available from

Irvin Girer
27436 Aberdeen St.
Southfield, Mich. 48076

This is an annotated checklist of stamps through December 1972, listing over twelve hundred postage stamps of Judaic interest. The listings are by subject and country, with an index to place-names and persons. The book is also illustrated with samplings of Judaica. Subjects include the Bible, synagogues, holidays, Jews on stamps, the tragic years (1933–45). This 180-page volume is the most comprehensive guide to the field yet produced. An excellent work.

2. *Great Jews in Stamps*, by Arieh Lindenbaum. $4.50. Available from

Amis Publishing Co.
38 W. 32nd St.
New York, N.Y. 10001

This book is organized by topic and gives an overview of some of the many Jews on stamps from around the world. Topics include music, theater, revolutionaries. Illustrations.

3. *A Glimpse into Jewish History through Philately*, by Emil Weitz. $2. Available from

Israel Coin Distributors Corp.
327 Park Ave. South
New York, N.Y. 10010

A history of the Jewish people as illustrated by stamps. Also contains a brief history of Judaica philately. This is a good introduction to the field.

4. *Scott's Standard Postage Stamp Catalog*. 3 volumes. Volume 1: $12.50. Volumes 2 and 3: $13.25 each.

Scott's Standard Postage Stamp Catalog
604 Fifth Ave.
New York, N.Y. 10020

These books include the most complete listing of stamps issued by every country. While there are other books published by other publishers that do the same, *Scott's* is the most popular, and the numbers that *Scott's* issues to every stamp have become a standard way of identifying each stamp. When all other sources of Judaica stamps are exhausted, or when you want to try to discover some on your own, a page by page search through these books will turn up some new material. This work is standard in most libraries.

5. "One Hundred Jews on Stamps," a stamp album for one hundred specific people ($17) and a monograph entitled "Concentration Camp and Ghetto Mail" ($2) are both available from

Judaica Historical Philatelic Society
P.O. Box 484 Cooper Sta.
New York, N.Y. 10003

Send to JHPS for other publications and current prices.

6. *Israeli Stamp Collecting Clubs* (Club Leader's Handbook), by Henry Stern. Available from

American Zionist Youth Foundation
515 Park Ave.
New York, N.Y. 10022

A wealth of information. Also valuable for adults.

7. *The Bible through Stamps*, by Ord Matek. New York Ktav, 1974. Clearly written with copious illustrations.

Periodicals

The following magazines have information of constant, frequent, or occasional interest to Judaica philatelists:

1. **Judaica Philatelic Journal**
P.O. Box 484 Cooper Sta.
New York, N.Y. 10003

A bimonthly, this is the most important journal in the field. There are reports on new stamps, special collections, new discoveries, and general information to the interested reader. Articles are often written by leaders in the field. A subscription is part of membership in JHPS.

2. The Israel Philatelist
27436 Aberdeen St.
Southfield, Mich. 48076

All members of Society of Israel Philatelists receive this. (Membership in SIP is $8 yearly.)

3. Topical Time
American Topical Association
3306 N. 50th St.
Milwaukee, Wis. 53216

This bimonthly is of occasional interest to Judaica philatelists. $6 per year.

4. Scott's Monthly Stamp Journal
604 Fifth Ave.
New York, N.Y. 10020

Published monthly, it lists new stamps issued for all countries each month. Also has a monthly listing of new stamps by topic—including some Judaica. $7.50 per year.

5. Linn's Weekly Stamp News
Sidney Printing and Publishing Co.
Box 29
Sidney, Ohio 45365

Runs articles periodically on Judaica. Often runs minutes of JHPS meetings. $6 per year.

6. Stamps
Weekly Magazine of Philately
153 Waverly Pl.
New York, N.Y. 10014

Of occasional interest, this is published weekly and costs $5 per year. The entire issue of March 17, 1973, was devoted exclusively to Judaica philately.

7. The Judaica Post
Holy Land Judaica
3018 Bathhurst St.
Toronto, Ont., Canada M6B   3B6

This bimonthly journal on the philately of Judaica has resumed publication. Information may be obtained from the publishers.

Where to obtain stamps

There are many ways to build a Judaica collection:

1. Join an organization and trade or buy from members.
2. Read the literature on new stamps and buy from local stamp dealers.
3. Read the literature on old stamps and send to companies listed in stamp magazines. For example, if you know of a Russian stamp that you want, send to a company that deals in Russian stamps.
4. The easiest way, however, is to deal with companies and individuals who specialize in Judaica. The following list, though not exhaustive, indicates leaders in the field:

1. **Ellen Shoshany Kaim**
P.O. Box 3820
New York, N.Y. 10017
(212) MO2-8458

In all probability, Ellen S. Kaim is the First Lady of Judaica Philately. A collector for years, her entire collection is for sale. Ms. Kaim is a full-time Judaica philatelist and possibly the only person doing this "more than full time." She is constantly researching in the field, finding obscure items of Jewish interest and selling them. She is willing to work with the beginner or the advanced collector and has material to offer both. Ms. Kaim has a huge inventory and will most probably be able to fill your orders. She considers herself to be in the business of "Jewish memorabilia," which includes stamps, postmarks, covers, letters, etc. All are for sale. She is a walking encyclopedia of Judaica information. Contacting her will be worth your while. Most importantly, her prices are very reasonable.

2. **Klutznick Exhibit Hall**
1640 Rhode Island Ave. N.W.
Washington, D.C. 20036

Has good selection of covers of Judaic interest. Send for complete list of offerings.

3. **Frank Steiner**
199 S. La Jolla Ave.
Los Angeles, Calif. 90048

Offers selection of covers from concentration camps and internment camps of World War II. Send for complete listing.

What will it cost?

A most important question to ask! Fortunately, this enjoyable and rewarding hobby of collecting stamps and other related items of Jewish interest does not have to be expensive. Most stamps, even older ones, are very inexpensive. It is only the exceptional stamp that is worth hundreds of dollars. Most stamps cost pennies to purchase. Although some do go a little higher, the point is that Judaica philately does not have to be expensive.

Even a budget of a few dollars a month will build a good collection in no time. So don't let cost discourage you from participating in a hobby that will prove exciting, educational, and fun.

Some first-day covers of Judaic interest

PLEASE INCLUDE WITH YOUR
ORDER BUSINESS-SIZE
STAMPED ENVELOPE,
SELF-ADDRESSED. PLEASE
SEND CASH, CHECK, OR MONEY
ORDER IN PAYMENT.

available from the

**Klutznick Exhibit Hall
1640 Rhode Island Ave. N.W.
Washington, D.C. 20036**

ISRAEL FIRST DAY COVERS

FEAST OF HANUKKAH, with 3 stamps depicting traditional Hanukkah menorot	.60
SHEARITH ISRAEL SYNAGOGUE, New York—notable world synagogues series	.50
SETTLEMENT OF EMEQ, fiftieth anniversary	.40
NINTH INTERNATIONAL HAPOEL GAMES—3 stamps: Running, Jumping, Basketball	1.00
MEMORIAL DAY, 1971	.50
MEMORIAL DAY, 1972	.40
MEMORIAL DAY, 1973	.40
MEMORIAL DAY, 1974	.50
INDEPENDENCE DAY SERIES	
New Gate and Jaffa Gate 1971	.40
Herod's Gate and Damascus Gate 1971	.50
Lion's Gate and Golden Gate 1972	.40
Zion Gate and Dung Gate 1972	.40
INDEPENDENCE DAY SERIES, 1972. Sheet with 4 stamps	1.00
DECLARATION OF INDEPENDENCE, 1973	.75
JETHRO'S TOMB	.40
ISRAEL THEATER SERIES, February 1971	
Inbal Dance Theater	.40
Twenty-fifth anniversary, Cameri Theater	.40
Israel National Opera	.40
ISRAEL LANDSCAPE SERIES	
The Negev	.30
Akko, Rosh Pinna, and Kinneret	.75
En Gedi, Netanya, Yafo	.75
Haifa, Judean Desert, Gan Ha-Shelosha, and En Avedat	1.50
Coral Island, Mount Hermon, and Disappearing Bay	1.25
Tel Dan and Plain of Zebulon (1973)	.40
Akko Aqueduct and Brekhat Ram (1974)	.75
EDUCATION SERIES	
Colorful designs, values: 0.15; 0.18; 0.20; 0.40 (on one cover)	.50
VOLCANI INSTITUTE OF AGRICULTURAL RESEARCH, fiftieth anniversary	.50
NOTABLE ISRAELI ARTISTS SERIES	
Menashem Shemi, "Zefat"	.40
Boris Schatz, "The Scribe"	.40
Abel Pann, "Sarah"	.40

PASSOVER COMMEMORATIVE COVER—3 stamps depict Seder, matzah making, Exodus	.75
SOVIET JEWRY "LET MY PEOPLE GO," with star of David	.40
400th ANNIVERSARY DEATH OF RABBI I. LURIA	.40
INTERNATIONAL BOOK YEAR	.40
SATELLITE COMMUNICATIONS	.40
FALL HOLIDAYS, 1972, 4 holy ark stamps	1.00
25th ANNIVERSARY OF ISRAEL INDEPENDENCE	.60
HEROES AND MARTYRS DAY, 1973	.30
9th MACCABIAH, 1973	.75
CHAGALL WINDOWS, jumbo stamps, 2 per cover (Series I)	
Judah and Levi	1.00
Simeon and Reuben	1.00
Issachar and Zebulon	1.00
CHAGALL WINDOWS (Series II)	
Naphtali and Asher	1.00
Benjamin and Joseph	1.00
Gad and Dan	1.00
ZIM ISRAEL NAVIGATION CO. 1957. 4 stamps	1.50
INTERNATIONAL STAMP EXPO. 1974	.75
CHILDREN'S DRAWINGS (3 stamps on one cover)	.30
EXODUS OF NORTH AFRICAN JEWS	.30
PROPHETS OF ISRAEL—cover with 3 stamps, depicting Ezekiel, Jeremiah, Isaiah	1.00
ISRAEL INSTITUTE OF TECHNOLOGY—"Technion Jubilee Year"	.60
DANISH RESCUE OF JEWS—thirtieth anniversary of rescue of 1,500 Jewish refugees	1.75
*HEBREW WRITERS ASSN.—fiftieth anniversary	.75
*PAINTINGS & SCULPTURE—3 stamps on 3 covers; values: 1.25; 2.00; 3.00	3.00
*WORKING YOUTH MOVEMENT—fiftieth anniversary	.30
*DOAR IVRI—set of 3 covers, each with souvenir sheet bearing a replica of one of Israel's first three stamps	6.00

New Items

25 YEARS FROM THE
BERGEN-BELSEN CONCENTRATION CAMP
LIBERATION 1945-1970

HEROES AND MARTYRS DAY

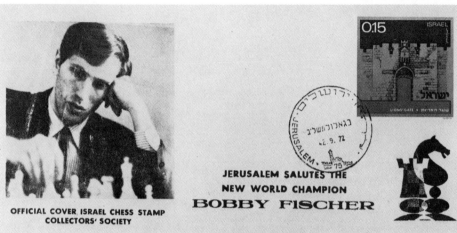

U.S. AND OTHER FIRST-DAY COVERS

GRANDMA MOSES, depicting Bnai Brith Senior Citizens
    Housing Project   .40
GEORGE WASHINGTON COMMEMORATIVE
    —Washington's letter to Newport Hebrew
    Congregation on cover   .40
AMERICAN REVOLUTION BICENTENNIAL SERIES
    (covers with biographical inserts)
    Covers with Bicentennial stamps feature notable
    Jews of the Revolution:
        Rev. Gershom M. Seixas, patriot and spiritual
          leader   .40
        Haym Salomon, patriot and broker to Office of
          Finance   .50
        Jonas Phillips, patriot merchant   .50
        Francis Salvador, first Jew to die in Revolution
          and first elected to public office   .50
        Aaron Lopez, Newport, R.I., patriot   .50
HISTORIC PRESERVATION COMMEMORATIVES
    Covers depicting three National Jewish Historic Sites
        Touro Synagogue, Newport, R.I.   .40
        Adas Israel Synagogue, Washington, D.C.   .40
        Moses Myers House, Norfolk, Va.   .40
TWENTY-FIFTH ANNIVERSARY OF PEACE CORPS
    Cover depicts "Shalom" sculpture and quotations from
    Hebrew Bible   .40
NATIONAL PARKS CENTENNIAL SERIES
    Yellowstone National Park, with insert facsimile of
      first map by Julius Bien   .50
    Cape Hatteras National Seashore with portrait of
      Bien on cover   .40

COLONIAL SILVERSMITH COMMEMORATIVE,
    features pair of rimmonim by Myer Myers, also
    insert biography   .50
MAIL ORDER CENTENNIAL, honoring Julius
    Rosenwald, with insert biography   .50
STAMP COLLECTING COMMEMORATIVE, honoring
    Jan Bart, with insert biography   .40
GEORGE GERSHWIN COMMEMORATIVE STAMP, 1973,
    with biography   .50
EINSTEIN—Notable Personalities Series, Switzerland   .60
AUSTRALIA—ISAAC ISAACS STAMP OF FDC,
    May 1973. First nativeborn governor   .75
AUSTRALIA—Cover with portraits and stamps of four
    honorees: Isaacs, Clarke, Gilmore, and Wentworth   1.00
H. S. TRUMAN COMMEMORATIVE, with facsimile
    of U.S. recognition of Israel document   .50
STATUE OF LIBERTY COMMEMORATIVE—Cover
    features Emma Lazarus   .50

WEST GERMANY—BREMERHAVEN PHILATELIC EXPO.
    Card in homage to the state of Israel, with facsimiles
    of three Israeli stamps   1.25

AUSTRIA—OTTO LOEWI 4S. One hundredth anniversary
    of birth of Nobel Prize winner   1.00
    MAX REINHARDT 2S. One hundredth anniversary
    of birth of noted theater director and producer   1.00
CURACAO—Cover with 3 stamps depicting oldest
    churches and synagogue on island   1.25

B.W.I.—Cover with stamps with portrait of Sigmund Freud,
    honoring United Nations World Health Organization   .65

Photo Credits

Where there is more than one credit on a page, the source is given in left-to-right order.

P. 10 Federation of Jewish Philanthropies; p. 12 Lauri Wolf; p. 14 Joseph Finkelstein; p. 15 The Jewish Encyclopedia; p. 16 Rabbi and Mrs. Richard Israel, Zionist Archives and Library; p. 17 National Jewish Welfare Board, Alan Gottlieb, Zionist Archives and Library; p. 20 Israel Government Tourist Office, Israel Government Tourist Office, Leonard Levin; p. 21 Zionist Archives and Library, Saul Nulman, National Jewish Welfare Board; p. 25 A. Thomas Koevary; p. 27 Danny Margolis; p. 28 The Jewish Encyclopedia, Jewish Agency; p. 30 Zionist Archives and Library; p. 31 Lauri Wolf, Sarah Finkelstein; p. 36 Israel Information Services, Zionist Archives and Library; p. 39 YIVO Institute for Jewish Research; p. 41 The Israel Museum (Jerusalem); p. 43 Zionist Archives and Library; p. 46 Leonard Levin, Lawrence Schiffman; p. 47 Alan Gottlieb, Zionist Archives and Library; p. 49 Israel Office of Information; p. 50 Jewish Agency, Zionist Archives and Library; p. 51 Lauri Wolf; p. 54 Federation of Jewish Philanthropies; p. 55 Federation of Jewish Philanthropies; p. 56 Zionist Archives and Library, YIVO Institute for Jewish Research; p. 59 Federation of Jewish Philanthropies; p. 60 Hella Hammid; p. 63 Israel Government Tourist Office; p. 65 Israel Government Tourist Office; p. 66 Hella Hammid; p. 68 Max Berne; p. 69 Max and Esther Ticktin; p. 70 Mae Rockland, Blu and Irving Greenberg, Mae Rockland; p. 71 from miniature in the Sarajevo Haggadah, 14th century (courtesy of Roselyn and Edwin Kolodny), Tamar and Samuel Fishman; p. 72 Annette Zimmerman; p. 73 Louise and Dan Franklin; p. 74 Sy Israel; p. 76 Dana Franklin, Solomon Mowhshowitz; p. 79 Leonard Levin; p. 81 A. Thomas Koevary; p. 85 Henry Gishner, Zionist Archives and Library, Zionist Archives and Library; p. 86 Zionist Archives and Library, Israel Government Tourist Office; p. 89 Leonard Levin; p. 90 Leonard Levin; p. 102 Zionist Archives and Library, Jewish Student Press Service, Yitzchak Ahren, Leonard Levin; p. 105 Yitzchak Ahren; p. 106 *Jewish Press*; p. 110 The Jewish Encyclopedia, The Jewish Encyclopedia, The Jewish Encyclopedia; p. 111 The Jewish Encyclopedia, The Jewish Encyclopedia; p. 116 from the film *Hester Street*, directed by Joan Micklin Silver; p. 124 Zionist Archives and Library; p. 127 Zionist Archives and Library; p. 128 The Jewish Encyclopedia; p. 131 The Jewish Theological Seminary of America; p. 133 Federation of Jewish Philanthropies; p. 139 The Jewish Theological Seminary of America; p. 148 Federation of Jewish Philanthropies; p. 152 Steve Cagan; p. 155 Steve Cagan; p. 156 Herbert Halweil; p. 159 New York Society for the Deaf; p. 160 Herbert Halweil; p. 161 Herbert Halweil; p. 167 Dr. Philip L. Levy; p. 169 Jewish Guild for the Blind, Herbert S. Sonnenfeld; p. 171 Jewish Guild for the Blind; p. 177 *Hadassah Magazine*; p. 178 Zionist Archives and Library, Jewish Agency; p. 179 Caudill Rowlett Scott, Zionist Archives and Library; p. 180 Board of Jewish Education; p. 181 Zionist Archives and Library, Solomon Mowshowitz; p. 183 Zionist Archives and Library, Hadassah; p. 186 Board of Jewish Education; p. 191 Zionist Archives and Library; p. 197 Zionist Archives and Library; p. 201 Zionist Archives and Library; p. 202 A. Thomas Koevary; p. 211 Torah Toys, Inc.; p. 212 Torah Toys, Inc.; p. 219 Zionist Archives and Library; p. 230 students of Bea Stadler; p. 231 students of Bea Stadler; p. 234 Daniel Boyarin, Leni Sonnenfeld; p. 236 *The Jews*, Louis Finkelstein, ed. (JPS), p. 242 Lauri Wolf, Amy Stone; p. 251 Whitestone Photo, Amy Stone; p. 257 Leni Sonnenfeld, A. Thomas Koevary; p. 265 Solomon Mowshowitz; p. 266 Hella Hammid; p. 267 National Jewish Welfare Board, Hella Hammid; p. 269 A. Thomas Koevary; p. 280 *Contemporary Synagogue Art* by Avram Kampf (JPS); p. 283 *Contemporary Synagogue Art* by Avram Kampf (JPS); p. 289 Linda Weltner/ARC; p. 290 Norma Harrop, Leni Sonnenfeld; p. 299 Jerome J. Shestack, Leni Sonnenfeld; p. 300 Leonard Levin; p. 302 The Jewish Encyclopedia; p. 305 Leni Sonnenfeld, Leonard Levin, Herbert S. Sonnenfeld; p. 312 A. Thomas Koevary; p. 313 A. Thomas Koevary; p. 314 Leni Sonnenfeld; p. 320 Zionist Archives and Library; p. 321 Zionist Archives and Library; p. 322 Linda Weltner/ARC; p. 323 Mae Rockland; p. 324 Mae Rockland and Jane Kahn; p. 325 Mae Rockland; p. 326 Jim McDonald; p. 327 Jim McDonald; p. 328 Mae Rockland, Jim McDonald; p. 329 Zionist Archives and Library; p. 332 Dona Rosenblatt; p. 333 Zionist Archives and Library; p. 334 Wagner International Photos; p. 335 Dona Rosenblatt; p. 336 Lesley Fox; p. 338 Israel Government Tourist Office; p. 339 A. Thomas Koevary; p. 340 Fred Berk, National Jewish Welfare Board, Zionist Archives and Library; p. 341 Dance Collection New York Public Library; p. 342 Zionist Archives and Library, Zionist Archives and Library, National Jewish Welfare Board; p. 343 Israel Office of Information, Israel Office of Information; p. 345 National Jewish Welfare Board, Margalit Oved, Margalit Oved; p. 346 Jewish Student Press Service; p. 347 Fred Berk; p. 348 Zionist Archives and Library; p. 350 Israel Office of Information; p. 352 Ron Katz; p. 353 Ron Katz, Linda Weltner/ARC; p. 354 Zionist Archives and Library; p. 355 Zionist Archives and Library; p. 356 Zionist Archives and Library; p. 357 Zionist Archives and Library; p. 359 Zionist Archives and Library; p. 362 National Jewish Welfare Board; p. 363 National Jewish Welfare Board, Zionist Archives and Library, Leonard Levin; p. 364 Zionist Archives and Library; p. 365 Solomon Mowshowitz; p. 367 National Jewish Welfare Board; p. 370 Aderet Records; p. 371 Neginah; p. 372 Solomon Mowshowitz; p. 376 RCA; p. 377 Ira Bejell; p. 379 National Jewish Welfare Board; p. 380 National Jewish Welfare Board; p. 384 Aaron Marcus; p. 385 Ira Bejell; p. 387 National Jewish Welfare Board; p. 388 National Jewish Welfare Board; p. 389 National Jewish Welfare Board; p. 390 National Jewish Welfare Board. *Inside Front Cover:* Alexis Bray, Israel Information Services, Leonard Levin, National Jewish Welfare Board, Fred Berk, Shapiro Studios, Jewish Guild for the Blind, Hella Hamid, Zionist Archives and Library, Keren Hayesod, Lauri Wolf, Jewish Guild for the Blind, Zionist Archives and Library, Alan Gottlieb, Zionist Archives and Library. *Inside Back Cover:* Zionist Archives and Library, Israel Information Services, National Jewish Welfare Board, Alan Gottlieb, Jewish Agency, Norma Harrop, Zionist Archives and Library, Leonard Levin, Joshua Morris Segal, Israel Information Services, Hella Hammid, A. Thomas Koevary, Zionist Archives and Library, Leonard Levin.